AMERICAN
POPULAR
MUSIC

AMERICAN POPULAR MUSIC

THE ROCK YEARS

Larry Starr

Christopher Waterman

New York   Oxford
Oxford University Press
2006

Oxford University Press, Inc., publishes works that further Oxford University's objective of excellence in research, scholarship, and education.

Oxford   New York
Auckland   Cape Town   Dar es Salaam   Hong Kong   Karachi
Kuala Lumpur   Madrid   Melbourne   Mexico City   Nairobi
New Delhi   Shanghai   Taipei   Toronto

With offices in
Argentina   Austria   Brazil   Chile   Czech Republic   France   Greece
Guatemala   Hungary   Italy   Japan Poland   Portugal   Singapore
South Korea   Switzerland   Thailand   Turkey   Ukraine   Vietnam

Published by Oxford University Press, Inc.
198 Madison Avenue, New York, New York 10016
http://www.oup.com

Oxford is a registered trademark of Oxford University Press

Library of Congress Cataloging-in-Publication Data
Starr, Larry.
  American popular music : the rock years / Larry Starr, Christopher Waterman.
    p. cm.
  "An abridged version of our comprehensive book American popular music : from minstrelsy to MTV"—Pref.
  Contents: "Choo choo ch' boogie" : the prehistory of rock 'n' roll, 1945–1955—"Rock around the clock" : rock 'n' roll, 1954–1959—"Good vibrations" : American pop and the British invasion, 1960s—"Papa's got a brand new bag" : country, soul, urgan folk, and the rise of rock, 1960s—The 1970s : rock music and the popular mainstream—Outsiders' music : progressive country, reggae, punk, funk, and disco, 1970s—The 1980s : digital technology, MTV, and the popular mainstream—"Smells like teen spirit" : hip-hop, "alternative" music, and the entertainment business—Conclusion.
  Includes bibliographical references (p.).
  ISBN 13: 978-0-19-530052-9 (pbk. : alk. paper)
  ISBN 0-19-530052-1 (pbk. : alk. paper)
  1. Rock music—United States—History and criticism.   I. Waterman, Christopher Alan, 1954– II. Title.
ML3534.3.S73 2005
781.66'0973—dc22   2005049894

Printing number: 9 8 7 6 5 4 3 2 1

Printed in the United States of America
on acid-free paper

CONTENTS

PREFACE   vii
LYRIC CREDITS   x

1   Themes and Streams of American Popular Music   1

2   "Choo Choo Ch' Boogie": The Prehistory of Rock 'n' Roll,
    1945–1955   18

3   "Rock around the Clock": Rock 'n' Roll, 1954–1959   53

4   "Good Vibrations": American Pop and the British Invasion, 1960s   92

5   "Papa's Got a Brand New Bag": Country, Soul, Urban Folk, and the
    Rise of Rock, 1960s   126

6   The 1970s: Rock Music and the Popular Mainstream   167

7   Outsiders' Music: Progressive Country, Reggae, Punk, Funk, and
    Disco, 1970s   196

8   The 1980s: Digital Technology, MTV, and the Popular Mainstream   231

9   "Smells Like Teen Spirit": Hip-Hop, "Alternative" Music, and the
    Entertainment Business   268

10 Conclusion   314

GLOSSARY   325
BIBLIOGRAPHY   331
INDEX   333

PREFACE

In presenting this survey of the rich terrain of American popular music during the rock era, we hope to have created a book capable of serving a number of purposes. It may be used as a text for introductory college-level courses, obviously, as it assumes a mature and literate reader but not one who necessarily has any specific background in music or in this particular area of musical study. These same assumptions will also make this book useful to the general reader who wishes a broad-based introduction to our subject. In addition, this volume will serve the interests of specialists—musicians, graduate students, teachers, and scholars—who need a one-volume overview, or review, of the topic. We have kept this wide potential audience constantly in mind as we strove to keep our book accessible and inviting, while always reflecting our own deep involvement in the music and in contemporary scholarly issues surrounding it.

American Popular Music: The Rock Years is an abridged version of our comprehensive book *American Popular Music: From Ministrelsy to MTV*. We have made every effort to retain the inclusive approach of the parent volume while producing a work of manageable size that can stand alone successfully as an internally consistent whole. Nevertheless, we must stress that this book inevitably tells just a portion of a huge and impressive story, and we direct those readers wishing to gain a thorough insight into the remarkable history of American popular music to our original, unabridged text.

What distinguishes our book from others in its rapidly growing field is that it combines two perspectives not often found in the same place: the study of cultural and social history on the one hand, and the analytical study of musical style on the other. Lest this sound disconcertingly heavy, let us assure our readers at the outset that we have brought to the treatment of our subject years of experience in teaching courses for a general student population and in lecturing on musical subjects to general audiences. This experience has taught us that it is neither necessary nor desirable to talk down, write down, or think down to such groups. People love music and can quickly grasp all kinds of intricacies and subtleties concerning music, so long as jargon is avoided and explanations kept clear and unpretentious. We love American popular music ourselves—that is why we have written this book—and we have attempted to foreground this love for the subject in our writing, realizing that it is the most valuable common bond we share with all potential readers of our work.

We fully expect that students, teachers, and readers of all kinds will enter into a creative dialogue with the material in this book. No general overview of a complex subject can begin to satisfy everyone. And since passions run high in the field of popular music, we anticipate that our particular perspectives, and particularly our choices of artists to emphasize and of specific examples to study, may well provoke some controversy at times, whether in the classroom or simply in the mind of the reader. We have felt it better to identify clearly our own viewpoints and enthusiasms than to try to hide behind a scrim of apparent "objectivity." The opening chapter outlines particular *themes* and *streams* that serve as recurring reference points throughout the book, so that our narrative focus and our strategy are put forward at the outset. While we feel that this text provides a sound and reliable starting point for the study and appreciation of American popular music, we claim no more than that. We hope and expect that teachers who use this book will share supplementary and contrasting perspectives on the material with their students, and that individual readers will use the bibliography as an enriching source of such perspectives as well. As white males who came to maturity in the days of rock 'n' roll and 1960s rock, we inevitably bring certain limitations, along with our passions, to the understanding of the broad trajectory of our subject, and it is certainly desirable for all readers to seek out other perspectives and modes of understanding as they pursue this subject further.

A brief word concerning methodology. We have sought to limit the use of specialized terms, to employ them only when clearly necessary, and to define them as they arise naturally in the course of study. The most important and frequently employed of these terms appear in **boldface** and are given extensive definitions in the glossary at the end of the book. The glossary is reserved for terms that recur throughout the book and that would not be defined adequately for our purposes in a standard college dictionary. (This means that terms like **producer,** which has a special meaning in popular music, will be found in the glossary, along with other expected terms such as **blues** and **syncopation.**) Significant terms that are relevant only to a limited section of material are *italicized* when they first occur, are defined in context, and may also be located by using the book's index.

An analogous strategy has been used for musical analyses. Rather than being separated out, or introduced independently, the main musical discussions are integrated into the text at the points where they become relevant to the developing narrative; this approach seemed to us both logical and functional. Listening charts are used to represent and summarize, in outline form, the most important elements of recordings that are discussed in some detail in the text. The fact that we are dealing here to an overwhelming extent with *songs*—texted music—has enabled us to treat musical issues with some sophistication without having to employ actual musical notation, since lyrics may be used as points of specific orientation in the musical discussions. This keeps the focus on *listening* and opens the musical analyses to the widest possible audience of readers without compromising depth of treatment.

Boxes are used occasionally in this book to provide further insight and information on significant individuals, recordings, and topics in cases where such material—albeit useful—would interrupt the flow of narrative. Important names are <u>underlined</u> throughout the book.

We would like to thank our families, who put up with a great deal as our work underwent its extensive prenatal development: Leslie, Dan, Sonya, and Gregory Starr; and Glennis and Max Waterman. We extend our gratitude to Maribeth Payne, our initial, ever-patient editor at Oxford University Press; to her gifted associates Maureen Buja and Ellen Welch; to Janet M. Beatty, executive editor at OUP; to Peter M. Labella, senior editor at OUP; to Christine D'Antonio, senior project editor at OUP; to Talia Krohn, associate editor at OUP; to Larry Hamberlin for his superb job of copyediting; and to Emily Pillars, development editor at OUP, for her essential preliminary review of the "rock years" project. We owe a substantial debt to the many anonymous readers who offered extensive and helpful comments on our work in its various stages. At the University of Washington, our valued colleague Tom Collier has been a consistent and selfless source of assistance and encouragement. The course on American popular music out of which this book grew was shaped not only by faculty members but by graduate students as well, among whom we especially wish to cite Jon Kertzer, Peter Davenport, Stuart Goosman, and Jun Akutsu. The many students who "road-tested" drafts of several chapters and offered their reactions to them also merit our sustained thanks. Graduate assistants Timothy Kinsella, Shelley Lawson, and Nathan Link at the University of Washington, and Sabrina Motley, Mark Eby, and Ann Mazzocca at UCLA gave invaluable and generous editorial assistance. We also owe a debt of gratitude to the folks at Joel Whitburn's Record Research for their series of books containing *Billboard* chart data. We could readily go on, like those CD inserts thanking everybody from the Almighty on down, but there's a story waiting to be told, and we'd best get on with it. If there's anybody out there we neglected to thank, let us know, and pray for a second edition so that we can do it next time!

Larry Starr, University of Washington
Christopher Waterman, UCLA

LYRIC CREDITS

AMERICAN POPULAR MUSIC

CHAPTER ONE

THEMES AND STREAMS OF AMERICAN POPULAR MUSIC

Welcome to Los Angeles! You picked up a cherry red rent-a-convertible at LAX, and you're searching the satellite radio for some sounds to accompany your drive north to the dance clubs on the Sunset Strip. Maybe a retro surf groove like "Misirlou" from the film *Pulp Fiction*; or a track from NWA's classic hip-hop album *Straight outta Compton*; or some L.A. punk, early stuff like X or Black Flag. Maybe you're a romantic at heart and want to cruise with the top down, blasting out a rock ballad from the latest Hollywood or Broadway blockbuster.

Whatever your preferences, as you fiddle with the dial it soon becomes apparent that the signals beamed into your car radio from outer space present a complex constellation of musical choices: 150 channels, from "Deep Classic Alternative" to "Urban Adult" and "Underground Dance," each representing a specialized branch of musical taste, each aimed at a particular audience. There are doubtless some channels that you might try only on occasion, and a few that you'd remove permanently from your radio if you knew how. That's the way popular music is, after all: some types of music attract us, others incite us to pitch the radio out the window, and yet others don't smell bad or good—they just don't smell like anything at all.

But think for a moment. Why all these stations? Who listens to them? Why are adjectives such as "soft" and "hard" applied to music? How do radio formats such as "classic rock," "album-oriented rock," "urban contemporary," and "adult alternative" take shape? What does this dividing up of styles and audiences tell us about contemporary American culture? And who's making money from all this?

We hope that this book will help you to think creatively and critically about such questions. Our goal is to get you to listen closely to popular music and to learn something about its history and about the people and institutions that have produced it. We cover a wide range of music, starting in the years after World War II and continuing up through the 1990s. Listening to music is an important part of this study, and we hope that you will enjoy the recordings that we have chosen to highlight. But be forewarned—we cannot possibly do justice to all the music you like, or all the musicians you admire (nor can we adequately denigrate the music you hate).

In this book we use the term "popular music" broadly, to indicate music that is mass-reproduced and disseminated via the mass media; that has at various times been listened to by large numbers of Americans; and that typically draws upon a variety of preexisting musical traditions. It is our view that popular music must be seen in relation to a broader musical landscape, in which various styles, audiences, and institutions interact in complex ways. This musical map is not static—it is always in motion, always evolving.

For our purposes, the designation "rock years" refers to a half century of musical history that begins in the mid-1950s with the emergence of rock 'n' roll as a group of musical styles and as a marketing category. The term "rock music" has generally been applied to a stream of popular music that flows from the pioneering rock 'n' roll recordings of Chuck Berry, Elvis Presley, and other musicians of the 1950s. Beginning in the 1960s, rock music differentiated into marketing categories such as country rock, folk rock, art rock, glam rock, southern rock, jazz rock, Latin rock, hard rock, and heavy metal, a process that continues to this day. By the mid-1970s a rebellion against mainstream corporate rock music yielded a genre called punk rock, a back-to-basics predecessor of today's "alternative rock." The continued importance of "rock" as an overarching category is indicated by the use of the term in contemporary radio programming, where rock music is divided into subcategories such as hard, soft, acoustic, classic, alternative, jam band/progressive, and punk/hardcore rock.

Our book also includes a wide range of musical styles that are typically not marketed under the heading of rock music. These include a variety of popular music styles grounded in the traditions and historical experiences of African Americans, including soul music and hip-hop. This is not to say that these styles of music have developed in isolation from rock music—it is hard, for example, to imagine the development of Motown or funk music without the influence of rock music. As we will see, there is often a big difference between the categories used to sell music and actual patterns of musical influence and exchange. By the same token, we will also pay attention to music typically marketed under the heading of "country" rather than rock music. Country music was one of the main roots of rock 'n' roll music, and most mainstream country music today has thoroughly internalized certain stylistic characteristics of rock music.

An important underlying issue here is that of race, and the division of people and the music they make and listen to into categories such as "black" and "white." Race and ethnicity have certainly played an important role in shaping the development of popular music in the United States, from the nineteenth-century minstrel show up to the record charts and radio formats of today, which remain partially segregated by "color." However, the history of American popular music also provides ample evidence of music's ability to overflow and complicate the boundaries of identity and prejudice.

It is important to remember that in many cases the sorts of stylistic categories we have been discussing here are themselves partly the product of marketing strategies by record companies, who in defining types of music hope to define types of fans to whom they can sell the music. Throughout this book we will find many examples of the complex relationships among musical styles, the preferences of audiences, and the efforts of the music industry to shape those preferences.

THEME ONE: LISTENING

Although this book covers a wide range of performers and styles, it is unified by several themes. First and foremost, we hope to encourage you to listen critically to a wide variety of rock music and its offshoots. The word "critical" doesn't imply adopting a negative attitude. Rather, critical listening is listening that consciously seeks out meaning in music, drawing on some knowledge of how music is put together, its cultural significance, and its historical development.

Even if you don't think of yourself as a musician, and don't have much—or any—experience at reading musical notation, it is likely that you know much more about music than you think. You know when a chord sounds "wrong," a note "out of tune," or a singer "off key," even if you can't come up with a technical explanation for your reaction. You have learned a lot about music just growing up as a member of society, although much of that knowledge rests below the level of conscious awareness.

In everyday life, people often do not think carefully about the music they hear. Much popular music is in fact designed not to call critical attention to itself (a good example of this is the multimillion-dollar "environmental music" industry, pioneered by the Muzak Corporation). Other types of popular music—funk, punk rock, hard rap, thrash metal—seek to grab your attention, but do not by and large encourage you to engage them analytically. The point of analyzing popular music is not to ruin your enjoyment of it. Rather, we want to encourage you to expand your tastes, to hear the roots of today's music in earlier styles, and in the final analysis, to be a more critically aware "consumer" of popular music.

Formal analysis—listening for musical structure, its basic building blocks and the ways in which they are combined—can tell us a lot about popular music. We can, for example, discover that recordings as different as Little Richard's rock 'n' roll anthem "Tutti Frutti," James Brown's "I Got You (I Feel Good)," The Doors' "Riders on the Storm," and the theme song of the 1960s TV show *Batman* all share the same basic musical structure, the twelve-bar blues form (to be discussed in Chapter 2). Similarly, tunes as diverse as Frank Sinatra's version of "Love and Marriage," the Penguins' 1955 doo-wop hit "Earth Angel," "Yesterday" by the Beatles, and the theme of the 1960s cartoon show (and the 1993 film) *The Flintstones* all have an AABA melodic structure. You don't have to worry about such technicalities yet; there will be ample opportunity to discuss them later on. The point here is simply to suggest that a lot of popular music draws on a limited number of basic formal structures.

Structure is not the only important dimension of music. In order to analyze the way popular music actually sounds—the grain of a singing voice, the flow of a dance groove, or the gritty sound of an electric guitar—we must complement formal analysis with the analysis of musical process. To adopt a biological analogy, there is an important difference between understanding the structure of an organism—

its constituent parts and how they are related—and the processes that bring these parts and relationships to life. Popular songs may be analyzed not only as composed "works" with their own internal characteristics but also as interpretations by particular performers: in other words, one must understand not only song but also singing.

Traditional musicology, which focuses on the written scores that serve as the model for performances in classical music, is often of little relevance in helping us to understand popular music. In this book we frequently use concepts directly relevant to popular music itself: for example, **riff,** a repeated pattern designed to generate rhythmic momentum; **hook,** a memorable musical phrase or riff; and **groove,** a term that evokes the channeled flow of "swinging" or "funky" or "phat" rhythms.

Another important aspect of musical process is **timbre,** the quality of a sound, sometimes called "tone color." Timbre plays an important role in establishing the "soundprint" of a performer. Play just five seconds of a recording by, say, Aretha Franklin, Bruce Springsteen, Bonnie Raitt, Dr. Dre, or Bono, and any knowledgeable listener will be able to identify the singer by the "grain" of his or her voice.

Instrumental performers may also have highly memorable "soundprints." Some—for example, Jimi Hendrix, Eric Clapton, and Eddie Van Halen—have become superstars. Others remain unknown to the general listening public, although their soundprints are very familiar: for example, James Jamerson, the master bassist of Motown; King Curtis, whose gritty tenor saxophone is featured on dozens of soul records from the 1960s; and Steve Gadd, studio drummer par excellence, who played on records by Aretha Franklin, Stevie Wonder, Barbra Streisand, Steely Dan, and Paul Simon during the 1970s.

Recording engineers, producers, arrangers, and record labels may also develop unique soundprints. We will encounter many examples of this: the distinctive **"slap-back"** echo of Elvis Presley's early recordings on Sun Records; the quasi-symphonic teen pop recordings produced by Phil Spector; the stripped-down, "back to basics" soul sound of Stax Records in Memphis; and the immense sampled bass drum explosions used by engineer Steve Ett of Chung House of Metal, one of the most influential hip-hop studios. You will learn more about the creative contributions of arrangers, engineers, and producers as we go along; for now, you should simply note that the production of a particular "sound" often involves many individuals performing different tasks.

Lyrics—the words of a song—are another important aspect of popular music. In many cases words are designed to be one of the most immediately accessible parts of a song. In other cases—for example, the songs of Bob Dylan, John Lennon and Paul McCartney, David Byrne, Prince, Beck, or Ice-T—the lyrics seem to demand interpretation, and fans take a great deal of pleasure from the process of figuring them out.

Dialect has also been a crucial factor in the history of American popular music. Some musical genres are strongly associated with particular dialects (country music with southern white dialects, rap music with certain urban black dialects, 1970s punk rock with working-class British dialects). The ability of African American artists such as Chuck Berry and Diana Ross to "cross over" to a white middle-class audience was to some degree predicated upon their adoption of a dialect widely used in the mass media. In other cases, the mutual incomprehensibility of varieties of English has been consciously emphasized, particularly in recordings aimed at consumption within ethnic communities. There are sometimes very good reasons not to be understood by the majority.

These are some of the dimensions of popular musical style to keep in mind as you work your way through this book. Think about what attracts you to the music you like: the texture of a voice, the power of a guitar, the emotional insight of a lyric, the satisfying predictability of a familiar tune, the physical momentum of a rhythm. This is what makes popular music important to people: its sound, the sense it makes, and the way it feels.

THEME TWO: MUSIC AND IDENTITY

None of us is born knowing who we are—we all learn to be human in particular ways, and music is one important medium through which we formulate and express our identity. Think back to the very first pop song you remember hearing as a little kid, when you were, say, five years old. Odds are you heard it at home, or maybe in a car, or (depending on your age) over a transistor radio or a portable CD player at the beach. The person playing it may have been one of your parents, or an older brother or sister. These are often the people who influence our early musical values, and it is they whose values we sometimes emphatically reject later in life. In elementary school, other kids begin to influence our taste, a development closely connected with the ways in which we form social groups based on gender, age, and other factors (boys versus girls, fifth graders versus first graders, cool kids versus nerds).

As we move into adolescence, popular music also enters our private lives, providing comfort and continuity during emotional crises and offering us the opportunity to fantasize about romance and rebellion. Pop music provides images of gender identity, culturally specific ways of being masculine and feminine. Ethnicity and race—including notions of how to act authentically "white" or "black" or "Latino"—are also powerfully represented in popular music.

As you grow older, a song or a singer's voice may suddenly transport you back to a specific moment and place in your life, sometimes many decades earlier. Like all human beings, we make stories out of our lives, and music plays an important role in bringing these narratives to life. Some popular songs—for example, the Beatles' "In My Life," Don McLean's "American Pie," Bob Seger's "Night Moves," and Missy Elliott's "Back in the Day"—are really about memory and the mixed feelings of warmth and loss that accompany a retrospective view of our own lives.

Popular music in America has from the very beginning been closely tied up with stereotypes, convenient ways of organizing people into categories. It is easy to find examples of stereotyping in American popular music: the common portrayal in song lyrics and music videos of women as sexual objects, and the association of men with violence; the image of African American men as playboys and gangsters; the stereotype of southern white musicians as illiterate, backwoods "rednecks"; the association of songs about money with supposedly Jewish musical characteristics; and the caricatures of Asian and Latin American people found in novelty songs right up through the 1960s.

Stereotyping is often a double-edged sword. In certain cases popular performers have helped to undermine the "commonsense" association of certain styles with

Aerosmith's **Steven Tyler** in concert. © Henry Ditz/CORBIS

certain types of people: the black country singer Charley Pride and the white blues musician Stevie Ray Vaughan are just two examples of performers whose styles challenge stereotyped conceptions of race and culture. The history of popular music in the United States is also replete with examples of minority groups who have reinterpreted derogatory stereotypes and made them the basis for distinctive forms of musical creativity and cultural pride—"Say It Loud, I'm Black and Proud," "Okie from Muskogee," "(At the) YMCA."

Why do people make and listen to music? What do they want from it, and what does it give them? These questions take us beyond the central concern of classic aesthetic theory, the creation and appreciation of "beauty for beauty's sake." People value music for many reasons, including a desire for beauty, but also a great deal more: they use music to escape from the rigors of the work week, to celebrate important events in their lives, to help them make money, war, and love. To understand the cultural significance of popular music, we must examine both the music—its tones and textures, rhythms and forms—and the broader patterns of social identity that have shaped Americans' tastes and values.

THEME THREE: MUSIC AND TECHNOLOGY

From the heyday of printed sheet music in the nineteenth century through the rise of the phonograph record, network radio, and sound film in the 1920s, right up to the present era of digital recording, computerized sampling, and Internet-based radio, technology has shaped popular music and has helped disseminate it, more and more rapidly, to more and more people. Technology doesn't determine the decisions made by a musician or an audience, but it can make a particular range of choices available to them.

It has often been argued that the mass media create a gap between musicians and their audiences, a distance that often encourages us to forget that the music we hear is made by other human beings. To what degree has technology affected our relationship to music and, more importantly, to other people? This is by no means a simple issue. Some critics of today's musical technology would say that a much higher percentage of Americans were able to perform music for their own enjoyment a century ago, when the only way of experiencing music was to hear it performed live or to make it yourself. This decline in personal music making is generally attributed to the influence of mass media, which are said to encourage passive listening. However, nationwide sales figures for musical instruments—including electronic instruments such as digital keyboards and drum pads—suggest that millions of people in the United States are busy making music.

In addition, although the mass media can encourage passivity, people aren't always passive when they listen to recorded music. Have you ever pretended to be a favorite musician while listening to music by yourself, perhaps even mimicking onstage movements (playing "air guitar" or "virtual drums")? Have you ever embarrassed yourself by unconsciously singing along with your iPod in a public setting? When you listen over headphones, don't you enter into the music in your imagination and in an important sense help to "make" the music?

Although we tend to associate the word "technology" with novelty and change, older technologies often take on important value as tokens of an earlier—and, it is often claimed, better—time. Old forms of musical "hardware" and "software"—music boxes, player pianos, phonographs, sheet music, and 78 r.p.m., 45 r.p.m., and long-playing (LP) discs—become the basis for subcultures made up of avid collectors. In some cases, older music technologies are regarded as qualitatively superior to the new. For example, some contemporary musicians make a point of using analog rather than digital recording technology. This decision is based on the aesthetic judgment that analog recordings, which directly mirror the energy fluctuations of sound waves, "sound better" than digital recordings, which break sound waves down into packets of information. Musicians who prefer analog recording say that it is "warmer," "richer-sounding," and somehow "more human" than digital recording.

Sometimes the rejection of electronic technology functions as an emblem of "authenticity," as, for example, in MTV's recently revived *Unplugged* series, where rockers such as Eric Clapton, R.E.M., and Nirvana demonstrate their "real" musical ability and sincerity by playing on acoustic instruments. However, there are also many examples of technologies being used in ways that encourage active involvement, including the manipulation of multiple record turntables by hip-hop **DJs** and the increasing popularity of karaoke singalong machines and computer software in American nightclubs and homes. If it is true that technology has been used in cynical ways to manipulate the public into buying certain kinds of music, it is also the case that people often exert creative control over the role of musical machines in their own lives.

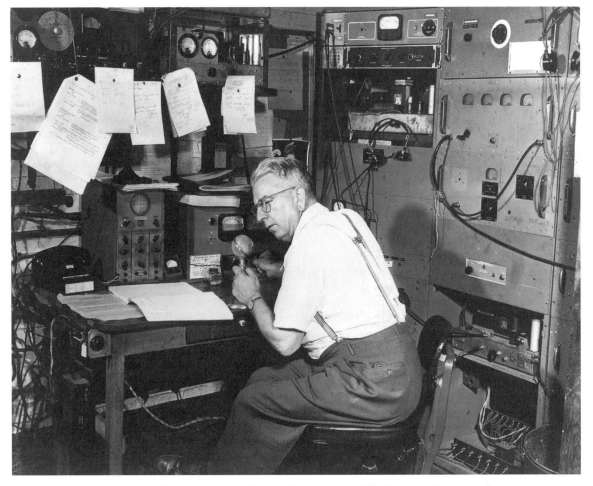

One of the earliest FM radio stations, Alpine, New Jersey, 1948. Courtesy Library of Congress.

THEME FOUR: THE MUSIC BUSINESS

To understand the history of American popular music, it is necessary that we learn about the workings of the music business. The production of popular music typically involves the work of many individuals performing different roles. From the nineteenth century until the 1920s, sheet music was the principal means of disseminating popular songs to a mass audience. This process typically involved a complex network of people and institutions: the **composer** and **lyricist** who wrote a song; the publishing company that bought the rights to it; song pluggers, who promoted the song in stores and convinced big stars to incorporate it into their acts; the stars themselves, who often worked in shows that toured along a circuit of theaters controlled by yet other organizations; and so on, right down to the consumer, who bought the sheet music and performed it at home.

The rise of radio, recording, and movies as the primary means for popularizing music added many layers of complexity to this process. Today hundreds of people will have had a hand in producing the music you listen to. In mainstream pop music, the composer and lyricist are still important; the songs they write are reworked to complement a particular performer's strengths by an **arranger,** who decides which instruments to use, what key the song should be in, how many times it should be repeated, and a host of other details. The **A&R** (artists and repertoire) personnel of a record company seek out talent, often visiting nightclubs and rehearsals to hear new groups. The **producer** of a record plays several roles: convincing the board of directors of a record company to back a particular project, shaping the development of new "talent," and often intervening directly in the recording process. Engineers work in the studio, making hundreds of important decisions about the balance between voice and instruments, the use of effects such as echo and **reverb,** and other factors that shape the overall "sound" of a record. The publicity department plans the advertising campaign, and the public relations department handles interactions with the press.

This is only the barest outline of the interlocking roles involved in the production and promotion of popular music today. Business agents, video producers, graphic artists, copy editors, record stores, stage hands, truck drivers, T-shirt companies, and the companies that produce musical hardware—often owned by the same corporations that produce the recordings—also play vital roles in this process. It is hard to know where to draw the boundaries of an industry that has extended itself into so many aspects of commerce and culture.

In addition, many of the roles described above have become intermingled in complex ways. A person such as Quincy Jones, for example, is a performer, a songwriter, an arranger, a producer (who makes lots of engineering decisions), and a record label executive. And the wider availability of digital recording equipment means that some performers may also act as their own arranger, producer, and engineer (Stevie Wonder and Prince are good examples of this collapsing of roles).

Theodor Adorno, a German philosopher who wrote in the 1940s and 1950s, powerfully criticized the effects of capitalism and industrialization on popular music. He suggested that the music industry promotes the illusion that we are all highly independent individuals defined by our personal tastes—"I'm a country fan," "You're a metalhead." In fact, Adorno argued, the industry manipulates the notion of personal taste to sucker us into buying its products. Emotional identification with the wealthy superstars portrayed on television and in film—the "Lifestyles of the Rich and Famous" syndrome—is, in Adorno's view, a poor substitute for the humane and ethical social relations that typify healthy communities.

In some ways Adorno was right: Americans are probably less individualistic than they like to think, and it is often true that record companies con us into buying the latest thing on the basis of tiny differences in musical style, rather like the little design changes that mark off different kinds of automobiles or tape decks or tennis shoes. And it is true that the private experience of listening over headphones—like the experience of driving alone in an automobile with the windows rolled up—can isolate people from one another.

But there's more to it than that. Just ask anyone who's worked in the music business and developed an ulcer trying to predict what the next trend will be. Compared to other industries that produce consumer products, the music business is quite unpredictable. Today, only about one out of eight recordings makes a profit. One platinum record—something like Michael Jackson's *Thriller*, Madonna's *Like a Virgin*, Nirvana's *Nevermind*, or Dr. Dre's *The Chronic*—must compensate for literally hundreds of unprofitable records made by unknown musicians or faded stars. As record company executives seek to guarantee their profits by producing variations on "the same old thing," they also nervously eye the margins to spot and take advantage of the latest trends.

The relationship between the "majors"—large record companies with lots of capital and power—and the "indies"—small independent labels operating in marginal markets—has been an important factor in the development of American popular music. In most cases, the majors have played a conservative role, seeking to ensure profits by producing predictable (some would say "bland") music for a large middle-class audience. The indies, run by entrepreneurs, have often had to be more daring, searching out new talent, creating specialized niches, and feeding new styles into the musical mainstream. It is mostly these small labels that initially popularized blues, country music, rhythm & blues, rock 'n' roll, funk, soul music, reggae, punk rock, rap, grunge, world beat, and other "alternative" styles. In some cases, indie labels have grown large and powerful; one example of this is Atlantic Records, which began as a small R&B label in the late 1940s and grew into a multimillion-dollar corporation.

Today, the relationship between indies and majors has been extended over the globe—five corporations (only one of them actually based in the United States) now control around 90 percent of the world's legal trade in commercially recorded music. Each of these transnational corporations has bought up many smaller labels, using them as incubators for new talent, a system reminiscent of the relationship between major and minor league teams in baseball.

THEME FIVE: CENTERS AND PERIPHERIES

The distinction between major and minor labels leads us to a final theme: the idea that the history of American popular music may be broadly conceptualized in terms of a center-periphery model. The "center"—actually several geographically distinct centers, including New York, Los Angeles, and Nashville—is where power, capital, and control over mass media are concentrated. The "periphery" is inhabited by smaller institutions and by people who have historically been excluded from the political and economic mainstream. This distinction is by no means intended to suggest that the center is normal and the periphery abnormal. Rather, it is a way of clarifying a process that has profoundly shaped the development of popular music in the United States: that is, the role of the musical "margins" in shaping mainstream popular taste and the workings of the music industry.

The stylistic mainstream of American popular music was, until at least the mid-1950s, largely oriented toward the tastes of white, middle- or upper-class, Protestant, urban people. In economic terms, this makes perfect sense, since it was these people who for many years made up the bulk of the expanding urban market for mass-reproduced music. From whom have the vital "peripheral" musical impulses of which we have been speaking come? The evidence is abundant: from African

Americans, poor southern whites, working-class people, Jewish and Latin American immigrants, adolescents, gays, and various other folks whose "difference" has at times weighed upon them as a burden.

The history of popular music in the United States shows us how supposedly marginal musics and musicians have repeatedly helped to invigorate the center of popular taste and the music industry. Regrettably, it has sometimes also been the case that the people most responsible for creating the music that people in the United States and elsewhere consider quintessentially American have not reaped an equitable share of the profits accumulated from the fruits of their labor.

STREAMS OF TRADITION: THE SOURCES OF POPULAR MUSIC

In 1937—at the height of the big band craze—the anthropologist Ralph Linton published an article entitled "One-Hundred Percent American." "There can be no question about the average American's Americanism or his desire to preserve his precious heritage at all costs," wrote Linton. "Nevertheless, some insidious foreign ideas have already wormed their way into his civilization without his realizing what was going on." These "insidious ideas"—derived from the cultures of Asia, the Near East, Europe, Africa, and Native America—include pajamas, the toilet, soap, the toothbrush, the chair, shoes, the mirror, coffee, fermented and distilled drinks, the cigar, and even the newspaper. On the train to work, Linton's "average American" reads the news of the day, imprinted in characters invented by the ancient Semites by a process invented in Germany on a material invented in China. As he scans the latest editorial pointing out the dire results to our institutions of accepting foreign ideas, he thanks a Hebrew God in an Indo-European language that he is 100 percent (decimal system invented by the Greeks) American (from Americus Vespucci, Italian geographer).

Similarly, every aspect of popular music that is today regarded as American in character has sprung from imported traditions. These source traditions may be classified into three broad "streams": European American music, African American music, and Latin American music. Each of these streams is made up of many styles of music, and each has profoundly influenced the others.

The European American Stream

Until the middle of the nineteenth century, American popular music was almost entirely European in character. The cultural and linguistic dominance of the English meant that their music—including folk ballads, popular songs printed as sheet music, and various types of dance music—established early on a kind of "mainstream" around which other styles circulated.

At the time of the American Revolution, professional composers of popular songs in England drew heavily upon the **ballad,** a type of song in which a series of **verses** telling a story, often about a historical event or personal tragedy, are sung to a repeating melody (this sort of musical form is called **strophic**). Originally an oral tradition, passed down in unwritten form, ballads were eventually circulated on large sheets of paper called broadsides, the ancestors of today's sheet music. While some broadside ballads were drawn from folk tradition, many were urban in origin and concerned with current events (much like today's tabloid newspapers). In most cases only the words were provided, with an indication of a traditional melody—for example, "Greensleeves"—to which they were to be sung. Balladmongers hawking the broadsides sang them on the streets, an early form of commercial song promotion. Composers of broadside ballads often added a catchy **chorus,** a repeated melody with fixed text inserted between verses.

The pleasure garden, a forerunner of today's theme parks, was the most important source of public entertainment in England between 1650 and 1850. Large urban parks filled with meandering tree-lined paths, the pleasure gardens provided an idyllic rural experience for an expanding urban audience. The pleasure gardens became one of the main venues for the dissemination of printed songs by professional composers, and many of the first widely popular songsheets were illustrated with sketches of the gardens and other romanticized rural scenes. In the 1760s the first American pleasure gardens opened in Charleston, New York, and other cities.

The English ballad opera tradition was also extremely popular in America during the early nineteenth century. These stage productions drew upon ballads, some of which had previously been circulated as broadsides. Perhaps the best known of the English ballad operas is John Gay's *The Beggar's Opera* (1728), designed to counter the domination of the British stage by Italian composers and musicians. The main characters in ballad operas were common people, rather than the kings and queens of imported operas; the songs were familiar in form and content; and the lyrics were all in English rather than Italian.

The pleasure gardens and ballad operas both featured songs produced by professional composers for large and diverse audiences. Melodies were designed to be simple and easy to remember, and the lyrics focused on romantic themes.

Dance music was another important aspect of the European influence on American popular music. Until the late nineteenth century European American dance was closely modeled on styles imported from England and the Continent. Country dances—in which dancers arranged themselves into circles, squares, or opposing rows—were popular. In the United States the country dance tradition developed into a plethora of urban and rural, elite and lower-class, black and white variants. It continues today in country and western line dances and in the contradances that form part of the modern folk music scene.

The nineteenth century also saw a move toward couple dances, including the **waltz,** the galop, the schottische, and the ballroom polka, the last based on a Bohemian dance that had already become the rage in the ballrooms of Paris and London before coming to America. Later, in the 1880s, a fast dance called the one-step, based in part on marching band music, became popular. These couple dances are direct predecessors of the African American–influenced popular dance styles of the early twentieth century, including the two-step, fox-trot, bunny hug, and Charleston.

Meanwhile, the English folk ballad tradition continued to thrive in America, and songs were reworked to suit the life circumstances of new immigrants. In the early twentieth century folklorists interested in continuities with English traditions were still able to record dozens of versions of old English ballads in the United States. While today these songs are preserved mainly by folk music enthusiasts, the core of the tradition—including its musical forms and storytelling techniques—lives on in contemporary country and western music. In addition, vocal qualities derived from the Anglo-American tradition—notably the thin, nasalized tone known as the "high lonesome sound"—continue today as markers of southern white identity.

The roots of country music lie in recordings of so-called **hillbilly music** made by record companies in the 1920s. This diverse body of music (later called "country and western" or simply "country music") developed mainly out of the folksongs, ballads, and dance music of immigrants from the British Isles. These early recordings of string bands (featuring some combination of fiddle, guitar, banjo, and mandolin), solo and duet singers (often accompanying themselves on stringed instruments or piano), white gospel ("Sacred Harp") singers, and championship yodelers were the predecessors of today's country music mega-hits. The first musicians to be commercially recorded in the rural South, while heavily steeped in earlier traditions, were also familiar with sentimental popular songs produced by professional songwriters in northern urban centers such as New York City. This cosmopolitan material became an important part of the country music repertoire, alongside the older Anglo-American ballads and fiddle tunes that still form such an important part of country music's identity and sense of tradition.

The mainstream of English-dominated popular song and dance music was from early on surrounded by a myriad of folk and popular styles brought by immigrants from other parts of Europe. The descendants of early French settlers in North America and the Caribbean maintained their own musical traditions. Millions of Irish and German immigrants came to the United States during the nineteenth century, seeking an escape from oppression, economic uncertainty, and—particularly during the potato famine of the 1840s—the threat of starvation. Between 1880 and 1910 an additional seventeen million immigrants entered the United States, mostly from eastern and southern Europe. These successive waves of migration contributed to the diversity of musical life in the United States. European-derived musical styles such as Cajun (Acadian) fiddling, Jewish klezmer music, and the Polish polka—an energetic dance, quite different from the "refined" style of polka discussed above—have each contributed to mainstream popular music while maintaining a core audience in their community of origin.

The African American Stream

Not all immigrants came willingly. Between one and two million people from Africa, about 10 percent of the total transatlantic traffic in slaves, were forcibly brought to the United States between the seventeenth and nineteenth centuries. The areas of western and central Africa from which slaves were drawn were home to hundreds of distinct societies, languages, and musical traditions.

The genesis of African American music in the United States involved two closely related processes. The first of these was syncretism, the selective blending of traditions derived from Africa and Europe. The second important process was the creation of institutions that became important centers of black musical life—the family, the church, the voluntary association, the school, and so on.

It is misleading to speak of "black music" as a homogeneous entity. African American culture took different forms in Brazil, Cuba, Haiti, Jamaica, and the United States, shaped by the particular mix of African and European (and in some cases American Indian) source traditions, and by local social conditions. In the United States, people from the Senegambia region of West Africa—the Wolof, Mandinka, and other groups—appear to have made up a large part of the slave population.

Kunta Kinte, the ancestor of *Roots* author Alex Haley, was a Wolof man from what is today the nation of Gambia; the banjo, an African American invention, was developed from stringed instruments common in the Senegambia region; and certain aspects of blues singing, including the role of the musician as a social critic, are derived from the griot (praise singer) traditions of the West African savannah.

Certain features of African music form the core of African American music and, by extension, of American popular music as a whole. **Call-and-response** forms, in which a lead singer and chorus alternate, the leader being allowed more freedom to elaborate his part, are a hallmark of African American musical traditions. In much African music making, repetition is regarded as an aesthetic strength, and many forms are constructed of relatively short phrases—often two to eight beats in length—that recur in a regular cycle. These short phrases are combined in various ways to produce music of great power and complexity. In African American music such repeated patterns are often called **riffs.**

The aesthetic interest of much African music lies in the interlocking of multiple repeating patterns to form dense **polyrhythms** (textures in which many rhythms are going on at the same time). This technique is evident in African American styles such as funk music, particularly the work of James Brown, and the instrumental accompaniments ("beats") for contemporary rap recordings. One common West African rhythm pattern has generated many variants in the Americas, including the "hambone" riff popularized during the rock 'n' roll era by Bo Diddley, Johnny Otis, and Buddy Holly.

In contrast to the aesthetics of Western art music, in which a "clear" tone is the ideal, African singers and instrumentalists often make use of a wide palette of timbres. Buzzing tones are often created by attaching a rattling device to an instrument, and singers frequently use growling and humming effects, a technique that can also frequently be heard in African American genres such as blues, gospel, and jazz. In West African drumming traditions the lead or master drummer often plays the lowest-pitched drum in the group. This emphasis on low-pitched sounds may be a predecessor of the prominent role of the bass drum in Mississippi black fife-and-drum ensembles and of the "sonic boom bass" aesthetic in rap music (the *whoooomp!* created by heavily amplified low-frequency signals). Kurtis Blow, a pioneering hip-hop artist, described the rap producer's goal in terms of breaking car speakers, house speakers, and boom boxes, identifying this as "African music"!

The influence of African musical aesthetics and techniques on American popular music has been profound. The history of this influence, which we shall examine in some detail, reveals both the creativity of black musicians and the persistence of racism in the music business and American society as a whole. The origins of a distinctively American style of popular entertainment lie in the minstrel show of the mid-nineteenth century, in which white performers artificially darkened their skin and mimicked black music, dance, and dialect. In the early twentieth century African American ragtime, the blues, and jazz profoundly shaped the mainstream of American popular song.

The record industry's "discovery" of black music can be traced to a set of recordings made in 1920 by the black vaudeville performer Mamie Smith (1883–1946). Her recording of "Crazy Blues" on OKeh Records sold an astounding seventy-five thousand copies within one month, mainly in black communities (at that time, five thousand sales of a given recording allowed a record company to recoup its production costs, meaning that any further record sales were almost all profit). Mamie Smith's records were soon available at music stores, drugstores, furniture stores, and other outlets in northern and midwestern cities, and throughout the Deep South.

The promotional catch-phrase "race music" was first applied by <u>Ralph Peer</u> (1892–1960), a white Missouri-born talent scout for OKeh Records, who had worked as an assistant on Mamie Smith's first recording sessions. Although it might sound derogatory today, the term *race* was used in a positive sense in urban African American communities during the 1920s and was an early example of black nationalism; an individual who wanted to express pride in his heritage might refer to himself as "a race man." The term was soon picked up by other companies and was also widely used by the black press. The performances released on "race records" included a variety of musical styles—blues, jazz, gospel choirs, vocal quartets, string bands, and jug-and-washboard bands—and verbal performances such as sermons, stories, and comic routines. However, not all recordings featuring African American artists were automatically classified as "race records." For example, recordings by black dance orchestras or jazz bands with a substantial white audience were listed in the mainstream pop record catalogs, and a few records by African American artists even found their way into the "hillbilly" or "country music" catalogs.

This raises an important point: despite the segregation and widespread racial prejudice of early twentieth-century America, neither the African American nor the European American streams of musical influence existed in isolation. Although country music is typically identified as a "white" style, some of its biggest stars—for example, Ray Charles and Charley Pride—have been black, and the styles of influential country musicians such as Hank Williams and Willie Nelson were strongly influenced by African American music. One could cite many more examples of the influence of black music on the musical "mainstream" of America: The "jazz age" of the 1920s and the "swing era" of the 1930s and 1940s involved the reworking of African American dance music so it would appeal to a predominantly white middle-class audience; 1950s rock 'n' roll was, in large part, rhythm & blues (R&B) music reworked for a predominantly white teen music market; the influence of 1960s soul music, rooted in black gospel and R&B, is heard in the vocal style of practically every pop singer, from Bonnie Raitt and Whitney Houston to Bruce Springsteen and Michael Jackson; the virtuoso guitar style of heavy metal owes a large debt to the urban blues of Muddy Waters and Howlin' Wolf; and rap music, based on African-derived musical and verbal traditions, continues to provide many white Americans with a vicarious experience of "listening in" on black urban culture.

We could say, then, that with every passing year American popular music has moved closer to the core aesthetic values and techniques of African music. Yet this way of phrasing the matter is somewhat misleading, for it directs attention away from the fact that African Americans are Americans, that the ancestors of black Americans arrived in the United States before the forebears of many white Americans. The complex history of interaction between European American and African American styles, musicians, and audiences demonstrates the absurdity of racism, just as it attests to the unfortunate tenacity of racial thinking in America.

The Latin American Stream

As in the United States, musicians in Latin America—those parts of the Americas colonized by Spain, Portugal, and France—developed a wide range of styles blending African music with the traditions of southern Europe. Over the course of the last century the diverse musical styles of the Caribbean, South America, and Mexico have exerted a steady, if often underrecognized, influence on popular music in the United States.

The first Latin American style to have a major international impact was the Cuban habanera, an African-influenced variant of the European country-dance tradition that swept the United States and Europe in the 1880s. The characteristic habanera rhythm—an eight-beat pattern divided 3–3–2—influenced late nineteenth-century ragtime music and was an important part of what the great New Orleans pianist Ferdinand "Jelly Roll" Morton called the "Latin tinge" in American jazz.

The next wave of Latin American influence on the music of the United States came from Argentina. The tango, initially played by musicians in the capital city of Buenos Aires, was influenced by the Cuban habanera rhythm, Italian and Spanish songs, and the songs of gauchos (cowboys). The tango reached Europe in the 1910s, where it was popularized by Carlos Gardel, a film and recording star who is today regarded as a national hero in Argentina. In the United States the ballroom version of the tango, a couple dance featuring close contact between partners and an insistent rhythm, was popularized around 1914 by the dance stars Irene and Vernon Castle. One of the first big tango stars was Rudolph Valentino, whose film persona somewhat indiscriminately mixed the stereotypes of the "Latin lover" and the proud and independent Middle Eastern sheik.

The next wave of Latin American musical influence was the rumba. The roots of the ballroom rumba style that became popular in the United States lie in 1920s Cuba. The rural *son*—a Cuban parallel of "country music"—moved to the city of Havana, where it was played by professional dance bands. These musicians created a more exciting style by adding rhythms from the rumba, an urban street drumming style strongly rooted in African traditions.

A "refined" version of rumba, developed by musicians working at tourist hotels in Cuba, was introduced to the world by Don Azpiazú and his Havana Casino Orchestra. Azpiazú's 1929 recording of "El Manicero" ("The Peanut Vendor") became a huge international hit. Within a few months of its release many dance orchestras in the United States had recorded their own versions of the song, a phenomenon later known as "covering" a hit song. The rumba reached a height of popularity in the United States during the 1930s and was succeeded by a series of Cuban-based ballroom dance fads, including the mambo (1940s) and cha-cha-chá (1950s).

Variants of Cuban-based music in the United States ranged from the exciting blend of modern jazz and rumba pioneered by Machito and Dizzy Gillespie in the 1940s to the tourist-oriented style performed by Desi Arnaz's orchestra on the *I Love Lucy* television show. The 1960s saw the emergence of salsa, a rumba-based style pioneered by Cuban and Puerto Rican migrants in New York City. The stars of salsa music include the great singer Celia Cruz and the bandleader Tito Puente. In the 1980s Miami Sound Machine created a commercially successful blend of salsa and disco music, and "world beat" musicians such as Paul Simon and David Byrne began to experiment with traditional Afro-Cuban rhythms.

The Brazilian samba is another dance style strongly rooted in African music. The variant of samba that had the biggest influence in the United States was the carioca, a smooth style developed in Rio de Janeiro. The carioca was boosted in the

1940s by the meteoric career of Carmen Miranda, who appeared in a series of popular musical films. A cool, sophisticated style of Brazilian music called the bossa nova ("new trend") became popular in United States during the early 1960s, eventually spawning hit songs such as "The Girl from Ipanema" (1964).

Mexican music has long had a symbiotic relationship with styles north of the Rio Grande. At the end of the nineteenth century Mexican musicians visited the World's Columbian Exposition in Chicago (an early example of the world's fair) and later toured throughout the United States. The two best-known Mexican-derived styles today are *conjunto acordeon* ("accordion band") music, played in northern Mexico and Texas, and mariachi music, a staple of the Mexican tourist trade, performed by ensembles made up of guitars, violins, and trumpets. Country and western music has been influenced by Mexican styles since at least the 1930s. Mexican immigrants in California (Chicanos) have also played an important role in the development of rock music. This continuing influence is exemplified by Ritchie Valens's 1959 hit "La Bamba," based on a folk tune from Veracruz; the mixture of salsa and guitar-based rock music developed in the late 1960s by the guitarist Carlos Santana; recordings of traditional Mexican songs by Linda Ronstadt; and the hard-rocking style of the Los Angeles–based band Los Lobos.

In this chapter we have discussed some unifying themes that run through the history of American popular music and described some of the diverse traditions that have contributed to this rich history. Now we want to turn to the decade following World War II, when the music industry began to notice a newly affluent teenage audience, and styles such as rhythm & blues and country and western music—the immediate ancestors of rock 'n' roll—began their move into the popular mainstream.

CHAPTER TWO

"CHOO CHOO CH' BOOGIE"
THE PREHISTORY OF ROCK 'N' ROLL, 1945–1955

The decade leading up to the emergence of rock 'n' roll is often portrayed as a period of musical stagnation or, at best, gestation. In fact, it could be argued that the decade after World War II was one of the most interesting, complex, and dynamic eras in the history of American popular music. The entertainment industry grew rapidly after the war, and in 1947 record companies achieved retail sales of over $214 million, finally surpassing the previous peak, established back in 1921, more than a quarter of a century earlier. This growth was supported by the booming postwar economy and by a corresponding increase in the disposable income of many American families.

In particular, record companies began for the first time to target young people, many of whom had more pocket money to spend on records than ever before. During World War II the demand for workers in military-related industries meant that many teenagers took on adult responsibilities, working for wages while continuing to attend high school. The idea that teenagers had the right to earn a salary of their own led after the war to the widespread practice of a weekly allowance in return for doing the household chores. Many young adults spent a considerable portion of their income on films, jukeboxes, and records. A survey of record retailers conducted in 1949 estimated that people under twenty-one constituted fully one-third of the total record-buying population of the United States, a great increase from previous eras. Although the music produced by the largest record companies was still mainly aimed at an older audience, the increasing importance of a new marketing category—the teenager—was a harbinger of the rock 'n' roll era.

Many of the hit records of the late 1940s and early 1950s were romantic songs, performed by crooners—sweet-voiced singers who used the microphone to create a sense of intimacy—with orchestral string backing. The sentimentality of these songs can be gleaned from their titles: "Prisoner of Love" and "(I Love You) For Sentimental Reasons" (1946), "My Darling, My Darling" and "You're Breaking My Heart" (1949), "Cold, Cold Heart" and "Cry" (1951), "No Other Love" and "You You You" (1953), all Number One pop hits. Big-band swing—the dominant jazz-based popular music style of the World War II era—was also supplanted by the romantic "light music" of Jackie Gleason, Percy Faith, and Mantovani and His Orchestra. These recordings typically featured string orchestras or choruses, with an occasional light touch of the exotic—maracas, castanets, a harpsichord, or a vaguely Latin rhythm. (These "easy listening" records soon became a mainstay of Muzak, a corporation that had since the late 1930s supplied businesses with recorded music, designed to subliminally encourage worker productivity.) Romantic vocal and orchestral recordings were interspersed on the hit charts with catchy, light-hearted novelty songs, including Number One hits such as "Woody Woodpecker" (Kay Kyser, 1948), "The Thing" (Phil Harris, 1950), "I Saw Mommy Kissing Santa Claus" (Jimmy Boyd, 1952), and "The Doggie in the Window" (Patti Page, 1953).

The roots of this musical conservatism are not difficult to pinpoint. Although there was a brief depression just after the war (see the discussion of "Choo Choo Ch' Boogie" below), the national economy expanded rapidly during the postwar decade, fueled by the lifting of wartime restrictions on the production of consumer goods, the increased availability of jobs in the industrial and service sectors of the economy, and the G.I. Bill, which provided educational and job opportunities for returning servicemen. After the uncertainty and personal sacrifice of the war years, many people simply wanted to settle down, raise a family, and focus on building their own futures. For millions of Americans who had served in the armed forces, or had come to the city in search of work during the war, or whose immigrant parents and grandparents had fled poverty earlier in the century, this represented the first opportunity to buy a home. If we also take into account the underlying uncertainties and tensions of the postwar era—including the threat of nuclear war and Cold War conflicts in Europe and Asia—it makes perfect sense that many new members of the American middle class preferred popular music that focused on romantic sentiments and helped to create a comforting sound environment in the home.

The economics of the music industry also played a role in this conservative trend and in the uneven quality of much mainstream pop music produced during this period. During the postwar decade we can see clearly for the first time a phenomenon that has helped to shape the development of popular music in the United States ever since: a constant tug-of-war between, on the one hand, the music business's efforts to predict (and therefore perchance control) the public's consumption of music, and on the other hand, the periodic eruption of new musical fads, usually based in youth culture. In general, the center of the music business—like many other sectors of corporate America—became increasingly routinized after the war. Music was now a product, sold in units, and listeners were consumers.

The idea of *Top 40 radio programming*—another attempt to control the uncertainty of the marketplace—was developed in the early 1950s by Todd Storz, a **disc jockey** in Omaha, Nebraska. Storz observed teenagers dropping coins in jukeboxes and noticed that they tended to play certain songs repeatedly. He applied this idea to radio programming, selecting a list of forty top hits, which he played over and over. The idea spread quickly, and within a few years many stations were playing the same set of songs. The ability of radio stations to control the public's exposure to new recordings led to a practice called **payola,** in which record companies paid DJs to put their records into "heavy rotation." By the mid-1950s this profitable practice had come under legal scrutiny, ending the careers of some prominent record executives and disc jockeys.

If the late 1940s and early 1950s were generally profitable for the music business—publishing firms, licensing agencies, record corporations, and radio networks—it was also a period of uncertainty. The executives who ran these powerful institutions, and who were therefore in charge of deciding how much and what sorts of music would be recorded and broadcast, were mainly veterans of an earlier era. Many of these men looked down their noses at the idea of producing music for a teenage audience, and this ultimately limited their ability to spot and exploit new trends.

At the same time, the increasingly rapid turnover of hit songs on the radio and jukebox meant that record companies started producing many more records than the public was willing to buy. In general, the big record companies competed by saturating the market with records, sometimes sending as many as one hundred thousand copies of a new record out to stores, with a guarantee that storekeepers could return all of the discs they didn't sell. This is clearly not a sound business strategy, and it adversely affected the overall quality of pop music during the early 1950s—one record company executive referred to the technique of market saturation as "throwing a lot of shit at the wall to see if anything sticks" (Clarke 1995, p. 311).

In general, the major record companies of the postwar period—RCA Victor, Columbia, Decca, and a new Los Angeles–based company, Capitol Records—experienced considerable growth. At the same time, however, musical genres regarded as marginal by the industry came to influence even more strongly the musical taste of middle-class white Americans. Back in the 1920s both the major record companies of the day and smaller upstart firms had begun to market recordings of musicians from the American South, performing music that drew upon a variety of rural folk music ultimately derived from ancestral traditions in Europe and Africa. The market for this music was broadly segregated by race, the recordings of white artists often being classified as "hillbilly music," and recordings of black artists as "race music." By the 1940s the pattern of racial segregation persisted, but the categories had been renamed, respectively, "country and western music" and "rhythm & blues."

Country and western music expanded its audience during World War II, and this trend continued through the early 1950s. The market for rhythm & blues also expanded as a result of postwar prosperity—the income of the average black family tripled during the war—and a growing (though still small) white audience, whose musical conversion had been prepared by the swing era. This market was supported by a new generation of music publishers and independent record labels, such as Chess (Chicago), Aladdin (Los Angeles), Atlantic (New York), King (Cincinnati), Sun (Memphis), and Duke/Peacock (Houston).

In addition, changes in the licensing of live and recorded music made it easier for country and western and rhythm & blues songwriters and music publishers to receive fees ("royalties") when their compositions were broadcast over the radio, used in movies and television shows, or performed live. *Licensing and copyright agencies* such as *ASCAP* (*The American Society of Composers, Authors, and Publishers*) and

BMI (*Broadcast Music, Incorporated*) control the flow of profits from the sale, broad-casting, and live performance of popular music. ASCAP was founded in 1914 in an attempt to force all business establishments that featured live music to pay royal-ties for the public use of music. By the 1920s almost all leading publishing houses and composers belonged to ASCAP, and by 1939 ASCAP had licensed around 90 percent of mainstream pop songs. As profits from radio broadcasts rose—partly stimulated by the big band craze—ASCAP turned up the legal pressure on the ra-dio networks (ABC, CBS, NBC, and Dumont) to turn over a larger portion of their revenues. In 1940 the radio networks counterattacked by forming BMI, a rival li-censing agency specifically designed to challenge ASCAP's monopoly. While BMI was not initially expected to survive for long, its "open door" policy allowed song-writers working outside of the mainstream pop to claim royalties from the use of their songs on the broadcast media, including radio and, increasingly, television. This gave a boost to musicians working in the idioms of country and western and rhythm & blues, genres which had largely been ignored by ASCAP and which rose in economic importance during and after World War II.

In retrospect, the music business of the late 1940s and early 1950s could be en-visioned as a Jurassic scenario, in which huge, slow, powerful carnivores ruled the roost, but only in continual competition with lighter, smaller, faster beasts. These little omnivores—independent record labels, renegade radio disc jockeys, talented musicians who had for various reasons been excluded from the wellsprings of profit, and entrepreneurs and hustlers of all stripes—shared a double advantage over the big guys. First, they were musically omnivorous, feeding on styles outside the main-stream of popular music; and second, they were more keenly attuned to changes in the environment, particularly the increasing importance of the teenage market for popular music. Although many of the little guys did get eaten, in the long run it was precisely these adaptive qualities that allowed them to play an indispensa-ble role in the development of American poplar music.

POPULAR MUSIC AND TECHNOLOGY IN THE POSTWAR ERA

During the decade following World War II the music industry was affected by the introduction of new technologies for the reproduction and transmission of musical sound and visual images. Magnetic tape recording, developed by the Germans and the Japanese during the 1930s, offered a number of advantages over the established means of recording music. In the recording studio, tape was better able to capture the full range of musical sounds than the older process of recording directly onto "master" phonograph discs. In addition, tape recording allowed musicians to rere-cord over the unsatisfactory parts of previous performances and to add layers of sound to a recording (a process called "overdubbing"). The best-known innovator in this field was the guitarist/inventor Les Paul (born 1915), who designed his own eight-track tape recorder and began in 1948 to release a series of popular record-ings featuring his own playing, overdubbed to sound like an ensemble of six or more guitars.

By the late 1940s recording studios were using audiotape, rather than "tran-scription discs," to produce most recordings, and some artists (notably the popular singer Bing Crosby) had begun to use tape to prerecord their appearances on radio. In 1948 the Ampex Corporation, backed by Crosby, introduced its first tape recorder, a machine that soon became a mainstay of the recording industry. The year 1949 saw the introduction of a two-track recorder, which could record simultaneous inputs from two microphones and thus produce stereo effects. While tape recorders were not initially successful as a home consumer item, the advantages of magnetic recording were felt immediately in the music industry.

The postwar era also saw a fierce competition over new disc technologies, known as the "Battle of the Speeds." In 1948 Columbia Records introduced the twelve-inch long-playing disc. Spinning at a speed of 33 1/3 revolutions per minute (r.p.m.), the LP could accommodate more than twenty minutes of music on each side, a great improvement over the three- to four-minute limitation of 78 r.p.m. discs. In addition, the LP was made of vinyl, a material at once more durable and less noisy than the shellac used to make 78s. In introducing the new discs at a Columbia Records board meeting, an executive put a fifteen-inch stack of LPs next to an eight-*foot* stack of 78s containing the same amount of music, in order to convince shareholders and the press to back the new technology. Interestingly, although the long-playing disc opened the possibility of longer uninterrupted recordings—a great advantage for fans of classical music and Broadway musicals—most pop music LPs were "albums" of three-minute performances. This suggests that what from the engineering point of view had seemed to be a technological restriction—the three-minute limit of 78 r.p.m. phonograph records—had long since become a musical habit. To this day, many pop music recordings are no longer than four minutes in length.

In 1949, responding to Columbia's innovation, the RCA Victor Corporation introduced yet another new disc format, the seven-inch 45 r.p.m. single. The "45," actually close to the old 78 r.p.m. discs in overall recording time, required a special mechanical record changer that fit the large hole at the center of the disc. However, 45s had at least one decided advantage from the consumer's viewpoint. Using a record changer, the listener could load a stack of singles, thus preprogramming a series of favorite recordings, each of which would begin less than fifteen seconds after the end of the previous record. This meant that consumers could focus their spending power on their favorite recordings, rather than buying a prepackaged series of songs by a single artist on an LP. Building on the basic principles of the jukebox, the marketing of 45s pointed the way forward to today's digital technologies, which allow consumers to program specific tracks in any order they choose.

In the end, the battle of the speeds was resolved by a technological compromise, in which turntables were set up to accommodate all three existing formats (78, 45, and 33 1/3 r.p.m.). LPs continued to serve as a medium for albums of pop songs and longer musical works such as Broadway cast recordings, while the 45 became the favored medium for distributing hit singles.

Radio broadcasting was also affected by technological change in the postwar period. In addition to the older AM (amplitude modulation) broadcasting technology that had dominated radio since the early 1920s, the postwar period saw the rapid growth of FM (frequency modulation) broadcasting. FM radio, which used higher frequencies than AM, had better sound quality and was not as easily subject to electrical disturbances such as lightning. The first commercial FM broadcast took place in 1939, and by 1949 around seven hundred FM stations were operating in the United States, along with well over one thousand AM stations. By the late 1950s FM was being used for stereo broadcasting.

Of all of the new electronic technologies of the postwar era, television exerted the most profound influence on American culture. The development of television broadcasting, foreseen by science fiction writers of the nineteenth century, started in earnest in the 1920s. At the 1939 New York World's Fair, RCA introduced its first fully electronic television system to the public. (At that time a television set cost $660, more than half the price of a new automobile!) During the war production of television was interrupted, but in the postwar years, with the economy booming and cheaper sets available, the new medium took off. In 1946 it was estimated that Americans owned six thousand television sets; this figure shot up to three million in 1948, then twelve million in 1951. For better or worse, by the early 1950s television had become the central focus of leisure time in millions of American households.

Television's massive success rested on its ability to fuse the forms and functions of previous media, including radio, the record player, and cinema. Like Hollywood film, television was a multiple medium, combining sound and moving images. Like radios and record players, the TV set could be brought into the family parlor (now called a "living room") and incorporated into the daily round of domestic life. TV quickly became the main outlet for corporate advertising, and by 1952 the four big networks—NBC, CBS, ABC, and Dumont—began to turn significant profits. TV broadcasters used a great deal of recorded and live music, and the postwar era saw the eruption of complex legal disputes over fees to be paid for use of songs on the air (a recapitulation of the battles between radio and the music business during the 1930s and 1940s). On the one hand, there can be no doubt that the new medium was perceived by the record industry as a threat: in 1949 retail sales of records fell drastically, while sales of television sets increased by some 400 percent. By the mid-1950s, however, television had become the most important medium for launching new performers and recordings, and established stars such as Perry Como, Nat "King" Cole, Tommy Dorsey, and Jackie Gleason hosted their own weekly variety shows.

LISTENING TO THREE BIG HITS FROM THE POSTWAR DECADE

We pause now to spend some sustained time with three representative hit records from the period under discussion. In doing so, we will not only become familiar with characteristic sounds of this decade but also begin to develop skills in listening critically to popular music, and to become familiar with terminology and concepts that will prove essential in our survey of the history of rock music. The conceptions of *rhythm, melody, harmony,* and *form* reflected in these examples have their roots in music that substantially predates these particular hits. Yet the influence of these conceptions also extended far into the future, as we shall soon see.

The three records, representing diverse styles, are "Goodnight, Irene" by the Weavers (1950), "Choo Choo Ch'Boogie" by Louis Jordan's Tympany Five (1946), and "Love and Marriage" by Frank Sinatra (1955). They will be considered in this order because, from the standpoint of musical form, "Goodnight, Irene" presents the simplest conception, while the other two present a somewhat more elaborate approach. (This in no way implies that the other two are either "better" records or that they are necessarily more "difficult" to understand or to enjoy!) In this section, we will deliberately isolate the musical aspects of these hits in order to concentrate on the listening experience they provide; the larger stylistic and cultural contexts of these recordings will emerge from the discussions that follow this section.

"Goodnight, Irene"

"Goodnight, Irene" is a perfect illustration of one of the oldest and most enduring of all musical forms: the **strophic** song. In a strophic song, a musical unit—which may be of any length, but typically is rather short—is heard and then repeated over and over again, to changing words. (The term is derived from the literary term *strophe,* indicating a poetic unit that contains a certain number of lines, usually with a set pattern of meter and rhyme.) The vocal *melody*, which is the pattern of pitches and rhythms to which the words are sung, remains the same in a strophic song for each of the poetic **strophes** in the song's lyrics.

Strophic songs are found in virtually all types and styles of music: in the folk cultures of many countries, in African American blues, in the early "hillbilly" music of the American rural South, and in all the periods of American popular song. It is easy to understand why this is true. Strophic songs, because of the repetitive nature of their music, are easy to learn and to remember. They can also readily be used by performers to encourage listeners to participate by singing along; the Weavers, in fact, made a habit of concluding their public appearances with "Goodnight, Irene," urging their audiences to sing with them. In addition, strophic songs can be almost infinitely adaptable, lending themselves to the spontaneous alteration of lyrics and to the creation of new poetic strophes to fit new occasions, new contexts, new performers, and new audiences—since everybody, presumably, either knows the tune to begin with or else can learn it in short order.

In "Goodnight, Irene" each strophe may be divided into two parts: the **verse,** in which the words change from strophe to strophe; and the **chorus,** in which both the music *and* the words remain the same from strophe to strophe. This offers a source of variety and interest within the strophic form, as each strophe presents one section that remains consistent and completely predictable, and another section in which the words change, revealing a new event or twist in the developing story. Again, it seems obvious why this verse-chorus arrangement became a favored approach to strophic form. The Weavers' recording of "Goodnight, Irene," clearly preserves a feeling for the basic verse-chorus strophe, while using the catchy chorus melody independently as a **hook** at the beginning of the record and as a means to facilitate a fade-out effect at the end. This formal arrangement is diagrammed below.

"Goodnight, Irene": OUTLINE OF THE FORM

[brief instrumental introduction]

CHORUS: *Irene, goodnight* . . .

[instruments, background voices repeat the chorus tune]

Strophe 1:   **VERSE:**   *Last Saturday night* . . .

CHORUS: *Irene, goodnight* . . .

Strophe 2:   **VERSE:**   *Sometimes I live* . . .

CHORUS: *Irene, goodnight* . . .

Strophe 3:   **VERSE:**   *Stop ramblin'* . . .

CHORUS: *Irene, goodnight* . . .

[chorus is repeated, fading out]

A closer look at the chorus of "Goodnight, Irene" will help introduce some basic concepts of melody and rhythm. The chorus may readily be subdivided into four *phrases*, brief melodic patterns separated from one another by breathing spaces (pauses or *rests*) in the vocal line:

Irene, goodnight; [vocal pause]
Irene, goodnight; [vocal pause]
Goodnight, Irene, goodnight, Irene, [brief vocal pause]
I'll see . . . dreams. [vocal pause]

Each phrase varies in pitch content, sometimes going higher and sometimes lower, in patterns that mimic the natural inflections of spoken words; phrases that "sing" naturally are generally a hallmark of effective songwriting. As is typical of most speech, the vocal melody tends to fall in pitch at the ends of phrases. Some phrase endings seem musically more conclusive than others; in the chorus of "Goodnight, Irene" this is true of the second and fourth phrases, both of which end on the same pitch. When the melody reaches such a temporary stopping point—what we might call the end of a musical "sentence"—musicians call this a **cadence**. The feeling of cadence will almost always be reinforced by events in the *harmony*, or the **chord** structure, of the music accompanying the melody, and this is certainly true in "Goodnight, Irene."

Attentive listening will reveal that each of the verses in "Goodnight, Irene" is constructed analogously to the chorus. Even though the melody for the verses is obviously not the same as the melody for the chorus, each verse also may be divided into four phrases, with clear cadences occurring at the ends of the second and fourth phrases.

We have considered melody, harmony, and form, but have left out what is probably the most basic of all musical elements, *rhythm*, the movement through time that in fact shapes melody, harmony, and form. In most popular music, the passage of time is marked by regular rhythmic pulses or *beats*. Beats are equal measurements of musical time; when you tap your foot or your finger to a tune, you are sensing and indicating its beats. In "Goodnight, Irene" the musical instruments start to articulate the beats shortly after the recording begins, and this regular beat then persists throughout the rest of the record, right through the fade-out. All beats are not equally intense, however, and a larger, regular rhythmic pattern is created by the significant *accent* given to every third beat:

One, two three; **One,** two three; **One,** two three; and so on.

These groups of three beats, defined by the regular accents, are called *measures*, or *bars*. (The three-beat bars—or triple *meter*—of "Goodnight, Irene" evoke the rhythm of the **waltz,** a dance whose popularity dates back to the nineteenth century.) It may also be noticed that the phrases of the vocal melody in this song all extend over a span four bars in length. Thus a great consistency characterizes the rhythmic patterns of this song at every level: a regular beat; constant three-beat measures; phrases that are all four bars in length (with cadences occurring regularly at the end of every other phrase); four-phrase verses and four-phrase choruses, producing in turn uniform eight-phrase strophes. Such regularity is typical of popular music, since it results in easily remembered, reassuringly predictable patterns that lend themselves readily to singing and dancing. Of course, too much regularity would result in boredom, so most popular records tread a fine line between what is predictable and what creates novelty and interest. In the Weavers' "Goodnight, Irene" the interest aroused by the changing words of the verses is reinforced musically by having a different member of the group sing each verse.

"Choo Choo Ch' Boogie"

"Choo Choo Ch' Boogie," while obviously very different in musical style from "Goodnight, Irene," is actually quite similar in musical form. It too is a strophic song with three verse-chorus strophes; see the accompanying listening chart. The fact that both of these songs share this basic form illustrates how useful and flexible a formal conception the strophic song with verses and a chorus can be.

The listening chart for "Choo Choo Ch' Boogie" is our first example of the fully detailed charts that will be presented regularly throughout this book to facilitate in-depth discussion of some particularly significant recordings. The reader is urged to refer to the chart to reinforce and supplement the discussion that follows, and also to use the chart as a visual aid when listening to the record.

One of the most immediately apparent and important differences between "Choo Choo Ch' Boogie" and "Goodnight, Irene" is that the rhythm of the former is based on regular *four-beat bars*, as opposed to the regular triple meter of "Irene." That is to say, the rhythmic accents in "Choo Choo Ch' Boogie" create the following steady pattern:

One, two three, four; **One,** two, three, four; **One,** two, three four; and so on.

(By far the most common meters found in all styles and periods of American popular music are quadruple meter, triple meter, and duple—a simple **one,** two—meter.) The four-beat bars of "Choo Choo Ch' Boogie" are arranged into two-bar phrases; each phrase corresponds to one line of the lyrics, as may be seen in the listening chart. The verses are all twelve bars (six phrases) in length, while the choruses are all eight bars (four phrases) in length, and this in turn creates consistent strophes of twenty bars each.

All this is hopefully straightforward enough to hear and to understand, but it is now important to pause briefly over the *internal* form of the twelve-bar verses.

This runs the risk of becoming slightly technical, but these verses exemplify the musical pattern of *twelve-bar* **blues**—an arrangement of rhythm and chords that has been employed so extensively in American popular music, especially in the rock era, that it demands our attention here.

Technical Note: Twelve-Bar Blues

Twelve-bar blues refers to a particular arrangement of four-beat bars. The bars are themselves grouped in phrases of two or four, with characteristic **chord** changes occurring at certain points. The issue of harmony in the twelve-bar blues is a complex one, especially since the chord progressions in a form as widespread and diverse as the blues will by no means be absolutely systematic or consistent from case to case. Still, the twelve-bar blues does tend to be marked by specific chord changes at particular points, and our present example—"Choo Choo Ch' Boogie"—offers a conveniently straightforward illustration of these changes in each of its verses. (The important thing to remember is that the chord changes in twelve-bar blues need not be limited only to these typical ones.)

If we call our starting chord the "home" chord (musicians would call it the **tonic**), this chart shows the most important, typical points of change in the twelve-bar blues pattern:

```
BARS:     1      2     3     4
CHORDS:   ↑ "Home" . . . . . . . .

BARS:     5      6     7     8
CHORDS:   ↑ Change 1   ↑ "Home"

BARS:     9      10    11    12
CHORDS:   ↑ Change 2   ↑ "Home"
```

Note that the chords at "changes" 1 and 2 are different from one another; thus, there are three essential chords that define the skeleton of the musical structure. (Musicians call the chord at bar 5 the *subdominant*, and the chord at bar 9 the *dominant*.) These are the same three chords that define the harmony in the verses of "Choo Choo Ch' Boogie," and they occur at precisely the rhythmic points shown above. To illustrate specifically, here is what happens in the first verse. The numbers of the bars show where the accent (the **one**) of the bar in question falls, and the chord changes always occur on the accented beats; remember to count the four beats in each bar:

```
BARS:     1                                2
LYRICS:   Headin' for the station with a pack on my back
CHORDS:   Home (tonic) . . . . . . . .

          3                                4
          I'm tired of transportation in the back of a hack
          [home (tonic)] . . . . . . . .

          5                                6
          I love to hear the rhythm of a clickety-clack
          Change 1 (subdominant) . . . . . . . .
```

7　　　　　　　　　　　　　　8
And hear the lonesome whistle, see the smoke from the stack
Home (tonic) . . . .

9　　　　　　　　　　　　　　10
And pal around with democratic fellows named Mac
Change 2 (dominant) . . . .

11　　　　　　　　　　　　　　12
So take me right back to the track, Jack.
Home (tonic) . . . .

Thus, "Choo Choo Ch' Boogie" integrates the twelve-bar blues progression into a verse-chorus strophic structure. Verses in twelve-bar blues form alternate with the eight-bar choruses. Additional variety is created in the recording by the employment of purely instrumental episodes: an introduction, a concluding "tag," and passages following the first and second occurrences of the chorus (see the listening chart). The instrumental introduction follows the chord pattern of the twelve-bar blues; the horns (a trumpet and two saxophones) imitate the sound of a train whistle, while the rhythm section (piano, bass, and drums) establishes a medium-tempo rhythm. (This infectious four-beat dance rhythm, common in Louis Jordan's recordings, is also sometimes called a *shuffle*.) After the introduction a verse is sung by Louis Jordan, backed by **riffs** (repeated patterns) in the horn section. Then a chorus, also sung by Jordan, is followed by a twelve-bar blues piano solo. The whole sequence of verse-chorus-instrumental solo is then repeated (with a twenty-bar saxophone solo, representing both verse and chorus, instead of a piano solo). A third strophe is sung, and a slight variation at the end of this chorus leads into the concluding ten-bar tag.

LISTENING CHART "CHOO CHOO CH' BOOGIE"

Music and lyrics by Milt Gabler, Denver Darling, and Vaughan Horton; as performed by Louis Jordan's Tympany Five; recorded 1946

FORM	LYRICS	DESCRIPTIVE COMMENTS
INSTRUMENTAL INTRODUCTION		**12-bar blues**
		During the first four bars, the horns imitate the sound of a train whistle
Verse 1	Headin' for the station with a pack on my back	**12-bar blues**
	I'm tired of transportation in the back of a hack	
	I love to hear the rhythm of a clickety-clack	
	And hear the lonesome whistle, see the smoke from the stack	
	And pal around with democratic fellows named Mac	
	So take me right back to the track, Jack.	
Chorus	Choo choo, choo choo, ch' boogie	**8 bars**
	Woo woo, woo woo, ch' boogie	
	Choo choo, choo choo, ch' boogie	
	Take me right back to the track, Jack.	

Piano solo	12-bar blues
Verse 2 You reach your destination, but alas and alack	12-bar blues
You need some compensation to get back in the black	
You take a morning paper from the top of the stack	
And read the situations from the front to the back	
The only job that's open needs a man with a knack	
So put it right back in the rack, Jack.	
Chorus [as before]	8 bars
Saxophone solo	20 bars (12-bar blues+
	8-bar "chorus")
Verse 3 Gonna settle down by the railroad track	12-bar blues
And live the life of Riley in a beaten-down shack	
So when I hear a whistle I can peep through the crack	
And watch the train a-rollin', when it's ballin' the jack	
Why, I just love the rhythm of the clickety-clack	
So take me right back to the track, Jack.	
Chorus [as before]	8 bars
Tag: Instruments (with brief vocal interjection)	10 bars

"Love and Marriage"

"Love and Marriage" introduces us to another venerable form in American popular music, the four-section **AABA** form. Songs constructed along these lines typically have sections of equal length, three of them presenting identical (or nearly identical) music to (usually) different words, while one—the B section—presents new words *and* new music. The repetitions of the A music assure that the song will quickly become familiar to the listener, while the B section offers some musical variety within the form. The principles behind this formal strategy seem obvious enough: state an effective musical idea to "hook" the listener; restate it (usually with new words) in order to fix it in the listener's mind; then sustain attention with a deviation from the established pattern; and conclude with the gratifying return of the now-familiar basic idea. It is not surprising that many songwriters have turned to AABA organization for the construction of memorable songs.

It is a simple matter to hear the AABA organization in "Love and Marriage," especially since each of the A sections begins with identical words: the words of the title, which thus serve as a recurring musical and verbal hook. After a brief instrumental introduction, the song proceeds as follows:

A	*Love and marriage, love and marriage, go together . . .*
A	*Love and marriage, love and marriage, it's an institute . . .*
B	*Try, try . . .*
A	*Love and marriage, love and marriage, go together . . .*

Following the completion of the form, an instrumental interlude presents the A music again, after which Frank Sinatra reenters and sings the last two sections, B and A, once more. A brief instrumental passage ends the recording.

"Love and Marriage" is typical of AABA songs of this period insofar as it is organized rhythmically in regular four-beat bars that are grouped into sections of eight-bar length. We may also call attention to a few formal subtleties that lend interest and distinction to this particular example of AABA song form. It will be noticed that the music of the second A section is indeed identical to that of the first A—with one small but important exception: it ends on a different pitch from the first. This is significant because, as a result of this alteration in the vocal melody (and in the accompanying chord), there is a **cadence** at the end of the second A whereas there was no cadence concluding the first A. In a sense, the first A section sets up the second A, which in turn musically rounds off the first. The beginning of the B section is marked by a particularly striking change in the harmony, that helps to set the music of this section strongly apart. In fact, the B section in an AABA form is frequently called a **release**—or, even more commonly, a **bridge** (presumably because it links two A sections). The final A of "Love and Marriage" restates not only the music but also the words of the opening section. Monotony is decisively avoided, however, for two reasons. First of all, this concluding section is extended beyond the expected eight bars to reach a length of eleven bars. Secondly, unlike the first A, this section does reach a cadence (although we are, effectively, forced to wait for it), so it provides a definitive feeling both of rounding and of conclusion to the overall form. Because of the differences among the three A sections in "Love and Marriage," the form is perhaps best represented as AA'BA".

Although AABA seems initially to represent a formal conception very different from that of the strophic song, a brief glance at the earlier history of American popular song establishes a link between them. The employment of AABA song forms was at its height in the first half of the twentieth century, especially in the 1920s, 1930s, and 1940s. This period is frequently called "the golden age of Tin Pan Alley"—named for the area in New York City where music publishing was centered, and where the great songwriters of this period such as Irving Berlin and George Gershwin plied their trade. Many **Tin Pan Alley** songs were in fact written in a strophic verse-chorus form; however, a favored form emerged for the chorus in these songs, and that was the 16- or 32-bar AABA arrangement (with equal sections of four or eight bars, respectively). What happened over time, as these songs gained wide currency through multiple performances and arrangements, is that their verses came increasingly to seem optional or even dispensable, and the choruses alone endured. One of the reasons this might have occurred is that a 16-bar or especially a 32-bar chorus with an interesting internal form has sufficient substance by itself to sustain a performance or a recording. (For a demonstration of the validity of this idea, we need look no further than the Sinatra recording of "Love and Marriage," which shows no traces of a verse.) The increasingly free-standing choruses of Tin Pan Alley songs were often called **refrains,** and this term proves useful to distinguish them from the choruses in strophic songs that are almost always performed with their verses. In addition to AABA, a common form for Tin Pan Alley refrains was the four-section arrangement ABAC or some variant thereof; in ABAC forms, the concluding C section, while introducing new music, frequently includes some direct or indirect reference back to A, for obvious reasons of rounding and conclusiveness.

It should not surprise us that "Love and Marriage" employs a form inherited from the heyday of Tin Pan Alley, since the men who wrote the song, Sammy Cahn and James Van Heusen, as well as Frank Sinatra himself, all began their careers in the 1930s. Indeed, the style of this recording would probably have struck many young listeners in 1955 as old-fashioned, especially since rock 'n' roll was beginning to achieve national prominence at this time. (It should be noted, however, that the AABA form itself proved quite durable, and was used in many songs in the later twentieth century that sounded nothing remotely like "Love and Marriage"—as we shall see.) Still, there is some reason to believe that the creators of this record wanted it to have a certain contemporary edge. The arrangement is unquestionably upbeat, and Sinatra does not burden this hymn to the traditional values of domesticity and monogamy with any feeling of excessive reverence; in fact, his delivery of the lyrics seems at points to take on an almost ironic quality. Certainly the concluding instrumental gesture, a deliberately deflated, off-kilter rendering of a musical cliché, is designed to leave the listener smiling, if not chuckling.

Now, fortified with some understanding of song forms and musical concepts, let us return to our historical narrative.

POP CROONERS

By 1946 the main focus of popular attention had shifted away from celebrity bandleaders of the swing era such as Benny Goodman, Count Basie, and Glenn Miller and toward a new generation of crooners. Many of the top singers of the postwar era—including Frank Sinatra, Perry Como, Nat "King" Cole, Frankie Laine, Peggy Lee, and Rosemary Clooney—had started their careers just before and during the war singing in front of big dance bands. By the early 1950s these pop stars had been joined by a younger generation of vocalists, who specialized in sentimental ballads, novelty numbers—cheerful, disposable songs that often resembled advertising jingles—and crooner-style **cover versions** of country and western and rhythm & blues hits. These vocalists were promoted to the expanding teenage audience.

The musicians' union recording ban of 1942–44—which had banned instrumentalists from recording but did not apply to even the most musically gifted vocalists—encouraged a number of big-band singers to begin recording under their own names, sometimes with choral accompaniment. Those singers with the most entrepreneurial savvy, or the best business agents, were able to parlay this opportunity into long-lasting success. In addition, the music industry's mastery of cross-media promotion—on radio, films, and television—reached new heights. Following in the footsteps of Bing Crosby, many of the biggest singing stars of the postwar era also became film stars (for example, Frank Sinatra and Doris Day) or hosted their own television shows (Perry Como and Nat "King" Cole).

<u>Frank (Francis Albert) Sinatra</u> (1915–98) was one of the first big-band singers to take advantage of changes in the music business. Born into a working-class Italian family in Hoboken, New Jersey, Sinatra attracted public attention in 1935 when he appeared as a member of a vocal quartet on a popular radio show called Major Bowes' Amateur Hour. From 1937 to 1939 he worked as a singing waiter at the Rustic Cabin, a nightclub in New Jersey. (Although the job paid little, Sinatra wisely

Waiting for Frankie outside, and celebrating his presence inside. Frank Driggs Collection.

kept it because the place was wired for radio broadcasts.) In 1939 the bandleader Harry James hired him, and later that same year he joined the Tommy Dorsey Orchestra.

Promoted on radio, at the movies, and in the press (including biographical comic books aimed at high school–age females), Sinatra's popularity soared, culminating in the first documented example of modern pop hysteria, the so-called Columbus Day Riot of 1944. The occasion was a return engagement at the Paramount Theater by Sinatra and the Benny Goodman band, and thirty thousand fans—including thousands of teenage girls, called "bobby soxers"—showed up to claim tickets. The Paramount could seat only thirty-six hundred people, and many fans refused to leave after the first show, triggering a riot among fans lined up outside the theater. In a sense, Sinatra was the direct predecessor of the teen idols of the rock 'n' roll era, and of the Beatles after them. Falling into a "Sinatrance," young women cried, screamed, and tore their hair. They followed the singer everywhere, fighting for pieces of his clothing and treating his used cigarette butts as sacred objects. The press and public bestowed nicknames on Sinatra: he was *Swoonatra*, *The Sultan of Swoon*, or, simply, *The Voice*. Although Sinatra's popularity took a nosedive in the early 1950s—largely as a result of well-publicized difficulties in his personal life—his success in later years was in no small part due to the connection his audience perceived between his voice and his personality, each involving a delicate balance between emotionalism and rationality, deep feeling and technical control.

While few postwar crooners were able to match Frank Sinatra's artistry or longevity, this does not mean that there was no serious competition. Despite the very small number of African American artists on the pop music charts of the early 1950s, it could be argued that the greatest postwar crooner—in both musical and commercial terms—was a black musician, Nat "King" Cole (1917–65). Nathaniel Coles was born in Montgomery, Alabama, and his family moved to the South Side of Chicago when he was only four years old. His father was pastor of a Baptist

Frank Sinatra: the ultimate cool "saloon singer" in the 1950s. Frank Driggs Collection.

Nat "King" Cole performs in a nightclub, 1954. Courtesy Library of Congress.

church, and young Nat was playing organ and singing in the choir by the age of twelve. He made his first recording in 1936, in the Solid Swingers, a jazz band led by his brother Eddie Cole. Nat Cole, a brilliant piano improviser, exerted a strong influence on later jazz pianists such as Oscar Peterson and Bill Evans. He moved from Chicago to Los Angeles in 1937 and formed his own group, the King Cole Trio.

Nat "King" Cole was by far the most successful black recording artist of the postwar era, placing a total of fourteen recordings in the Top 10 pop charts between 1946 and 1954. Along with the Mills Brothers and Louis Jordan, Cole was one of the first African American musicians to cross over regularly to the predominantly white pop charts. Although he continued to record a range of material—including jazz performances with the King Cole Trio—Cole's biggest commercial successes were sentimental ballads, accompanied by elaborate orchestral arrangements: "(I Love You) For Sentimental Reasons" (1946); "Nature Boy" (1948); "Unforgettable" (1950); his biggest hit, "Mona Lisa" (1950), which sold over five million copies; and "Too Young" (1951), perhaps the first teenage love ballad.

Given the racial prejudice prevalent in the American music industry, and in society as a whole, Nat "King" Cole's professional success was truly remarkable, comparable to the baseball career of Jackie Robinson, who became the first black player in the major leagues in 1947. Promoted by Capitol Records as a "sepia Sinatra," Cole was the first black musician to host his own weekly radio series (1948–49) and the first to have a network television show (1956–57). He recorded hundreds of songs for Capitol Records, helping to keep the new Los Angeles–based company afloat during its early years. Nat "King" Cole entered a field dominated exclusively by white artists and bested all but the most popular of them in both artistic and commercial terms. And unlike many pop crooners of the time, Cole thought of himself first and foremost as a musician, a musician who sang because his public wanted him to sing. In response to jazz critics who lambasted him for his success as a pop crooner, Cole noted that critics weren't the ones who bought records: "They get 'em free."

URBAN FOLK MUSIC: THE WEAVERS

During the early 1950s a new genre of popular music, called "urban folk," showed up on the pop charts. This genre combined a number of seemingly contradictory tendencies. It was inspired by rural folk music, yet performed by urban intellectuals. While embracing populist, presumably anticommercial values, it was used by the record industry to generate millions of dollars in profits. Many urban folk recordings were seemingly harmless singalongs, designed to invite audience participation. Yet, only a few years after the initial burst of public interest in this music, some of its best-known practitioners were being persecuted for their political beliefs. And the record industry really didn't know what to do with urban folk music. Was it "folk music"? Or "country and western"? Or perhaps "novelty music"?

The first urban folk group to achieve commercial success was the Weavers, a quartet led by the singer, banjo player, and political activist Pete Seeger (b. 1919). The Weavers developed a repertoire based on American and international folk songs

Leadbelly, the composer of "Goodnight Irene," and **the Weavers** (Pete Seeger, Lee Hays, Fred Hellerman, Ronnie Gilbert). Courtesy Library of Congress.

and performed at union rallies, college concerts, and urban coffeehouses. The group was "discovered" at a New York City nightclub by Gordon Jenkins, the managing director of Decca Records, and between 1950 and 1954 they placed eleven records in the Top 40. It is difficult to gauge what impact the Weavers might have had on pop music had they been allowed to sustain their early success. Three members of the group, including Seeger, were accused of being Communists during the early 1950s.[1] (Their main accuser later admitted that he had fabricated the charges and went to prison for perjury.) Decca Records, unwilling to withstand the heat, dropped their contract, and the Weavers never again appeared on the pop music charts. Seeger, however, continued to play a leading role as a champion of folk music and a populist activist; he has been called "America's tuning fork."

The Weavers' singalong version of "Goodnight Irene," composed by the Louisiana-born musician Huddie Ledbetter (a.k.a. Leadbelly, 1889–1949), was the most successful of their recordings, reaching the Number One position on the pop charts in 1950. Of course, this is not folk music in any strict sense. On "Goodnight Irene" the Weavers were accompanied by the orchestral arrangement of Gordon Jenkins, who also worked with Frank Sinatra, Nat "King" Cole, and other pop stars. Despite their folksy informality, "Goodnight Irene" and the Weavers' other hits are pop records, through and through. They helped to define a niche in the popular market for folk-based popular music, including the later work of the Kingston Trio; Peter, Paul, and Mary; and Bob Dylan. In addition, the Weavers' use of international materials—including Israeli, Cuban, and South African songs—make them the first world beat artists, a category of popular music that would not emerge in defined form for another thirty years.

SOUTHERN MUSIC IN THE POSTWAR ERA

As we have already indicated, the market for forms of popular music rooted in the traditions of the American South emerged with new vigor after World War II. The old categories "race music" and "hillbilly music" underwent a series of name changes, reflecting shifts in social attitudes and in the music industry's perception of the economic potential of southern music. In 1942 *Billboard* (a music industry magazine that publishes weekly "charts" tracking the nationwide popularity of recordings) began for the first time to list these records, subsuming them under the single category "Western and Race," a hybrid designation that was soon changed to "American Folk Records." In 1949 *Billboard* began using the terms "Rhythm & Blues" and "Country and Western" as more dignified and up-to-date replacements for "Race" and "Hillbilly," respectively.

During the late 1930s and 1940s millions of people had migrated from the rural South in search of employment in defense-related industries. Cities such as

---

1. In the environment of the Cold War there was an upsurge of anticommunist sentiment in the United States. This led to hearings in the House of Representatives by the so-called Un-American Activities Committee, in which many people were targeted for alleged subversive activities and intentions. In the entertainment business, many careers were temporarily derailed or totally destroyed by this process.

Chicago, Detroit, Pittsburgh, New York, Washington, D.C., Nashville, Atlanta, and Los Angeles were all home to large populations of transplanted southerners, whose musical tastes were doubly shaped not only by their experience of rural traditions but also by the desire to forge new, urbanized identities (and thereby distance themselves from the stereotyped image of the "hick" or "rube"). This migrant population greatly expanded the target audience for southern-derived music, providing a steady source of support for the urban honky-tonks, juke joints, and lounges where country and western and rhythm & blues groups played.

Radio also played a crucial role in the popularization of these types of music. There was a substantial increase in the number of radio stations catering specially to transplanted southerners, some capable of saturating the entire country's airwaves, others low-wattage affairs with a broadcasting radius of only a few miles. The country music radio business was positively booming in the late 1940s and early 1950s, with new shows modeled on Nashville's *Grand Ole Opry* coming on the air in all of America's major cities and on hundreds of small stations that sprouted in rural areas. During the war a number of white disc jockeys began to mix black popular music in with their usual diet of pop records, and 1949 saw the inauguration of the first radio station dedicated exclusively to playing music for a black audience—WDIA in Memphis, Tennessee, featuring the popular blues musician and disc jockey B. B. King. (Although this station catered to a predominantly black audience in the Mississippi Delta area, it was in fact owned by white businessmen.) In 1953 a nationwide survey in *Billboard* reported that pop music accounted for an average of thirty-one hours a week of radio programming, with country music occupying eleven and a half hours, and **R&B** two and a half. (The rest of the time was taken up with news, sports, comedy, and drama.) While these figures may not seem impressive at first glance, the fact that country music was being heard more than an hour a day on average, and that R&B recordings were getting any airplay at all on mainstream pop radio stations, is an indication of the expanding audiences for these styles.

The jukebox business—which had expanded greatly during and just after the war—also played an important role in promoting country and western and rhythm & blues records. In addition, the Movieola—a type of jukebox that played short musical films or "soundies" on demand and was thus an ancestor of today's music videos—also played a part in popularizing southern-based musicians. The musicians' union recording ban of 1942–44 provided many southern-born musicians with new opportunities for recording. Because many of these performers did not belong to the musicians' union, the ban on studio recording did not apply to them, and they were free to continue making records.

Finally, the success of country and western and rhythm & blues music (and other nonmainstream styles such as the polka and Mexican-American music) was indebted to the reemergence, during and just after the war, of dozens of small independent record labels. As in the 1920s, this new generation of "indies" was made possible by a strong national economy and by the activity of small-scale entrepreneurs, eager to create new market niches, develop specialized audiences, and exploit areas of America's musical map that the major companies did not perceive as significant. These small record companies played an important role in country music and, as we shall see, almost completely dominated the R&B field.

RHYTHM & BLUES

Although *Billboard* adopted a new designation in 1949 for what had formerly been called "race records," in some ways the commercial logic underlying the category hadn't really changed much since the 1920s and 1930s. Like the older term, "rhythm & blues" described music performed almost exclusively by black artists and produced in the main (at least at first) for sale to African American audiences.

R&B, as the genre came to be known, was a loose cluster of styles, rooted in southern folk traditions and shaped by the experience of returning military personnel and hundreds of thousands of black Americans who had migrated to urban centers such as New York, Chicago, Detroit, and Los Angeles during and just after the war. The top R&B recordings of the late 1940s and early 1950s included swing-influenced "jump bands," Tin Pan Alley–style love songs performed by black crooners, various styles of urban blues, and gospel-influenced vocal harmony groups.

The reappearance of small independent record labels during and just after the war provided an outlet for performers who were ignored by major record companies such as Columbia, RCA Victor, and Capitol. The development of portable tape recorders made record producers and studio owners out of entrepreneurs who could not previously have afforded the equipment necessary to produce master recordings. Each company was centered on one or two individuals, who located talent, oversaw the recording process, and handled publicity, distribution, and a variety of other tasks. These label owners worked the system in as many ways as time, energy, and ingenuity allowed. They paid radio DJs **payola** to promote their records on the handful of stations that played black music. They visited nightclubs to find new talent, hustled copies of their records to local record store owners, and occasionally attempted to interest a major label in a particular recording or artist with crossover potential.

Most "indie" label owners worked a particular piece of musical and geographical territory. However, they also had dreams of the huge financial success that would accrue to the label that found a way to cross R&B records over to the pop music charts. The middle-class white audience for this music, and the big record companies' and radio networks' interest in it, were growing—but the competition was fiercer than ever. By 1951 there were over one hundred independent labels slugging it out for a piece of the R&B market, and few of them lasted more than a few months.

Indie owners often put their names down for composer credits on songs they recorded and thereby often earned more royalties from a given song than the actual composer. In the postwar era the importance of composers' credits was based on the fact that mainstream pop artists and record companies often tried to cash in on the potential popularity of an R&B recording by creating their own (sometimes almost indistinguishable) versions of it. Although the most famous examples of this practice involve white musicians (and major record companies) exploiting songs first recorded by black artists (and independent record companies), the profit motive led to a variety of interactions, including pop versions of hillbilly songs and black versions of Tin Pan Alley songs. In general, this practice—called covering a song or making a **cover version**—was crucial to the increasing crossover success of black music (and, to a lesser degree, black musicians) during the 1950s.

Jump blues, the first commercially successful category of rhythm & blues, flourished during and just after World War II. During the war, as shortages made it more difficult to maintain a lucrative touring schedule, the leaders of some big bands were forced to downsize. They formed smaller combos, generally made up of a rhythm section (bass, piano, drums, and sometimes guitar) and one or more horn players. These jump bands specialized in hard-swinging party music, spiced with humorous lyrics and wild stage performances.

The most successful and influential jump band was the Tympany Five, led by Louis Jordan (1908–75), an Arkansas-born saxophone player and singer who began making recordings for Decca Records in 1939. Jordan was tremendously popular with black listeners and, like Nat "King" Cole, was able to build an extensive white audience during and after the war. But Jordan himself regarded Cole as being in "another field"—the pop field. Although Cole enjoyed greater financial success, in the end Jordan had a bigger impact on the future of popular music, inspiring a number of the first rock 'n' roll artists. As the rock 'n' roll pioneer Chuck Berry put it, "I identify myself with Louis Jordan more than any other artist" (Shaw 1986, p. 64).

Louis Jordan and His Tympany Five, 1946. Frank Driggs Collection.

James Brown, the godfather of soul music, was once asked if Louis Jordan had been an influence on him: "He was everything," Brown replied (Chilton 1994, p. 126).

The fact that his music appealed to an interracial audience should not lead us to assume that Jordan's career was unaffected by racism. An article published in 1944 described what was to become a standard practice for booking popular black musicians: "Due to the Louis Jordan band's popularity with both white and colored audiences, promoters in larger cities are booking the quintet for two evenings, one to play a white dance and the other a colored dance" (Chilton 1994, p. 107). As R&B artists like Jordan began to attract a more diverse audience, the separation between white and black fans was maintained in various ways. Sometimes white R&B fans sat in the balcony of a segregated theater or dance hall, watching the black dancers below in order to pick up the latest steps. At other times a rope was stretched across the middle of the dance floor to "maintain order." Then, as at other times, the circulation of popular music across racial boundaries did not necessarily signify an amelioration of racism in everyday life.

"Choo Choo Ch' Boogie," which we have already examined in detail, was Louis Jordan's biggest hit, and it exemplifies key elements of the jump blues style of R&B. Released in 1946 by Decca Records, the song topped the R&B charts for an amazing eighteen weeks, reached Number Seven on *Billboard*'s pop hit list, and sold over two million copies. "Choo Choo Ch' Boogie" was cowritten by Milt Gabler, Jordan's producer, and two country and western musicians who worked at a radio station in New York City. The title of the song draws a parallel between the motion of a railroad train—a metaphor of mobility and change long established in both country music and the blues—and the rocking rhythm of boogie-woogie music. *Boogie-woogie*, a style of piano music which originated in black communities in the southwest during the 1920s and triggered a national craze during the 1930s, provided an important link between rhythm & blues and country music during the postwar period, a connection that was to prove important in the formation of rock 'n' roll.

The song's lyric (see listening chart) describes a situation that would have been familiar to many Americans, particularly to ex-GIs returning to the United States during the postwar economic downturn of 1946, when jobs were temporarily scarce and the future seemed uncertain. The song brings back a character from the Great Depression era, the poor but honest hobo, hopping freight trains and traveling from city to city in search of work. The protagonist arrives home, weary of riding in the back of an army truck, and heads for the railroad station. His initial optimism is tempered as he searches the employment notices in the newspaper and realizes that he does not have the technical skills for the few positions that are open. (African American listeners may have interpreted the line "the only job that's open needs a man with a knack" as a comment on the employment practices of the many businesses that favored white over black veterans.) Despite his misfortune, however, our hero remains cheerful, and the lyric ends with an idyllic description of life in a shack by the railroad track.

If jump bands represented the hot end of the R&B spectrum, the cool end was dominated by a blend of blues and pop singing sometimes called the *blues crooner* style. The most successful blues crooner of the late 1940s and early 1950s was a soft-spoken Texas-born pianist and singer named <u>Charles Brown</u> (1922–99). His smooth, sensitive, somewhat forlorn vocal style (sometimes called "cocktail blues") attracted attention, and he began to develop a national reputation with the release of "Drifting Blues," one of the top-selling R&B records of 1945 and 1946. In the 1980s Brown was rediscovered by a new generation of R&B fans and went on to develop a successful international touring career, culminating in a Grammy nomination.

"Black Night," one of Charles Brown's most successful recordings, held the Number One position on the R&B charts for fourteen weeks in 1951. The fact that "Black Night" did not show up on the pop charts can in part be attributed to the record's dark mood, slow tempo, and somber lyrics:

Nobody cares about me, ain't even got a friend
Baby's gone an' left me, when will my troubles end?
Black night is falling, oh how I hate to be alone
I keep crying for my baby, but now another day is gone.

I've got no one to talk with, to tell my troubles to
Don't even know I'm living since I lost you
Black night is falling, oh how I hate to be alone
I keep crying for my baby, but now another day is gone.

My mother has her troubles, my father has his, too
My brother's in Korea, and I don't know just what to do
Black night, black night is falling, oh how I hate to be alone
I keep crying for my baby, but now another day is gone.

In formal terms, "Black Night" is a twelve-bar blues, although the very slow tempo can make it hard to hear the overall structure of the song at first. It also exemplifies the continuing importance of the blues in black popular music, not only as a musical form, but also an emotional state and a perspective on the world. After 1952 Brown's blues ballad style became less popular, as the urban black audience's taste shifted toward more hard-edged singers, perhaps reflecting the growth of active resistance to racial segregation.

A very different urban blues tradition of the postwar era, *Chicago electric blues*, derived more directly from the rural Mississippi Delta tradition of artists like Charley Patton and Robert Johnson, whose music was originally released on "race records" back in the 1920s and 1930s. Chicago was the terminus of the Illinois Central railroad line, which ran up through the Midwest from the Mississippi Delta. Although Chicago's black neighborhoods were well established before World War II, they grew particularly rapidly during the 1940s, as millions of rural migrants came north in search of employment in the city's industrial plants, railroad shops, and slaughterhouses. The South Side's nightclubs were the center of a lively black music scene that rivaled New York's Harlem and L.A.'s Central Avenue. The musical taste of black Chicagoans, many of them recent migrants from the Deep South, tended toward rougher, grittier styles, closely linked to African American folk traditions but also reflective of their new, urban orientation. The career of <u>Muddy Waters (McKinley Morganfield)</u> (1915–83) exemplifies these developments.

Waters was "discovered" in the Mississippi Delta by the folk music scholars John and Alan Lomax, who recorded him in the late 1930s for the Library of Congress. (Waters apparently had some difficulty in getting copies of these recordings, but when he did they were played on jukeboxes in the delta and became regional hits.) In 1943 he moved to Chicago and found work in a paper mill while continuing to work as a musician at nightclubs and parties. In response to the noisy crowds, and to the demand for dance music, Waters soon switched from the acoustic to the electric guitar (1944) and eventually expanded his group to include a second electric guitar, piano, bass, amplified harmonica ("blues harp"), and drum set. During the late 1940s and early 1950s he was the most popular blues musician in Chicago, with a sizable following among black listeners nationwide.

Waters's approach to the blues is different from that of blues crooners like Charles Brown. Like many of the great Mississippi guitarists, Waters was a master of bottleneck slide guitar technique. He used his guitar to create a rock-steady, churning rhythm, interspersed with blues licks, which were counterpoised with his voice in a kind of musical conversation. The electric guitar, which could be used to create dense, buzzing tone colors (by using **distortion**) and long sustained notes that sounded like screaming or crying (by employing **feedback**), was the perfect tool for extending the Mississippi blues guitar tradition. Waters's singing style—rough, growling, moaning, and intensely emotional—was also rooted in the Delta blues. And the songs he sang were based on themes long central to the tradition: on the one hand, loneliness, frustration, and misfortune ("I Feel Like Going Home" and "Still a Fool"), and on the other, independence and sexual braggadocio ("Just Make Love to Me" and "Mannish Boy").

"Hoochie Coochie Man," composed by <u>Willie Dixon</u> (1915–92), Chess Records' house songwriter, bass player, producer, and arranger, is perhaps the best example of the latter theme. The song was Waters's biggest hit for Chess Records, reaching Number Three on the R&B charts in 1954. (Although none of Waters's recordings crossed over to the pop charts, his music was later to play an important role in inspiring rock musicians such as Eric Clapton and the Rolling Stones—who adopted their name from one of his songs.) This recording typifies Chicago urban blues, with its loud volume and dense textures, its buzzing, growling tone colors, and its insistent beat. "Hoochie Coochie Man" is also an example of a common variation on the blues form, a sixteen-bar blues. The first eight bars of the song feature a technique called *stoptime,* in which the beat is suspended in order to focus attention on the singer's voice. (In essence, this is equivalent to the first four bars of a twelve-bar blues, made twice as long by application of the stoptime technique.) Then the regular pulse is reestablished, and the last eight bars are played. Because the lyric of the stoptime section changes each time (like a **verse**), while the words in the second eight-bar section are repeated (like a **chorus**), the song combines the blues form with a strophic verse-chorus structure.

The lyric of "Hoochie Coochie Man" is essentially an extended boast, related to the African American tradition of "toasts," fantastic narratives emphasizing the performer's personal power, sexual prowess, and ability to outwit authority.

> *I got a black cat bone, I got a mojo too*
> *I got the John the Conkaroo, I'm gonna mess wit' you*
> *I'm gonna make you girls lead me by my hand*
> *Then the world'll know the hoochie coochie man*

The song draws a direct link between the personal power of the singer (quintessentially expressed through sex) and the southern folk tradition of mojo, a system of magical charms and medicines, including the black cat bone and John the Conquerer root. This image of supernatural power applied in the service of personal goals was ultimately derived from the cultures of West Africa, and it tapped a common reservoir of experience among Waters's listeners, many of whom were not many years removed from the folk culture of the rural South. In essence, the lyric of "Hoochie Coochie Man" is an argument for the continuing relevance of deep traditional knowledge in the new urban setting, and it is easy to see why this would have been an attractive message for recent urban migrants. "Hoochie Coochie Man" can also be heard as a direct ancestor of contemporary "gangsta rap" recordings, which project a similar outlaw image as a response to the challenging conditions of urban life.

Another important thread in the tapestry of postwar rhythm & blues was *vocal harmony groups*. (Although this tradition is today sometimes called "doo-wop," the earliest performers did not use this term.) Many of these vocal groups were made up of high school kids from the black neighborhoods of cities such as New York and Washington, D.C., and interviews with the singers indicate that these groups served a number of functions: a means of musical expression, an alternative or adjunct to urban gangs, and a route to popularity. Few members of these groups initially saw singing as a way to make a living; this perception changed rapidly after the first vocal R&B groups achieved commercial success.

The vocal harmony group most responsible for creating a new, harder-edged sound more closely linked to black gospel music was the Dominoes, led by vocal coach Billy Ward, a strict disciplinarian and savvy entrepreneur. In 1950 Ward started rehearsing with a number of his most promising students. Their first big hit was "Sixty Minute Man," recorded in New York City and released by the independent label Federal Records in 1951. A large part of the song's popularity was due to its lyric, which catalogued the singer's lovemaking technique in some detail:

> There'll be fifteen minutes of kissin',
> Then you holler please don't stop
> (GROUP: Don't stop!)
> There'll be fifteen minutes of teasin'
> And fifteen minutes of pleasin'
> And fifteen minutes of blowin' my top!

The combination of a naughty lyric, rocking dance rhythm, and bass lead vocal caught the attention of the R&B audience, and "Sixty Minute Man" monopolized the Number One spot on the R&B charts for fourteen weeks during the summer of 1951. It was also one of the first vocal-group R&B records to cross over to the pop charts, where it reached the Number Seventeen position—doubtless without the assistance of AM pop radio.

But it was the Dominoes' next big hit, "Have Mercy Baby," that pushed vocal-group R&B firmly in the direction of a harder-edged, more explicitly emotional sound. Recorded in Cincinnati, Ohio, and released by Federal Records in 1952, "Have Mercy Baby" was the first record to combine the twelve-bar blues form and the driving beat of dance-oriented rhythm & blues with the intensely emotional flavor of black gospel singing. The song's commercial success (Number One R&B for ten weeks in 1952) was in large part due to the passionate performance of the Dominoes' lead tenor, Clyde McPhatter (1932–72), a former gospel singer from North Carolina. McPhatter, the son of a Baptist preacher and a church organist, was like many other R&B musicians insofar as the black church played a major role in shaping his musical sensibility. While in formal terms "Have Mercy Baby" is a twelve-bar blues, it is essentially a gospel performance dressed up in R&B clothing. With a few changes in the lyrics—perhaps substituting the word "Lord" for "baby"—McPhatter's performance would have been perfectly at home in a black Baptist church anywhere in America. The sheer intensity of McPhatter's plea for redemption—you can actually hear him weeping during the fadeout ending—spoke directly to the core audience for R&B, many of whom had grown up within the African American gospel music tradition.

To be sure, this mixing of church music with popular music was controversial in some quarters, and McPhatter and later gospel-based R&B singers faced occasional opposition from some church leaders. But in retrospect the postwar confluence of the sacred and secular aspects of black music, and its commercial exploitation by the music business, seem almost inevitable. Although it did not appear on the pop music charts, "Have Mercy Baby" attracted an audience among many white teenagers, who were drawn by its rocking beat and emotional directness. In addition, the Dominoes were featured on some of the earliest rock 'n' roll tours, which typically attracted a racially mixed audience. Although McPhatter soon left the Dominoes to form a new group called the Drifters, the impact of his rendition of "Have Mercy Baby" was profound and lasting—the record is a direct predecessor of the soul music movement of the 1960s, and of the recordings of Ray Charles, James Brown, and Aretha Franklin.

WOMEN IN R&B: RUTH BROWN AND BIG MAMA THORNTON

Like many other genres of popular music, rhythm & blues played an important role as a stylized medium for enacting sexual politics. This was particularly important during the postwar period, as black families came under the disintegrating pressures of social change and individuals sought to cope with the sometimes alienating experience of urban life. We have already seen several portrayals of male identity in R&B, including Charles Brown's dejected lover and Muddy Waters's magically charged mojo man. Here we want to examine briefly images of male-female relationships in the work of two influential female R&B singers, Ruth Brown and Willie Mae "Big Mama" Thornton.

Ruth Brown (b. 1928), also known as "Miss Rhythm," was born in Virginia. As a child she participated in two streams of the black church tradition, the AME (African Methodist Episcopal) and Baptist denominations. In musical terms, the Methodist services she attended were relatively restrained, with the accompaniment of a piano and big church organ, while the Baptist ceremonies, held in a rough-hewn country church, were often ecstatically emotional and featured only hand clapping and tambourine as accompaniment. Both of these streams can be detected in Brown's later work, which ranged from crooner-style ballads to jump band blues songs.

Although her parents initially resisted the idea of her singing outside the church, Brown began her professional career at the age of sixteen and in 1949 signed with the new independent label Atlantic Records. Chart figures suggest that Ruth Brown was the most popular black female vocalist in America between 1951 and 1954, and it is said that she almost single-handedly kept Atlantic Records alive during its pre-

Circa 1955: Promotional headshot of American R&B singer **Ruth Brown** wearing hoop earrings and a strapless dress. Photo by Frank Driggs Collection/Getty Images.

carious early years. The song with which Ruth Brown was most closely associated was "Mama, He Treats Your Daughter Mean," which held the Number One position on the R&B charts for five weeks in 1953 and reached as high as Number Twenty-three on the pop charts. Brown, the daughter of a respectable, churchgoing family, did not feel comfortable with the song at first:

> That tune, I didn't want to do. I thought, when I first heard it, "That's the silliest mess I have ever heard." At that time, I wasn't having too much of a problem [with men], so I felt like, "What is she talking about, Mama he treats your daughter mean. . . . Mama, the man is lazy, almost drives me crazy." I wasn't dealing with that kind of a lifestyle, so it didn't make sense to me. (Deffaa 1996, p. 35)

According to Brown, the song was recorded quickly, without much rehearsal, and its crossover success on the R&B and pop charts came as something of a surprise. The form of "Mama, He Treats Your Daughter Mean" is an example of the blending of blues and Tin Pan Alley–derived forms. The song's A section (Mama, he treats your daughter mean . . .) is a sixteen-bar blues. (Unlike Willie Dixon's "Hoochie Coochie Man," the twelve-bar form here is expanded by adding four extra bars in the middle of the song. The B section (Mama, he treats me badly . . .) is also sixteen bars in length. The band plays the song at a medium tempo, with the horns (saxophones and trumpets) riffing behind the singer. Certain characteristics of Brown's vocal style are clearly evident on this record, including a warm, somewhat husky tone, a strong rhythmic feeling, and the little upward squeals she places at the ends of words such as "mama," "man," and "understand." This fits the somewhat complaining tone of the song, in which a young woman turns to her mother for help in dealing with a good-for-nothing lover. One of the most memorable features of the recording—and a link to the church music of Brown's youth—is the solo tambourine, which starts the record and continues throughout.

Brown was paid less than seventy dollars for recording the song, in addition to a promised royalty of 5 percent of sales. As was often the case in the R&B business, she received few of her royalties, since the cost of studio time, hiring musicians, and the songwriters' royalties were charged to her account. One of the biggest stars of the postwar era, Brown ended up leaving the music business entirely for a decade and working as a domestic servant in order to raise her children. She was rediscovered in the 1970s and worked to publicize the plight of older rhythm & blues artists who had been denied their share of profits by record companies. In the 1980s she appeared in the Broadway show *Black and Blue* and won a Tony Award in 1989.

Big Mama Thornton (1926–84), born in Montgomery, Alabama, was the daughter of a Baptist minister. She began her professional career as a singer, drummer, harmonica player, and comic on the black vaudeville circuit and later settled in Houston, Texas, working as a singer in black nightclubs. Her imposing physique and sometimes malevolent personality helped to ensure her survival in the rough-and-tumble world of con artists and gangsters. One producer and songwriter who worked with Big Mama described her in vivid terms (in the liner notes to the 1992 MCA release *Big Mama Thornton: Hound Dog/The Peacock Recordings*):

> In rehearsal she'd fool around, pick up one of those old microphones with a heavy, steel base with one hand and turn it upside down with the base in the air and sing like that. She was a powerful, powerful woman. She had a few scars, looked like knife scars on her face, and she had a very beautiful smile. But most of the time she looked pretty salty.

In the early 1950s Thornton arrived in Los Angeles and began working with Johnny Otis (Veliotes), a Greek-American drummer, promoter, bandleader, and nightclub owner who lived in the black community and was a major force in the R&B scene. Looking for material for Big Mama to record, Otis decided to consult two white college kids who had been pestering him to use some of the songs they had written. After hearing Thornton's powerful singing, Jerry Leiber and Mike Stoller ran home and composed a song that they felt suited her style: "Hound Dog." The combination of Leiber and Stoller's humorous country-tinged lyric, Johnny Otis's drumming, and Thornton's powerful, raspy singing produced one of the top-selling R&B records of 1953: Number One for seven weeks. (This was the first hit written and produced by the team of Leiber and Stoller, who were to become a major force in early rock 'n' roll music.)

Of course, most people today know "Hound Dog" through Elvis Presley's version of the song, recorded by RCA Victor in 1956. If you are familiar only with Presley's version, then the original recording may come as something of a revelation. From the very first phrase (You . . . ain't . . . *nothin'* . . . but a houn' dog . . .) Thornton lays claim to the song, and to our attention. Her deep, raspy, commanding voice, reprimanding a ne'er-do-well lover, projects a stark image of female power rarely expressed in popular music of the 1950s. The bluntness of the lyric is reinforced by the musical accompaniment, which includes a bluesy electric guitar, a simple drum part played mainly on the tom-toms, and hand clapping on beats 2 and 4. The tempo is relaxed, and the performance is energetic but loose.

The basic form of "Hound Dog" is a twelve-bar blues with an AAB text, in which the first line of each verse (A) is repeated (A again) and the verse concludes with a contrasting line (B). The opening verse of Big Mama's performance illustrates this form clearly:

A   You ain't nothin' . . .
A   You ain't nothin' . . .
B   You can wag your tail . . .

Each line of the text corresponds to four bars of music, yielding a total of twelve bars for each verse. (This twelve-bar form with AAB text is often referred to as the "standard" blues form, although, as we have already seen, popular musicians often rework the structure of the blues to suit their own expressive purposes.) The band adds a few extra beats here and there in response to Thornton's phrasing, another feature that links this urban recording to the rural origins of the blues. The final touch, with the all-male band howling and barking in response to Big Mama's commands, reinforces not only the humor of the record but also its feeling of informality, the sense that these are not distant pop stars but people you could get to know and maybe even party with.

Although both records are intended to create a humorous effect, the defiant attitude of "Hound Dog" does make an interesting comparison with the complaining tone of "Mama, He Treats Your Daughter Mean," a quality that Ruth Brown herself apparently did not find particularly appealing. Both songs were composed by men and sung by women; and both implicitly rely on the "offstage" presence of a male persona, a lazy, deceitful jerk. But the similarities between the two songs and performances end there. "Hound Dog" was designed specifically to fit Thornton's strong, rough-hewn persona. "Mama," written by professional tunesmiths with no particular singer in mind, presents the image of a female narrator unable to deal with the male problem in her life. One woman expresses her frustration with cute little squeals, the other growls her anger. One gossips, the other threatens to inflict physical harm. One—we might imagine—is a somewhat spoiled middle-class teenager, the other an older woman from a working-class background. Of course, these are stylized images, exaggerated for dramatic effect; but it is their very exaggeration that allows them to convey popular conceptions of sexuality and gender identity in a particular place and time.

COUNTRY AND WESTERN MUSIC

Country and western, the industry's new name for what used to be called hillbilly music, mushroomed in popularity after World War II. Although the South remained a lucrative area for touring performers, the wartime migration of millions of white southerners meant that huge and enthusiastic audiences for country and western music had also been established in the cities and towns of Pennsylvania, Ohio, Michigan, and California. The postwar era saw the rapid spread of country music programming on radio, and by 1949 over 650 radio stations were making live broadcasts of country performers. The continuing success of WSM's *Grand Ole Opry*, broadcast from Nashville, inspired a new generation of country music shows, including Shreveport's *Louisiana Hayride*, Dallas's *Saturday Night Shindig*, Boston's *Hayloft Jamboree*, and *Hometown Jamboree*, broadcast from Los Angeles. As in the R&B field, dozens of independent record labels specializing in country music sprang up after the war, and Nashville, Tennessee, and southern California began to assert themselves as centers for the production of country music. In 1950—when Capitol Records became the first major company to set up its country music operation in Nashville—it was estimated that country music accounted for fully one-third of all record sales nationwide.

As country music's core audience moved north, west, and upward into the urban middle class, the "mainstreaming" of country music continued apace. Pop artists such as Bing Crosby ("Sioux City Sue," Number Three pop in 1946) and Tony Bennett ("Cold, Cold Heart," Number One pop in 1951) had huge chart successes with their adaptations of country material. Since the 1920s the New York–based music industry had underestimated—and often seemed embarrassed by—the popularity of popular styles based in southern folk music. But by 1950, when a pop-style rendition of the country song "Tennessee Waltz" became the fastest-selling record in twenty-five years, the record company executives had no choice—country music was off the porch and sitting in the living room.

Patti Page (b. 1927 in Oklahoma) sold more records than any other female singer of the early 1950s. She had success with love songs ("All My Love," Number One pop in 1950) and novelty items like "The Doggie in the Window" (Number One pop in 1953), but her biggest hit was a recording of "Tennessee Waltz." Page's version of the song—previously recorded by one of its writers, *Grand Ole Opry* star Pee Wee King—held the Number One position on the pop charts for thirteen weeks in 1950 and eventually went on to sell more than six million copies. In some ways this was a recording that pointed back toward the nineteenth century—a sentimental **waltz** song packed with nostalgic references to the South. However, the popular appeal of this record was also apparently boosted by two technological innovations: the use of multitrack tape recording, which allowed Page to sing a duet with herself, and the fact that this was one of the first songs to be issued as a 45 r.p.m. single. "Tennessee Waltz" helped to make Mercury Records into a major label, spawned a rash of cover versions by other artists, and served notice that a pop-styled approach to country and western music could not only penetrate but actually dominate the mainstream.

In some ways, the range of country music styles during the postwar era resembles contemporaneous developments in rhythm & blues. There were *country crooners*, who specialized in a smooth, pop-oriented style; *bluegrass* musicians, who focused on the adaptation of traditional southern music in a package suitable to the times; and *honky-tonk* music, a hard-edged, electronically amplified style featuring songs about the trials and tribulations of migrants to the city and gender roles and male-female relationships during a period of intense social change.

Honky-tonk music—sometimes called "hard country" or "beer-drinking music"—conveyed the sound and ethos of the roadside bar or juke joint. During the Great Depression of the 1930s the oil fields of Texas and Oklahoma had provided a lucrative (and rare) source of steady, well-paid work, attracting thousands of men from the American southwest and farther afield. When the prohibition of alcohol was repealed in 1933, the formerly illegal drinking establishments that serviced these men multiplied and became a major source of employment for country and western musicians. These honky-tonks, as the people who frequented them called them, provided relief from the daily pressures of work on the oilfields, in the form of drinking and dancing. (The practice of going from bar to bar on a Saturday night is still called "honky-tonking.") By the postwar period thousands of these rowdy

Patti Page, May 1956. © Bettmann/ CORBIS

nightspots were sprinkled across the American southwest and further afield, ranging from small, dimly lit dives to big, neon-lit roadhouses.

Country and western music, both recorded and performed live, was crucial to the profitability of honky-tonks. Many of them featured colorfully glowing (and loud) jukeboxes, the mechanical record players that had spread rapidly in popularity during and after World War II. In adjusting to the honky-tonk milieu, country musicians made a number of changes in their performance practice. First, many of the old-time songs about family and the church seemed out of place in the new setting. Musicians began to compose songs about aspects of life directly relevant to their patrons: family instability, the unpredictability of male-female relationships, the attractions and dangers of alcohol, and the importance of enjoying the present. When the rural past was referred to, it was usually through a veil of nostalgia and longing. Honky-tonk vocal styles were often directly emotional, making use of "cracks" in the voice and stylistic features from black music, such as **melisma** and **blue notes.** Like urban blues musicians such as Muddy Waters, country musicians adapted traditional instruments and playing techniques to the rowdy atmosphere of the juke joint. The typical instrumentation of a honky-tonk band included a fiddle, a steel guitar, a "takeoff" (lead) guitar, a string bass, and a piano. The guitars were electronically amplified, and the musicians played with a percussive, insistent beat (sometimes called "sock rhythm") well suited to dancing.

When today's musicians talk about playing "good old country music," they are most often referring to the postwar honky-tonk style rather than to the rural folk music of the South. Honky-tonk stars such as Ernest Tubb, Hank Williams, Lefty Frizzell, Hank Snow, George Jones, and Webb Pierce dominated the country and western charts during the early and mid-1950s. Although their fortunes declined somewhat after the emergence of rock 'n' roll—especially a country-tinged variety of rock 'n' roll called **rockabilly**—honky-tonk music remains the heart and soul of modern country music.

HANK WILLIAMS

Hank Williams (1923–53) was the most significant figure to emerge in country music during the immediate post–World War II period. Williams wrote and sang many songs in the course of his brief career that were enormously popular with country audiences at the time; between 1947 and 1953 he amassed an astounding thirty-six Top 10 records on the country charts, including such Number One hits as "Lovesick Blues," "Cold, Cold Heart," "Jambalaya (On the Bayou)," and "Your Cheatin' Heart." All of these Number One hits—along with many other Williams songs—have remained long-term country favorites and are established "standards" of their genre. In addition, his songs were successfully covered by contemporary mainstream pop artists, thus demonstrating the wide-ranging appeal of the new country material. "Cold, Cold Heart" helped launch the career of Tony Bennett when the young crooner scored a huge success with it in 1951 (Number One pop for six weeks).

Hank Williams represented for postwar country audience the enduring myth of the hard-living, hard-loving rambler. Although the details of Williams's life seem in retrospect to have custom-designed him for legendary status, it is important to realize that these were the actual facts of his life: born into crushing poverty in Alabama, this son of a sharecropper learned to make his way at an early age by performing on the street, learning a great deal from a black street singer named Rufe "Tee-Tot" Payne. By the time he was sixteen, Williams, now called "the Singing Kid," had his own local radio show; shortly thereafter he formed a band, the Drifting Cowboys, and began touring throughout Alabama. Enormous success came to Williams by the time he was in his midtwenties, but it did not come without its problems. By 1952 he was divorced, had been fired from the *Grand Ole Opry* (for numerous failures to appear), and was seriously dependent on alcohol and painkilling drugs. He was dead on New Year's Day 1953 at age twenty-nine, having suffered a heart attack in the back of his car while en route to a performance.

Williams affirmed the importance of religious traditions in country music by recording some gospel material. The fact that he recorded his sacred tunes under a pseudonym, rather than under his own name, however, ties him more closely to the practices of black secular singers than to those of most white artists. (Then again, his actual choice of pseudonym, "Luke the Drifter," links these records back to the rambler image projected by the bulk of Williams's secular work.)

A brief look at two of the most famous songs written and performed by Hank Williams will demonstrate his debts to country music traditions as well as the progressive elements in his music. "I'm So Lonesome I Could Cry" is a timeless lament that builds clearly on earlier models in both its words and its music, while "Hey, Good Lookin'" is an almost startling anticipation of the style that, in the later 1950s, would come to be called **rockabilly.**

Like the song "Goodnight Irene" (analyzed earlier in this chapter), "I'm So Lonesome I Could Cry" evokes the flavor of "old-timey" country music with its waltzlike triple meter and its straightforward strophic structure. The lyrics too refer to traditional country images. The "wide open spaces" are called up with pictures of

Hank Williams performs, while Chet Atkins—soon to be a hugely influential figure in country music himself, as a guitarist and producer—looks on admiringly. Ernie Newton is playing bass. Courtesy of Country Music Hall of Fame and Museum.

birds, of the moon going behind the clouds, and of the "silence of a falling star" that illuminates the sky, while the presence of the "midnight train . . . whining low" affirms Williams's ties to the spirits of the ramblers who came before him. Against the steady rhythmic backdrop of guitars and bass, the sound of the fiddle asserts Williams's kinship with earlier country music. On the other hand, the prominent steel guitar throughout helped create a sense of modernity for Williams's audience and assured that the essence of his music would be a feeling of utter immediacy— of a song for the here-and-now.

Like much of the finest rurally based music, black and white, "I'm So Lonesome I Could Cry" is structured to capitalize on the regional characteristics of the singer-composer's performance style. The abundance of sustained vowel sounds placed on the downbeats of measures, as in "Hear that lonesome whippoorwill," or "The silence of a falling star," draws out the characteristic twang of Williams's accent and lends a particular expressivity to the actual sound of the lyrics that underlines their dark emotional content. Williams's drawl also leads him naturally to delay somewhat the full force of those vowel sounds, so that he seems rhythmically behind the beat. Again, this beautifully reinforces the mournful essence of the song— as if it is a constant effort for the singer to rise to the high notes on those vowels (and this makes the fall in pitch that marks the end of every phrase in the song seem that much more inevitable, and that much sadder). When he approaches the end of the song, the almost-break in Williams's voice as he sings "and as I wonder where you are" is heartbreaking; there seems to be no separation between the singer and the song, or between the sound of his country voice and the meaning of its expression. It's no wonder Williams evoked such a response in the burgeoning country music audience after World War II.

Along with a few of Williams's other records, the jaunty "Hey, Good Lookin'" was actually something of a minor crossover hit for him (Number Twenty-nine pop, but Number One on the country chart—for eight weeks—in 1951). This should not seem surprising, given its danceable character and its pop-friendly thirty-two-bar AABA form borrowed from Tin Pan Alley models. With its prominent steel guitar and fiddle parts, not to mention the character of Williams's vocal, there's still no mistaking the record's basis in country music. What is most arresting here, however, is the specific targeting of a youthful audience. The lyrics address cars, dancing, and young romance, and the use of terms like "hot-rod Ford," "soda pop," "go steady," and "date book" create what would—about five years later—have been called a "teen-friendly" piece of material.

In a sense, "Hey, Good Lookin'" came a little too early, and Hank Williams of course died much too young. Had Williams been able to bring this same song, or something like it, to a savvy record producer in late 1955 or early 1956—to a producer aware of the noise being made by the young Elvis Presley or by Carl Perkins at the time—that cynical producer might have said something like this: "Hank, you've got something there. Please throw out those fiddles, though—too hillbilly. And replace the steel guitar with a regular electric guitar played R&B-style. Add some R&B-based drumming too. I think you'll have a hit rock 'n' roll record." And had Williams been interested, which is questionable, his name might well have been added to the rockabilly roster, perhaps even close to the top of it. As it is, Williams's early death leaves us pondering what might have been; but in any case, a song like "Hey, Good Lookin'" attests to the forward-looking character of his creativity.

———————

The decade following World War II saw important changes in the popular music business, including the introduction of new technologies such as tape recording; the "covering" of rhythm & blues and country and western songs by mainstream pop artists; and the entertainment industry's increasingly sophisticated application of marketing techniques. All of these were preconditions for the rise of rock 'n' roll and the rapid transformation of American popular music that took place in the mid-1950s, the subject of our next chapter.

CHAPTER THREE

"ROCK AROUND THE CLOCK"
Rock 'n' Roll, 1954–1959

The advent of rock 'n' roll music in the mid-1950s brought enormous changes to American popular music, and eventually to world popular music—changes whose impact is still being felt today. Most significantly, styles that previously had remained on the margins of pop music from a marketing standpoint now began to infiltrate the center and eventually to dominate the center completely. Rhythm & blues and country music recordings were no longer necessarily directed to specialized and regionalized markets; they now began to be heard in significant numbers on mainstream pop radio, and many could be purchased in music stores nationwide that catered to the broadest general public.

The emergence of rock 'n' roll was surely an event of great significance in cultural terms. Because of its importance, we must be careful not to mythologize it or to endorse common misconceptions about it. In particular, the following issues demand our attention: first, rock 'n' roll was neither a "new" style of music, nor was it any single style of music; second, the era of rock 'n' roll does not mark the first time that music was written specifically to appeal to young people; third, rock 'n' roll is certainly not the first American music to bring black and white popular styles into close interaction. In fact, the designation "rock 'n' roll"—like "Tin Pan Alley," "hillbilly music," or "rhythm & blues"—was introduced as a commercial and marketing term, for the purpose of identifying a new target audience for musical products.

This new audience was dominated by those born into the so-called baby boom generation at the end of, and immediately following, World War II. It was a much younger audience than had ever before constituted a target market for music, and it was a large audience that shared some specific and important characteristics of group cultural identity. These were kids growing up in the 1950s, a period of relative economic stability and prosperity, but also a period marked by a self-conscious return to "normalcy" defined in socially and politically conservative ways, following the enormous destabilizing traumas of world war. In terms of the entertainment industry, this was the first generation to grow up with television as a readily available part of its culture; this powerful new mass medium proved a force of incalculable influence and offered another outlet for the instantaneous nationwide distribution of music.

Yet the 1950s was a period characterized by its own political and cultural traumas. Cold War tension between the United States and the Soviet Union fed an intense anticommunism in America that resulted in such controversial phenomena as congressional hearings concerning "un-American activities" and the blacklisting of many writers, musicians, and entertainment personalities who had been involved in suspect left-wing groups and actions in the 1930s, 1940s, and 1950s. During these years, children grew up amid fears induced by the introduction of atomic weapons and their further development by the American and Soviet—and eventually other—superpowers. Furthermore, new levels of racial awareness and tension in America emerged in the wake of the 1954 Supreme Court decision in the case of *Brown v. Board of Education,* which mandated the end of racial segregation in public schools.

Perhaps the most important factor of all for adolescents during the 1950s was simply their identification by the larger culture itself as a unique generational group, even as they were growing up. Thus they quickly developed a sense of self-identification as teenagers (this category was not necessarily limited to young people between the ages of thirteen and nineteen; many ten-, eleven-, and twelve-year-olds participated fully in "teen" culture). Naturally such a group, from a young age, had to have its own distinctive emblems of identity, including dance steps, fashions, ways of speaking, and music. The prosperity of the 1950s gave these young people an unprecedented collective purchasing power, as the allowances of millions of kids went toward leisure and entertainment products geared especially to this generation's tastes and sense of identity. What resulted was an increasingly volatile give-and-take between, on the one hand, products and trends that were prefabricated for teens by the adult commercial culture, and on the other hand, products and trends chosen and developed unpredictably by the members of the new generation themselves. Rock 'n' roll music was at the center of this give-and-take. It emerged as an unexpected musical choice by increasing numbers of young people in the early to mid-1950s; it then became a mass-market phenomenon exploited by the mainstream music industry in the later 1950s; and eventually it was to some extent reclaimed by these teenagers themselves in the 1960s as they grew old enough to make their own music and, increasingly, to assume some control of the production and marketing of it.

The term "rock 'n' roll" was probably first used for commercial and generational purposes by disc jockey Alan Freed (1922–65). In the early 1950s Freed discovered that increasing numbers of young white kids were listening to and requesting the rhythm & blues records he played on his *Moondog Show* nighttime program in Cleveland—records he then began to call "rock 'n' roll" records. Freed also promoted concert tours featuring black artists, playing to a young, racially mixed audience, and promoted them as "rock 'n' roll revues." The term "rock 'n' roll" itself was derived from the many references to "rockin'" and "rollin'" (sometimes separately, sometimes together) that may be found in rhythm & blues songs,

Teenagers study the offerings on a jukebox, 1957. Courtesy Library of Congress.

and on race records dating back at least to the late 1920s. Among the relevant recordings that would have been known to Freed and his audience were the late-1940s rhythm & blues hit "Good Rockin' Tonight" (recorded by a number of different artists after first becoming a hit for its composer, Roy Brown) and the huge 1951 hit by the Dominoes, "Sixty Minute Man" (which featured the lyric "I rock 'em, roll 'em, all night long, I'm a sixty-minute man"). "Rock" and "roll" are clearly associated in these and other songs with sexual implications, but like the similar original implications of the word "jazz," these implications faded as "rock 'n' roll" increasingly came to refer simply to a type of music.

In 1954 Freed moved to station WINS in the larger New York radio market, taking the phrase "rock 'n' roll" with him to identify both the music he played and his target audience. Freed continued to promote African American musicians, in the face of considerable resistance in the society as a whole to the idea of racial integration. In 1957 a TV show sponsored by Freed was canceled after the black teenage singer Frankie Lymon was shown dancing with a white girl. In 1958 Freed himself was arrested for anarchy and incitement to riot after a fight broke out at one of his rock 'n' roll concerts in Boston. In the early 1960s Freed was prosecuted for accepting **payola**—the illegal practice, common throughout the music industry, of paying bribes to radio disc jockeys in order to get certain artists' records played more frequently—while promoters like Dick Clark (who handled mainly white rock 'n' roll artists) escaped relatively unscathed. Freed was blackballed within the music business, and he died a few years later, a broken man.

Disc jockey **Alan Freed** in Cleveland. Courtesy Library of Congress.

Whatever his indiscretions, Alan Freed was clearly in the vanguard of an increasing number of disc jockeys, all over the country, who wished to capture the new, large audience of young radio listeners and potential record buyers, and who consequently embraced the term "rock 'n' roll" to refer to virtually any kind of music pitched to that audience. This included records that would previously have been marketed purely as rhythm & blues or as country and western, along with an expanding group of hybrid records that drew freely on multiple stylistic influences, including those associated with mainstream Tin Pan Alley–type music. Strange as it now seems, in the early heyday of rock 'n' roll Chuck Berry, Pat Boone, Fats Domino, Ricky Nelson, the Everly Brothers, and Elvis Presley were all lumped together as "rock 'n' roll singers"—meaning simply that they all had records being listened to and purchased by large numbers of teenagers. This was a period of remarkable heterogeneity on radio and on the record charts, as all of the above singers, along with the likes of Frank Sinatra and Patti Page, could be heard jostling each other on Top 40 radio stations and seen nudging each other on the pop charts. In the marketing confusion that resulted, rock 'n' roll records appeared on different, previously exclusive, charts simultaneously; early in 1956 Carl Perkins's "Blue Suede Shoes" and Elvis Presley's "Heartbreak Hotel" both made chart history by climbing to the upper reaches of the country and western, rhythm & blues, and pop charts all at the same time.

The purchase of rock 'n' roll records by kids in the 1950s proved a relatively safe and affordable way for kids to assert generational identity through rebellion against previous adult standards and restrictions of musical style and taste. (The original associations of the term "rock 'n' roll" with marginalized African American musical styles and with sexually risqué lyrics obviously didn't hurt the sense of rebellion at all, for those familiar with the associations—whether they were the kids themselves, or their parents!) Thus the experience of growing up with rock 'n' roll music became an early and defining characteristic of the baby boom generation. Rock 'n' roll records accompanied the boomers in their progress from preadolescence through their teenage years. It is consequently not surprising that this music increasingly and specifically catered to this age group, which by the late 1950s had its own distinctive culture (made possible by abundant leisure time and economic prosperity) and its associated rituals: school and vacation (represented in rock 'n' roll songs such as "School Day" and "Summertime Blues"), fashions ("Black Denim Trousers and Motorcycle Boots" and "Itsy Bitsy Teenie Weenie Yellow Polkadot Bikini"), social dancing ("At the Hop" and "Save the Last Dance for Me"), and courtship ("Teen-Age Crush," "Puppy Love," "A Teenager in Love," and "Poor Little Fool"). Some rock 'n' roll songs—for example, "Roll over Beethoven" and "Rock and Roll Is Here to Stay"—self-consciously announced themselves as emblems of a new aesthetic and cultural order, dominated by the tastes and aspirations of youth.

It would not be an exaggeration to say that the 1950s essentially invented the teenager as a commercial and cultural entity, and that rock 'n' roll music, along with television and, to some extent, movies, played an essential role in this invention. Although popular music of all eras has reached out to young audiences with plentiful songs about love and courtship, the virtually exclusive emphasis on appeal to one particular, extremely young, generation is what most distinguishes the phenomenon of rock 'n' roll. It is thus not surprising that teenagers themselves were recruited, with increasing frequency, as performers to market this music, beginning with the popular group Frankie Lymon and the Teenagers (who scored their first and biggest hit "Why Do Fools Fall in Love?" early in 1956, when lead singer Lymon himself was only thirteen years old), and continuing in the following years with a string of "teen idols" like Ricky Nelson, Paul Anka, and Annette Funicello. (The popularity of both Nelson and Funicello was closely linked to television; the former was already well known to audiences as the younger son on *The Adventures of Ozzie and Harriet* show before he started making records, and the latter was prominently featured on *The Mickey Mouse Club*—a show obviously aimed at the baby boomer audience.) The association of rock 'n' roll with adolescence and adolescents was so complete that, in the 1960s, practitioners of the music who had grown out of their adolescent years, and who wanted to appeal to a maturing audience of their peers, rechristened their music simply *rock.*

For all this appropriate emphasis on the generational culture of rock 'n' roll, we should not ignore that the shift in musical marketing away from primarily racial and regional considerations (and their associated class-related aspects) toward primarily generational considerations had some unforeseen and extremely significant consequences that profoundly affected the American cultural landscape. There was a period in the later 1950s when much of the same popular music—rock 'n' roll records—would be played for dances at inner-city, primarily black, public schools, for parties at exclusive white suburban private schools, and for socials in rural settings catering to young people. This was a new kind of situation, especially in the society of the 1950s, which was in most respects polarized in terms of race, class, and region. Influences and interactions among supposedly exclusive groups of musicians (black and white, rural and urban, upper and lower class) have occurred throughout the history of American popular music. But rock 'n' roll music seemed to offer a bridge connecting supposedly exclusive *audiences*. If you were young in the 1950s, no matter where you lived, no matter what your race or class, rock 'n' roll was *your* music. An important, if ultimately fragile, potential of popular music to create new connections and relationships among audiences in a highly fragmented society was first glimpsed on a large scale in the period of rock 'n' roll.

COVER VERSIONS AND EARLY ROCK 'N' ROLL

One of the most important precedents for the rise of rock 'n' roll was a commercial and musical phenomenon known as the *cover version*. In the broadest sense, this term simply refers to the practice of recording a song that has previously been recorded by another artist or group. However, practitioners, merchants, and scholars of popular music have usually used the term in a more restricted sense, to refer to a version—sometimes an almost exact copy—of a previously recorded performance, often involving an adaptation of the original's style and sensibility, and usually aimed at cashing in on its success. Of course, the process of musical borrowing is no doubt as old as music itself. But this process takes on new significance when the element of financial profit is introduced, and when issues of social inequality are involved. In such contexts, the influence of one tradition, style, or performer on another can also be seen as a kind of musical appropriation, and borrowing becomes something more akin to stealing.

The practice of covering often worked in both directions, and country and rhythm & blues musicians sometimes recorded their own stylized renditions of Tin Pan Alley songs that had previously been popularized by pop crooners. However, the most notorious examples—and those most important for understanding the rise of rock 'n' roll in the mid-1950s—involved white performers covering the work of African American recording artists. This was a relationship not simply between individual musicians but also between competing institutions, since the underlying motivation for covering a recording typically involved the major record companies' attempt to capitalize on the musical discoveries of small independent record labels. The practice also represented a new stage in the evolution of white fascination with black music.

To better our understanding of this phenomenon, let's look at specific examples of cover versions. In 1947 a black singer and pianist named Paula Watson recorded a song called "A Little Bird Told Me" for the independent label Supreme. Watson's version of the song, released in 1948, reached Number Two on the R&B charts and made an impact on the pop charts, peaking at Number Six. This early crossover hit attracted the attention of Decca Records, which immediately issued a cover version of the song performed by a white singer named Evelyn Knight. Knight's version of the song reached Number One on the pop charts, in large part owing to the promotional power of Decca Records and the fact that white performers enjoyed privileged access to radio and television play.

The tiny Supreme label sued Decca Records, claiming that its copyright to the original had been infringed. In this case the crux of the matter was not the song per se—its author, Harvey Brooks, collected composer's royalties from both record companies. Rather, Supreme claimed that Decca had stolen aspects of the original recording, including its arrangement, texture, and vocal style. Although Evelyn Knight had indeed copied Paula Watson's singing precisely—to the degree that it fooled musical experts brought in as witnesses—the judge ultimately decided in favor of the larger company, ruling that musical arrangements were not copyrighted property and therefore not under legal protection. This decision affirmed the legal principle that the song (published in the form of sheet music) was a copyrightable form of intellectual property, but that individual interpretations or arrangements of a given song could not be protected under the law. This meant the continuation of an older conception of music's legal status—focused on the written document—in an era when recordings, rather than sheet music, had become the dominant means of transmission. (Today, in the era of digital **sampling**, these questions continue to loom large in court cases concerning the ownership of popular music. In certain instances, specific aspects of a recorded performance have been deemed protectable by copyright. See Chapter 9.)

The "Little Bird Told Me" decision opened the floodgates for cover versions during the 1950s, for better or worse. Now let's take a closer look at three more examples of cover versions, each of which gives us a different perspective on the complex musical, economic, and social forces that converged to create rock 'n' roll in the mid-1950s.

Cover Version 1: "Shake, Rattle, and Roll"

Original version performed by Big Joe Turner (Number One R&B, Number Twenty-two pop, 1954); cover version performed by Bill Haley and the Comets (Number Seven pop, 1954)

Perhaps the most famous example of a mid-1950s cover version is the song "Shake, Rattle, and Roll," composed in 1954 by Jesse Stone, the black producer and talent scout for Atlantic Records. (The song was actually published under the pseudonym Charles Calhoun.) "Shake, Rattle, and Roll" is a twelve-bar blues, with a repeated section that functions like a chorus (*Shake, rattle, and roll . . .*). The original recording of the song, released by Atlantic in 1954, is in the jump blues R&B style. It features Big Joe Turner (1911–85), a forty-three-year old vocalist who had begun his career as a singing bartender in the depression-era nightclubs of Kansas City and had sung with various big bands during the swing era. Turner was one of Atlantic's early stars, and his recording of "Shake, Rattle, and Roll" not only held the Number One position on the R&B charts but also crossed over to the pop charts, where it reached Number Twenty-two.

This crossover hit soon caught the attention of executives at Decca Records and of a former country and western bandleader named Bill Haley (see Box 3.1). Later in 1954 Bill Haley and the Comets recorded a rendition of "Shake, Rattle, and Roll" that was clearly indebted to Turner's original but also departed from it in significant ways. While the Atlantic recording features a band made up of veteran jazz musicians, playing a medium-tempo shuffle rhythm, the Haley recording emphasizes guitars rather than saxophones and has a rhythmic feeling more akin to western swing than jump blues R&B. One of the most obvious differences between the two versions lies in the song's text. The original lyric, as written by

Jesse Stone and embellished by Big Joe Turner, is full of fairly obvious sexual references:

> *Well, you wear those dresses, the sun come shinin' through*
> *Well, you wear those dresses, the sun come shinin' through*
> *I cain' believe my eyes, all that mess belong to you*
>
> *I'm like a one-eyed cat, peepin' in a seafood store*
> *I'm like a one-eyed cat, peepin' in a seafood store*
> *Well I can look at you, tell you ain' no child no more*

Presumably because these lyrics would have proved too wild for AM radio and offended many in the predominantly white pop music audience, Haley sang a bowdlerized (censored) version of the song:

> *Wearin' those dresses, your hair done up so nice*
> *Wearin' those dresses, your hair done up so nice*
> *You look so warm, but your heart is cold as ice.*
>
> *I'm like a one-eyed cat, peepin' in a seafood store,*
> *I'm like a one-eyed cat, peepin' in a seafood store*
> *I can look at you, tell you don't love me no more*

That the "one-eyed cat, peepin' in a seafood store" line survived the censor's blade is surprising, since it is a fairly obvious double-entendre reference to the male and female sexual organs. The person charged with rewriting the lyric may have been a bit too square to catch the sexual reference, a fact that must have delighted those who knew the original version.

The other major difference between Turner's and Haley's versions of "Shake, Rattle, and Roll" is the level of profit generated by the two recordings. In fact, this is not the most egregious example of a white band and major record company reaping profits from a song originally recorded by black musicians for an independent label, since both versions appeared on the pop charts, and each sold over a million copies. There are crucial differences between the two, however. While Big Joe Turner's version crossed over to the pop chart (and the expanding white teenage audience for black popular music), the majority of Atlantic's sales was nonetheless focused in the black community. Haley's version reached Number Seven on the pop chart but did not appear on the R&B charts at all, indicating that black audiences preferred Turner's jump band–style approach to the country-tinged style of the Comets. While Haley built on his early hit success, going on to become the first "king" of rock 'n' roll music, Turner was never again able to score a Top 40 pop hit or a Number One R&B hit. Atlantic sought to promote the middle-aged blues shouter to the teen audience for rock 'n' roll, but his time had passed. Turner himself claimed that "rock 'n' roll" was just another name for the same music he had always sung, but that he got "knocked down" in the traffic of a newly crowded scene.

The two versions of "Shake, Rattle, and Roll" represent a pivot point between early 1950s R&B and later 1950s rock 'n' roll. And they are also a junction at which two popular musicians crossed paths—Big Joe Turner on his way down, and Bill Haley on his way up.

Original version com-
posed and performed
by the Chords (Num-
ber Two R&B, Num-
ber Five pop, 1954);
cover version per-
formed by the Crew
Cuts (Number One
pop for nine weeks,
1954)

Cover Version 2: "Sh-Boom"

"Sh-Boom" is one of the most famous cover versions of the early rock 'n' roll era.
In fact, its original recording by the Chords is often cited as one of the very first
rock 'n' roll records. Certainly the Chords' "Sh-Boom" is a prime example of the
rhythm & blues black vocal group style and, as a Top 10 pop hit, was also one of
the first records to demonstrate the huge appeal that style could have to a mass audience. It is particularly significant that the Chords managed to place their record
near the top of the pop charts in spite of a massively successful cover version of the
tune by the white group the Crew Cuts. The Crew Cuts' "Sh-Boom" was one of the
two biggest pop hits of 1954 and thus offers a particularly instructive example of
the "cover record" phenomenon. A splendid irony underlying all this is the fact
that the Chords' original "Sh-Boom" was in fact on the "flip" side of their own cover
version (for the R&B market) of white pop singer Patti Page's hit "Cross over the
Bridge"! If some discerning listeners and some enterprising disc jockeys hadn't
turned the Chords' record over and enthused over the apparent throwaway number on the B-side, you wouldn't be reading this right now.

The Chords' "Sh-Boom" also illustrates how the presence of unexpected elements
in the arrangement and performance of a rather ordinary tune can help create an extraordinary and original pop record. Essentially, the song is a standard AABA love
ballad whose sentimental lyrics and stereotypical chord changes would suggest, on
paper, either a slow rhythm & blues ballad or some grist for a latter-day pop crooner's
mill. However, the Chords made the striking decision to treat the song as an uptempo
number and to add some novel touches that were appropriate to an uptempo record
but that also made this one really stand out. Among these novel touches on the Chords'
recording (see the outline below) are: an **a cappella** vocal introduction; the incorporation of brief passages of **scat singing** (nonsense syllables), borrowed from jazz, at
strategic points in the performance; a long and sizzling instrumental break, in the
form of a saxophone solo—accompanied by the vocal group's rhythmic nonsense syllables in the background—right in the middle of the record; and an unexpected ending on the term "sh-boom" itself, intoned by the group on an especially rich chord.
This record anticipates the kind of unexpected syntheses from different musical styles
that would come to characterize the most inventive rock 'n' roll records. For example, the sax solo would have been typical of an uptempo urban blues or dance-
oriented R&B recording, but would probably not have been expected in a record with
love ballad lyrics, while nonsense vocal sounds—expected in R&B love ballads—were
not typically paired with hot instrumental solos. The association made in the record
between jazz-related scat vocal solos and the nonsense syllables of vocal group "doo-
wop," while logical, was also quite original.

There are novel touches in the Crew Cuts' recording as well, which help account for its great popular success. As shown in the outline below, this version begins with scat singing. In the middle of the record, instead of a saxophone solo,
there are two brief sections of group nonsense-syllable singing—each of which is
punctuated by an isolated, loud, and humorous kettledrum stroke. Toward the end
of the recording there are not one but *two* "false" endings (see outline). Arguably,
all these effects tend to push this version into the category of a full-fledged novelty
record (whereas the Chords' version comes across as an uptempo R&B record with
some novel aspects).

In terms of singing style, the Crew Cuts are crooners. The alternation between phrases where a solo voice takes the lead and phrases that are sung by the full group produces some agreeable variety in their arrangement, but there is really no difference in vocal coloration between the solo and the group; that is to say, the group passages are, in effect, "crooning times four." In contrast, the Chords' vocal arrangement is typical of a rhythm & blues approach insofar as it exploits differences in vocal **timbre** among the group's members, as well as the opposition between solo and group singing. This is heard most clearly in the B section **(bridge)** of the Chords' version, where the lead is taken by a solo bass voice that presents a strong contrast to the sound of the lead tenor heard in the first two A sections. Of course, the Chords' general approach throughout is rougher in sound than that of the Crew Cuts, underlining the much more aggressive rhythmic feeling of their recording as a whole. And the overriding difference between the Chords' and the Crew Cuts' recordings of "Sh-Boom" has to do precisely with that rhythmic feeling: simply put, the former swings hard and the latter does not.

OUTLINE: THE CHORDS' "SH-BOOM"

Introduction (full group a cappella, then band enters)

A ("Life could . . . "; tenor lead)
  (Scat singing interlude)
A ("Life could . . . "; tenor lead)
B ("Every time . . . "; bass lead)
A ("Life could . . . "; full group)
  (Scat singing interlude)
Sax Solo (with group "doo-wop" sounds in
  background; this is the length of two
  A sections)
A (full group; same words as first A section)
  (Scat singing interlude, leading to
  sudden ending with the full group)

OUTLINE: THE CREW CUTS' "SH-BOOM"

Introduction (scat singing)

A (tenor lead)
A (tenor lead)
B (tenor lead, then full group)
A (tenor lead)
Group "nonsense" singing (two sections,
  each the length of an A section,
  punctuated by kettledrum strokes)
B (full group)
A (full group, then tenor lead; same words
  as first A section)
  (Scat singing interlude, leading to
  first "false" ending, then to:)
A (full group, then tenor lead; same words
  as the second A section)
("False" fadeout leads to sudden loud
  conclusion with the full group)

Original version composed and performed by Junior Parker (no chart appearance, 1953); cover version performed by Elvis Presley (Number Eleven country and western, 1955)

Cover Version 3: "Mystery Train"

The biggest star of the rock 'n' roll era—and arguably of the entire history of American popular music—was Elvis Presley (1935–77). Presley was born in Tupelo, Mississippi, the only child of a poor family, and his musical taste was shaped at a young age by the white gospel music he heard at church, by radio broadcasts of country music and rhythm & blues, and by the popular crooners of the postwar era, especially Dean Martin. (At the age of eight Presley won a talent contest at a Mississippi county fair, singing an old country song called "Old Shep.") As a teenager he moved to Memphis, took a job as a truck driver, and nurtured his ambition to become a singing film star.

In 1954 Presley came to the attention of Sam Phillips, the owner of Sun Records, a small independent label in Memphis, Tennessee, that specialized in country and rhythm & blues recordings and had scored a few regional hits. Phillips teamed Presley with two musicians from a local country band called the Starlite Wranglers, Scotty Moore (b. 1931) on electric guitar and Bill Black (1926–65) on string bass. Presley made a series of recordings with an R&B cover version on one side and a country song on the other. In essence, Sam Phillips was fishing with Elvis as bait, trying to see if he could develop a single artist who could sell to both white and black audiences. In his early live appearances, Elvis was billed as "the King of Country Bop," an attempt to indicate his idiosyncratic combination of black and white influences. The last record that Elvis made with Sam Phillips—just before he signed with RCA Victor and went on to become a national celebrity—was a cover version of an R&B song called "Mystery Train," and it is this recording that we want to examine in some detail.

In 1953 Herman ("Little Junior") Parker (1927–71), a singer, songwriter, and harmonica player who was achieving some success with his rhythm & blues band Little Junior's Blue Flames, had recorded a tune called "Mystery Train" for Sam Phillips's Sun label. The song received little attention at the time of its release, but at some point the young Elvis Presley must have noticed it, for he recorded "Mystery Train" early in 1955—also for Sun Record Company. Examining these two versions of "Mystery Train" will assist us in understanding the developing synergy between rhythm & blues and country music that led to the phenomenon called rock 'n' roll. It will also serve to underline the essential role of small independent record labels in disseminating "marginal" music and thus in contributing to this synergy. And it will help trace the origins of Elvis Presley's unique style, illuminating what Sam Phillips (who worked extensively with both black and white artists during the heyday of Sun Record Company) had in mind when he made his oft-quoted, oft-paraphrased observation that if he could find a white man with "the Negro sound and the Negro feel," then he could become a millionaire.

"Mystery Train" as a composition is credited to Parker and Phillips, and it is a strophic twelve-bar blues structure, at least in its original version (with one harmonic irregularity: some strophes begin on the subdominant chord rather than on the **tonic,** so that the first two four-bar phrases of these particular strophes are harmonically identical). Both Parker's original performance and Presley's cover version are individually fine recordings. What is most remarkable, however, is how *different* they are from one another. Although Presley obviously learned a great deal from listening to Parker, and to dozens of other fine rhythm & blues artists, Presley's "Mystery Train" is arguably less a traditional cover than a reconceptualization of the song—a reconceptualization that reflects both Presley's distinctive self-awareness as a performer and his emerging (if probably implicit) ideas regarding his listening audience and how to engage it.

Junior Parker's original "Mystery Train" is a darkly evocative record with obvious roots both in rural blues and in rhythm & blues traditions. The train was a favorite subject and image for country blues singers, and the spare, nonlinear lyrics in Parker's song are clearly aligned with country blues traditions; this train is certainly "mysterious." In the first strophe, the "long black train," with its "sixteen coaches" taking the singer's "baby" away, paints a funereal picture. By the time we reach the third and final strophe, the train is bringing "baby" back to the singer, and the mood has brightened. But that brightening is darkened by the certainty already communicated in the second strophe: the train that took her away will "do it again." Parker's "Mystery Train" articulates a pessimistic worldview characteristic of the blues by asserting that the singer may triumph over adversity, but only temporarily—that is to say, life is a cycle of misfortunes offering, at best, periodic relief, but no permanent reprieve. (Two out of the three strophes portray "baby"'s departure, while only one depicts her anticipated return.)

Parker's band constitutes a fairly typical rhythm & blues lineup for its time: electric guitar, acoustic bass, piano, drums, and saxophone. The "chugging" rhythm conveys a perfect sense of the train's steady, inexorable momentum. The saxophone is confined basically to long, low notes that evoke the train's whistle, while an additional atmospheric touch is added at the end of the recording, with a vocal imitation of the sound of the train's brakes as it finally comes to a stop (an event marked by the concluding guitar chord and the cessation of the "chugging" rhythm).

Elvis Presley's "Mystery Train," recorded when the "hillbilly cat" was barely twenty years old, conveys a breathless sense of intensity, excitement, and even enthusiasm (listen to Presley's spontaneous-sounding, triumphant "whoop" at the end of the recording!) that makes for a totally different experience from that offered by Parker's rendition. The much faster tempo of the Presley record is of course a decisive factor, but it is only the most obvious of many reasons that may be cited for the essential transformation "Mystery Train" undergoes here. There is little, if any, attempt at naturalistic evocation of the train by Presley's band, which consists simply of electric guitar, acoustic guitar, acoustic bass, and drums. One might hear a trainlike rhythm in the pattern of the drumsticks, but the speed of the recording encourages one to imagine a roller coaster rather than a train (especially by 1955 standards). In fact, unlike Parker's record, Presley's version focuses on the singer rather than the train. Parker's protagonist seems ultimately at the mercy of the train, which has taken away his "baby" and will do so again, even if it occasionally brings her back. But Presley's vocal portrays a confident protagonist who projects control over his own future.

Presley's version presents significant alterations of Parker's original in the internal structuring of both the words and the music. In the lyrics to the second strophe, Presley makes a crucial substitution, asserting that while the train took his "baby," "*it never will again*"! As if to emphasize this essential change, Presley repeats this second strophe, with its altered lyrics, at the end of his record, so that now there are a total of four strophes, three of which look toward the return of his "baby," while only one (the first one) emphasizes her departure. That departure now becomes a one-time occurrence, as the song assumes a linear narrative shape that it did not have in Parker's original version. Even more importantly, this revision of the lyrics expresses and underlines the singer's feeling of control over the situation—definitely not an attitude traditionally associated with the blues. (It would be hard to imagine Parker asserting that the train will never take his lover away again.) In Parker's "Mystery Train," the instrumental break occurs between the second and third strophes, emphasizing, and allowing the listener to ponder, the singer's assertion that the train is going to take his "baby" again; arguably, this structural arrangement colors significantly our entire perception of the song. In Presley's version, by contrast, the instrumental break occurs after the third strophe, leaving the singer's words "she's mine, all mine" resonating in the listener's ears.

While Parker's "Mystery Train" follows the standard format of twelve-bar blues in the rhythmic arrangement of all its phrases and strophes, Presley's version is highly irregular by comparison. Many of the phrases in Presley's "Mystery Train" are longer than they "should" be; if we attempted to notate his performance in terms of a twelve-bar blues paradigm, we would find ourselves constantly having to add "half-bar" extensions (two extra beats) to many phrases. While there seems to be a general pattern formed by these extensions throughout the first three strophes, Presley breaks free of even this suggested pattern in his final strophe, extending one of the phrases yet further than before, while constricting another. (One of the truly remarkable things about this "Mystery Train" is that Presley's band was able to follow the apparent spontaneity, and consequent unpredictability, of his phrasing—especially given the breakneck speed of the performance.) Clearly, this singer is constrained by nothing; the rhythmic freedom of the music itself is reflective of his apparently limitless confidence.

With all these differences, we still should not ignore Presley's obvious debts to the blues and rhythm & blues traditions represented by Parker's original composition and recording. It is not difficult to hear strong aspects of what Sam Phillips called "the Negro sound and the Negro feel" in Presley's performance: in particular, the strong regional accent and the frequency of **blue notes** and of sliding between pitches. These characteristics are points of intersection between black blues and white country traditions. What is important is to understand how Presley emphasized these common elements to form a style that sounded significantly "blacker" (particularly to white audiences) than that of virtually any other white singer who had emerged in the post–World War II era. (Presley also incorporated some vocal effects more specifically associated with white traditions—especially the kind of rapid stuttering, "hiccuping" effect heard in lines like "comin' dow-*how*n the li-*hine*" or "she's mine, a-*hall* mine.") Even the kind of rhythmic freedom that we have observed in Presley's "Mystery Train" reflects practices common in African American music, although one would have to go back to rural blues recordings to find anything comparably irregular, as most rhythm & blues records were tied to the kind of regularity in phrasing that was usually expected in music designed to be suitable for dancing.

This observation brings us to our final point. In sum, Elvis Presley's "Mystery Train" is unique in our experience of cover records thus far because it is more aggressive and "raw" than the original on which it was modeled. But the freedom and rawness of Presley's version is not primarily in the service of a vision that seeks to return us to the original flavor and context of rural blues—far from it. Rather, Presley's "Mystery Train" is the expression of a young white singer who is looking with optimism toward an essentially unbounded future, flush with new possibilities for stylistic synthesis that would help assure both intensely satisfying personal expression and an unprecedented degree of popular success. Unlike Parker's "Mystery Train," which is the expression of a man working knowledgeably within a tradition that both defines and confines the outlines of his music, and of his worldview, Presley's "Mystery Train" offers a totally new kind of ride, a ride without preconceived limits or conditions. No wonder so many other young singers, and a remarkably large young audience, wanted to climb aboard!

THE ROCK 'N' ROLL BUSINESS

To comprehend the emergence of rock 'n' roll as a musical genre and a commercial category, it is important that we gain some understanding of the economics of the music business in the mid-1950s. The overall vitality of the American economy after World War II helped push the entertainment industry's profits to new levels. Sales of record players and radios expanded significantly after the war. Total annual record sales in the United States rose from $191 million in 1951 to $514 million in 1959.

This expansion was accompanied by a gradual diversification of mainstream popular taste, and by the reemergence of independent ("indie") record companies, whose predecessors had been wiped out twenty years before by the Great Depression. Most of these smaller companies—established by entrepreneurs in New York and Los Angeles, and in secondary centers such as Chicago, Cincinnati, Nashville, Memphis, and New Orleans—specialized in rhythm & blues and country and western recordings, which had begun to attract a national mass audience. This process was viewed with a mixture of interest and alarm by the directors of the "majors" (large record companies such as RCA Victor, Capitol, Mercury, Columbia, MGM, and Decca), which still specialized mainly in the music of Tin Pan Alley, performed by crooners. A few of the majors—for example, Decca, which had already made millions from the sale of R&B and country records—did manage to produce some early rock 'n' roll hits. Other large record companies took a couple of years to react to the emergence of rock 'n' roll. RCA Victor, for example, scored a Number One hit in 1956 with Kay Starr's rendition of "Rock and Roll Waltz" (a song that described a teenager watching her parents try to dance to the new music, accompanied by music more akin to a ballroom waltz than to rock 'n' roll). But RCA also signed the **rockabilly** singer Elvis Presley and set to work transforming him into a Hollywood matinee idol and rock 'n' roll's first bonafide superstar.

The sales charts published in industry periodicals like *Billboard* and *Cashbox* during the 1950s chronicle changes in popular taste, the role of the indies in channeling previously marginal types of music into the pop mainstream, and the emergence of a new teenage market. The charts also reveal a complex pattern of competition among musical styles. As an example, let's have a look at the *Billboard* charts for July 9, 1955, when Bill Haley and the Comets' "Rock around the Clock" became the first rock 'n' roll hit to reach the Number One position on the "Best Sellers in Stores" chart (see Box 3.1). This event is cited by rock historians as a revolutionary event, the beginning of a new era in American popular culture. However, two very different recordings, reminiscent of earlier styles of popular music, held the Number One positions on the jukebox and radio airplay charts on July 9—the Latin American ballroom dance hit "Cherry Pink and Apple Blossom White," by Perez Prado and His Orchestra, and "Learning the Blues," performed by the former big-band crooner Frank Sinatra with the accompaniment of Nelson Riddle and His Orchestra. And lest we assume that this contrast in styles represented a titanic struggle between small and large record companies, it should be noted that all three of the above records were released by majors (Decca, RCA Victor, and Capitol, respectively).

The record that pushed "Rock around the Clock" out of the Number One position two months later was "The Yellow Rose of Texas" (a nineteenth-century minstrel song), performed in a deliberately old-fashioned singalong style by the Mitch Miller Singers. Miller was the powerful director of the **A&R** (artists and repertoire) department at Columbia Records, and in that role had helped to establish the careers of pop crooners such as Doris Day, Tony Bennett, and Frankie Laine. He was also an arch-enemy of rock 'n' roll music and of its increasing influence on AM radio programming, which he derided as being geared to "the eight- to fourteen-year-olds, to the pre-shave crowd that make up twelve percent of the country's population and zero percent of its buying power" (Clarke 1995, p. 410). It is not hard to understand Miller's anger over the domination of radio by Top 40 playlists—predetermined lists of records by a limited number of artists, often backed up by bribes from record company officials to radio station personnel. One could see the free-form FM broadcasts of the late 1960s (Chapter 5) and the rise of alternative stations in the 1980s and 1990s as similar reactions against the playlist concept. But his refusal to recognize the teenage market was nothing if not short-sighted. A 1958 survey of the purchasing patterns of the nineteen million teenagers in the United States showed that they spent a total of nine million dollars a year and strongly influenced their parents' choices of everything from toothpaste and canned food to automobiles and phonographs. And, of course, they bought millions and millions of records.

Bill Haley and the Comets shake up a crowd at the Sports Arena, Hershey, Pennsylvania, 1956. Courtesy Library of Congress.

Box 3.1 Bill Haley and "Rock around the Clock" (1955)

Bill Haley (1925–81) would seem an unlikely candidate for the first big rock 'n' roll star, but in the early 1950s this leader of various obscure western swing groups was seeking a style that would capture the enthusiasm of the growing audience of young listeners and dancers, and he accurately sensed which way the wind was blowing. He dropped his cowboy image, changed the name of his accompanying group from the Saddlemen to the Comets, and in 1953 wrote and recorded a song, "Crazy, Man, Crazy," that offered a reasonable emulation of dance-oriented black rhythm & blues music. The record, released by a small indie label, rose as high as Number Twelve on the pop charts. In 1954 the Comets were signed by Decca Records, where they worked in the studio with A&R man Milt Gabler. Gabler, who had produced a series of hit records with Louis Jordan and His Tympany Five (see Chapter 2), helped to push Haley's style further in the direction of jump band rhythm & blues—"I'd sing Jordan riffs to the group that would be picked up by the electric guitars and tenor sax," he later said.

As we have already mentioned, Bill Haley and the Comets recorded commercially successful cover versions of rhythm & blues hits in the mid-1950s, notably "Shake, Rattle, and Roll" (Number Seven, 1954) and "See You Later, Alligator" (Number Six, 1956). But they attained their unique status in pop music history when their record of "Rock around the Clock" became, in 1955, the first rock 'n' roll record to be a Number One pop hit. It stayed in the top spot for eight consecutive weeks during the summer of 1955 and eventually sold over twenty-two million copies worldwide.

"Rock around the Clock," written by Max C. Freedman and Jimmy DeKnight, was actually recorded in 1954 and was not a big hit when first released. But then the record was prominently featured in the opening credits of the 1955 movie *Blackboard Jungle*, which dealt with inner-city teenagers and juvenile delinquency, and "Rock around the Clock" quickly achieved massive popularity—and forged an enduring link that has connected teenagers, rock 'n' roll, and movies ever since. Bill Haley's claim to have "invented" rock 'n' roll deserves little credibility. But Haley proved to be an important popularizer of previously marginalized musical sounds and ideas, and he paved the way for the widespread acceptance of many more creative artists working with rock 'n' roll.

"Rock around the Clock" demonstrated the unprecedented success that a white group with a country background could achieve playing a twelve-bar blues song driven by the sounds of electric guitar, bass, and drums. It proved a portent of the enormous changes that were about to overtake American popular music and opened the floodgates for artists like Elvis Presley, Carl Perkins, and Buddy Holly. "Rock around the Clock" also helped prepare a receptive mass audience for the sounds of rhythm & blues, and for black artists building on the rhythm & blues tradition. While the song was still at the top of the pop chart in 1955, Chuck Berry's trailblazing "Maybellene" made its appearance on the same chart, and before long was itself in the Top 10.

Box 3.2 The Electric Guitar

It is almost impossible to conjure up a mental image of Chuck Berry—or Buddy Holly, or Jimi Hendrix—without an electric guitar in his hands. Certainly, one of rock 'n' roll's most significant effects on popular music was its elevation of the electric guitar to the position of centrality that the instrument still enjoys in most genres of popular music today. The development of the electric guitar is a good example of the complex relationship between technological developments and changing musical styles. Up through the end of World War II, the guitar was found mainly in popular music that originated in the South (blues and hillbilly music), and in various "exotic" genres (Hawai'ian and Latin American guitar records were quite popular in the 1920s and 1930s). Because of its low volume, the acoustic guitar was difficult to use in large dance bands and equally difficult to record. Engineers began to experiment with electronically amplified guitars in the 1920s, and in 1931 the Electro String Instrument Company (better known as Rickenbacker) introduced the first commercially produced electric guitars. Laid across the player's knees like the steel or Hawai'ian guitars used in country music and blues, these instruments were called "frying pans" because of their distinctive round bodies and long necks. By the mid-1930s the Gibson Company had introduced a hollow-body guitar with a new type of pickup—a magnetic plate or coil attached to the body of the guitar, which converts the physical vibrations of its strings into patterns of electric energy. This pickup later became known as the <u>Charlie Christian</u> pickup, after the young African American guitarist from Texas (1916–42) who introduced the guitar into Benny Goodman's band and helped to pioneer the modern jazz style called *bebop*. Despite Christian's innovations with the Goodman band, few of the popular big bands introduced the instrument, and none allowed it to play a prominent role.

The *solid-body electric guitar* was developed after World War II and was first used in rhythm & blues, blues, and country bands—the country musician <u>Merle Travis</u> (1917–83) had one designed for him as early as 1946, and blues musicians such as <u>T-Bone Walker</u> (1910–75) and Muddy Waters were also recording with electric guitars by the late 1940s. The first commercially produced solid-body electric guitar was the Fender Broadcaster (soon renamed the Telecaster), brainchild of Leo Fender and George Fullerton. This model, released in 1948, featured two electronic pickups, knobs to control volume and tone (timbre), and a switch that allowed the two pickups to be used alone or together, allowing the player to create a palette of different sounds. In 1954 Fender released the Stratocaster, the first guitar with three pickups, and the first with a "whammy bar" or "vibrato bar," a metal rod attached to the guitar's bridge that allowed the player to bend pitches with his right as well as his left hand. Fender's most successful competitor, the Gibson Company, released a solid body guitar in 1952, christening it the Les Paul in honor of the popular guitarist who helped to popularize the new instrument and the use of multiple track tape recording. The first widely popular electric bass guitar, the Fender Precision Bass, was introduced in 1951.

What is it about electric guitars that makes them such an object of fascination—sometimes bordering on fetishism—for musicians and fans alike? Like any kind of influential technology—say, the automobile or the phonograph—the meaning of the guitar is a complex matter. To begin with, the instrument came into the popular mainstream with a somewhat dubious reputation, perhaps a carryover from the medieval European association of stringed instruments with the Devil, and associated with the music of marginalized regions (the South, Latin America) and people (sailors and railway men, sharecroppers and hobos, blacks, Latinos, and poor southern whites). A lot of the put-downs aimed at young rock 'n' rollers by the mainstream music press of the 1950s ridiculed the guitar, suggesting that it was an instrument that anyone could play (if you believe *that*, we suggest that you take a few guitar lessons!). The electric guitar became a symbol of the energetic diversity that was elbowing its way into the mainstream of American popular music during this period. This feeling of excess and invasion was reinforced by the development of portable tube amplifiers, which, if pushed hard enough, could provide a dense, sizzling, and very loud sound, eventually augmented by special effects devices such as wah-wah pedals and "fuzz boxes," and perfectly designed to drive parents and other authority figures nuts. In addition, the suitability of the guitar for use as a phallic symbol—a formerly male practice more recently appropriated by female rockers—has added to the instrument's aura of danger and excitement.

LISTENING AND ANALYSIS   "MAYBELLENE"

Basic Description

Charles Edward Anderson ("Chuck") Berry (b. 1926) burst precipitously onto the pop music scene with his first record, "Maybellene." It was a novel synthesis that did not sound precisely like anything before it, and it introduced listeners to an already fully formed style of songwriting, singing, and guitar playing that would exercise a primal influence on virtually all the rock 'n' roll to follow.

Berry was born in California but grew up in St. Louis, where he absorbed blues and rhythm & blues styles. He was one of the first black musicians to consciously forge his own version of these styles for appeal to the mass market—and he was certainly the most successful of his generation in this effort. Like many other black musicians, Berry also knew country music, and he found that his performances of country songs in clubs appealed strongly to the white members of his audience. He put this knowledge and experience to good use: "Maybellene" was distantly modeled on a country number called "Ida Red." Nevertheless, the primary elements of "Maybellene" trace their roots clearly to rhythm & blues: the thick, buzzing timbre of Berry's electric guitar (see Box 3.2); the blue notes and slides in both voice and guitar; the socking backbeat of the drum; and the form, derived from twelve-bar blues structures.

Chuck Berry in 1959. Courtesy Library of Congress.

What, then, made "Maybellene" sound so startlingly new? The explosive tempo, for one thing; while bands occasionally may have played for dancing at a tempo like this, no vocal-based rhythm & blues had ever gone at this pace, because it's exceptionally hard to articulate words, and have time to breathe, when trying to sing at this tempo. But Berry pulls it off, articulating the words with clarity and remarkable force. This brings up another essential aspect of the record's novelty and appeal, which is the lyrics themselves. The lyrics to "Maybellene" provide an original and clever description of a lovers' quarrel in the form of a car chase, complete with a punning invented verb form (*motorvatin'*), humorous details ("Rain water blowin'" under the automobile hood, which is "doin' my motor good"), and a breathless ending in which the singer catches Maybellene in her Cadillac at the top of a hill—an ending that still leaves listeners room to imagine a wide range of sequels. And what could reach out to a young audience more effectively than a story featuring both cars and sex appeal?

In addition, we shouldn't miss the implied class distinction the lyrics make between Maybellene, in her top-of-the-line Cadillac Coupe de Ville, and the narrator, in his more humble, middle-class, but eminently functional "V-8 Ford." As he chases and finally catches the Cadillac (and Maybellene), there is a sense of the underdog's triumphing in the race, and the boastful claim of the first verse, that nothing could outrun his V-8 Ford, is vindicated. (Cars have long been an important status symbol in American culture, and African American culture is certainly no exception to this. A song recorded by Bessie Smith in 1928, a generation before "Maybellene," called "Put It Right Here (Or Keep It Out There)," described the singer's deadbeat lover as follows: "Once he was like a Cadillac, now he's like an old worn-out Ford." The concern with cars persists into contemporary rap music; an early example of this is "Sucker M.C.'s," a 1983 hit by Run-D.M.C.).

All the basic ingredients that would inform a string of successive, successful Chuck Berry records are present in "Maybellene." These elements became his trademarks: an arresting instrumental introduction for unaccompanied electric guitar; relentless intensity produced by a very fast tempo and a very loud volume level; formal and stylistic elements strongly related to earlier rhythm & blues music; and witty lyrics, clearly enunciated and designed to appeal to the lifestyle and aspirations of his young audience.

Form

The form of "Maybellene" is clearly based on the twelve-bar blues. The **chorus** ("Maybellene, why can't you be true?") adheres to the traditional twelve-bar structure in every respect: three four-bar phrases, standard chord pattern, and even a traditional three-line poetic arrangement where the second line is a repetition of the first. But the **verses,** while twelve bars long, completely suppress chord changes, remaining on the "home" (or **tonic**) chord throughout while the voice delivers rapid-fire lyrics using brief, repetitive patterns of notes (see listening chart). Ironically, by eliminating chord changes and restricting melodic interest in the verses, Berry turns what could have been a static, purely strophic form into something more dynamic. Instead of a string of standard twelve-bar blues stanzas, we hear an alternating verse-chorus structure that allows Berry to tell his story, and to build his record, in a more exciting way.

The stripped-down music of the verses focuses all attention on their lyrics—which is appropriate, as it is the verses that relate the ongoing progress of the car chase. Their repetitive melodic formulas allow Berry to concentrate on articulating the densely packed words; the continuous verbal activity more than compensates for the lack of musical variety. Actually, the verses build enormous tension, so that when the choruses at last bring some chord changes—basic as they are—there is a feeling of release and expansion. The pace of the lyrics also slows down momentarily for the choruses, which reinforces this effect of expansion and allows Berry to lean expressively on the crucial name "Maybel*lene.*" Yet, while the choruses provide variety and release, they create tension of another sort, as they postpone the continuation of the story being told in the verses. This same effect is created on a larger scale by the instrumental break before the final verse: variety and release on the one hand (and an opportunity for Berry to showcase his considerable guitar chops), along with a real sense of racing along down the highway, but tension and postponement of the story's climax on the other.

The manipulation of a limited set of musical materials to achieve maximal results of variety, novelty, and excitement is the essence of effective rock 'n' roll. "Maybellene" is an outstanding case in point. The formal issues discussed above may seem either obvious or all but lost in the pure visceral intensity of the record, but the seamlessness of Chuck Berry's artistry should not blind us to the man's brilliance. Above all, "Maybellene" is a beautifully formed record, building inexorably from start to finish, where everything is made to count, without a single word or note wasted.

The Song/The Recording

In Chuck Berry's "Maybellene," the song *is* the recording. When people think of or cite "Maybellene," they are referring to Berry's original recording of it—the ultimate, and really the only important, source material. The culture of rock 'n' roll centered to an unprecedented extent on records: records played on the radio, records played at dances, records purchased for home listening. Studio recordings thus increasingly came to represent the original, primary documents of the music, often preceding and generally taking precedence over any live performances of the material. Baby boomers went to hear rock 'n' roll stars perform the hits they already knew from the records they heard and bought; on the nationally broadcast television program *American Bandstand,* singers came without accompanying bands and lip-synched their songs while the records played in the background. The issuing of sheet music was becoming an afterthought, an ancillary to the recording. In many future discussions, consequently, we will be discussing the song and the recording as one, rather than as separate entities.

The record opens arrestingly with the sound of Berry's hollow-body electric guitar playing a bluesy lick that literally sizzles with sonic energy. The impact of "Maybellene" is in no small part due to the infectious rhythmic **groove** and texture established by Berry and a gifted group of sidemen, including the great blues composer and bassist Willie Dixon, an integral part of Muddy Waters's recordings for Chess Records (see Chapter 2); Jerome Green, playing maracas; and pianist Johnny Johnson, who may well have played a role in the creation of Berry's songs. Some credit for the overall sound of the recording must also go to Phil and Leonard Chess, who in their years of recording Chicago blues musicians such as Muddy Waters and Howlin' Wolf had learned how to stay out of the way of a good recording. They sometimes offered advice but never tried to radically alter a musician's style for commercial effect.

Amid the numerous elements borrowed from rhythm & blues and urban blues, we may hear in "Maybellene" a prominent, very regular bass line, alternating between two notes on beats 1 and 3 of each bar. The rhythmic feel of this bass line is stylistically much more suggestive of country music than of anything found typically in rhythm & blues, and its presence here points to Berry's knowledge of country music and to what Berry himself has identified as the country origins of "Maybellene." As we shall see repeatedly, rock 'n' roll music is often based on a synthesis of widely diverse stylistic elements.

LISTENING CHART "MAYBELLENE"

Music and lyrics by Chuck Berry (also credited to disc jockeys Russel Fratto and Alan Freed);[1] as performed by Chuck Berry and His Combo; recorded 1955

FORM	LYRICS	DESCRIPTIVE COMMENTS
Instrumental intro		Solo electric guitar "hook" establishes characteristic sound (suggesting auto horns) and tempo.
Chorus	*Maybellene . . .*	Twelve-bar blues.
Verse 1	*As I was . . .*	Twelve bars, without any chord changes; very fast pacing of lyrics.
Chorus	*Maybellene . . .*	As before.
Verse 2	*The Cadillac . . .*	As in verse 1.
Chorus	*Maybellene . . .*	As before.
Instrumental break		Two successive twelve-bar sections.
Chorus	*Maybellene . . .*	As before.
Verse 3	*The motor . . .*	As in verse 1.
Chorus	*Maybellene . . .*	As before.
Instrumental coda		Fades out.

EARLY ROCK 'N' ROLL STARS ON THE R&B SIDE

We will represent the rhythm & blues–based side of rock 'n' roll with the three most prominent African Americans to be identified with the new music. Of the three, Chuck Berry was the songwriter/performer who most obviously addressed his songs to teenage America (white and black) in the 1950s; Little Richard was the cultivator of a deliberately outrageous performance style that appealed on the basis of its strangeness, novelty, and sexual ambiguity; and Fats Domino's work most directly embodied the continuity of rhythm & blues with rock 'n' roll. As might be expected from this description, Domino was the earliest of the three to become an established performer (although he was slightly younger than Berry)—he cut his first rhythm & blues hit, "The Fat Man," in 1949 at the age of twenty-one. But all three crossed over to the

---

1. In the early years of rock 'n' roll, the record market was fluid and unpredictable, and agents, promoters, distributors, and disc jockeys were often given (or would take) songwriting credits in exchange for the "favor" of pushing particular artists or records. There was nothing new in this practice; it just became much more widespread. In any case, it is doubtful that Fratto and Freed had anything substantial to do with the creation of "Maybellene," although they certainly helped it to be heard and to become popular.

pop charts and mainstream success within the first few months following the massive success of Bill Haley's "Rock around the Clock" (see Box 3.1).

Chuck Berry

After the success of "Maybellene," Chuck Berry went on to write and record other excellent rock 'n' roll songs that became more and more explicit celebrations of American teenage culture and its music. "Roll Over Beethoven" (1956) praises rhythm & blues at the expense of classical music. "School Day" (Number Eight pop, Number One R&B in 1957) describes drudgery relieved by an after-school trip to the "juke joint," at which point the record becomes literally an advertisement for itself and an anthem for the music it represents: "Hail! Hail! Rock 'n' roll! Deliver me from the days of old!" "Rock and Roll Music" (Number Eight pop, Number Six R&B, also in 1957) articulates the virtues of its subject, as opposed to the limitations of "modern jazz" or a "symphony." "Sweet Little Sixteen" (Number Two pop, Number One R&B in 1958) wittily describes the young collector of "famed autographs," coping with growing up ("tight dresses and lipstick"), for whom a rock 'n' roll show becomes—in her mind, at least—a national party where all the "cats" want to dance with her.

Berry's consummate statement on rock 'n' roll mythology is doubtless "Johnny B. Goode" (Number Eight pop, Number Five R&B in 1958). Here he relates the story of a "country boy" who "never learned to read or write so well" but who "could play a guitar just like a-ringin' a bell." (Berry's autobiography states that the "country boy" was originally a "colored boy," but Berry opted to make his tale color-blind, recognizing the diversity of his audience and the potential universality of his myth.) The boy's mother predicts his coming success as a bandleader with his "name in lights, saying 'Johnny B. Goode tonight' "—as one of pop music's greatest verbal puns embodies the dream of every teenager with a guitar and a wish to succeed as a rock 'n' roller (with parental approval and appreciation, no less)!

It cannot be known how many careers in music were inspired or encouraged by "Johnny B. Goode," but a list of pop musicians who have been obviously and singularly influenced by Chuck Berry would read like a who's who of rock stars from the 1960s and beyond. He is probably the only musician of his generation to be inescapably influential on three different, and essential, fronts: as a brilliantly clever and articulate lyricist and songwriter; as a fine rock 'n' roll vocal stylist; and as a pioneering electric guitarist. The mass adulation belonged to Elvis Presley, but the greatest influence on musicians unquestionably was made by Berry.

Little Richard

The centrality of records to the culture of rock 'n' roll didn't negate the significance of live performances. Indeed, live performances disseminated via the new mass medium of television, or on the movie screen, assumed a new importance for performers of rock 'n' roll music, and individual artists and vocal groups sought to cultivate visual characteristics or mannerisms that would set them apart from others and encourage listeners to remember them—and to go out and buy their records. Chuck Berry had his famous "duck walk" as a stage device. But no performer in the early years of rock 'n' roll was as visually flamboyant as Little Richard.

Richard Wayne Penniman ("Little Richard") (b. 1932) spent several lackluster years as a journeyman rhythm & blues performer before hitting the pop charts early

Little Richard in 1957. Frank Driggs Collection.

in 1956 with his wild performance of the nonsensical song "Tutti-Frutti." Based on the twelve-bar blues, "Tutti-Frutti" alternated nonsense choruses ("Tutti-frutti, au rutti, a-wop-bop-a-loom-op a-lop-bam-boom!"—and variants thereof) with non-specific but obviously leering verses ("I got a gal named Sue, she knows just what to do"), all delivered by Little Richard in an uninhibited shouting style complete with falsetto whoops and accompanied with a pounding band led by Little Richard's equally uninhibited piano. In retrospect, it seems surprising that records like "Tutti-Frutti" and its even more successful—and more obviously salacious—follow-up, "Long Tall Sally" (see listening chart, p. 86) got played on mainstream radio at all. It must have been assumed by programmers that Little Richard was a novelty act and that therefore nobody would pay attention to, or understand, the words of his songs. But teenage listeners in the 1950s certainly understood that Little Richard embodied the new spirit of rock 'n' roll music in the most extroverted, outrageous, and original way.

Any doubts on the matter would surely have been resolved by seeing Little Richard's performances in any of the three rock 'n' roll movies in which he appeared during the two years of his greatest popular success, 1956–57: *Don't Knock the Rock, The Girl Can't Help It,* and *Mister Rock 'n' Roll.* Heavily made up, with his hair in an enormous pompadour, rolling his eyes, playing the piano while standing and gyrating wildly, Little Richard epitomized the abandon celebrated in rock 'n' roll lyrics and music. (Although new to his audiences, Richard's appearance and approach to performance had clear antecedents, going back to earlier styles of stage performance.) Both the sound of his recordings and the visual characteristics of his performances made Little Richard an exceptionally strong influence

on later performers; the white rockabilly singer-pianist Jerry Lee Lewis was ines-
timably in his debt, and in the 1960s the English Beatles and the American Creedence Clearwater Revival—along with many other bands—played music whose
roots could readily be traced back to Little Richard. Moreover, the lingering (and
carefully crafted) ambiguity of Little Richard's sexual identity—available evidence
suggests that he might best have been classified in the early days as an omnivore—
paved the way for the image of performers such as David Bowie, Elton John, and
Prince.

Our representative example of Little Richard's music is "Long Tall Sally" (see
the listening chart). Like most of Little Richard's songs, this one is built on the
twelve-bar blues. Like Chuck Berry and other artists who came out of rhythm &
blues to seek pop stardom, Little Richard adapted the twelve-bar blues structure so
as to reflect the more traditionally pop-friendly format of verse-chorus. Here, the
first four bars of each blues stanza are set to changing words—**verses**—while the
remaining eight bars, with unchanging words, function as a repeated **chorus.** This
simple but surprisingly effective formal arrangement is reflected in both identical
and varied ways in many rock 'n' roll songs of the period; for examples of variations on this structure, see the listening charts for Elvis Presley's "Don't Be Cruel"
and for the Coasters' "Charlie Brown."

Fats Domino

Antoine "Fats" Domino (b. 1928), a singer, pianist, and songwriter, had been an established presence on the rhythm & blues charts for several years by the time he
scored his first large-scale pop breakthrough with "Ain't It a Shame" in 1955 (Number Ten pop, Number One R&B). In this case, mainstream success was simply the
result of the market's catching up with Domino; there is no significant stylistic difference between his earlier rhythm & blues hits and his rock 'n' roll bestsellers like
"I'm in Love Again" and "I'm Walkin'." Domino himself remarked that he was always playing the same music, that they called it "rhythm & blues" first and "rock
'n' roll" later, and that it made no difference to him—although it surely did make
a difference to him when the rock 'n' roll market catapulted his record sales into
the millions and eventually made him the second biggest-selling recording artist of
the 1950s, right behind Elvis Presley.

Domino was born in New Orleans and grew up bathed in the rich and diverse
musical traditions of that city. His distinctive regional style best exemplifies the
strong connections between rock 'n' roll and earlier pop music. Jazz was a strong
early influence on him, along with the rhythm & blues piano style of Professor Longhair (1918–80; real name Henry Roeland Byrd) and the jump band style of trum-
peter Dave Bartholomew's ensemble. Bartholomew became Domino's arranger, producer, and songwriting partner, and their collaboration produced a remarkable
string of consistently fine and successful records. Their "New Orleans" sound was
also widely admired and imitated among musicians; Domino played piano on hit
records by other artists, and Little Richard recorded in New Orleans to use the city's
distinctive sidemen and thus try to capture some of the city's rock 'n' roll magic.
(Little Richard's "Long Tall Sally" is modeled directly on Domino's "Ain't It a
Shame," both in formal layout and musical arrangement.)

Given his strong links to tradition, it is not surprising that Fats Domino recorded
a number of standards—in contradistinction to artists like Chuck Berry and Little

Fats Domino and his band, in a scene from the 1958 movie *The Big Beat*. Courtesy Library of Congress.

Richard, who concentrated on novel songs and styles to appeal to their new audience. In fact, Domino's 1956 remake of "Blueberry Hill" proved to be his most popular record, reaching the Number Two position on the pop charts and topping the R&B charts. "Blueberry Hill" was a Tin Pan Alley tune that had originally been a big hit in 1940 for the Glenn Miller Orchestra (with vocal by Ray Eberle). Domino preserved his own rhythm & blues–based style when performing "Blueberry Hill" and other standards, however, thus bringing a new kind of musical hybrid to mass-market attention, and with this phenomenon a new and important musical bridge was crossed. We might say that, rather than crossing over himself, Domino made the music cross over to him. Smooth Tin Pan Alley–style crooning and uninflected urban diction were replaced by Domino's rhythmically accented, full-throated singing in his characteristic New Orleans accent, and it certainly wasn't the sound of a sweet band backing him or shaping his own piano accompaniment. Another pop success for Domino was his rocking uptempo version of "My Blue Heaven," a huge Tin Pan Alley hit from the 1920s.

Fats Domino, Little Richard, and Chuck Berry all achieved their successes recording on independent labels, thus demonstrating the great importance of the indies to the popularization of rock 'n' roll. Domino recorded for Imperial, a Los Angeles–based concern headed by Lew Chudd, that also issued records by the important rhythm & blues electric guitar stylist Aaron "T-Bone" Walker. Little Richard was an artist for Specialty Records, Art Rupe's Hollywood label, that had on its

Box 3.3   Tin Pan Alley Lives! The "Standard" in the Age of Rock 'n' Roll

The advent of rock 'n' roll is often viewed as the death of Tin Pan Alley. It is easy to see why this would seem to be so. Country- and rhythm & blues–based musical styles were moving to the center of the pop world from the peripheries, and Tin Pan Alley music was the mainstream music of the generation that the baby boomers were rebelling against: it was their parents' music. However, the Tin Pan Alley style proved versatile enough to survive, and even to flourish, in a number of different guises during the early years of rock 'n' roll.

Fats Domino was not the only rock 'n' roller to successfully adapt "standard" songs to a rhythm & blues–based style. The procedure was a stock in trade of many black vocal groups; the Platters virtually made a career of it, scoring Number One hits with "My Prayer" (1956), "Twilight Time" (1958), and "Smoke Gets in Your Eyes" (1959). These were all Tin Pan Alley tunes, dressed up with strong backbeats and a commanding, extroverted lead vocal, that were accepted by young listeners as rock 'n' roll ballads. From the country side, Elvis Presley included Tin Pan Alley standards in his performing repertoire from the beginning of his career with Sun Records, and in 1959 the country artist Carl Mann achieved a pop hit with his rockabilly version of "Mona Lisa," a song that had been a huge success in 1950 for Nat "King" Cole as a Tin Pan Alley–style ballad.

Furthermore, new songs in the old Tin Pan Alley style could be found on the pop charts even in the late 1950s, right along with the new rock 'n' roll hits. In what might seem one of the unlikeliest musical success stories of the era, the young singer <u>Johnny Mathis</u> (born 1935, the same year as Elvis Presley) began a career in 1957 as a latter-day crooner with gentle pop ballads like "It's Not for Me to Say" and "Chances Are," and soon found himself a best-selling recording artist who appealed as much to the rock 'n' roll generation as he did to their parents. Mathis's widespread acceptance makes one hesitate to call his approach anachronistic and demonstrates again the fluidity of pop music styles and trends during this period.

Perhaps the most remarkable manifestation of Tin Pan Alley endurance may be found in the career and recordings of Frank Sinatra during the 1950s. Sinatra's status as *the* pop icon of the 1940s seemed well on the wane in the opening years of the new decade; his records were no longer selling well, and by 1952 Columbia had allowed his contract to lapse. Reluctantly picked up by Capitol Records, Sinatra turned to the adult audience and to the new medium of the long-playing record album to reinvent himself, and he spectacularly revived his career. This involved a rethinking of the standard Tin Pan Alley repertoire, along with some novel ideas about the possibilities inherent in the pop album format.

Working with distinguished arranger/conductors like Billy May and Nelson Riddle, Sinatra conceived fresh interpretations of "standards" that renovated these old songs and, in some cases, brought new and unexpected meanings to them. One of the most famous examples of this is Sinatra's 1956 recording of "I've Got You under My Skin," a Cole Porter composition from the 1930s. The song most readily suggests a mood of acquiescence—of giving in to the condition of being obsessed by, and possessed by, another. But Sinatra's interpretation brings a novel and occasionally aggressive intensity to the song, as if the singer is surprised and even somewhat at war with his own newly discovered sense of vulnerability. This version uncovers new layers of richness and potential in a song that other singers and listeners might just have taken for granted in the 1950s, and Sinatra managed to do this with many of the standards he recorded during this decade. Furthermore, Sinatra presented these standards not as single records but in groups, in albums that were designed by him and his arranger/conductors as complete and integrated listening experiences, as opposed to essentially random collections of single songs. For example, "I've Got You under My Skin" was on the album *Songs for Swingin' Lovers*, where Sinatra's distinctive interpretation of Cole Porter's standard clearly meshed with the active, worldly implications of the album's theme. Among other Sinatra albums from this period that present standards in thematically unified groups are *In the Wee Small Hours* (1955, a collection of world-weary "saloon" songs) and *Come Dance with Me* (1959). Although the term did not come into common use until the mid-1960s, it is arguable that Sinatra's are the first real *concept albums* (see Chapter 5). Like the songs within them, these albums have themselves become "standards" of pop excellence and innovation.

Spurred by his new success as an album artist, Sinatra also sought out good new material in the Tin Pan Alley mold to reestablish a strong presence on the pop singles charts. Many of these songs came from movies—a medium through which Sinatra also reinvigorated his career in the 1950s, by appearing successfully as a dramatic actor in nonmusical films, in addition to starring in musicals. One of Sinatra's major hits of this period, "Love and Marriage" (see Chapter 2), which he introduced in 1955 on a television production of the Thornton Wilder play *Our Town*, found new life—and a new audience—as the theme song for another television show in the 1980s, the long-running comedy *Married with Children*. By this time, Sinatra, in his seventies, was himself the longest-running superstar in the history of American popular music.

roster such rhythm & blues stars as Percy Mayfield, Lloyd Price, and Guitar Slim, along with important African American gospel groups and soloists. Berry's records were issued on Chess, the Chicago label of the Chess brothers Leonard and Phil, that also served as home for an impressive list of blues-based artists like Muddy Waters, Howlin' Wolf, and Willie Dixon, along with other rock 'n' rollers like Bo Diddley and the Moonglows.

EARLY ROCK 'N' ROLL STARS ON THE COUNTRY SIDE

Elvis Presley

The biggest rock 'n' roll star to come from the country side of the music world was of course Elvis Presley. Presley's early career with the independent label Sun

Records was briefly considered in the previous discussion of "Mystery Train." When RCA Victor bought out Presley's contract from Sun in late 1955, at the then-extravagant price of thirty-five thousand dollars, this mainstream major label set about consciously trying to turn the "hillbilly cat" into a mainstream performer without compromising the strength of his appeal to teenagers. In this they were assisted by two major players. First, there was Presley's manager, Colonel Thomas Parker, who saw to it that Presley was seen repeatedly on television variety shows and in a series of romantic Hollywood films. Second was RCA's Nashville **producer** Chet Atkins, who saw to it that Presley's records for the label were made pop-friendly, according to Atkins's standards. (In the 1960s Atkins became the producer most credited with developing the "Nashville Sound" of pop-oriented country music; see Chapter 5.) They succeeded beyond anyone's expectations. Although Presley's television performances were denounced by authorities as vulgar because of the singer's hip-shaking gyrations, the shows were attended by hordes of screaming young fans and were admired on the screen by millions of young viewers. And Presley's records racked up astronomical sales as he dominated the top of the pop charts steadily from 1956 on into the early 1960s, quickly establishing himself as the biggest-selling solo artist of rock 'n' roll, and then as the biggest-selling solo recording artist of *any* period and style—a title he still holds at the beginning of the twenty-first century!

Presley's biggest hit, "Don't Be Cruel," topped the charts for eleven weeks in the late summer and fall of 1956, eventually yielding pride of place to another Presley record, "Love Me Tender." "Don't Be Cruel" is based on the twelve-bar blues (see the listening chart below). Presley's vocal is heavy with blues-derived and country inflections; we hear a striking regional accent, and the occasional "hiccuping" effect ("baby, it's just you I'm *a*-thinkin' of") is one associated particularly with rockabilly singers like Presley, Gene Vincent, and Buddy Holly. The strong backbeat throughout evokes rhythm & blues. Imposed on all these diverse and intense stylistic elements is a wash of electronic **reverb**—an attempt by the engineers at RCA's Nashville studios to emulate the distinctive (and decidedly low-tech) **"slap-back"** echo sound of Presley's previous recordings on Sun Records. There is also the sweetening sound of the backing vocal group, the Jordanaires, whose precise "bop, bop"s and crooning "aah"s and "ooo"s are doubly rooted in white gospel music and in the most genteel, established, mainstream pop style. Whether this odd amalgam is deemed to work as a source of stylistic enrichment, or whether listening to Presley and the Jordanaires together on this record seems like listening to the Chords and the Crew Cuts *simultaneously* performing "Sh-Boom" (see the preceding discussion of cover versions) will obviously be a matter of personal taste. It can never be known how much the Jordanaires added, or if they added at all, to the appeal of this and many other records Presley made with them for RCA. But the commercial success of these records was unprecedented, and their mixture of styles was yet another indication of the extent to which the traditional barriers in pop music were falling down. (Major labels often tended to sweeten recordings by rock 'n' roll singers for the mass market, while the indies went for a rawer, more basic sound. For example, many of Jackie Wilson's rhythm & blues–based recordings for the Brunswick label—a subsidiary of the major Decca—featured elaborately arranged backing choruses and orchestral arrangements.)

Frank Sinatra and **Elvis Presley** on television together in 1960: it looks like the young "idol" is trying to teach the older "idol" some new moves. Frank Driggs Collection.

On the other side of "Don't Be Cruel" was Presley's version of "Hound Dog," a song that had been a major rhythm & blues hit in 1953 for Big Mama Thornton. Comparing Presley's cover of "Hound Dog" for RCA with the earlier cover he did for Sun of the rhythm & blues tune "Mystery Train" sheds further light on the shaping of Elvis's image for mainstream consumption. Whereas his rockabilly "Mystery Train" is noticeably faster, looser, and wilder than Junior Parker's original, his "Hound Dog" has lost some of its teeth—so to speak—as a result of the bowdlerization of the original words. Big Mama Thornton's version is full of sexual innuendo, making it clear that the term "hound dog" is being used metaphorically, not literally ("daddy, I know you ain't no real cool cat"; "you can wag your tail, but I ain't gonna feed you no more"; see the discussion in Chapter 2). Such sexual implications are gone in Presley's rendition, which seems to be literally about a pathetic mutt who is "cryin' all the time" and "ain't never caught a rabbit." With the lyrics cleaned up in this way for mass consumption, the undeniable passion of Presley's performance seems a bit over the top for the subject matter, turning the record into a kind of novelty song. But this certainly didn't bother the singer's audience, most of whom could not have been familiar with Thornton's original anyway; "Hound Dog" proved just about as popular as "Don't Be Cruel" itself.

Presley's extraordinary popularity established rock 'n' roll as an unprecedented mass-market phenomenon. His reputation as a performer and recording artist endured up to his death in 1977 at the age of forty-two—and continues beyond the grave; Graceland, his home in Memphis, Tennessee, is now a public museum dedicated to his memory and it is visited by upwards of 600,000 people annually. Presley gave strong performances and made fine records at many points throughout his career, and he starred in many movies. But it cannot be denied that Elvis Presley's principal importance as a musical influence and innovator—like that of Chuck Berry, Little Richard, and Fats Domino—rests upon his achievements during the early years of rock 'n' roll. In 1956 Presley cut a handful of records that literally changed the world for himself and for those around him, and the unbridled exuberance of his live performances at that time were the model for every white kid who wanted to move mountains by strumming a guitar, shaking his hips, and lifting his voice.

Buddy Holly

Buddy Holly (Charles Hardin Holley) (1936–59) offered an image virtually the opposite of Presley's intense, aggressive, suggestively sexual stage persona. Here was a clean-cut, lanky, bespectacled young man—obviously nobody's idea of a matinee idol, but one who certainly knew his way around a guitar and a recording studio. The Texas-born Holly began his career with country music but soon fell under the influence of Presley's musical style and success and formed a rock 'n' roll band, the Crickets.

Holly's first record in his new style, "That'll Be the Day," rose to Number One on the pop charts in late 1957 and established his characteristic and highly influential sound. "That'll Be the Day" combined elements of country, rhythm & blues, and mainstream pop in the kind of synthesis that typified rock 'n' roll in a general sense, but which nevertheless projected a distinctive approach and sensibility. Holly's vocal style, full of country twang and hiccups, along with expressive **blue notes,** projected that mixture of toughness and vulnerability that forms the essence of both fine country singing and fine blues singing. The Crickets' instrumental lineup of two electric guitars (lead and rhythm), electric bass, and drums provided an intense support for Holly's voice, and during instrumental breaks, Holly's lead guitar playing was active, riff-based, and hard-edged in a way that reflected the in-

Buddy Holly. Frank Driggs Collection.

fluence of Chuck Berry. "That'll Be the Day" is structured like a typical pop song, alternating verses and choruses of eight bars each; but when it comes time to provide an instrumental break, the Crickets play a twelve-bar blues pattern. This works, because important aspects of both vocal and instrumental style throughout the record are based on blues- and rhythm & blues–derived elements. On some later records, like "Oh, Boy!" and "Peggy Sue," Holly used a twelve-bar blues structure for the song itself.

Buddy Holly's career was tragically cut short when he was twenty-two by a plane crash that also claimed the lives of two other prominent rock 'n' roll personalities: the promising seventeen-year-old Chicano singer and songwriter Ritchie Valens, and the Big Bopper (J. P. Richardson), who had achieved success with novelty records. A measure of Holly's importance for later pop music may be seen in the fact that the Beatles modeled their insect-based name, their four-piece instrumental lineup, and aspects of their vocal style on the Crickets—and through the Beatles, of course, the influence passed on to innumerable bands. Holly was also, like Chuck Berry, an important rock 'n' roll songwriter; in addition to the songs already mentioned, he wrote and recorded "Everyday," "Not Fade Away," "Rave On," and others, which became increasingly popular in the years after his death and were covered by rock bands. Furthermore, Holly's work with arrangements and studio effects looked forward to some of the recording techniques of the 1960s. He frequently used *double-tracking* on his recordings—a technique in which two nearly identical versions of the same vocal or instrumental part are recorded on top of one another, foregrounding that part so that it seems to come right out of the speaker at the listener—and some of his last records used orchestral strings.

LISTENING COMPARISON OF TWO BLUES-BASED ROCK 'N' ROLL SONGS: "LONG TALL SALLY" AND "DON'T BE CRUEL"

LISTENING CHART "LONG TALL SALLY"

Music and lyrics credited to Enotris Johnson, Richard Penniman, and Robert Blackwell; as performed by Little Richard and unidentified band; recorded 1956

FORM	LYRICS	DESCRIPTIVE COMMENTS
Verse 1	*Gonna tell Aunt Mary . . .*	Underlying rhythmic and chord structure is that of the twelve-bar blues, with the first four bars constituting the verse and the final eight bars the chorus; loud,
Chorus	*Oh, baby . . .*	flamboyant vocal style throughout.
Verse 2	*Well, Long Tall Sally . . .*	Twelve-bar blues pattern persists throughout the song.
Chorus	*Oh, baby . . .*	
Verse 3	*Well, I saw Uncle John . . .*	
Chorus	*Oh, baby . . .*	
Instrumental break		Two twelve-bar blues sections; intense saxophone solo reflects the mood of the vocal.
Repetition of verse 2 + chorus, then verse 3 + chorus		
Conclusion	*We're gonna have some fun tonight . . .*	Extended choruslike section; twelve-bar blues structure.

LISTENING CHART "DON'T BE CRUEL"

Music and lyrics by Otis Blackwell and Elvis Presley;[2] as performed by Elvis Presley, vocal and guitar, with the Jordanaires and backing instrumentalists; recorded 1956

FORM	LYRICS	DESCRIPTIVE COMMENTS
Instrumental intro		Repetitive guitar hook, strong backbeat (four bars long)
Verse 1	*If you know . . .*	Twelve-bar blues structure, arranged to suggest a verse-chorus pattern, with the first eight bars constituting the verse and
Chorus	*Don't be cruel . . .*	the final four bars the chorus.

[2]Presley, though not generally known as a songwriter, was credited as coauthor of a handful of his early hits for RCA.

Verse 2	*Baby, if I made you mad . . .*	Twelve-bar blues structure, with an extension added (six bars in length) to the chorus.
Chorus + extension	*Don't be cruel . . .* *I don't want . . .*	
Verse 3	*Don't stop a-thinkin' of me . . .*	Twelve-bar blues, plus extension (as before).
Chorus + extension	*Don't be cruel . . .* *Why should we . . .*	
Verse 4	*Let's walk up . . .*	Twelve-bar blues, plus extension (as before).
Chorus + extension	*Don't be cruel . . .* *I don't want . . .*	
Concluding chorus +	*Don't be cruel . . .*	
Additional extension	*Don't be cruel . . .* *I don't want . . .*	

SONGWRITERS AND PRODUCERS OF EARLY ROCK 'N' ROLL

The relatively clear lines of division between songwriters and performers that characterized the world of mainstream pop music up to around 1955 no longer held up in the early years of rock 'n' roll's mainstream success. This is because the roots of rock 'n' roll lie with rhythm & blues and country music, areas of activity where performers often wrote their own songs and, conversely, songwriters frequently performed and recorded their own works. Of the five early rock 'n' roll stars we have discussed in detail, only Elvis Presley did not regularly write his own material. This diminishing importance of the independent songwriter represented another major shift brought about by the rock 'n' roll revolution. In time, it came to be expected that performers would be the composers of their own songs, and this led to a correspondingly stronger identification of artists with specific material. Here lie the origins of the mystique of the pop music personality as a creative artist, rather than as merely an interpreter—a mystique that came into its own in the later 1960s.

None of this meant that important nonperforming songwriters ceased to exist, of course. As we shall see in the next chapter, the early 1960s actually brought a renewed emphasis on songwriting as an independent craft, prior to the heyday of songwriting bands like the Beatles and songwriter-performers like Bob Dylan. And with the increasing importance of the recording itself as the basic document of rock 'n' roll music, another behind-the-scenes job grew steadily in importance in the later 1950s and the early 1960s: that of the record **producer.** Producers could be responsible for many things, from booking time in the recording studio, to hiring backup singers and instrumentalists, to assisting with the engineering process. Essentially, though, the producer was responsible for the characteristic *sound* of the finished record, and the best producers left as strong a sense of individual personality on their products as did the recording artists themselves. When the producer and the songwriter were the same person (or persons), his or her importance and influence could be powerful indeed.

This was the case with the most innovative songwriting/producing team of the early rock 'n' roll years, <u>Jerry Leiber</u> and <u>Mike Stoller</u> (both born 1933). Leiber and Stoller were not recording artists, but they were already writing rhythm & blues songs when they were teenagers. Eventually they wrote and produced many hits for Elvis Presley, and they did the same for one of the most popular vocal groups of this period, the Coasters. (They also produced and did occasional writing for the Drifters, and the elaborately produced orchestral sound of these records in the early 1960s was possibly even more influential than Leiber and Stoller's previous records had been in the later 1950s.) The team constructed what they called "playlets" for the Coasters, scenes from teenage life of the 1950s distilled into brilliantly funny rock 'n' roll records. Like many by Chuck Berry, the Coasters' hits were specifically about, and for, their intended audience. An examination of "Charlie Brown" will enable us to appreciate in detail this targeting of the teenage audience, along with the vocal artistry of the Coasters and the behind-the-scenes writing and production artistry of Leiber and Stoller.

LISTENING AND ANALYSIS "CHARLIE BROWN"

Basic Description

"Charlie Brown" presents an indelible portrait of a ubiquitous figure, the class clown. Although such a song topic would probably not have occurred to anyone prior to the 1950s, it certainly made an effective choice at a point when, for the first time ever, the biggest market of potential record buyers consisted of schoolkids: the junior high schoolers and high schoolers, even elementary schoolers, each of whom probably knew a "Charlie Brown" in at least one of his or her classes. The specific time period and culture of the 1950s is evoked through a sparing but telling use of then-current slang terms like "cool" and "daddy-o."

From the first arresting vocal **hook,** "Fee fee, fie fie, fo fo, fum," the record brims with unrelenting high energy. Like Chuck Berry, the Coasters were adept at delivering a dense, cleverly worded text very clearly at a fast tempo. The intensity of the Coasters' vocal style owes much to rhythm & blues, although certain comic effects—like the low bass voice repeatedly asking, "Why's everybody always pickin' on me?" and asking, "Who, me?" in the bridge—suggest roots going back to much earlier stage routines. (The low bass voice was also a staple element of rhythm & blues group singing style; see the discussion of the Chords' "Sh-Boom" previously in this chapter.) Highly effective are the contrasts between passages that are essentially vocal solos, with occasional, minimal contributions by the rhythm instruments (at the start of each A section—see the listening chart that follows), and the following passages where the full band offers a steady accompaniment and the saxophone engages in call-and-response with the vocal group.

Form

"Charlie Brown" combines aspects of two different formal designs we have seen in previous musical examples. The song reveals its mainstream pop roots in its

Box 3.4 The Kingston Trio: Folk Music in the Age of Rock 'n' Roll

One of the later hits of the 1950s was "Tom Dooley," an adaptation of an old ballad song, at once a throwback to an earlier era and a harbinger of important currents in American popular music of the 1960s. Even as the taste of most young people was attracted to the electrified sounds of rock 'n' roll, the urban folk-pop tradition that had been pioneered by the Weavers in the early 1950s (see Chapter 2) continued to expand its appeal. The most popular of the folk groups was the Kingston Trio, composed of Dave Guard, Nick Reynolds, and Bob Shane. Formed in 1957, the group was named after the capital of Jamaica—a gesture in the direction of the Caribbean calypso-pop hits of Harry Belafonte and other folk singers of the mid-1950s. The group featured smooth, pop-style performances of folk songs and accompanied themselves on acoustic instruments (guitar, banjo, and string bass). In a sense the Kingston Trio—three bright, smiling, well-scrubbed young white men in collegiate sweaters—represented a neatened-up and depoliticized version of the Weavers. Operating in a middle zone between the abandon of Elvis Presley and the nostalgia of Frank Sinatra, they were able to appeal to many younger listeners while not scaring Mom and Dad.

While their music may have lacked the creativity and social engagement of the Weavers or later folk artists such as Bob Dylan, the Kingston Trio were responsible for keeping public interest in folk music alive through the late 1950s and early 1960s. In addition, their hit records represent a new trend in the record business, the hit LP. While only two of their single releases made it into the Top 10, the Kingston Trio dominated the sales of $33\frac{1}{3}$ r.p.m. LP albums. They had five Number One albums on the pop charts between 1958 and 1960; fifteen Top 10 albums between 1958 and 1963; and four of their LPs stayed on the *Billboard* charts for over two years, an astonishing feat.

The Kingston Trio's only Number One hit single was their adaptation of "Tom Dula," a nineteenth-century American ballad about an innocent man hanged to death for allegedly murdering his girlfriend. The trio's adaptation of this old song, "Tom Dooley," reached Number One on the pop charts in 1958, sold more than three million copies, and was the most popular song on their debut LP, *The Kingston Trio*, which stayed on the *Billboard* album charts for over three and a half years. (The song even inspired a movie, *The Legend of Tom Dooley*.) The form of "Tom Dooley" should be familiar to you by now—it is a **strophic ballad,** with a series of verses telling a story and a chorus that comes back between the verses. There is a strange contrast between the grim tale told by the lyrics—that of an innocent man waiting to be hung—and the cheerful, upbeat tone of the trio's performance. When they sing, "Hang down your head, Tom Dooley, poor boy, you're bound to die" they almost sound happy about it. While the contrast between the content and style in this recording may strike you as a bit odd, this approach was an important element of the Kingston Trio's huge success in the late 1950s and early 1960s—they were optimistic, enthusiastic, and not given to deep philosophical exploration or political experimentation, just nice boys, and fun to sing along with in the bargain.

overall AABA structure. But the A sections are twelve-bar blues stanzas, which would not of course be typical of a Tin Pan Alley tune; furthermore, each A section divides the twelve bars into a little verse-chorus structure of the type we have seen in "Long Tall Sally" and "Don't Be Cruel." The most direct kinship is with "Long Tall Sally": four bars of verse, followed by eight bars of chorus. The kinship is that much more marked because of an additional similarity between the two; in both "Charlie Brown" and "Long Tall Sally" the twelve-bar blues stanzas start off with vocal solos, and a continuous full accompaniment does not join in until the chorus portions at the fifth bar of the structure. The B section, in contrast, is eight bars in length, providing a harmonic and rhythmic **release** from the succession of blues structures.

LISTENING CHART   "CHARLIE BROWN"

Music and lyrics by Jerry Leiber and Mike Stoller; as performed by the Coasters with accompanying band (King Curtis, sax solo); recorded 1958

FORM	LYRICS	DESCRIPTIVE COMMENTS
A (verse)	*Fee, fee, fie, fie, fo, fo, fum,* *I smell smoke in the auditorium!*	Twelve-bar blues stanza, divided into a four-bar verse (vocal solo) and an eight-bar chorus with full accompaniment and call and response between the voices and the saxophone.
(chorus)	*Charlie Brown, Charlie Brown,* *He's a clown, that Charlie Brown.* *He's gonna get caught, just you wait* * and see.* *"Why's everybody always pickin' on me?"*	
A (verse)	*That's him on his knees, I know that's him,* *Yellin' "seven come eleven" down in* * the boys' gym.*	As before.
(chorus)	*Charlie Brown . . .*	
B	*Who's always writing on the wall?* *Who's always goofin' in the hall?* *Who's always throwing spitballs?* *Guess who? ("Who, me?") Yeah, you!*	Bridge section.
A (verse)	*Who walks in the classroom cool* * and slow?* *Who calls the English teacher "Daddy-o"?*	As before.
(chorus)	*Charlie Brown . . .*	
Instrumental break		Twelve-bar blues stanza, constructed exactly like the A sections, but with the voices absent and the saxophone freely improvising over the rhythmic and chordal structure; blue notes are noticeable in the sax solo.
Repetition of final A section		
Instrumental fade-out		

The Song/The Recording

As songwriters, Leiber and Stoller always had an interest in mixing—even scrambling—elements derived from rhythm & blues music, which they knew well and loved, with elements derived from mainstream pop. This interest is evident in the form of "Charlie Brown" itself, as we have discussed, but it may also be seen in certain details. For example, the twelve-bar blues stanzas in the song are noticeably *lacking* in blue notes; Leiber and Stoller wrote a simple pop-oriented melody and just directed the bass singer to speak his solo line. But as producers, Leiber and Stoller brought in King Curtis, a Texas-born rhythm & blues saxophonist, to play on the record. In his twelve-bar instrumental break Curtis emphasized blue notes, jumping in front of and behind the beat in a complex manner evocative of stuttering (this style, as much indebted to country hoedown music as to R&B, was also used successfully by the country and western saxophonist Boots Randolph). Curtis's "yackety sax" sound links the Coasters' record to both rhythm & blues and country music, and creates a humorous, goofy effect perfectly suited to the comic tale of Charlie Brown.

Apart from the sparkling clarity of the recording, there is only one prominent production effect in "Charlie Brown": the artificially high voices in the bridge on "Yeah, you!" This effect was produced by playing a tape of normal voices at double speed, a device that was popular on novelty records at this time. Here we see the modest beginnings of the kind of artificial studio effects that would be found on more and more records as producers took increasing advantage of increasingly sophisticated recording studios and techniques.

The rise of rock 'n' roll in the mid-1950s transformed the landscape of American popular music, further cementing the popularity of southern-derived styles ultimately derived from the blues and country music, and transforming the teenager into both a marketing concept and a cultural icon. The dominance of youth culture—and of the music industry's sometimes clumsy attempts to interpret and shape it—was to become even more predominant during the following decade, as rock 'n' roll gave way to rock. In the next two chapters we will follow this story in some detail, from the emergence of a new generation of American teen pop stars and the onset of the so-called British Invasion through the rise of soul music and the musical experimentalism of the late 1960s **counterculture**.

"GOOD VIBRATIONS"

American Pop and the British Invasion, 1960s

Few eras in American history have been as disruptive, controversial, and violent as the decade of the 1960s. The Civil Rights Movement, the Vietnam War, and the assassinations of President John F. Kennedy and the Reverend Martin Luther King Jr. are events that still inspire impassioned debate among both historians and everyday citizens at the beginning of the twenty-first century. But one claim about the decade that could scarcely be contested is this: popular music played a role of unprecedented centrality and importance in defining the character and spirit of the 1960s. This is because the baby boom generation played a vital role in the essential political and cultural events of this period—and the boomers were a generation identified, by themselves and by others, and to a remarkable degree, with their own popular music: rock 'n' roll. As rock 'n' roll developed and changed with the times, eventually becoming "rock," it came increasingly to serve as an outlet for expression of the hopes and fears of a generation coming to terms with American politics, the racial climate in the country, and a controversial war in Southeast Asia.

The decade surely began innocently enough, however. In fact, the Number One song in the country at the turn of the decade—as the innovative, rockin' 1950s gave way to the revolutionary, rockin' 1960s—was an acoustic, deliberately old-fashioned cowboy ballad, "El Paso," written and performed by the country singer Marty Robbins. This historically inconvenient fact is worth pausing over, for a number of reasons. It reminds us of the extent to which popular views of history inevitably entail simplification and the neatening out of the complex and disorderly details that form much of the substance of life and culture in any period and place. It also reveals once again how diverse and unpredictable the pop music market remained, in 1960 and beyond. Furthermore, the popularity of "El Paso" attests to the pull that country music—and not just rockabilly!—continued to exert on mainstream pop at this time. This is important, because the significant contributions of country music to mainstream American pop of the 1950s and 1960s tend to be largely underestimated and undervalued by most historians and critics. The sudden reemergence of country music as a major market force in the late 1980s and the 1990s came as a surprise only to those who had been ignoring the full picture for a long time; country has surely gained commercial strength recently, but it has never been absent from the pop scene since the beginnings of hillbilly recordings in the 1920s.

THE EARLY 1960s: DANCE MUSIC AND "TEENAGE SYMPHONIES"

The early 1960s are often described as a lackluster period in the development of American popular music: a time of relative stasis between the excitement of the early rock 'n' roll years and the coming of the Beatles to America in 1964. But at least three important trends emerged in the early 1960s. A new kind of social dancing developed, inspired by "The Twist" and a spate of other dance-oriented records, that gave rock 'n' roll music for the first time a new and distinctive set of movements and social customs to accompany it. Members of the first generation to grow up with rock 'n' roll began to assume positions of shaping power in the music industry as writers and producers, as the Tin Pan Alley system was reinvented for the new music and its new audiences at the Brill Building in New York, at Gold Star Studios in Los Angeles, and at the Motown headquarters in Detroit. And new stylistic possibilities (and cultural contexts) for rock 'n' roll began to emerge out of California, spearheaded by the Beach Boys, whose leader, Brian Wilson, established a model for many to follow by being an innovative performer, writer, and producer all rolled into one.

The Twist

"The Twist" began its popular career inauspiciously, as the B-side of a 1959 single by the veteran rhythm & blues group Hank Ballard and the Midnighters. Ballard was convinced that he had written a smash hit with "The Twist," a teen-oriented rock 'n' roll song using a twelve-bar blues structure; it celebrated a simple, hip-swiveling dance step that was gaining some popularity among young African Americans. But the decision makers at Ballard's indie label, King, didn't agree and promoted the other side of the record, a perfectly fine but more old-fashioned rhythm & blues ballad called "Teardrops on Your Letter." This tune peaked at Number Eighty-nine on *Billboard*'s "Hot 100" chart (although both sides of the record enjoyed popularity among rhythm & blues fans) and promptly disappeared from view—along with, one would have assumed, "The Twist." However, the dance named in Ballard's song continued its still somewhat obscure existence.

Meanwhile, somebody must have paid serious attention to that flip side of "Teardrops on Your Letter," somebody with connections at another indie label, Parkway. Since Parkway was based in Philadelphia, its artists had particularly easy access to *American Bandstand*, the teen-oriented, nationally broadcast television show that originated in the same city. *American Bandstand* was all about dancing: rock 'n' roll records were played, and the camera showed the teenagers in the studio dancing to them. It was the perfect venue for promoting a new dance record, and a new dance, to the broad rock 'n' roll audience.

Parkway recording artist <u>Chubby Checker</u> was himself all of eighteen when he cut a cover of Hank Ballard's "The Twist" in 1960. (His real name was Ernest Evans; his stage name had in fact been suggested by the wife of *American Bandstand* host Dick Clark, based on Evans's resemblance to a young Fats Domino.) This record was heavily promoted, and this time around Ballard's conviction about the song proved justified: it reached the Number One position on the charts. Checker's version adhered so closely to the vocal inflections and the arrangement of the original that Ballard (when interviewed for the 1993 documentary movie *Twist*) claimed he mistook it for his own record the first time he heard it on the radio!

Even more than the song, the dance itself caught the imagination of young people nationwide as they had the opportunity to observe it on *American Bandstand.* (In fact, Ballard's original recording also entered the pop charts at this time, swept there by the wave of enthusiasm engendered by the dance.) The twist was essentially an individual, noncontact dance without any real steps. Although it was generally done by a boy-and-girl couple facing one another, there was no inherent reason why it had to be restricted to this format; it could at least hypothetically be performed by any number of people, including one, in any dance floor pattern, in any gender combination. The twist was not the first noncontact, free-form dance to emerge in the history of American social dancing, but its enormous popularity signaled a sea change in the entire culture of popular dance. Against all apparent odds, it turned out to be much more than a passing novelty.

Soon adults of all ages and classes and races were doing the twist, along with the teenagers. In turn, the popularity and wide social acceptance of this free-form dancing brought rock 'n' roll music to a significantly broader audience than ever before: it was no longer just music for teenagers but an accepted fact of American social life. Clubs called *discotheques*, dedicated to the twist and other free-form dances that followed in its wake—the pony, the mashed potatoes, the monkey, and countless others—sprang up all over; one of the most famous, New York's Peppermint Lounge, gave its name to one of the biggest hits of early 1962, "Peppermint Twist," recorded by the club's house band, Joey Dee and the Starliters. Less than a year after it completed its first chart run, Chubby Checker's "The Twist" was back on the Hot 100 for another go-round and reached Number One a second time. (This feat has been accomplished by only two records in the history of the pop charts; that the other one is Bing Crosby's "White Christmas" gives some indication of the extraordinary level of popularity of both the twist as a dance and "The Twist" as a record.) Live rock 'n' roll shows began to include female "go-go" dancers along with the singing acts; in the later 1960s these dancers also began to be featured, with or without their clothes, in clubs where recorded rock music was played.

The free-form dances that have accompanied, and in some cases inspired, so much of American popular music from the 1960s to the present thus all find their point of origin in the twist. The discotheques of the 1960s were the ancestors of the discos of the 1970s, and the spirit of bodily freedom represented by those institutions persisted in the mosh pits and related venues of the 1990s and beyond. Rock 'n' roll had found a social body language that matched the novelty of the music and the feeling of liberation that it celebrated.

It should come as no surprise that, in the wake of "The Twist," many other popular songs of the early 1960s were dance-oriented. To cite only a few represen-

In 1961 *everybody* did the twist! Teenagers on *American Bandstand*; **Chubby Checker** (center), with country singer **Conway Twitty** (left) and *American Bandstand* host **Dick Clark.** Courtesy Library of Congress.

tative examples: Chubby Checker recorded "Let's Twist Again" in 1961; teenager Dee Dee Sharp cut a duet with Chubby Checker, "Slow Twistin'," as well as "Mashed Potato Time" (both 1962) and "Do the Bird" (1963); songwriter Carole King tapped her babysitter, sixteen-year-old Little Eva (Eva Narcissus Boyd), to record her song "The Loco-Motion" in 1962; and the Motown group the Miracles sang about "Mickey's Monkey" (1963). (As we will see, the later disco craze of the 1970s inspired an analogous flood of dance-oriented songs—see Chapter 6. Popular music designed specifically for dancing remained popular through the 1980s into the 1990s; at the time of this writing, "dance" is treated by the music trade magazines as a separate and substantial genre of American and world pop music.) For the most part, the dance songs of the 1960s, like their later counterparts, were catchy and functional and tended to break no new ground musically or lyrically—which may account, at least somewhat, for the poor reputation of this period in many histories of American pop. Simple verse-chorus formats predominated. But if the songs were not in themselves novel or important, the new dance culture to which they contributed certainly was. And a few of these songs have retained the affection of a large public for a surprisingly long time: Chubby Checker joined with the rap group Fat Boys in a successful revival of "The Twist" (subtitled "Yo, Twist!") in 1988, and "The Loco-Motion" was a Number One song for the hard-rock group Grand Funk in 1974 and for the Australian singer Kylie Minogue in 1988.

Phil Spector

As we have seen, many teenagers achieved success as recording artists in the early years of rock 'n' roll. At the age of seventeen, Phil Spector (b. 1940) had a Number One record as a member of a vocal group, the Teddy Bears, whose hit song "To Know Him Is to Love Him" was also composed and produced by Spector. (The multitalented young man also played guitar and piano on the record, which was the first one he ever made!) It may initially seem surprising, then, that Spector elected not to follow the path of songwriting performers like Chuck Berry and Buddy Holly. Instead he emulated Jerry Leiber and Mike Stoller (see Chapter 3), with whom he apprenticed, and by the early 1960s Spector had established himself as a songwriter-producer, working behind the scenes of rock 'n' roll rather than in

Phil Spector in 1965. Library of Congress.

its spotlights. But Spector must have sensed where the real emerging power was in this young music business: with the people who actually shaped the sounds of the records. The wisdom of his decision is reflected in the fact that his name today is probably better known, and certainly more widely revered among pop musicians, than that of Chubby Checker, Little Eva, and any number of young performers active in the early 1960s.

By the time he was twenty-one years old, Spector was in charge of his own independent label, Philles Records, and he brought a new depth of meaning to the phrase "in charge." Working with personally selected songwriters (and often serving as a collaborator in their writing) and with hand-picked vocalists, instrumentalists, arrangers, and engineers, he supervised every aspect of a record's sound. Spector's level of involvement, and his obsession with detail, became legendary; as a result a Philles record has a distinctive kind of sonority, tied more closely to Spector's personal talents and vision than to the contributions of any other songwriters, or of the technicians, or even of the actual performers. That is to say, more than records by the Crystals or the Ronettes, these are "Phil Spector records." It is indicative that Spector is, at the time of this writing, the only American pop music producer to have had a CD box set issued under his own name; in fact, if you want to hear the hits of the Crystals or the Ronettes, you need to buy *Phil Spector: Back to Mono (1958–1969)*, a set of four compact discs issued in 1991.

The characteristic Philles sound was at once remarkably dense and remarkably clear, and it became known as the "wall of sound." Spector achieved this effect by having multiple instruments—pianos, guitars, and so forth—doubling each individual part in the arrangement, and by using a huge amount of echo, while carefully controlling the overall balance of the record so that the vocals were pushed clearly to the front. The thick texture and the presence of strings on these records led them to be called "teenage symphonies." A perfect example is "Be My Baby," to be discussed in detail shortly. However, Spector explored many different types of sound textures on his recordings, and a record like "Uptown," also discussed below, has a decidedly different and more intimate—while no less impressive—impact.

Philles Records helped establish a new and important model for the production and marketing of pop records. Many indie companies, mimicking the practice of major labels with earlier styles of pop music, rushed as many records as they could into the rock 'n' roll market, often without much thought for quality control, hoping for the occasional hit. In contrast, as would be expected from the description provided above, Phil Spector turned out an exceptionally small number of records, about twenty in a two-year period, an astoundingly large percentage of which were hits. Of course, the increasingly high profile of record producers through the later 1960s and up to the present (one need only recall the importance of George Martin's work with the Beatles) is a direct outgrowth of Spector's contribution and notoriety; a 1965 essay by the noted writer Tom Wolfe dubbed the then-twenty-four-year-old millionaire "the first tycoon of teen." And when today's bands labor painstakingly for a year or more over the studio production of a disc, they are demonstrating, knowingly or not, Spector's legacy at work.

It is also significant that Spector's own preferred recording venue was Gold Star Studios in Los Angeles; this was an early indication of the coming shift away from New York as the dominant power center of the pop music industry. The studio musicians with whom Spector worked regularly at Gold Star Studios came to be known as the "wrecking crew"; individually and collectively they made essential contributions to a remarkable number of hit records from the 1960s on. Among the best known of these musicians are Hal Blaine, drummer; Carol Kaye, bassist; and Jack Nitzsche, arranger and percussionist.

Phil Spector preferred to work with vocal groups over individual artists (although he did do some work with soloists), and his output as producer helped assure, as a result both of its own quality and of its influence, that the early 1960s were a golden age for rock 'n' roll vocal groups. Spector's predilection for vocal groups—shared by many songwriters and producers at the time—was probably due to a couple of factors. The groups offered great potential for intricate and varied vocal textures, of course. But the groups also had a kind of anonymity, as far as the listening public was concerned: they had no star leaders known by name, and their personnel could be reduced, augmented, or otherwise altered at the will of the producer. The increased power of the producer in this situation was most likely the critical issue here. Cultural historians would also attach significance to the fact that the producers of vocal group rock 'n' roll in this period tended to be, like Phil Spector, male and white, while a large proportion of the most popular vocal groups were female (the so-called *girl groups*), and of these, a significant number were composed exclusively of African Americans. In effect, the increased specialization and resulting hierarchical arrangement of power and influence that occurred in an operation like Philles Records restored a Tin Pan Alley–like model to the creation and marketing of some of the most successful rock 'n' roll. The parallel even extends to the fact that a large number of the most important songwriters and producers of this period, including Spector himself, were Jews born in New York.

To list the songwriters with whom Spector worked is to list some of the most prodigious talents of the early 1960s, including the teams of Carole King and Gerry Goffin, Barry Mann and Cynthia Weil, and Jeff Barry and Ellie Greenwich. For these and many other aspiring songwriters of the time, New York's *Brill Building* (at 1619 Broadway) served as a base of operations, where they worked in little cubicles with pianos, all packed tightly together, turning out songs for large numbers of artists and (mostly indie) labels. Producers and label executives were constantly in attendance or close at hand, and the Brill Building became quite literally rock 'n' roll's vertical Tin Pan Alley. The successful songwriters were often working with a number of different artists, producers, and labels at the same time, and consequently could hope to have several hits on the charts simultaneously; the regular work at a stable location and the promise of considerable royalty income made this type of work seem both more reliable and more potentially lucrative than that of performers. (Some of the Brill Building songwriters did perform occasionally on records, playing instruments, providing background vocals, and sometimes even doing a lead vocal, but this was not a regular thing. In the early 1960s the only one of this group to have a name as a recording artist was Neil Sedaka, who generally performed his own material; Carole King's performing career took off much later.)

Like Phil Spector, a large proportion of the Brill Building songwriters tailored their output toward vocal groups, and many of the resulting records remain classics of their period. The Drifters performed "Save the Last Dance for Me" by Doc Pomus and Mort Shuman (Number One, 1960), "Up on the Roof" by Goffin and King (Number Five, 1963), and "On Broadway" by Mann and Weil and Leiber and

Songwriters at work in New York City's Brill Building: **Barry Mann, Cynthia Weil,** and **Carole King**. Frank Driggs Collection.

Stoller (Number Nine, 1963); the Shirelles—one of the first successful girl groups—recorded "Will You Love Me Tomorrow?" by Goffin and King (Number One, 1961); the Dixie Cups sang "Chapel of Love" by Barry and Greenwich and Spector (Number One, 1964); and the list could go on and on. Talented hopefuls flocked to the Brill Building. In addition to those already mentioned, Neil Diamond also got his start as a writer there before becoming a superstar singer-songwriter in the late 1960s and 1970s.

Phil Spector retired from steady writing and production work in 1966. But he has periodically resurfaced to work on special projects that attract his interest. The best-known of these involved the Beatles; he worked on the last album released by the group, *Let It Be* (1970), and then assisted individual members with solo albums in the early 1970s.

LISTENING TO TWO PHIL SPECTOR PRODUCTIONS

"Be My Baby," composed by Phil Spector, Ellie Greenwich, and Jeff Barry, performed by the Ronettes (Number Two, 1963); "Uptown," composed by Barry Mann and Cynthia Weil, performed by the Crystals (Number Thirteen, 1962)

"Be My Baby" was one of the biggest hits among the many produced by Spector, and it remains a favorite to this day on oldies radio. With its employment of a full orchestral string section, pianos, an array of rhythm instruments, and a background chorus behind the lead vocal, it is an opulent "teenage symphony" and a fine illustration of Spector's "wall of sound" at full tilt. It is certainly the arrangement and production that gives this record its individual and enduring character. As a composition, the song itself is a simple if effective vehicle, expressing the most basic romantic sentiments in a straightforward verse-chorus framework. But the listener is hooked from the first, as an aggressive, distinctive rhythmic pattern on the solo drum gives the record its beat from the get-go and draws us immediately into the song. (Notice also the spectacular effect achieved by the surprise recurrence of this drum introduction just before the final repetitions of the song's chorus; this sudden crack in the wall of sound has an explosive impact!)

"Uptown" is an earlier, very different Philles record (one of the first to be issued) that serves well to illustrate another aspect of Spector's production talents. "Uptown" is a song quite unlike "Be My Baby," and Spector appropriately provided it with a highly individual arrangement and production. Although "Uptown" uses orchestral strings and percussion effects in as sophisticated a manner as "Be My Baby," the earlier song conveys a much more open, spacious feeling, as if illustrating in sound the relief experienced by the protagonist when he leaves work each evening and goes uptown.

"Uptown" deals with class inequalities and economic injustice; the fact that it does this gently makes it no less remarkable for 1962, when pop songs on such subjects were virtually nonexistent. (These subjects would have been regarded as appropriate for urban folk music at this time, but not for the pop market; see Chapter 5.) The hero of the song works downtown, where he "don't get no breaks," and it is only when he comes uptown in the evening to his lover's "tenement," where they "don't have to pay much rent," that he can feel like a "king" with the world "at his feet." The contrast between downtown and uptown is captured in the music as well. The downtown sections are in a **minor** key (also unusual for this period), while the uptown sections move to a **major** key. Note also the striking effect of the flexible tempo of the opening section on the record, which helps establish the unusual atmosphere and functions as a kind of atypical **hook**, by setting up a high degree of anticipation in the listener. The suspense is relieved when a steady tempo is established at the first occurrence of the word "uptown."

Spector recorded "Uptown" in New York. Given his own New York background, which he shared with the songwriters Mann and Weil, it is hard to escape the conviction that "Uptown" is indeed about New York, where uptown and downtown Manhattan exemplify the economic and class distinctions depicted in the lyrics. Furthermore, given the many "Spanish"-sounding features of this recording, one suspects that the specific uptown location is probably New York's Spanish Harlem, a largely Puerto Rican enclave that had gained pop music notoriety just a year before the release of "Uptown" through a song actually called "Spanish Harlem"—a Top 10 hit for Ben E. King that was cowritten by Phil Spector himself.

Several factors contribute to the general Latin feeling of "Uptown." (Like so much pop music, "Uptown" is concerned with the general evocation of an "exotic" locale, not with any kind of ethnomusicological accuracy. The "exotic" stylistic effects in "Uptown" are actually not specifically characteristic of Puerto Rican music at all.) The ornate guitar figures heard as accompaniment to the opening verse are obviously reminiscent of flamenco guitar style. The prominent use of castanets (also present in "Be My Baby," but just as part of the wall of sound, not as a specifically evocative presence) for percussion, and the general rhythmic feeling of Latin American dance throughout the record (aspects of *baion* rhythm in the accompaniment, and aspects of Cuban *bolero* rhythm in the song's melody) also contribute strongly to the exotic coloration of "Uptown." We dwell on this because "Uptown" has to serve as the basic example here of an important trend—the incorporation of Latin American elements into the fabric of 1960s rock 'n' roll. The trend is also clearly evident in "Spanish Harlem" and in many records of the early 1960s by the Drifters (the most famous of which is "Save the Last Dance for Me").

Berry Gordy and Motown

Meanwhile, in Detroit, <u>Berry Gordy Jr.</u> (b. 1929) was creating his own songwriting/producing/marketing organization along lines directly analogous to Philles Records. But Motown (named after the "Motor town" or "Motor city"—i.e., Detroit, the automobile production capital of America) came to be a success story that surpassed even that of Philles; more importantly, it came to be the most stunning success story in the entire history of African American businesses in this country. Motown was not the first black-owned record company by a long shot (first was the Black Swan company in 1921). The intensity and duration of its commercial success (and it is still an important market presence at the time of this writing) may be attributed to the distinctive dual thrust of Gordy's vision.

First of all, he was determined to keep all of the creative *and* financial aspects of the business under African American control—which effectively meant under *his* control. This worked because Gordy had an uncanny ability to surround himself with first-rate musical talent in all areas of the record-making process, and to maintain the loyalty of his musicians for substantial periods of time. It also worked, of course, because Gordy had a shrewd head for business as well as for music, and this leads us to the second element of his visionary plan. Unlike the music of earlier black-owned record companies, Motown's music was not directed primarily at black audiences. Gordy unapologetically sought to make an African American pop music addressed to the widest possible listening public. The only segregation Gordy permitted his product was geared to age; like rock 'n' roll itself, Motown's music was designed to cut across divisions of race, region, and class, but it definitely was—as the label itself proclaimed—"the sound of young America."

It is almost as if Gordy launched his enterprise as a kind of counteroffensive against the expropriation of African American music and the exploitation of African

American musicians that had been as much a part of the early history of rock 'n' roll as it had been of other periods in the development of American popular music. And the unique genius of Gordy—and of his entire Motown organization—was the ability to create a black music aimed right at the commercial mainstream that somehow never evoked the feeling, or provoked the charge, of having sold out. With remarkably few exceptions, Motown recordings avoided direct evocations of earlier rhythm & blues forms and styles; twelve-bar blues patterns are strikingly rare, as are the typical devices of doo-wop or anything suggestive of the 1950s sounds of Chuck Berry, Fats Domino, or Little Richard. Yet a generalized blues or gospel manner remained a defining characteristic of Motown's performers; sometimes it could be very subtle, as is often the case with William "Smokey" Robinson, and sometimes much more overt, as is the case with Martha Reeves. And this manner proved sufficient to give a definite African American slant to the pop-structured, pop-flavored songs that were characteristic of Motown.

Like Phil Spector, Berry Gordy Jr. started his career as a songwriter (he cowrote a number of pop and rhythm & blues hits performed by Jackie Wilson in the late 1950s), although unlike Spector he did not perform on records. Motown, which began its operations in 1959 but at first grew very slowly, was reaching its commercial peak just at the point when Spector folded Philles in 1966. The Motown model was strikingly similar to that employed by Philles: tight quality control on all levels of creation and production, and the concentration on a small number of records to yield a high proportion of hits. It is impossible to determine direct influence, one way or the other, between the Philles and Motown organizations; it seems to be a case of two remarkable talents having similar ideas, and similar success, at around the same time. However, Gordy's organization was noticeably larger in its scope and ambition than Spector's.

From the beginning, Gordy planned a group of labels rather than just one: records under the Motown, Tamla, Gordy, and Soul names were all issued from his Detroit headquarters, and each label boasted its own roster of hitmakers. Furthermore, whereas Spector was essentially interested only in the records themselves, Gordy specifically chose and developed his recording artists to be charismatic and sophisticated live performers, complete with characteristic modes of dress and distinctive stage choreography—not to mention strict codes of conduct on and off stage that apparently were enforced quite vigorously. There were complaints about the iron hand with which Gordy ruled his roost, just as there were complaints about Spector's passion for control. But there can be no doubt that Gordy's active encouragement of his artists to be more than just recording acts made it possible for both individuals and groups from the organization to develop long-term careers. It is no accident that groups like the Supremes and the Temptations are significantly better known to a wide public than are the Crystals or the Ronettes—or that individuals like Smokey Robinson and Diana Ross were able to win the kind of name recognition that enabled them eventually to branch off from the groups with which they initially were associated (the Miracles and the Supremes, respectively) and to forge hugely successful solo careers.

The Motown records of the early 1960s exemplify the rock 'n' roll trends of their time. Among the biggest of Motown's early hits were "Please Mr. Postman" by the Marvelettes (Number One, 1961), a quintessential girl group record, and "Do You Love Me" by the Contours (Number Three, 1962), a hard-driving dance record that linked success in romance to the ability to perform currently popular dance steps, such as the twist and the mashed potatoes. (The Contours' "Do You Love Me" found renewed chart success in 1988, on the strength of its prominent employment on the soundtrack of the movie *Dirty Dancing*, which is set in the early 1960s.) By the mid-1960s a more complex, occasionally lush sound came to characterize Motown's productions. Surely the Temptations' "My Girl" (see the "Listening To" section) is as much a "teenage symphony" as any of Phil Spector's most elaborate offerings. Just like Spector, however, Motown never lost touch with a danceable beat, and although the Supremes' "You Can't Hurry Love" (see the "Listening To" section) has a much more sophisticated sound and arrangement than "Please Mr. Postman" from five years earlier, both records share an irresistible **groove.** Gordy's touch seemed never to falter, and his organization steadily increased its share of the hit record market throughout the 1960s; in the year 1970 alone, Motown and its affiliated labels placed sixteen records in the Top 10 and scored seven Number One records (out of the year's total of twenty-one Number One songs)!

Motown's headquarters in Detroit (which Gordy named "Hitsville, USA") served as a magnet for a spectacular array of talented individuals, some of whom did session work or even office work until they finally managed to get the attention of Gordy. Among performers, Gordy—like so many other producers—tended to favor vocal groups, although he did have important solo acts from early on, such as Marvin Gaye, Mary Wells, and Stevie Wonder, and did eventually wean some solo performers from the groups that they fronted. Important Motown groups not yet mentioned include Martha (Reeves) and the Vandellas, Junior Walker and the All Stars, the Four Tops, Gladys Knight and the Pips, and the Jackson Five; the last-named group made their first record for Motown in 1969, when lead singer Michael was all of eleven years old, and their string of hits for the label helped assure Motown's fortunes well into the 1970s. Gordy's organization was also blessed with remarkable songwriting and production talent, and Gordy would often have his teams of songwriting producers compete for the privilege of working with particular hot recording acts. Among the most famous of these Motown writing/production teams were (Eddie) Holland–(Lamont) Dozier–(Brian) Holland, Norman Whitfield and Barrett Strong, and Nickolas Ashford and Valerie Simpson. Smokey Robinson was unusual among the earlier Motown artists in being both a performer and a songwriter/producer; he furnished material not just to his own group, the Miracles, but also to Mary Wells, the Marvelettes, and the Temptations. Later on, in the 1970s, Marvin Gaye and Stevie Wonder also took on writing and production responsibilities for their own records.

Finally, but certainly not least in importance, Motown had a sterling house band, the so-called Funk Brothers, in every sense a match for Phil Spector's Wrecking Crew in assuring that the highest level of instrumental musicianship was always present to back up and inspire the vocal performers. Bass player James Jamerson, drummer Benny Benjamin, and keyboardist Earl Van Dyke were among the most important contributors to the Motown sound.

In 1971 Berry Gordy moved the Motown headquarters to Los Angeles, at last joining the "westward migration" that had been playing an important role in American pop music, and in American culture generally, since the early 1960s. We now turn our attention specifically to California, to surf music, and to Brian Wilson—who did more than any other single person to make California the new focus of America's rock 'n' roll mythology.

LISTENING TO THE MOTOWN SOUND

"My Girl," composed and produced by Smokey Robinson and Ronald White, performed by the Temptations (Number One, 1965); "You Can't Hurry Love," composed by Holland-Dozier-Holland, produced by Brian Holland and Lamont Dozier, performed by the Supremes (Number One, 1966)

"My Girl" is a moderate-tempo love ballad. As a composition, it is a song of sweetly conventional romantic sentiment in a straightforward verse-chorus form. But as a recording, it is lifted emphatically beyond the ordinary by virtue of the Temptations' thoroughly engaging performance and by virtue of Motown's spectacular production values.

From the outset, the arrangement hooks the listener: a repeating solo bass motive establishes the beat, over which a lead guitar enters with a memorable melodic figure. (Both of these instrumental hooks are also used later on in the recording, so that they are firmly fixed in the listener's mind after one hearing of the song.) Then the drums and lead voice enter, followed subtly by background vocals; by the time the first chorus is reached, brass instruments are present in the accompaniment, to which are then added orchestral strings. The cumulative layering of sounds gives a sense of steadily increasing passion and intensity to the song, as the singer's words metaphorically detail his feelings for his "girl." The second verse brings new brass fanfares in response to the lead vocalist's calls. There is a sumptuous instrumental interlude before the third (last) verse, dominated by the strings, which play a new melodic figure over the song's characteristic chord progressions. Then, as a final intensifying gesture, a dramatic upward key change takes place just before the concluding verse and chorus.

If "My Girl" showcases the brilliance of Motown's arranging and producing staff, "You Can't Hurry Love" demonstrates that Motown's writers could also come up with clever, innovatively structured pop songs. The listening outline below conveys the intricacies of this Holland-Dozier-Holland composition, although the most casual hearing of the record will affirm that—as with so much of the finest pop music—catchiness was absolutely not sacrificed to the cause of sophistication.

The opening A section of "You Can't Hurry Love" is extremely short, just half the length of each of the ensuing B and C sections. The function of this A is at first unclear, both because of its brevity (is it a kind of introduction? or is it a very short verse?) and because of its similarity to the music of B; the basic chord progressions underlying both A and B are virtually identical, even though their vocal melodies differ. C brings a striking chord change and another change of melody, which might initially suggest a kind of **bridge** section. But when A fails to return after C, and instead B and C alternate with one another, we seem to be in an unorthodox verse-chorus type of situation, in which we hear the first verse (C) after the chorus (B), and in which the words of the chorus aren't always exactly the same. Just when a pattern seems to have been established, A unexpectedly returns with a vengeance. Instead of proceeding right to B, it is played

The Supremes (Diana Ross is on the right). Frank Driggs Collection.

twice through, creating a composite section that is now as long as B or C. Then, in the most clever formal maneuver of all in this already complex song, an ambiguous section is inserted, as the composers take advantage of the chord progression shared by A and B; with minimal melodic activity from the voice, which keeps "waitin'," we can't tell for sure which of the two sections we're actually hearing! The instruments tease us briefly here by playing the melodic motive associated with B, "you can't hurry love." But the voice holds back until we're at the top of the chord progression again, at which point it finally begins a proper, full repetition of B, toward the end of which the record fades out.

All this play with form would be just so much intellectual busywork if it didn't reflect on the meaning of the song. "You Can't Hurry Love" is a song about the importance of waiting. Formally, the song keeps us guessing—waiting for clarification of the functional relationships among the different sections. When the A section at last returns, it keeps us waiting extensively for B and its restatement of the song's essential message. On the level of detail, notice also in the second and third B sections how the lead vocalist avoids or postpones singing the words "you can't hurry love," again forcing the listener to wait. This makes the final B that much more of a release of tension, as it behaves in an expected manner at last.

Like all the great Motown hits, "You Can't Hurry Love" submerges its many subtleties beneath an irresistible pop-friendly surface. Maybe this is why you don't tend to find it, or other Motown records, the subject of discussion when matters turn toward innovative aspects of 1960s music. Still, any list of the significant music of this period that omits a record like "You Can't Hurry Love" is surely missing something important.

LISTENING OUTLINE: "YOU CAN'T HURRY LOVE"

Form	Lyrics
Instrumental intro	
A	I need love . . .
B: b	You can't hurry love . . .
b	You can't hurry love . . .
C	But how many heartaches . . .
B: b	(You can't hurry love—) no . . .
b	How long must I wait? . . .
C	No, I can't bear . . .
B: b	(You can't hurry love—) no . . .
b	You can't hurry love . . .
Brief instrumental break	
A	No, love, love don't come easy . . .
A	for that soft voice . . .
A or B?	I keep waitin' . . .
B: b	You can't hurry love . . .
b	You can't hurry love . . .

Brian Wilson and the Beach Boys

Brian Wilson (b. 1942) formed the Beach Boys with his two brothers, a cousin, and a friend in Hawthorne, California, in 1961. The band was achieving national chart hits within a year and thrived right through the period of the "British Invasion" to become not only the bestselling American group of the 1960s but probably the most nationally and internationally celebrated American rock group ever—and certainly the one with the longest history of chart success. (They scored a Number One hit as late as 1988, with "Kokomo.") As songwriter, arranger, producer, and performer, Brian Wilson was the guiding spirit of the Beach Boys during the first decade of the group's existence, when their artistic and commercial importance and influence were at a peak. Wilson's clear, and stated, model was Phil Spector, and Wilson worked regularly in the Los Angeles recording studios with many of the same musicians who graced Spector's productions. Unlike Spector, however, Wilson was always an essential performing presence on the records he wrote, arranged, and produced for the Beach Boys. Even after he stopped touring with the group in 1964, the sound of Wilson's clear, intense falsetto remained a defining element of the Beach Boys' studio recordings.

By participating significantly in the creation of beautifully produced "teenage symphonies" featuring vocal groups, Wilson and the Beach Boys obviously contributed to one of the central trends of the early 1960s. But if we wish to understand why their importance and influence went well beyond this, we have to look at even broader issues.

If we were to conceptualize a defining model for the career of a self-sustaining, trend-setting rock group of the 1960s, it would look something like this:

- Start out by demonstrating a mastery of the basic early rock 'n' roll ballad and uptempo styles
- Create original material based on, and extending, those styles
- Eventually branch out totally beyond the traditional forms, sounds, and lyric content of rock 'n' roll to create something truly different and unique

The Beach Boys, with Brian Wilson in the car, leaning back. Capitol Records.

The reference point that most people would use for constructing a model like this would probably, and understandably, be the career of the Beatles—the shape of their career is surely encapsulated in the description above—or possibly one of the other "British Invasion" groups. But the group that first established this model, and did so with outstanding success, was the Beach Boys. The Beach Boys were in fact a clear, and stated, model for the Beatles, especially during the remarkably productive and innovative years (for both groups) of 1965–67.

In a sense, Brian Wilson was the first self-conscious second-generation rock 'n' roller. By this we mean two things. First, that Wilson explicitly acknowledged his reliance on, and reverence for, his predecessors in the rock 'n' roll field—by covering, and quoting from, their records. Second, that at the same time, Wilson carved out distinctive new ground—by deliberately moving the lyrics, and eventually the music, of his own songs beyond the territory carved out by his predecessors, into novel areas that were of particular meaning to him, to his time, and to his place in America. (The Beatles, the Rolling Stones, and other bands were also self-conscious second-generation rock 'n' rollers in this sense, but it is important to realize that Brian Wilson was, in all essential respects, the first fully realized representative of this type of pop musician.)

Brian Wilson's place in America was, of course, southern California, and that land of sun and surf was celebrated in song after song by the Beach Boys. These songs enshrined Wilson's somewhat mythical version of California indelibly in the consciousness of young Americans—to such an extent that still, for legions of pop music fans, merely the titles are sufficient to summon an entire state of mind: "Surfin' Safari," "Surfer Girl," "The Warmth of the Sun," "California Girls," and so forth. Wilson's vision was appealingly inclusive, even as it remained place-specific; "I wish they all could be California girls," he sang. (One also thinks of the opening lines of "Surfin' USA": "If everybody had an ocean, across the USA, then everybody'd be surfin' like Californ-i-ay.") Cars retained their importance to status and young romance in Wilson's California mythology, the models suitably modernized and spruced up to serve the new time and place, as in "409," "Little Deuce Coupe," "Little Honda," and other songs.

A few examples may suffice to trace Wilson's journey from imitation, through emulation, to innovation. The Beach Boys' first Top 10 hit, the famous "Surfin' USA" (Number Three, 1963), simply borrows the music of Chuck Berry's 1958 hit "Sweet Little Sixteen" as a setting for Brian Wilson's paean to California's—and America's—new beach craze. While the words are all new, they also embody an indirect homage to Berry's original lyrics, insofar as Wilson adopts Berry's idea of national celebration while changing its mode of expression from dancing to surfing. The many listeners who knew "Sweet Little Sixteen" encountered in "Surfin' USA" an unusual hybrid: musically a cover record that shortened and simplified the form of Chuck Berry's original, lyrically a tribute to the spirit of Berry that reworked and updated his approach to writing rock 'n' roll anthems to suit the requirements of a new time and place. The B-side of "Surfin' USA," "Shut Down," was a substantial hit as well. In "Shut Down," Wilson employed an established rock 'n' roll song form, the AABA pattern in which the A sections are twelve-bar blues structures (see the discussion of "Charlie Brown" in Chapter 3), to tell the story of a drag race between two high-powered automobiles. Needless to say, it is the singer's car that wins!

The Beach Boys' next hit, "Surfer Girl" (Number Seven, 1963), reinvigorated the sound and spirit of the doo-wop ballad by infusing it with California beach content. "Fun, Fun, Fun," the group's first hit of 1964, evoked Chuck Berry again, in an initially overt but ultimately more subtle way. The solo guitar introduction cops its twelve-bar blues licks directly from Berry's "Roll Over Beethoven" and "Johnny B. Goode." But after paying its respects (or its dues?) to Berry in this way, the main body of the song pursues an original path. It's a strophic form, with newly composed music and words, whose sixteen-bar strophes have nothing to do with the structure of the blues—but everything to do with what Brian Wilson learned from Chuck Berry about how to write and perform rock 'n' roll anthems. That is to say, after acknowledging Berry by quoting his signature manner of beginning a record, Wilson surprises his listeners and proceeds to pay his mentor the best possible tribute: not by copying him, but by revealing how well his lessons have been absorbed. "Fun, Fun, Fun" turns imitation into emulation. With its rapid-fire, clearly articulated lyrics, that manage to compress a remarkable number of deeply resonant references to youth culture (fancy cars, car radios, fast driving, hamburger stands, schoolwork, parents, the pursuit of romance and—naturally—fun) into two minutes' time, and its eminently catchy and danceable music, "Fun, Fun, Fun" is the kind of song Chuck Berry might have written had he been born sixteen years later, in southern California. (In the song "Do You Remember?"—an album track from the Beach Boys' *All Summer Long* [1964]— Berry is mentioned as "the greatest" of the early rock 'n' rollers to whom Brian Wilson pays tribute.)

By mid-1964 Wilson had moved past obvious emulation into a period of aggressive experimentation with his inherited styles and forms. "I Get Around," the Beach Boys' first Number One record, turns the uptempo rock 'n' roll anthem into a thoroughly individual kind of expression; the song's adventurous chord changes and quirky phrase structure take it well beyond the boundaries of 1950s rock 'n' roll, without ever sacrificing the immediate appeal and accessibility so essential to the genre. On the other hand, an album track like "The Warmth of the Sun" (from *Shut Down, Volume 2,* released in 1964), while clearly a descendent of the doo-wop ballad in sound, rhythm, and vocal texture, presents lyrics that probe the dissolution of young romance in a newly poignant and personal way, set to music that so enlarges the melodic and harmonic boundaries of the style that one quickly forgets the song's antecedents and focuses instead on its remarkable individuality. While it is questionable whether a song like "Warmth of the Sun" would have been successful as a single, it is unquestionable that songs like this were heard and appreciated, both by listeners and by those involved in the making of pop music, and thus contributed significantly to the evolution of musical style. We can also see here the beginnings of a significant trend: namely, the increasing importance of album tracks, and eventually of albums themselves, in the development of adventurous popular music. Rock 'n' roll was on its way to becoming rock.

By 1965 Brian Wilson was achieving international acclaim as a composer and recording studio wizard who produced brilliant singles and albums, and the Beach Boys were being viewed as the most serious creative and commercial threat—in America *and* in England—to the dominance of the Beatles, whose American triumph in 1964 had turned the entire world of pop music upside down. Let us now catch

Box 4.1 Other "Surf Music"

The Beach Boys were not the only representatives of a distinctive "California sound" in the early 1960s. The popular duo Jan (Berry) and Dean (Torrence) worked with Brian Wilson and the Beach Boys on a number of mutual projects; Wilson in fact cowrote Jan and Dean's biggest hit, "Surf City" (Number One, 1963). In addition, a highly influential style of guitar-dominated instrumental rock 'n' roll was pioneered in southern California, principally by Dick Dale (b. 1937), who performed with his band, the Del-Tones. Dale employed a solid-body guitar, a high-wattage Fender amplifier, and lots of **reverb** to achieve the "wet" sound of what came to be known as "surf guitar." A characteristic device was Dale's rapid, descending **tremolo**—borrowed by a group called the Chantays to open their recording of what became the most famous surf instrumental, "Pipeline" (the title is a surfing term for the curl of a wave before it breaks). Sustained national recognition eluded Dick Dale in the 1960s, but it finally became his in the 1990s, when his recording of "Misirlou," from 1962, was used as opening music for the hit film *Pulp Fiction*. The most successful instrumental group associated with surf rock was, paradoxically, a Seattle-based ensemble, the Ventures, who adopted aspects of the style after it became popular in California.

up with the Beatles, whose music in its turn was providing Brian Wilson, and many, many others, with creative stimulation and challenges.

THE BEATLES, THE BRITISH INVASION, AND THE AMERICAN RESPONSE

By the time the Beatles had their first Number One record in America, "I Want to Hold Your Hand," which topped the charts at the beginning of February 1964, they were established stars in Great Britain and were widely known throughout Europe. Already in 1963, spurred by the mass adulation surrounding the group across the Atlantic that had come to be known as "Beatlemania," some small American indie companies had licensed Beatles recordings for stateside release—but the group's British hits did not catch on here at first.

Much ink has been spilled over conjectures regarding the timing of the Beatles' remarkable success on American shores. Many historians of pop culture point to the impact of the assassination of President John F. Kennedy on November 22, 1963, claiming that as a new year began, young people were hungry for a change in the prevailing national mood of solemnity, and that the Beatles provided just the ticket in the form of something novel, "exotic," uplifting, and fun. This seems a convenient but facile explanation. A more practical, if also more cynical, one might be that the Beatles really "hit" in America only when a major label, Capitol (the American label officially linked to the Beatles' British label, EMI), launched a major promotional campaign behind the first Beatles single they chose to release here, "I Want to Hold Your Hand," and its accompanying album, *Meet the Beatles*. But outpourings of mass enthusiasm for entertainers were nothing new in the America of 1964; one thinks of the manias for Frank Sinatra in the 1940s and for Elvis Presley in the 1950s. Arguably the chief common element in these and other related phenomena in the entertainment business is their unpredictability.

Still, although America has retained a cultural fascination with things British throughout its history, American Beatlemania does represent the first time this degree of adulation was bestowed on non-native pop musicians. America had been exporting its popular music to Great Britain, to Europe, and increasingly throughout the industrialized world with enormous success for a long time, but the impact of the Beatles in this country marked the significant beginning of an aggressively reciprocal process. Of course, the reciprocities involved here are deep and complex. As we have seen, American popular music, especially that of the twentieth century, is built on a complex amalgam of influences that may be traced to a variety of world sources. And the most direct, formative influences on the music of the Beatles themselves—and of countless other British bands of the 1960s—were those of 1950s American rock 'n' roll.

One immediate result of the Beatles' popularity in America was to unleash a flood of recordings by British bands on the American market, an astoundingly large number of which were successful. Although the impact of many of these "British Invasion" bands was short-lived, other groups have retained substantial, long-term importance in the pop culture of this country; one thinks particularly of the Rolling Stones, the Who, and the Kinks. Another immediate result was the formation—or adaptation—of American groups to mimic distinctive aspects of "British" style, which of course included fashion (particularly Beatles-style, "mop-top" haircuts) and pseudo-English accents along with the musical characteristics that were supposed to evoke the Beatles or their countrymen. An extreme example of the effect of the British Invasion may be found in the career of the Walker Brothers, an American group that actually went to England in 1964 to record. They became popular in England and achieved some American hits—after being marketed here as a British Invasion band! (They weren't really brothers either!)

The close interconnections between American and British pop music that were established in the wake of the Beatles' stateside success continue to this day; among the most successful artists on the American charts in the 1990s were British acts like Eric Clapton, Elton John, Sting, and the group Oasis. Even more significantly, the British Invasion was the first of many developments that may be seen as indicative of an accelerating receptivity in America to *overt* pop music influences from all over the world. The Beatles themselves modeled such receptivity in their own embrace of influences from Indian music—first heard as a surface element in their employment of an Indian instrument, the *sitar*, in "Norwegian Wood" (a track from the album *Rubber Soul,* 1965), and later heard as a more profound influence on both the sound and structure of "Within You without You" from *Sgt. Pepper's Lonely Hearts Club Band* (1967; see the discussion of this album in Chapter 5). At present, "world music" is important enough in the culture of American pop to represent a distinctive marketing category, a category responsible for the sale in this country of increasing numbers of albums from international sources. And the mingling of

The Beatles in an open rehearsal for their first television appearance in the United States, February 1964. Left to right: Paul McCartney, George Harrison (both also shown on the monitor), Ringo Starr, John Lennon. Courtesy Library of Congress.

American and world popular musics, with all their attendant reciprocal influences, continues to accelerate.

This may seem a rather elaborate heritage to trace ultimately to one group, a group that had an American chart run of just over six years before they announced their disbandment. But the remarkable thing about the Beatles is that they proved truly worthy of the early adulation heaped upon them: up to the end of their career as a group, they continued to evolve in new and unexpected directions and to challenge themselves and their wide audience. They altered the character of pop music profoundly and bequeathed to popular culture a remarkably rich, and complex, inheritance.

We can trace the evolution of the Beatles by using the model advanced for describing the career of the Beach Boys. They started out as a performing band

Box 4.2 Other British Invasion Bands

It was not only the Beatles' immense popularity but also the wide-ranging and eclectic character of their musical output that made their influence on American pop so great. No other 1960s band—British or American—had the range or reach of the Beatles. The other British Invasion acts that did make a long-term impact in America started as the Beatles did: with firm roots in American rhythm & blues and rock 'n' roll. But the Rolling Stones, the Animals, the Who, the Kinks, and Eric Clapton all remained closer to these roots, on the whole, during their careers than did the Beatles. Indeed, it was just at the point that the Beatles became a studio band and began producing music that was essentially uncategorizable, like "Eleanor Rigby" and many of the songs on the album *Sgt. Pepper's Lonely Hearts Club Band* (see Chapter 5), that the Rolling Stones—who to this day play international live tours—began to call themselves the "World's Greatest Rock 'n' Roll Band." Regardless of one's feelings about that claim, there is no doubt that, of all the British Invasion acts other than the Beatles, the Rolling Stones have had the greatest cumulative influence in America.

The Rolling Stones excelled in presenting covers and original songs of an intense, gritty, and often dark character. They cultivated an image as "bad boys," in deliberate contrast to the friendly public image projected by the Beatles. Perhaps their most famous hit record is "(I Can't Get No) Satisfaction" (Number One, 1965, composed by band members Mick Jagger and Keith Richards); with its memorable buzzing guitar "hook," its unrelenting beat, and its unabashedly self-oriented and ultimately sexual lyrics, the song perfectly exemplifies the distinctive low-down, hard-rocking essence both of the Rolling Stones themselves and of their music. The Rolling Stones experimented occasionally in the later 1960s with unusual instrumentation and unconventional forms, as did virtually every other major British and American group—one had, after all, to keep up with the Beatles in some sense. But while a record like "As Tears Go By" (Number Six, 1966) is undeniably affecting and effective, its gently somber atmosphere and employment of orchestral strings render it a highly atypical Stones opus. The ultimate importance of the Rolling Stones lies in the power and longevity with which they kept, and continue to keep, the spirit of basic rock 'n' roll alive. (As late as 1986, the group achieved a Top 10 hit with "Harlem Shuffle," their faithful remake of a neglected American rhythm & blues hit from 1964 by Bob and Earl.)

It is obviously impossible to do justice in this book to the Rolling Stones or to many other important British acts of the 1960s and beyond—although we will return to the Stones for a while in Chapter 6. Although the importance of these artists to the stylistic development of American pop may not be extensive, their presence on the American and world pop music landscape has been, and continues to be, a formidable one.

modeled on Buddy Holly's group, the Crickets (see Chapter 3); after some initial shifts in personnel, the Beatles achieved a stable lineup by 1962 consisting of John Lennon and George Harrison (lead and rhythm guitars and vocals), Paul McCartney (bass and vocals), and Ringo Starr (drums and occasional vocals). During their extended apprenticeship period, the Beatles played at clubs in their home town of Liverpool and elsewhere—most famously in Hamburg, Germany—performing an imitative repertoire that centered on covers of songs by the American rock 'n' roll artists they most admired, such as Chuck Berry, Little Richard, Carl Perkins, and naturally Buddy Holly. (The country/rock 'n' roll duo the Everly Brothers also exercised a significant influence on the Beatles' group singing style.) Several such covers found their way onto early Beatles albums, once their manager Brian Epstein managed, after much difficulty, to get them a recording contract (in 1962). A few of these cover recordings were also eventually chart hits for the Beatles in America, among them "Matchbox," a Carl Perkins tune (Number Seventeen, 1964) and the Beatles' best-known cover record, "Twist and Shout" (Number Two, 1964), a rhythm & blues dance number composed by Phil Medley and Bert Russell that the Beatles doubtless learned from the 1962 hit recording by the Isley Brothers.

"Twist and Shout" was on the Beatles' first album, *Please Please Me*, released in Great Britain in 1963. By the time of this recording the Beatles were entering a period of emulation by writing some of their own songs; *Please Please Me* contains six covers and eight original selections. The Beatles' chief songwriters were Lennon and McCartney, who, at least at first, worked as a team, but eventually Harrison began to contribute songs as well, and by the end of the Beatles' career even Starr had emerged occasionally as a songwriter. This brings up an important point. Unlike the Beach Boys in the 1960s, whose creative center was unquestionably found in one member of the group, the Beatles throughout their prime years were a kind of multiple-threat team. The many creative and performing abilities shared among the four Beatles allowed the group to achieve a wonderful collective synergy, a whole both greater than and different from the sum of its parts. (The after-the-fact proof of this statement may be seen in the four contrasting solo careers the individual members of the group had after the Beatles broke up in 1970.) The Beatles were also blessed with a sympathetic and encouraging producer in George Martin. Martin was sometimes called "the fifth Beatle" in acknowledgment of his increasingly essential role in the recording studio in the later 1960s, as the Beatles came to attempt more and more sophisticated arrangements and electronic engineering effects on their recordings.

Four representative songs will serve well to chart the Beatles' career as songwriting performers from 1962 to 1966, the year that they quit touring, gave up live performance, and went on to become the world's first famous studio rock band. These four songs demonstrate their development from emulators to innovators; the final phase of their career will be discussed in the next chapter. From very early on, the Beatles' original songs showed considerable individuality and creativity in dealing with the inherited materials of rock 'n' roll. By 1965, with the appropriately titled "Yesterday," they were revealing an ability to emulate Tin Pan Alley as well as American rockers. And with "Eleanor Rigby" in 1966, the Beatles achieved a song that was—and is—truly "beyond category," a song that helped certify their new status as not only the most popular band in the history of rock 'n' roll but also the most innovative one.

LISTENING TO FOUR SONGS BY THE BEATLES, 1962–1966

"Please Please Me" was recorded in late 1962. It was the Beatles' first Top 10 hit in Britain and was one of the songs unsuccessfully released in America in 1963. But indie label Vee-Jay rereleased the single when "I Want to Hold Your Hand" began its rapid ascent on the American charts in early 1964, and before long "Please Please Me" was up in the Top 3 along with "I Want to Hold Your Hand" and another Beatles hit, "She Loves You," which had also initially been released in this country in 1963. (During a now-famous week in early April 1964 the Beatles achieved the unprecedented and still unique feat of having all of the top five records on the American charts for the week—an index of the intensity of American Beatlemania at the time.)

"Please Please Me," a fine example of the early Beatles' songwriting and performing, is a straightforward uptempo love song in a typical AABA form. The group sings and plays it crisply, energetically, and efficiently—once through the song, and it's over, in just two minutes' time.

Still, individualistic features in the song already point to the creative energy at work in the group. The lyrics contain some clever internal rhymes, as when "com*plainin*" is rhymed with "*rain in* [my heart]" at the beginning of the B section. The title itself plays with the word "please," using it both as verb and adverb. Effective rhymes and wordplay would become two trademarks of the Beatles' songwriting.

Musically, as shown in the listening chart, the A sections have their own distinctive internal form that proves a source of considerable interest. First there are two identical phrases (*a, a*) to set the poetic couplets that open these sections. These *a* phrases have a basically descending melodic motion over minimal chord changes. In the rather unexpected third phrase, *b,* where the text consists simply of the repeated words "Come on, come on," the music becomes the focus of interest, with continuous chord changes and a steadily ascending melodic line depicting the intensity that underlies the unchanging lyrics. With the final phrase, *c,* a melodic high point is reached as the lyrics arrive at the words of the song's title, "Please please me," after which the melody descends once again and the harmony presents a conclusive **cadence**. The musical form of the A sections, a-a-b-c, also delineates the rhyme scheme in the four-line stanzas of the lyrics.

"A Hard Day's Night," a Number One hit in 1964, was the title song from the Beatles' first movie. It shares a few surface characteristics with "Please Please Me." The name of the song once again demonstrates wordplay, in characterizing the work experience of those who do their "hard day's work" at night— like members of a rock band. The overall form of the song is once again AABA. But the considerably more subtle and elaborate playing with formal characteristics and expectations clearly demonstrates the increasing sophistication of

LISTENING CHART "PLEASE PLEASE ME" (1962)

Written by John Lennon and Paul McCartney; performed by the Beatles

FORM	LYRICS	DESCRIPTIVE COMMENTS
Instrumental intro		As a hook, the lead guitar and harmonica play the melody of the first two phrases of A.
A: a	*Last night . . .*	
a	*I know . . .*	Same melody line, new words.
b	*Come on . . .*	Note steady chord changes, ascending melody.
c	*Please please me . . .*	High point of melody comes on words of the title.
A: a	*You don't . . .*	Same music as before, with new words for
a	*Why do I . . .*	the first two lines of the stanza.
b	*Come on . . .*	
c	*Please please me . . .*	
B: d	*I don't . . .*	Bridge section; new music.
d′	*I do . . .*	Note change and extension at the end of this phrase, leading back to the final A.
A	*Last night . . . (etc.)*	Exact repetition of the opening A, with brief extension at the end.

the Beatles' songwriting. And while the performance of the song is fully as energetic and engaging as that of "Please Please Me," some novel touches reveal the group's increasing attention to details of sound and arrangement.

In a sense, "A Hard Day's Night" may be heard as the Beatles' updating of the old Tin Pan Alley classic "My Blue Heaven": it similarly portrays the delights of returning home to a rewarding domestic relationship. (It is not at all unthinkable that the Beatles knew "My Blue Heaven," especially since Fats Domino had revived it and made it a hit again, in rock 'n' roll style of course, in 1956. Domino was very popular in Britain, and the Beatles eventually created an implicit tribute to his New Orleans style by writing and recording "Lady Madonna" in 1968. Domino appreciated the compliment and returned it by recording the song himself the same year.) Musically, "A Hard Day's Night" is clearly modeled on those AABA song forms in which the A sections are twelve-bar blues stanzas. But while the A sections are indeed twelve bars in length, have three four-bar phrases, and incorporate **blue notes,** they are not exactly traditional twelve-bar blues structures. In the lyrics, the Beatles begin by making a reference to the traditional a-a-b poetic stanza found in many blues, by having the second line begin with the same words as the first (see listening chart). But that second line ends with different words, and the following A stanza features three completely independent lines. In the music of these A sections, the Beatles do not follow the traditional chord structure of twelve-bar blues. There are **chords** used in addition to the traditional three (**tonic,** subdominant, and dominant—see the discussion of twelve-bar blues in Chapter 2), and the traditional chords do not always occur in the expected places. In particular, the usual chord change at the start of the second

LISTENING CHART "A HARD DAY'S NIGHT" (1964)

Written by John Lennon and Paul McCartney; performed by the Beatles

FORM	LYRICS	DESCRIPTIVE COMMENTS
Introductory guitar chord, then pause		Dissonance followed by open space creates anticipatory tension.
A	*It's been a hard day's night . . .* *It's been a hard day's night . . .* *But when I get home to you . . .*	Music and lyrics of A sections are modeled on twelve-bar blues patterns but introduce significant variations.
A	*You know I work all day . . .* *And it's worth it . . .* *So why on earth should I moan . . .*	Same music, new lyrics.
B	*When I'm home . . .*	Bridge section; new music, consisting of two similar phrases.
A	*It's been a hard day's night . . .*	Exact repetition of the first A section.
A	*[Instrumental interlude]* *So why on earth should I moan . . .*	Guitar solo for the first eight bars, then voices return for the last phrase (four bars) of the section.
B	*When I'm home . . .*	As before.
A	*It's been a hard day's night . . .*	As before.
Instrumental coda		Fades out.

phrase (the move to the subdominant chord) is postponed to the start of the third and final phrase of the twelve-bar section. This yields an interesting result: although the lyrics to the A sections do not conform to the a-a-b pattern, the *musical* phrases do.

These musical alterations are not merely technical details, for they serve the meaning of the lyrics. It is the third line in each of the A stanzas that describes the trip home from work and the actual reuniting with the loved one. Thus it is entirely appropriate that the harmony should wait until this point to make its own anticipated move. (The harmony does return to the **tonic** at the expected point—in the eleventh bar—as the singer settles down with his lover at home and feels "all right," or "okay.")

Lastly, we may mention three aspects of the song's arrangement. The song begins literally with a bang: a loud, isolated guitar chord whose unexpected harsh **dissonance** is permitted to ring in the air before the song actually gets going. This is the most effective and efficient of hooks, and it also perfectly prepares the tense feelings described in the opening words of the song. Notice also the unique guitar **timbre** employed for the instrumental solo in the middle of the record, which allows this solo on the twelve-string guitar to stand out from the many other guitar sounds heard elsewhere throughout the performance. The very end brings an unexpected instrumental **coda,** as a solo guitar gently strums a repeating figure that fades out. The abrupt cessation of drums and accompanying chords underlines the relaxed character of this ending, which creates an effective counterbalance to the song's unnerving opening and surely signifies the final lifting of tension after the "hard day's night" and the settling in to the delights of being home.

"Yesterday," which reached the Number One position on the pop charts in 1965, may be the Beatles song with the most wide-ranging and enduring popularity; certainly it has been the one most performed by other artists, and its appeal cuts across generational and stylistic divides. The song comes across with a remarkable directness and simplicity, so natural in its verbal and melodic expression that it seems hardly to have been consciously composed. But, as we know from many previous examples of fine popular music, such an effect is difficult to achieve and almost invariably conceals much art.

As a composition, "Yesterday" obviously evokes Tin Pan Alley models. Musically, it employs a standard AABA form. Its lyrics approach the time-honored theme of broken romance in a gentle, general, and straightforward manner, such that virtually anyone could understand and empathize, and virtually nobody could take offense. (One aspect of the song's appeal is that the feelings involved are utterly clear, whereas the specific situation remains vague enough to stimulate the imagination of many different listeners: "Why she had to go I don't know, she wouldn't say.") But the song may assert its kinship with Tin Pan Alley most tellingly in its emphasis on a distinctive and expressive melodic line, a line that fits the words beautifully. The melody is accompanied by equally expressive harmonies, which explore a wider range of chords than was typical for rock music at this time. The moderate tempo, and the general avoidance of any intense rhythmic effects, also distance "Yesterday" from the rock mainstream and edge it closer in spirit to Tin Pan Alley.

The Beatles' recording of "Yesterday" underlines the song's unexpected character in every way. The use of a solo voice throughout, the similarity of Paul McCartney's lyrical and unaffected style of delivery to Tin Pan Alley–style crooning, the choice of acoustic (rather than electric) guitar, the employment of orchestral string instruments to augment the accompaniment, the lack of any drums or percussion instruments, the prevailingly soft dynamic level—all these elements set the record apart from others of its time, including other records by the Beatles, as if to emphasize that this song is a deliberate venture into new musical territory. While anyone who had been listening carefully to the Beatles knew by 1965 that they were capable of writing beautifully melodic love ballads (such as "And I Love Her" and "If I Fell," both from the Beatles' 1964 movie *A Hard Day's Night*), "Yesterday" was designed to—and did—make listeners really sit up and take notice. Maybe the Beatles were more than just a good old rock 'n' roll band, or even more than a good new rock band. Maybe they were just something else entirely.

As you listen to "Yesterday," try to notice some of the artistry that went in to the creation and performance of this famous song. Each of the A sections begins with an isolated, essential word that serves as a decisive hook into the story (see listening chart); these single opening words are set to foreshortened musical phrases (one bar in length, as opposed to the standard two bars) that func-

LISTENING CHART "YESTERDAY" (1965)

Written by John Lennon and Paul McCartney; performed by the Beatles (actually Paul McCartney, vocal solo, accompanied by guitar and string ensemble)

FORM	LYRICS	DESCRIPTIVE COMMENTS
Brief intro: acoustic guitar vamp		
A	*Yesterday . . .*	Guitar accompaniment continues.
A	*Suddenly . . .*	String ensemble joins the guitar; fuller sound.
B	*Why she had to go . . .* *I said something wrong . . .*	Bridge section; new music, consisting of two similar phrases.
A	*Yesterday . . .*	

Repetition of B and final A sections, followed by brief coda, in which the voice hums the closing melodic phrase of A accompanied by the strings.

tion equally as focusing hooks. The ascending gestures in the melody always depict the receding past ("all my troubles seemed so far away," "I'm not half the man I used to be," and so forth), while the immediately following descending gestures always bring us back down to earth in the present ("Now it looks as though they're here to stay," "There's a shadow hanging over me," etc.). The lyrics to the bridge section reveal again the Beatles' adeptness at internal rhyming: "I said something *wrong,* now I *long* for yesterday." And the final word in the bridge, "yesterday," links this B section effectively to the final A, which begins with the same word. In terms of the arrangement, we can admire how withholding the entrance of the orchestral strings until the second A section makes their arrival a wonderfully rich, intense surprise that goes splendidly with the word "suddenly."

"Eleanor Rigby," a Number Eleven pop hit in 1966, was not quite the smash hit the preceding three songs were. Actually, it was issued as the B-side of "Yellow Submarine," a novelty number that went to the Number Two position on the charts; it is a tribute to the impact of "Eleanor Rigby" that it made the charts at all, let alone that it reached nearly as high as the Top 10.

"Eleanor Rigby" is a startling song right from the outset. Without any preparation, the voices enter with a high, loud cry of "Ah," accompanied by an active string ensemble (violins, violas, and cellos). Orchestral strings are traditionally associated with soothing music—an association exemplified by a song like "Yesterday"—but here they are confined to steady, repeated chords and brief rhythmic figures, assuming functions much like those of the rhythm guitar and drums in a more typical rock configuration. The harmony is equally dislocating. The song opens on a big **major** chord, but after the initial vocal phrase it settles onto an unexpected **minor** chord. These two chords alternate throughout the song, and they are in fact the only two chords used. The restriction of the chordal vocabulary (which beautifully suits the story of repression told by the song), the oscillation between two chords that do not share a traditional harmonic rela-tionship, and the fact that it is the second, minor chord (rather than the opening major chord) that proves to be the central focus (or **tonic**) of the song as a whole, are all factors contributing strongly to the unique atmosphere of "Eleanor Rigby."

The subject matter of the song, loneliness, is not in itself an unusual one in pop music, but "Eleanor Rigby" looks at loneliness and the lack of human con-nection from a uniquely philosophical, even spiritual, viewpoint rather than from a romantic viewpoint. Eleanor Rigby and Father McKenzie, introduced in two sep-arate verses of the song, remain isolated from one another—and from other peo-ple—in their lives. And even in death! Only Father McKenzie is even aware of Eleanor's passing; they "meet" in the third and final verse only in a graveyard that finalizes their nonrelationship, and the "good" Father can only wipe dirt from his hands as he walks away from the site of Eleanor's burial. As the lyrics say, so succinctly and eloquently, "No one was saved." This is somber stuff indeed, and it is to the Beatles' credit that the song conveys its despairing message in an efficient and utterly unsentimental way, which of course maximizes the effect.

Apart from the striking introduction, the form of the song suggests that of the traditional folk **ballad,** with verses that tell a developing story alternating with a repeated chorus (see the listening chart). By the mid-1960s the urban folk re-vival had already been in full swing for years (see Chapter 5), so it was not sur-prising to see the Beatles laying claim to the folk ballad form as they continued to expand their musical horizons. What was, and remains, surprising is their unique take on this tradition. The ballad form was conventionally used as a means of telling a large-scale, dramatic, often tragic story. And many of the urban folk performers, such as Bob Dylan, adapted the form in their original songs to serve the same kind of dramatic purpose. In "Eleanor Rigby," on the other hand, *noth-ing* happens in the lives of the protagonists. And that, the Beatles tell us, is the source of this tragedy.

The bowed strings take over the role of a strumming guitar in the "ballad" of "Eleanor Rigby," paradoxically giving the song a much harder edge. As you listen, notice the slight variations in the string parts from verse to verse and even in the repetitions of the chorus; they help maintain interest in the emerg-ing story.

A few more musical details deserve mention here. The phrase structure of the verses is distinctive: a long initial phrase (of four bars): "Eleanor Rigby picks up the rice in a church where a wedding has been," is answered by a very short (one-bar) phrase: "Lives in a dream." The consistent, atypical, extreme asym-metry of these paired phrases gives the song an unquiet quality of continual in-completion—especially since the shorter phrases are left to hang melodically at a relatively high point, without any conventional feeling of resolution. This is a perfect musical illustration of the incompleteness that characterizes the lives be-ing described. (In a sense, this kind of phrase structure is the reverse of that used in "Yesterday," where the opening phrase of each section is foreshortened while the ensuing phrases blossom out to traditional lengths.) Also, in the chorus, no-

LISTENING CHART   "ELEANOR RIGBY" (1966)

Written by John Lennon and Paul McCartney; performed by the Beatles, with accompanying string ensemble

FORM		LYRICS	DESCRIPTIVE COMMENTS
Introduction		*Ah, look at all . . .*	Voices and strings enter at once.
		Ah, look at all . . .	Exact repetition.
Verse 1:	**a**	*Eleanor Rigby . . .*	Solo voice, accompanied by strings marking
		Lives in a dream.	each beat with a chord; unusual phrase structure
	a	*Waits at the window . . .*	creates a striking effect.
		Who is it for?	
Chorus:	**b**	*All the lonely people . . .*	
	b'	*All the lonely people . . .*	Second phrase of chorus changes the melody
			to go higher than the first phrase.
Verse 2:	**a**	*Father McKenzie . . .*	As before.
		No one comes near.	
	a	*Look at him working . . .*	
		What does he care?	
Chorus:	**b**	*All the lonely people . . .*	
	b'	*All the lonely people . . .*	
Introduction recurs		*Ah, look at all . . .*	As before.
		Ah, look at all . . .	
Verse 3:	**a**	*Eleanor Rigby . . .*	As before.
		Nobody came.	
	a	*Father McKenzie . . .*	
		No one was saved.	
Chorus:	**b**	*All the lonely people . . .*	As a conclusion, the melody and lyrics of the
	b'	*All the lonely people . . .*	Introduction are sung in counterpoint against
			the melody and lyrics of the chorus, then
			strings bring the song to an abrupt ending.

tice how the second phrase goes higher than the first, making the question it asks ("Where do they all belong?") even more intense and insistent.

Finally, the Beatles find extremely imaginative uses for their introductory material later on in the song, demonstrating again their originality and mastery of form. Just at the point when two successive verse-chorus sections have us convinced that we are listening to a straightforward **strophic** form, the introduction is unexpectedly brought back. The renewed cry of "Ah, look at all the lonely people!" underlines the song's theme and helps set off the crucial third verse. Then, at the very end, the final chorus is rendered climactic rather than simply repetitive because the introduction's words and melody are sung simultaneously with it in **counterpoint**. This brings the song full circle; there is nothing left to say, and the strings bring "Eleanor Rigby" to a quick, brusque conclusion.

The Beatles and their music have been discussed in such detail in this book simply because the impact of their popularity and originality on American popular music has been incalculable; the group was *the* central fact of American pop culture in the 1960s. Brian Wilson viewed them as his principal rivals in the creation of innovative pop music, and even Motown's Temptations acknowledged, in their own hit song "Ball of Confusion," that "the Beatles' new record's a gas"! Thus the Beatles are an essential part of the history of American pop; or, put another way, with the arrival of the Beatles on our shores and on our charts, the history of American pop becomes unavoidably international.

Meanwhile, Back in California . . .

While the other Beach Boys were out on tour, Brian Wilson was preparing his response and challenge to the Beatles, whose late 1965 album *Rubber Soul* had particularly inspired him, in the form of an elaborately produced and strikingly unconventional album called *Pet Sounds*. Less a work of rock 'n' roll than a nearly symphonic cycle of songs, *Pet Sounds* charts a progression from youthful optimism ("Wouldn't It Be Nice" and "You Still Believe in Me") to philosophical and emotional disillusionment ("I Just Wasn't Made for These Times" and "Caroline, No"). Released in mid-1966, *Pet Sounds* was arguably rock's first *concept album*—that is, an album conceived as an integrated whole, with interrelated songs arranged in a deliberate sequence. (The listening sequence was easier to mandate, obviously, in the days of long-playing records with two numbered sides, played on phonographs without remote controls, than in today's world of single-sided compact discs whose contents listeners may readily program, and edit, for themselves by pushing a few buttons.) *Pet Sounds* was a modest seller compared to some other Beach Boys albums, but it had an enormous impact on musicians who heard it. With its display of diverse and unusual instrumentation, including orchestral wind instruments as well as strings; its virtuosic vocal arrangements, showcasing the songs' advanced harmonies; and its occasional formal experiments, exemplified by the AA'BCC' form of the remarkable instrumental "Let's Go Away for Awhile," the album was state-of-the-art pop music in every sense, designed to push at the boundaries of what had been considered possible. Its historical importance is certified by Paul McCartney's affirmation that *Pet Sounds* was the single greatest influence on the Beatles' landmark 1967 album *Sgt. Pepper's Lonely Hearts Club Band* (see next chapter).

Wilson furthered his experimentation with the late 1966 single "Good Vibrations," which reached Number One on the charts and has remained probably the Beach Boys' most famous song (see the "Listening and Analysis" section). By this time, Wilson was also at work on an album to be called *Smile*. Eagerly anticipated for many months, *Smile* was abandoned in 1967, and the collapse of what was evidently a strikingly novel and ambitious project—even by Wilson's exceptionally high standards—marked the onset of a decline in his productivity and achievement from which he has only recently recovered. The material from the *Smile* sessions occasionally surfaced on later albums and CD compilations by the Beach Boys, hinting at how unprecedented and stunning the album was intended to be. The promise of *Smile* was finally fufilled when Wilson returned to and completed the project in 2004.

LISTENING AND ANALYSIS "GOOD VIBRATIONS"

Basic Description

"Good Vibrations" may well be the most thoroughly innovative single from the singular decade of the 1960s. Virtually every aspect of the record is unusual, from the vocal arrangement to the instrumentation, from the chordal vocabulary to the overall form. Beginning with a gentle, unaccompanied sigh in a high solo voice right at the outset (which might be an anticipation of the opening word, "I," but could also be just the sighing sound "ah"), "Good Vibrations" establishes a unique world of sounds, textures, and feelings.

Probably the only remotely conventional thing about the song is its lyrics, with their admiring references to the beloved's "colorful clothes," hair, perfume, smile, and eyes. But there is something otherworldly about the lyrics as well—at least when they claim, "I don't know where, but she sends me there," or when they refer to "a blossom world," not to mention the "good vibrations" themselves. Notice also the extensive periods on the recording where lyrics are of secondary importance, or of no importance at all: the C section, the following instrumental transition, and the concluding "variations on B" section (see listening chart). These are in no sense secondary or unimportant portions of the record itself; it is just that here *sound* becomes more significant than *sense* (literally speaking)—or better, here the sound *becomes* the sense of the song. The sound is the way in which Wilson musically communicates the sensuous experience that is the essential subject matter of "Good Vibrations."

Form

There is no name for the form of "Good Vibrations"; it is as individual and distinctive as everything else about this recording. The best way to follow it is with the listening chart. The formal freedom is that much more effective because Wilson sets the listener up at first to expect a straightforward, predictable verse-chorus form with his initial ABAB pattern—since the lyrics to A change but those to B remain the same—and then goes on to present the unexpected. The C section could seem at first like a bridge, but instead of any return to A we get totally new material in D. In fact, the A music never returns at all, which is probably the second most surprising thing about this formal structure. The most surprising thing is that Wilson somehow manages to make this unconventional form work so effectively.

It works because of subtle interconnections that are established among the different musical sections. The C section has overlapping vocal textures that are reminiscent of the vocal textures in B sections, even though the specific music and the words are different. In the unexpected D section, the organ and percussion accompaniment maintains a kinship with the A sections, which also prominently feature those instruments. In addition, the clear presence of the words "good vibrations" in the D section provides a textual link between it and the preceding B sections, and also ties D to the concluding section, which we are calling "variations on B."

This final section requires a few comments. Its relationship with the earlier B sections is textually and musically obvious, but it is also clear that this is not a literal repetition, nor is it the kind of slight modification that would mandate a B' label. Rather, Wilson is taking verbal, musical, and textural ideas from his B material and arranging them in new ways to create a section that sounds evolutionary rather than stable. We could borrow a term from classical music and call this a kind of "development" of the ideas; "development" is a term rarely if ever needed to describe formal sections of popular songs, but then most popular songs do not behave like "Good Vibrations." (Wilson employs one particularly sophisticated music device here. At the beginning of the "variations on B" he plays the characteristic chord progression of the earlier B sections, but in *reverse* order, starting on the final chord and ending on the opening chord. This allows him to proceed by then taking the opening chord again and playing the chords in the original order—but with new, textless vocal parts. The material is constantly in flux.) Remarkably, the song fades out while immersed in this development section, never having returned to its point of origin or to any other stable reference point. In a way, this is a perfect ending for a record so thoroughly liberated from traditional formal constraints.

The Song/The Recording

As a composition, "Good Vibrations" boasts memorable melodic hooks and a wide and colorful palette of chords. Both the high opening minor-key melody of the A section (which first ascends, and then descends) and the major-key bass line "I'm pickin' up good vibrations" of the B section (which first descends, and then ascends) are instantly memorable tunes—and beautifully contrasting ones. Consequently, they serve as effective landmarks for the listener who is journeying for the first time through this complex musical landscape. The D section offers a new but equally memorable melody. Some details of the harmony are indicated on the listening chart, for those who may wish to follow them.

The instrumentation of "Good Vibrations" is perhaps the most unusual ever employed on a hit record. Organ, flutes, solo cello, and colorful percussion instruments are all in evidence, clearly differentiating the sound of this recording from anything commonly associated with rock 'n' roll. But the ultimate exotic touch is provided by the *theremin*—the whirring, sirenlike, otherworldly instrument that appropriately illustrates the "good vibrations" in the B sections. (There is some question about whether the recording actually employed a theremin or a somewhat different instrument that sounds very much like one. But such questions are not of great significance to listeners; the exotic effect is certainly achieved!) Notice how Wilson also uses the voices of the Beach Boys as an additional choir of sound colors, pitting solo against group sounds, high voices against low, and so forth. Some prominent details of both the instrumental and vocal parts are indicated in the descriptive comments on the listening chart.

"Good Vibrations" was an extremely costly recording to produce, in terms of both time and money. Wilson tried out many different instrumental and vocal arrangements and a number of different formal schemes, committing hours and hours of rehearsal time to tape before he finally settled on the version we can hear today on record—which is actually a composite of several tapes made at various times. Thus, "Good Vibrations," which Brian Wilson called his "pocket symphony," is an important milestone in the developing history of rock pro-duction, as well as a landmark hit record of the 1960s.

LISTENING CHART "GOOD VIBRATIONS"

Music by Brian Wilson; lyrics by Mike Love; produced by Brian Wilson; as performed by the Beach Boys with instrumental accompaniment; recorded 1966

FORM	LYRICS	DESCRIPTIVE COMMENTS
A	*I love the colorful clothes . . .*	High solo voice, with delicate, high-range accompaniment of organ, flutes, and eventually percussion; minor key.
B	*I'm pickin' up good vibrations . . .*	Bass voice enters, accompanied by cello, theremin, and percussion, then rest of group comes in with overlapping vocal parts; major key.
A	*Close my eyes, she's somehow closer now . . .*	As before.
B	*I'm pickin' up good vibrations . . .*	As before; formal structure up to to this point suggests verse-chorus form.
C	[soft humming at first, then more vocal activity, then:] *I don't know where, but she sends me there . . .*	Steadily building tension; no stable key.
Brief instrumental transition: organ and percussion		New key established (major).
D	*Gotta keep those lovin' good vibrations happenin' with her.*	Solo voice, then group, with organ accompaniment; the line of text repeats, then fades out while organ finishes the section.
Transition	[*Aah!*]	
Variations on B	*I'm pickin' up good vibrations . . .*	Full group texture, with overlapping vocal parts; major key; then voices drop out, leaving cello and theremin, which are joined by percussion before fading out; no stable key.

By the mid-1960s the transition from rock 'n' roll to rock music was well under way, under the influence of performers such as the Beach Boys, the Beatles, and Bob Dy-lan. In the following chapter we will follow American popular music into the cultur-ally and politically turbulent period of the late 1960s, tracing the development of coun-try and western, soul music, and the urban folk movement; the rise of psychedelia and the counterculture; and the diversification of rock—now positioned at the center of the popular mainstream—into dozens of subcategories and specialized audiences.

CHAPTER FIVE

"PAPA'S GOT A BRAND NEW BAG"

Country, Soul, Urban Folk, and the Rise of Rock, 1960s

In Chapter 3 we stressed the integration of country- and rhythm & blues–based styles into the mix that came to be known as rock 'n' roll. Rhythm & blues was an obvious influence on virtually all the music discussed in Chapter 4. While the country influences on 1960s rock 'n' roll were far less obvious, they remained present as well. In particular, the Beatles' close harmony singing owed not a little to the model of the Everly Brothers—and thus to the whole history of country's "high lonesome" duet and group sounds. One of the Beatles' chart-making cover recordings was of "Act Naturally"; issued on the B-side of "Yesterday," the song had originally been a Number One hit on the country charts in 1963 for Buck Owens.

However, this mentioning of the country charts brings us to the fact that the pre–rock 'n' roll distinctions among genres and audiences did not simply collapse after 1955, although the situation was much more fluid than it had been. One still finds much significantly popular music that did *not* cross over into the mainstream during the late 1950s and 1960s, even though eclectic influences were everywhere present on the pop charts. Artists and records that appealed to select or regional audiences were much less likely to find their way onto the pop charts than those that managed to cut across such distinctions. Listeners to pop- and rock-oriented radio stations in New York City or Detroit could probably have gone through the whole decade of the 1960s totally unaware of performers like Buck Owens or Merle Haggard. Yet these performers—along with many others who would not have been heard on those urban radio stations, such as George Jones, Sonny James, Webb Pierce, Kitty Wells, and Loretta Lynn—were the bread and butter of country stations in the southern and western parts of the United States during this same period. Thus we have the striking anomaly that, among all the artists just mentioned, only one achieved a national Top 40 pop hit during the entire decade, and he did so only once: Buck Owens's "I've Got a Tiger by the Tail" got up to Number Twenty-five in 1965. Yet the same record occupied the Number One spot on *Billboard*'s country charts for five weeks, and was just one of *twenty-one* Number One country songs for Owens during the decade. Sonny James had twelve Number One country hits during this same period, Merle Haggard had seven, and the list could go on.

But the anomalies don't end there. Those same listeners in New York or Detroit might in turn have heard rhythm & blues–oriented music on their radios that, while popular locally, failed to make much of a dent in the national pop charts. Although Motown's records had no trouble crossing over—they were, as we have seen, designed to do so—a record like Freddie Scott's "Are You Lonely for Me," issued on the small Shout label, could hold the Number One spot on *Billboard*'s R&B chart for four weeks in 1967, while climbing no higher than Number Thirty-nine (and then for one week only) on the pop chart.

Just how much weight should be given to all this chart data is, of course, a justifiable question. But regardless of the actual numbers, it seems clear that such data does reflect some clear and persistent divisions among markets and audiences for popular music, divisions that had at least something to do with racial and ethnic factors, geographical location, and distance from major urban centers. The especially large differences between the country and the pop charts for much of the 1960s might have resulted, to a certain extent, from some inherent bias on the part of the data collectors toward the large radio stations and record retailers centered in the big cities of the North.[1] But these differences also reflected the authentic, and increasingly wide, gulf between the lingeringly rural cultures of the South and Southwest and the urban cultures that dominated much of the North. (The feeling of separateness that characterized much of the country audience was articulated memorably in Merle Haggard's controversial 1969 recording "Okie from Muskogee"—a critique of the late 1960s **counterculture** that may or may not have been made with deeply serious intent—that rose to Number One country, Number Forty-one pop.) In spite of all this, country music did have a much wider impact on the pop music of the 1960s than is generally acknowledged.

Many of the younger country artists at this time, while not directly embracing the **rockabilly** styles of Elvis Presley or Buddy Holly, wanted to update the sound of their honky-tonk roots. Starting with a basis in the **ballad** style of Hank Williams—taking, we might say, a song like "I'm So Lonesome I Could Cry" instead of "Hey, Good Lookin'" as their point of orientation (see the discussion of Hank Williams in Chapter 2)—they opted for a newly sophisticated approach to the vocal presentation and instrumental arrangement of country music, a highly influential approach that came to be known as *countrypolitan,* a fusion of "country" and "cosmopolitan." Nashville was at the center of this development, and the style

---

1. Such a bias would also help explain the relatively much greater congruence between the R&B and pop charts during this time, as R&B is a largely urban (albeit not exclusively northern) music. The R&B and pop charts were getting close enough to each other that *Billboard,* over-optimistically, briefly dropped the separate R&B charts for a little over a year, from late 1963 to early 1965; then the R&B charts resumed their appearance. Significantly, when *Billboard* changed its methods of gathering data in the early 1990s, relying on electronically generated data of actual record sales and radio play instead of accepting reports from selected outlets, the presence of country records on the pop charts increased dramatically.

was also often called the "Nashville sound." Among its most important manifestations were the recordings of Patsy Cline.

PATSY CLINE AND THE NASHVILLE SOUND

Patsy Cline (1932–63) began her career as a hit maker in 1957 with her recording of
"Walkin' after Midnight," which was indicative of her future achievements and importance insofar as it was successful on both the country (Number Two) and the
pop charts (Number Twelve). Such crossover success from country to pop was of
course not uncommon in the fluid record market of 1957. But it was noteworthy
when Cline achieved even greater crossover success in 1961, at a time of vastly increasing segregation between the country and pop markets. Her two big hits of that
year, "I Fall to Pieces," which reached Number One country and Number Twelve
pop, and "Crazy" (Number Two country, Number Nine pop) reflected a particular
kind of sensibility: they were ballads of broad appeal, in no sense "teen" records,
performed by Cline in a manner that, while sophisticated in phrasing and articula-
tion, had sufficient hints of rural and bluesy inflections to show where her roots
lay. The crooning background voices gave these records a pop sheen, while the
high-register piano remained evocative of the honky-tonk origins of this type of
music. Cline continued to be a significant presence on both country and pop charts
until her premature death in a plane crash in early 1963.

Other recordings of the early 1960s that demonstrated the crossover appeal of
the Nashville sound were those of Jim Reeves and Floyd Cramer. A ballad like
Reeves's "He'll Have to Go" (Number Two pop, Number One country—for fourteen weeks!—in 1960) demonstrates a similar mixture of elements to those that made
Cline's records so successful; Reeves possessed a fine, full, deep baritone voice that
was particularly well suited for mainstream pop appeal. Floyd Cramer was a
Nashville session pianist who combined his honky-tonk-derived style with orchestral strings to produce the huge instrumental hit "Last Date" (Number Two pop,
Number Eleven country, 1960).

The impact of the Nashville sound on 1960s pop is clear if we consider certain
records by artists not primarily identified with country music. Connie Francis and
Brenda Lee, the two most popular female vocalists of the early 1960s, depended
mainly on the young rock 'n' roll audience for their reputation and record sales,
and both certainly made uptempo records obviously addressed to the new teenage
audience (such as Francis's 1962 hit "Vacation" and Lee's 1960 smash "Sweet
Nothin's"). But Connie Francis's two biggest hits, "Everybody's Somebody's Fool"
and "My Heart Has a Mind of Its Own"—both of which made it to Number One
on the pop charts in 1960—betray a significant Nashville sound influence, and
Brenda Lee's own biggest hit, the 1960 Number One "I'm Sorry," shows that influence even more transparently. Indeed, "I'm Sorry," with its strings and crooning chorus backing Lee's mournful and blues-inflected vocal performance, features
a type of sound that has been prominent on the country charts for much of the latter part of the twentieth century. These mainstream pop hits by Francis and Lee
may well have paved the way for Patsy Cline's crossover successes in 1961.

The records made by rock 'n' roller Elvis Presley from 1960 on (after he returned
from a tour of duty in the army) reflected an increasingly eclectic set of influences,

but the Nashville sound is especially prominent among them. Good illustrations of this would be his 1961 hit "Can't Help Falling in Love" and his 1965 recording of "Crying in the Chapel," originally a country hit in 1953.

It might seem initially surprising that the Nashville sound's influence extended into rhythm & blues in the early 1960s, but given the constant interchanges between white and black musicians throughout the history of American popular music, this really shouldn't strike us as unexpected. Two hits by Solomon Burke, "Just Out of Reach (Of My Two Open Arms)" (Number Twenty-four pop, Number Seven R&B, 1961), and "Cry to Me" (Number Forty-four pop, Number Five R&B, 1962) sound for all the world like country records performed by a black vocalist, and a large number of similar-sounding records were made in the wake of their success, by Burke and by other artists associated with rhythm & blues. By the later 1960s the career of Charley Pride—an African American who set out to appeal principally to the country audience—was in full swing; by 1983 Pride had racked up an astonishing twenty-nine Number One country hits (none of which even dented the rhythm & blues charts), thus illustrating once again how color-blind music and its audiences really can be some of the time.

But the most remarkable and unexpected synthesis of country with rhythm & blues elements was probably achieved by Ray Charles. Charles's achievement looms so large in the annals of American popular music that we must stop here to consider his career in some detail.

RAY CHARLES AND SOUL MUSIC

Ray Charles (born Ray Charles Robinson, 1930–2004) was a constant presence on the rhythm & blues charts during the 1950s, but major crossover success eluded him until 1959, which is why we have not grouped him with early African American rock 'n' roll stars like Chuck Berry, Little Richard, and Fats Domino. In any case, Charles was never interested in being typecast as a rock 'n' roller, and he never consciously addressed his recordings to the teen market—or to any obviously de-limited market, for that matter. Characteristically, as soon as he established himself as a mass-market artist with the stunning blues-based and gospel-drenched "What'd I Say" (Number Six pop, Number One R&B, 1959), he immediately sought new worlds to conquer; his next record was a highly individual cover of Hank Snow's 1950 hit "I'm Movin' On," one of the biggest country records of all time. Within a year, Charles had achieved his first Number One pop hit with his version of the old **Tin Pan Alley** standard "Georgia on My Mind" (by Stuart Gorrell and Hoagy Carmichael), which also made it to Number Three on the rhythm & blues chart. But Charles's most astounding success was with his version of country artist Don Gibson's "I Can't Stop Loving You," which brought Charles's unique take on country music to the top spot on *both* the pop and rhythm & blues charts (five weeks Number One pop, ten weeks Number One R&B) in 1962 and gave him the biggest hit record of that entire year.

Ray Charles was certainly not the first artist to assay many different genres of American popular music, and he was of course only one of many to achieve remarkable crossover success. What is it then that made his career so distinctive, that made him such a universally admired pop musician—by audiences, critics, and

Ray Charles in 1960. Courtesy Library of Congress.

other musicians—that the appellation "genius" has clung to his name for decades, as if he had been born to the title?

Part of it is the astounding range of talents Charles cultivated. He was a fine songwriter, having written many of his early rhythm & blues hits, including classics of the genre like "I've Got a Woman" and "Hallelujah I Love Her So." He was a highly skilled arranger, as well as an exceptionally fine keyboard player who was fluent in jazz as well as mainstream pop idioms. And above all he was an outstanding vocalist, with a timbre so distinctive as to be instantly recognizable and an expressive intensity that, once heard, is difficult to forget. But this still is not the whole story. Charles's most characteristic recordings are not only distinguished, individual statements but also unique and encompassing statements about American popular music *style.*

After an apprenticeship period, during which he emulated the pop-friendly vocal and instrumental approach of Nat "King" Cole (see Chapter 2), Ray Charles established a style that immediately expressed his interest in synthesis. Charles's first Number One rhythm & blues recording, "I've Got a Woman" (recorded in 1954), is an obviously secular song based on gospel models, performed by Charles in a manner clearly related to gospel vocal stylings. Although black gospel music had been a long-term influence on aspects of secular "race" records and rhythm & blues, arguably nobody before Charles had brought the sacred and secular idioms into such a direct and intimate relationship; by the time of "Hallelujah I Love Her So" (Number Five R&B, 1956) he was expressing the connection in the song's very title! Needless to say, some people were scandalized by this. The final portion of "What'd I Say," in which Charles shouts and groans in call and response with a female chorus to produce music that simultaneously evokes a wild Southern Baptist service and the sounds of a very earthly sexual ecstasy, was banned on many radio stations in spite of the record's status as a national hit.

Although the term "soul music" would not enter the common vocabulary until the later 1960s, it is clearly soul music that Ray Charles was pioneering in his gospel-blues synthesis of the 1950s. He is now widely acknowledged as the first important soul artist, and his work proved an incalculable influence on James Brown, Aretha Franklin, Curtis Mayfield, Otis Redding, Sly Stone, and innumerable others. When Charles went on to record Tin Pan Alley and country material in the 1960s, far from leaving his soul stylings behind, he brought them along to help him forge new, wider-ranging, and arguably even braver combinations of styles.

When Charles recorded "Georgia on My Mind," he did not attempt to turn the Tin Pan Alley standard into a rhythm & blues song (the way Fats Domino did with "My Blue Heaven"). Neither did he remake himself into a crooner (the way Elvis Presley often did when performing mainstream pop-oriented material). Rather than using the jump band group that had backed him on most of his earlier records— and then perhaps adding some superficial sweetening with strings and crooning background chorus—Charles wholeheartedly embraced the Tin Pan Alley heritage of the song and presided over a sumptuous arrangement of it, with orchestral strings and accompanying chorus, that virtually outdid Tin Pan Alley itself in its elaborateness and unrestrained sentiment. But against this smooth and beautifully performed backdrop (Charles always insisted on the highest musical standards from all personnel involved in his performances), Charles sang "Georgia on My Mind" as if he were performing a deeply personal blues. While the original words, melody, and phrasing of the song were clearly conveyed, Charles employed an intense and sometimes rough-edged vocal timbre, used constant **syncopation**, and selectively added shakes, moans, and other improvised touches ("*I said-a*, Georgia") to reflect what was at this point his natural, individual vocal approach, rooted in gospel and blues. And he occasionally provided jazz-based fills in his piano part between vocal phrases, to evoke call and response within his own performance, while the backing chorus echoed his words at strategic intervals, producing call and response between them and Charles himself.

The result of all this was an extraordinary and unprecedented juxtaposition and dialogue of styles within a single recording. And as the description above indicates, this was no haphazard jumble of different elements; it came across as expressive and utterly purposeful. In effect, Ray Charles did more than reinterpret "Georgia on My Mind"; he virtually reinvented the song for a new generation of listeners and left his mark on the song permanently. It seems only appropriate that in 1979 his recording was named "the official song of the state of Georgia."

In 1962 Charles cast his stylistic net still wider, producing a concept album, *Modern Sounds in Country and Western Music*, that stands as a milestone in the history of American popular music. When Charles first announced to his record company that he wanted to do an album of country songs, the project was derisively labeled "Ray's folly"; it was thought that he would lose his audience. Charles is not a man to be crossed, however, and he persevered, with the result of course that he enlarged his audience even further—and beyond anyone's expectations. By this point, Charles was aggressively and creativity playing with stylistic mixtures, and the album essentially redrew the map of American popular music, both appealing to and challenging fans of radically different genres.

Every song on *Modern Sounds in Country and Western Music* was transformed from its origins into something rich and strange. The Everly Brothers' "Bye, Bye, Love" and Hank Williams's "Hey, Good Lookin'" became big-band shouts to book-end the album, while other songs received orchestral treatments worthy of the best Tin Pan Alley arrangements—or of Charles's "Georgia on My Mind." It's hard to think of any major aspect of American pop that isn't represented, or at least implied, somewhere on this amazingly generous record, which weaves a tapestry of stylistic and historical associations, reaching across space, time, and race to build radically new bridges. The enormously popular "I Can't Stop Loving You" merges aspects of country, Tin Pan Alley, gospel, and blues, and even (as in "Georgia") a hint of jazz piano. Here Charles engages in stylistic call and response with the large background chorus, personalizing the lyrics that they sing in smooth massed harmony. The deliberateness of this dialogue is clearly revealed toward the end of the record by Charles's seemingly offhand, but illuminating, aside to the chorus: "Sing the song, children" (a remark that also confirms, as if there could be any doubt, exactly who's in charge here).

Although Ray Charles's many country-oriented records of the 1960s did extremely well on both the pop and rhythm & blues charts, they did not register on the country charts of the time. Perhaps Charles's genre-bending approach was a bit too exotic for the typical country music fan at the time. Still, these records were heard and deeply appreciated by many country musicians. We can take the word of no less an authority than Willie Nelson, who is quoted in the booklet accompanying the Ray Charles box set *Genius & Soul:* "With his recording of 'I Can't Stop Loving You,' Ray Charles did more for country music than any other artist." Charles finally did crack the country charts in the 1980s with some of his later efforts in the genre.

Ray Charles remained active almost until his death, performing and recording in all the many genres (and mixed styles) of which he was a seasoned master. In summarizing an astounding career that steadfastly resists summarizing, we might paraphrase what songwriter Jerome Kern reportedly said about Irving Berlin: this man has no "place" in American music; he *is* American music! Or perhaps we can leave the last word to Charles himself (as quoted by Quincy Jones in the booklet accompanying *Genius & Soul*): "It's all music, man. We can play it all."

JAMES BROWN AND ARETHA FRANKLIN

Among many significant artists whose names became linked with the concept of "soul music" in the 1960s, James Brown and Aretha Franklin may be selected as representative. Like Ray Charles, Brown and Franklin are exceptionally popular performers with multidecade careers; in fact, *Joel Whitburn's Top R&B Singles, 1942–1995* lists Brown and Franklin as the top two rhythm & blues artists of this entire time period. Both Brown (known as "Soul Brother Number One") and Franklin (known as "Lady Soul") brought experience with gospel singing to bear upon their performances of secular material. In so doing, they each developed an intense, flamboyant, gritty, and highly individual approach to the singing of pop music, and their approaches represented distinctive analogues to the "soul" style of Ray Charles.

James Brown

If Charles employed "soul" as an avenue of approach to the most diverse kinds of material, James Brown (b. 1933) revealed different tendencies virtually from the beginning. His first record, "Please, Please, Please" (Number Five R&B, 1956), which Brown wrote himself, is indicative: while the song is in the general format of a strophic 1950s R&B ballad, Brown's vocal clings obsessively to repetitions of individual words (the title "please," or even a simple "I") so that sometimes the activity of an entire strophe will center around the syncopated, violently accented reiterations of a single syllable. The result is startling and hypnotic. Like a secular version of a transfixed preacher, Brown shows himself willing to leave the traditional notions of verbal grammar, and even meaning, behind, in an effort to convey a heightened emotional condition through the effective employment of rhythm and vocal timbre, animating repetitive ideas. Later on, Brown would leave the structures of 1950s R&B far behind and eventually would abandon chord changes entirely in many of his pieces. By the later 1960s a characteristic Brown tune like "There Was a Time" (Number Three R&B, Number Thirty-six pop, 1968) offered music focused almost exclusively on the play of rhythm and timbre, in the instrumental

James Brown in action, 1964. Courtesy Library of Congress.

parts as well as in the vocal. While the singer does tell a story in this song, the vocal melody is little more than informal reiterations of a small number of brief, formulaic pitch shapes; the harmony is completely static, with the instrumental parts reduced to repeating **riffs** or held **chords**. But this description does the song scant justice—when performed by Brown and his band, its effect is mesmerizing. James Brown's fully developed version of soul is a music of exquisitely focused intensity, devoted to demonstrating the truth of the saying "less is more."

In the politically charged "Say It Loud—I'm Black and I'm Proud," which reached Number One on the R&B and Number Ten on the pop charts in 1968, Brown pares his vocal down to highly rhythmic speech, backed once again by a harmonically static but rhythmically active accompaniment. Although the term would not be in use for at least a decade, "Say It Loud—I'm Black and I'm Proud" is for all intents and purposes a *rap* number, a striking anticipation of important black music to come (both in its musical style and in its emphasis on the black experience as subject matter) and a telling illustration of Brown's pivotal role in the history of pop culture generally. In the wake of the urban folk movement of the early 1960s and the subsequent folk rock (which we will discuss below), in which white singers presented themselves as spokespeople for the political and social concerns of their generation, Brown led black musicians in assuming a comparable role for the black community, especially in the time of enormous unrest and political instability that followed the assassination of the Reverend Martin Luther King Jr. in 1968. For his constructive contributions to the politics of his time, Brown was publicly honored by both Vice President Hubert Humphrey and President Lyndon Johnson. Thus soul musicians came to be seen not merely as entertainers but as essential contributors to—and articulators of—African American life and experience, and this was the view not only of the black community but also of the national political leadership.

From the late 1960s through the disco music of the 1970s, from the beginnings of rap on through the flowering of hip-hop in the 1990s, no other single musician has proven to be as influential on the sound and style of black music as James Brown. His repetitive, riff-based instrumental style, which elevated rhythm far above harmony as the primary source of interest, provided the foundation on which most of the dance-oriented music of this entire period has been based. His records are **sampled** by hip-hop artists more than those of any other musician—which is not surprising, given his achievement as a pioneer of rap style.

Brown's focus on rhythm and timbre, and in particular the complex, interlocking **polyrhythms** present in many of his songs, have been cited as demonstrating his strong conceptual links with African music styles. Certainly, the minimizing or elimination of chord changes and the consequent deemphasis on harmony makes Brown's music seem, both in conception and in actual sound, a lot less "Western" in orientation than a good deal of the African American music that preceded it. On the one hand, this quality in Brown's work resonated with many aspects of African American culture in the late 1960s and the 1970s, when there was a marked concern with the awareness of African "roots." On the other hand, one could argue that the acceptance and wide influence of the "non-Western" aspects of Brown's music helped provide a foundation for the recent explosion of interest in world musics of many sorts, which was such a significant and distinguishing characteristic of the cultural scene in the 1980s and 1990s.

One additional and fascinating aspect of Brown's work is the relationship it suggests to the "minimalist" music by avant-garde "art music" composers, such as Philip Glass and Steve Reich, that was developing simultaneously if independently in the late 1960s in New York. This was also music based on repetitive rhythmic patterns with a deemphasis on traditional harmonic movement. There is no issue of direct influence here, one way or the other. But it could be argued that only old cultural habits and snobbery have kept James Brown out of discussions of minimalism in scholarly forums and journals.

As influential as his recordings were and are, Brown is above all an artist who exults and excels in live performance, where his acrobatic physicality and remarkable personal charisma add great excitement to the vocal improvisations he can spin over the ever tight accompaniment of his band. A typical Brown show ends with the singer on his knees, evoking once again the intensity of the gospel preacher as he exhorts his "congregation," "Please, please, please"! Although he was not the first pop artist to release a "live" album, Brown's *Live at the Apollo,* recorded in concert at the famed Apollo Theater in Harlem in late 1962, proved an important pop breakthrough both for him and for the idea of the concert album, as it reached the Number Two position on the *Billboard* chart of bestselling albums in 1963 and remained on that chart for well over a year. In particular, the album allowed the listener to experience without interruption an example of one of Brown's remarkable extended "medleys," in which several of his songs would be strung directly together, without dropping a single beat, to produce a cumulative effect of steadily mounting excitement. Many pop artists since have released "live" albums—in fact, the "live" album has become virtually an expected event in the recording career of any artist with a significant following—but few have matched the sheer visceral thrill of James Brown's *Live at the Apollo.*

Aretha Franklin

Like Ray Charles and James Brown, <u>Aretha Franklin</u> (b. 1942) underwent a long period of "apprenticeship" before she achieved her definitive breakthrough as a pop star in 1967. After an unfocused and less than stellar career as a Columbia Records artist from 1960 to 1966, during which time she recorded a mixture of Tin Pan Alley standards and unremarkable rhythm & blues material, she went over to Atlantic Records. Atlantic, an indie label with a long history of R&B success, knew what to do with Franklin. Atlantic producers Ahmet Ertegun and Jerry Wexler encouraged her to record strong material well suited to her spectacular voice and engaged stellar and empathetic musicians to back her up (usually the Muscle Shoals Sound Rhythm Section, based in Alabama). The rest, as they say, is history. Beginning with "I Never Loved a Man (The Way I Love You)" (Number One R&B, Number Nine pop, 1967), Franklin produced an extraordinary and virtually uninterrupted stream of hit records over a five-year period that included thirteen million-sellers and thirteen Top 10 pop hits. Although the later 1970s and early 1980s witnessed a decline in Franklin's status as a top hit maker, she was never completely absent from the charts, and the mid-1980s brought her a resurgence of popularity, with hits like "Freeway of Love" (Number One R&B, Number Three pop, 1985) and a duet with George Michael, "I Knew You Were Waiting (For Me)" (Number One pop, Number Five R&B, 1987). As of 1994 Franklin was still a presence on the R&B charts and the pop album charts.

Aretha Franklin performs on television, 1967. Courtesy Library of Congress.

Unlike Ray Charles and James Brown, Franklin literally grew up with gospel music; her father was the Reverend C. L. Franklin, the pastor for a large Baptist congregation in Detroit and himself an acclaimed gospel singer. Aretha Franklin's first recordings were as a gospel singer, at the age of fourteen, and she occasionally returned to recording gospel music even in the midst of her career as a pop singer—most spectacularly with the live album *Amazing Grace* (1972), which was actually recorded in a church. *Amazing Grace* built on Franklin's established popularity to introduce legions of pop music fans to the power of gospel music. The album was a Top 10 bestseller and the most successful album of Franklin's entire career; it sold over two million copies.

What is most important about Aretha Franklin is the overwhelming power and intensity of her vocal delivery. Into a pop culture that had almost totally identified female singers with gentility, docility, and sentimentality, her voice blew huge gusts of revisionist fresh air. When she demanded "respect" (see the "Listening To" section), or exhorted her audience to "think about what you're trying to do to me" (in the hit recording "Think" of 1968, which she cowrote), the strength of her interpretations arguably moved her songs beyond the traditional realm of personal intimate relationships and into the larger political and social spheres. Especially in the context of the late 1960s, with the civil rights and black power movements at their heights, and the movement for women's empowerment undergoing its initial stirrings, it was difficult *not* to hear large-scale ramifications in the records of this extraordinary African American woman. Although Aretha Franklin did not become an overtly political figure in the way that James Brown did, it may be claimed that she nevertheless made strong political and social statements just through the very character of her performances.

Directly tied to this issue is the fact that Franklin was not only a vocal interpreter on her records but also—like Charles and Brown—a major player in many aspects of their sound and production. She wrote or cowrote a significant portion of her repertoire (this involvement goes back to her early days at Columbia). In addition, Franklin is a powerful keyboard player; her piano is heard to great advantage on many of her recordings. And she also provided vocal arrangements, which were colored by the call and response of the gospel traditions in which she was raised.

In other words, Franklin not only symbolized female empowerment in the sound of her records but also actualized female empowerment in the process of making them. By the time she recorded a tune called "Sisters Are Doin' It for Themselves" (with Eurythmics) in 1985, she was, in effect, telling a story that had been personally true of her for a long time. But in the 1960s female empowerment was something quite new and important in the history of pop music. And neither its novelty nor its importance was lost on the rising generation of female singer-songwriters, such as Laura Nyro, Joni Mitchell, and Carole King, whose ascent to prominence began directly in the wake of Aretha Franklin's conquest of the pop charts.

LISTENING TO   TWO CLASSICS OF SOUL MUSIC

"Papa's Got a Brand New Bag," composed by James Brown, performed by James Brown and the Famous Flames (Number Eight pop, Number One R&B, 1965); "Respect," composed by Otis Redding, performed by Aretha Franklin (Number One pop, Number One R&B, 1967)

Both of these recordings exemplify the intense vocal performance and use of call-and-response technique characteristic of soul music. In Brown's case, the call and response takes place between his solo vocal and the instrumental accompaniment, while on Franklin's recording a female singing group provides the responses to her lead vocal. Each of the records under discussion was career-defining for its respective artist. "Papa's Got a Brand New Bag" was Brown's first Top 10 pop hit and the biggest R&B hit of his entire career, while "Respect" was for Franklin both her first Number One pop hit and the biggest R&B hit of *her* entire career.

"Papa's Got a Brand New Bag" is an excellent representative example for James Brown, as it is a record that, in a sense, looks both forward and back in his career. In terms of its form, the song uses the time-tested twelve-bar blues pattern as its basis, breaking up the pattern after two strophes with an eight-bar bridge section (a device we have also seen before; see the discussion of "Charlie Brown" in Chapter 3) before continuing with further blues-based stanzas. In terms of subject matter, the song's lyrics obviously recall the dance-oriented rock 'n' roll songs of the early 1960s, as the singer praises "Papa's"—presumably Brown's—ability to do the jerk, the fly, the monkey, the mashed potatoes, the twist (naturally), and even the "boomerang"; Brown's dancing was a legendary aspect of his live shows. However, the title tells us that "Papa's Got a Brand *New* Bag," and even if the song itself looks toward the past in its form and its lyrics, Brown's actual recording sounds nothing like a typical blues-based R&B record of its time or a typical teen-oriented dance song. Instead, the record looks forward to the riff-dominated records by Brown and others that would virtually define dance-oriented soul music in the later 1960s and the 1970s.

The critical factor here is the repeating instrumental riff, which embodies a kind of call-and-response pattern, as two strong, short, rhythmic "stabs" on successive beats are answered by a four-note figure in the horn section of the band, landing on an accented final note (da-da-da-*dum*). This riff is used for all of the twelve-bar blues sections in "Papa's Got a Brand New Bag." The pitches change slightly to accommodate the chord change at the fifth bar of these sections (see the discussion of twelve-bar blues in Chapter 2), but the really arresting event occurs at the tenth bar, where the instrumental accompaniment stops entirely for a few beats, creating a passage of what jazz musicians call "stoptime." This produces enormous tension, and after Brown completes his next vocal phrase, the lead guitar bursts back in with an aggressive pattern of rapidly strummed chords that prepares the return of the riff and of the rhythm section. Thus the listener's attention is directed away from the harmonic changes in the twelve-bar blues pattern and more toward events defined by *rhythm*: the presence or absence of the riff, and stoptime as opposed to rhythmic continuity. Even the sense of a separate bridge section is downplayed considerably on this recording, as the harmony remains fairly static throughout the bridge (whereas typically it would wander, and change, if anything, more rapidly than elsewhere), while a slightly different—but nonetheless clearly related—three-note horn riff is heard in every bar.

When listening to "Papa's Got a Brand New Bag," then, one experiences musical shaping created more emphatically by rhythmic patterns than by chord changes or melodic lines. In terms of the sound and the **groove** of the recording, we are here well on our way toward the minimizing or even elimination of chord changes that would characterize much of Brown's later work. It is this aspect of the record that is so arrestingly novel, and that represents such a significant discovery on Brown's part.

James Brown's "Papa's Got a Brand New Bag" is worthy of its title and of its enduring popularity. In 1965 it represented a enormous flying leap into the future of soul, a musical analogy to Brown's own daring acrobatic leaps onstage.

Merely by undertaking to record "Respect," Aretha Franklin took a daring step. The song had already been a significant hit for its composer, Otis Redding, in 1965 (Number Four R&B, Number Thirty-five pop); by covering it, Franklin was, in a sense, going head to head with one of the most impressive and powerful soul singers of the day—and on his home turf, so to speak, by taking on a song he had written for himself. But the implications of Franklin's cover extend well beyond this, because Redding's song is a demand for "respect" from one's lover, and by putting the song in a woman's voice Franklin radically shifts the sense of who is in control in the relationship. In her version, it is *she*—the woman—who has "what you want" and "what you need," not to mention "money" as well! And Franklin makes a telling change in the lyrics of the second strophe. In Redding's original, he acknowledges that his woman might do him wrong, yet it's all right with him so long as she only does so "while I'm gone." But Franklin tells her lover that "I ain't gonna do you wrong while you're gone" (presumably his doing *her* wrong is not even in question), but only "'cause I don't wanna." It could not be clearer just who is holding all the cards in Franklin's version!

Of course, none of Franklin's play with the gender issues implicit in "Respect" would have any effect if it weren't for the overwhelming power and assurance with which she delivers the song and makes it her own. Each strophe of the song builds effectively to the crucial word "respect," at which point the backing group joins in call and response with Franklin. But Franklin is also careful to structure her entire performance around a steadily building intensity, so that the listener hears something much more than a song with four identical strophes. By the time we reach the third strophe, she is improvising variants on the basic melody, and the call and response is varied as well ("just a, just a, just a, just a, just a, just a, just a, just a, just a little bit"). After this a brief but completely unexpected instrumental break, with totally unexpected chords new to the song, raises the emotional temperature in preparation for the final strophe. The last time around, Franklin reaches her highest note yet in the song on "All I want you to *do* for me," and the backing group matches her new intensity with its own new response: "re-re-re-re-re-re-re-re-*spect*." Then, instead of ending, this final strophe is extended with a stoptime solo for Franklin, after which the group responds with a shot heard 'round the world ("sock it to me, sock it to me, sock it to me . . .") and the record fades with Franklin and her backing singers trading shout for shout.

After the daring and achievement of this recording, Aretha Franklin never had to demand "respect," at least from musicians and audiences, again. It was hers wherever and whenever she brought her great and insightful gifts of song.

URBAN FOLK MUSIC IN THE 1960s: BOB DYLAN

Urban folk music continued to flourish during the early days of rock 'n' roll and into the 1960s. We have not been discussing it because, to a large extent, it followed an independent course through the early 1960s, remaining an acoustic guitar–based music aloof from the new styles and the large-scale changes that characterized much of the pop music of this time. In the early 1960s it was even fashionable for urban folk performers to look down their noses at rock 'n' roll as "unserious"; the dour liner notes to the hugely successful first album by Peter, Paul, and Mary (1962) exhorted readers, "No dancing, please!" But by 1967 electric instruments and drums had joined Peter, Paul, and Mary's acoustic guitars, and they were in the pop Top 10 singing (somewhat ironically, but with a firm bid for continuing relevance) "I Dig Rock and Roll Music"! The individual most responsible for this shift was not Peter or Paul or Mary, but the man who had written their biggest acoustic hit, "Blowin' in the Wind" (Number Two, 1963). He was also the man who, virtually single-handedly, dragged urban folk music—with some people kicking and screaming—into the modern era of rock. His name was Bob Dylan (b. 1941).

Dylan (born Robert Zimmerman) first established himself as an acoustic singer-songwriter in New York City's burgeoning urban folk scene. The early 1960s was a period of explosive growth for acoustic urban folk music. The baby boomers were reaching college age, demonstrating increasing cultural and political interests and awareness, and they represented an expanding audience both for traditionally based folk music and for newly composed "broadsides" on the issues of the day (such as the Cold War with the Soviet Union, the testing and stockpiling of nuclear arms, and racial bigotry). Encouragement and a sense of history were provided by elder statesmen of the urban folk scene, such as Pete Seeger and the Weavers, whose careers in turn were reinvigorated by the thawing of the political climate after the blacklisting days of the 1950s (see Chapter 2) and by the enthusiasm of younger folk performers and their audiences. By 1962 even the extremely popular Kingston Trio (see Box 3.4)—whose acoustic folk repertoire almost always stayed within the bounds of safe traditional material or the occasional novelty number—ventured to record Pete Seeger's poignant antiwar song "Where Have All the Flowers Gone," unexpectedly scoring a pop hit with it (Number Twenty-one). This attests to the increasing politicization of the urban folk movement and its audiences at this time; the success of "Where Have All the Flowers Gone" doubtless helped pave the way for that of "Blowin' in the Wind" the following year.

Bob Dylan's contemporaries in the urban folk scene included such gifted performers as Joan Baez and Judy Collins, and such talented songwriters as Tom Paxton and Phil Ochs. But Dylan stood out early for two basic reasons. First was the remarkable quality of his original songs, which reflected from the beginning a strong gift for poetic imagery and metaphor and a frequently searing intensity of feeling, sometimes moderated by a quirky sense of irony. (His interest in poetry was manifest in the choice of his new last name, borrowed from the Welsh poet Dylan Thomas.) Second was Dylan's own style of performance, which eschewed the deliberate and straightforward homeliness of the Weavers, the smooth and pop-friendly approach of the Kingston Trio and Peter, Paul, and Mary, and the lyrical beauty of Joan Baez and Judy Collins, in favor of a rough-hewn, occasionally aggressive vocal, guitar, and harmonica style that demonstrated strong affinities to rural models in blues and earlier country music. Dylan's performance style was sufficiently idiosyncratic in the context of the urban folk scene to keep him from being truly pop-marketable for years; his early songs were introduced to Top 40 audiences by other, smoother performers. Still, it may be claimed that Dylan's own performances serve the distinctive intensity of his songs more tellingly than the inevitably sweeter versions of other singers.

Bob Dylan the songwriter was introduced to many pop fans through Peter, Paul, and Mary's recording of his "Blowin' in the Wind," and to this day the song remains probably Dylan's best-known work. The opening strophe clearly reveals Dylan's gift for concise, evocative, and highly poetic lyric writing, the ability to suggest much with a few finely tuned images:

> *How many roads must a man walk down*
> *Before you call him a man?*
> *Yes, 'n' how many seas must a white dove sail*
> *Before she sleeps in the sand?*
> *Yes, 'n' how many times must the cannon balls fly*
> *Before they're forever banned?*
> *The answer, my friend, is blowin' in the wind,*
> *The answer is blowin' in the wind.*

The three successive questions build in specificity and intensity. The first question could imply many different things having to do with maturity and experience. The image of the "white dove" in the second question is one traditionally associated with the idea of peace. With the third question, the subject of war becomes inescapable, and it becomes clear that Dylan is asking, in three different ways, just what it will take, and how long it will take, before humankind develops the maturity to put a stop to wars. What makes the song so poignantly effective, though, is that Dylan leaves the answer—and even the issue of whether there *is* an answer—up to us, and in our hands: the phrase "The answer is blowin' in the wind" returns to the deliberate, thoroughgoing ambiguity of the opening question. This effectively sets up the two additional strophes of the song, which are similarly structured as three increasingly pointed questions followed by the same ambiguous answer. Dylan's avoidance of any specific political agenda in "Blowin' in the Wind" is typical of many of his best "protest songs" and is actually a source of strength, as it helps assure their continuing relevance despite changes in the political climate. In any case, the questions posed in "Blowin' in the Wind" surely—if unfortunately—ring with a resonance not limited by the time and place of the song's creation.

As is the case with many of the finest folk songs, whether traditional or newly composed, the melody of "Blowin' in the Wind" provides a simple, functional, and immediately memorable setting for the words. In this **strophic** form, notice how Dylan's melody makes each of the three questions hang unresolved; a final feeling of **cadence** in the melody is delayed until we reach the "answer" on the last word of each strophe.

It is illuminating to compare the Peter, Paul, and Mary recording of "Blowin' in the Wind" with Dylan's own performance as heard on his second album, *The Freewheelin' Bob Dylan* (1963). The folk trio performs the song with a touching sincerity and simplicity; the various questions posed in the lyrics are sung by different numbers and combinations of voices, at varying levels of intensity, while the "answer" is always provided by Mary's gentle solo sound. One might initially find Dylan's rendition monochromatic in comparison. But his syncopation of the melodic line—a performance approach utterly lacking in the Peter, Paul, and Mary interpretation—throws rhythmic weight on the most pointed words in the song (such as, in the opening stanza, "be*fore* they're *forever* *banned*") and the resulting feeling of angularity, reinforced by the intense and unpretty timbre of Dylan's voice, arguably presses the listener to ponder the lyrics that much more seriously.

In addition to writing impressive topical songs like "Blowin' in the Wind," Dylan quickly distinguished himself as a composer of more intimate but highly original songs about human relationships. One hesitates to call a song like "Don't Think Twice, It's All Right" (also on *The Freewheelin' Bob Dylan*, and also a Top 10 single for Peter, Paul, and Mary—their followup hit to "Blowin' in the Wind") a "love song," however. Dylan himself is quoted in the liner notes to the *Freewheelin'* album concerning this song: "A lot of people make it a sort of a love song—slow and easygoing. [Was he thinking of a performance like Peter, Paul, and Mary's?] But it isn't a love song. It's a statement that maybe you can say to make yourself feel better." Dylan's gift for irony, to which we have previously referred, is exemplified memorably in the lyrics of "Don't Think Twice, It's All Right":

Box 5.1 Tin Pan Alley <u>Still</u> Lives!
Dionne Warwick and the Songs of Burt Bacharach and Hal David

We have already seen how the Tin Pan Alley model for the creation and marketing of popular music was adopted for rock 'n' roll by 1960s organizations like Philles and Motown. And performers based in Tin Pan Alley traditions, both older (Frank Sinatra and Tony Bennett) and younger (Johnny Mathis), continued to command substantial audiences throughout the 1960s. However, arguably the most remarkable testament to the resilience of the Tin Pan Alley aesthetic in the 1960s was the extensive series of hit songs written for singer <u>Dionne Warwick</u> (b. 1940) by composer <u>Burt Bacharach</u> (b. 1928) and lyricist Hal David. In Warwick, the two songwriters found a distinctive young African American vocalist who, despite a training in gospel music that might have more typically prepared her for a career as an R&B–oriented performer, was willing to cultivate more of a crooning approach to performance that proved perfect for the convincing delivery of their work. (This is not to say that Warwick couldn't shout soulfully when needed, as any listener who has enjoyed the explosive endings of "Anyone Who Had a Heart" and "Promises, Promises" can affirm.)

The kinship of the Bacharach-David songs to Tin Pan Alley models is the result of a number of factors. David's lyrics are almost always intelligent and adult-oriented, and they can exhibit a cleverness of structure and rhyme akin to that found in a song like "Love and Marriage" (as in "Do You Know the way to San Jose"). Bacharach's music generally owes little to rock in terms of direct influence; its emphasis is rather on melodic and harmonic sophistication of a nature that clearly links him to the tradition of someone like George Gershwin (as may be heard in songs like "Alfie" and "Promises, Promises," in particular). Yet Bacharach is not an imitator, and therein lies his importance and achievement. His use of **minor** keys—in songs like "Walk on By" and "The Look of Love"—is noteworthy, but perhaps most distinctive is Bacharach's way of incorporating highly original phrasing and rhythms into his songs. His novel rhythms are not those of rock, but are related rather to complexities of meter found more often in modernistic art music or in the jazz of a rhythmic innovator like Dave Brubeck than in pop song. (The chorus section of "I Say a Little Prayer" may serve as a good example of Bacharach's rhythmic gifts; a listener attempting to count out the patterns here will have a pleasantly dizzying experience!)

Every virtue of the Bacharach-David songs is emphasized in Dionne Warwick's elegant recordings of them, as Warwick is both melodically expressive and rhythmically precise, while articulating the lyrics with clarity and intensity. These recordings are among the glories of 1960s music. Although the Bacharach-David team provided excellent material to other artists as well ("What the World Needs Now Is Love," recorded by Jackie DeShannon, and "One Less Bell to Answer," performed by the Fifth Dimension, are two famous and outstanding examples), and although Dionne Warwick also found success with songs by other writers, a certain synergic magic was undeniably lost when the singer and the songwriters parted company early in the 1970s.

Still I wish there was somethin' you would do or say
To try and make me change my mind and stay.
We never did too much talkin' anyway,
But don't think twice, it's all right.

Clearly, this situation is not "all right" at all, and the blunt realism underlying Dylan's view of romantic relationships, as expressed in this song and in many others, sounded a refreshingly original note in a pop landscape where the typical treatment of relationships was still that reflected in a song like "Be My Baby," and where a relationship crisis might be represented by a date's inability to do the twist or the mashed potatoes. Dylan's own performance of "Don't Think Twice, It's All Right" does the song full justice by conveying a deep, underlying sense of personal injury.

We have been stressing the innovative character of Dylan's songwriting, but he maintained important ties with folk traditions as well. Many of his original compositions were modeled, implicitly or explicitly, on the musical and poetic content of preexisting folk material. For example, one of his most famous "protest" songs,

Bob Dylan as urban folkie (c. 1964) and as folk rocker (c. 1966). Courtesy Library of Congress.

"A Hard Rain's A-Gonna Fall," is clearly based on the old English ballad "Lord Randall"; both employ a strophic pattern, in which each strophe opens with a pair of questions addressed by a mother to her son, followed by the son's answer or answers, ending always with the same concluding line. Even the melodic lines of "Lord Randall" and "A Hard Rain's A-Gonna Fall" are distinctly similar. But Dylan is never merely a mimic, and "A Hard Rain's A-Gonna Fall" introduces a highly original structural device that has no parallel in "Lord Randall": its strophes are of widely varying lengths, depending on the number of times the third melodic phrase is repeated to changing words. (The son offers anywhere from five to twelve answers to the individual questions posed by his mother.) The concept of the "variable strophe," as we might call it, is found in a number of Dylan's finest songs, notably "Mr. Tambourine Man" and—as we shall see shortly—"Like a Rolling Stone."

The year 1965 was the pivotal one in Bob Dylan's career, the year in which he moved from being the most distinctive songwriter among American urban folk artists to being an epochal influence on the entirety of American popular culture. We may cite four major events that proved decisive in this extraordinary development, involving the release of an album, two hit singles (one by the Byrds and one by Dylan himself), and a live performance.

Early in 1965 Dylan released his fifth album, *Bringing It All Back Home,* in which acoustic numbers demonstrating Dylan's now-familiar style shared disc space with songs using electric guitar and drums. In addition to adumbrating a radical shift in Dylan's sound, the album featured several songs that carried Dylan's flair for intense and unusual poetic imagery into the realm of the surreal. One such song, "Mr. Tambourine Man," which was not one of those performed by Dylan in a rock-oriented style, was covered by the fledgling California rock group the Byrds; their truncated version of "Mr. Tambourine Man," adapted to fit the customary length for radio play, soared remarkably to Number One in June 1965, thus becoming the first landmark *folk-rock* hit. The Byrds' combination of Dylan's lyrics and melody with a musical accompaniment that included tambourine (naturally), drums, and their own trademark electric Rickenbacker twelve-string guitar sound was unique, memorable, and—obviously, if unexpectedly—marketable. The lesson was not lost on Dylan himself, who returned to the recording studio early in the summer with a rock band to cut his own breakthrough single, "Like a Rolling Stone." This six-minute, epic pop single, which made it to Number Two on the charts, certified that a sea change was taking place in American popular culture. (See the detailed discussion of this song below.) As if to affirm that there would be no turning back, Dylan then appeared at the famous Newport Folk Festival in late July with an electric band. Many folk purists were appalled by this assault on their home turf, and Dylan was booed off the stage (returning later to do an acoustic set). But he had the last laugh, of course, as it was not long before many urban folk artists had followed his lead into the electric wonderland of rock music.

From our latter-day vantage point, all the fuss about Dylan's "going electric" can seem quite silly. We have seen that the entire history of American popular music has been a story of influences, interactions, and syntheses among its various streams. The steadily increasing popularity of both urban folk music and rock 'n' roll in the early 1960s made it inevitable that these two supposedly independent styles would eventually interact with one another, and even fuse to some extent.

But the boost given to this fusion by the fact that the most individual and creative of the young urban folk artists, Bob Dylan, was the first to promote it—and to promote it aggressively and enthusiastically at that—cannot be underestimated.

From Dylan's own point of view, he was probably just following a model already well established by performers in the genres of blues and country music, genres to which his personal performing style had always demonstrated obvious ties. Rural blues artists like Muddy Waters and Howlin' Wolf had long ago made their way to the city and developed electric blues, just as country artists like Hank Williams had developed the honky-tonk style (see Chapter 2). And these newer blues- and country-based styles had themselves played an essential role in the 1950s synthesis that is called rock 'n' roll. Why, then, was there such a shock wave produced by the concept of Bob Dylan as a rock 'n' roll star?

It probably had to do with the differing cultural roles assigned by most people to urban folk music on the one hand and to rock 'n' roll on the other. Urban folk in the early 1960s was, as we have seen, an increasingly topical, political, socially conscious music. Even the singing of traditional folk songs often carried with it a subtext of political identification—with labor, with the poor, with minority groups and other peoples seen as oppressed, with a movement for international peace and understanding—depending on the nature and origins of the particular songs chosen. Thus the words were of paramount importance in urban folk music, and the acoustic guitar accompaniments enabled the words to be heard clearly. Besides, acoustic guitars were easily portable, readily accessible, and presented no elaborate barrier between performers and audiences. It was a relatively simple matter to bring an acoustic guitar along to a political meeting or demonstration, and to set it up and play it there when and if the occasion presented itself, which surely cannot be said of rock 'n' roll band equipment. And of course rock 'n' roll was identified—even, perhaps especially, by those who enjoyed it—as a "fun" music, a music to accompany dancing and other socializing, whose lyric content was by definition light, amusing, sometimes clever, often generic, but virtually never serious.

By the mid-1960s changes within rock 'n' roll were already in the wind, as we have seen in previous discussions of music by the Beatles and the Beach Boys. But Bob Dylan's electric style and other manifestations of folk rock had the effect of an enormous injection of growth hormones into the pop music scene. Suddenly, it was all right—expected, even—for rock 'n' roll to be as "adult" as its baby boomer audience was now becoming itself, and rock 'n' roll abruptly grew up into rock. Pop records on serious subjects, with political and poetical lyrics, sprang up everywhere; before long, this impulse carried over into the making of ambitious concept albums, as we shall see. The later 1960s flowered into a period of intense and remarkable innovation and creativity in pop music. (Of course, the pressure to be adult and creative also inevitably led to the production of a lot of pretentious music as well.)

Dylan was, naturally, the main man to emulate. In the summer and fall of 1965 it seemed that almost everybody was either making cover records of Dylan songs or producing imitations of Dylan's songs and style. For example, both the Byrds and the pop singer Cher were on the charts during the summer with competing versions of Dylan's "All I Really Want to Do," and the first Number One pop hit of the fall was the politically charged, folk-rock "Eve of Destruction"—composed by the Los Angeles songwriter P. F. Sloan in an obviously Dylanesque style, complete with variable strophes, and sung in a gruff Dylanesque voice by Barry McGuire, who had been a member of the acoustic urban folk group the New Christy Minstrels.

Despite the popularity of "Like a Rolling Stone" and of a few singles that followed, Bob Dylan never really established himself as primarily a "singles artist." Rather, he was the first important representative of yet another pop phenomenon: the rock musician whose career was sustained essentially by albums. (Among many prominent figures who followed in these particular footsteps of Dylan, we could cite Frank Zappa, Joni Mitchell, Led Zeppelin, and the Grateful Dead.) Every single Bob Dylan album except his very first one has appeared on *Billboard* magazine's "Top Pop Albums" chart. Although his influence was at its peak in the 1960s—and one way to measure that peak is to remember that Dylan was the choice of the then-new *Rolling Stone* magazine for president of the United States in 1968!—Dylan has continued to be a widely admired and closely followed artist into the new century. Never content to be pigeonholed or to fall into a predictable role as elder statesman for any particular movement or musical style, Bob Dylan has over the course of his career produced a distinctive, heterogeneous, and erratic output of albums that, taken together, represent a singular testament to the spirit of pop music invention. Among these albums may be found examples of country rock (*Nashville Skyline,* 1969), what would later be termed Christian rock (*Slow Train Coming,* 1979), and even latter-day forays back into traditional acoustic folk material (*Good as I Been to You,* 1992)—along with many examples of the folk-rock approach that initially sealed his place in the pantheon of American music. As of this writing, Dylan is still touring and recording tirelessly, and challenging his audiences to guess what his next move might be.

LISTENING AND ANALYSIS   "LIKE A ROLLING STONE"

Composed and performed by Bob Dylan (with unidentified instrumental accompaniment); recorded 1965

Basic Description

"Like a Rolling Stone" is one of a handful of watershed recordings in the history of American popular music. It effectively put an end to previous restrictions on length, subject matter, and poetic diction that had exercised a controlling influence on the creation of pop records. Although surely other recordings had mounted some challenges to these restrictions before Dylan cut "Like a Rolling Stone," no other pop record had attacked them so comprehensively or with such complete success. After the huge acceptance of "Like a Rolling Stone," literally nothing was the same again.

In discussing the impact of this recording, its sheer *sound* must not be neglected. "Like a Rolling Stone" has an overall timbre and a sonic density that were unique for its time, owing to the exceptional prominence of *two* keyboard instruments—organ and piano—that dominate the texture even more than the electric guitars, bass, and drums. And the distinctive sound of Dylan's vocal cuts aggressively through this thick instrumental texture like a knife. It is difficult to say which was more influential on the future sound of rock: the keyboard-dominated band, or Dylan's in-your-face vocal style, which was positioned on the cutting edge between rhythmic speech and pitched song.

The density of sound and the aggressiveness of the vocal style are clearly suited to this fierce song about a young woman's fall from a state of oblivious privilege into one of desperation. The lyrics range from the bluntest realism:

> *You've gone to the finest school—all right, Miss Lonely, but you know you only used to get . . .*
> > *juiced in it.*
> *Nobody's ever taught you how to live out on the street, and now you're gonna have to get . . .*
> > *used to it.*

to the kind of novel surrealistic imagery that Dylan was pioneering in many of his lyrics at this time:

> *You used to ride on a chrome horse with your diplomat,*
> *Who carried on his shoulder a Siamese cat.*

The chorus that concludes each strophe is typical of Dylan insofar as it provides no resolution or answers; instead, it hurls a defiant question at the song's protagonist—and at the listener:

> *How does it feel*
> *To be without a home*
> *Like a complete unknown,*
> *Like a rolling stone?*

Doubtless for many of those in Dylan's audience, reaching adulthood and venturing out on their own for the first time, this question possessed a profound and pointed relevance.

Form

"Like a Rolling Stone" reveals its antecedents in Dylan's acoustic folk style in a number of ways, the most obvious of which relate to form. Like "Blowin' in the Wind" and many of Dylan's other early compositions, "Like a Rolling Stone" falls into a strophic verse-chorus pattern (see the listening outline). But the strophes in "Like a Rolling Stone" are extremely long; it is as if every formal aspect present in "Blowin' in the Wind" has been enlarged to create an effect of great intensity and expansion. In the strophes of "Blowin' in the Wind" each verse consists of three questions, which are followed by the "answer" of the chorus. Each of the questions, as well as the "answer," is eight bars long; the result is a rather typical thirty-two bar formal unit. In "Like a Rolling Stone," however, the verse portions alone are forty bars in length. In the chorus portions, Dylan employs his "variable strophe" idea on a small scale but to considerable effect: the chorus in the first strophe is twenty bars long (five four-bar phrases), while in succeeding strophes the chorus expands to twenty-four bars in length (*six* four-bar phrases, the result of an additional repetition of a musical phrase, accompanying added words).

This formal expansion is necessary to accommodate the song's poetic content. The remarkable thing is that "Like a Rolling Stone" feels denser, not looser, than "Blowin' in the Wind"; compare a typical phrase in the lyrics of the latter:

> *How many roads must a man walk down*
> *Before you call him a man?*

with the opening phrase of the former:

> *Once upon a time you dressed so fine; you threw the bums a dime in your prime*
> *Didn't you?*

Obviously, the lyrics are packed more tightly in an eight-bar phrase of "Like a Rolling Stone" than they are in a comparable eight-bar phrase of "Blowin' in the Wind." The combination of greater verbal density (note the internal rhymes in the line quoted above, which are not atypical of "Like a Rolling Stone" and add considerably to the effect) with overall formal expansion creates an ongoing, coiled-spring intensity. This is the more marked because Dylan's choruses in "Like a Rolling Stone" don't even afford the listener the comfort of an ambiguous "answer"; they only ask questions. Poetically, "Like a Rolling Stone" takes the question-answer format of "Blowin' in the Wind" and in effect turns it on its head.

The Song/The Recording

In a strophic form, it is obviously the lyrics that must supply a sense of continuing development. Each succeeding strophe of "Like a Rolling Stone" widens its focus, as the alienation of the protagonist from her earlier realm of privilege becomes more and more marked and painful. The opening strophe basically describes the protagonist and her behavior. The second strophe mentions the school she used to attend; the third refers to "the jugglers and the clowns" who entertained her and the "diplomat" with whom she consorted. With the final strophe, we are given a wide-angle picture of "all the pretty people" who are "drinkin', thinkin' that they got it made"—a party at which the protagonist is no longer welcome.

Dylan's music serves its purpose of reinforcing the tension embodied in the content of the lyrics. We have already discussed this in terms of the overall sound of the recording. Notice also how every phrase in the verse portions ends with a sense of melodic incompletion, keeping the tension alive. This is another structural similarity to "Blowin' in the Wind." And, again as in the earlier song, a cadence is reached only in the chorus portions—although this arguably has an ironic effect in "Like a Rolling Stone," since the words offer no sense of completion whatsoever at these points. (Dylan's recording of "Like a Rolling Stone" fades out rather than actually concluding—like a typical rock 'n' roll song—while his "Blowin' in the Wind" comes to a formal ending, like a typical acoustic folk song.)

One further connection with acoustic folk traditions in the recording of "Like a Rolling Stone" lies in the fact that this record is, for all intents and purposes, simply a document of a live studio performance—with minimal, if any, editing or obvious "production" effects. Dylan has remained true to this kind of sound ideal throughout his recording career, eschewing the highly produced sound typical of so much 1960s (and later) rock.

At a duration of six minutes, "Like a Rolling Stone" was by far the longest 45 r.p.m. pop single ever released up to that time. Dylan's record company knew they were making history; the time "*6:00*" was emblazoned on the label in huge black numerals, demanding as much attention as the title of the song and the name of the artist! At first, some record stations pared the record down to conventional length by playing only the first two of the song's four strophes. But before long the complete single was being heard widely on national radio, and an important barrier in pop music had been broken. By the end of the 1960s, pop singles lasting over seven minutes had been made—the Beatles' "Hey Jude" (1968), the biggest chart hit of the entire decade, clocked in at seven minutes, eleven seconds.

LISTENING OUTLINE: "LIKE A ROLLING STONE"

Form	Lyrics
Strophe 1: *Verse*	*Once upon a time . . .*
Chorus	*How does it feel . . .*
Strophe 2: *Verse*	*You've gone to the finest school . . .*
Chorus [expanded]	*How does it feel . . .*
Strophe 3: *Verse*	*You never turned around to see the frowns on the jugglers and the clowns . . .*
Chorus [expanded]	*How does it feel . . .*
Strophe 4: *Verse*	*Princess on the steeple and all the pretty people . . .*
Chorus [expanded]	*How does it feel . . .*

THE COUNTERCULTURE AND PSYCHEDELIC ROCK

The explosive entrance of folk rock into the wide arena of American popular culture coincided, as we have seen, with the development of increasingly innovative approaches to rock 'n' roll itself (exemplified most forcefully in the work of the Beatles and the Beach Boys in 1965–66). Both of these phenomena were abetted, of course, by the maturation into early adulthood of the baby boomer audience, and by the maturation of many of those actually making the music. This was also a period of increasing political restlessness and ferment in the United States. America's engagement in the Vietnamese civil war was steadily escalating, while the civil rights movement was challenging the persistence of racial segregation and inequality everywhere on the home front. There were many who sensed a relationship between these two volatile political issues, linking what they viewed as external

Box 5.2 Simon and Garfunkel

Perhaps nothing illustrates the changes wrought by the phenomenon of folk rock so well as the story of Simon and Garfunkel's first hit record, "The Sounds of Silence." In early 1965 Paul Simon and Arthur Garfunkel were an urban folk duo with a fine acoustic album to their credit, *Wednesday Morning, 3 A.M.,* that was causing no excitement whatsoever in the marketplace. When folk rock hit the scene in midyear and Bob Dylan went electric, Simon and Garfunkel's producer, Tom Wilson—who was also the producer for Bob Dylan's records at the time—had a "bright idea." He took one of Simon's original compositions from the *Wednesday Morning* album, a highly poetic song about urban alienation called "The Sound of Silence," overdubbed a rock band accompaniment of electric guitars, bass, and drums onto the original recording, speeded it up very slightly, changed the title for some reason to "The Sounds of Silence," and released it as a single—all without Simon or Garfunkel's prior knowledge or permission! The duo found little to complain about, however, as they found themselves with a Number One pop hit on New Year's Day

Art Garfunkel (left) and **Paul Simon** in a recording studio, 1966. Courtesy Library of Congress.

1966. Needless to say, they never looked back. Simon and Garfunkel became one of the most enduringly popular acts ever to perform in a folk-rock style. Although the duo broke up in 1970 (they have occasionally reunited for special occasions), their songs and albums continue to be popular to this day.

We will meet Paul Simon again later on, as he is among the few singer-songwriters to come to prominence in the 1960s who arguably achieved his creative peak considerably later on. To say this is not to denigrate Simon's work with Simon and Garfunkel, which includes such memorable and varied songs as "A Hazy Shade of Winter," "America," and "Bridge over Troubled Water"; it is simply to claim that these earlier compositions would probably not lead one to suspect that Simon would eventually go on to produce such adventurous works of world music as *Graceland* and *The Rhythm of the Saints* (see Chapter 8).

colonialism—an inappropriate involvement with the affairs of a so-called Third World country—with internal colonialism—that is, the systematic oppression of minority peoples and cultures within the United States itself. This connection was made the more readily because of the large proportion of African American soldiers serving in the U.S. forces in Vietnam.

The youth audience for pop culture was directly implicated in the politics of the Vietnam War, as all young American men between the ages of eighteen and twenty-six were eligible to be drafted into the armed forces—and increasing numbers of them were drafted. Antiwar groups and organizations began to multiply, attracting large numbers of young—especially college-aged—men and women. In addition, a significant number of young people were involved in various ways with the many organizations, demonstrations, and legal initiatives that formed the civil rights movement.

In the later 1960s the meeting of the culture surrounding new rock music with the political and social discontents that largely defined the era resulted in a famous, if slippery, phenomenon: the emergence of what was called the **counterculture.** This was never the kind of systematic, highly organized movement that many liked to claim it was at the time (and later on). Although the mythic typical member of the counterculture was a young rock music fan who supported the civil rights movement and opposed the Vietnam War, it is important to remember that many older folks opposed the Vietnam War, and many of these probably had no special fondness for the new rock music; that many young rock music fans were apolitical, or even supporters of conservative political agendas; and that many of the same movements that promulgated utopian visions of a new, more just social order excluded most women and people of color from leadership positions. In other words, the notion of a counterculture, while it provides us with a convenient label for the more innovative, rebellious, and radical aspects of 1960s musical, political, and social culture taken all together, is inevitably a simplification, and unless we are careful, it may involve us in a number of dubious historical fictions. What is probably most significant here, for our purposes, is to note that rock music—the 1960s descendent of 1950s rock 'n' roll—was an essential part of the definition of the counterculture, which demonstrates once again the remarkable degree of identification between the baby boomer generation and the music they chose to make and hear.

Along with rock music and radical politics, the counterculture developed its own characteristic jargon, fads, and fashions: long hair for both women and men; beards; beads; "peasant," "eastern," and tie-dyed shirts; and blue jeans. The slang terms most often associated with hippies—"groovy," "far out," "stoned," and so on—were mainly derived from black English, a continuation of a historical pattern that goes back to the nineteenth century. In addition, the counterculture's fascination with "exotic" cultures—as reflected in the popularity of Indian classical music, Nehru jackets, and African dashikis—also has deep historical roots. At the same time, a distinctive openness and sense of freedom regarding sexual activity also emerged—encouraged to no small extent by the successful development and marketing of the first birth-control pills for women.

Many members of the counterculture were members of the American middle class, born into families that were predominantly white, Christian or Jewish, and financially solvent. It is thus understandable that the rebellious attitude of young people during the late 1960s—as during earlier periods—focused as much on a critique of the values and social habits of the middle-class family as they did on resistance to government policies or the operations of big industry. This critical attitude toward bourgeois values and attitudes was perhaps quintessentially embodied in the concept of communal living, regarded as an antidote to the psychological pathologies of the nuclear family. (Some prominent San Francisco rock bands, including the Grateful Dead, actually *were* communes.) These communitarian values were embodied in large, loosely bounded public events called "be-ins," which emphasized informal musical performance, spontaneity, and camaraderie. This communal, "let it all hang out" ethos spilled over into the large concert venues where rock music was typically played in the late 1960s, including San Francisco's Avalon Ballroom and the Fillmore West. The countercultural commitment to antiestablishment values included a variety of anarchist and libertarian philosophies. This commitment was correlated with a rejection of the romanticism of mainstream pop music, and a rejection of the commercial motivations of the big corporations that marketed pop music. (Ironically, some rock bands associated closely with the counterculture—including the Jefferson Airplane—had enough business savvy to secure lucrative contracts with major labels. Some of the biggest record corporations—for example, Columbia Records—actually promoted themselves as specializing in countercultural music.)

The issues surrounding free love—or liberated sexuality—in the 1960s have become so controversial and mythologized (especially in light of our more recent, ongoing crises with AIDS) that straightforward discussion of them is still nearly impossible. In fact, the sexual mores of the period had surprisingly little direct effect on the style or substance of pop music. Surely there was much intricate and newly poetic probing of the *emotional* nature of relationships in the song lyrics of the era, owing chiefly to the influence of Dylan and other folk rockers. But apart from isolated, and slightly later, examples (one could cite "Love the One You're With," a hit for both Stephen Stills and the Isley Brothers in 1971, or "The Pill," a 1975 recording by country star Loretta Lynn), the sexual revolution of the 1960s seems not to have been significantly documented in the music of the time. Of course, it could also be claimed that sexuality has been at least an implicit subject in most of the popular love songs of any period—including those of the Tin Pan Alley and of the rock 'n' roll years—and that consequently there was little need to change the basic character of love song lyrics in the 1960s to accommodate a new generation.

Presumably, everybody who needed to know knew what was being sung about when a singer pleaded "I want you," whether that singer was Elvis Presley in the culturally conservative 1950s ("I Want You, I Need You, I Love You," 1956) or Bob Dylan in the culturally radical 1960s ("I Want You," 1966).

Similarly, the contemporary dilemma of drug use in American society—including the abuse of drugs by very young people—makes it hard to provide a simple, unambiguous evaluation of the counterculture's relationship to intoxicants and recreational chemicals. The vulgar catchphrase was "sex, *drugs,* and rock and roll"; and instead of (or in addition to) the alcohol of their parents' generation many young people in the 1960s came to favor psychedelic substances, particularly marijuana and LSD (lysergic acid diethylamide, or "acid"). Unquestionably there was lots of drug use, both by musicians and by their audiences, in the later 1960s. Many recordings and concerts were experienced by "stoned" young people; at least some of those recordings and concerts were probably intended by the musicians to be experienced in that way; and some of the musicians involved made the music while stoned themselves. There is, for example, no possible dispute about the subject matter of a song with a title like "Don't Bogart That Joint." But when questioned about the Beatles' song "Lucy in the Sky with Diamonds," whose title and psychedelic imagery was widely assumed to be connected to LSD, John Lennon replied that the song had been inspired by a picture drawn by his four-year-old son that the little boy had himself called "Lucy in the sky with diamonds," and Lennon disclaimed any connection between the song and drugs. (Of course, one could choose to be skeptical about Lennon's statement as well; the point is that there is no absolute "truth" that can be determined here.) Certainly the flamboyant, colorful visual effects used on rock music posters and record jackets and in the light shows at rock concerts were to some degree modeled on the experience of tripping. In the end, however, it is not easy to determine to what degree the characteristic open-endedness of many rock music performances—including the hours-long musical explorations of bands like Jefferson Airplane and the Grateful Dead—is directly attributable to drug use.

In order to put the drug culture of the 1960s into perspective, it is necessary to remember a number of things. The use and abuse of alcohol, marijuana, cocaine, heroin, and other drugs has formed a part of the culture of musicians and their audiences in this country for a very long time. The pressures and doldrums of a performer's life have led many musicians to use stimulants, depressants, and intoxicants of various kinds, and unhealthy dependencies have naturally resulted all too frequently, prematurely snuffing out some of the brightest lights in America's musical history. (A partial list would include Charlie Parker, Hank Williams Sr., Elvis Presley, Janis Joplin, and Jimi Hendrix, among many others.) Furthermore, the venues in which pop music is heard live are most commonly those in which the legal—and sometimes illegal—consumption of intoxicants forms an essential aspect of the audience's "good time." In this connection, it is important to recall that during the era of Prohibition, 1919–33, the manufacture and sale of alcoholic beverages were illegal in the United States. Thus many adults who were nonplussed by younger people's consumption of illegal marijuana and LSD in the 1960s had doubtless themselves enjoyed the new pop music and jazz of the 1920s and early 1930s to the accompaniment, in speakeasy clubs or at home, of illegal bootleg liquor.

An appropriate perspective on the drug use of the 1960s would also take into account that many participants in the counterculture, including musicians and members of the rock audience, were not involved with drugs. Furthermore, along with the pleasure seekers who sought only to enjoy themselves and follow fashion while repeating the slogans of the time about "mind expansion" and "turning on," there were those who were quite seriously seeking alternatives to the prevailing American bourgeois lifestyle, who may have employed hallucinogens such as peyote, psilocybin mushrooms, and LSD carefully and sparingly as an aspect of spiritual exploration (in a manner akin to that found in certain nonwestern cultures—there was, for example, a good deal of interest in Indian culture among members of the counterculture, some of it superficial and trendy but some of it assuredly serious). In the end, it appears that the value of psychoactive substances depends on the context and manner of their use; and that the drug culture of the 1960s was, at various times, both an enabler and a destroyer of musical creativity. Interviews with rock musicians of the late 1960s—now in their fifties and sixties—are notable for their lack of nostalgia in relation to drug use.

It was, and is, easy to poke fun at stereotypical images of the counterculture. Frank Zappa, assuredly a participant in the counterculture (and reportedly a non-drug user), wrote a savagely satirical song in 1967 called "Who Needs the Peace Corps?" that targeted "phony hippies" and their "psychedelic dungeons." Yet the greatest virtue of the 1960s counterculture, for all its naïveté and excesses, may be that it gave birth to and encouraged some innovative and remarkable creative manifestations, among which are certainly the works of Zappa himself. We will now look at a few of these creative reflections of, and influences on, the "age of psychedelia."

SGT. PEPPER'S LONELY HEARTS CLUB BAND

Summer 1967 was the so-called Summer of Love, when many young participants in the newly self-aware counterculture were following the advice of a pop hit that told them to head for San Francisco (whose Haight-Ashbury district was already a legendary center of countercultural activity), wearing flowers in their hair. But the group celebrations called "love-ins" were not limited to San Francisco. In fact, a sense of participation in the counterculture was readily available that summer to anyone who had a phonograph and the spending money to purchase the Beatles' new album, *Sgt. Pepper's Lonely Hearts Club Band,* as revolutionary a work of pop musical art as had ever been made.

The countercultural ambience of *Sgt. Pepper* was obvious in a number of ways. The unprecedented and now-famous album cover, a wild collage of faces and figures surrounding the four Beatles dressed in full formal band regalia, pictured a number of people from many different time periods who were associated with aspects of the counterculture: Karl Marx, Oscar Wilde, Marlon Brando, James Dean, not to mention Bob Dylan. (The figure of a young girl off to the side was dressed in a sweater that read "Welcome the Rolling Stones"!) The song that opened the second side of the record, "Within You without You," was the most thoroughgoing of the Beatles' attempts to evoke the sound and spirit of Indian music; it featured Indian instruments (sitar and tabla, in lieu of guitars and Western drums), unusual meters and phrase structures, and deeply meditative, philosophical lyrics.

The lyrics to a number of other songs had what could easily be interpreted as drug references, for those so inclined. We have already mentioned "Lucy in the Sky with Diamonds," but among other examples well noted at the time were "A Little Help from My Friends," which features the repeated line "I get high with a little help from my friends," and the concluding song "A Day in the Life," which ends the album with the famous line "I'd love to turn you on." Furthermore, the record had many musical sounds and sound effects that could be—and were—interpreted as psychedelic in inspiration. Among the most celebrated of these were the electronically distorted voices in "Lucy in the Sky with Diamonds" and the chaotic orchestral sweep upward that occurs twice in "A Day in the Life."

Arguably more important than any specific countercultural references in *Sgt. Pepper* was the way in which the album was structured to invite its listeners' participation in an implied community. The record is a clearly and cleverly organized performance that reflects an awareness of, and actually addresses, its audience. The

The *Sgt. Pepper*–era **Beatles.** Frank Driggs Collection.

opening song, "Sgt. Pepper's Lonely Hearts Club Band," formally introduces the "show" to come and acknowledges the listener(s) with lines like "We hope you will enjoy the show," and "You're such a lovely audience, we'd love to take you home with us." This song is reprised, with different words ("We hope you have enjoyed the show") as the penultimate selection on the album, after which the "performance" ends and the performers return to "reality" with "A Day in the Life" ("I read the news today, oh boy"). Yet even in this final song, the continued presence of the listener(s) is acknowledged, at least implicitly, with the line "I'd love to turn you on."

The Beatles' brilliant conceit of *Sgt. Pepper* as a "performance" is evident even before the music begins: the opening sounds on the record are those of a restless audience. Audience sounds of laughter and applause are heard at schematic points in both the initial presentation and the reprise of the song "Sgt. Pepper's Lonely Hearts Club Band." Yet this is clearly not a recording of an actual live performance. Virtually every song on the album features a unique instrumental arrangement significantly different from that of the songs that precede and follow it—in other words, the songs are arranged to provide maximum variety and contrast on a record album, not as a practical sequence for a live performance situation. Even more obviously, the album is full of studio-produced effects, the most spectacular of which are the sound collage that actually overlaps the ending of "Good Morning Good Morning" with the reprise of "Sgt. Pepper's Lonely Hearts Club Band," and the explosively distorted final chord of "A Day in the Life," which very gradually fades out over a duration of about forty-five seconds. In the employment of these effects, and in many other aspects of the album, the hand of the producer George Martin is clearly evident.

There is a profound irony in the fact that the first album made by the Beatles after they decided to abandon live performing and assume an identity solely as a recording act is an album that, in effect, mimics and creatively reimagines the concept of performing before an audience. This irony would, of course, not be lost on Beatles fans, who were well aware of the group's highly publicized decision, and who had to wait longer for this album than for any previous one by the group. (More than nine months separated the release of *Sgt. Pepper* from that of the Beatles' immediately preceding album, *Revolver*, and that was a long time in those days.) But *Sgt. Pepper* in turn so widened and enriched the idea of what a rock album could be that, it could be argued, the gain at least somewhat balanced the loss of the Beatles as a touring group.

Rock 'n' roll had always communicated to its widest audience by means of records. *Sgt. Pepper* simply turned that established fact into a basis for brilliantly self-conscious artifice. When the Beatles sang "We'd love to take you home with us" in the opening song of the album, they must have done so with ironic recognition of the fact that it was actually their audience that takes *them* home—in the form of their records. As we have already attempted to show, everything about *Sgt. Pepper* is inclusionary; it posits the rock album as the creator of an audience community, a community for which that album also serves as a means of communication and identity. And in fact the album achieved unprecedented success in reaching a large community, even by the Beatles' standards: it sold eight million copies and remained on *Billboard*'s album charts for more than three years.

The most historically significant fact about *Sgt. Pepper* is the way in which it definitively redirected attention from the single-song recording to the record album as the focus of where important new pop music was being made. That *Sgt. Pepper* was conceived as a totality, rather than as a collection of single songs, is apparent in many ways, but most indicative perhaps was the unprecedented marketing decision not to release any of the songs on the album as singles. (The singles gap was filled by the Beatles' release of "All You Need Is Love" in the summer of 1967, a song that would only later be collected on an album.) *Sgt. Pepper* was not the first concept album, but it was the first album to present itself to the public as a complete and unified marketing package, with a distinctive and interrelated collection of parts, all of which were unavailable in any other form: not just the songs on the record itself, but also the cover art and the inside photograph of the Beatles in their band uniforms, the complete song lyrics printed on the back of the album jacket (a first, and a precedent-setting one), the extra page of "Sgt. Pepper cut-outs" supplied with the album, and even (with the earlier pressings) a unique inner sleeve to hold the record that was adorned with "psychedelic" swirls of pink and red coloring!

Sgt. Pepper did for the rock album what Dylan's "Like a Rolling Stone" had done for the rock single. It rewrote all the rules, and things were never the same again. Countless albums appearing in the wake of *Sgt. Pepper* imitated aspects of the Beatles' tour de force, from its cover art to its printed lyrics to its use of a musical reprise, but few could approach its real substance and achievement. To their credit, the Beatles themselves did not try to imitate it but went on to other things, continuing to produce innovative music on albums and singles until they disbanded early in 1970. As of the present writing, interest in the Beatles continues unabated; their three *Anthology* collections (on discs and videos) of previously unreleased material have all been recent best-sellers, and in 2000 a new compilation of their top-selling singles, entitled simply *1*, was released and proved extremely popular.

SAN FRANCISCO ROCK: JEFFERSON AIRPLANE, JANIS JOPLIN, AND THE GRATEFUL DEAD

During the late 1960s an "alternative" rock music scene, inspired in part by the Beatles' experimentalism, established itself in San Francisco. The city had already long been a center for artistic communities and subcultures, including the "beat" literary movement of the 1950s, a lively urban folk music scene, and a highly visible and vocal gay community. "Psychedelic rock," as the music played by San Francisco bands was sometimes called, encompassed a variety of styles and musical influences, including folk rock, blues, "hard rock," Latin music, and Indian classical music. In geographical terms, San Francisco's psychedelic music scene was focused on the Haight-Ashbury neighborhood, center of the hippie movement.

A number of musical entrepreneurs and institutions supported the growth of the San Francisco rock music scene. Tom Donahue, a local radio **DJ,** challenged the mainstream Top 40 AM pop music format on San Francisco's KYA and later pioneered a new, open-ended, and eclectic broadcasting format on FM station KMPX. (Donahue is the spiritual forefather of today's alternative FM formats, including many college stations.) The foremost promoter of the new rock bands—and the first to cash in on the music's popularity—was Bill Graham. Graham, a European immigrant who had worked as a taxi driver to support his business studies, began staging rock concerts in San Francisco in 1965. For one of his first rock concerts

Graham rented a skating rink, which he later renamed the Fillmore. The Fillmore—renamed the Fillmore West when Graham opened the Fillmore East in New York City—was a symbolic center of the counterculture, and psychedelic posters advertising its concerts are today worth thousands of dollars. Other individuals built professional careers out of the job of creating psychedelic atmosphere for rock concerts: Chet Helms, for example, was responsible for developing the multimedia aesthetic of light shows at the Fillmore and Avalon Ballroom.

Jefferson Airplane was the first nationally successful band to emerge out of the San Francisco psychedelic scene. Founded in 1965, the Airplane was originally a semiacoustic folk-rock band, performing blues and songs by Bob Dylan. Eventually they began to develop a louder, harder-edged style with a greater emphasis on open forms, instrumental improvisation, and visionary lyrics. Along with the Quicksilver Messenger Service and the Grateful Dead (see below), Jefferson Airplane was one of the original triumvirate of San Francisco "acid rock" bands, playing at the Matrix Club (center of the San Francisco alternative nightclub scene), larger concert venues such as the Avalon Ballroom and Fillmore, and at communal outdoor events such as happenings and be-ins. In late 1965 the Airplane received an unprecedented twenty-thousand-dollar advance from RCA, one of the largest and most powerful corporations in the world. (Despite the anticommercial rhetoric of the counterculture, this event was responsible for sparking off the formation of dozens of psychedelic bands in the Bay Area eager to cash in on the Airplane's success. Parallels to this seemingly paradoxical link between countercultural values and the good old profit motive may sometimes be observed in connection with today's "alternative" music movements.) The Airplane's 1967 LP *Surrealistic Pillow* sold over one million copies, reaching Number Three on the pop album charts and spawning two Top 10 singles. The biggest celebrity in the group was vocalist <u>Grace Slick</u> (b. 1939), who—along with Janis Joplin—was the most important female musician on the San Francisco scene.

Jefferson Airplane were introduced to a national audience by their recording of "Somebody to Love," which reached Number Five on the national pop charts in 1967. "Somebody to Love" exemplifies the acid rock approach, including a dense musical texture with plenty of volume and lots of electronic **distortion**. (The process of making hit singles encouraged the band to trim its normally extended, improvised performances down to a manageable—and AM radio–friendly—three minutes.) The song itself, which originated in an act of familial composition by Grace Slick, her husband, and her brother-in-law, exemplifies the tendency of late 1960s rock musicians to compose their own material. (Another paradox of the psychedelic rock movement was that it combined the urban folk musicians' emphasis on communal creativity with the influential rock-musician-as-artist ideology represented in the work of the Beatles, Bob Dylan, and Brian Wilson.)

Grace Slick's only serious competition as queen of the San Francisco rock scene came from <u>Janis Joplin</u> (1943–70), the most successful white blues singer of the 1960s. Born in Port Arthur, Texas, Joplin came to San Francisco in the mid-1960s and joined a band called Big Brother and the Holding Company. Their appearance at the Monterey Pop Festival in 1967 led to a contract with Columbia Records, eager to cash in on RCA's success with Jefferson Airplane, and on the growing national audience for acid rock. Big Brother's 1968 album *Cheap Thrills*—graced with a cover design by the underground comic book artist Robert Crumb—reached Number One on the pop charts and included a Number Twelve hit single (the song "Piece of My Heart," a cover version of a 1960s R&B hit by Erma Franklin).

Joplin's full-tilt singing style and directness of expression were inspired by blues singers such as Bessie Smith, and by the R&B recordings of Big Mama Thornton. (Joplin rediscovered Big Mama in the late 1960s and helped to revive her performing career.) She pushed her voice unmercifully, reportedly saying that she would prefer a short, exceptional career to a long career as an unexceptional performer. Although her growling, bluesy style made her an icon for the mainly white audience for rock music, Joplin was not a success with black audiences, and she never managed to cross over to the R&B charts.

One of Joplin's most moving performances is her rendition of the George Gershwin composition "Summertime," written in 1935 for the American folk opera *Porgy and Bess.* Although this recording was criticized for the less-than-polished accompaniment provided by Big Brother and the Holding Company, Joplin's performance is riveting. She squeezes every last drop of emotion out of the song, pushing her voice to the limit, and creating not only the rough, rasping tones expected of a blues singer but also multipitched sounds called "multiphonics." The impression one retains of Janis Joplin—an impression reinforced by listening to her

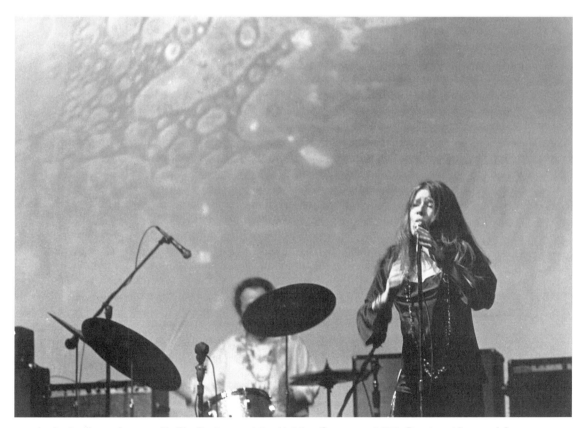

Janis Joplin performs with Big Brother and the Holding Company, 1968. Courtesy Library of Congress.

recordings—is actually that of a sweet, vulnerable person, whose tough exterior and heavy reliance on drugs functioned as defense mechanisms, and as armor against life's disappointments.

No survey of the 1960s San Francisco rock scene would be complete without mention of the Grateful Dead, a thoroughly idiosyncratic band—actually as much an experience or institution as a band in the usual sense—whose career spanned more than three decades. (Although it is often stated that the Grateful Dead were not a commercially successful band, eight of their LPs reached the Top 20, including 1987's *In the Dark,* which held the Number Nine position on *Billboard*'s album charts.) "The Dead," as they are known to their passionately devoted followers, grew out of a series of bands involving Jerry Garcia (1942–95), a guitarist, banjoist, and singer who had played in various urban folk groups during the early 1960s. This shifting collective of musicians gradually took firmer shape and in 1967 was christened the Grateful Dead (a phrase Garcia apparently ran across in an ancient Egyptian prayer book). The Dead helped to pioneer the transition from urban folk music to folk rock to acid rock, adopting electric instruments, living communally in the Haight-Ashbury district, and participating in public LSD parties ("acid tests") before the drug was outlawed. (These experiences were chronicled in Tom Wolfe's book *The Electric Kool-Aid Acid Test.*)

In musical terms, it is hard to classify the Grateful Dead's work. For one thing, their records do not for the most part do them justice. The Dead were the quintessential "live" rock band, specializing in long jams that wander through diverse musical styles and grooves and typically terminate in unexpected places. The influence of folk music—prominent on some of their early recordings—was usually just below the surface, and a patient listener may expect to hear a kind of "sketch-map" of American popular music—including folk, blues, R&B, and country music, as well as rock 'n' roll—with occasional gestures in the direction of African or Asian music. Their repertoire of songs was huge; in any given live performance, one might have heard diverse songs from different periods in the band's existence. (This means that each performance was also a unique musical version of the band's history, at least for those who had studied it.)

If the Grateful Dead were a unique musical institution, their devoted fans—"Deadheads"—were a social phenomenon unparalleled in the history of American popular music. Traveling incessantly in psychedelically decorated buses and vans, setting up camp in every town along the tour, and generally pursuing a peaceful mode of coexistence with local authorities, hardcore Deadheads literally lived for their band. While it has been pointed out that much of the satisfaction of this mobile/communal lifestyle has to do with the creation of a special social ethos, there can be no denying that the core source of appeal for serious Deadheads was the band's music. They taped the band's performances—were often *encouraged* to tape the band's performances, something quite unusual in the popular music business—and then circulated these tapes (called *bootlegs*), building up extensive lists that chronicle every concert the band ever played. There are now entire sites devoted to this purpose on the World Wide Web, with precise descriptions of the repertoires played at particular concerts and statistical breakdowns of the frequency of certain songs and certain sequences of songs. Although other popular musicians have certainly inspired adoration—Frank Sinatra, Elvis Presley, and the Beatles come immediately to mind—the devotion of Deadheads remains truly unique.

Box 5.3 "Cloud Nine": The Motown Response to Psychedelia

With its gaze always fixed firmly on the commercial mainstream, the Motown organization was never one that could directly be associated with the conception of a counterculture. But Motown was also "the sound of young America," and Berry Gordy Jr. was pop-savvy enough to realize that completely ignoring the influence of artists like Bob Dylan and the Beatles on the rock audience would relegate Motown's music to the dreaded realm of the irrelevant and unhip. Sure enough, the Supremes' "summer of love" hit in 1967, "Reflections," opened with the sounds of a strange, repeated electronic beep, followed by an explosion! After this tip of the hat to psychedelia, the record proceeded in a style basically identical to that of the Supremes' earlier efforts—except for the occasional recurrence of the strange beep.

A more thoroughgoing, serious attempt by Motown to respond to currents in the counterculture is represented by the late 1960s and early 1970s records of the Temptations. Producer Norman Whitfield, who was cowriting songs for the Temptations with Barrett Strong, actually caused some controversy within the Motown organization when he came up with "Cloud Nine" in late 1968. The "cloud nine" of the song, where "you can be what you want to be" and "you're a million miles from reality," is obviously a drug reference, but the context is far removed from that of blissful, mind-expanding psychedelia; the reality of the song is that of the urban slums, where people turn to drugs out of desperation. The gritty depiction of slum life in the lyrics of "Cloud Nine" related the song much more closely to the spirit of socially conscious urban folk rock than to the spirit usually associated with psychedelia. The sound of the record was also quite novel for Motown, with distorted electric guitars and echolike effects setting off a vocal arrangement that made a point of contrasting the varied vocal timbres and ranges represented among the members of the Temptations. In effect, "Cloud Nine" represented a new kind of hybrid for Motown, one that fused elements of the new rock and folk rock with the potent synthesis of pop and rhythm & blues that had always characterized its music. (A parallel may be drawn with the music being developed at this same time by the San Francisco–based interracial "psychedelic soul" group Sly and the Family Stone, which was attempting a similar kind of complex fusion. This group was headed by the African American songwriter/producer Sylvester Stewart.)

The success of "Cloud Nine" (Number Six pop, Number Two R&B) established the marketability of Whitfield's new approach and led, naturally enough, to other hit records by the Temptations along analogous lines, like "Run Away Child, Running Wild," "Psychedelic Shack," "Ball of Confusion (That's What The World Is Today)," and "Papa Was a Rollin' Stone." Other Motown acts also made their contributions to the organization's hipper image; 1970 brought Edwin Starr's protest song "War"—another Whitfield-Strong composition that reached Number One on the pop charts—and a record by the Supremes called "Stoned Love."

Jerry Garcia died in 1995—partly as a result of longtime drug and alcohol use—and the band has officially broken up, but the remaining members still assemble periodically to hit the road, with their huge entourage in tow. And although in the span of more than three decades the band placed only one single in the Top 40 ("Touch of Gray," a Number Nine pop hit in 1987), the thirty-odd albums recorded by the Grateful Dead continue, year by year, to sell hundreds of thousands of copies to one of the most loyal audiences in the history of American popular music.

GUITAR HEROES: HENDRIX AND CLAPTON

The 1960s saw the rise of a new generation of electric guitarists who functioned as culture heroes for their young fans. Their achievements were built on the shoulders of previous generations of electric guitar virtuosos—Les Paul, whose innovative tinkering with electronic technology inspired a new generation of amplifier tweakers; T-Bone Walker, who introduced the electric guitar to R&B music in the late 1940s; urban blues musicians such as Muddy Waters and B. B. King, whose raw sound and emotional directness inspired rock guitarists; and early masters of rock 'n' roll guitar, including Chuck Berry and Buddy Holly. Beginning in the mid-1960s, the new guitarists—including Jimi Hendrix, Eric Clapton, Jimmy Page, Jeff Beck, and the Beatles' George Harrison—took these influences and pushed them farther than ever before in terms of technique, sheer volume, and improvisational brilliance.

The Jimi Hendrix Experience. Frank Driggs Collection.

Jimi Hendrix (1942–70) was the most original, inventive, and influential guitarist of the rock era, and the most prominent African American rock musician of the late 1960s. His early experience as a guitarist was gained touring with rhythm & blues bands. In 1966 he moved to London, where, at the suggestion of the producer Chas Chandler, he joined up with two English musicians, bassist Noel Redding and drummer Mitch Mitchell, eventually forming a band called the Jimi Hendrix Experience. The Experience was first seen in America in 1967 at the Monterey Pop Festival, where Hendrix stunned the audience with his flamboyant performance style, which involved playing the guitar with his teeth and behind his back, stroking its neck along his microphone stand, pretending to make love to it, and setting it on fire with lighter fluid and praying to it. (This sort of guitar-focused showmanship, soon to become commonplace at rock concerts, was not unrelated to the wild stage antics of some rhythm & blues performers. Viewing the Hendrix segment of the documentary film *Monterey Pop*, it is clear that some people in the self-consciously hip and mainly middle-class white audience found themselves shocked and therefore delighted by Hendrix's boldness.)

Jimi Hendrix's creative employment of **feedback, distortion,** and sound-manipulating devices like the wah-wah pedal and fuzz box, coupled with his fondness for aggressive **dissonance** and incredibly loud volume—all of these characteristics represented important additions to the musical techniques and materials available to guitarists. Hendrix was a sound sculptor, who seemed at times to be consciously exploring the borderline between traditional conceptions of music and noise, a pursuit that links him in certain ways to composers exploring electronic sounds and media in the world of art music at around the same time. (One of the most famous examples of Hendrix's experimentation with electronically generated sound was his performance of the American national anthem at the Woodstock Festival in 1969. Between each phrase of the melody, Hendrix soared into an elaborate electronic fantasy, imitating "the rockets' red glare, the bombs bursting in air," and then landing precisely on the beginning of next phrase, like a virtuoso jazz musician. This was widely taken as an antiwar commentary, though Hendrix had himself served in the U.S. Army paratroopers.) All of these cited characteristics, along with any number of striking studio effects, may be heard on the first album by the Experience, *Are You Experienced?* (1967), and particularly on its famous opening cut, "Purple Haze."

In one limited sense, "Purple Haze" is a strophic song with clear roots in blues-based melodic figures, harmonies, and chord progressions. But to regard the extraordinary instrumental introduction, the guitar solo between the second and third strophes, and the violently distorted instrumental conclusion all as mere effects added to a strophic tune is really to miss the point. In fact, it could be argued that the strophic tune serves as a mere scaffolding for the instrumental passages; but at the least, the effects are equal in importance to the elements of the tune itself. The radical character and depth of Hendrix's contribution may be seen in the extent to which he requires us to readjust our thinking and terminology in the effort to describe appropriately what constitutes the real essence of his song. When we add in the impact of the lyrics, with their reference to "blowin' my mind" and lines like "'scuse me while I kiss the sky," it is easy to see why Hendrix became an iconic figure for the counterculture, as well as a role model for rock musicians.

It is emblematic of how far Hendrix had strayed from his rhythm & blues roots in music like "Purple Haze" that neither this song, nor any other released by Hendrix as a single, ever made a dent in the R&B charts. Hendrix was not a singles artist in any case, and his real kinship was with the new rock audience that viewed the record album as its essential source of musical enlightenment. In a sense, this made him a new kind of crossover artist. His audience rewarded him by elevating all of the five albums he designed for release in his all-too-brief lifetime into the Top 10.

We have noted that Hendrix's notoriety as a creative force first developed in England, and this was no accident. On the one hand, it was arguably difficult for an African American musician who neither fit into nor cared much about popular definitions of black musical style to find acceptance in the American popular music scene. And the way toward Hendrix's success in London was also paved by a thriving British pop culture scene, including boutiques, nightclubs, and youth movements such as the "mods"—who wore elaborate clothing reminiscent of centuries-old fashions and listened to American soul music—and the "rockers"—leather-jacketed rock 'n' roll fans. As we have seen, British youth seized upon American popular music with a passion during the 1960s, and an important part of this fascination was focused on the electric guitar.

Eric Clapton (b. 1945) was the most influential of the young British guitarists who emerged during the mid-1960s. Influenced by the blues recordings of Robert Johnson and B. B. King, he first attracted notice as a member of the Yardbirds, a band that had little pop success but served as a training ground for young guitarists, including Clapton, Jeff Beck, and Jimmy Page (later a member of Led Zeppelin). Clapton soon began to attract the adulation of young blues and R&B fans, largely as a result of his long, flowing blues-based guitar solos. (The most common graffiti slogan in mid-1960s London was "Clapton is God," an index of his popularity.) From 1966 to 1968 Clapton played in a band called Cream, featuring the drummer Ginger Baker and bassist Jack Bruce. Cream, the first in a line of rock "power trios" that formed during the late 1960s and early 1970s, exerted a major influence on early heavy metal music (see Chapter 6). Their performances were more akin to avant-garde jazz than to pop music, using "songs" as quickly discardable excuses for long, open-ended improvised solos. Cream took the United States by storm in the late 1960s, selling millions of LPs in the space of three years and placing two singles in the Top 10.

Although it is difficult to summarize the work of a musical improviser in a single recording, Cream's version of rural blues artist Robert Johnson's "Cross Road Blues," retitled "Crossroads," recorded live at the Fillmore West in San Francisco, does convey a sense of the power and passion of Eric Clapton's guitar playing. While this song represents the deep respect that many rock guitarists held for Robert Johnson, the original 1936 and Cream's 1968 recordings are in many ways light-years apart. In stylistic terms, Cream's performance is more indebted to postwar urban blues and R&B than to the rural blues. Johnson's complex guitar accompaniment has been reduced to a single powerful riff, played in unison by the electric guitar and bass guitar, and projected by a veritable wall of amplifiers. Clearly, the recordings of Robert Johnson were an inspiration and not a direct musical model for young guitarists like Clapton.

Still, there is at least one similarity between the musical challenges faced by the two master guitarists, playing some thirty years apart: both men's performances are highly exposed, Johnson playing solo and Clapton with only bass and drum set ac-

Box 5.4 Roots Rock: Creedence Clearwater Revival

In 1969, a year when the influence of the counterculture seemed to be at a new height—what with domestic political turmoil on the one hand, and the Woodstock music festival attracting nearly half a million fans on the other— the pop charts were ruled by Creedence Clearwater Revival. This seems initially like another of pop music's great historical ironies. Creedence was a deliberately old-fashioned rock 'n' roll band, consisting of two guitarists, a bass player, and a drummer, performing both original material and some old 1950s rock 'n' roll tunes in a musical style essentially untouched by the trappings of the psychedelic era: no exotic instruments, no unusual or extended guitar solos, no studio effects, no self-conscious experimentation with novel harmonies, rhythms, or song forms. Creedence was one of the all-time great singles bands, turning out a spate of incredibly catchy, uptempo two- to three-minute pop records that cut right through all the psychedelic haze and scored major hits for the group one after the other. Given these songs' lack of pretension, they were as effective as live performance vehicles as they were as pop recordings. In addition, the albums put out by Creedence were all huge sellers, despite—or perhaps we should say because of—the fact that they were essentially just old-fashioned collections of great singles.

Creedence Clearwater Revival restored to rock music a sense of its roots at precisely the point when the majority of important rock musicians seemed to be pushing the envelope of novel possibilities as far and as rapidly as they could. Creedence was in no sense a reactionary phenomenon, however; the group's choice of the word "revival" was an astute one. The many original songs in their repertoire, all written by lead singer and guitarist John Fogerty, possessed solid musical virtues, and several of them also reflected a decidedly up-to-date political awareness (such as "Bad Moon Rising" and "Fortunate Son") that nevertheless was not tied to any specific agenda (much like the kind of awareness found in Bob Dylan's lyrics). In fact, Creedence's best songs have arguably stood the test of time better than a lot of other music from the 1960s that might have seemed much more adventurous and relevant at the time.

Creedence Clearwater Revival was the first widely successful "roots" rock 'n' roll band. Perhaps owing to their extraordinary popularity, many other roots artists have appeared as rock has continued to evolve. But Creedence set the standard in this realm, and it is one that has yet to be approached by anyone else.

companiment. This has the effect of focusing attention on the guitarist and requiring that he play more or less constantly to keep the performance moving. Clapton's approach to this task involves not only the application of highly developed technical skills but also the use of electronic **feedback,** which allows him to sustain long notes and create flowing streams of shorter notes. The performance opens with Clapton singing a few strophes of Johnson's song, then launching into an escalating series of improvised twelve-bar choruses. This is "busy" music, designed to showcase the virtuosity of the performers, and Baker and Bruce play constantly throughout, driving Clapton along to higher and higher emotional peaks. Although some rock critics regard Cream as an example of the self-indulgence and showiness of some late-1960s rock music, there can be no disputing that Clapton, Baker, and Bruce both upped the technical ante for rock musicians and paved the way for later guitar-focused bands. And they also helped to establish the importance of the concert as a venue for experiencing rock music—hardcore fans argued that unless you heard Clapton play live, you hadn't really heard him at all.

———————

During the second half of the 1960s, the popular music favored by many young Americans took on a harder-edged, more emphatic tone. African American soul musicians reemphasized the gritty, down-to-earth side of rhythm & blues and made its political dimensions more explicit. And a new generation of musicians—raised on a diet of blues, R&B, urban folk music, and rock 'n' roll—helped to create rock, the loud, unruly, and increasingly profitable child of the music pioneered by Chuck Berry, Elvis Presley, and others in the 1950s.

In Chapter 6 we will follow rock music's transformation from an experimentalist, countercultural movement into a profit-making center of the American entertainment industry. It was during the 1970s that the tension between commercialism and authenticity that characterizes rock music right up to the present day arose in a clear form. In addition, the 1970s saw the first appearance of rock 'n' roll nostalgia, a sign both that the baby boomers were aging and that rock music had begun to develop a sense of its own history.

CHAPTER SIX

THE 1970s

Rock Music and the Popular Mainstream

One of the most pervasive stereotypes about the 1970s—famously captured in novelist Tom Wolfe's epithet, "The Me Decade"—has to do with a shift in the values of young adults, away from the communitarian, politically engaged ideals of the 1960s **counterculture,** toward more materialistic and conservative attitudes. While this generalization should be taken with a large grain of salt, it is undeniable that the early 1970s did see a kind of turning inward in American culture. The majority of Americans had grown weary of the military conflict in Vietnam, which drew to a close with the U.S. withdrawal from Saigon in 1975. Around the same time, popular attention was focused on domestic problems, including the oil crisis (1973) and economic inflation, which threatened the financial security of millions of Americans. If the assassination of President Kennedy in 1963 had robbed many Americans of a certain political idealism, the Watergate hearings—viewed by millions on television—and the subsequent resignation of President Nixon (1974) occasioned a growing cynicism about politics.

Meanwhile, the ideological polarization of the late 1960s continued unabated, and popular music remained a favorite target of conservative politicians and commentators, much as it had been during the jazz and rock 'n' roll eras of the 1920s and 1950s. It is interesting that in 1970, just as America was taking a conservative turn, hippie dress and slang, psychedelic imagery, and rock music had begun to enter the cultural mainstream of AM radio, network television, and Hollywood movies. (This suggests an analogy to the 1920s, when the "jazz age" was born in a period of strong political conservatism.) In the early 1970s the market for popular music became focused on two main categories of consumers: a new generation of teenagers, born in the late 1950s and early 1960s; and adults aged twenty-five to forty, who had grown up with rock 'n' roll and were looking for more mature (i.e., more conservative) material. Nostalgic fare such as the film *American Graffiti* (1973), the Broadway musical and film *Grease* (1972 and 1978, respectively), and the popular television series *Happy Days* used early rock 'n' roll—now nearly twenty years old—to evoke the so-called Golden Age of 1950s America, before the Kennedy assassination, the invasion of the Beatles, the rise of the counterculture, and the escalating social conflicts of the late 1960s.

If many Americans wished that the 1960s would just go away, others mourned the decade's passing. For rock fans, the end of the counterculture was poignantly symbolized by the deaths of Jimi Hendrix (1970), Janis Joplin (1970), and Jim Morrison of the Doors (1971), and by the breakup of the Beatles, who, more than any other group, inspired the triumphs (and excesses) of rock music. On December 31, 1970, Paul McCartney filed the legal brief that was to formally dissolve the business partnership of the Beatles. For many rock fans, the demise of the "Fab Four" was incontrovertible proof that the 1960s were dead and gone. But this certainly didn't mean that rock music itself was moribund. If in the late 1960s rock was the music of the counterculture, defined by its opposition to the mainstream of popular music, by the 1970s it had helped to redefine the popular mainstream, becoming the primary source of profit for an expanding and ever more centralized entertainment industry.

During the 1970s the music industry reached new heights of consolidation. Six huge corporations—Columbia/CBS, Warner Communications, RCA Victor, Capitol-EMI, MCA, and United Artists–MGM—were responsible for over 80 percent of record sales in the United States by the end of the decade. Total profits from the sale of recorded music reached new levels—two billion dollars in 1973 and four billion dollars in 1978—in part owing to the increasing popularity of prerecorded tapes. (The eight-track cartridge and cassette tape formats had initially been introduced during the mid-1960s, and their popularity expanded rapidly during the early 1970s. By 1975 sales of prerecorded tapes accounted for almost one-third of all music sales in the United States.)

However, the music industry had also become increasingly risky. During the 1970s the industry came to depend on a relatively small number of million-selling ("platinum") LPs to turn a profit. A small number of "multiplatinum" superstars—including Paul McCartney, Elton John, and Stevie Wonder—were able to negotiate multimillion-dollar contracts with the major record companies. Unable to compete in this high-end market, small independent labels of the sort that had pioneered rock 'n' roll in the 1950s accounted for only about one out of every ten records sold in the early 1970s. (The energy crisis of 1973 created a shortage of polyvinyl chloride, the petroleum-based substance from which tapes and discs were made, and this also helped to drive many small record companies out of business.) Yet, as we shall see in Chapter 7, the indies came back to exert an important musical influence in the second half of the decade, introducing new genres such as disco, punk rock, funk, and reggae.

Like other big businesses, the record industry was increasingly impelled to present more choices (or at least to create the impression of choice) for its customers. This imperative led to the emergence of dozens of specialized types of popular music—middle of the road (MOR), easy listening, adult contemporary, singer-songwriters, country pop, soft soul, urban contemporary, funk, disco, reggae, oldies, and lots of subgenres of rock music, including country rock, folk rock, soft rock, hard rock, pop rock, heavy metal, southern rock, jazz rock, blues rock, Latin rock, art rock, glam rock, punk rock, and so on—each with its own constellation of stars and target audience. Record stores were organized in more complex patterns, with dozens of distinct categories listed on the labels of record bins.

On the other hand, the Top 40 playlist format, based on nationally distributed, pretaped sequences of hit songs, increasingly dominated the AM radio airwaves, resulting in a diminished range of choices, at least for AM radio listeners. By the mid-1970s most AM radio stations relied heavily on professional programming consultants, who provided lists of records that had done well in various parts of the country. Throughout the decade, these radio playlists grew more and more restricted, making it difficult for bands without the backing of a major label to break into the Top 40.

While some hard rock or progressive rock bands were able to get singles onto Top 40 radio, the primary medium for broadcasting rock music was FM radio. During the 1970s the number of FM radio stations in the United States increased by almost a thousand, and the popularity of FM—with its capability for high-fidelity stereo broadcasting—surpassed that of AM radio. The eclectic free-form FM programming of the late 1960s—in which a **DJ** might follow a psychedelic rock record with a jazz or folk record—became restricted mainly to community- or college-based stations situated at the left end of the dial (where many such stations remain today). Seeking to boost their advertising revenues, many FM stations moved to a format called *AOR* (album-oriented rock), aimed at young white males aged thirteen to twenty-five. The AOR format featured hard rock bands, such as Led Zeppelin and Deep Purple, and art rock bands like King Crimson; Emerson, Lake, and Palmer; and Pink Floyd. AOR generally excluded black artists, who were featured on a radio format called urban contemporary. (The only exceptions to this rule seem to have been Marvin Gaye, Stevie Wonder, and Sly and the Family Stone, whose music transcended the boundary between soul and rock.) While these changes led to greater economic efficiency, the definition of rock as white music, and the increasingly strict split between black and white popular music formats, reflected the general conservatism of the radio business and of the music industry as a whole.

A survey of *Billboard* charts during the 1970s reveals a complex picture in which the various traditions discussed throughout this book—Tin Pan Alley, black popular music (now called "soul"), and country music—continued to intermingle with one another, as well as with rock music. The commercial mainstream, as defined mostly by AM radio, featured a variety of styles, each designed to reach a mass audience:

- *Pop rock,* an upbeat variety of rock music (represented by artists such as Elton John, Paul McCartney, Rod Stewart, Chicago, Peter Frampton)
- *Adult contemporary,* an extension of the old crooner tradition, with varying degrees of rock influence (Barbra Streisand, Neil Diamond, Roberta Flack, the Carpenters)
- *Singer-songwriters,* a cross between the urban folk music of Peter, Paul, and Mary and Bob Dylan and the commercial pop style of the Brill Building tunesmiths (Paul Simon, Carole King, James Taylor)[1]

---

1. Of course, performing artists can and did write their own material in all kinds of styles, but singer-songwriters were most frequently identified with the style indicated here.

- *Soft soul,* a slick variety of rhythm & blues, often with lush orchestral accompaniment (the O'Jays, the Spinners, Al Green, Barry White)
- *Country pop,* a style of soft rock, lightly tinged with country music influences (John Denver, Olivia Newton-John, Kenny Rogers)
- *Bubble gum,* cheerful songs aimed mainly at a preteen audience (the Jackson Five, the Osmonds)
- *Disco,* a new form of dance music in the late 1970s characterized by elaborate studio production and an insistent beat (Donna Summer, Chic, the Village People, the Bee Gees)

The 1970s also saw the beginnings of "oldies radio," which played hits of the 1950s and early 1960s. This is a further instance of the nostalgic tendencies that characterized the period—tendencies also symbolized by the renewed popularity of Elvis Presley, who scored more than twenty Top 40 hits during the 1970s, and of Chuck Berry, who charted his first Number One pop record in 1972, the double-entendre song "My Ding-a-Ling."

It is worth taking a moment to consider what these changes meant for African American musicians, who had, after all, provided much of the inspiration for new forms of popular music. By the mid-1970s older soul and R&B stars such as Aretha Franklin and James Brown, though still popular among black listeners, found it more difficult to penetrate the pop- and rock-dominated Top 40 charts. (However, both Franklin and Brown staged big comebacks during the 1980s.) Atlantic Records, a pioneer in the field of R&B and soul music, increasingly turned its attention to grooming and promoting white rock acts such as Led Zeppelin. Motown Records continued to score successes on Top 40 radio and the pop singles charts with artists such as Diana Ross (who left the Supremes to become a solo act in 1970), the "soul bubblegum" group Jackson Five, the Spinners, and Marvin Gaye. But Motown no longer enjoyed its former dominance of the crossover market.

Many of the black performers featured on the AM radio airwaves and Top 40 charts specialized in a smooth, romantic style called "soft soul," clearly indebted to the Motown sound of the early to mid-1960s. One of the most commercially successful forms of soul music during the 1970s was the so-called Philadelphia sound, produced by the team of Kenny Gamble and Leon Huff, and performed by groups such as the O'Jays ("Love Train") and Harold Melvin and the Blue Notes ("If You Don't Know Me by Now"). These groups had a great deal of crossover success in the 1970s, regularly scoring Top 10 hits on the pop charts and the soul (the equivalent of the old R&B) charts. In retrospect, it does seem that much 1970s soul music was less assertive in its lyrics and its rhythms than its 1960s counterpart, and some observers have suggested that this was a strategic counterreaction on the part of radio stations and record companies to the racial violence that had erupted on the streets of Watts, Detroit, and Newark during the late 1960s.

Watching today's cable television advertisements for collections of "classic seventies hits," one could come to the conclusion that rock music had by 1970 pushed the old Tin Pan Alley songwriting tradition off the map entirely. That would be inaccurate, however, for the first Number One single of the 1970s was a throwback to the Brill Building era of the early 1960s (see Chapter 4), a sprightly and thoroughly escapist pop song entitled "Raindrops Keep Fallin' on My Head," performed by former country singer B. J. Thomas. This record—which stayed on the charts for nearly six months, in no small part owing to its being featured in the soundtrack of a popular film, *Butch Cassidy and the Sundance Kid*—was composed by Hal David and Burt Bacharach, third-generation Tin Pan Alley songwriters (see Box 5.1), and the song was shopped around to various other singers (including Bob Dylan!) before Thomas was chosen to record it. (Interestingly, the song was a crossover hit, reaching Number Thirty-eight on the R&B charts in 1970, in a cover version by the black soul singer Barbara Mason.) Several Number One singles of the 1970s—such as Roberta Flack's "Killing Me Softly with His Song" (1973), Debby Boone's "You Light Up My Life" (1977), Barbra Streisand's film theme "The Way We Were" (1973), and her romantic duet with Neil Diamond on "You Don't Bring Me Flowers" (1978)—attest to the continuing popularity of an approach to composing and performing songs directly derived from the Tin Pan Alley tradition. While rock critics tend to regard most "soft rock" and "adult contemporary" as the musical equivalent of pond scum, there is no denying their mass popularity throughout the 1970s.

COUNTRY MUSIC AND THE POP MAINSTREAM

During the 1970s, country and western music—now generally just called "country"—became a huge business, reaching out to young and middle-class listeners while at the same time reinforcing its traditional southern and white working-class audience base. In 1974 the *Grand Ole Opry* moved from the run-down Nashville theater where it had been broadcasting since 1941 into a multimillion-dollar facility, complete with a 110-acre theme park called "Opryland." The national weekly magazines *Newsweek* and *Time* ran sympathetic cover stories on country stars Loretta Lynn and Merle Haggard; three country music shows were being featured on network television in the early 1970s (*The Glen Campbell Goodtime Hour, The Johnny Cash Show*, and *Hee-Haw*); and eventually Hollywood films such as *Nashville* (1975) and *Coal Miner's Daughter* (1980, a depiction of Loretta Lynn's life story) helped to broaden country's audience and to ameliorate long-standing stereotypes of country fans as "rednecks." The generally conservative mood of the country—reflected in Richard Nixon's landslide victory over George McGovern in the 1972 presidential election—helped to reinforce country's popularity among the American middle class.

The country-pop crossover of the 1970s—an updated version of the success enjoyed by an artist like Patti Page during the 1950s (see Chapter 2)—was accomplished by a new generation of musicians, many of whom had developed their careers in the fields of pop, urban folk music, and rock 'n' roll. During the mid-1970s a number of records reached the Number One position on both the pop and country charts—Charlie Rich's ballad "The Most Beautiful Girl" (1973), John Denver's "Thank God I'm a Country Boy" (1975; see below), Glen Campbell's rendition of "Rhinestone Cowboy" (1975), and the truckers' anthem "Convoy," recorded by C. W. McCall in 1975 in the midst of nationwide fuel shortages and a Teamsters' Union strike. The last record helped to spread the popularity of citizens band (CB) radio, part of a more general "redneck chic" movement, in which millions of middle-class Americans adopted southern working-class cultural practices.

These "country pop" stars came from diverse musical and social backgrounds. <u>Glen Campbell</u> was born in Arkansas in 1936. He worked with western dance bands

Box 6.1 Hardcore Country: Merle Haggard and the Bakersfield Sound

During the 1970s, as country music became a multimillion dollar business dominated by various blends of country and pop music, some musicians returned to the straightforward, emotionally direct approach of postwar honky-tonk musicians like Hank Williams and Ernest Tubb (see Chapter 2). The "back to the basics" spirit of so-called hardcore country is perhaps best captured in the recordings of Merle Haggard, born near Bakersfield, California, in 1937. The son of migrants from Oklahoma (the "Okies," whose lives formed the basis for John Steinbeck's novel *The Grapes of Wrath*), Haggard wandered from place to place as a child, spending time in a series of juvenile homes and reform schools. When as a nineteen-year-old he began serving three years for burglary in San Quentin Prison, it did not appear that Merle Haggard had much of a future.

However, Haggard's talents as a musician and songwriter, and his new-found gift for being in the right place at the right time, eventually bailed him out. In the early 1960s, after his release, Haggard worked odd jobs around Bakersfield, playing at night in local honky-tonks. Bakersfield was at precisely this moment emerging as the center of a distinctive style of country music, an outgrowth of the **rockabilly** style of the 1950s (see Chapter 3). Defined by a spare, twangy sound, electric instrumentation, and a strong backbeat, the "Bakersfield sound" stood in direct opposition to the slick sound of much Nashville country music. Popularized by musicians like Haggard and Buck Owens, this was one of the most influential country genres of the late 1960s, reviving the spirit of postwar honky-tonk and setting the stage for subsequent movements such as country rock and outlaw country.

In 1965 Haggard scored a Top 10 country hit with the song "(My Friends Are Gonna Be) Strangers," which established the name for his band (the Strangers), and led to a recording contract with Capitol Records. In the late 1960s Haggard capitalized on his experience as a convict to write songs about life outside the law (e.g., "The Fugitive," a Number One country hit in 1967). An important aspect of Haggard's work as a songwriter is his commitment to chronicling the lives and attitudes of everyday people in gritty, realistic language. The central character of many Haggard songs is a white male worker, struggling to achieve the comfort and security of middle-class life. Hardworking, beer-drinking, patriotic, and politically conservative, this character's voice is perhaps most famously heard in Haggard's 1969 recording of his song "Okie from Muskogee," which reached Number One on the country charts and Number Forty-one on the pop charts and garnered him an invitation to Richard Nixon's White House:

> We don't smoke marijuana in Muskogee
> We don't take our trips on LSD
> We don't burn our draft cards down on Main Street
> We like livin' right, and bein' free. . . .

> *We don't make a party out of lovin'*
> *We like holdin' hands and pitchin' woo*
> *We don't let our hair grow long and shaggy*
> *Like the hippies out in San Francisco do. . . .*
>
> *We still wave Old Glory down at the courthouse,*
> *In Muskogee, Oklahoma, USA.*

Although this song alienated many liberal listeners who had previously lauded Merle Haggard as a "poet of the common man" and therefore expected him to share their own political sentiments, there is no denying that Haggard's songs reflected the real concerns and aspirations of millions of Americans, particularly migrants from the South who struggled to support their families through the shifting economic climate of the 1970s. Songs like "If We Make it through December" (Number One country, Number Twenty-eight pop in 1973) captured the real-life dilemmas of working-class Americans struggling to create secure lives for their families in a hostile world:

> *Got laid off down at the factory*
> *And their timing's not the greatest in the world*
> *Heaven knows I been working hard*
> *Wanted Christmas to be right for Daddy's girl*
> *I don't mean to hate December, it's meant to be the happy time of year*
> *And my little girl don't understand why Daddy can't afford no Christmas*
> *   here.*
>
> *If we make it through December everything's gonna be all right, I know*
> *It's the coldest time of year and I shiver when I see the falling snow . . .*
> *If we make it through December we'll be fine.*

in the Southwest as a teenager and moved to Los Angeles in 1958, where he developed a career as a studio session guitarist and vocalist. Starting in the late 1960s he had a string of crossover hits on the country and pop charts, including "Gentle on My Mind" (1967), "By the Time I Get to Phoenix" (1967), and "Wichita Lineman" (1968). In 1969 he began hosting his own network television series, and his genial, laid-back style helped to expand his national popularity. Charlie Rich, the "Silver Fox," was also born in Arkansas, in 1932. Rich was a talented jazz and blues pianist whose career started as part of the stable of rockabilly performers at Sam Phillips's Sun Records. By the 1960s he had switched to the pop-oriented country-politan style, and he scored a series of Number One crossover hits during the mid-1970s, winning the Country Music Association's award as Entertainer of the Year in 1974. At the following year's CMA awards ceremony, Rich announced the country-tinged pop singer John Denver as his successor for Entertainer of the Year and demonstrated his distaste by setting fire to the envelope. Denver was born John Henry Deutschendorf in New Mexico, in 1943. Denver's work will be discussed later in this chapter in connection with Top 40 music. Here it suffices simply to note that many in the traditional audience for country music despised Denver and his pop-oriented hit records even more than Charlie Rich did.

The dichotomy between pop performers who capitalized on the popularity of country music, on the one hand, and established country musicians who moved toward the pop mainstream, on the other, is well illustrated by the careers of two female recording stars of the 1970s: Olivia Newton-John and Dolly Parton. Newton-John was born in England in 1948 and grew up in Australia. During the mid-1970s she scored a series of Top 10 country pop crossover hits—"Let Me Be There," "If You Love Me (Let Me Know)," and "Have You Never Been Mellow"—and in 1974 won the Country Music Association's award for Female Singer of the Year. After the awards ceremony, a group of veteran country musicians met to form a new association—the Association of Country Entertainers—dedicated to resisting the perceived invasion of pop singers like Olivia Newton-John and John Denver, who were eager to capitalize on country's burgeoning popularity but ambivalent about identifying themselves too exclusively with the genre. The suspicions of hardcore country fans seemed justified when in the late 1970s Newton-John abandoned country music to jump on the oldies rock 'n' roll bandwagon, appearing in the film *Grease* and on its bestselling soundtrack album (1978). In fairness, however, it must be noted that pop opportunists such as Newton-John and Denver played a major role in widening the national audience for country music during the 1970s.

At about the same time that Newton-John was moving out of country music, Dolly Parton, an established country music star, was making her first major inroads into pop. Born in the hill country of Tennessee in 1946, Parton began her recording career at the age of eleven, moved to Nashville in 1964, and built her career with regular appearances on country music radio and television, including the *Grand Ole Opry.* Parton's flexible soprano voice, songwriting ability, and carefully crafted image as a cheerful sex symbol combined to gain her a loyal following among country fans. (Parton succeeded Olivia Newton-John as the CMA's Female Singer of the Year in 1975 and 1976, and later on, in the 1980s, was the first female country musician to host her own national television series.) Although she scored a series of Number One hits on the country charts during this period, it was not until the late 1970s that Parton was able to get a record into the Top 40 pop charts. (Her rendition of "Here You Come Again"—written by veteran Brill Building composers Barry Mann and Cynthia Weil—reached Number Three pop and Number One country in 1977.) Between them, Olivia Newton-John and Dolly Parton illustrate the extremes of the seventies country pop continuum—one a pop performer seeking to capitalize on the rising popularity of country music, and the other a country singer seeking to maintain her loyal following in that market while extending her appeal to a wider audience.

A 1970s JUKEBOX: SOME CHARACTERISTIC SOUNDS OF THE DECADE

Although the jukebox was in decline as an outlet for disseminating pop music in the 1970s, we are using the image of a jukebox here for our overview of six representative hit singles that, taken together, may be said to typify many aspects of the that decade's music. These six recordings differ widely in style, but they were all hugely popular—all were Number One singles—and thus can serve to demonstrate the diversity that was embraced by "mainstream pop" audiences during this period. All are records by artists who had multiple hit singles *and* hit albums during the 1970s. For all these artists, that decade was also the period of their maximum influence and popular success; all of them are still principally identified with the music that they recorded during this period.

Although some of these selections reflect the influence of the music of the 1960s, this influence tends to be felt in relatively subtle ways. None of these records are overtly novel or experimental in character, in the way that was characteristic of such representative 1960s artists as the Beatles or Bob Dylan. This conservatism typifies the nature of most mainstream pop in the 1970s, which tended to avoid the self-conscious tendency to "push the envelope" that is evident in much of the popular music from the preceding decade. In particular, we may observe that the six selections in our "1970s jukebox," regardless of their length, all display straightforward and readily accessible song forms. Except for the instrumental "Love's Theme," which is in the venerable AABA form, all the songs are clearly based on the simple and time-honored verse-chorus principle.

Yet the changes wrought by the 1960s have left unmistakable traces on this group of hits. With the sole exception of "Thank God I'm a Country Boy," these records reflect the move toward longer singles that became manifest during the second half of the 1960s: "It's Too Late," "Superstition," "Crocodile Rock," and "Love's Theme" are all well over three minutes in duration, and "Hotel California" exceeds six minutes of playing time. All of these songs were also featured cuts on top-selling albums by their respective artists—albums whose release was closely coordinated with that of the singles. Obviously, the singles were designed not only to be big sellers in their own right but also to call attention to the new albums from which they were drawn and to encourage the purchase of those albums. Thus the increasing prominence of the album over the single as a prime vehicle for marketing pop music performers—another trend that began in the 1960s—continued unabated throughout the 1970s. Finally, all of the artists represented here are closely identified with material that they wrote (or cowrote) themselves, primarily for their own performance; that is to say, like so many of the most representative individuals and groups from the 1960s, they are *singer-songwriters.* (Although John Denver's "Thank God I'm a Country Boy" is not his own composition, it is once again "the exception that proves the rule," as all of his other big hits were self-penned, and all of the other five songs showcased here were written or cowritten by the artists who perform them.)

"It's Too Late" (1971)

Performed by Carole King; written by Carole King and Toni Sterne

The career of <u>Carole King</u> in the 1970s illustrates, perhaps better than any other example could, the central prominence of singer-songwriters during this period. King had been an important songwriter for more than a decade (in the 1960s, she wrote many hits with Gerry Goffin, her husband at that time; see Chapter 4) but was virtually unknown as a performer until she released the album *Tapestry,* from which the single "It's Too Late" was drawn, in 1971. The astounding popularity of both the single and the album established Carole King as a major recording star. In the aftermath of King's success as a performer, relatively few songwriters were content to remain behind the scenes; it came to be expected that most pop songwriters would want to perform their own material and, conversely, that most pop singers would want to record material that they had written themselves. Just the same, few singer-songwriters at this time were able to achieve the degree of success won by King. "It's Too Late" held the Number One spot for five weeks, and even its flip side, "I Feel the Earth Move"—also a cut from *Tapestry*—proved popular in its own right and was frequently played on the radio. (Both songs remained long-term favorites of King's fans.) *Tapestry* itself was an unprecedented hit. It was the Number One album for fifteen weeks, remained on the charts for nearly six years, and sold in excess of ten million copies, more than any album by the Beatles.

Carole King was approaching the age of thirty when she recorded "It's Too Late." Clearly she was far from being the teenager who had written such songs as "Will You Love Me Tomorrow?" and "Take Good Care of My Baby" for a market consisting principally of other teenagers; King had matured, and her audience had matured along with her. "It's Too Late" is clearly an *adult* relationship song, written from the point of view of someone who has long left behind teenage crushes, insecurities, and desperate heartbreak. The singer describes the ending stage of a significant relationship with a feeling of sadness, but also with a mature philosophical acceptance that people can change and grow apart, and an understanding that this does not represent the end of the world for either of them.

The music of "It's Too Late" also reflects King's maturity. Her acoustic piano is the song's backbone, and it leads us through a sophisticated progression of relatively complex chords that portray a musical world far removed from the harmonic simplicity of early rock 'n' roll. When, toward the end of the substantial instrumental interlude preceding the final verse of the song, the saxophone enters to play a melody, the context evokes a kind of light jazz, rather than earlier rock. (The recording as a whole epitomizes the kind of sound that came to be known—fortunately or otherwise—as "soft rock.") Like the words of the song, the sound of its music was clearly geared toward an audience of maturing young adults. It is equally clear that the audience was out there and more than ready to appreciate a recording like this one.

"Superstition" (1972)

Performed and written by Stevie Wonder

Stevie Wonder was a highly successful singer and songwriter during his teenage years with Motown in the 1960s. But he established a new benchmark of achievement for a pop music figure in 1971 when, at the age of twenty-one, he negotiated a new contract with the Motown organization that guaranteed him full artistic control over all aspects of his music. As a master of all trades—singer, songwriter, multi-instrumentalist, arranger, and producer—Wonder was able to use this control to his utmost advantage, and he made all his subsequent recordings his *own* to a degree that has rarely been approached by other artists in the field. We can hear the results of this on an incredibly tight cut like "Superstition," on which Wonder plays most of the instruments (synchronizing the performance by *overdubbing* several tracks on the recording tape) to accompany his own singing of his own composition. "Superstition" was the first featured single from the album *Talking Book,* which also achieved tremendous popularity.

"Superstition" blends elements borrowed from different aspects of African American musical traditions and adds its own distinctive flavorings to the mix. The use of a repeated riff over an unchanging chord as the song's hook—a riff heard right from the outset, and which persists throughout all three verse sections of the song—obviously reflects the influence of James Brown's brand of late 1960s soul music (see Chapter 5). But Wonder gives this music his own inflection through his employment of the electric keyboard instrument called the *Clavinet*—a novelty at the time—to play the riff. (Throughout the early 1970s, Wonder was a pioneer in the use of new electronic instruments, including *synthesizers,* in pop music.) The chorus section ("When you believe . . .") introduces chord changes that are suggestive of blues influence; taken as a whole, the large verse-chorus unit of the song may be heard as an expanded variant of the twelve-bar blues in terms of both phrase structure and harmonic vocabulary. The persistence and flexibility of blues traditions in American popular music remains a source of wonder. The lyrics, however, take a thoroughly modern, sophisticated stand ("Superstition ain't the way"); in "Superstition," Stevie Wonder thus fused something old and something blue with the borrowed and the new to create an irresistible pop hit.

"Crocodile Rock" (1972)

Performed by Elton John; written by Elton John and Bernie Taupin

By the 1970s the "British invasion" of the 1960s had turned into a long-running "British occupation" of the American pop charts, as numerous artists from across the Atlantic achieved hit singles and albums in the United States on a regular basis. No artist illustrates this trend better than <u>Elton John</u> (Reginald Kenneth Dwight), named in Joel Whitburn's *Top Pop* books as "the #1 Pop artist of the 70s" in America. "Crocodile Rock," which was released late in 1972 and topped the charts in February 1973, was the first of six Number One hits for John during this decade. It was a featured single on his album *Don't Shoot Me I'm Only the Piano Player,* the second of seven consecutive million-selling Number One albums for John during this same period.

Like Carole King and Stevie Wonder, Elton John was a keyboard-playing singer-songwriter; the sound of John's piano is essential to the character of "Crocodile Rock," and to many of his other hits. Lyricist Bernie Taupin was John's songwriting partner not only for "Crocodile Rock" but for all of John's major hits of the 1970s.

"Crocodile Rock" reveals how thoroughly Elton John had assimilated the basic sounds and feelings of American rock 'n' roll while still being able to add his personal touch. The song capitalizes in a savvy way on the nostalgia that seemed to be sweeping the pop music landscape at the time of its release. In late 1972 Chuck Berry and Ricky Nelson were both back in the Top 10 for the first time in many years, while Elvis Presley was enjoying his biggest hit in a long time and the last Top 10 hit of his career ("Burning Love"). This was also the period when aging baby boomers began to flock to rock 'n' roll "revival" shows, in which artists from the 1950s and early 1960s (frequently including vocal groups with old names but lots of new faces) appeared to play their original, now "classic," hits. (Note the sly reference to the old Bill Haley hit "Rock around the Clock" in the opening verse of "Crocodile Rock.") Not insignificantly, just a year before "Crocodile Rock" hit Number One, the singer-songwriter Don McLean made an enormous impact with his own Number One hit "American Pie"—a record whose subject matter was nostalgia for the early years of rock 'n' roll and the conviction that something of great

innocence and promise had been lost amid the tumult and violence that marked
the end of the 1960s.

Like "American Pie," "Crocodile Rock" deals with nostalgia and the sense of
loss, but in a much more lighthearted fashion. It seems to emphasize the happy
memories ("I remember when rock was young, me and Susie had so much fun")
over the unhappy present ("But the years went by and rock just died"); in fact, the
second verse ends up affirming the persistence of remembered joy ("But they'll
never kill the thrills we've got"), and the final verse is simply a return back to the
first, "when rock was young." Musically, the flavor is clearly that of an upbeat
teenage dance song, and even though there never actually was a famous rock 'n'
roll dance called the "crocodile," the song may be deliberately evoking the memory of other "animal" dances, like the monkey. The chord progressions of "Crocodile Rock" obviously recall those of early rock 'n' roll songs without duplicating
them exactly, and an element of novelty is added in the wordless part of the chorus with the kazoo-like sound of John's Farfisa organ.

No single record could be cited to represent an artist's entire career when the
artist's musical output has been as substantial and as varied as that of Elton John.

Elton John receives an obviously unexpected hug from a grinning **Barry White** in California, c. 1975. James Fortune/Hulton Archive.

But "Crocodile Rock" can surely serve as a representation of John's characteristic good humor, and of the way in which he typically is able to link commercial smarts with musical intelligence.

"Love's Theme" (1973)

Performed by the Love Unlimited Orchestra, conducted by Barry White; written by Barry White

A dizzying upward sweep in the strings; the pulse kicks in, subtly at first, but becoming progressively stronger; and a downward lunge on the keyboard ushers in "Love's Theme," one of the biggest instrumental hits of the 1970s. The Love Unlimited Orchestra, a forty-piece studio ensemble, was the brainchild of <u>Barry White</u>, a multitalented African American singer, songwriter, arranger, conductor, and producer, who had already begun to have a string of solo vocal hits by the time that "Love's Theme" hit the Number One spot on the pop chart in February 1974. Originally formed to back the female trio Love Unlimited, which was yet another one of White's projects as a writer and producer, the Love Unlimited Orchestra also played on some of White's solo recordings, in addition to having hit instrumental records under its own name. ("Love's Theme" was featured on *Rhapsody in White,* the cleverly titled Top 10 album by the Love Unlimited Orchestra.)

The instrumental pop hit, which reached its pinnacle as a genre during the big band years (1935–45), never totally died out during the early years of rock 'n' roll or during the emergence of rock in the 1960s. In fact, as we have seen, instrumental virtuosity on the electric guitar became one of the defining elements of late 1960s and 1970s rock. Still, "Love's Theme" represented a different kind of instrumental for the 1970s; guitar pyrotechnics play no part in the arrangement, although the use of the "scratch" guitar sound as a recurring percussive element throughout the recording does constitute a nod to the more advanced guitar styles of the period cultivated by artists such as Jimi Hendrix. Instead, the emphasis in "Love's Theme" is on two things: danceability on the one hand, and the sweet sound of string-dominated melody on the other. Its successful synthesis of these two elements, which might seem at first to be unlikely bedfellows, is one of the strikingly original—and very influential—aspects of this record.

The danceability of "Love's Theme" made it one of the earliest *disco*-styled hits (see Chapter 7), as it quickly became a favorite in dance clubs. This recording was the first in a long line of instrumental, or largely instrumental, disco records. These records followed the lead of "Love's Theme" insofar as they typically presented a similar combination of a strong beat with an elaborate arrangement featuring bowed string instruments; examples include the Number One hits "TSOP (The Sound of Philadelphia)" by MFSB (which topped the charts later in 1974), "The Hustle" by Van McCoy and the Soul City Symphony (1975), and "Fly, Robin, Fly" by Silver Convention (also 1975). In addition, the lush arrangement of "Love's Theme," featuring a melody designed to take full advantage of the way orchestral string instruments can hold long notes, links this instrumental in a general way to the sound of what was called "soft soul," a popular genre in the later 1960s and throughout the 1970s, exemplified by languid or midtempo love songs with similarly "romantic" arrangements. (Examples include recordings by the Delfonics, the Spinners, the Stylistics, and by Barry White himself as a solo vocalist.) In a sense, "Love's Theme" has it both ways; it's like a love ballad for instruments with a double-time dance beat. The steady, syncopated dance groove keeps the string sounds from spilling over into sentimentality, while the smooth string melody prevents the dance pulse from seeming overly mechanical or depersonalized.

While listening to "Love's Theme," it is a relatively simple matter to pick out the tune's basic AABA structure—yet another testament to the remarkable durability of this formal arrangement. Note how the **bridge** section (B) is slightly longer than the others, and how effective this extension of the bridge is, as we wait for the return of A.

Barry White was best known for his full, deep voice, which he could employ to great and seductive effect, not only in actually singing his love songs, but also in the spoken introductions he sometimes provided for them (as in his 1974 Number One solo hit, "Can't Get Enough of Your Love, Babe"). Still, the single biggest hit record with which White was associated remains "Love's Theme," and in terms of the long-range impact of its sound on the pop music market, it may also be his most influential recording. It is no accident that the lead-off cut on *The Disco Box,* a four-CD compilation of the dance-oriented music of the 1970s and early 1980s (issued by Rhino in 1999) is "Love's Theme."

"Thank God I'm a Country Boy" (1975)

Performed by John Denver; written by John Martin Sommers

Throughout the 1970s it was fashionable in certain hip circles to praise the virtues and alleged simplicity of rural life. Country-flavored rock was popular during this period, as is demonstrated by much of the recorded output of the Eagles (see below). Obviously a recording like John Denver's "Thank God I'm a Country Boy" partook of, and benefited from, this trend, even if John Denver himself was generally not regarded as being particularly hip by the standards of the day.

The late John Denver got his start in the 1960s in the urban folk movement (as a member of the Chad Mitchell Trio), and the sound of the acoustic guitar remained a prime element in many of the records he made as a solo artist in the 1970s. Several of his early hits, including his first two Top 10 records ("Take Me Home, Coun-

John Denver. Frank Driggs Collection.

try Roads" and "Rocky Mountain High," from 1971 and 1972 respectively) were "country" records more in terms of their subject matter than in terms of their actual musical style, which might best be described as an urban folk style flavored with some pop elements. By the time he achieved his third Number One hit with "Thank God I'm a Country Boy" in 1975, however, Denver was obviously going all-out to portray himself as a country artist musically as well. In this he was obviously successful, insofar as he was a significant presence on the country charts as well as on the pop charts in the mid-1970s—the only artist in our jukebox for whom this is true. (The Eagles scored an isolated hit on the country charts with their "Lyin' Eyes" in 1975; aside from this, only John Denver among our jukebox artists ever even made it into the country music Top 40.) This demonstrates that the strong sense of separation between the country and the mainstream pop charts that we noted as characteristic of the 1960s continued, in many ways, into the 1970s.

"Thank God I'm a Country Boy" is a cut taken from Denver's live album *An Evening with John Denver,* which documented his concert performances in Los Angeles during the summer of 1974. Although live albums were commonplace by this time, live singles were still relatively uncommon, but the sense of immediacy and spontaneity so essential to the character and appeal of this recording obviously results directly from the presence of an actual, enthusiastic concert audience. The opening, with Denver singing unaccompanied except for the rhythmic hand-clapping of his audience, captures something of the ambience of a real country dance party. The rural flavor of Denver's vocal of course adds to this impression; it should be noted that Denver came by this flavor naturally, having been raised in the South and the Southwest. When the instruments enter on the second verse of the song, the fiddle-led ensemble directly evokes the general sound and feeling of the old-time acoustic country string bands. The lyrics also make continual reference to the fiddle as a marker of country culture, and the second verse even mentions directly the classic country fiddle tune "Sally Goodin."

A cynic might call a recording like "Thank God I'm a Country Boy" an example of "country lite," and certainly there is no trace of hardship in the lyrics' description of "life on a farm," where things are "kinda laid back" and "life ain't nothin' but a funny, funny riddle"; the joyful music and singing also lie quite a distance from the "high lonesome" sound of much early country music. Still, even if this record is regarded as the musical equivalent of a city dweller's Sunday drive into the country (and we should remember that it was recorded in Los Angeles), John Denver and his accompanying musicians make the drive an exhilarating one, and there is no trace of condescension either in their deliberate evocation of country style or in the singer's exuberant delivery of the song's message.

"Hotel California" (1976)

Performed by the Eagles; written by Don Felder, Don Henley, and Glenn Frey (all members of the Eagles)

California in the 1970s retained the central position in American popular culture that it had attained during the 1960s, and if the Beach Boys epitomized the culture of southern California in the earlier decade, then the Eagles were the group that most obviously inherited that distinction. Indeed, the close association of this Los Angeles–based group with the Golden State was so well established at the time of their peak popularity (1975–80) that it lent particular authority to their ambitious saga of "Hotel California"—the million-selling single from the extraordinarily successful album of the same name (which has sold in excess of fourteen million copies).

The Eagles serve as an excellent case in point to illustrate the accelerating ascendancy in importance of albums over singles during the 1970s. When the Eagles issued their first compilation of singles in album form, *Eagles/Their Greatest Hits, 1971–1975,* the album achieved sales far beyond those of all its hit singles taken together; it was, in fact, the first recording to be certified by the Recording Industry Association of America (RIAA) as a million-selling ("platinum") album, and it went on to sell more than twenty-six million copies.

Starting out in 1971 with feet firmly planted in what was called "country rock," the Eagles had moved from laid-back tunes like "Take It Easy" and "Peaceful Easy Feeling," and songs that evoked traditional Western imagery like "Desperado" and "Tequila Sunrise," to harder-hitting material like "One of These Nights" by 1975. "Hotel California" was the fourth of their five Number One singles, and it introduced a new, complex, poetic tone into the Eagles' work. Indeed, of all the selections in our 1970s jukebox, "Hotel California" sounds closest to an ambitious late-1960s record. This is due to several factors: its length, its minor-key harmonies, and its rather unusual overall shape (with extended guitar solos at the *end* of the record) all contribute to the effect, but surely it is the highly metaphoric lyrics that establish the most obvious kinship with the songwriting trends of the 1960s.

The tone of "Hotel California," however, is pure 1970s. The sense of loss and disillusionment that is treated so casually in "Crocodile Rock" here assumes a desperate, almost apocalyptic, character:

> *Her mind is Tiffany twisted. She got the Mercedes bends.*
> *She got a lot of pretty, pretty boys, that she calls friends.*
> *How they dance in the courtyard; sweet summer sweat.*
> *Some dance to remember; some dance to forget.*

When the visitor asks the hotel captain to bring up some wine, he is told, "We haven't had that spirit here since nineteen sixty-nine." Finally, as the last verse ends, the fleeing visitor is told by the "night man" at the door that "you can check out any time you like, but you can never leave." As if to illustrate all the implications of this memorable line, the song neither proceeds to the now-expected chorus ("Welcome to the Hotel California," whose pop-friendly major-key music assumes an increasingly ironic edge as the record progresses) nor fades out quickly. Instead, those words become the final words we hear, and the Eagles launch into lengthy guitar solos—over the chords of the verses, *not* those of the chorus—as if to underline our "stuck" situation and to eliminate anything that remotely suggests "welcoming." California, that sun-blessed beacon to the generation of "peace and love" in the 1960s, has here become a sinister trap for those who have no place left to go.

ROCK COMES OF AGE

During the 1970s rock music, the brash child of rock 'n' roll, diffused into every corner of the music industry. Influenced by the Beatles, Bob Dylan, Brian Wilson, and Jimi Hendrix, many progressive rock musicians had come to view themselves as Artists, and their recordings as works of Art. While this occasionally led to the production of self-indulgent dross, some musicians used the medium of the long-playing record album to create innovative and challenging work. At the same time, the music industry moved to co-opt the appeal of rock music, creating genres like "pop rock" and "soft rock," designed to appeal to the widest possible demographic and promoted on Top 40 radio and television. Musicians as diverse as Led Zeppelin; Stevie Wonder; Elton John; Carole King; Pink Floyd; Paul Simon; Neil Diamond; Crosby, Stills, and Nash; the Rolling Stones; Frank Zappa and the Mothers of Invention; and Santana were promoted by record companies under the general heading of rock music. Even Frank Sinatra, scarcely a rock musician, tried his hand at a Beatles song or two.

There were, however, some important exceptions to the general popular appeal of rock music. Record sales in black communities, as reflected in the *Billboard* soul charts during the 1970s, do not suggest much interest in rock music. (The Rolling Stones managed to get only one of their singles into *Billboard*'s soul Top 40 chart during the decade, and multiplatinum rock acts such as Led Zeppelin, Deep Purple, and Pink Floyd made no dent whatsoever.) While the Monterey and Woodstock rock festivals had featured performances by African American artists, the promise of rock music as a zone of interracial interaction seemed to have largely vanished by the early 1970s. Many of the white rock stars who had formed their styles through exposure to earlier styles of blues and R&B seemed to have little interest in contemporary black popular music of the 1970s. As one critic put it in 1971, "Black musicians are now implicitly regarded as precursors who, having taught the white men all they know, must gradually recede into the distance" (Morse 1971, p. 108).

While there was no clear successor to Jimi Hendrix in the decade following Woodstock—that is, no single artist who could champion the presence of black musicians in rock music—we can point to a number of interestingly diverse interactions between soul music and rock. Several prominent black musicians—Sly Stone, Stevie Wonder, Marvin Gaye, and George Clinton—were able to connect long-standing aspects of African American musical traditions with elements from rock, including the notion of the musician as an artistic mastermind and of the LP record album as a work of art. In addition to their intrinsic importance, the varied work of these musicians paved the way for later artists such as Prince and Michael Jackson.

Early rock festivals such as Monterey (1967) and Woodstock (1969), regarded as the climax of the 1960s counterculture, had by the early 1970s mutated into highly profitable mass-audience concerts, held in civic centers and sports arenas across the country. In 1973 the British hard rock group Led Zeppelin (see below) toured the United States, breaking the world record for live concert attendance set by the Beatles during their tours of the mid-1960s. A whole series of bands that sprang up in the early 1970s—Styx, Journey, Kansas, REO Speedwagon, ZZ Top, Rush, and others—tailored their performances to the concert context, touring the country with elaborate light shows, spectacular sets, and powerful amplification systems, transported in caravans of semi trucks. For most rock fans, the live concert was the peak of musical experience—you hadn't really heard Led Zeppelin, it was said, until you'd heard and seen them live (and spent a little money on a poster or T-shirt, imprinted with the band's image). Of course, the relationship between rock stars and their devotees at these concerts was anything but intimate. Nonetheless, the sheer enormity, the sound and spectacle of a rock concert, helped to create a visceral sensation of belonging to a larger community, a temporary city formed by fans.

In the 1960s recordings such as the Beach Boys' *Pet Sounds* (1966), the Beatles' *Sgt. Pepper's Lonely Hearts Club Band* (1967), and the Who's "rock opera" *Tommy* (1969) established the idea of the record album as a thematically and aesthetically unified work and not simply a collection of otherwise unrelated cuts. By the early 1970s the twelve-inch high-fidelity LP had become established as the primary medium for rock music.

What makes a rock album more than a mere collection of singles? Let's start with a basic fact about the medium, its capacity: a twelve-inch disc, played at $33\frac{1}{3}$ r.p.m., could accommodate more than forty minutes of music, over twenty minutes per side. In the 1950s and early 1960s little creative use was made of this additional real estate—most rock 'n' roll–era LPs consist of a few hit singles, interspersed with a lot of less carefully produced filler. During the second half of the 1960s rock musicians began to treat the time span of the LP as a total entity, a field of potentiality akin to a painter's canvas. They also began to put more effort into *all* of the songs on an album, and to think of creative ways to link songs together, creating an overall progression of peaks and valleys. (Of course, old habits die hard, and most progressive rock albums still used songs, each approximately three to six minutes in length, as basic building blocks.)

The development of studio technology also encouraged musicians to experiment with novel techniques. High-fidelity stereo sound, heard over good speakers or headphones, placed the listener in the middle of the music (and the music in the middle of the listener!) and allowed sound sources to be "moved around." The advent of 16-, 24-, and 32-track recording consoles and electronic sound devices allowed musicians—and the record producers and studio engineers with whom they worked—to create complex aural textures, and to construct a given track on an LP over a period of time, adding and subtracting (or "punching in" and "punching out") individual instruments and voices. Innovations in the electronic synthesis of sound led to instruments like the Melotron, which could imitate the sound of a string orchestra in the studio and at live performances.

The musical response to the opportunities provided by these technological changes varied widely. Some rock bands became famous for spending many months (and tons of money) in the studio to create a single rock "masterpiece." A few multitalented musicians, such as Stevie Wonder and Edgar Winter, took advantage of multitracking to play all of the instruments on a given track. Other musicians reacted against the dependence on studio technology, recording their albums the old-fashioned way, with little overdubbing. (As we shall see, when punk rock arose in the late 1970s as a reaction against the pretentiousness of studio-bound progressive rock, musicians insisted on doing recordings in one take to create the sense of a live performance experience.) Studio technology could even be used to create the impression that studio technology was not being used, as in many folk rock albums.

Although the idea of creating some sort of continuity between the individual tracks, and of creating an inclusive structure that could provide the listener with a sense of progression, was shared widely, rock musicians took a range of approaches to this problem. One way to get a sense of this range is to listen to a handful of classic rock LPs from the early 1970s.

Some rock albums are centered on a fictitious character whose identity is analogous to that of one or more musicians in the band. Perhaps the best-known example of this strategy is *The Rise and Fall of Ziggy Stardust and the Spiders from Mars* (1972), the creation of "glam rock" pioneer David Bowie. (Glam—short for *glamour*—rock emphasized the elaborate, showy personal appearance and costuming of its practitioners.) In this case, the coherence of the album derives more from the imaginative and magnetic persona of the singer and his character than from the music itself. As Bowie put it, "I packaged a totally credible plastic rock star," an alien who comes to visit Earth and becomes first a superstar and finally a "Rock 'n' Roll Suicide," perishing under the weight of his own fame. Much of the LP's effect was connected with the striking image of Bowie playing the role of Ziggy, decked out in futuristic clothing and heavy facial makeup, a sensitive rocker, sexy in an androgynous, cosmic way. The *Ziggy Stardust* concert tour was a theatrical tour de force, with special lighting effects and spectacular costumes, and set the standard for later rock acts, ranging from "new wave" bands like the Talking Heads (see Chapter 7) to hard rockers like Kiss. Bowie's unique ability to create quasi-fictional stage personae, and to change them with every new album, was a precedent for the image manipulation of 1980s stars like Michael Jackson, Prince, and Madonna.

Other successful rock albums were held together not by a central character or coherent plotline, but by an emotional, philosophical, or political theme. The album *Blue* (1971), composed and performed by the singer-songwriter Joni Mitchell, consists of a cycle of songs about the complexities of love. The album is carefully designed to create a strong emotional focus, which is in turn clearly related to the autobiography of the singer herself. In some ways *Blue* is a culmination of the tendency inherent in the folk rock and singer-songwriter genres toward self-revelation. Even the most optimistic songs on the album—"All I Want," "My Old Man," and "Carey"—have a bittersweet flavor. Some—such as "Little Green," about a child given up for adoption, and the concluding track "The Last Time I Saw Richard"—are delicate yet powerful testimonials to the shared human experience of emotional loss. The sound of the LP is spare and beautiful, focusing on Mitchell's voice and acoustic guitar. This is a case where studio technology is used to create a feeling of simplicity and immediacy.

Dark Side of the Moon (1973), an album by the British rock band Pink Floyd is based on the theme of madness and the things that drive us to it—time, work, money, war, and fear of death. The LP opens with the sound of a beating heart, then a ticking clock, a typewriter, a cash register, gunfire, and the voices of members of Pink Floyd's stage crew, discussing their own experiences with insanity. The album's feeling of unity has something to do with its languid, carefully measured pace—most of the songs are slow to midtempo—as well as its musical texture and mood. In terms of style, the progression moves from spacey, neo-psychedelic sound textures to jazz and blues-influenced songs and then back to psychedelia. The sound of the record, produced by Alan Parsons, is complex but clear, and interesting use is made of sound effects, as in the song "Money," with its sampled sounds of clinking coins and cash registers, treated as rhythmic accompaniment. (This achievement is particularly impressive when we recall that 1973 was before the advent of digital recording techniques.)

If there was ever an antidote to the notion that popular music must be cheerful and upbeat in order to be successful, *Dark Side of the Moon* is it. This meditation on insanity stayed on the *Billboard* Top LPs charts for over fourteen years, longer than any other LP in history, and sold twenty-five million copies worldwide. In recent years, various mythologies have grown up around *Dark Side of the Moon*. For example, it is claimed that the album can be synchronized with the 1939 film *The Wizard of Oz*. Many people maintain that if you start the album up after the MGM Lion's third roar there are some amazing synchronicities. (For example, the song "Brain Damage" begins playing just as the Scarecrow starts to sing "If I Only Had a Brain"). Whatever the merit of these claims, it is clear that Pink Floyd's *Dark Side of the Moon* continues to exert a powerful, if somewhat dark, fascination upon millions of rock fans.

A final example of the "theme album" is <u>Marvin Gaye</u>'s bestselling LP *What's Going On* (1971), which fused soul music and gospel influence with the political impetus of progressive rock. The basic unifying theme of this album is social justice. The title track, inspired by the return of Gaye's brother from Vietnam, is a plea for nonviolence, released during the peak of antiwar protests in the United States. Other songs focus on ecology, the welfare of children, and the suffering of poor people in America's urban centers. Gaye cowrote the songs and produced the album himself, supporting his voice—overdubbed to sound like an entire vocal group—with layers of percussion, strings, and horns. Once again, the producer's consideration of the overall sound texture of the album had a great deal to do with its aesthetic effect and commercial success.

Motown owner Berry Gordy initially didn't want to release *What's Going On*, thinking it had no commercial potential. This was a rare case of misjudgment on Gordy's part; the album reached Number Two on the LP charts and generated three Number One singles on the soul charts, all of which crossed over to the pop Top 10: the title song, "Mercy Mercy Me (The Ecology)," and "Inner City Blues (Make Me Wanna Holler)." Two other tracks, "Wholy Holy" and "Save the Children," inspired hit cover versions by Aretha Franklin and Diana Ross. But the significance of this album, and of Marvin Gaye's commitment to a socially responsible aesthetic vision, surpasses any measure of commercial success. Along with Stevie Wonder and Sly Stone, Marvin Gaye showed that soul and R&B albums could provide artistic coherence that transcended the three-minute single, managed to bridge the divide between AM Top 40, FM album-oriented radio, and the soul music market, and held open the possibility that popular music might still have something to do with social change, as well as money making and artistic self-expression.

A strategy that was fairly unusual in rock music was the adoption of elements of large-scale structure from European classical music. The live album *Pictures at an Exhibition* (1971), recorded by the art rock band Emerson, Lake, and Palmer, adopts its main themes and some of its structural elements from a suite of piano pieces by the Russian composer Modest Musorgsky (1839–81). This was a canny choice, since Musorgsky's composition—inspired by a walk through an art gallery—consists of a sequence of accessible, reasonably short, easily digestible "paintings," a parallel with the song format of much popular music. Some sections of the LP are reorchestrations of the original score (making prominent use of Keith Emerson's virtuosity on organ and synthesizer), while others are improvisations on the borrowed materials, and still others new songs by the band, musing on ideas in the music. The album concludes with "Nutrocker," a rock 'n' roll version of Tchaikovsky's *Nutcracker Suite*.

In the end, however, rock music is less centrally concerned with large-scale, architectural structures than with the immediate experience of musical texture, rhythmic momentum, and emotional intensity. Many of the most effective rock albums do not have an overarching structural logic, a story to tell, or a single organizing image, but rather find their unity in a visceral cohesion of musical style, texture, and attitude. *Exile on Main Street* (1972), now often cited as the best album ever recorded by the Rolling Stones, had decidedly mixed reviews when it first came out, because of its impenetrable sound and the inaudibility of its lyrics. Even the

Box 6.2 Album Art

If the rock LP was a container for music, it was also an art object in its own right. LP dust jackets often featured a printed version of the lyrics and a range of highly imaginative designs. Covers conveyed a lot, not only about a rock group's physical appearance, but also about their aesthetic aims and personality. Some showed concert photos of the artists at work; Jimi Hendrix's *Band of Gypsys* (1970) and Deep Purple's *Made in Japan* (1973) were bestselling examples. Others revealed some aspect of the musicians' private lives; the eponymous LP *Crosby Stills and Nash* (1969) has a cover photo of the three folk rock musicians lounging on an old sofa on the front porch of a house, while the inside of Marvin Gaye's *What's Going On* (1971) contains a photo collage of his family. The sexuality of rock stars was often emphasized, as on the Rolling Stones' quadruple-platinum LP *Sticky Fingers* (1971), which featured a close-up photograph of the crotch of Mick Jagger's blue jeans, complete with a working zipper! Other covers, particularly of hard rock and heavy metal albums, tapping into the sexual fantasies of the young male audience for rock music, featured scantily clad women in suggestive poses. Alternative models of sexuality also found their way onto album covers, the most notorious example being David Bowie's *Diamond Dogs* (1975), which featured an androgynous Bowie-canine creature with its genitals exposed. (The cover created a furor and was soon yanked from the shelves of record stores and replaced with a tamer alternative.)

Record companies often gave dust-jacket artists wide latitude to invent visual analogues to the music inside. The cover of *Brain Salad Surgery* (1973), a Top 10 LP by the art rock band Emerson, Lake, and Palmer, was designed by the Swiss artist H. R. Giger, who went on create the nightmarish creature in the film *Alien*. The Latin rock band Santana's second LP, *Abraxas* (1970), presented a colorful psychedelic rendering of the fusion of European and African cultural influences. Even reissues of oldies from the 1950s and 1960s were given imaginative treatments, as on the Drifters' *Greatest Recordings* album cover (1971), which took an old publicity photo and turned it into a psychedelic image. Finally, some album designs featured a minimalist approach, the prototypical example being *The Beatles* (1968), whose stark white cover earned it the nickname "the White Album."

cover art for the LP—a photographic collage of freaks and misfits—seemed designed to repel many in the Stones' loyal audience, who had followed the band since their early days as the slightly nasty counterpart of the Beatles. In *Exile on Main Street* we have an album—actually a double album, containing two LPs and eighteen songs—that is held together by its texture (dense, dark, guitar-based rock 'n' roll), its rough, unpolished studio sound (reminiscent on some tracks of Elvis Presley's early work with Sun Records), and its bad attitude (personified by the sneering, mumbling Mick Jagger). The material is strongly oriented toward the Stones' musical roots, as it consists mainly of blues-based rockers like "Rocks Off," "Shake Your Hips," and "Tumbling Dice," with a few examples of country and folk music influence ("Sweet Virginia" and "Sweet Black Angel").

Exile on Main Street was recorded in the basement of guitarist Keith Richards's home in France—where the Stones were living in tax exile at the time—and Jagger's voice is purposefully buried in the mix, under the gritty guitars, bass, and drums, and the occasional horn section. (The producer Jimmy Miller was largely responsible for creating the LPs cohesive sound palette.) The overall impression is one of bleakness and desolation, a reflection of the Stones' state at the time. The band's abuse of drugs and alcohol was so intense that members of the band have since wondered aloud how they ever got the record made. *Exile on Main Street* is at once an apotheosis of the Stones' image as bad boys, and a tip of the hat to the influences that formed their style, including urban blues, soul, and country music.

LISTENING AND ANALYSIS   "STAIRWAY TO HEAVEN" AND "OYE COMO VA"

To gain a better sense of the variety of rock music during the early 1970s, we are going to take a closer look at two tracks from highly successful albums: "Stairway to Heaven," from *Led Zeppelin IV* (1971); and "Oye Como Va," a Top 20 hit from Santana's quadruple-platinum album *Abraxas* (1970). These two examples will suffice to show the diversity of music that was produced, promoted, and consumed under the general label of rock music during this period. One was the granddaddy of heavy metal music, a bombastic fusion of guitar-driven rock 'n' roll, psychedelia, art rock, and folk music; and the other a fascinating amalgam of blues, jazz, rock, and Latin American popular music, a progenitor of the world beat movement of the 1980s and 1990s (see Chapter 9).

Led Zeppelin and Heavy Metal

By the early 1970s the British hard rock band Led Zeppelin, formed in London in 1968, was well on its way to becoming the most profitable and influential act in rock music. "Zep," as its fans called it, was made up of Jimmy Page, a brilliant guitarist who had honed his skills as Eric Clapton's successor in a pioneering British band called the Yardbirds; John Bonham, who established the thunderous sound of heavy metal drumming; John Paul Jones, who provided the band's solid bottom, doubling on electric bass and organ; and Robert Plant, whose agile high tenor voice established the norm for subsequent heavy metal singers. Zeppelin's sledgehammer style of guitar-focused rock music drew on various influences, including urban blues, San Francisco psychedelia, and the virtuoso guitar playing of Jimi Hendrix. Although Led Zeppelin is usually associated with the heavy textures and extremely loud volume of their hard rock repertoire, their recordings also included another important stream—an interest in folk music, particularly the traditions of the British Isles.

"Stairway to Heaven" is Led Zeppelin's most famous recording, and it reflects certain unique features of the band's musical approach, as well as its position vis-à-vis the commercial mainstream of pop music. To begin with, the song presents us with a fascinating marketing strategy, at first glance perverse, but actually quite brilliant. Although "Stairway to Heaven" was the most frequently requested song on FM radio during the 1970s, the eight-minute track was never released as a single. In other words, to own a copy of "Stairway to Heaven," you had to buy the album. Of course, that could prove difficult for the uninitiated consumer, since the band insisted on an album cover that bore neither the name of the album, nor the name of the band, nor the name of the record company. (Atlantic Records was horrified by this design, but the band held the master tapes for the album hostage, and the record company had no choice but to go along.) Driven in part by the popularity of "Stairway to Heaven," the LP *Led Zeppelin IV* reached the Number Two position on the *Billboard* Top LP charts and stayed on the charts for five years, eventually selling fourteen million copies.

"Stairway to Heaven" has been called the "anthem" of heavy metal music, a genre that developed out of hard rock in the 1970s and achieved mainstream success in the 1980s (see Chapter 8; other examples of early proto-metal bands include Deep Purple and Black Sabbath). What accounts for this recording's tremendous commercial success and its ability to ignite the imaginations and inspire the loyalty of millions of fans? To begin with, "Stairway" skillfully juxtaposes two dimensions of Led Zeppelin's musical persona—the bone-crushing rock band, known for inspiring riots and dismantling hotel rooms, and the folk music aficionados, steeped in a reverence for ancient English and Celtic mythology. While these two sensibilities might seem diametrically opposed, the twin musical threads of sonic aggression and acoustic intimacy run through the entire history of heavy metal. (Most heavy metal albums include at least one "ballad," a term that in this context usually implies the use of acoustic guitar.) For many fans in Zeppelin's predominantly young, male audience, the combination of rock physicality and folk mysticism in "Stairway to Heaven" created something akin to a sacred experience. The somewhat inscrutable song text, composed by singer Robert Plant during a rehearsal, was also an important source of the recording's attraction. Both Plant and Jimmy Page were at the time exploring the writings of the noted English mystic Aleister Crowley—into whose house Page eventually moved—and reading scholarly tomes like *Magic Arts in Celtic Britain*, which Plant later said influenced the lyrics for "Stairway." The text's

LISTENING CHART "STAIRWAY TO HEAVEN"

Music and lyrics by Jimmy Page and Robert Plant; performed by Led Zeppelin; recorded 1971

FORM	LYRICS	DESCRIPTIVE COMMENTS
Section One (0:00)		
A (8 measures)	Instrumental	Six-string acoustic guitar; double-tracked recorder (flute) duet enters in measure 5; Slow tempo (72 beats per minute).
B (8)		Guitar and recorders continue.
A (8)	*There's a lady . . . When she gets there . . .*	Vocal enters.
B (4)	*Ooo . . . And she's buying . . .*	
A (8)	*There's a sign . . . In a tree . . .*	
A' (4)	Instrumental	Six-string guitar and recorders continue.
Section Two (2:14)		Twelve-string guitar, soft electric guitar, electric piano; intensity increases, tempo slightly faster (80 b.p.m.).
B (8)	*Oooo, It makes . . . Oooo, It makes . . .*	
A (8)	*There's a feeling . . . In my thoughts . . .*	
X (1)	Instrumental	One-measure linking section; electric guitar becomes more dominant.
B (8)	*Oooo, It makes . . . Oooo, really makes . . .*	Texture thickens, volume and tempo increase slightly.
A (8)	*And it's whispered . . . And a new day . . .*	
X (1)	Instrumental	Linking section.
B (8)		Slight crescendo, slight tempo increase. Drums enter at end, leading us into next section.
Section Three (4:19)		
C (8)	*If there's a bustle . . . Yes there are . . .*	New minor chord progression; electric guitar, twelve-string acoustic guitar, plus electric bass and drum set; tempo faster (84 b.p.m.).
X (1)	Instrumental	Linking section.
B (8)	*And it makes . . .*	
C (8)	*Your head . . . Dear lady . . .*	
X—(2)	Instrumental	Linking section, plus one measure pause.
D (8)		Instrumental fanfare using chords from C; Tempo speeds up, leading us into next section.

Guitar Solo (20)	| | | | |	Chord pattern continues; tempo faster (ca. 98 b.p.m.); multitracked guitar plays supporting pattern under solo (last 8 measures).
C (18)	*And as we . . . (4)* *There walks . . . (4)* *How everything . . . (4)* *The tune . . . (4)* *To be a rock . . . (2)*	
C (8)	Instrumental	Tempo slows down, intensity decreases.
B (3)	*And she's buying . . .*	Solo voice (rubato).

references to mythological beings—the May Queen and the Piper—and rural images—paths and roads, rings of smoke through the forest, a songbird by a brook, the whispering wind—helped to create a cumulative mood of mystery and enchantment.

Although the basic building blocks of "Stairway to Heaven" are straightforward four- and eight-bar phrases, the overall arrangement is quite complex in formal terms (see the listening chart). There are three main sections. Section One alternates two eight-measure phrases, which we are calling A and B. The basic form of Section One is ABABAA' (the last section being an abridged version of A). Section Two reverses the order of the phrases and inserts a brief one-measure linking phrase (which we are calling X). The form of Section Two is BAXBAXB. Section Three, which takes up almost half of the total eight minutes of recording time, introduces a new (though closely related) chord progression and melody, which we are calling C.[1] The first part of Section Three has the form CXBCX. After a one-measure pause, this is followed by an instrumental fanfare that propels us into Jimmy Page's guitar solo. Robert Plant's voice then reenters, and there is an extended vocal section, using the harmonies from phrase C. The arrangement concludes with an instrumental phrase, slowing down and becoming much quieter in the last two measures. The track concludes quietly, with Robert Plant repeating the key line of the text: *And she's buying a stairway to heaven*. The arrangement of "Stairway to Heaven" is constructed to create a continual escalation in density, volume, and speed. (The tempo increases from around 72 beats per minute at the opening of the recording to 84 beats per minute at the beginning of Section Three, and peaking at around 98 b.p.m. during the guitar solo. This substantial, though gradual, increase in speed is crucial to the overall impact of the recording.)

If "Stairway" seems complex in purely structural terms, this may be because the logic of its organization is fundamentally emotional and metaphoric. The recording can itself be seen as an analogue of the heavenly stairway, springing

---

1. Throughout "Stairway to Heaven," the harmonies circle around a set of closely related chords, including A minor, C major, and F major, giving the performance an additional sense of continuity.

from the rural, mythological past (symbolized by acoustic instruments), soaring on jet-powered wings of metal, and finally coming to rest on a high, peaceful plateau. Similarly, the outer cover of the original album juxtaposes the sepia image of a peasant with that of a modern skyscraper rising over the formerly rustic landscape. The inner jacket portrays a mysterious hooded figure standing atop an icy peak with a staff and a lantern, looking down at a bell-bottomed seeker of knowledge who struggles to reach the top. Also included inside the album's dust jacket are the lyrics to "Stairway to Heaven" and a set of mystical symbols, or runes, one of which inspired the informal name for the album, "zoso." In seeking to understand what a recording like "Stairway" meant to its fans, the analysis of musical form must be coupled with a consideration of its other expressive dimensions, including the song text and the graphic design of the album on which it appeared.

Santana: The Roots of Rock Multiculturalism

If rock was quintessentially defined for many listeners by white bands like Led Zeppelin, Pink Floyd, and the Rolling Stones, the San Francisco–based group Santana reveals a nascent trend within rock music toward multicultural engagement. The band was led by guitarist Carlos Santana (b. 1947, in Mexico), who began his musical career playing guitar in the nightspots of Tijuana. As a kid he was exposed to the sounds of rock 'n' roll, including the music of Mexican American musicians such as Ritchie Valens, whose version of the folk song "La Bamba" had broken into the *Billboard* Top 40 in early 1959. Santana moved to San Francisco at age fifteen, where he was exposed to other forms of music that were to play a profound part in shaping the style and sensibility of his music: jazz, particularly the experimental music of John Coltrane and Miles Davis; salsa, a New York–based style of Latin dance music strongly rooted in Afro-Cuban traditions; and in the late 1960s, San Francisco rock, including artists as diverse as Janis Joplin, Jimi Hendrix, and Sly and the Family Stone (see Chapter 5). Around 1968 Santana put together a group of middle- and working-class Latino, black, and white musicians from varied cultural backgrounds. The band's eponymous first album, *Santana*, released in 1969, reached Number Four on the Top LPs chart, in large part due to the band's spectacular performance in the film and soundtrack LP of *Woodstock*.

In 1970 Columbia Records released Santana's second LP, which firmly established both the band itself and a strong Latin American substream within rock music. *Abraxas* held the Number One position on the LP charts for six weeks, spent a total of eighty-eight weeks on the charts, and sold over four million copies in the United States alone. The album also produced two Top 40 singles: "Black Magic Woman" (Number Four pop in 1970), originally recorded by the English blues rock band Fleetwood Mac; and the infectious "Oye Como Va" (Number Thirteen pop, Number Thirty-two R&B in 1971), composed by New York Latin percussionist and dance music king Tito Puente. These two singles, which had a great deal to do with the success of the album, were shorter versions of the tracks found on the LP. (This was a typical strategy, given the duration of tracks on many rock LPs.) Tying blues, rock, and salsa together in one multicultural

Carlos Santana. Frank Driggs Collection.

package, *Abraxas* also featured less commercial tracks such as "Gypsy Queen" (composed by the jazz guitarist Gabor Szabo), and the impressionistic "Singing Winds, Crying Beasts."

We will take a closer look at the LP version of "Oye Como Va," since it allows the band to stretch out a bit and best illustrates certain features of Santana's style. To appreciate what goes into a recording like "Oye Como Va," we must consider not only the instrumentation—essentially a guitar-bass-keyboards-drums rock band plus Latin percussion—but also the recording's "mix," that is, the precise tonal quality, balancing, and positioning of sounds recorded on various tracks in the studio. (*Abraxas* was coproduced by the band and Fred Catero, whose straightforward approach to studio production can also be heard on early LPs of the jazz rock band Chicago.) Santana's instantly recognizable sound focused on the fluid lead guitar style of Carlos Santana and the churning grooves created by the drummer (Mike Shrieve), the bass player (Dave Brown), and two Latin percussionists (Jose Areas and Mike Carabello). The rhythmic complexity of "Oye Como Va"—essentially an electrified version of an Afro-Cuban dance rhythm—required that the recording be mixed to create a "clean" stereo image, so that the various instruments and interlocking rhythm patterns could be clearly heard. Listening over headphones or good speakers, you should be able to hear where the various instruments are positioned in the mix. The electric bass is in the middle, acting as the band's rhythmic anchor; the guitar and keyboards are placed slightly to the left and right of center, respectively, and thus kept out of each other's way; and the percussion instruments (including guiro, a ridged gourd scraped with a small stick; *timbales*, a set of two drums played with flexible sticks; *agogo*, a metal bell; and *congas*, hand-played drums) are positioned even farther out to the left and right.

The track opens with the electric bass and Hammond B-3 organ—one of the most characteristic sounds of 1970s rock music—playing the interlocking pattern that functions as the core of the groove throughout the recording. (In a salsa band, this two-measure pattern would be called the *tumbao*.) In the background we hear someone say "Sabor!" ("Flavor!") and at the end of the fourth measure the *timbales* and *agogo* enter, bringing in the rest of the instruments at the beginning of the fifth measure. At this point all of the interlocking repeated patterns—bass, organ, bell, scraper, and congas—have been established. The signature sound of Carlos Santana's guitar enters in the ninth measure, as he plays a two-measure melodic theme four times. This is followed by the first of four sections in which the whole band plays a single rhythmic and melodic pattern in unison (in the listening chart we call these sections B and B', respectively). Throughout the track, the rhythm functions as the heart of the music. As if to remind us of the importance of this deep connection with Afro-Latin tradition, all of the other layers are periodically stripped away, laying bare the pulsing heart of the music.

At the most general level, we can make a few observations about how the four minutes and seventeen seconds of "Oye Como Va" are organized. The whole arrangement is 136 measures in length; out of that total only 16 measures (about 12 percent of the total) is devoted to singing, which in this context seems almost a pretext for the instrumental music. In general, song lyrics are less important than the musical groove and texture in most of Santana's early recordings. (The lyric for this song consists of a short phrase in Spanish, repeated over and over, in which the singer boasts about the potency of his "groove" to a brown-skinned female dancer.)

Taking away the other obviously precomposed elements—the guitar melody (phrase A), unison figures played by the whole band (B, B', and the call-and-response figure after the first guitar solo), and the other interlude sections—we find that nearly half of the recording (66 measures) is devoted to improvised solos by the guitar and organ. The other elements of the arrangement—including the dramatic group crescendos that lead into the last two solos—seem designed to support improvisation. In essence, then, "Oye Como Va" is a vehicle for instrumental soloing, more like a jazz performance than a Top 40 pop song. (Of course, it is precisely the solos that Columbia Records chose to cut when they edited the track for AM radio airplay.) In particular, Carlos Santana's solos on "Oye Como Va" provide us with a good example of the work of a talented rock improviser. Rather than playing torrents of fast notes to show off his guitar technique (which was and remains considerable), Santana uses the electric guitar's ability to sustain notes for long periods of time to create long, flowing melodic lines that gradually rise in intensity, lifting the whole band with him. In live performance, of course, Santana and other instrumental soloists could stretch out for much more than four and a half minutes. If the soft side of rock often worked within the restricted time format imposed by Top 40 radio, progressive rock bands such as Santana, the Allman Brothers, and the Grateful Dead kept alive the notion of extended, open-ended performance, an important part of the legacy of the San Francisco rock scene of the late 1960s (see Chapter 5).

LISTENING CHART "OYE COMO VA"

Music and lyrics by Tito Puente; performed by Santana; recorded 1971

FORM	LYRICS	DESCRIPTIVE COMMENTS
Groove (8)	Instrumental	The basic *cha-cha* rhythm is established on organ, electric bass, and (from the fifth measure) percussion.
A (8)		The guitar states a two-measure melodic phrase four times (with minor embellishments).
B (4)		A unison figure, played by the whole band.
C (8)	*Oye como va . . .*	Vocals (two four-measure phrases)
B' (2)	Instrumental	The unison figure again (first half only).
Guitar Solo (20)		Extended solo by Carlos Santana.
Interlude (6)		Call-and-response exchange between guitar and band.
Groove (4)		Stripped down to the basics again.
Interlude (8)		Suddenly quieter; organ and guitar play chord pattern; gradual crescendo.
Organ solo (22)		
Groove (4)		One more time!
B' (2)		The unison figure again (first half only).
C (8)	*Oye como va . . .*	Vocals (two four-measure phrases)
Interlude (4)	Instrumental	Suddenly quieter, then crescendo.
Guitar solo (24)		Another solo by Carlos Santana.
B (4)		The unison figure again, functioning as a tag.

Although the 1970s are often portrayed as a time of corporate consolidation and conservatism in popular music, that was only one dimension of a more complex story. In the next chapter we will examine a number of developments that extend a pattern we have discerned in earlier periods: the continual refreshing of popular music by performers and styles situated at the margins of the commercial mainstream. In the creativity and energy of genres such as progressive country, reggae, punk, funk, and disco, we will find affirmation both of changes in the business of music and of deep continuities underlying the history of American popular music.

CHAPTER SEVEN

OUTSIDERS' MUSIC

Progressive Country, Reggae, Punk, Funk, and Disco, 1970s

Although the 1970s are often described as a period of stylistic conservatism and corporate consolidation in popular music, the decade also fostered music that did not fit neatly into the frameworks of Top 40 radio, album-oriented rock, or the Nashville sound. The genres we will be discussing in this chapter arose, for the most part, as a response to the conservatism of the music industry; the exception is reggae music, which came from completely outside the commercial mainstream of the American music industry. Each of these genres embodied in its own way the contradictions built into the popular music industry, and the complex processes by which the mainstream and the margins of popular music are continually redefined.

THE OUTLAWS: PROGRESSIVE COUNTRY MUSIC

During the late 1960s and early 1970s, mainstream country music was dominated by the slick Nashville sound, by the hardcore country of artists like Merle Haggard, and by various blends of country and pop promoted on AM Top 40 radio (see Chapter 6). But a new generation of country musicians at this time began to embrace the music and attitudes that had grown out of the 1960s **counterculture**. *Progressive country,* as this movement came to be known, was inspired by the honky-tonk and **rockabilly** amalgam of Bakersfield country music, the singer-songwriter genre (especially the work of Bob Dylan), and the country rock style of musicians like Gram Parsons, who was a member of the Byrds for a brief time in the late 1960s. In general, progressive country performers wrote songs that were more intellectual and liberal in outlook than their contemporaries and were more concerned with testing the limits of the country music tradition than with scoring hits. Many of the movement's key artists—including Willie Nelson, Kris Kristofferson, Tom T. Hall, and Townes Van Zandt—were not polished singers by conventional standards, yet they wrote distinctive, individualistic songs and had compelling voices. Such artists developed a sizable cult following, and progressive country began to inch its way into the mainstream, usually in the form of cover versions. Tom T. Hall's "Harper Valley PTA" was a Number One pop and country hit for Jeannie C. Riley as early as 1968, while Sammi Smith took Kris Kristofferson's "Help Me Make It through the Night" to the top of the country charts and into the pop Top 10 in 1971.

One of the most influential figures in the progressive country movement was Willie Nelson (born in Texas in 1933). Nelson had already developed a successful career as a professional songwriter when he left Nashville to return to Texas in 1971. (Nelson's song "Crazy" had been a Top 10 country and pop hit for Patsy Cline in 1961.) He settled in Austin, a university town and home to one of the most energetic and eclectic live music scenes in the country. At "cosmic cowboy" venues such as the Armadillo World Headquarters, and on Austin radio station KOKE-FM, a fusion of country music and countercultural sensibilities was already well under way. Nelson fit right in to the Austin scene, letting his hair and beard grow long and donning a headband, an earring, jogging shoes, and bluejeans (one of the few markers of cultural identity shared by rednecks, cowboys, and hippies!). Singing in an unpolished, almost conversational voice—an approach that had frustrated his attempts to gain success as a recording artist in Nashville—Willie Nelson bridged the gap between rock and country without losing touch with his honky-tonk roots. In the summer of 1971 he organized the first of a series of outdoor festivals that included older country musicians (e.g., Roy Acuff and Earl Scruggs) as well as younger musicians who were experimenting with a blend of country and rock music. These "picnics," closer in ethos to Woodstock than to the *Grand Ole Opry*, brought thousands of rock fans into the fold of country music and prepared the way for Nelson's ascendance as the preeminent male country music star of the 1980s.

Willie Nelson's initial rise to national fame came in the mid-1970s, through his association with a group of musicians collectively known as "the Outlaws." The centerpiece of the Outlaws was another Texas-born musician, Waylon Jennings (1937–2002). Jennings began his career as a musician and disk jockey and in 1958 joined Buddy Holly's rock 'n' roll group, the Crickets. In the early 1960s he set up shop at a nightclub in Phoenix, Arizona, where the clientele included businessmen, college students, and cowboys, a diverse audience that encouraged him to develop a broad repertoire. In 1965 he was signed by RCA Victor and relocated to Nashville. Although RCA producer Chet Atkins—who had remolded Elvis into a pop star in 1956—attempted to push him in the direction of the countrypolitan sound popular at the time, Jennings resisted these efforts, eventually winning substantial leeway in his choice of material. (His early 1970s LPs included Beatles songs such as "Norwegian Wood" and "You've Got to Hide Your Love Away.")

While he chose to remain close to the music industry in Nashville rather than return to Texas, Jennings cultivated an image as a rebel, and in 1972 recorded an album called *Ladies Love Outlaws*. On the cover he appeared in "bad guy" dress, complete with a black cowboy hat and a six-shooter. The commercial potential of the outlaw image was soon recognized by music publicists in Nashville, who lost

Box 7.1 A Country Concept Album: *Red-Headed Stranger* (1975)

One of the ideas that progressive country musicians adopted from rock music during the 1970s was that of the concept album. The central medium for the transmission of country music during the 1970s was still the individual song, and although some country LPs sold well, 45 r.p.m. singles remained the bread and butter of the industry. During the mid-1970s, however, progressive country musicians began to create albums unified around a single theme or dramatic character. Perhaps the best example of this trend is Willie Nelson's album *Red-Headed Stranger* (1975), which sold over two million copies and reached Number Twenty-eight on *Billboard*'s Top LPs chart. (*Billboard* had no separate LP charts for country or soul music, since these genres were assumed by definition to be singles-oriented.) *Red-Headed Stranger* included Nelson's first big crossover hit as a singer, rather than as a songwriter—"Blue Eyes Crying in the Rain," Number Twenty-one pop and Number One country—and established the notion of the country concept album.

Of course, the technique of telling stories through song had long been part of the Anglo-American ballad tradition, one of the main taproots of country music. In putting together *Red-Headed Stranger*, a meticulously crafted song cycle outlining the saga of a broken-hearted cowboy, Nelson stuck close to the traditional time limit of three minutes per song, alternating songs with shorter bits of material that established the narrative context (for example, dance music to give us the feeling of a turn-of-the-century saloon in Denver). The musical accompaniment—acoustic guitar, electric guitar, mandolin, piano, harmonica, electric bass, and drums—is strikingly spare and restrained, and some tracks use only acoustic guitar and piano (played by Nelson's sister). The jacket sleeve featured excerpts from the lyrics, accompanied by paintings of the red-headed stranger in the various scenarios portrayed by the songs.

The album opens with the song "Time of the Preacher":

> *It was a time of the preacher, when the story began*
> *Of a choice of a lady, and the love of a man*
> *How he loved her so dearly, he went out of his mind*
> *When she left him for someone that she'd left behind*
>
> *He cried like a baby, and he screamed like a panther in the middle of the*
>   *night*
> *And he saddled his pony, and he went for a ride*
> *It was a time of the preacher, in the year of '01*
> *Now the preaching is over, and the lesson's begun.*

In the next song, only a minute and a half in length, Nelson adopts the first-person voice of the jilted cowboy, who discovers his wife's infidelity—"I couldn't believe it was true." This is followed by a reappearance of the "Time of the Preacher" song, which functions throughout the album as a thematic refrain, connecting the various songs. As the story unfolds, we observe the red-headed stranger tracking down his wife and her lover, shooting them dead in a tavern, and riding off on his black stallion. As in rock concept albums based on a dramatic character—say, *The Rise and Fall of Ziggy Stardust and the Spiders from Mars*—the line dividing the fictional persona in the song and the musician who sings the song is thin indeed. The album cover of *Red-Headed Stranger* portrays Nelson in cowboy dress, with a beard and long, ragged red-tinted hair, an image clearly intended to reinforce the longtime Nashville songwriter's public image as an outlaw musician.

no time turning it into a commercial term. The Outlaws were never a cohesive performing group: in fact, the label "outlaw country" was largely a product of the record industry's search for a way to capitalize on the overlap between audiences for rock and country music.

In 1976, after musicians such as Willie Nelson and Waylon Jennings had begun to receive substantial radio airplay, RCA Victor released a compilation of their early 1970s recordings entitled *Wanted: The Outlaws*. This LP included a mix of material, ranging from a version of the country music classic "T for Texas," first recorded under the title "Blue Yodel" by Jimmie Rodgers in 1927, to a cover of an Elvis Presley hit ("Suspicious Minds"), to Willie Nelson's humorous song "Me and Paul," in which the country singer compares his problems on the road to those of rock star Paul McCartney. The album was a huge success—it reached the Top 10 on *Billboard*'s Top LPs chart, soon became the first platinum country music LP, and eventually sold over two million copies. Though the Outlaws—like most "alternative"

Willie Nelson, looking very much the country outlaw. Frank Driggs Collection.

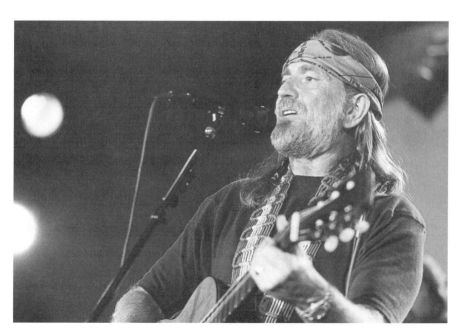

music movements—had a commercial dimension, they did represent a heartfelt rebellion against the conservatism of the country music establishment. Their approach found common ground in the past and the future of country music, managed to challenge briefly country pop's hold on the charts in the mid-1970s, and paved the way for later alternative country artists such as k.d. lang, Dwight Yoakam, and Lyle Lovett.

The song "Pancho and Lefty," performed by its composer, <u>Townes Van Zandt</u> (born 1944 in Ft. Worth, Texas, died 1997), is an instructive example of the idiosyncratic sensibility of much progressive country. Van Zandt was a singer-songwriter who became a cult hero of the progressive country movement. Though Van Zandt never placed a record on the country Top 40 charts, his fifteen LPs became underground classics, and his songs were covered by prominent country musicians. (Willie Nelson and Merle Haggard took a version of "Pancho and Lefty" to the top of the country charts in 1983.)

Van Zandt's performance of "Pancho and Lefty," from his 1972 LP *The Late, Great Townes Van Zandt,* is typical of his work: a spare, unpolished vocal style, with guitar accompaniment that often uses more complex harmonies than are typical in country music. (The use of Mexican mariachi-style trumpets at some points in the arrangement evokes the story's location, near the Rio Grande River.) In structural terms, this song fits within the European-derived ballad tradition that was such an important influence upon early country music. More specifically, "Pancho and Lefty" evokes an old Spanish ballad tradition that took root in Mexico, where it developed into a genre known as the *corrido.* Typical *corridos* exhibit the familiar ballad form, a series of four-line stanzas that tell a story about famous heroes and villains, historical events, or tragic romances, sung to a repeated melody and interrupted at regular intervals by a chorus.

Since the very beginnings of recorded country music songwriters have drawn on the themes and images of the Anglo-American cowboy ballad and the Mexican *corrido* in singing their stories of the exploits of heroes and outlaws along the Rio Grande. In a manner typical of progressive country songwriters, however, Van Zandt manages to put some new twists into an old form. The tale of Pancho and Lefty begins with a four-line stanza that functions as a framing device, in which the singer seems to be addressing one of the characters in the story in a direct, second-person voice:

> *Livin' on the road my friend, was gonna keep you free and clean*
> *Now you wear your skin like iron, and your breath's as hard as kerosene.*
> *You weren't your mama's only boy, but her favorite one it seems*
> *She began to cry when you said good-bye, and sank into your dreams.*

Van Zandt then sinks into the typical third-person voice of the ballad singer, an observer recounting a sequence of events. In a series of carefully constructed stanzas he describes the outlaw team of Pancho and Lefty, the former a young Mexican bandit who dies at the beginning of the story, the latter his Anglo accomplice, who through a series of misfortunes ends up in a flophouse in Cleveland, Ohio, wasting away as an old man.

> *Well the poets tell how Pancho fell, and Lefty's living in a cheap hotel*
> *The desert's quiet and Cleveland's cold, so the story ends we're told*

Pancho needs your prayers it's true, but save a few for Lefty, too
He just did what he had to do, and now he's growing old.

This is not the usual fate of outlaw heroes in the ballad tradition, who typically either meet their end in a hail of bullets or, through sheer wits, manage to escape to fight another day. As Van Zandt moves through the song, it becomes increasingly apparent that Lefty isn't such a hero after all, a point driven home by the chorus which describes the "kindness" shown Lefty by the federal marshals (*Federales*) who were his natural enemies:

And all the Federales say they could have had him any day
They only let him hang around out of kindness, I suppose.

The chorus becomes the object of a subtle manipulation, in which just a few words are altered each time through. After we find out that Lefty has fled to Ohio, the chorus informs us that the *federales* claim to have purposefully allowed the pitiful sap to escape with his life, out of kindness. By the end of the song, the federal marshals too have aged, and the chorus takes on an ironic tone:

A few grey Federales say they could have had him any day
They only let him go so wrong out of kindness, I suppose.

In the end, the listener is left uncertain—did Lefty betray his Mexican partner, leaving him at the mercy of the federal marshals, or is the whole story simply the dreamlike fantasy of a lonely old man, as the first stanza suggests?

Townes Van Zandt died prematurely at the age of fifty-two. However, his songs—which combine the straightforwardness of traditional country music with the poetic subtlety of singer-songwriters such as Bob Dylan—have inspired country and rock musicians ranging from Lyle Lovett to Neil Young.

"I SHOT THE SHERIFF": THE RISE OF REGGAE

Reggae—a potent mixture of Caribbean folk music and American rhythm & blues—was the first style of the rock era to originate in the so-called Third World. The popularity of reggae in America may be related both to earlier "exotic" music crazes—the Argentine tango and the Cuban rumba—and to the coming world beat movement of the 1980s and 1990s. Born in the impoverished shantytowns of Kingston, Jamaica, reggae first became popular in the United States in 1973, after the release of the Jamaican film *The Harder They Come* and its soundtrack album. (This is yet another example of the importance of film as a medium for promoting popular music, exemplified by the Hollywood musicals of the 1930s and rock 'n' roll films of the 1950s.) During the 1970s a handful of Jamaican musicians—notably Bob Marley and Jimmy Cliff—achieved a measure of commercial success in the United States, while numerous American and British rock musicians—including Eric Clapton, Paul Simon, the Police, and Elvis Costello—found inspiration (and profit) in the style. In addition, rap music of the 1980s was strongly influenced by Jamaican "dub," a branch of the reggae tradition in which verbal performances are improvised over prerecorded musical accompaniments.

Reggae music was itself a complex composite of influences, some of them from the United States. The history of reggae thus gives us an opportunity to examine not only the burgeoning interest of American musicians in "world music" but also the influence of American forms on local music elsewhere, a fascinating story that mainly lies outside the scope of this book. The roots of reggae lie in the Jamaican equivalent of country music, a genre called *mento*. Mento—a mixture of Jamaican folk songs, church hymns, sailor's shanties, and Cuban influences—arose in rural Jamaica during the late nineteenth century. By World War II, mento had lost its popularity among the thousands of young Jamaicans who were migrating to the capital city of Kingston. (Today's tourist resorts on Jamaica's north coast are among the last places where mento can be heard.) During the 1940s and early 1950s dance bands from the United States—including those of Benny Goodman, Count Basie, and Glenn Miller—became popular in the dance halls of Kingston. Jamaican musicians formed what they called "road bands," local bands that toured from town to town, playing public dances.

Starting in the 1950s American rhythm & blues—broadcast by powerful radio stations in Miami and New Orleans—became popular among youth in Kingston. Migrant Jamaican workers in Costa Rica, Panama, Cuba, and the United States brought back the hit recordings of American artists such as Louis Jordan and Fats Domino, and local entrepreneurs set up portable sound systems to play **R&B** records for dances and parties, driving the road bands out of business. In the 1960s a shortage of U.S. records encouraged some sound system operators to set up their own recording studios in Kingston. Some of these men—including Coxsone Dodd and Leslie Kong—became leading producers in the Jamaican popular music business.

During the 1960s a succession of new popular genres emerged out of the intersection of Jamaican folk music and American rhythm & blues. The first of these was *ska* (an onomatopoeic term derived from the style's typical sharp offbeat accents). The instrumentation of ska bands was derived from R&B, with a rhythm section of piano, bass, guitar, and drums and a horn section including some combination of brass instruments and saxophones. Ska music was usually played at fast tempos, with the bass playing a steady four-beat pattern and the piano, guitar, and drums emphasizing beats two and four. The singing on ska records was strongly influenced by R&B, ranging from rougher blues-influenced styles to romantic crooning. The biggest star of Jamaican ska was Don Drummond, a trombonist and leader of a band called the Skatalites. The Skatalites also worked as a studio band, backing many of the most popular singers of the time and exerting a substantial influence on the youth culture of Kingston, particularly when several members of the band joined the Rastafarian religious movement.

It is worth taking a moment here to discuss the Rastafarian movement, since it is such a prominent theme in reggae music. Rastafarianism was founded by Josiah Marcus Garvey (1887–1940), a Jamaican writer and political leader who inspired a "Back to Africa" repatriation movement among black Americans in the 1920s. Before leaving Jamaica for the United States in 1916, Garvey wrote, "Look to Africa for the crowning of a black king; he shall be the redeemer," a phrase that was taken quite literally as prophecy by Garvey's followers. In 1930, when Haile Selassie ("Power of the Trinity") was crowned king of the African nation of Ethiopia, preachers in Kingston saw this as confirmation of Garvey's prediction and proceeded to scrutinize the Old Testament in search of passages that supported the authenticity of Selassie's divinity. The Rastafarians' reinterpretation of the Bible focused on passages that dealt with slavery, salvation, and the apocalyptic consequences that would eventually be visited upon the oppressors (collectively referred to as Babylon). Rastafarianism became associated with a unique set of cultural practices, including special terminology (for example, "I-and-I" is substituted for "we"), the use of marijuana (*ganja*) as a sacramental herb, and the wearing of a distinctive hairstyle called "dreadlocks."

The Rastafarian movement spread rapidly, through an extensive network of neighborhood churches and informal prayer meetings, where music and dance were used to "give praise and thanks" (*satta amassanga*) and to "chant down Babylon." In the mountainous interior of Jamaica, where communities of escaped slaves called "maroons" had been living since the nineteenth century, Rastafarian songs and chants were mixed with an African-derived style of drumming called *burru*, creating a heavier, slower sound. This style in turn fed back into urban popular music, resulting around 1966 in an updated version of ska called *rock steady*. Rock steady was considerably slower in tempo than ska, reflecting the aforementioned influence of *burru* drumming, and some of its leading exponents—notably Alton Ellis, who had the first big rock steady hit in 1966—began to record songs with social and political content.

The main patrons of rock steady were the Rude Boys, a social category that included anyone against "the system": urban Rastas, thugs hired by competing political parties, and lower-class youth generally. An informal and unruly Jamaican youth movement, halfway between the Black Panthers and urban street gangs in the United States, Rude Boys increasingly came into conflict with the Jamaican police, and media coverage of their exploits helped to create the image of romantic outlaw heroes. The film that initiated reggae music's popularity in the United States, *The Harder They Come* (1972), was in fact a thinly disguised biography of one such ghetto hero (Vincent Martin, a.k.a. Rhygin', a Jamaican outlaw of the early 1960s). Bob Marley's song "I Shot the Sheriff" (see Box 7.2) is about a young man who is persecuted by the local sheriff and then accused of murdering both the sheriff and his deputy in cold blood.

Under the influence of Rastafarian religiosity and Rude Boy street politics, a new genre called reggae took shape in Kingston during the late 1960s. (The word "reggae" is derived from "raggay," a Kingston slang term meaning "raggedy, everyday stuff.") In musical terms reggae was a further extension of the evolution from ska to rock steady. In reggae music the tempo was slowed down even further, creating wide spaces between notes, allowing the music to breathe and emphasizing the **polyrhythmic** heritage of Afro-Jamaican traditions. Each instrument in a reggae band has its own carefully defined role to play. The heart of reggae music consists of "riddims," interlocking rhythmic patterns played by the guitar, bass, and drums. The guitar often plays short, choppy **chords** on the second and fourth beat of each measure, giving the music a bouncy, up-and-down feeling. The bass-drum combination is the irreducible core of a reggae band, sometimes called the "riddim pair." (The most famous of these are the brothers Aston and Carlton Barrett, who played in Bob Marley's band, and Sly Dunbar and Robbie Shakespeare, who have appeared on literally hundreds of reggae recordings, and on the LPs of rock artists such as Bob Dylan, Mick Jagger, and Peter Gabriel.) This musical mixture was further enlivened by the influence of contemporary black American popular music, particularly the soul recordings of James Brown and Aretha Franklin. Political messages were central to reggae music—while ska musicians of the early 1960s, like their American R&B counterparts, sang mainly about love and heartbreak, the most popular reggae artists focused their attention on issues such as social injustice and racism.

The film *The Harder They Come* featured reggae songs by a number of the most popular Jamaican musicians. The star of the film, and the vocalist on the title track of the soundtrack LP, was Jimmy Cliff (b. 1948). Like Ivan, the outlaw character he portrayed in the film, Cliff was only a teenager when he left the rural Jamaican town of St. James for the city of Kingston. Cliff arrived in Kingston in 1962 and made his first record within a year. Working with the producer Leslie Kong, he recorded a series of Jamaican Top 10 hits during the mid-1960s. While performing at the 1964 World's Fair in New York City, Cliff met Chris Blackwell of the English independent label Island Records, who convinced him to move to London. After working as a backup singer and scoring a few hits on the European charts, he returned to Jamaica in 1969 and recorded the song "Many Rivers to Cross," which inspired the director Perry Henzel to offer him the lead role in *The Harder They Come*. Although the film did not reach the mass audience commanded by many Hollywood movies, it did create a devoted audience for reggae music in the United States, particularly among young, college-educated adults, who were attracted by the rebellious spirit of the music and its associations with Rastafarianism and *ganja* smoking. (The film played for seven years straight at a movie theater in Boston, Massachusetts, sustained mainly by the enthusiasm of that city's large student population.)

Jimmy Cliff's 1972 recording of "The Harder They Come" exemplifies the reggae style of the early 1970s: a moderate tempo; strong guitar chords on the second and fourth beats of each measure; R&B-influenced singing; and a gritty lyric about the individual's struggle against oppression.

> *I keep on fighting for the things I want*
> *Though I know that when you're dead you can't*
> *But I'd rather be a free man in my grave*
> *Than living as a puppet or a slave*
>
> *So as sure as the sun will shine*
> *I'm gonna get my share now what is mine*
> *And then the harder they come, the harder they fall*
> *One and all*

Although Cliff was the first Jamaican musician to gain recognition in the United States, his contemporary Bob Marley (1945–81), leader of the Wailers, quickly surpassed Cliff in popularity. A national hero in his native Jamaica, Marley was reggae's most effective international ambassador. His songs of determination, rebellion, and faith, rooted in the Rastafarian belief system, found a worldwide audience that reached from America to Japan and from Europe to Africa. The son of a British naval officer who deserted his family when Bob was six years old, Marley migrated to Kingston from the rural parish of St. Ann at the age of fourteen. His early career reflects the economic precariousness of the music industry in a Third World country. After making a few singles for the Chinese-Jamaican producer Leslie Kong, Marley formed the Wailers in 1963 and signed with Coxsone Dodd's studios. Following a long period with little financial success (including a year of factory work

Bob Marley.
© S. I. N./Corbis.

for Marley in Wilmington, Delaware), the Wailers signed with the producer Lee Perry, who added Aston and Carlton Barrett, a masterful bassist-and-drummer "riddim pair."

In 1972 Chris Blackwell, who had launched Jimmy Cliff's international career, signed Bob Marley and the Wailers to Island Records and advanced them the money to record at their independent Tuff Gong studio in Jamaica. Marley's recognition abroad was boosted by the success of Eric Clapton's cover of "I Shot the Sheriff," from the Wailers' second LP for Island Records (see Box 7.2). The Wailers' first major concert in the United States took place in 1974 in Boston, where for a year and a half over a thousand young people a day had been viewing *The Harder They Come*. Between 1975 and 1980 Marley recorded six gold LPs for Island Records, including *Rastaman Vibration*, which reached Number Eight on the *Billboard* Top LPs charts in 1976. Wounded in a politically motivated assassination attempt in 1976,

Box 7.2 The Popularization of Reggae

Although the majority of American listeners became conscious of reggae as a distinctive musical style only in the mid to late 1970s, with the steadily increasing popularity in this country of Bob Marley and the Wailers, there are individual instances long before this of Jamaican music appearing on the American charts. In fact, among the many imported hits during the British Invasion year of 1964 was a ska-flavored recording by the Jamaican teenager Millie Small called "My Boy Lollipop," which climbed all the way up to Number Two on *Billboard*'s list of top singles. In 1968 Johnny Nash, an African American pop singer who established a recording studio in Jamaica, had a Top 5 hit with the reggae-influenced "Hold Me Tight," and 1969 saw the American success of two reggae records by Jamaican artists: "Israelites" by Desmond Dekker and the Aces (Number Nine pop), and "Wonderful World, Beautiful People," by Jimmy Cliff (Number Twenty-five pop).

Both Johnny Nash and Jimmy Cliff went on to bigger things in the early 1970s. Nash hit the Number One spot for four weeks in 1972 with another reggae-flavored tune, "I Can See Clearly Now." Nash wrote this song himself (as was also the case with "Hold Me Tight"), but he assured a sense of Jamaican authenticity by arranging for members of the Wailers to provide his instrumental support on the track. He then followed this up with a cover of Bob Marley's "Stir It Up" (Number Twelve pop, 1973). As for Jimmy Cliff, his starring role in the 1972 movie *The Harder They Come* introduced both him and the Jamaican music scene to a significant American audience previously unaware of both. (We might recall here the significance of another movie, *Blackboard Jungle*, in popularizing another music from the margins, rock 'n' roll, in 1955; see Chapter 3.) In a fine illustration of the reciprocal relationships that tend to characterize so much of pop music history, Cliff returned to the charts for the first time in many years, and hit the American Top 20 for the first time, in the early 1990s with nothing other than his own cover of Nash's "I Can See Clearly Now" (Number Eighteen pop, 1994), which was also featured in a movie, *Cool Runnings*.

Surely the best-known cover version of any reggae number is Eric Clapton's million-selling recording of Bob Marley's "I Shot the Sheriff," a Number One hit in 1974, which appears on Clapton's Number One album from the same year, *461 Ocean Boulevard*. Clapton's name on the label, along with his easygoing vocal delivery, doubtless helped to propel the single to the top of the charts; considered in terms of the song's lyrics and music, "I Shot the Sheriff" seems an unlikely 1970s hit. It is clearly a political song, but for anyone not thoroughly versed in contemporary Jamaican politics, its precise significance is difficult to grasp. This is an example of a "coded" lyric, (a phenomenon also found in **blues** lyrics), that communicates something extra to members of a specific group who are attuned to its message. Furthermore, the music of the song is appropriately dark in color, with a predominance of minor chords.

It is instructive to compare Clapton's version with Bob Marley's own recording of "I Shot the Sheriff," which may be found on the 1973 album

Burnin' and on compilations issued after Marley's death in 1981. Marley's version sounds much more insistently rhythmic and intense than Clapton's. Actually, Marley's tempo is only a hairbreadth faster than Clapton's, but the greater prominence of both bass and percussion in Marley's recording emphasizes the distinctive "riddims" of Jamaican reggae and creates the illusion of a considerably faster performance. (The recording closes with just the bass guitar and drums—the heartbeat of reggae—played by the riddim pair of Aston and Carlton Barrett.) In addition, the high range of the Wailers' voices creates a strong element of urgency that is lacking in the Clapton recording. Marley and the Wailers add small but effective and apparently spontaneous variations in the vocal lines of the successive verses of the song, giving a sense of familiarity and freedom with the material that also has no real counterpart in the cover version. And there is of course no substitute for the Jamaican patois (a **dialect** of English with strong African influence) in Marley's original ("Ev'ry day the bucket a-go-a well; one day the bottom a-go drop out"). It is to Clapton's credit, however, that he doesn't even try to mimic Marley's rendition of a Jamaican proverb about the eventual triumph of the oppressed (he sings "Every day the bucket goes to the well, but one day the bottom will drop out").

In sum, Clapton made an effective 1970s pop single out of Marley's "I Shot the Sheriff" by smoothing out its sound. The traditional rock backbeat (emphasizing with the drums the second and fourth beats of the four-beat measures), clearly to be heard on Clapton's recording, ties it to the rock mainstream, while the basic rhythmic character of Marley's version is decidedly outside that mainstream (with all the beats much more evenly emphasized, and the **syncopated** patterns imposed over them brought strongly forward). It may seem ironic to find a hero of the 1960s counterculture like Eric Clapton cast in the role of mainstream popularizer for a new marginal music in the 1970s, but the history of American popular music is full of such ironies, as one decade's rebel becomes the next decade's establishment.

Marley died of cancer in 1981, at the age of thirty-six. His appeal and popularity, both in America and worldwide, has only grown in the years since his death: the 1984 LP compilation *Legend* has sold over eight million copies in the United States alone.

"PSYCHO KILLER": 1970s PUNK AND NEW WAVE

During the 1970s the first "alternative" movements emerged within rock music. While rock had begun as a vital part of the 1960s counterculture, by 1975 it had come perilously close to occupying the center of popular taste, a development that left some young musicians feeling that its rebellious, innovative potential had been squandered by pampered, pretentious rock stars and the major record companies that promoted them. The golden age of *punk rock*—a "back to basics" rebellion against the perceived artifice and pretension of corporate rock music—lasted from around 1975 to 1978, but both the musical genre and the sensibility with which it was associated continue to exert a strong influence today on alternative rock musicians. *New wave* music, which developed alongside punk rock, approached the critique of corporate rock in more self-consciously artistic and experimental terms. (The term "new wave" was soon picked up by record companies themselves, who began using it in the late 1970s to refer to pop-influenced performers such as Blondie). Although the initial energy of the punk and new wave scene was largely expended by the start of the 1980s, young musicians inspired by the raw energy and minimalism of this movement went on to create distinctive regional music scenes in Los Angeles; Minneapolis; Seattle; Athens, Georgia; and elsewhere.

Punk was as much a cultural style—an attitude defined by a rebellion against authority and a deliberate rejection of middle-class values—as it was a musical genre. The contrarian impulse of punk culture is evoked (and parodied) in the song "I'm against It," recorded by the Ramones in 1978.

I don't like sex and drugs
I don't like waterbugs
I don't care about poverty
All I care about is me

I don't like playing Ping-Pong
I don't like the Viet Cong
I don't like Burger King
I don't like anything

Well I'm against it, I'm against it

In its automatic gainsaying of everything from sex and drugs to the Viet Cong and Burger King, this song evokes the motorcycle gang leader played by Marlon Brando in the archetypal teen rebellion film *The Wild One* (1954). When asked by a young woman, "What are you rebelling against?" the Brando character responds, "Whaddaya got?"

Punk was in fact both the apotheosis and the ultimate exploitation of rock 'n' roll as a symbol of rebellion, a tradition that began in the 1950s with white teenagers gleefully co-opting the energy and overt sexuality of black rhythm & blues to annoy their parents, and continued through the 1960s with songs like the Who's 1966 youth anthem "My Generation" ("Why don't you all just f-f-fade away?"). To many of its fans, punk rock represented a turn toward the authentic, risk-taking spirit of early rock 'n' roll and away from the pomposity and self-conscious artistry of album-oriented rock. On the other hand, like all alternative styles of popular music, punk rock was riven through with contradictions.

To begin with, if punk was explicitly against the standards of traditional commercial fashion, it was also a fashion system in its own right, with a very particular look: torn blue jeans, ripped stockings, outfits patched with ragged bits of contrasting materials, and perhaps a safety pin through the cheek. If some punk musicians framed their challenge to established authority in terms of progressive social values, others flirted with fascist imagery, attaching Nazi swastikas to their clothing and associating with the racist "skinhead" movement. Many in the punk movement—including musicians, fans, and those rock critics who championed the music—saw punk as a progressive response to the conservatism of the record industry. Yet the nihilism of much punk rock—the music's basic "I don't give a f——" stance—posed a crucial question that still resonates in today's alternative rock music: is it possible to make music that is "authentic" or "real" while at the same time loudly proclaiming that you don't care about anything?

In musical terms, punk rock turned progressive rock—with its artistic aspirations and corporate backing—on its head. As the drummer for the Ramones, widely regarded as the first punk rock band, put it:

> We took the rock sound into a psychotic world and narrowed it down into a straight line of energy. In an era of progressive rock, with its complexities and counterpoints, we had a perspective of non-musicality and intelligence that took over from musicianship. (Laing 1985, p. 23)

Punk was a stripped-down and often purposefully "nonmusical" version of rock music, in some sense a return to the wildness of early rock 'n' roll stars like Jerry Lee Lewis and Little Richard, but with lyrics that stressed the ironic or dark dimensions of human existence—drug addiction, despair, suicide, lust, and violence. As David Byrne, the leader of the new wave band Talking Heads, put it (on the PBS television series *Rock & Roll*):

> Punk . . . was more a kind of do-it-yourself, anyone-can-do-it attitude. If you only played two notes on the guitar, you could figure out a way to make a song out of that, and that's what it was all about.

Punk rock and its more commercial cousin, new wave, took shape in New York City during the mid-1970s. One of the predecessors of punk rock was an American musical institution called the *garage band*, typically a neighborhood operation, made up of young men who played mainly for themselves, their friends, and the occasional high school dance. A few of these local groups went on to enjoy some commercial success, including the Los Angeles–based Standells (whose "Dirty Water" was a Number Eleven pop hit in 1966); ? and the Mysterians, from the industrial town of Flint, Michigan (who took "96 Tears" to the top of the charts in the same year); and Portland, Oregon's Kingsmen, best known for their cover version of the 1950s R&B song "Louie, Louie" (Number Two pop in 1963). The rough-and-ready, do-it-yourself attitude of the garage bands—something akin to a rock 'n' roll–based folk music movement—paved the way for punk rock.

Three groups, none of them very successful in commercial terms, are frequently cited as ancestors of 1970s punk music, and of later genres such as new wave, hardcore, industrial, and alternative rock: the Velvet Underground, the Stooges, and the New York Dolls. The Velvet Underground, a New York group, was promoted by the pop art superstar Andy Warhol, who painted the famous cartoonlike image of a banana on the cover of their first LP. Their music was rough-edged and chaotic, extremely loud, and deliberately anticommercial, and the lyrics of their songs focused on topics such as sexual deviancy, drug addiction, violence, and social alienation. The leaders of the Velvet Underground were singer and guitarist Lou Reed— who had worked previously as a pop songwriter in a Brill Building–style "music factory"—and John Cale, a viola player active in the avant-garde art music scene in New York, who introduced experimental musical elements into the mix, including electronic noise and recorded industrial sounds.

If the Velvet Underground represented the self-consciously experimentalist roots of 1970s new wave music, the Stooges, formed in Ann Arbor, Michigan, in 1967, were the working-class, motorcycle-riding, leather-jacketed ancestors of punk rock. The lead singer of the Stooges, Iggy Stooge (a.k.a. <u>Iggy Pop</u>, James Osterburg), was famous for his outrageous stage performances, which included flinging himself into the crowd, cutting himself with beer bottles, and rubbing himself with raw meat. Guitarist Ron Asheton has described the Stooges' approach:

> Usually we got up there and jammed one riff and built into an energy freak-out, until finally we'd broken a guitar, or one of my hands would be twice as big as the other and my guitar would be covered in blood. (Palmer 1995, p. 263)

The Stooges' eponymous first album (1969), produced by the Velvet Underground's John Cale, created a devoted if small national audience for the Stooges' demented "garage band" sound. A good example of the sensibility that underlay much of the Stooges' work—the depression of unemployed Michigan youth caught in the middle of a severe economic recession—is the song "1969," which evokes a world light-years distant from the utopianism of the hippie movement and the Woodstock festival, held that same summer:

The New York Dolls make a fashion statement. Frank Driggs Collection.

Well it's 1969 OK all across the USA
It's another year for me and you
Another year with nothing to do
Last year I was 21 I didn't have a lot of fun
And now I'm gonna be 22 I say oh my and a boo-hoo

Another year with nothing to do
It's 1969, 1969, 1969, 1969, 1969, baby

Another band that exerted a major influence on the musical and visual style of the punk rock movement was the New York Dolls, formed in New York City in 1971. Dressed in fishnet stockings, bright red lipstick, cellophane tutus, ostrich feathers, and army boots, the all-male Dolls were an American response to the English glam rock movement, typified by the reigning master of rock gender bending, David Bowie (see Chapter 6). Their professional career began inauspiciously—at a Christmas party in a seedy welfare hotel in Manhattan—but by late 1972 they had built a small and devoted following. Although the New York Dolls soon succumbed to drug and alcohol abuse, they did establish certain core features of punk antifashion and helped to create a new underground rock music scene in New York City.

The amateur energy of garage band rock'n' roll, the artsy nihilism of the Velvet Underground, the raw energy and abandon of the Stooges, and the antifashion of the New York Dolls converged in the mid-1970s in New York City's burgeoning club scene. The locus of this activity was a converted folk music club called CBGB & OMFUG ("Country, Bluegrass, Blues & Other Music for Urban Gourmandizers"), located in the run-down Bowery area of Manhattan. The first rock musician to perform regularly at CBGBs was Patti Smith (b. 1946), a New York–based poet, journalist, and singer who had been experimenting with combining the spoken word and rock accompaniment. In 1975 Smith began a stint at CBGBs, establishing a beachhead for punk and new wave bands, and signed a contract with Arista, a new label headed by Clive Davis, the former head of Columbia Records. (Her critically acclaimed album *Horses* reached Number Forty-seven on the *Billboard* charts in 1976.) Other influential groups who played at CBGBs during the mid-1970s included Television—whose lengthy instrumental improvisations were inspired by the Velvet Underground and avant-garde jazz saxophonist Albert Ayler—Blondie, and the Voidoids, featuring the alienated lyrics and howling voice of lead singer Richard Hell, one of the original members of Television.

The first bonafide punk rock band was the Ramones, formed in 1974 in New York City. The Ramones' high-speed, energetic, and extremely loud sound influenced English punk groups such as the Sex Pistols and the Clash and also became a blueprint for 1980s L.A. hardcore bands. Although they projected a street-tough image, all of the band's members were from middle-class families in the New York City borough of Queens. The band—not a family enterprise, despite their stage names—consisted of Jeffrey Hyman (a.k.a. Joey Ramone) on vocals; John Cummings (Johnny Ramone) on guitar; Douglas Colvin (Dee Dee Ramone) on bass; and Tom Erdelyi (Tommy Ramone) on drums. The band's first manager, Danny Fields, had previously worked with the Stooges and Lou Reed and thus had a good sense of the Ramones' potential audience.

Taking the stage in blue jeans and black leather jackets—a look calculated to evoke the sneering, rebellious ethos of 1950s rock 'n' rollers—the Ramones began playing regularly at CBGBs in 1975. By the end of the year they had secured a recording contract with Sire Records, an independent label that signed a number of early punk groups. Their eponymous debut album was recorded in 1976 for just over six thousand dollars, an incredibly small amount of money in an era of expensive and time-consuming studio sessions. The album gained some critical attention and managed to reach Number 111 on the *Billboard* album charts.

Later that year the Ramones staged a British Invasion in reverse. Their concerts in English cities, where their records had already created an underground sensation, were attended by future members of almost every important British punk band, including the Sex Pistols (see Box 7.3), the Clash, and the Damned. In 1977 the Ramones scored a U.K. Top 40 hit with the song "Sheena Is a Punk Rocker" (Number Eighty-one U.S.), which announced that the center of the rock 'n' roll universe had shifted from the beaches of southern California to the lower east side of Manhattan:

> *Well the kids are all hopped up and ready to go*
> *They're ready to go now*
> *They've got their surfboards*
> *And they're going to the discotheque au go go*

The Ramones: Johnny, Dee Dee, Tommy, and Joey. Frank Driggs Collection.

But she just couldn't stay
She had to break away
Well New York City really has it all
Oh yeah, oh yeah.

Sheena is a punk rocker, Sheena is a punk rocker, Sheena is a punk rocker now.

The Ramones' music reflected their origins as a garage band made up of neighborhood friends. As the guitarist Johnny Ramone phrased it in an interview with the popular music scholar Robert Palmer:

> I had bought my first guitar just prior to starting the Ramones. . . . It was all very new; we put records on, but we couldn't figure out how to play the songs, so we decided to start writing songs that were within our capabilities. (Palmer 1995, p. 274)

These songs had catchy, pop-inspired melodies, were played at extremely fast tempos, and generally lasted no more than two and a half minutes. (In live performances, the Ramones managed to squeeze twelve or thirteen songs into a half-hour set.) The band's raw, hard-edged sound was anchored by a steady barrage of notes, played on drums, bass, and guitar. Johnny Ramone rarely if ever took a guitar solo, but this makes sense when you consider the band's technical limitations and the aesthetic goal of the music—a rejection of the flashy virtuosity of progressive rock music, with its extended and sometimes self-indulgent solos.

The song "I Wanna Be Sedated," from the band's fourth album, *Road to Ruin* (1978), is a good example of the Ramones' style, and of their mordant—one is tempted to say twisted—sense of humor:

Twenty-twenty-twenty-four hours to go, I wanna be sedated
Nothin' to do and nowhere to go-o-o, I wanna be sedated
Just put me in a wheelchair, get me to the show
Hurry hurry hurry, before I gotta go
I can't control my fingers, I can't control my toes
Oh no no no no no

Ba-ba-bamp-ba ba-ba-ba-bamp-ba, I wanna be sedated
Ba-ba-bamp-ba ba-ba-ba-bamp-ba, I wanna be sedated

The song text's images of drug-induced insanity (and its putative antidote, drug-induced paralysis) are juxtaposed with a catchy pop melody and Beach Boys–like chorus, a combination that affirms Joey Ramone's early description of the band's style as "sick bubblegum music."

It is, in fact, hard to know how seriously to take the Ramones. Although they played alongside self-consciously "cutting-edge" bands like the Patti Smith Group and Television, the Ramones identified themselves as a band that was "able to just play and be song-oriented and sound great, people who play real rock 'n' roll." Nonetheless, some of their recordings did provide grim "news flashes" on the facts of life in many working-class and middle-class homes during a period of severe economic recession. The song "I Wanted Everything" (1978) is a kind of punk counterpart to Merle Haggard's hardcore country song "If We Make It through December" (1973, see Chapter 6), sung, however, by a dispossessed son rather than a struggling father. The stark realism of this tale of a good boy gone wrong is

Box 7.3 "The End of Rock 'n' Roll": The Sex Pistols

We have already mentioned the impression made by the Ramones on musicians in the United Kingdom, an "American Invasion" that began some twelve years after the Beatles stormed New York City. The English stream of punk rock bubbled up during the summer of 1976, an unusually hot summer and a high point of unemployment, inflation, and racial tension in cities like London, Birmingham, Manchester, and Liverpool. In England, more than the United States, punk rock was associated with a mainly white working-class youth subculture. More explicitly political and less artsy than some of the New York bands, groups like the Sex Pistols, the Clash, and the Damned succeeded in outraging the British political establishment and the mainstream media while at the same time achieving a modicum of commercial success in the late 1970s.

The most outrageous—and therefore famous—punk band was the Sex Pistols, formed in 1975 in London. They were the creation of Malcolm McLaren, owner of a London "antifashion" boutique called *Sex*, which specialized in leather and rubber clothing. (McLaren had begun his career in the music business in 1974, when he managed unsuccessfully the short-lived New York Dolls.) Upon his return to London, McLaren conceived the idea of a rock 'n' roll band that would subvert the pop music industry and horrify England's staid middle class. Glen Matlock (bass), Paul Cook (drums), and Steve Jones (guitar) were regular customers at the shop, and they were looking for a singer. McLaren introduced them to John Lydon, a young man who hung around listening to the jukebox at *Sex* and had never sung in public before. (Lydon's inconsistent approach to personal hygiene led Steve Jones to christen him <u>Johnny Rotten</u>, a stage name that stuck.) The Sex Pistols got their first gigs by showing up and posing as the opening band. Given the nature of Johnny Rotten's stage act—sneering and screaming obscenities at the audience, commanding them to applaud, and throwing beer on them when they didn't—it is perhaps not surprising that they were banned from many nightclubs.

The trajectory of this band's rapid ascent and implosion is complex, and we can present only a summary here. EMI Records, England's biggest and most conservative label, signed the Sex Pistols for around sixty thousand dollars in 1976, releasing their first single, "Anarchy in the UK," in December. The single was a Top 40 hit in the U.K. but was withdrawn from record shops after Rotten uttered an obscenity during a television interview. At an annual meeting of shareholders in December 1976, the chairman of EMI, Sir John Read, made the following statement (as recorded in the Report of the EMI General Meeting, 12/7/76):

> Sex Pistols is the only "punk rock" group that EMI Records currently has under direct recording contract and whether EMI does in fact release any more of their records will have to be very carefully considered. I need hardly add that we shall do everything we can to restrain their public behavior, although this is a matter over which we have no real control.

The resulting uproar caused EMI to terminate the Sex Pistols' contract in January 1977, and all but five out of twenty-one dates on a planned concert tour of the U.K. were promptly canceled. In March the bassist Glen Matlock was replaced by John Ritchie, a nonmusician friend of John Lydon, who went by the stage name <u>Sid Vicious</u>. The American label A&M Records then signed the Pistols for over $200,000, only to fire them the very next week. In May Virgin Records signed them and released their second single, "God Save the Queen (It's a Fascist Regime)." Despite being banned from airplay, the song went to Number Two (cited as a blank on the U.K. charts). The band was featured in a 1978 film called *The Great Rock 'n' Roll Swindle*, a title that some critics thought captured perfectly the essence of the band's exercise in manipulation. The Sex Pistols broke up that same year, during their only U.S. tour, a tour undertaken to support the release of their only studio album, *Never Mind the Bollocks, Here's the Sex Pistols* (1977). In 1979 Sid Vicious was imprisoned in New York on charges of stabbing his girlfriend to death, and he died of a heroin overdose while out on bail. In 1986 the surviving members of the group sued Malcolm McLaren for cheating them of royalties and were awarded around $1.5 million. Though they did not represent "the end of rock 'n' roll," the Sex Pistols did manage to do away with themselves quite efficiently.

The Sex Pistols.
Frank Driggs Collection.

reminiscent of the work of Bruce Springsteen, often regarded as a working-class rock 'n' roll hero of the 1980s (see Chapter 8), and this realism suggests that American punk rock was not a totally nihilistic movement.

If the Ramones and the Sex Pistols epitomized punk rock's connections to the rebellious energy of early rock 'n' roll, another band, Talking Heads, represented the more self-consciously artistic and exploratory side of the alternative rock scene of the mid-1970s. Talking Heads was formed in 1974 by David Byrne (born in Scotland in 1952), Chris Frantz, and Tina Weymouth, who met as art students at the Rhode Island School of Design. They first appeared at CBGBs in 1975 as the opening act for the Ramones, though they attracted a somewhat different audience, made up of college students, artists, and music critics. In 1976 they were signed to a recording contract by Sire Records, and their first album, *Talking Heads: 77*, achieved critical acclaim and broke into the Top 100 on the *Billboard* album charts. The band's style reflected their interest in an aesthetic called minimalism, which stresses the use of combinations of a limited number of basic elements—colors, shapes, sounds, or words. This approach was popular in the New York art music scene of the 1960s and 1970s, as represented in the work of composers such as Steve Reich, Terry Riley, and Philip Glass, who made use of simple musical patterns, repeated and combined in various ways. The Talking Heads' instrumental arrangements fused this approach with the interlocking, riff-based rhythms pioneered by African American popular musicians, particularly James Brown (see the discussion of funk music below). Clarity is another important aspect of the minimalist aesthetic, and the Talking Heads' songs were generally quite simple in structural terms, with strong pop hooks and contrasting sections marked off by carefully arranged changes in instrumental texture.

In their visual presentation and stage demeanor, the Talking Heads were from another universe than the other CBGBs bands—they dressed in slacks, sweaters, and vests, projecting the image of cerebral but nerdy college students. David Byrne's stage demeanor was described by reviewer Michael Aron for *Rolling Stone* magazine (11/17/77):

> Everything about him is uncool: his socks and shoes, his body language, his self-conscious announcements of song titles, the way he wiggles his hips when he's carried away onstage (imagine an out-of-it kid practicing Buddy Holly moves in front of a mirror).

Just as the punk rockers' antifashion became a new kind of fashion, so David Byrne's studied awkwardness established a new kind of cool, one still much in evidence on college campuses today.

The center of attention on most Talking Heads recordings was David Byrne's trembling, high-pitched voice and his eclectic songwriting. Byrne often delivered his lyrics in a nervous, almost schizophrenic stream-of-consciousness voice, like overheard fragments from a psychiatrist's office. A good example of this approach—as well as the only single from the Heads' first LP to appear on the singles charts (peaking at Number Ninety-two)—was the song "Psycho Killer," inspired by Norman Bates, the schizophrenic murderer in Alfred Hitchcock's film *Psycho*. Although it now seems like an ironic commentary on mass media portrayals of "the serial killer," this song had a darker, more immediate resonance when it was released in

1977, during the Son of Sam killing spree, in which a deranged man shot thirteen people in New York City.

The recording opens with Tina Weymouth's electric bass, playing a simple riff reminiscent of mid-1970s funk or disco music (see below). She is soon joined by two guitars, playing crisply articulated, interlocking chord patterns. David Byrne's voice enters in the thirteenth bar, enunciating the lyrics in a half-spoken, half-sung style, over a simple melody that uses only a few pitches and stays mainly on the **tonic** note. The first verse (A^1) gives us a glimpse into the psychosis of the narrator:

> *I can't seem to face up to the facts*
> *I'm tense and nervous and I can't relax*
> *I can't sleep 'cause my bed's on fire*
> *Don't touch me I'm a real live wire*

This verse is followed by two statements of the chorus (B), which references the title of the song, dips abruptly and somewhat schizophrenically into a second language (French), and ends with a stuttered warning to the listener:

> *Psycho Killer, Qu'est-ce que c'est* [What is it?]
> *Fa fa fa fa fa fa fa fa fa far better*
> *Run run run run run run run away*

The chorus blends into a four-bar vocal interlude, with Byrne's voice leaping up an octave and emitting a distressed "Ay yai yai yai," and a two-bar instrumental section that reestablishes the basic **groove**. In the second verse (A^2), Byrne shifts from singing to speech, becoming more agitated as he expresses his anger at people who talk a lot, despite having nothing to say, and at his own inability to communicate with others:

> *You start a conversation, you can't even finish it.*
> *You're talking a lot, but you're not saying anything.*
> *When I have nothing to say, my lips are sealed.*
> *Say something once, why say it again?*

The chorus (B) is heard two more times, followed by the interlude, and then by a new section (C), in which Byrne struggles to confess his crime in an awkward, strangled variant of French:

> *Ce que j'ai fais, ce soir la* [The things I did on that night]
> *Ce qu'elle a dit, ce soir la* [The things she said on that night]
> *Realisant mon espoir* [Realizing my hope]
> *Je me lance vers la gloire . . . Okay* [I throw myself toward glory . . . Okay]

Eventually Byrne switches back into English, focusing obsessively on a single pitch and revealing more of his character's motivation for committing an unspecified though presumably horrific act:

> *We are vain and we are blind*
> *I hate people when they're not polite*

After final repetitions of the "Psycho Killer" chorus (B) and interlude, the band moves into a concluding twenty-four-bar instrumental section (or **coda)**, in which the basic groove is elaborated with distorted textures, wavering pitches on the guitars, strange vocal sounds from Byrne, and the panning of one guitar back and forth from left to right speaker, like the unanchored movement of a madman's thoughts. The last sound we hear is the squeal of **feedback** from one of the microphones, fading into silence and darkness.

LISTENING CHART "PSYCHO KILLER"

Music and lyrics by David Byrne, Chris Frantz, Tina Weymouth; performed by Talking Heads; recorded 1977

FORM	LYRICS	DESCRIPTIVE COMMENTS
Intro (12)	Instrumental	Bars 1–4: The electric bass plays a simple two-bar pattern two times.
		Bars 5–8: The bass drum enters with a steady pulse, and electric guitar plays sustained chords.
		Bars 9–12: The second electric guitar enters, completing the basic groove—the two guitars play choppy, rhythmically interlocking chords (à la James Brown).
A^1 (8)	*I can't seem to face up . . .* *I'm tense and nervous . . .* *I can't sleep . . .* *Don't touch me . . .*	Vocal enters; simple melody, centered on tonic pitch; instrumental accompaniment is based on interlocking riffs.
B (8)	*Psycho Killer, Qu'est-ce que c'est?* *Fa fa fa fa fa fa fa fa fa far better* *Run run run run run run run away* *Oh-oh-oh-oh . . .*	New harmonies, sustained chords on guitar mark beginning of chorus; bass and drums continue pulse.
B (8)	Lyric repeats	
Interlude (6)	*Oh . . . Ai yai yai yai yai (4)*	Byrne sings nonsense syllables, makes muffled vocal sounds in background.
	Instrumental (2)	Bass, drums and guitars play basic groove for last two bars.
A^2 (8)	*You start a conversation . . .* *You're talking a lot . . .* *When I have nothing to say . . .* *Say something once . . .*	Byrne moves from singing into speech mode; uses vocal quality to evoke psychotic persona.
B (8)	*Psycho Killer, Qu'est-ce que c'est?* *Fa fa fa fa fa fa fa fa fa far better* *Run run run run run run run away* *Oh-oh-oh-oh . . .*	
B (8)	Lyric repeats	
Interlude (2)	*Oh . . . Ai yai yai yai yai*	First part only.

C (20)	*Ce que j'ai fais, ce soir la*	Rhythm section plays marchlike pulse in unison for first eight bars, while Byrne speaks the lyrics.
	Ce qu'elle a dit, ce soir la	
	Realisant mon espoir	Guitar plays sustained chords (four bars).
	Je me lance, vers la gloire . . . Okay	Rhythm section reestablishes basic groove (four bars).
	Ya ya ya ya ya ya ya	
	We are vain and we are blind	Groove continues (four bars).
	I hate people when they're not polite	
B (8)	*Psycho Killer, Qu'est-ce que c'est?*	
	Fa fa fa fa fa fa fa fa fa far better	
	Run run run run run run run away	
	Oh-oh-oh-oh . . .	
B (8)	*Lyric repeats*	
Interlude (4)	*Oh . . . Ai yai yai yai yai*	Byrne sings nonsense syllables, makes vocal sounds in background.
Coda (3 × 8 = 24)	Instrumental	Bass, drums and guitars elaborate on basic groove for last twenty-four bars, building in intensity.
		Last eight bars feature stereo effect, guitar moving back and forth from left to right speaker.

Rather like David Bowie's Ziggy Stardust, the persona projected in "Psycho Killer"—tongue-tied, nervous, emotionally distant, and obsessively intellectual—provided David Byrne with a durable stage persona. In a review of the 1984 Talking Heads concert film *Stop Making Sense,* one critic remarked on Byrne's ability to project "a variant on his basic 'Psycho Killer' self for each song; he demonstrates over and over that a public self is a Frankenstein self, a monster put together from bits and pieces of image tissue." Throughout the late 1970s and 1980s Talking Heads recorded a series of critically acclaimed albums, most of which reached *Billboard*'s Top 40 and achieved either gold or platinum status. The commercial success was linked to the accessibility of Talking Heads' music, which mixed in influences from rhythm and blues and funk music, and from West African music, with its complexly interlocking but catchy polyrhythmic patterns. David Byrne went on to become a major figure in the world beat movement of the 1980s and 1990s, introducing American audiences to recording artists from Africa, Brazil, and the Caribbean.

"TEAR THE ROOF OFF THE SUCKER": FUNK MUSIC

Punk rock was a reaction against the pretentiousness of progressive rock and its multimillionaire superstars, hidden behind designer sunglasses, limousine windows, and mansion walls. *Funk music* represented yet another back-to-basics impetus, the impulse to dance. Most album-oriented rock music was aimed at a predominantly white male audience and was designed for listening rather than dancing. (While rock fans certainly engaged in free-form movement, the idea of organized social dancing was anathema to the "do your own thing" ethos of the counterculture and to the "high art" aspirations of some rock musicians.) In urban black communities across America, however, dance remained a backbone of social life, a primary means for transmitting traditional values and for generating a sense of novelty and excitement. And for the first time since the twist craze of the early 1960s, funk music—and its commercial offspring, disco—brought this intensive focus on dancing back into the pop mainstream.

The word "funky"—probably derived from the (central African) BaKongo term *funki*, meaning "healthy sweat"—was already in wide use by New Orleans jazz musicians during the first decade of the twentieth century. Today "funky" carries the same ambivalent meaning that it did a century ago—strong body odors (particularly those related to sex), and a quality of earthiness and authenticity, quintessentially expressed in music. If the concept of soul symbolized the spiritual, uplifting side of black consciousness, then funk was its profane and decidedly down-to-earth counterpart.

By the early 1970s the term "funk" was being used as a label for a genre of popular music characterized by strong, dance-oriented rhythms, catchy melodies, call-and-response exchanges between voices and instruments, and heavy reliance on repeated, rhythmically interlocking patterns. Most funk bands, echoing the instrumentation of James Brown's hits of the late 1960s, consisted of a rhythm section (guitar, keyboards, electric bass, and drums) and a horn section, which effectively functioned as part of the rhythm section and occasionally supplied jazz-influenced solos. Although funk music was initially targeted mostly at the predominantly urban black audience for soul music, funk groups such as Kool and the Gang, Ohio Players, and Chic were able to score Number One pop hits during the 1970s. Funk represented a vigorous reassertion of African American musical values in the face of soft soul's dominance of the R&B/pop crossover market, and it paved the way for the more commercialized sounds of disco music in the mid-1970s (see next section).

As we have suggested, James Brown was one of the prime inspirations for funk musicians. During the early 1970s Brown continued to score successes with dance-oriented hits, including "Super Bad" (Number Thirteen pop, Number One R&B in 1970), "Hot Pants (She Got to Use What She Got to Get What She Wants)" (Number Fifteen pop, Number One R&B, 1971), "Get on the Good Foot" (Number Eighteen pop, Number One R&B, 1972), and "The Payback" (Number Twenty-six pop, Number One R&B, 1974). Brown's ranking on the pop charts declined gradually throughout this period, however, in large part owing to competition from a new generation of musicians who played variations on the basic style he had established the decade before. This approach—the core of funk music—centered on the creation of a strong rhythmic momentum or groove, with the electric bass and bass drum often playing on all four main beats of the measure, the snare drum and other instruments playing equally strongly on the second and fourth beats (the backbeats), and interlocking ostinato patterns distributed among other instruments, including guitar, keyboards, and horns.

Another important influence on 1970s funk music was the group Sly and the Family Stone, an interracial "psychedelic soul" band whose recordings bridged the gap between rock music and soul music. Sly Stone (Sylvester Stewart) was born in Dallas, Texas, in 1944, and moved to San Francisco with his family in the 1950s. He began his musical career at the age of four as a gospel singer, went on to study

Sly and the Family Stone. Frank Driggs Collection.

trumpet, music theory, and composition in college, and later worked as a disc jockey at both R&B and rock-oriented radio stations in the San Francisco Bay Area. Sly formed his first band (the Stoners) in 1966 and gradually developed a style that reflected his own diverse musical experience, a blend of jazz, soul music, San Francisco psychedelia, and the socially engaged lyrics of folk rock. The Family Stone's national popularity was boosted by their fiery performance at the Woodstock Festival in 1969, which appeared in the film and soundtrack album *Woodstock.*

Between 1968 and 1971 Sly and the Family Stone recorded a series of albums and singles that reached the top of both the pop and soul charts. Recordings like "Dance to the Music" (Number Eight pop and Number Nine R&B in 1968), the double-sided hit singles "Everyday People"/"Sing a Simple Song" (Number One pop and R&B in 1969) and "Thank You (Falletinme Be Mice Elf Again)"/"Everybody is a Star" (Number One pop and R&B in 1970), and their last big crossover hit, "Family Affair" (Number One pop and R&B, 1971) exerted a big influence on funk music. The sound of the Family Stone was anchored by the electric bass of Larry Graham—positioned prominently in the studio mix—and by an approach to arranging that made the whole band, including the horn section, into a collective rhythm section.

By 1973 funk music had burst onto the pop music scene, pushed to the top of the charts by a large and heterogeneous audience, united by their thirst for rhythmically propulsive dance music. Crossover gold records such as Kool and the Gang's "Jungle Boogie" (Number Four pop and Number Two R&B in 1973) and "Hollywood Swinging" (Number Six pop and Number One R&B in 1974), The Ohio Players' "Fire" (Number One pop and R&B, 1974) and "Love Rollercoaster" (Number One pop and R&B in 1975), and the multimillion-selling "Play That Funky Music" (Number One pop and R&B in 1976) by the white band Wild Cherry were played constantly on AM radio and in nightclubs and discotheques. These bands kept the spirit and style of James Brown and Sly Stone alive, albeit in a commercialized and decidedly nonpolitical manner. The image of black "funkmasters," dancing in Afro hairdos, sunglasses, and brightly colored clothing on television shows like *American Bandstand* and *Soul Train*, occasionally came uncomfortably close to racial stereotyping. Certainly, the record industry's packaging of black "authenticity"—as symbolized by strongly rhythmic, body-oriented music—had a great deal to do with the sudden crossover success enjoyed by bands such as Kool and the Gang and the Ohio Players (who had struggled for success as an R&B band since 1959). However, if the success of funk music in the mainstream pop market capitalized to some degree upon long-standing white American fantasies about black culture, white funk bands such as Wild Cherry and the Average White Band were also able to place records in the R&B Top 10.

Although they did not share the huge commercial success of the groups just mentioned, the apotheosis of 1970s funk music was a loose aggregate of around forty musicians (variously called Parliament or Funkadelic), led by <u>George Clinton</u> (a.k.a. Dr. Funkenstein). Clinton (b. 1940), an ex-R&B vocal group leader and songwriter, hung out with Detroit hippies, listened to the Stooges, and altered his style (as well as his consciousness) during the late 1960s. Enlisting some former members of James Brown's band (bassist William "Bootsy" Collins and saxophone players Maceo Parker and Fred Wesley), he developed a mixture of compelling polyrhythms, psychedelic guitar solos, jazz-influenced horn arrangements, and R&B vocal harmonies. Recording for the independent record company Casablanca (also a major player in the field of disco music), Parliament/Funkadelic placed five LPs in the *Billboard* Top 40 between 1976 and 1978, two of which went platinum.

The band's reputation was in substantial measure based on their spectacular concert shows, which featured wild costumes and elaborate sets (including a huge flying saucer called "the Mothership"), and their innovative concept albums, which expressed an alternative black sensibility, embodied in a patois of street talk, psychedelic imagery, and science fiction–derived images of intergalactic travel. George Clinton took racial and musical stereotypes and played with them, reconfiguring black popular music as a positive moral force. On his albums, Clinton wove mythological narratives of a primordial conflict between the "Cro-Nasal Sapiens" (who "slicked their hair and lost all sense of the groove") and the "Thumpasorus People," who buried the secret of funk in the Egyptian pyramids and left Earth for the Chocolate Milky Way, under the wise leadership of "Dr. Funkenstein." Parliament concerts featured a cast of characters such as "Star Child" (a.k.a. "Sir Lollipop Man"), the cosmic defender of funk, and "Sir Nose D'VoidOfFunk," a spoof of commercialized, soulless, rhythmically challenged pop music and its fans. Clinton's blend of social criticism, wacky humor, and psychedelic imagination is perhaps best captured in his revolutionary manifesto for the funk movement: "Free Your Mind, and Your Ass Will Follow."

"Give Up the Funk (Tear the Roof off the Sucker)," from the million-selling LP *Mothership Connection*, was Parliament's biggest crossover single (Number Five R&B, Number Fifteen pop in 1976). It exemplifies the band's approach to ensemble style, known to fans as "P-Funk": heavy, syncopated electric bass lines; interlocking rhythms underlain by a strong pulse on each beat of each measure; long, multisectioned arrangements featuring call-and-response patterns between the horn sections and keyboard synthesizer; R&B-styled vocal harmonies; and verbal mottoes designed to be chanted by fans ("We want the funk, give up the funk; We need the funk, we gotta have the funk"). Arranged by Clinton, bass player Bootsy Collins, and keyboardist Bernie Worrell, the recording is constructed out of these basic elements, alternated and layered on top of one another to create a series of shifting sound textures, anchored in the strong pulse of bass and drums.

Clinton and other former Parliament/Funkadelic musicians continued to tour and record throughout the 1980s, but public and critical disdain for 1970s popular culture—especially disco and the dance-oriented music that preceded and inspired it—had a negative impact on the band's fortunes. During the early 1990s the rise of funk-inspired rap (e.g., Dr. Dre) and rock music (e.g., Red Hot Chili Peppers) established the status of George Clinton and his colleagues as one of the most important—and most frequently **sampled**—forces in the recent history of black music. Discovered by a new generation of listeners, Clinton is still performing as of this writing, having appeared to great acclaim at the 1999 reincarnation of the Woodstock festival.

"NIGHT FEVER": THE RISE OF DISCO

If funk music heralded the return of black social dance music to the mainstream of American popular music, the era of *disco*—roughly 1975 to 1980—represents the commercial apotheosis (and sudden, though temporary decline) of this trend. Like punk rock, disco music represented a reaction against two of the central ideas of album-oriented rock: the LP as Art and the rock group as Artists. Unlike punk, disco deemphasized the importance of the band—which, in disco music, was usually a concatenation of professional session musicians—and focused attention on the producers who oversaw the making of recordings, the **DJs** who played them in nightclubs, and a handful of glamorous stars, who sang with the backing of anonymous studio musicians and often had quite short-lived careers. Disco also rejected the idea of the rock album as an architecturally designed collection of individual pieces. Working night after night for audiences who demanded music that would keep them dancing for hours at a stretch, DJs rediscovered the single, expanded it to fill the time frame offered by the twelve-inch long-playing vinyl disc, and developed techniques for blending one record into the next without interruption. (These turntable techniques paved the way for the use of recordings in popular genres of the 1980s and 1990s, such as hip-hop, house, acid jazz, and techno.)

The term "disco" was derived from "discotheque," a term first used in Europe during the 1960s to refer to nightclubs devoted to the playing of recorded music for dancing. By the mid-1970s clubs featuring an uninterrupted stream of dance music were increasingly common in the United States, particularly in urban black and Latino communities, where going out to dance on a weekend night was a well-established tradition, and in the increasingly visible gay communities of cities such as New York and San Francisco. The rise of disco and its invasion of the Top 40 pop music mainstream were driven by several factors: the inspiration of black popular music, particularly Motown, soul, and funk; the rise in popularity of social dancing among middle-class Americans; new technologies, including synthesizers, drum machines, and synchronized turntables; the role of the Hollywood film industry in promoting musical trends; and the economic recession of the late 1970s, which encouraged many nightclub owners to hire disc jockeys rather than live musicians.

The archetypal early disco hit is Donna Summer's "Love to Love You Baby" (Number Two pop, Number Three R&B, 1975), recorded in Germany and released in the United States by Casablanca Records, the independent label that also released LPs by Parliament/Funkadelic. "Love to Love You Baby" reflects the genre's strong reliance on musical technologies of the mid-1970s and the central importance of the record producer in shaping the sound texture of disco recordings. Producer Giorgio Moroder's careful mix takes full advantage of multitrack recording technology (which allows Summer's voice to appear in several places at the same time), clear stereo separation of instruments, keyboard synthesizers with the ability to play more than one note at a time and to imitate other musical instruments, and electronic **reverb,** which plays a crucial role in establishing the spatial qualities of a recording. The original recording is much longer than the usual pop single—almost seventeen minutes long—and was produced specifically for use in discotheques, where customers demanded unbroken sequences of dance music. (The version that made the *Billboard* singles charts was edited down to under five minutes in length, to fit the framework of Top 40 radio.) The performance is clearly seductive in intent, an impression created not only by the lyrics themselves but also by Summer's languorous and sexy whispers, moans, and growls. (This impression is reinforced by the nicknames bestowed on Donna Summer at the time by the popular music press, including "First Lady of Lust" and "Disco's Aphrodite.")

The recording opens with an intake of breath and Summer's voice singing the hook of the song ("Ahhhh, love to love you baby") in an intimate, almost whispering voice, accompanied by the gentle sound of a closed hi-hat cymbal (a pair of cymbals opened and closed by the drummer's left foot). The next sounds to appear are the electric guitar, played with a wah-wah pedal (a foot-operated device that allows the guitarist to change the **timbre** of his instrument), and the bass drum, playing a solid four-to-the-bar beat. The core elements of early disco music are thus presented within the first few measures of the recording: a sexy, studio-enhanced female voice, and a rhythm track that is borrowed in large part from funk music and anchored by a hypnotic steady pulse. The overall arrangement is made up of two basic phrases, which are alternated, always returning to the hook. Working with his then state-of-the-art multitrack recording board, Giorgio Moroder gradually builds up layers of sound texture and then strips them away to reveal the basic pulse of the music.

By the late 1970s disco had taken over the popular mainstream, owing in large part to the success of the film *Saturday Night Fever* (1977), the story of a working-class Italian kid from New York who rises to become a championship dancer. *Saturday Night Fever*—shot on location at a Brooklyn discotheque—strengthened interest in disco stars like Donna Summer and Gloria Gaynor. The film also launched the second career of the Bee Gees, an Australian group known theretofore mainly for sentimental pop songs like "Lonely Days" (a Number Three pop hit from 1970) and "How Can You Mend a Broken Heart" (Number One in 1971). The Bee Gees reinvented themselves by combining their polished Beatle-derived vocal harmonies with funk-influenced rhythms, played by Miami studio musicians, and created a mix that appealed both to committed disco fans and a broader pop audience; their songs from the *Saturday Night Fever* soundtrack, such as "Stayin' Alive" and "Night Fever," were among the most popular singles of the late 1970s. At a more general level, *Saturday Night Fever* also helped to link disco music and dancing to a traditional American cultural theme, that of upward mobility. Spreading from the urban communities where it first took flower, disco dancing offered millions of working-class and middle-class Americans, from the most varied of cultural and economic backgrounds, access to glamour that hadn't been experienced widely since the days of the grand ballrooms.

The strict dress codes employed by the most famous discotheques implied a rejection of the torn T-shirt and jeans regalia of rock music, and the reinstatement of notions of hierarchy and classiness—if you (and your clothes) could pass muster at the velvet rope, you were allowed access to the inner sanctum. Walking through the front door of a disco in full swing was like entering a sensory maelstrom, with thundering music driven by an incessant bass pulse; flashing lights and mirrors on the ceiling, walls, and floor; and—most important—a mass of sweaty and beautifully adorned bodies packed onto the always limited space of a dance floor. For its adepts, the discotheque was a shrine to hedonism, an escape from the drudgery of everyday life, and a fountain of youth. (The death throes of this scene are evocatively rendered in the 1998 film *The Last Days of Disco*.)

A few examples must suffice here to give a sense of how thoroughly disco had penetrated popular musical taste by the late 1970s. One important stream of influence involved a continuation of the old category of novelty records, done up in disco style. A band called Rick Dees and his Gang of Idiots came out of nowhere to score a Number One hit with the goofy "Disco Duck" (1976), followed by the less successful zoo-disco song "Dis-Gorilla" (1977). The Village People—a group built from scratch by the French record producer Jacques Morali and promoted by Casablanca Records—specialized in over-the-top burlesques of gay life and scored Top 40 hits with songs like "Macho Man" (Number Twenty-five, 1978), "YMCA" (Number Two, 1978) and "In the Navy" (Number Three, 1979). For those who caught the inside references to gay culture, the Village People's recordings were charming, if simple-minded parodies; for many in disco's new mass audience, they were simply novelty records with a disco beat. Morali's double-entendre strategy paid off—for a short while in the late 1970s, the Village People were the bestselling pop group in North America.

For a few years everyone seemed to be jumping on the disco bandwagon. Barbra Streisand teamed up with disco artists, including the Bee Gees' Barry Gibb, who produced her multiplatinum 1980 album *Guilty*, and Donna Summer for the single "No More Tears" (Number One in 1979). Disco met the surf sound when Bruce Johnston of the Beach Boys produced a disco arrangement of "Pipeline," which had been a Number Four instrumental hit for the Chantays back in 1963. Even hard rock musicians like the Rolling Stones released disco singles (such as "Miss You," Number One in 1978). On the other side of the Atlantic a genre called Eurodisco developed, featuring prominent use of electronic synthesizers and long compositions with repetitive rhythm tracks, designed to fill the entire side of an LP. (This sound, as developed by bands like Germany's Kraftwerk, was to become one important root of techno.) And black musicians, who had provided the basic material of which disco was constructed, were presented with new audiences, opportunities, and challenges. Motown diva Diana Ross scored several disco-influenced hits (e.g., "Love Hangover," Number One in 1976, and "Upside Down," Number One in 1980). And James Brown, who was knocked off the pop charts by disco music, responded in the late 1970s by promoting himself as the "Original Disco Man." (His R&B hit "It's Too Funky in Here," released in 1979, is a clear gesture in this direction.)

Few styles of popular music have inspired such passionate loyalty, or such utter revulsion, as disco music, and it is worth taking a few moments to consider the negative side of this equation. If you were a loyal fan of Led Zeppelin, Pink Floyd, and other album-oriented rock groups of the 1970s, disco was likely to represent a self-indulgent, pretentious, and vaguely suspect musical orientation. The rejection of disco by rock fans reached its peak during a 1979 baseball game in Chicago, where several hundred disco records were blown up and a riot ensued. (This mass passion is reminiscent of the Beatle record burnings organized during the 1960s by fundamentalist Christian preachers.) After all, disco is only music—what on earth could inspire such a violent reaction?

Some critics connect the antidisco reaction of the 1970s with the genre's links to gay culture. The disco movement initially emerged in Manhattan nightclubs such as the Loft and the Tenth Floor, which served as social gathering spots for homosexual men. According to this interpretation, gays found it difficult to get live acts to perform for them. The disc jockeys who worked these clubs responded to the demands of customers by rummaging through the bins of record stores for good dance records, often coming up with singles that had been successful some years earlier in the black and Puerto Rican communities of New York.

That disco was to some degree associated in the public imagination with homosexuality has suggested to some observers that the phrase "Disco Sucks!"—the rallying cry of the antidisco movement—evinces a strain of homophobia among the core audience for album-oriented rock, young, middle- and working-class, and presumably heterosexual white men. Certainly disco's associations with a contemporary version of ballroom dancing did not conform to contemporary models of masculine behavior. The tradition of dancing to prefigured steps, and to music specifically designed to support dancing, which had found its last expression in the early 1960s with dance crazes like the twist, had fallen out of favor during the rock era. It may therefore have seemed to many rock fans that there was something suspect—even effeminate—about men who engaged in ballroom dancing.

Still, it can safely be assumed that the audience for album-oriented rock wasn't entirely straight, and that heterosexuals did patronize discos with large homosexual clienteles, at least in the big cities. The initial rejection of disco by many rock fans may have had as much to do with racism as with homophobia, since the genre's roots lay predominantly in black dance music. In addition, the musical values predominant among rock fans—including an appreciation of instrumental virtuosity, as represented in the guitar playing of Jimi Hendrix, Eric Clapton, or Jimmy Page—would not have inclined them toward a positive regard of disco, which relied heavily on studio overdubbing and consisted mainly of fairly predictable patterns designed for dancing. And the fact that millions of sports fans of all descriptions today enthusiastically mimic the movements of a popular—and, for some listeners, explicitly gay—disco record like the Village People's multimillion-selling single "YMCA" complicates the picture even further. Although disco cannot simply be identified as "gay music," there is no doubt that the genre's mixed reception during the late 1970s provides additional evidence of the transformative effect of marginalized musical styles and communities on the commercial mainstream of American popular music.

LISTENING TO "BAD GIRLS" AND "GOOD TIMES"

Dance-oriented music dominated the American pop charts in the late 1970s. The titles of the Number One pop records from the end of 1977 through the summer of 1979 would read, with few exceptions, like a track listing for a "Disco's Greatest Hits" album. Disco's spectacular hold on the Number One spot ended with two splendid examples of the genre: "Bad Girls," performed by Donna Summer, and "Good Times," performed by Chic. A brief consideration of the similarities shared by these records, and of the differences between them, will offer us a useful look at the essential characteristics, as well as the diversity, of disco music.

What Makes Both These Records "Disco"?

1. ***The BEAT!*** This is dance music, of course, and the pounding beat defines the music as disco. Indeed, the beat is established immediately on both "Bad Girls" and "Good Times," and it never lets up, persisting right through the fade-outs that end these recordings. The beat constitutes the essential hook on all disco records. It is characteristic of disco that every pulse is rhythmically articulated by the bass and/or the drums. There is no such thing as stoptime in this music, and the signature *thump!—thump!—thump!—thump!* of disco creates and maintains an irresistible dance groove; disco dancers literally never have to skip a beat. Consequently, although there are many changes in the musical texture during "Bad Girls," the rhythm never lets up, regardless of whatever other instruments or vocal parts enter or leave the mix. On the other hand, the fact that there are only slight alterations in texture throughout "Good Times" helps assure that attention remains focused on the rhythm itself, and the minimal feel of this particular recording offers an excellent example of how hypnotic a basic rhythm-propelled track can be.

2. ***A steady, medium-fast tempo.*** Like most social dance music, disco recordings maintain an unvarying tempo throughout. Above and beyond this obvious characteristic, however, the tempos of most disco records tend also to be fairly similar to one another, to accord with the active dance styles preferred by the patrons of discotheques. The tempo of "Bad Girls" is slightly faster than that of "Good Times," but obviously the same kinds of steps and body movements would fit both records equally well. Recordings intended for use in discotheques often bore indications of their tempos in the form of beats per minute (*b.p.m.*), to assist the club disc jockeys in arranging relatively seamless sequences of dance numbers, and if the DJ had an adjustable-speed turntable, it was possible to adjust the tempos of individual records slightly so that the dance beat wouldn't vary at all from one to the next—then, even when the song changed, the dancers still would never have to skip a beat.

3. ***Straightforward, repetitive song forms.*** With the emphasis on dancing, it would obviously be pointless for disco records to employ complex,

Chic and Donna Summer: kings and queens of disco. Frank Driggs Collection

intricate song forms, such as those developed by some artists in the late 1960s and the 1970s. Such niceties suggest an entirely different kind of listening environment and, if they weren't just missed entirely by disco fans, might prove distracting and even annoying on the dance floor. Both "Bad Girls" and "Good Times" are based clearly on a verse-chorus kind of form. Furthermore, in both, the chorus is heard first, and this serves a number of purposes. Each song's chorus begins with the title words ("Bad girls," "Good times"), identifying the song immediately and functioning as a concise, and extremely effective, verbal and musical hook. Counting the initial statement, the chorus in each of these recordings is heard a total of three times, which results in a readily accessible, repetitive kind of structure that assures memorability.

4. ***Straightforward subject matter and lyrics.*** No Dylanesque imagery or poetic obscurities, please—again, for obvious reasons. There is no doubt what either "Bad Girls" or "Good Times" is about. This is not to say that the lyrics to disco songs are without interest, however; see the further discussion, especially in reference to "Bad Girls," below.

5. ***Limited harmonic vocabulary.*** In essence, the harmony of "Good Times" simply oscillates between two chords, with the change occurring on the downbeat of every other measure. "Bad Girls" has only a slightly wider harmonic vocabulary, but it too gives the sense of being built around two basic, alternating chords much of the time; these two chords underlie the entire chorus and do not shift when the choruses give way to the verses. Both records thus achieve a highly focused, almost hypnotic, effect in the harmonic realm that is analogous to—and abets—their virtually obsessive rhythmic character. (The conceptual debt that recordings of this type owe to the late 1960s music of James Brown should be obvious; see Chapter 5.)

Note: The five characteristics listed above—emphasis on the beat; steady, relatively fast, tempo; avoidance of formal complexity; direct lyrics; and a limited chord vocabulary—clearly do not apply only to typical disco music. They also would serve well in a general way, for example, in describing much typical early rock 'n' roll. The point to be made here is that, in the context of album-oriented rock, the output of singer-songwriters, and several other manifestations of 1970s pop music, the "return to basics" (that is, the return to danceable music)—with a new twist—that disco represented came across, to many, as both novel and refreshing. It is also important to emphasize here that disco music proved, in certain ways, to be forward-looking. The most immediate example of this is the fact that the chords and rhythmic patterns of "Good Times" were borrowed wholesale to constitute the instrumental backing for the single that broke rap music into the commercial mainstream for the first time: "Rapper's Delight," by the Sugarhill Gang (see Chapter 9).

Some Distinguishing Characteristics of "Bad Girls" and "Good Times"

We have already noted the greater textural variety of "Bad Girls." Donna Summer's lead vocal, responding voices, brass instruments, and even a police whistle appear, disappear, and reappear—sometimes expectedly, sometimes not—over the course of the recording, creating a feeling that is evocative of the action, excitement, and occasional unpredictability of a busy street scene. It also seems appropriate that "Bad Girls" is more elaborate from a formal point of view than "Good Times." The verse sections of "Bad Girls" fall into two distinct parts, the second part marked by a pause in the vocals and the interjection of short, accented chords on the brass instruments. (This part has a formal effect somewhat similar to that of a **bridge** section in other song structures.) In addition, after the third and final verse, there is a coda in place of the expected concluding chorus. In this coda, the lead vocalist abandons at last her position as observer of the scene and actually joins the "bad girls" with a shout of "Hey, mister, have you got a dime?"—acting, in effect, upon her earlier realization (in the third verse) that she and the "bad girls" are "both the same," even though the others are called "a different name."

The vocal styles used in the two recordings are decidedly different. Donna Summer's emphatic, expansive style clearly derives from roots in R&B and gospel; her background, like that of so many African American pop stars, included church singing. Summer's personal intensity solicits our involvement in, and concern with, the story of the "bad girls." In short, "Bad Girls" is a brilliantly performed pop record that is enhanced by an elaborate and clever production. Yet the question suggests itself: can any recording so irresistibly danceable, with such an upbeat rhythmic feeling, really convey a downbeat social "message"—especially about an issue as thorny and complex as prostitution? Won't people be too busy dancing to notice? And doesn't it sound as if these "bad girls" are really just out for, and having, "good times"?

In a way, the inverse situation applies to "Good Times." This apparently carefree anthem is intoned by a small group of voices singing in unison in a clipped, unornamented, basically uninflected kind of style that comes across as intentionally depersonalized. Is there ultimately something just a little too mechanistic about the voices, and the obsessive chords and rhythms, in these "good times"? Some rock critics have suggested that the song has an ironic edge to it, and they could certainly support this idea by pointing to those occasional darker phrases that pop up in the lyrics like momentary flickering shadows: "A rumor has it that it's getting late," and "You silly fool, you can't change your fate." On the other hand, it might be claimed that those looking for hidden depths in a song like "Good Times" are those who have simply lost the ability to enjoy a superb party record.

On the one hand, the popular music of the 1970s provides rich evidence of the continuing vitality of venerable musical forms and techniques—including the African-derived polyrhythms of funk music and reggae, the twelve-bar blues form in rock music, and the Euro-American ballad form in country music—and of the capacity of marginalized communities and musical traditions to revitalize the commercial mainstream of popular music. On the other hand, the 1970s also saw the consolidation—on an unprecedented worldwide scale—of corporate control over the production of musical products. By the close of the decade, a handful of major transnational companies were responsible for the majority of record sales—in America and worldwide—and were busy swallowing up smaller companies. At the same time that the major record companies sought to make the market more predictable, however, the audience for popular music fragmented into dozens of specialized taste communities, creating a complex musical landscape bound to elude the predictive efforts of even the most experienced record producer or corporate CEO. The margins and the mainstream; corporate control and consumer unpredictability; ancient traditions and new technologies—these are the themes that will now carry us into the decades of the 1980s and 1990s, as we conclude our journey through the history of the rock years.

CHAPTER EIGHT

THE 1980s

Digital Technology, MTV, and the Popular Mainstream

From the viewpoint of the American music industry, the 1980s began on a sour note. Following a period of rapid expansion in the mid-1970s, 1979 saw an 11 percent drop in annual record sales nationwide, the first major recession in the industry in thirty years. Profits from the sale of recorded music hit rock bottom in 1982 ($4.6 billion), down half a billion dollars from the peak year of 1978 ($5.1 billion). The major record companies—now subdivisions of huge transnational conglomerates—trimmed their staffs, cut back expenses, signed fewer new acts, raised the prices of LPs and cassette tapes, and searched for new promotional and audience-targeting techniques. The pattern of relying on a small number of multiplatinum artists to create profits became more pronounced in the 1980s. By the mid-1980s, when the industry began to climb out of its hole, it was clear that the recovery was due more to the megasuccess of a few recordings by superstar musicians—Michael Jackson, Madonna, Prince, Bruce Springsteen, Whitney Houston, Phil Collins, Janet Jackson, and others—than to any across-the-board improvement in record sales.

A number of reasons have been adduced for the crash of the early 1980s—the onset of a national recession brought on by the laissez-faire economic policies of the Reagan administration; competition from new forms of entertainment, including home video, cable television, and video games; the decline of disco, which had driven the rapid expansion of the record business in the late 1970s; and an increase in illegal copying ("pirating") of commercial recordings by consumers with cassette tape decks. In 1984 sales of prerecorded cassettes, boosted by the popularity of the Sony Walkman personal tape player and larger portable tape players called "boomboxes," surpassed those of vinyl discs for the first time in history. (The introduction of digital audio tape, or DAT, in the early 1990s, and of writable compact discs, or CD-Rs, at the turn of the century, provided consumers with the ability to make near-perfect copies of commercial recordings, a development that prompted the music industry to respond with new anticopying technologies.)

The 1980s also saw the rise of technologies that would revolutionize the production of popular music. The development of *digital sound recording* led to the introduction of the five-inch *compact disc* (CD), and the rapid decline of the vinyl disc. The sounds encoded on a compact disc are read by a laser beam and not by a diamond needle, meaning that CDs are not subject to the same wear and tear as vinyl discs. The first compact discs went on sale in 1983, and by 1988 sales of CDs surpassed those of vinyl discs for the first time. Although CDs cost about the same as vinyl LPs to manufacture, the demand for the new medium allowed record companies to generate higher profits by pricing them at thirteen dollars or more, rather than the eight or nine dollars charged for LPs. Digital technology also spawned new and more affordable devices for producing and manipulating sound—such as *drum machines* and *sequencers,* and *samplers* for digital **sampling**—and the *musical instrument digital interface* (MIDI) specification, which standardized these technologies, allowing devices produced by different manufacturers to "communicate" with one another. Digital technology—portable and relatively cheap—and the rapid expansion of the *personal computer* (PC) market in the early 1990s allowed musicians to set up their own home studios and stimulated the growth of genres like *hip-hop* and *techno,* both of which rely heavily on digitally constructed sound *samples, loops,* and *grooves.* For the first time, satellite technology allowed the worldwide simultaneous broadcast of live concerts, and the development of fiber optics allowed musicians in recording studios thousands of miles apart to work together in real time.

Deregulation of the entertainment industry led to an explosion in the growth of cable television, one by-product of which was the launching of *Music Television* (MTV) in 1981. MTV changed the way the industry operated, rapidly becoming the preferred method for launching a new act or promoting the latest release of a major superstar. (The advent of videos designed to promote rock recordings is often traced to the band Queen's mock-operatic hard rock extravaganza "Bohemian Rhapsody," released in 1975. However, such early music videos were essentially advertisements for the sound recordings and not viewed as products that might be sold on their own merits.) Although the first song broadcast on MTV bore the title "Video Killed the Radio Star," it is more accurate to say that MTV—and its spin-off VH-1, aimed at an older, twenty-five- to thirty-five-year old audience—worked synergistically with radio and other media to boost record sales and create a new generation of rock superstars. It also strongly influenced the direction of popular music in the early 1980s, sparking what has been called a second British Invasion by promoting English artists such as Eurythmics, Flock of Seagulls, Adam Ant, Billy Idol, and Thomas Dolby. (In July 1983 eighteen of the singles in *Billboard*'s Top 40 chart were by English artists, topping the previous record of fourteen, set in 1965 during the first British Invasion.) By the mid-1980s the impact of MTV had been felt throughout the music industry.

MTV's relentless focus on white rock artists reminded many critics of the exclusionary practices of album-oriented rock radio in the 1970s. Out of more than 750 videos shown on MTV during the channel's first eighteen months, only about twenty featured black musicians (a figure that includes racially mixed bands). At a time when black artists such as Michael Jackson and Rick James were making multiplatinum LPs, they could not break into MTV, which put Phil Collins's cover version of the

Supremes' "You Can't Hurry Love" into heavy rotation, but played no videos by Motown artists themselves. Executives at MTV responded to widespread criticism of their policy with the argument that their format focused on rock, a style played by few black artists. Of course, this was a tautological argument—the restrictive format of MTV was the cause, and not merely a by-product, of the problem.

The mammoth success of Michael Jackson's *Thriller*, released by Columbia Records in 1982, forced a change in MTV's essentially all-white rock music format. The three videos made to promote the *Thriller* LP through three of its hit singles—"Billie Jean," "Beat It," and "Thriller"—set new standards for production quality, creativity, and cost and established the medium as the primary means of promoting popular music. "Thriller"—a horror movie *cum* musical directed by John Landis, who had previously made the feature film *An American Werewolf in London*—metamorphosed into a sixty-minute home video entitled *The Making of Michael Jackson's Thriller*, with the original fifteen-minute video and lots of filler material, including interviews with the star. *The Making of Michael Jackson's Thriller* sold 350,000 copies in the first six months, yet MTV still refused to air Jackson's videos. Finally, after Columbia Records threatened to ban its white rock groups from performing on MTV, the channel relented, putting Jackson's videos into heavy rotation. (*Thriller* will be discussed in more detail later; for now we will simply note that Jackson did not share the segregationist sentiments of MTV executives, going out of his way to include white rock stars such as Paul McCartney and Eddie Van Halen on his LP.)

The process of corporate consolidation (sometimes called "horizontal integration"), which has emerged at intervals throughout the history of American popular music, once again reared its head during the late 1980s and early 1990s. To a greater extent than ever before, record labels could no longer be considered stand-alone institutions but rather subdepartments of huge transnational corporations. By 1990 six corporations collectively controlled over two-thirds of global sales of recorded music: the Dutch *Polygram* conglomerate (owner of Mercury, Polydor, Island, A&M and other labels); the Japanese corporations *Sony* (Columbia Records) and *Matsushita* (MCA and Geffen Records); the British firm *Thorn* (EMI, Virgin, Capitol); the German *Bertelsmann* conglomerate (BMG and RCA Records); and *Time-Warner*, the only American-based corporation in this list (Warner, Elektra, and Atlantic Records). Similarly, the American market for recorded music now had to be seen as part of a wider global market that transcended national borders. In 1990 the largest market for recorded music in the world remained the United States, which, at $7.5 billion, accounted for approximately 31 percent of world trade, followed at some distance by Japan (12 percent), the United Kingdom and Germany (9 percent each), and France (7 percent). Even in the United States, however, the record company executives concerned themselves to an unprecedented degree with global sales and promotion.

This move toward global corporate consolidation of the music business was accompanied by a further fragmentation of the marketplace for popular music and the creation of dozens of new musical genres, marketing categories, and radio formats. Some of these were more novel than others, but all bore some relationship to musical forms of the past. Country music continued its six-decade journey from the margins to the center of popular taste, becoming the bestselling genre of music in the United States with rock- and pop-influenced country superstars such as Garth

Brooks, Clint Black, and Reba McEntire. Rock music, which had undergone a process of fragmentation in the early 1970s, shattered into a hundred specialized genres and subgenres, some with huge audiences (adult contemporary and heavy metal), and others supported by smaller but devoted groups of fans (hardcore, thrash, and techno, the respective children of punk rock, heavy metal, and Eurodisco). Rap music, which had emerged during the mid-1970s from the hip-hop culture of black, Latino, and Caribbean American youth in New York City, had by the late 1980s grown into a multimillion-dollar business. During the 1990s the relationship between the center and periphery of the music business, and between mainstream and marginalized types of music, became even more complicated, with self-consciously anticommercial genres like gangsta rap, speed metal, and grunge reaching the top of the *Billboard* LP and singles charts and generating huge profits for the music industry, and with musicians from Latin America (Ricky Martin) and French Canada (Celine Dion) ranking among the most profitable superstars in the United States at the end of the second millennium.

The core themes that we have traced throughout this book—the intimate relationship between social identity and musical style; the links between music, economics, and technology; and the interaction of various streams of musical tradition—were just as evident at the close of the twentieth century as they were at its inception. On the other hand, much has changed over the past hundred years; old, deep patterns of American musical culture have been profoundly shaped by the advent of new technologies and institutions, new social movements, and profound shifts in the self-definition and values of musicians and their audiences. In this chapter we will begin our consideration of the popular music of the 1980s and 1990s with a look at the changing nature of the musical mainstream.

DIGITAL TECHNOLOGY AND POPULAR MUSIC

During the 1980s new technologies—including digital tape recorders, compact discs, synthesizers, samplers, and sequencers—became central to the production, promotion, and consumption of popular music. These devices were the fruit of a long history of interactions between the electronics and music industries and between individual inventors and musicians.

Analog recording—the norm since the introduction of recording in the nineteenth century—transforms the energy of sound waves into physical imprints (as in pre-1925 acoustic recordings) or into electronic waveforms that closely follow (and can be used to reproduce) the shape of the sound waves themselves. *Digital recording*, on the other hand, samples the sound waves and breaks them down into a stream of numbers (0s and 1s). A device called an *analog-to-digital converter* does the conversion. To play back the music, the stream of numbers is converted back to an analog wave by a *digital-to-analog converter* (DAC). The analog wave produced by the DAC is amplified and fed to speakers to produce the sound. There have been many arguments among musicians and audiophiles over the relative quality of the two technologies: initially, many musicians found digital recording too "cold" (perhaps a metaphor for the process itself, which disassembles a sound into millions of constituent bits). Today, however, almost all popular recordings are digitally recorded.

Synthesizers—devices that allow musicians to create or "synthesize" musical sounds—began to appear on rock records during the early 1970s, but their history begins much earlier. One important predecessor of the synthesizer was the *theremin,* a sound generator named after the Russian inventor who developed it in 1919. This instrument used electronic oscillators to produce sound, and its pitch was controlled by the player's waving his or her hands in front of two antennae. The theremin was never used much in popular music, although its familiar sound can be heard in the soundtracks of 1950s science fiction films such as *The Day the Earth Stood Still,* and on the Beach Boys' 1966 hit "Good Vibrations."

Another important stage in the interaction between scientific invention and musical technology was the *Hammond organ,* introduced in 1935 by the inventor Laurens Hammond. The sound of the Hammond B-3 organ was common on jazz, R&B, and rock records (e.g., Santana's "Oye Como Va"), and its rich, fat sound is frequently sampled in contemporary popular music. The player could alter the **timbre** of the organ through control devices called "tone bars," and a variety of rhythm patterns and percussive effects were added later. Although the Hammond organ was not a true synthesizer, it is certainly a close ancestor.

In the early 1970s the first synthesizers aimed at a mass consumer market were introduced. These devices, which used electronic oscillators to produce musical tones, were clumsy and limited by today's standards, yet their characteristic sounds are viewed with some nostalgia and are often sampled in contemporary recordings. The first synthesizers to be sold in music stores alongside guitars and pianos were the *Minimoog,* which had the limitation of being able to play only one pitch at a time, and the *Arp* synthesizer, which could play simple **chords**. The *Synclavier,* a high-end (and expensive) digital synthesizer, was introduced to the market in 1976. The more affordable *Prophet-5,* introduced in 1978, was an analog synthesizer that incorporated aspects of digital technology, including the ability to store a limited number of sampled sounds.

The 1980s saw the introduction of the first completely digital synthesizers—including the widely popular Yamaha *DX-7*—capable of playing dozens of "voices" at the same time. The *MIDI* (Musical Instrument Digital Interface) specification, introduced in 1983, allowed synthesizers built by different manufacturers to be connected with and communicate with one another, introducing compatibility into a highly competitive marketplace. *Digital samplers*—for example, the *Mirage* keyboard sampler, introduced by Ensoniq in 1984—were capable of storing both prerecorded and synthesized sounds. (The latter were often called "patches," a nostalgic reference to the wires or "patch cords" that were used to connect the various components of early synthesizers.) *Digital sequencers,* introduced to the marketplace at around the same time, are devices that record musical data rather than musical sound and allow the creation of repeated sound sequences (loops), the manipulation of rhythmic grooves, and the transmission of recorded data from one program or device to another. *Drum machines* such as the *Roland TR 808* and the *Linn LM-1*—almost ubiquitous on 1980s dance music and rap recordings—rely on "drum pads" that can be struck and activated by the performer, and which act as a trigger for the production of sampled sounds (including not only conventional percussion instruments but also glass smashing, cars screeching, and guns firing).

Digital technology has given musicians the ability to create complex 128-voice textures, to create sophisticated synthesized sounds that exist nowhere in nature, and to sample and manipulate any sound source, creating sound loops that can be controlled with great precision. With compact, highly portable, and increasingly affordable music equipment and software, a recording studio can be set up literally anywhere—in a basement, or on a roof. As the individual musician gains more and more control over the production of a complete musical recording, distinctions between the composer, the performer, and the producer sometimes melt down entirely.

Certain contemporary genres make particularly frequent and effective use of digital technologies, particularly rap/hip-hop and various genres of electronic dance music (electronica or techno). The technology of digital sampling allows musicians to assemble preexisting sound sources and to cite performers and music from various styles and historical eras. During the 1980s musicians began to reach back into their record collections for sounds from the 1960s and 1970s. It has been suggested that this reflects a more general cultural shift toward a "cut-and-paste" approach to history, in which pop music cannibalizes its own past. However, it is worth remembering that, while the technology is new, the idea of recycling old materials (and thereby selectively reinventing the past) is probably as old as music itself.

Some interesting legal dilemmas are connected with the widespread use of digital sampling. American intellectual property law has always made it difficult to claim ownership of a groove, style, or sound, precisely those things that are most distinctive about popular music—like the timbre of James Brown's voice, the electric bass sound of Parliament/Funkadelic's Bootsy Collins, or the distinctive snare drum sound used on many of Phil Collins's hit recordings (a sound constructed in the studio out of a combination of sampled and synthesized sources). In recent years many lawsuits have centered on these issues, in which musicians and producers claim that their sound has been stolen by means of digital sampling. George Clinton has responded to the wholesale sampling of his albums by rap musicians by releasing a collection of sounds and previously unreleased recordings called *Sample Some of Disc, Sample Some of D.A.T.* The collection comes with a copyright clearance guide and a guarantee that users will only be "charged per record sold, so if your single flops, you won't be in the red."

Of course, no technology is inherently good or evil—it's what humans do with their tools that counts. On the one hand, many musicians mourn the replacement of acoustic musical instruments—and the physical discipline and craft involved in mastering them—by machines. Others tout the democratization of popular music made possible by more affordable technologies. And still others point out that, no matter how good the technology, only a small percentage of musicians are able to gain access to the powerful corporations that control the music industry. The odds that a musician will succeed have not changed much, precisely because almost everyone now has access to the new technology. While high-quality demonstration tapes ("demos") used to be a luxury available to only those musicians who could afford to rent a professional recording studio, now every kid on the block has a demo.

A 1980s CD CHANGER

Although the single disc had gone into decline as a primary medium for distributing popular music—replaced first by the LP, and then by the CD and music video— it nonetheless remained true that, as one record company executive put it, "nobody goes around humming albums." Songs remained the basic currency of popular music throughout the 1980s and into the 1990s. As we did in our attempt to sketch the stylistic range of Number One pop singles during the 1970s (Chapter 6), we will again use the metaphor of the jukebox—or, more apropos to the 1980s, the multidisc CD player—to discuss a series of recordings that illustrate the diversity of materials and performers that topped the charts.

We have chosen to focus on five recordings, each of which reached the Number One position on the pop charts during the 1980s. Taken as a group, they give us a sense of the diversity of styles embraced by the mass audience for popular music. As in our examples from the 1970s, the majority of these songs were written by the performers themselves. The two exceptions are Kenny Rogers's version of "Lady," a song penned by fellow pop superstar Lionel Richie, and Tina Turner's performance of "What's Love Got to Do with It," written by a pair of professional tunesmiths.

Taken individually, each of these recordings reveals a distinctive dimension of the subject matter that, more than any other, has dominated American popular music for over a century: love (and its profane cousin, sex). If during the 1980s consumers were faced with an ever broader choice of musical styles, they were also bombarded by a great diversity of mass-mediated images of intimate relationships. From the romantic chivalry of Kenny Rogers's "Lady" (1980) to the world-weariness of Tina Turner's "What's Love Got to Do with It" (1984) and the playful blues-derived bravado of Peter Gabriel's "Sledgehammer" (1986), popular music in the 1980s remained an important forum for public discourse about the nature of love and sexuality.

"Lady" (1980)

Performed by Kenny Rogers; written by Lionel Richie

The blend of country and pop music that had helped to create huge crossover hits for Nashville during the 1970s continued apace throughout the following decade, paving the way for country music's spectacular invasion of the mainstream during the 1990s. Texas-born Kenny Rogers (b. 1938)—a veteran of folk pop groups such as the New Christy Minstrels and the First Edition, and the star of made-for-TV movies such as *The Gambler* and *Coward of the County*—was one of the main beneficiaries of country pop's increasing mainstream appeal. As a renegade from pop music, Rogers was not considered authentic by conservative country music fans, but he did receive a number of awards from the Country Music Association, including Male Vocalist of the Year (1979). From 1977 to 1984 he sold an estimated $250 million worth of records, including a total of six gold and twelve platinum albums.

The song "Lady" appeared on *Kenny Rogers's Greatest Hits*, the bestselling country album of the 1980s, and was the tenth bestselling single of the entire decade. In addition, it was one of very few singles during the decade to appear on all of the major *Billboard* charts, topping the pop (*Hot 100*), adult contemporary, and country charts, and reaching Number Forty-two on the rhythm & blues chart. Only a few other recordings in the history of American popular music accomplished this feat, including Elvis Presley's "Hound Dog" and "Don't Be Cruel" (1956). In style and sensibility, however, Rogers's performance of "Lady" is light-years away from Presley's crossover hits. Whereas Presley found common ground between the blues and country music in the musical heritage of the South, Rogers was first and foremost a creature of the pop mainstream, and more particularly of a category called "adult contemporary" (that did not even exist as a marketing category in 1956), mainly romantic songs aimed at a twenty-five- to forty-five-year-old audience.

"Lady" was written and produced by another superstar of the 1980s, <u>Lionel Richie</u>. Richie, a former member of a vocal R&B group called the Commodores, is an African American singer and songwriter whose career overarches conventional genre boundaries. Although his own big hits of the 1980s were soul-tinged variants of adult contemporary music, Richie also placed two singles in the country Top 40 during the 1980s and was the composer of "Sail On," a song covered by a number of prominent country artists. (In the mid-1980s Richie became one of the few black musicians admitted to the Country Music Association during a period when country and black popular music had less overlap then ever before.)

"Lady" is a sentimental song that has much in common with popular songs of the nineteenth century, such as Stephen Foster's well-known "Jeanie with the Light Brown Hair." The song follows a verse-chorus structure and uses the image of a knight in shining armor, ultimately derived from the Crusades of the Middle Ages, to profess the singer's deep and undying love. Lionel Richie, who produced the recording, followed a strategy of keeping it simple, avoiding "gimmicks," and foregrounding Rogers's sincere delivery of the lyrics.

The musical accompaniment for Rogers's husky voice is delicate, opening with a solo acoustic piano, and only gradually introducing additional layers of orchestration—an oboe, strings, a suggestion of pedal steel guitar (evocative of country music). Finally, just as the chorus arrives, the whole rhythm section joins in, energetically supporting the emotional climax of the whole song. This structure repeats with the same pattern of quiet reflection giving way to the more explicitly emotional chorus, which is repeated at the end.

In many ways "Lady" seems a throwback to the prerock era: a soft and sentimental song, couched in a determinedly bland arrangement calculated both to create an air of intimacy and to offend as few people as possible. The crossover success of "Lady" is particularly interesting in that it took place in the 1980s, a period when the country and R&B charts each overlapped frequently with the pop charts but rarely with each other. By the early 1980s it may have been that the one thing that country music and soul fans had in common was the old tradition of the romantic "torch song."

"Sweet Dreams (Are Made of This)" (1983)

Written and performed by Eurythmics

This Number One single from the early 1980s exemplifies one of the directions dance music took in the postdisco era. With its heavy reliance on electronically synthesized sounds, sequenced loops, and what has been described as a cool or austere emotional tone, Eurythmics' "Sweet Dreams" points the way toward later technology-centered music styles such as techno. Like some of the most successful techno groups of the 1990s (see Chapter 9), Eurythmics consisted of a core of only two musicians—the singer <u>Annie Lennox</u> (b. 1954 in Scotland) and keyboardist and technical whiz <u>Dave Stewart</u> (b. 1952 in England).

Eurythmics' first chart appearance in the United States came with the release of their second album, *Sweet Dreams (Are Made of This),* in 1983. The title track was released as a single soon after the album, rocketed to Number Two on the English charts, and shortly afterward climbed to Number One on the American charts. The popularity of "Sweet Dreams (Are Made of This)" in the United States was boosted enormously by a video produced to promote the record, which was placed into heavy rotation by the fledgling MTV channel. In particular, the stylishly androgynous image of Annie Lennox—a female David Bowie, in a business suit and close-cropped orange hair—is often identified as an important ingredient in Eurythmics' success.

"Sweet Dreams" is a good example of commercial new wave music of the early 1980s, an outgrowth of the 1970s new wave/punk scene promoted by major record labels. It also exemplifies a more specific genre label that began to be used about this time: "synth-pop," the first type of popular music explicitly defined by its use of electronic sound synthesis. Although synth-pop died out by the end of the 1980s, it helped to establish the centrality of the synthesizer in popular dance music.

"Sweet Dreams" is built around a hypnotic digital loop: a repeated pattern established abruptly at the beginning of the record, as though the listener were dropped into the flow of a synthetic river of sound. A booming steady pulse, synthesized on a digital drum machine and reminiscent of disco music, underlies the melodic portion of the loop. Annie Lennox's singing alternates between an R&B- and soul-influenced **melismatic** style and the flatter, more deadpan tone that she adopts on the verses. The verses themselves consist of two four-line blocks of text, sung by Lennox in overdubbed harmonies. The singer seems to be expressing an unsettling—and titillating—combination of cynicism, sensuality, and—in the chorus—hope for the future. Some lines of the text ("some of them want . . . ") hint darkly at sadomasochistic relationships, suggesting that the singer's sophistication has perhaps been won at some emotional cost. In the call-and-response chorus—which uses multitracking technology to alternate Lennox as lead singer with Lennox as choir—the mood changes, and the listener is exhorted to "hold your head up," while the multitracked voices urge us to keep "movin' on."

Combined with Lennox's carefully cultivated sexual ambiguity—in a subsequent music video, "Who's That Girl," she plays male and female characters, and ends up kissing herself/himself—the lyrics and musical textures of "Sweet Dreams" suggest a sophisticated, even worldweary take on the nature of love, far removed from the naïve romanticism of Kenny Rogers's recording of "Lady."

Finally, although "Sweet Dreams" is sometimes regarded to as an example of the emerging technological sophistication of the early 1980s, the recording was made under less than optimum conditions. The studio rented by Stewart was a dingy, V-shaped warehouse attic, without any of the amenities of a professional studio (such as acoustical tiles or isolation booths for recording separate instrumental tracks). Their equipment was rudimentary—an eight-track tape recorder and a cheap mixer, two microphones, an early version of a digital drum machine available in England at the time, and a handful of old sound effects devices. "It sounded so sophisticated," reported Stewart in a 1983 feature in *Billboard,* "but often we had to wait for the timber factory downstairs to turn off their machinery before we could record the vocals." In fact, not all of the instrumental sounds on the recording are electronic in origin: the clinking **counterpoint** under the chorus of "Sweet Dreams" was played on milk bottles pitched to the right notes by filling them with different levels of water. In this sense "Sweet Dreams" both hearkens back to the "do it yourself" ethic of 1970s punk and new wave music and points forward to the experiments of 1990s techno musicians, who often introduce natural environmental sounds into their recordings.

"What's Love Got to Do with It" (1984)

Performed by Tina Turner; written by Terry Britten and Graham Lyle

By the time Tina Turner (née Annie Mae Bullock, b. 1939 in Tennessee) recorded "What's Love Got to Do with It," she had been in the popular music limelight for over twenty years. Her recording debut took place in 1960 as a member of the Ike and Tina Turner Revue. Tina's husband, Ike Turner, had begun his recording ca-

Tina Turner in action. Frank Driggs Collection.

reer much earlier, as a performer on Jackie Brenston's "Rocket 88" (1951), some-times credited as the first rock 'n' roll record. Ike and Tina scored big crossover hits during the 1960s with "A Fool in Love" (Number Two R&B and Number Twenty-seven pop in 1960), "It's Gonna Work Out Fine" (Number Two R&B and Number Fourteen pop in 1961), and a gold record version of Creedence Clearwater Revival's 1969 hit "Proud Mary" (Number Four pop and Number Five R&B in 1971).

As recounted in her 1986 bestselling autobiography, *I, Tina,* Tina Turner eventu-ally tired of the abusive behavior of her husband, leaving him in 1976 to start her own career. The first years were tough, but by 1981 the Rolling Stones and Rod Stewart, old fans of the Ike and Tina Revue, had hired her as an opening act on their concert tours. In 1983 she was offered a contract by Capitol Records. Her first album, entitled *Private Dancer* (1984), reached Number Three on the album charts, stayed in the Top 40 for seventy-one weeks, spawned five hit singles, and eventually went on to attain worldwide sales in excess of eleven million copies. In succeeding years Turner con-tinued to build her career, releasing a series of platinum albums and appearing in movies such as *Mad Max beyond Thunderdome* (1985). In 1993 a film version of her au-tobiography was produced, entitled *What's Love Got to Do with It.*

The crossover hit "What's Love Got to Do with It" (Number One pop and Num-ber Two R&B in 1984) stayed on the charts for twenty-eight weeks, and earned Grammy awards in 1984 for Best Female Pop Vocalist, Song of the Year, and Record of the Year. Turner did not like the song at first and did not hesitate in conveying this sentiment to Terry Britten, its coauthor and producer of the *Private Dancer* al-bum. "[Terry] said that when a song is given to an artist it's changed for the artists," Turner reminisced. "He said for me to make it a bit rougher, a bit more sharp around the edges. All of a sudden, just sitting there with him in the studio, the song be-came mine" (Wynn 1985, p. 132).

The lyric of "What's Love Got to Do with It" sets up an ambivalent relationship between the overwhelming sexual attraction described in the verses and the singer's cynicism about romantic love, derided in the song's chorus as a "secondhand emo-tion." This dynamic in the song's text is reinforced by the musical accompaniment. Though the tempo remains fairly constant (a relaxed pace of 98 beats per minute), the instrumental arrangement alternates between the rich, continuous texture, dom-inated by flute- and stringlike synthesizer sounds, that underlies the verses, and a more bouncy, reggae-like groove established by the electric bass and guitars on the chorus, the lyrics of which begin with the song's title.

The whole arrangement itself is carefully constructed—an eight-bar instrumen-tal introduction; a unusual thirteen-bar verse ("You must understand . . . "), com-prising seven- and six-bar sections (A); an eight-bar chorus (B); then another verse (A) ("It may seem . . . "), followed by another chorus (B). The middle point of the arrangement in structural terms is a synthesizer solo of seven and a half bars, us-ing the harmonies of the chorus (B'). This is followed by an eight-bar section (C) with new harmonies, where the singer reveals her fear of heartbreak more explic-itly ("I've been taking . . . "). The arrangement concludes with three repetitions of the chorus (minus one bar, thanks to the early entrance of the chorus each time through), fading away at the very end.

For many in her audience, the character in this song—an experienced, cyni-cal, yet still vulnerable woman—was Turner herself, a case where the boundary between the public and private lives of a recording artist seems to have dissolved almost entirely. (In the case of a David Bowie or—as we shall discuss—Madonna, a sense of ironic distance between the celebrity image and the individual behind it is carefully maintained. In Tina Turner's case, this distinction between image and identity is much less certain.) The combination of poignancy and toughness projected in Turner's recordings and live performances was linked by her fans to the details of her biography and helps to explain her appeal as the first black woman to attain major status in the predominantly white male field of arena rock music.

"Jump" (1984)

Performed by Van Halen, written by Eddie Van Halen, Alex Van Halen, Michael Anthony, and David Lee Roth

Heavy metal music, pioneered in the late 1960s and early 1970s by bands such as Led Zeppelin and Deep Purple, went into a period of relative decline during the late 1970s, partly as a result of the disco craze. By the early 1980s most hit singles—particularly those promoted on MTV—were oriented more toward postdisco dance music played on keyboard synthesizers than toward the electric guitar virtuosity of heavy metal bands. The music industry tended to ignore heavy metal music, regarding it and its core audience of adolescent white males as something of an embarrassment.

During the 1980s, however, heavy metal came back with a vengeance. A slew of metal albums topped the singles and album charts, ranging from the pop metal sounds of bands like Van Halen, Bon Jovi, Mötley Crüe, and Def Leppard to the harder sound of speed metal bands such as Metallica, Slayer, Anthrax, and Megadeath. One of the most important moments in the mainstreaming of heavy metal was the release of Van Halen's album *1984*, which featured the Number One pop single "Jump."

"Jump" was in some ways a remarkable departure from standard heavy metal practice. To begin with, its main instrumental melody was played on a synthesizer rather than an electric guitar. This may seem like a minor detail, but it was an important symbolic and aesthetic issue for hardcore metal fans, many of whom focus closely on the technical virtuosity of guitarists like <u>Eddie Van Halen</u>. From this perspective, the keyboard synthesizer (like disco music) is viewed as a somewhat questionable, perhaps even effeminate instrument. As Philip Bashe, an expert on heavy metal music, has put it, the fact that Eddie Van Halen played the bombastic opening theme of "Jump" on a synthesizer rather than a guitar was "a brave test of the Van Halen audience's loyalty" (Bashe 1985, p. 137). The success of the single was boosted by its corresponding music video, which was shot in home-movie style and featured the athletic prowess and oddball sense of humor of David Lee Roth—at that time Van Halen's lead singer.

On "Jump," the song itself, in the conventional sense of words-plus-melody, is not a core focus of attention for the musicians or their listeners. (Eddie Van Halen, when asked by an interviewer what his mother would think of the lyrics to his band's songs, said that he had no idea at all what they were!) The text of "Jump"—a casual come-on to a girl from a guy leaning against a jukebox—seems almost an afterthought, apart, perhaps, from the clever "go ahead and jump!" hook phrase, which sounds rather as though David Lee Roth were counseling the object of his affections to jump off a high ledge, rather than into his arms. The notion of love as risk taking—so strongly portrayed in Tina Turner's "What's Love Got to Do with It"—is present here as well, though from a decidedly male point of view.

The chief significance of a recording like "Jump," however, lies not in the song per se but in the musical textures created by the band and the studio engineer, and in the sensibility that they evoke. As we have mentioned, one of the main points of attention for heavy metal fans is the virtuosity of the genre's master guitarists, a tradition that they trace back to pioneers such as Jimi Hendrix and Led Zeppelin's Jimmy Page. Eddie Van Halen, widely recognized as a primary innovator in electric guitar performance, is famous for developing widely used techniques ("pull-offs" and "tapping") and for performing various operations on his guitars and amplifiers to modify their sound.

Although "Jump" relies heavily on the keyboard synthesizer for its effect, the sounds generated by Eddie Van Halen are in fact closely analogous to his guitar style. In particular, he uses the synthesizer to create something akin to "power chords," two-note combinations that, when played at high volume on an electric guitar, create the massive, distorted, bone-crunching sound associated with heavy metal bands. "Jump" opens with a synthesized power chord, as if to announce right from the beginning that the sheer sound of the music is more important than the specific instruments used to produce it. Thick textures and a strong pulse, played on keyboards, bass, and drums, propel us through the first two verses of the song. The arrival of the chorus is marked by a sudden opening up, in which the synthesizer plays long sustained chords, the electric guitar plays a sizzling counterpoint to the vocal melody, and the drums and bass play an interesting irregular rhythmic pattern that first suspends the beat and then, after four bars, unleashes it with even greater energy. After another verse- and-chorus section, we are transported into the midst of a virtuoso guitar solo that uses Eddie Van Halen's famed techniques. The guitar solo is followed by a longer synthesizer solo, which develops an elaborate melodic improvisation that closely parallels the style of Van Halen's guitar playing.

Although some hardcore metal fans criticized Van Halen for moving away from the guitar-centered model of heavy metal musicianship, the band succeeded in introducing synthesizers into the genre, and in helping to spread metal's popularity to a larger and more diverse audience. In 1983 only 8 percent of records sold in the United States were heavy metal; a year later that total had risen to 20 percent, making metal one of the most popular genres of popular music. This process continued in 1986 when the pop metal band Bon Jovi released the album *Slippery When Wet*, which held the Number One spot for eight weeks and went on to sell over twelve million copies worldwide. By the end of 1986 MTV had launched *Headbangers' Ball*, a show designed specifically for metal fans, which soon became the most-watched show on the channel. In the late 1980s heavy metal music accounted for around half of the Top 20 albums on the *Billboard* charts on any given week.

"Sledgehammer" (1986)

Written and performed by Peter Gabriel

<u>Peter Gabriel</u> (b. 1950 in England) first achieved celebrity as a member of the art rock group Genesis. After leaving Genesis in 1976, Gabriel released four solo albums, all of them titled *Peter Gabriel*. Partly in an effort to clear up the consumer confusion that followed in the wake of this unusual strategy, he gave his next album a distinctive-if brief-title: *So*. *So* was an interesting and accessible amalgam of various musical styles, reflecting Gabriel's knowledge of the new digital technologies, his budding interest in world music (see Chapter 9), and his indebtedness to black music, particularly R&B and soul music of the 1960s. The album peaked at

Number Two on the Top LPs chart, sold four million copies, and produced Gabriel's
bestselling single "Sledgehammer" (Number One pop, Number Sixty-one R&B in
1986).

"Sledgehammer" features a horn section led by the trumpet player Wayne Jackson, who, as a member of the Memphis Horns, had played on many of the biggest
soul music hits of the 1960s ("Knock on Wood," "Soul Man," etc.). Jackson had
deeply impressed sixteen-year-old Peter Gabriel during an appearance with the Otis
Redding Soul Revue at a London R&B club in 1966. Gabriel described "Sledgehammer" as

> an attempt to recreate some of the spirit and style of the music that most excited me
> as a teenager—60s soul. The lyrics of many of those songs were full of playful sex-
> ual innuendo and this is my contribution to that songwriting tradition. It is also
> about the use of sex as a means of getting through a breakdown in communication.
> (Bright 1999, p. 267)

The lyrics to "Sledgehammer"—packed with double-entendre references to sledge-
hammers, big dippers, steam trains, the female "fruitcake" and the male "honey-
bee"—are in fact a G-rated variant of the sexual metaphors that have long been a
part of the blues tradition.

The formal building blocks of "Sledgehammer" are twelve-bar and eight-bar
sections, with the former predominating in the first half of the arrangement. While
most pop music recordings are concerned to establish the beat or groove as quickly

as possible, "Sledgehammer" opens with an exotic touch, a digital keyboard sample of a Japanese flute called the shakuhachi, as a hint of Gabriel's budding interest in world music. The funk-influenced groove—with strong backbeats on the snare drum, the keyboard bass landing strongly on the first beat of each measure, and the guitar playing a bouncy upbeat pattern similar to ska—is introduced by the horn section, backed by synthesizers. After eight bars the horns drop out and the rhythm takes four measures to establish the groove that will carry us through the rest of the recording.

Following the introduction, Peter Gabriel sings two verses (beginning with the lines "You could have a steam train" and "You could have a big dipper"), each of which is twelve bars in length. Though his intent to evoke the blues form seems clear, he does not strictly observe the a-a-b lyric form found often in **blues** (that is to say, he does not repeat the first line of the text in the verses). In addition, he dispenses with the traditional approach to blues harmonies, staying on the **tonic** chord for a full eight measures, moving to a related chord (which musicians call the relative minor) for two bars, and then returning to the tonic for the last two bars. (Although many traditional blues linger on the tonic chord in a manner similar to this, they rarely if ever move to the relative minor chord, a harmony more in keeping with **Tin Pan Alley** music.)

After singing two of these twelve-bar verses, Gabriel moves to the eight-bar chorus ("I want to be your sledgehammer"). Once again, the song takes an interesting turn in harmonic terms, shifting from the **major** key of the verse to a **minor** key based on the same tonic note. (More precisely, the B section begins on a chord closely related to the tonic major, and then shifts to the tonic minor chord itself.) Listen closely for the shift between the A and the B section, and see if you can hear the different color or feeling of the harmonies.

The arrangement continues with a four-bar instrumental section taking us back to the major-key harmonies of the verse; another verse ("Show me round your fruitcakes"), shortened to eight instead of twelve bars; and two presentations of the chorus ("I want to be your sledgehammer"). The last section of the arrangement relies on a minor-key harmonic pattern closely related to that of the chorus, moving back and forth between the tonic minor chord and another, closely related chord; it begins with a keyboard synthesizer solo. Finally, a series of eight-bar sections ("I will show for you") are heard, in which Gabriel's vocal phrases alternate with a choir of gospel-style singers. The arrangement reaches a peak here, with Gabriel improvising solo phrases against the responses of the choir ("Show for me, Show for you"). Gabriel's attempt to "recreate some of the spirit and style" of 1960s soul music may be successful precisely because he does not try to produce an exact copy of the black musical styles that inspired him. Rather, he uses fundamental elements such as the twelve-bar blues form, call-and-response singing, strong funk-derived **polyrhythms**, and an R&B style horn section as the basis for a performance that reflects his own musical experience and taste, including references to world music and harmonies that take the blues in new directions.

The success of "Sledgehammer" was in no small part due to the massive exposure it received on MTV in the mid-1980s. The video version of "Sledgehammer" was an eye-catching, witty, and technically innovative work that pushed the frontiers of the medium. It won nine MTV Awards (more than any video in history), including Best Video and the prestigious Video Vanguard Award for career achievement in 1987, and was ranked the fourth best video of all time in a 1999 retrospective aired on MTV. The making of the video, which combined stop-motion techniques and live action, required Gabriel to spend eight painful sixteen-hour days lying under glass with his head supported by a steel pole. (Aardman Animations, the outfit that produced the "Sledgehammer" video, went on to work on the *Wallace and Gromit* videos and the talking car ads aired by Chevron in the late 1990s.)

One key to the success of any music video is the relationship it establishes between the sound of the original recording (which, except in the case of live concert videos, is always made first) and the flow of visual images. The video of "Sledgehammer"—directed by Steven Johnston—opens with enlarged microscopic images of human sperm cells impregnating an egg, which develops into a fetus, accompanied by the exotic sound of the synthesized flute. As the groove is established, we see Gabriel's face in close-up, moving to the groove, wiggling his eyebrows, ears, and mouth in time to the music. The stop-motion technique—in which the camera is halted and restarted in order to create the illusion of inanimate objects moving under their own power—creates a jerky stop-start effect that establishes a kind of parallel reality, carefully coordinated to match the rhythms of the music. The lyrics of the song are also reflected in the video images: when Gabriel sings "You could have a steam train," a toy locomotive circles his head on miniature tracks; when he sings "You could have a bumper car bumping, this amusement never ends," two smiling (and singing) bumper cars appear next to his ears, mountains of popcorn pile up behind him, and his hair turns to pink cotton candy. After a series of stop-motion sequences featuring everything from singing fruits and vegetables to dancing furniture, Gabriel is transformed into a "starman" and walks off into the night sky. Thus the video takes us from the microscopic origins of life to the vastness of the galaxy, with many diverting stops in between. As Gabriel himself admitted some years later, although the recording of "Sledgehammer" would probably have done well on its own, the ambitious and highly creative video of the song, played endlessly on MTV, introduced the song to millions of Americans who might otherwise never have purchased a Peter Gabriel record.

A TALE OF THREE ALBUMS

A brief look at three multimillion-selling albums of the 1980s will help document the variety of styles that characterized this period. Each of these albums represents the biggest commercial success in its artist's solo career. *Thriller*, in fact, ranks as the top-selling album in history as of this writing, having achieved worldwide sales in excess of forty million copies; it was the Number One album for thirty-seven weeks during 1983.

In the case of Michael Jackson, *Thriller* was the zenith of a career as a solo artist that had been gathering momentum throughout the 1970s, even while Jackson continued to be a pivotal member of the tremendously successful group the Jackson Five (which changed its name to the Jacksons with its departure from the Motown organization in 1976, a departure that caused no substantial interruption in its long-running success story). *Thriller* was state-of-the-art pop music, an album dedicated not so much to breaking new ground as to consolidating Michael Jackson's dominance of the contemporary pop scene by showcasing his versatility as a performer of a stylistically wide range of up-to-date material.

Like Jackson, Paul Simon got his start in the 1960s as a member of a group, in this case the famous folk rock duo Simon and Garfunkel (see Chapter 5). When Simon went on to a productive solo career in the 1970s, however, the duo disbanded. *Graceland* revived a career that had seemed to be in decline in the early 1980s (Simon's two preceding albums had neither the critical nor the commercial success that greeted most of his work of the 1970s) and—with its employment of African musicians, African music, and (occasionally) African subject matter, along with other "exotic" touches—suddenly thrust Simon into the forefront of the new category called world music.

On the other hand, Bruce Springsteen's *Born in the U.S.A.* seemed more concerned with this country's past in its depiction of adult working-class Americans whose better days are behind them, and the album's music is drenched appropriately in Springsteen's typical roots-based rock sound. The glitzy, consciously "modern" sound and production values of *Thriller* clearly were not for Springsteen; neither was he trying in any way to change the basic direction of his career and his music, as Simon was in *Graceland.* In *Born in the U.S.A.* Springsteen was simply continuing to make the kind of music, and to voice the kinds of concerns, that had characterized his career from its beginning in the 1970s. The unexpected megasuccess of the album (it sold over fifteen million copies, whereas the best selling album among Springsteen's previous efforts—*Born to Run* from 1975—had sold less than five million) took the artist himself somewhat by surprise and left him anxious to ascertain whether his newly enlarged audience was truly understanding the less-than-cheerful messages he wished to convey, as we shall see.

Thriller (Michael Jackson, 1982)

In fashioning *Thriller,* Michael Jackson (b. 1958) worked with the veteran producer Quincy Jones to create an album that achieved boundary-crossing popularity to an unprecedented degree. At a time when the pop music audience seemed to be fragmenting to a greater extent perhaps than ever before, *Thriller* demonstrated a kind of across-the-board appeal that established new and still unduplicated heights of commercial success. In a sense, Jackson here revived the goal that had animated his old boss at Motown, Berry Gordy Jr. (see Chapter 4): to create an African American–based pop music that was aimed squarely at the mainstream center of the market. That Jackson met his goal in such a mind-boggling fashion proved conclusively that there indeed still was a mainstream in the pop music of the early 1980s, and that Jackson had positioned himself unquestionably in the center of it.

To do this, Jackson had to be more than just "the sound of young America" (to quote Motown's memorable phrase from the 1960s). It is of course true that teenagers, preteenagers, and young adults made up a substantial portion of the 1980s market. But members of the baby boom generation, along with the many who came to maturity during the 1970s, were also still major consumers of pop music. And age was far from the only basis on which segmentation of the audience seemed to be taking place; fans of soft rock, heavy metal, funk, and new wave music, for instance, appeared to want less and less to do with one another. A disturbing subtext of all this was a tendency toward increasing resegregation along racial lines of the various audiences for pop. Heavy metal and new wave fans—and bands—were overwhelmingly white, while funk and the emerging genre of rap were associated with black performers and listeners.

Thriller represented an effort to find ways to mediate among the various genres of early 1980s pop music, to create points of effective synthesis from the welter of apparently competing styles, and to bridge the divides—actual or potential—separating different segments of the pop music audience. Jackson confronted the racial divide head-on by collaborating with two very popular, and very different, white artists: ex-Beatle Paul McCartney joined Jackson for a lyrical vocal duet on "The Girl Is Mine," while Eddie Van Halen of the heavy metal group Van Halen contributed the stinging guitar solo on the intense "Beat It." Both of these radically different songs, along with two others on *Thriller*, were written by Jackson himself; his versatility and his gift for crossing genres extended also into the domain of songwriting. It is also clear that "The Girl Is Mine" and "Beat It" were fashioned to attract different segments of the white audience. The mere presence of Paul McCartney was a draw for many listeners who had been fans of the Beatles in the 1960s, as well as for those who admired McCartney's 1970s band Wings; as a song, "The Girl Is Mine" combines a gentle melodic flow with a feeling of rhythmic vitality, effectively echoing the virtues of the best Beatles and Wings ballads. "The Girl Is Mine" captured this essentially soft rock ambience—and its audience—especially well: the single release of this song held the Number One spot on *Billboard*'s "Top Adult Contemporary" chart for four weeks. Moreover, "The Girl Is Mine" had sufficient crossover appeal to top the R&B chart (now called "Hot Black Singles") for three weeks as well. As the first single to come out of the *Thriller* album, "The Girl Is Mine" demonstrated immediately how well Michael Jackson's new music could break down preconceptions about marketability.

"Beat It," on the other hand, has nothing to do with soft rock and was a gesture obviously extended to "metal-heads," who must have been struck by the novelty of a collaboration between a celebrated heavy metal guitarist and an African American pop icon. But this door also could, and did, swing both ways. "Beat It" joined "The Girl Is Mine" on the list of Number One black singles in 1983.

Much of *Thriller* consists of uptempo, synthesizer- and bass-driven, danceable music that occupies a (probably conscious) middle ground between the heavy funk of an artist like George Clinton and the brighter but still beat-obsessed sound that characterized many new wave bands (of which Blondie would be a good example). Perhaps the outstanding—and, in this case, unexpected and highly original—example of the album's successful synthesis of diverse stylistic elements may be found in the title song. "Thriller" starts out depicting a horror-movie scene, which eventually turns out to be on the television screen being watched by two lovers, providing them with an excuse for cuddling "close together" and creating their own kind of thrills. In a conclusion that pairs an old white voice with a new black style, horror-movie star Vincent Price comes from out of nowhere to perform a "rap" about the terrors of the night. (This "rap" describes some typical horror-film situations, but its language is occasionally spiced up with current pop-oriented slang—as when Price refers to "the funk of forty thousand years.")

In the early years of long-playing records, the pop music album was typically a collection of individual songs, several (and sometimes all) of which had previously been released as singles. In our discussions of the 1960s and 1970s, we have remarked on the steadily increasing importance of the album over the single, as pop artists began more and more to conceive of the album as their principal creative medium. *Thriller* is a unique landmark in this evolutionary process. *Thriller* is not a concept album—unless the "concept" was to demonstrate that an album could be made to engender hit singles, rather than vice versa. For out of the nine songs on *Thriller,* seven were released as singles, one by one, starting with "The Girl Is Mine" (the only one to be released prior to the album itself), and all seven were Top 10 hits. (Both "Billie Jean" and "Beat It" were Number One pop hits; these two and "Thriller" sold over two million copies each as singles, while "The Girl Is Mine" was a million-selling single. The only songs from *Thriller* that were not turned into hit singles are "Baby Be Mine" and "The Lady in My Life.")

Visual media both old and new played a significant role in the *Thriller* saga. In May 1983 Jackson appeared on the television special *25 Years of Motown* and introduced what came to be known as his "moonwalk" dance while performing "Billie Jean" from *Thriller;* the performance was a sensation and doubtless added to the continuing popularity of the album. By this time, the videos for *Thriller* songs that Jackson had made were being shown regularly on MTV. Jackson's embrace of the relatively new medium of music video reflected his foresight in realizing its potential. While bringing his work to the attention of yet another segment of the music public, his videos in turn helped boost the power and prestige of MTV itself, because they were so carefully, creatively, and elaborately produced. Because Jackson was the first African American artist to be programmed with any degree of frequency on MTV, *Thriller* thus contributed to the breakdown of yet another emerging color line in pop culture. (Significantly, in the video of "Beat It," Jackson is seen breaking up a racially charged gang fight.)

Born in the U.S.A. (Bruce Springsteen, 1984)

Throughout the 1970s <u>Bruce Springsteen</u> (b. 1949) had been forging a progressively more successful career in pop music while continuing to cast both his music and his personal image in the light of the rebellious rock 'n' rollers of the 1950s and the socially conscious folk rockers of the 1960s. Springsteen's songs reflected his working-class origins and sympathies, relating the stories of still young but aging men and women with deadend jobs (or no jobs at all), who are looking for romance and excitement in the face of repeated disappointments and seeking meaningful outlets for their seething energies and hopes in an America that seems to have no pieces of the American dream left to offer them. Some of the song titles from his first few albums are indicative: "Born to Run," "Darkness on the Edge of Town," "Hungry Heart," "Racing in the Street," "Wreck on the Highway," and so on. Springsteen performed with his E Street Band, and their music was characterized by a strong, roots-rock sound that emphasized Springsteen's connections to 1950s and 1960s music. The band even included a saxophone—virtually an anachronism in the pop music of this period—to mark the link with the rhythm & blues and rock 'n' roll of earlier eras. (In this connection, it is worth noting that one of the songs on *Born in the U.S.A.*, "Cover Me," is based on a twelve-bar blues progression. Twelve-bar blues form was also all but an anachronism in the mainstream pop music of the 1980s, but it was part of Springsteen's musical heritage and style, and his continuing employment of this form represented another obvious homage to the roots of rock.) Still, the emphasis in Springsteen's music was predominantly on the traditional rock ensemble of guitars, bass, and drums, with keyboard instruments occasionally used prominently.

Bruce Springsteen. Frank Driggs Collection.

The album immediately preceding *Born in the U.S.A.* represented a departure for Springsteen: *Nebraska* (1982) featured him in a solo, "unplugged" setting that underlined the particular bleakness of this collection of songs. Consequently, many fans may have celebrated *Born in the U.S.A.*, which brought back the E Street Band with an actual as well as a symbolic bang, as a kind of "return to form" for Springsteen. Certainly the album is dominated by uptempo, rocking songs, with Springsteen shouting away in full voice and grand style, and the band playing full tilt behind him. Still, listening at the record (or tape or CD) player with the album's lyric sheet in hand, it is hard to see how anybody could have regarded *Born in the U.S.A.* as anything other than a typically dire commentary by Springsteen on the current state of the union. Indeed, the very first lyrics of the title song, which opens the album, set the tone decisively:

> *Born down in a dead man's town,*
> *The first kick I took was when I hit the ground.*
> *You end up like a dog that's been beat too much*
> *Till you spend half your life just covering up.*

"Born in the U.S.A." tells the story of a returning Vietnam veteran unable to get a job or to rebuild his life, and its despairing message is characteristic of most of the songs on the album.

But maybe many people weren't listening to the words. In the wake of this album's rapid and enormous popularity, Springsteen found himself and his band on tour playing to huge, sold-out stadiums where—given the amplification levels and the crowd noise—most people probably couldn't even *hear* the words. Confronted with hordes of fans waving American flags, and the exploitation of his image in the presidential election year of 1984 by political forces for which he had little sympathy, Springsteen periodically found himself having to explain that he was not associated with "feel-good" politics or uncritical "America first" boosterism. Was Springsteen a victim of his own success, forced into a stadium rock culture that ill served the purpose and meaning of his songs? (Had rock music gained the world, so to speak, only to lose its soul?) Or was there actually some fundamental dichotomy between Springsteen's message and the energetic, crowd-pleasing music in which he was couching it?

There is of course no objectively "correct" answer to such questions. But when listening to *Born in the U.S.A.* as a recording, and as a whole, Springsteen's sincerity seems as apparent as his intensity, and it is hard not to sense, and hard not to be affected by, the prevailing dark ambience. In a general way, *Born in the U.S.A.* is a concept album: a series of musical snapshots of working-class Americans, all of whom seem to be somewhere around Springsteen's age (he turned thirty-five the year he released this album, the same age as his protagonist in the song "My Hometown"), many of whom are having economic or personal difficulties, and all of whom sense the better times of their lives slipping into the past. In the album's original LP form, each of the two sides starts out with a strong, aggressive song and winds down to a final cut that is softer in sound but, if anything, even darker in mood. The first side ends with the low-key but eerie "I'm on Fire," whose protagonist seems about to explode from the weight and pain of his own "bad desire"; in terms of the listening experience, the spooky urgency of this song appears to speak to the cumulative hard luck and frustration of all the different characters described in the songs of Side One. Side Two starts off with an extroverted rebound in musical energy and a cry of "No Surrender." But disillusionment and resignation come to characterize the songs on this side of the record as well, until the "fire" image reappears strikingly in the penultimate song, "Dancing in the Dark." Finally comes "My Hometown"; Springsteen, his voice drained of energy, sings of the decay of his place of birth and of possibly "getting out" with his wife and child, heading toward—it isn't clear what. In this poignant finale, Springsteen comes as close as any pop artist ever has to embracing and conveying an authentically tragic vision.

Amazingly, "My Hometown" was a major hit as a single recording, reaching Number Six on the pop chart in early 1986 (and Number One on the adult contemporary chart). It was the last of seven consecutive singles to be culled from the album, all of which were Top 10 pop hits; in this respect, *Born in the U.S.A.* followed in the footsteps of *Thriller* as an album that spawned a parade of hit singles. The album itself sold over fifteen million copies, as we have already noted, and stayed on the album charts for over two years. Like Michael Jackson, Springsteen produced a series of music videos to go with several of the songs released as singles from *Born in the U.S.A.*; these videos proved popular in their own right and further enhanced the popularity of the album. Thus Springsteen stayed abreast of the changing music scene at the same time that he tried to speak, through his songs, to the values and attitudes that for him lay at the core of all that was worthwhile and enduring in rock.

Graceland (Paul Simon, 1986)

Paul Simon's interest in music that was not indigenous to the United States manifested itself long before he recorded *Graceland*. When he was still singing with Garfunkel, Simon (b. 1941) recorded "El Condor Pasa," a song that paired his own lyrics

Paul Simon. Frank Driggs Collection.

with a backing instrumental track based on an old Peruvian folk melody, performed in "native" style by a group called Los Incas. "El Condor Pasa" appeared on the 1970 Simon and Garfunkel album *Bridge over Troubled Water* and was released as a single that same year. The song was indicative of the path Simon would later pursue much more systematically and thoroughly in *Graceland,* in which many of the songs present Simon's vocals and lyrics over an accompaniment performed in South African style by South African musicians.

A considerable portion of the music for *Graceland* was actually recorded in South Africa, and that resulted in some awkward political issues for Simon. Like *Born in the U.S.A.,* this album became a focus of political attention for fans, skeptics, and, with reluctance, its creator. At the time, a United Nations boycott on performing and recording in South Africa was in effect as part of an international attempt to isolate and ostracize the government of that country, which was still enforcing the widely despised policy of apartheid (separation of the races). Simon could not deny that he broke the boycott, but he claimed that he was in no sense supporting the ideology of the South African government by making music with black South Africans on their native soil. In fact, the success of *Graceland* helped bring black South African musicians and styles to a much wider and racially more diverse audience than they had ever been able to reach before; this proved to be true within South Africa itself, as well as in America and many other parts of the world. It could well be argued that Simon ultimately made, through his racially integrated music, a forceful statement about the virtues of free intermingling and cultural exchange.

In any case, Simon came to a mutual understanding with the United Nations and the opponents of apartheid in relatively short order, and he stopped performing in South Africa until apartheid was dismantled several years later.

A truly "global" album from a geographical point of view, *Graceland* was recorded in five different locations on three different continents: in addition to Johannesburg, South Africa, tracks were cut in London, England; New York City; Los Angeles; and Crowley, Louisiana. Many of the selections on the album combine elements that were recorded at different times in different places, but others were the result of sessions where all the participants were present in the same place at the same time. While Simon flew to South Africa to work on several songs with musicians there, at another time he brought South African musicians to New York to work with him, and on yet another occasion Simon and the South African vocal group Ladysmith Black Mambazo recorded together in London.

What ultimately distinguishes *Graceland* from earlier forays into world music, whether by Simon or by other pop musicians, is the extent to which the album explores the concept of *collaboration*—collaboration among artists of different races, regions, nationalities, and ethnicities, which produced in turn collaboration among diverse musical styles and approaches to songwriting. This provides a conceptual basis for *Graceland*, to be sure, but Simon's album is quite different from the usual concept album. There is certainly no explicit or implicit story line that connects the songs, nor is there any single, central subject that links them all together—unless one is willing to view collaboration itself (primarily *musical* collaboration but also, in two instances, collaboration on lyrics as well) as the album's "subject matter." But the idea of an album designed to explore collaboration seems a perfectly logical, if unusual, concept to embrace in understanding *Graceland*.

The various approaches to the concept of collaboration that are found among the songs on *Graceland* run a gamut from "Homeless," in which both the words (in Zulu and English) and the music were cowritten by Simon and Joseph Shabalala of Ladysmith Black Mambazo, to a cut like "I Know What I Know," in which Simon added his own lyrics and vocal melody to preexisting music (originally not written for Simon) by General M. D. Shirinda and the Gaza Sisters. In the case of "Homeless," the song makes a unified and gently poignant impression; the images of poor people could refer to South Africa or to America, or to both, and the slow-moving, harmonious vocal music encourages us to take their plight seriously. In "I Know What I Know," on the other hand, Simon deliberately makes no attempt to match the tone of his lyrics to the culture or to the implied locale of the original South African music. Instead, the lyrics seem to portray an encounter between two worldly wise and cynical people at an upper-crust cocktail party (or some such gathering), and their mood and subject both stand in remarkable, ironic contrast to the jubilant, uninhibited sound of the danceable South African instrumental music and to the Gaza Sisters' voices. The result is a virtual embodiment, in words and sounds, of a profound clash of cultures—as if some characters typical of Simon's earlier, sophisticated urban songs of late twentieth-century anxiety (such as those found on an album like *Still Crazy after All These Years*, from 1975) were suddenly dropped into the middle of a busy South African village on a day of celebration.

That the uneasy mismatch of music and lyrics in "I Know What I Know" is neither accidental nor careless on Simon's part is signaled by the presence on the album of songs that, occupying a middle ground between "Homeless" and "I Know

What I Know," make cultural diversity an aspect of their stated subject matter and of their music. The third verse of "You Can Call Me Al" describes a man who is uncomfortable in a foreign culture:

> *A man walks down the street*
> *It's a street in a strange world*
> *Maybe it's the Third World*
> *Maybe it's his first time around*
> *He doesn't speak the language*
> *He holds no currency*
> *He is a foreign man*
> *He is surrounded by the sound*
> *The sound*

The "sound" here is being produced by a group of black South African musicians playing with Simon and American session musicians in New York City; significantly, the multicultural group is joined on this cut by Morris Goldberg, who (Simon's liner notes pointedly inform us) is a *white* South African emigrant based in New York, and who contributes a striking pennywhistle solo. Members of this same diverse ensemble also play on "Under African Skies," the verses of which actually shift location from Africa to Tucson, Arizona, and back again. Here Simon is joined in vocal duet by Linda Ronstadt—from Tucson, Arizona.

In both the music and the words of *Graceland,* the meanings and implications can be allusive and elusive, often seeming to change color or to shift in midphrase. Yet the lilt of Simon's melodies and the dynamic rhythms provided by his diverse collaborators keep the album from ever sounding "difficult" or arcane. It is to Simon's credit that he never attempts to sound like anybody but himself, nor does he require his fellow musicians to adapt their style perforce to his; this is why the songs on *Graceland* are true collaborations, and such unusually successful ones. In the largest sense, one might say that *Graceland* is "about" the joys, complexities, and perplexities of living in an increasingly diverse, multicultural world. (This is a subject that also informs the words and music of Simon's next album, *The Rhythm of the Saints,* from 1990.)

That one need not venture to other continents, or even to other countries, to find "other" cultures is a point made, in effect, by the last two cuts on *Graceland*: "That Was Your Mother," in which Simon is joined by the Zydeco band Good Rockin' Dopsie and the Twisters, from Louisiana; and "All Around the World, or The Myth of Fingerprints," in which Simon plays with Los Lobos, the well-known Mexican American band from Los Angeles. On both of these selections, the prominent employment of accordion and saxophone creates aural links with the sounds of South African ensembles on other songs from *Graceland,* demonstrating musically that the world is indeed a shrinking place. (Conversely, Simon remarks in his liner notes how the South African instrumentalists he recorded in Johannesburg for the title song produced a sound that reminded him in certain ways of American country music.) At the end, then, Paul Simon comes home, only to find himself still, and always, a musical "citizen of the world."

Graceland, although not exactly the kind of smash-hit album that both *Thriller* and *Born in the U.S.A.* were (it never hit Number One on the album chart), eventually sold over five million copies. As the Grammy Award winner for Album of the

Year in 1986, it spectacularly revived Simon's then-flagging career and garnered a great deal of attention, not only for Simon himself, but also for many of the musicians who played on the album with him. *Graceland* did not prove to be a major source of hit singles, but a concert video featuring much of its music, taped in Africa with African musicians, was very popular. It is the album responsible, more than any other, for introducing a wide audience to the idea of world music, and for this reason alone the importance and influence of *Graceland* cannot be underestimated.

"BABY I'M A STAR": PRINCE, MADONNA, AND THE PRODUCTION OF CELEBRITY

The production of celebrity may be as central to the workings of the American music industry as the production of music itself. In the 1910s and 1920s dancers Irene and Vernon Castle were made into national figures through a combination of theater tours, silent film appearances, magazine stories, and mass-produced "how-to" guides to ballroom dancing. In the 1930s and 1940s crooners such as Bing Crosby and Frank Sinatra were turned into media stars through increasingly sophisticated promotional techniques involving sound film, network radio, and the print media. During the postwar years network television became an indispensable tool for the promotion of popular music and the production of celebrity—it is, for example, hard to imagine the careers of Elvis Presley or the Beatles without the initial boost provided by network television appearances.

By the 1980s the "star-making machinery behind the popular song" (to quote a lyric by singer-songwriter Joni Mitchell) had grown to unprecedented proportions. Since the profitability of the music industry depended on the sales generated by a relatively limited number of multiplatinum recordings, the coordination of publicity surrounding the release of such recordings was crucial. The release of a potential hit album—and of those individual tracks on the album thought to have potential as hit singles—was cross-promoted in music videos, television talk show appearances, Hollywood films, and newspaper, magazine, and radio interviews, creating the overall appearance of a multifront military campaign run by a staff of corporate generals.

The power of mass-mediated charisma is rooted in the idea that an individual fan can enter into a personal relationship with a superstar via images and sounds that are simultaneously disseminated to millions of people. The space between the public image of the star and the private life and personality of the musician who fills this role is where the contemporary industry of celebrity magazines, television exposés, "unauthorized" biographies, and paparazzi photographers flourishes, providing fans with provocative tidbits of information concerning the glamour, habits, and character traits of their favorite celebrities. This field of popular discourse is dominated by certain well-worn narratives. In what is perhaps the most common of these storylines, the artist, born into humble circumstances, rises to fame, is overtaken by the triple demons of greed, power lust, and self-indulgence, falls into a deep pit (of despair, depression, drug addiction, alcoholism), and then repents his or her sins and is accepted (in a newly humbled status) by the media and millions of fans. Other celebrities manage to flaunt convention and maintain their "bad boy" or "bad girl" image throughout their careers, while still others are portrayed as good-hearted and generous (if a bit bland) from the get-go. Of course, these story lines are as much about the fans themselves—and the combination of admiration and envy they feel toward their favorite celebrities—as about the particular musicians in question.

While stars such as Bing Crosby, the Beatles, and Bob Dylan had played an important role in shaping their own public image, the 1980s saw the rise of a new breed of music superstar particularly adept at manipulating the mass media, and at stimulating public fascination with their personal characteristics, as well as with their music. Certainly, no analysis of celebrity in late twentieth-century America would be complete without discussion of <u>Madonna</u> and <u>Prince</u>. Like their contemporary Michael Jackson, Madonna Louise Veronica Ciccone and Prince Rogers Nelson were born in the industrial north-midwestern United States during the summer of 1958. (All three of these 1980s superstars were only six years old in 1964, when the Beatles stormed America, and barely ten years old during the first Woodstock festival.) Despite the proximity of their geographical origins, Ciccone and Nelson followed quite distinctive career paths. To begin with, Ciccone was a dancer and photographic model who moved into music almost by accident, while Nelson had been making music professionally since the age of thirteen, as an occasional member of his father's jazz trio. Madonna first emerged out of New York's thriving dance club scene, while Prince's career developed in the regional metropolis of Minneapolis, Minnesota. Madonna's hit recordings—like most pop recordings—depended on a high degree of collaborative interaction between the singer, the songwriter(s), the producer, the recording engineers, studio session musicians, and others. But many of Prince's hit recordings, inspired by the early 1970s example of Stevie Wonder, were composed, produced, engineered, and performed solely by Nelson himself, many at his own studio in Minneapolis (Paisley Park, Inc.).

Despite these obvious differences, however, Madonna and Prince have much in common. Both are self-conscious authors of their own celebrity, creators of multi-

Superstars of the 1980s:
Prince and Madonna.
Frank Driggs Collection

ple artistic alter egos, and highly skilled manipulators of the mass media. Both experienced a meteoric rise to fame during the early 1980s and were dependent on mass media such as cable television and film. And both Madonna and Prince have sought to blur the conventional boundaries of race, religion, and sexuality and periodically sought to rekindle their fans' interest by shifting shape, changing strategy, and coming up with new and controversial songs and images. Early, sexually explicit recordings by Madonna and Prince played a primary role in stimulating the formation of the Parents' Music Resource Center (PMRC), a watchdog organization founded in 1985. During the second half of the 1980s, the PMRC—bolstered by its alliance with the Parent/Teachers Association (PTA)—pressured the recording industry to institute a rating system parallel to that used in the film industry. Although popular musicians ranging from Frank Zappa to John Denver argued against the adoption of a ratings system, the industry began to place parental warning labels on recordings during the late 1980s.

Madonna

From the late 1980s through the 1990s Madonna's popularity was second only to that of Michael Jackson. Between 1984 and 1994 Madonna scored twenty-eight Top 10 singles, eleven of which reached the top spot on the charts. During the same ten year period she recorded eight Top 10 albums, including the Number One hits *Like a Virgin* (1984), *True Blue* (1986), and *Like a Prayer* (1989). Over the course of her career, Madonna has sold in excess of fifty million albums and has been one of the most reliable sources of profit for Warner Entertainment, corporate owner of the Sire record label, for which she records. She also paved the way for female dance music superstars of the 1990s such as Paula Abdul.

As a purposefully controversial figure, Madonna has tended to elicit strongly polarized reactions. The 1987 *Rolling Stone* readers' poll awarded her second place for Best Female Singer and first place for Worst Female Singer. (In the same poll she also scored third place for Best-Dressed Female and first place for Worst-Dressed Female.) Jacques Chirac, the president of France, once described Madonna as "a great and beautiful artist," while the political philosopher Camille Paglia asserted that she represented "the future of feminism." The author Luc Sante's distaste for Madonna (as articulated in his article, "Unlike a Virgin," published in *The New Republic*, 8/20/90) was based largely on aesthetic criteria:

> Madonna . . . is a bad actress, a barely adequate singer, a graceless dancer, a boring interview subject, a workmanlike but uninspired (co-)songwriter, and a dynamo of hard work and ferocious ambition.

Other observers are ambivalent about Madonna, perhaps feeling—as the satirist Merrill Markoe once put it—"I keep trying to like her, but she keeps pissing me off!" (Sexton 1993, p. 14). In the academic field of popular culture studies, scholars have created a veritable cottage industry out of analyzing Madonna's social significance, variously interpreting her as a reactionary committed to turning back the advances of feminism, a postmodern performance artist, a politically savvy cultural subversive, and a "container for multiple images." Whatever one's view of these various characterizations, the fact that it is difficult to find anyone who (a) has never heard of Madonna, or (b) harbors no opinion of her at all, is an indication that her career strategy has by and large been most effective.

Madonna Louise Veronica Ciccone was born into an Italian American family in Rochester, Michigan, a suburb of Detroit. She moved to New York City in 1977, worked as a photographic model, studied dance, and became a presence at Manhattan discotheques such as Danceteria, where the DJ, Mark Kamins, played her demo tapes. (It was Kamins who introduced Madonna to executives at Sire Records, the label of the Ramones and Talking Heads, and who in 1982 produced her first dance club hit, "Everybody.") In 1983 Madonna's breakthrough single "Holiday" (Number Sixteen pop, Number Twenty-five R&B) established certain elements of a distinctive studio sound, rooted in the synth-pop dance music of the early 1980s (see the discussion of "Sweet Dreams (Are Made of This)" earlier in this chapter). In addition, Madonna took a page from Michael Jackson's book, enlisting the services of manager Freddie DeMann, who had guided Jackson's career in the years leading up to the megasuccess of 1982's *Thriller*. DeMann oversaw the production of Madonna's first two music videos, "Borderline" and "Lucky Star," the latter of which featured glimpses of the young star's navel, setting a precedent for subsequent, ever more explicit sexual provocations. The choice of Freddie DeMann also points toward an important aspect of Madonna's modus operandi—the ability to enlist a collaborative network of talented professionals, including producers, recording engineers, designers, and videographers.

In 1984 her second album—*Like a Virgin*, produced by Nile Rodgers, who was involved with the writing and production of a number of disco-era hits, including Chic's "Good Times" (see Chapter 7)—shot to top of the album charts, eventually selling more than ten million copies. The album spawned a series of hit singles: "Like a Virgin" (Number One for six weeks in 1984 and early 1985), "Material Girl" (Number Two in 1985), "Angel," and "Dress You Up" (both Number Five in 1985). *Like a Virgin* was promoted on MTV with a series of videos and formed the basis for an elaborately staged concert tour (the "Virgin Tour"), all carefully coordinated as part of a campaign to establish Madonna as a national celebrity. In 1985 Madonna also played a leading role in the film *Desperately Seeking Susan*, receiving generally positive reviews. In an industry where women are often treated as attractive but essentially noncreative "objects," Madonna began early on in her career to exert an unusual degree of control, not only over her music (writing or cowriting many of the songs on her early albums and playing an active role in the production process), but also over the creation and promulgation of her media image. Even seemingly uncontrollable events—like the ubiquitous tabloid accounts of her tempestuous and short-lived marriage to actor Sean Penn—seemed only to feed Madonna's growing notoriety.

During the second half of the 1980s Madonna began to write and record songs with deeper—and more controversial—lyric content. These included "Papa Don't Preach" (1986), in which a pregnant young woman declares her determination to keep her baby and urges her father to lend his moral support; "Open Your Heart" (1986), the video version of which portrays Madonna on display at a sleazy peepshow attended by dozens of men; "Express Yourself" (1989), in which she appears alternatively as a cross-dressing figure, dominating a tableau of male industrial workers, and as a submissive female stereotype, crawling under a table with a collar around her neck; and "Like a Prayer" (1989), the video of which included images of group and interracial sex, burning crosses, and an eroticized black Jesus. (This last video was censured by the Vatican and caused the Pepsi-Cola Corporation to cancel a lucrative endorsement deal with Madonna.)

The controversy-and-commercialism ante was upped even further in 1992 with the publication of *Sex,* a 128-page coffeetable book featuring nude and S&M-garbed photographs of Madonna and other celebrities, and the synchronized release of the album *Erotica,* which peaked at Number Two on the *Billboard* album chart and produced five major hit singles. The year 1994 saw the release of a warmer and more subtly sexual album, *Bedtime Stories,* which spawned "Take a Bow," her biggest single hit ever (Number One for seven weeks in 1994). Toward the end of the 1990s Madonna once again refined her public image, winning a Golden Globe award for her leading role in the film *Evita* (1996) and releasing an album of love ballads (*Something to Remember,* 1996) aimed at a more mature audience. But in 1998 she returned to the disco-derived synth-pop sound that had dominated her early recordings, with the release of *Ray of Light,* which debuted at Number Two on the album charts.

Madonna has frequently challenged the accusation—leveled at her by critics on both the left and the right—that her recordings, videos, and concert productions reinforce old, negative stereotypes of women. In a 1991 interview Madonna responded to these criticisms:

> I may be dressing like the typical bimbo, whatever, but I'm in charge. You know. I'm in charge of my fantasies. I put myself in these situations with men, you know, and everybody knows, in terms of my image in the public, people don't think of me as a person who's not in charge of my career or my life, okay? And isn't that what feminism is all about, you know, equality for men and women? And aren't I in charge of my life, doing the things I want to do? Making my own decisions? (Sexton 1993, p. 286)

Madonna's rhetorical question pulls us into the middle space between the public image and the private life: between the international superstar, Madonna, and Madonna Louise Veronica Ciccone, a talented and ambitious Italian American woman from the suburbs of industrial Detroit. Throughout her career, Madonna Ciccone has released tidbits of information about her private life, attitudes, and values that invite her fans (and her detractors) to imagine what the woman behind the "star-making machinery" is "really" like.

LISTENING TO "LIKE A VIRGIN" (1984)

The core dichotomy of Madonna's public persona—the innocent, emotionally vulnerable, cheerful girl versus the tough-minded, sexually experienced, self-directed woman—was established in the hit single that propelled her to superstar status: "Like a Virgin" (Number One pop and Number Nine R&B in 1984). "Like a Virgin" was not written by Madonna herself but by a pair of male songwriters, Billy Steinberg and Tom Kelly. As Steinburg himself put it, this is not a song about a virgin in any narrowly technical sense—rather, it is about the feeling that someone who has grown pessimistic about love gets from a new relationship. (We have already encountered this theme in Tina Turner's rendition of "What's Love Got to Do with It.") "Like a Virgin" is a good example of the mileage that Madonna and her producer, Nile Rodgers, were able to get out of a fairly simple set of musical elements.

The form of "Like a Virgin" is straightforward. After a four-bar instrumental introduction that establishes the dance groove, there is an eight-bar verse, which we are calling A^1 ("I made it through the wilderness . . . "); a ten-bar version of the verse with somewhat different harmonies, which we call A^2 ("I was beat, incomplete . . . "); and a chorus featuring the hook of the song, which we call B ("Like a virgin . . . "). The only additional structural element is an eight-bar interlude near the middle of the arrangement. The basic structure of the recording is thus

A^1A^2B
A^1A^2B
Eight-bar interlude
A^2BBB (etc., with a gradual fade out)

As in much popular music, the timbre, texture, and rhythmic momentum of "Like a Virgin" are more important to the listener's experience than the song's structure. The studio mix—overseen by Madonna's longtime collaborator Shep Pettibone—is clean, with clear stereo separation, heavy reliance on synthesized sound textures, and the singer's voice strongly foregrounded over the instruments. (As on many dance-oriented hit singles of the 1980s, the characteristic lead guitar sound of rock music is absent here.) Synthesizers are indispensable to the overall effect of this recording—this is a studio sound that simply could not have been created ten years before. Throughout the recording, however, the producer and engineers are careful not to make the instrumental parts too busy or complex, so that Madonna's voice remains the undisputed center of the listener's attention.

As we have discussed, Madonna's persona on recordings and videos and in concert depends on the ironic manipulation of long-standing stereotypes about females. Her vocal style in "Like a Virgin" reflects this aspect of her persona clearly and deliberately, ranging from the soft, intimate breathiness associated with Hollywood sex symbols like Marilyn Monroe to the throaty, tougher sound of 1960s singers like Ronnie Spector, the lead singer on the Ronettes' "Be My Baby." (The contrast between these two vocal personas is reinforced in the video version of "Like a Virgin" by an alternation between images of one Madonna as a bride dressed in white, about to be taken to bed by her groom, and another Madonna dressed in a tight black skirt and top and blue tights, dancing sexily in a gondola moving down the canals of Venice.) During the verses Madonna uses a breathy, somewhat reedy "little girl" voice, occasionally interspersing little squeals, sighs, and intakes of breath at the ends of phrases. Throughout the recording, Madonna shifts back and forth between the two personas, the innocent virgin and the experienced, worldly wise woman, each signified by a distinctive set of vocal timbres.

Of course, how a song's lyrics are interpreted is strongly influenced by their musical setting and by the visual images that accompany the words and music in a video or live concert. When Madonna revived "Like a Virgin" for her 1990

Blonde Ambition tour, the song was placed in a more complex and provocative context, with Madonna clad like an ancient Egyptian princess, reclining on a huge bed, and framed on either side by black male dancers wearing cone-shaped brassieres. Whatever one's interpretation of the sexual and religious symbolism of Madonna's performances and its relationship to her own experience growing up as a Catholic, it is clear that she has a talent for recycling her repertoire in controversial and thought-provoking ways.

Prince

Between 1982 and 1992 Prince (a.k.a. the Artist) placed nine albums in the Top 10, reaching the top of the charts with three of them (*Purple Rain* in 1984, *Around the World in a Day* in 1985, and *Batman* in 1989). During the same decade he placed twenty-six singles in the Top 40 and produced five Number One hits. Over the course of his career, Prince has sold almost forty million recordings, making him one of the most popular music superstars of the last two decades of the twentieth century. More importantly, Prince is one of the most talented musicians ever to achieve mass commercial success in the field of popular music.

Prince Rogers Nelson was born in Minneapolis, Minnesota, the child of parents who migrated from Louisiana to the north and identify themselves as African Americans while acknowledging a mixed-race heritage that includes Italian and Native American ancestry. Prince has stated that growing up in a middle-class Minneapolis neighborhood exposed him to a wide range of music, and that his early influences included everything from James Brown and Santana to Joni Mitchell. As he testified in a 1985 interview on MTV (also transcribed in *Rock & Soul*, 4/86):

> I was brought up in a black-and-white world and, yes, black and white, night and day, rich and poor. I listened to all kinds of music when I was young, and when I was younger, I always said that one day I would play all kinds of music and not be judged for the color of my skin but the quality of my work.

When he was seven his mother and father separated, and Prince spent much of his adolescence being shunted from one home to another. Various statements by Prince suggest that the instability of that period in his life, and the ambivalence of his relationships with his estranged parents, have formed the source material for some of his best-known songs.

One of the first things that strikes one about Prince's career is his amazing productivity. Throughout the 1980s and 1990s, when most superstars released an album every two or three years, Prince's output averaged over an album per year. During the 1980s he composed, performed, and recorded more than seventy-five songs each year. Only about three hundred of these songs have been released; the studio vault at Paisley Park is said to contain more than one thousand unreleased songs, more than ten thousand hours of material. Prince's compositions have been recorded by a wide range of artists, including George Clinton, Miles Davis, Joni Mitchell, Madonna, Bonnie Raitt, and Celine Dion. In addition to recordings released under his own name, Prince has developed a variety of satellite projects, groups or artists who have served in part as outlets for his music (for example, the Time, Apollonia 6, and Sheila E).

In stylistic terms, Prince's recorded output has encompassed a wide range of musical inspirations, from funk and guitar-based rock 'n' roll to urban folk music, new wave, and psychedelic rock. While the dominant impression of Prince's musical approach is that of a thoroughgoing open-mindedness, he has from the beginning sought to exert tight control over his music and his business. Prince owns his own studio (Paisley Park Studios, in Minneapolis) and produces his own recordings; plays most of the instruments on his albums; and struggled for years to wrest control of his music from Warner Brothers, eventually signing an agreement with Capitol-EMI that let him retain control over the master tapes recorded in his studio. (The basis of this dispute seems to have been that Warner Brothers could not release and promote Prince's new material as quickly as he wanted. As of this writing, Prince is rerecording and rereleasing all of the material that was originally released by Warner.) By the late 1990s he was releasing music exclusively—and extensively—on his own independent label, NPG Records, through his Web site, and via his direct-selling telephone hotline, which receives some seven thousand calls a month.

Descriptions of Prince's personality in the popular press present a series of opposed images: he is portrayed as a flower child and as a dictator; a male chauvinist who can form close personal relationships only with women; an intensely private person and a shrewd self-promoter; a sexual satyr and a steadfastly pious man, who has dedicated many of his albums to God. These discussions of Prince draw many comparisons with earlier figures in the history of popular music: the extroverted and sexually ambiguous rock 'n' roll star Little Richard; the guitar virtuoso Jimi Hendrix; the groundbreaking and idiosyncratic bandleader Sly Stone; and the brilliant songwriter and multi-instrumentalist Stevie Wonder. Prince has been critical of the tendency of journalists and record company publicists to identify him only with black artists. In response to the question "What do you think about the comparisons between you and Jimi Hendrix?" he responded, "It's only because he's black. That's really the only thing we have in common. He plays different guitar than I do. If they really listened to my stuff, they'd hear more of a Santana influence than Jimi Hendrix" (Karlen, 1985)

Prince's British biographer Barney Hoskyns christened Prince "the Imp of the Perverse," referring to his apparent delight in confounding the expectations and assumptions of his audience, music critics, and the record industry. Certainly, Prince's relationship to the "star-making machinery" of the entertainment industry is as complex as his racial identity, sexual orientation, and musical style. As a public celebrity, Prince occupies a middle ground between the hermitlike reclusiveness of Michael Jackson and the exuberant exhibitionism of Madonna. Throughout his career, Prince has granted few press interviews yet has for the most part managed to keep himself in the limelight. In the early 1990s Prince changed his name to a cryptic and unpronounceable symbol that blended male and female elements, engaged in a series of public battles with Warner over control of his music, and produced a compact disc recording that could only be played in the order in which it was originally programmed, a reassertion of the principle of the rock album as a complete artistic work. It is hard to imagine another celebrity who would willingly relinquish his nom de plume, publicly (and successfully) defy the will of the transnational corporation that had initially helped to launch his career, and deny his fans the right to consume his songs in whatever order they might choose.

Perhaps the best example of Prince's skill at manipulating the boundary between the public and the private are the film and soundtrack album *Purple Rain* (1984), which established him as a pop superstar. *Purple Rain* was the bestselling album of 1984, bumping Bruce Springsteen's *Born in the U.S.A.* out of the top position on *Billboard*'s pop album chart, holding the Number One position for twenty-four weeks, and producing five hit singles, including "When Doves Cry," "Let's Go Crazy" and "Purple Rain." Since 1984 the album has sold more than thirteen million copies, making it one of the ten bestselling albums of all time. The film did reasonably well at the box office, although it did not succeed in establishing Prince as a matinee idol. Reviews varied widely, some critics regarding the film as a self-indulgent, poorly written, badly acted attempt to promote a music album, while *Rolling Stone* numbered it among the best rock movies ever made. The film and the album were cross-promoted by Warner Entertainment, which spent $3.5 million for television ads, and by MTV, which ran footage from the celebrity-packed premiere party in Hollywood. The single of "When Doves Cry" was released a few weeks before *Purple Rain* appeared in theaters and helped to boost the film's popularity, which in turn helped several other songs on the soundtrack to reach the Top 40.

The plot and characters of *Purple Rain* draw heavily on the details of Prince's life, both personal and professional. Prince stars as "the Kid," a young, gifted musician struggling to establish himself in the nightclub scene of Minneapolis. His main competition in the musical arena is Morris Day, the real-life leader of one of Prince's "satellite" projects, the Time. The Kid is attracted to a beautiful young singer named Apollonia (another of Prince's real-life protégés), who in the film is also being pursued by Morris Day. The Kid's parents—the only characters in the film portrayed by professional actors—are to some degree based on Prince's mother and father. Another subplot has to do with the Kid's inability to accept creative input from the musicians in his band, the Revolution. The film concludes on a relatively upbeat note as the Kid adopts one of his father's compositions, incorporating a rhythm track created by members of the Revolution, and creates the song "Purple Rain," which wins over his audience, the band, Apollonia, and even Morris Day.

As with any semiautobiographical work, it is not easy to draw boundaries between the fictional character (the Kid), the celebrity persona (Prince), and the private individual (Prince Rogers Nelson). The character of the Kid—talented, self-absorbed, obsessed with exerting control over his music and his career, troubled by family conflicts and an inability to sustain intimate relationships—seems consonant with the accounts offered by Prince's family and professional associates. Apart from the Academy Award–winning soundtrack, a major source of the film's attraction for Prince's fans no doubt lay in the idea that this was a form of public psychoanalysis, a tantalizing opportunity to catch a glimpse of the "man behind the curtain." If *Purple Rain* is a film with genuinely confessional aspects, it is also a product of the increasingly sophisticated marketing strategies applied by entertainment corporations during the 1980s.

LISTENING TO "WHEN DOVES CRY" (1984)

"When Doves Cry"—a last-minute addition to the *Purple Rain* soundtrack—is an unusual pop recording in a number of regards. To begin with, the album track runs almost six minutes, a length that, although not without precedent, was much longer than the typical Top 40 hit of the 1980s. (A shortened version was released as a single.) Pop music recordings of the 1980s—such as Madonna's "Like a Virgin"—were typically the product of collaboration among the singer, songwriter(s), producer, studio engineers, session musicians, and others. "When Doves Cry," on the other hand, is essentially the work of a single person—Prince wrote the song, produced the recording, sang all of the vocal parts, and played all of the instruments, including electric guitar, keyboard synthesizers, and the Linn LM-1 digital drum machine. The lyric of "When Doves Cry," with its striking imagery and psychoanalytical implications, certainly does not conform to the usual formulas of romantic pop song. In addition, this recording crosses over the boundaries of established pop genres, fusing a funk rhythm with the lead guitar sound of heavy metal, the digitally synthesized and sampled textures of post-disco dance music, and the aesthetic focus and control of progressive rock and the singer-songwriter tradition. In this sense it is a good example both of Prince's desire to avoid being typecast as a traditional R&B artist and of the creative eclecticism that led music critics to come up with labels such as "dance rock," "funk rock," or "new wave funk" to describe his music.

The instrumentation of "When Doves Cry" is also somewhat unusual, as it lacks a bass part. Usually the bass helps to establish the tonality (or key) of a given piece of music and combines with the drums to provide the rhythmic bedrock of a recording. Prince's decision to "punch out" (exclude) the bass track that he had already recorded—apparently a spur-of-the-moment experiment during the process of mixing—gives the recording an unusually open feeling. In addition, Prince's composition avoids the tendency, pronounced in many rock and pop recordings, to establish a clear distinction between a verse and a chorus, each having its own distinctive melody and harmonies. "When Doves Cry" does use the verse-and-chorus form, but the melody and supporting harmonies are almost identical in the two sections, making the distinction between them much less fixed. While many pop recordings use the verse-chorus structure to build to a final climax, followed by a relatively rapid fade-out, the musical intensity of "When Doves Cry" rises and falls continuously, creating a complex succession of peaks and valleys. (One critic has interpreted this "ebbing and flowing of pleasure" as embodying a female rather than male pattern of sexual excitement and has connected this musical approach to Prince's embracing of female qualities in his own personality.) Finally, the studio mix is also unusual, relatively spare and dry, and quite unlike the lush, reverb-laden studio sound of most 1980s dance music recordings (including Madonna's hit singles). Prince does use studio effects such as echo and digital processing, but they are tightly controlled and focused.

The arrangement of "When Doves Cry" can be divided into two major sections. Section One, about three and a half minutes in length, is basically a presentation of the song, with its alternation of verse (A) and chorus (B). Section Two consists of a series of eight-bar phrases in which the background texture is subtly varied while instrumental solos (guitar and keyboard synthesizer), sung phrases (both solo and overdubbed in harmony), and other vocal effects (breathing, screaming, sighing, groaning) are sometimes juxtaposed or layered on top of one another, and sometimes alternated one after the other. Perhaps the best analogy for the overall effect of this recording is that of a weaving, made up of patches of subtly shifting textural effects and tone colors, held together by the strong threads of a funk-derived dance groove, and strung on a formal loom made up of eight-bar sections. This is a recording that rewards repeated listening, not least because one musician has created every sound that you hear throughout.

"When Doves Cry" opens abruptly with a virtuoso burst of lead guitar, establishing from the very first moment Prince's mastery of the hard rock idiom. (We could say that Prince was able to do for himself what Michael Jackson needed Eddie Van Halen's help to accomplish on his *Thriller* album.) As the main dance groove is established on the Linn LM-1 digital drum machine, the guitar plays five more bars. We then hear a strange yet recognizably human sound, a pattern created by running Prince's voice through a digital processor and turning it into a repeating loop. As the keyboard synthesizer introduces a chord pattern that interlocks rhythmically with the drum machine (completing the basic groove that will carry us through most of the recording), Prince's voice moves across the stereo space of the recording from left to right and then fades out. Only sixteen bars into the recording, it is clear that this is not your normal pop single.

The first half of the arrangement (Section One) begins by placing equal weight on the verse and the chorus material (sixteen bars each) and then gradually deemphasizes the verse (A), which finally disappears altogether (see the listening chart). The chorus is always followed by an eight-bar groove section, in which the underlying drum machine–and–synthesizer dance rhythm is brought to the fore. The presentation of the song, with its weakly contrasted verse-chorus structure, makes full use of studio technology, and of Prince's remarkable abilities as a singer. In the first verse he sings alone, in a middle-register voice. The second verse introduces a second copy of Prince, another middle-register voice that overlaps slightly with the first one; as this concludes, the two Princes sing together, first in unison, then in overdubbed harmony. In the chorus ("How can you . . .") these two voices are joined by a third, low-register, growling voice; eventually ("Maybe you're . . . "), we are presented with four Princes singing in harmony with one another, plus a fifth Prince who interjects solo responses.

The second half of "When Doves Cry" (Section Two) presents an even more complex palette of timbral and textural variations, playing with combinations of the drum machine–plus–synthesizer groove, sustained orchestral sounds, instrumental solos (including a keyboard solo that resembles eighteenth-century music), and an astonishing variety of vocal timbres. If you listen closely you should be able to distinguish as many as a dozen unique voices in the studio mix, positioned to the left, right, and center, some heavily modified by digital technology, and others closer to the natural sound of Prince's singing voice. In addition to the complex patterns of harmony and call-and-response singing, Prince uses a variety of vocal effects, including a James Brown–like scream, rhythmic breathing, sighs, and groans. These sounds lend a sense of physical intimacy to the recording and enhance its aura of sexuality.

If "Like a Virgin" can be interpreted as a musical analogue to Madonna's "split personality," "When Doves Cry" may represent an even more complex set of psychological relations between the public persona and private personality of a pop superstar. In a 1996 television interview, Prince Rogers Nelson revealed that he, like millions of other children, had created an alternative personality, an imaginary companion who had not only helped him through the dislocations of his youth but also continued to offer him guidance as an adult. It may not be too much of a reach to suggest that the "multiple Princes" of "When Doves Cry"— a song that wears its Oedipal heart on its sleeve, so to speak—are not only an experiment in musical polyphony but also a conscious representation of the continuous inner dialogue that has shaped Prince's career. (In interviews, Prince has described how his "spirit" has advised him to change course, abandon projects, and even alter his name.) In its rich layering of instrumental textures and vocal personalities, "When Doves Cry" imparted to the public image of Prince a complexity and psychological depth that is in fact not typical of mass-media celebrities. And in the process, it established his reputation as one of the most creative and influential musicians of the 1980s.

LISTENING CHART   "WHEN DOVES CRY" (ALBUM VERSION)

Composed, performed and produced by Prince; recorded 1984

FORM	LYRICS	DESCRIPTIVE COMMENTS
Intro		Lead guitar solo, no accompaniment
Section One [0:03–3:19]		
Groove (8)		Dance tempo established on drum machine; guitar stops at end of bar 5; digitized loop of Prince's voice enters in bar 6 (L side).
Groove (8)		Keyboard synthesizer enters, playing main riff; Prince's voice loop moves [L to R], then fades (bars 1–4).
A (8)	*Dig if you will . . .*	Keyboard drops out; solo voice and drum machine only.
A (8)	*Dream if you can . . .*	Second solo voice enters (overlaps with first voice); two voices combined (overdubbed), bars 5–8; vocal harmony in bars 7–8 ("They feel the heat").
B: (8)	*How can you . . .*	New vocal timbre added (growling bass voice); solo voice responds in bar 4 ("So cold"); new synthesizer pattern added (offbeats).
+		
(8)	*Maybe you're . . .*	More overdubbed voices added; four-part vocal harmony; solo voice responds in bar 4 ("She's never satisfied").
Groove (8) [1:34]		Drum machine and keyboard synthesizer.
A (8) [1:50]	*Touch . . .*	Vocal sounds in background (groans, sighs).
B: (8) [2:05]	*How can you . . .*	New vocal timbre added (bass voice, growling); vocal responses in harmony.
+		
(8) [2:20]	*Maybe you're . . .*	More overdubbed voices added; four-part vocal harmony.

Groove (8) [2:35]			Drum machine and keyboard synthesizer; voices drift in and out (high falsetto timbre); vocal harmony riff (bars 7–8).
B: (8)	**[2:50]**	*How can you . . .*	Synthesized string sounds added in background; four-part vocal harmony with solo voice responses.
+			
(8)	**[3:05]**	*Maybe you're . . .*	Four-part vocal harmony with solo voice responses.

Section Two [3:20–5:51]

Interlude (8)	Synthesizer riff drops out; drum machine plus synthesized string sounds; Prince's "voices" overlap ("When doves cry").
Groove (8)	Groove reestablished; lead guitar solo begins; solo and duet voices drift in and out.

[NOTE: The single version of the song fades out and ends at this point.]

Groove (8)	Guitar solo; solo and duet voices drift in and out.
Groove (8) [4:06]	Guitar solo; solo and duet voices drift in and out; James Brown–style scream begins bar 5.
Groove (8)	Guitar solo ends; vocal sounds float over the groove (breathing, sighs, screams, groans).
Groove (8) [4:37]	Vocal sounds float over groove.
Groove (8)	Stoptime in rhythm section with vocal harmony response; keyboard solo begins bar 5.
Groove (8)	Keyboard solo continues with vocal riff background; groove reestablished in bar 5.
Groove (8)	Prince's "voices" overlap ("When doves cry"); synthesized strings.
Groove (8)	Prince's "voices" overlap ("Don't cry").
Coda	Rising melodic pattern on keyboard; synthesized strings in background.

The decade of the 1980s saw important shifts in the music business, starting with a precipitous decline in record sales unprecedented since the Great Depression; the introduction of digital technologies, including samplers and the compact disc; the increasing reliance of corporations on a small number of multiplatinum albums by megastars, promoted on the new medium of music video; and the continued splintering of the market for popular music into dozens of specialized audiences and genres. In Chapter 9 we will follow the development of alternative music movements such as hip-hop, hardcore, alternative rock, techno, and world beat from the 1980s into the 1990s, paying particular attention to conflicts over authenticity and commercialism (or "keeping it real" and "selling out").

CHAPTER NINE

"SMELLS LIKE TEEN SPIRIT"

Hip-Hop, "Alternative" Music, and the Entertainment Business

Preceding the dawn of the rock era the market for popular music was clearly divided into a stylistic core—**Tin Pan Alley** love songs and jazz-influenced dance music, with the occasional touch of Latin American exoticism—and a periphery, including types of music that came to be known as rhythm & blues, country music, and folk music. By the end of the twentieth century, it had become almost impossible to sustain a clear-cut dichotomy between the center of American popular music and its margins.

For one thing, the most economically successful popular music (in terms of record sales and radio airplay) no longer presented a coherent stylistic thumbprint. The bestselling albums of the 1990s featured an extraordinary variety of artists, ranging from "adult contemporary" divas such as Celine Dion, Janet Jackson, and Mariah Carey (the biggest-selling pop and R&B recording artist of the decade) to country music stars like Clint Black, Reba McEntire, Shania Twain, and Garth Brooks (the biggest-selling male artist of the decade), the R&B vocal quartet Boyz II Men, gangsta rappers such as Snoop Doggy Dogg, 2Pac Shakur, and the Notorious B.I.G., hard rock and heavy metal bands like Aerosmith and Metallica, punk-influenced alternative rock bands such as Nirvana, Pearl Jam, and the Red Hot Chili Peppers, the confessional "alternative singer-songwriter" Alanis Morissette, and hugely popular lush, romantic soundtrack albums for films such as *The Bodyguard* (1993) and *Titanic* (1996). Albums by new artists were very successful, as the record companies sought to identify and promote a new generation of pop superstars (in the process spending hundreds of millions of dollars on recording deals, in the hope of repeating the ever elusive Michael Jackson phenomenon). Five of the annual bestselling albums of the 1990s were in fact debut albums by previously unknown artists: Mariah Carey's eponymous debut album (1991); *The Sign* by the Swedish Euro-disco group Ace of Base (1994); the southern blues rock album *Cracked Rear View* by Hootie and the Blowfish (1995); Alanis Morissette's angst-ridden *Jagged Little Pill,* the best-selling album of the entire decade (1996); and *Spice* (1997), by teenybopper girl idols the Spice Girls.

Although the singles market as a whole continued to shrink, the 1990s did produce a number of the bestselling singles in history, including "One Sweet Day," an R&B-flavored love song by Mariah Carey and Boyz II Men, which held the Number One position for a record sixteen weeks in 1995; "Candle in the Wind 1997," retro-rocker Elton John's multiplatinum tribute to the late Princess Diana; and a Latin novelty number called "The Macarena," which swept the nation in a matter of weeks in 1996, inspiring a dance fad and supplementing the repertoire of songs performed by audiences at massive sporting events (a diverse corpus that also includes "Take Me Out to the Ballgame," composed in 1908 by Tin Pan Alley songwriters Albert von Tilzer and Jack Norworth, "We Will Rock You," by the 1970s arena rock band Queen, and the Village People's disco hit "YMCA").

Taken as a whole, then, the popular mainstream of the 1990s includes a jumble of old and new styles, slick pop and R&B, rock-influenced country music, and rough-edged, in-your-face alternative rock and rap music. It is these last two categories on which we wish to focus in this chapter. Throughout this book we have traced the relationship between mainstream popular music—the music that in any given era attracts the broadest audience, receives the widest dissemination via the mass media, and generates the bulk of profits for the music industry—and varieties of music that originate on the margins of the musical economy, where survival is predicated on patronage from particular regional or ethnic communities. Many of the strongest influences in the history of popular music have come from people historically excluded from power, wealth, and social mobility, including African Americans, the working class, rural southerners, and immigrant communities. More recently, ironically, the very notion of outsider, alternative, or marginal music has itself become a means of promoting music to a mass audience hungry for novelty, excitement, and a sense of authenticity.

In this chapter we will examine a group of genres and styles that originated outside the mainstream in one way or another. First, we will look at the history of *hip-hop*—the first street-based movement in black popular music since vocal-group R&B of the 1950s—and its transformation from a local outgrowth of minority youth culture in New York City into a multimillion-dollar global industry. Then, in the second half of the chapter, we will examine the concept of *alternative music,* a term that is used across a wide range of popular genres, including rock, rap, adult contemporary, dance, folk, and country music. We will begin this half of the discussion with a consideration of alternative rock, which emerged as a more-or-less underground movement in the early 1980s, combined the rebellious spirit and youth appeal of rock 'n' roll with the nihilism of punk rock, and during the 1990s led to the confounding spectacle of vociferously anticommercial artists playing at corporate-sponsored rock festivals and releasing multiplatinum albums for major record companies. We will then examine the meaning of the term "alternative" as it is applied to other genres, including urban folk music (Ani DiFranco), hip-hop (Lauryn Hill), and country music (k.d. lang), and we will take a brief look at the development of postdisco electronic dance music, or *techno*. Finally, our focus will turn to one of the few truly novel developments of the 1980s and 1990s: the emergence of so-called world music or world beat, a heterogeneous category that includes artists from Africa, the Near East, and Asia—the ultimate margins of the American music industry (and of the American musical imagination). While this category covers a great diversity of musical styles, we will focus on two examples of collaboration between American and non-Western artists.

Each of these musical genres or movements—hip-hop, alternative music, techno, world music—exemplifies the tensions and contradictions created when music is marketed to a mass audience specifically on the basis of its difference from or opposition to the popular mainstream, and taken as a whole, they give us a glimpse of the diversity and complexity of American popular music at the end of the twentieth century.

"DROPPIN' SCIENCE": HIP-HOP CULTURE AND RAP MUSIC

Of all the genres of popular music surveyed in this book, none has spurred more vigorous public debate than rap music. Rap has been characterized as a vital link in the centuries-old chain of cultural and musical connections between Africa and the Americas; as the authentic voice of an oppressed urban underclass; and as a form that exploits long-standing stereotypes of black people. In fact, each of these perspectives has something to tell us about the history and significance of rap music. Rap is indeed based on principles ultimately derived from African musical and verbal traditions. Evidence of these deep continuities may be found in features familiar throughout the history of African American music: an emphasis on rhythmic momentum and creativity; a preference for complex tone colors and dense textures; a keen appreciation of improvisational skill (in words and music); and an incorporative, innovative approach to musical technologies. Much rap music does constitute a cultural response to oppression and racism, a system for communication among black communities throughout the United States ("Black America's CNN," as rapper Chuck D once put it), and a source of insight into the values, perceptions, and conditions of people living in America's beleaguered urban communities. And finally, although rap music's origins and inspirations flow from black culture, the genre's audience has become decidedly multiracial, multicultural, and transnational. As rap has been transformed from a local phenomenon, located in a few neighborhoods in New York City, to a multimillion-dollar industry and a global cultural phenomenon, it has grown ever more complex and multifaceted.

The Origins of Hip-Hop, 1975–1979

Rap initially emerged during the 1970s as one part of a cultural complex called *hip-hop*. Hip-hop culture, forged by African American and Caribbean American youth in New York City, included distinctive styles of visual art (graffiti), dance (an acrobatic solo style called breakdancing and an energetic couple dance called the freak), music, dress, and speech. Hip-hop was at first a local phenomenon, centered in certain neighborhoods in the Bronx, the most economically devastated area of New York City. Federal budget cuts caused a severe decline in low-income housing and social services for the residents of America's inner cities during the mid-1970s. By 1977, when President Carter conducted a highly publicized motorcade tour through New York's most devastated neighborhoods, the South Bronx had become, as the *New York Times* put it, "a symbol of America's woes."

The youth culture that spawned hip-hop can on one level be interpreted as a response to the destruction of traditional family- and neighborhood-based institutions and the cutting of funding for public institutions such as community centers, and as an attempt to lay claim to—and, in a way, to "civilize"—an alienating and hostile urban environment. The young adults who pioneered hip-hop styles such as breakdancing, graffiti art, and rap music at nightclubs, block parties and in city parks often belonged to informal social groups called "crews" or "posses," each associated with a particular neighborhood or block. It is important to understand that hip-hop culture began as an expression of local identities. Even today's multiplatinum rap recordings, marketed worldwide, are filled with inside references to particular neighborhoods, features of the urban landscape, and social groups and networks.

If hip-hop music was a rejection of mainstream dance music by young black and Puerto Rican listeners, it was also profoundly shaped by the techniques of disco **DJ**s. The first celebrities of hip-hop music—<u>Kool Herc</u> (Clive Campbell, born in Jamaica, 1955), <u>Grandmaster Flash</u> (Joseph Saddler, born in Barbados, 1958), and <u>Afrika Bambaata</u> (Kevin Donovan, born in the Bronx, 1960)— were DJs who began their careers in the mid-1970s, spinning records at neighborhood block parties, gym dances, and dance clubs, and in public spaces such as community centers and parks. These three young men—and dozens of lesser-known DJs scattered throughout the Bronx, Harlem, and other areas of New York City and New Jersey—developed their personal styles within a grid of fierce competition for celebrity and neighborhood pride. As Fab Five Freddie, an early graffiti artist and rapper, put it:

> You make a new style. That's what life on the street is all about. What's at stake is honor and position on the street. That's what makes it so important, that's what makes it feel so good—the pressure on you to be the best . . . to develop a new style nobody can deal with. (George 1985, p. 111)

The disco DJ's technique of "mixing" between two turntables to create smooth transitions between records was first adapted to the hip-hop aesthetic by Kool Herc, who had migrated from Kingston, Jamaica, to New York City at the age of twelve. Herc noticed that the young dancers in his audiences responded most energetically during the so-called breaks on funk and salsa records, brief sections where the melody was stripped away to feature the rhythm section. Herc responded by isolating the breaks of certain popular records—such as James Brown's "Get on the Good Foot"—and mixing them into the middle of other dance records. These rhythmic sound collages came to be known as "breakbeat" music, a term subsequently transferred to "breakdancing," acrobatic solo performances improvised by the young "B-boys" who attended hip-hop dances.

Another innovation helped to shape the sound and sensibility of early hip-hop: the transformation of the turntable from a medium for playing back recorded sound into a playable musical instrument. Sometime in the mid-1970s Kool Herc began to put two copies of the same record on his turntables. Switching back and forth between the turntables, Herc found that he could "backspin" one disc (i.e., turn it backwards, or counterclockwise, with his hand) while the other continued to play over the loudspeakers. This allowed him to repeat a given break over and over, by switching back and forth between the two discs and backspinning to the beginning of the break. This technique was refined by Grandmaster Flash, who adopted the mixing techniques of disco DJs, particularly their use of headphones to synchronize the tempos of recordings and to create smooth transitions from one dance groove to the next. Using headphones, Flash could more precisely pinpoint the beginning of a break by listening to the sound of the disc being turned backward on the turntable. Flash spent many hours practicing this technique and gained local fame for his ability to "punch in" brief, machine gun-like segments of sound.

A new technique called "scratching" was developed by Flash's young protégé, Theodore, who broke away and formed his own hip-hop crew at the tender age of thirteen. In 1978 Theodore debuted a new technique that quickly spread through the community of DJs. While practicing backspinning in his room, Theodore began to pay closer attention to the sounds created in his headphones as he turned the disc counterclockwise. He soon discovered that this technique yielded scratchy, percussive sound effects, which could be punched in to the dance groove. At first Theodore wasn't sure how people would react:

> The Third Avenue Ballroom was packed, and I figured I might as well give it a try. So, I put on two copies of [James Brown's] "Sex Machine" and started scratching up one. The crowd loved it . . . they went wild. (Hager 1984, p. 38)

The distinctive sound of scratching became an important part of the sonic palette of hip-hop music—even in the 1990s, after digital **sampling** had largely displaced turntables as a means of creating the musical textures and grooves on rap records, producers frequently used these sounds as a way of signaling a connection to the "old school" origins of hip-hop.

Although all DJs used microphones to make announcements, Kool Herc was also one of the first DJs to recite rhyming phrases over the "breakbeats" produced on his turntables. Some of Herc's "raps" were based on a tradition of verbal performance called "toasting," a form of poetic storytelling with roots in the trickster tales of West Africa. The trickster—a sly character whose main goal in life is to defy authority and upset the normal order of things—became a common figure in the storytelling traditions of black slaves in the United States, where he took on additional significance as a symbol of cultural survival and covert resistance. After the Civil War the figure of the trickster was in part supplanted by more aggressive male figures, the focus of long, semi-improvised poetic stories called "toasts." The toasting tradition frequently focused on "bad men," hard, merciless bandits and spurned lovers who vanquished their enemies, sometimes by virtue of their wits, but more often through physical violence.

Although the toasting tradition had largely disappeared from black communities by the 1970s, it took root in prisons, where black inmates found that the old narrative form suited their life experiences and present circumstances. One of the main sources for the rhymes composed by early hip-hop DJs in the Bronx was the album *Hustler's Convention* (1973), by Jala Uridin, leader of a group of militant ex-convicts known as the Last Poets. *Hustler's Convention* was a compelling portrait of "the life"—the urban underworld of gamblers, pimps, and hustlers—comprising prison toasts with titles like "Four Bitches Is What I Got" and "Sentenced to the

Chair." The record, featuring musical accompaniment by an all-star lineup of funk, soul, and jazz musicians, became enormously popular in the Bronx and inspired Kool Herc and other DJs to compose their own rhymes. Soon DJs were recruiting members of their posses to serve as verbal performers, or "MCs" (an abbreviation of the term "master of ceremonies"). MCs played an important role in controlling crowd behavior at the increasingly large dances where DJs performed and soon became more important celebrities than the DJs themselves. If DJs are the predecessors of today's rap producers—responsible for shaping musical texture and groove—MCs are the ancestors of contemporary rappers.

Hip-Hop Breaks Out, 1979–1988

Until 1979 hip-hop music remained primarily a local phenomenon. The first indication of the genre's broader commercial potential was the twelve-inch dance single "Rapper's Delight," recorded by the Sugarhill Gang, a crew based in Harlem. This record, which popularized the use of the term "rapper" as an equivalent for MC, established Sugar Hill Records—a black-owned independent label based in New Jersey—as the predominant institutional force in rap music during the early 1980s. The recording recycled the rhythm section track from Chic's "Good Times" (see Chapter 7), played in the studio by session musicians usually hired by Sugar Hill to back R&B singers. The three rappers—Michael "Wonder Mike" Wright, Guy "Master Gee" O'Brien, and Henry "Big Bank Hank" Jackson—recited a rapid-fire succession of rhymes, typical of the performances of MCs at hip-hop dances.

Well it's on-n-on-n-on-on-n-on
The beat don't stop until the break of dawn

I said M-A-S, T-E-R, a G with a double E
I said I go by the unforgettable name
Of the man they call the Master Gee

Well, my name is known all over the world
By all the foxy ladies and the pretty girls

I'm goin' down in history
As the baddest rapper there could ever be

The text of "Rapper's Delight" alternates the braggadocio of the three MCs with descriptions of dance movements, exhortations to the audience, and humorous stories and references. One particularly memorable segment describes the consternation of a guest who is served rotting food by his friend's mother, seeks a polite way to refuse it, and finally escapes by crashing through the apartment door. The record reached Number Four on the R&B chart and Number Thirty-six on the pop chart and introduced hip-hop to millions of people throughout the United States and abroad. The unexpected success of "Rapper's Delight" ushered in a series of million-selling twelve-inch singles by New York rappers, including Kurtis Blow's "The Breaks" (Number Four R&B, Number Eighty-seven pop in 1980), "Planet Rock," by Afrika Bambaata and the Soul Sonic Force (Number Four R&B, Number Forty-eight pop in 1982), and "The Message", by Grandmaster Flash and the Furious Five (Number Four R&B, Number Sixty-two pop in 1982).

While most of the early hip-hop crossover hits featured relatively predictable party-oriented raps, "The Message" established a new (and, in the end, profoundly influential) trend in rap music: social realism. In a recording that links the rhythmic intensity of funk music with the toast-derived images of ghetto life in *Hustler's Convention,* "The Message" is a grim, almost cinematic portrait of life in the South Bronx. The rap on the first half of the recording was cowritten by Sylvia Robinson, a former R&B singer and co-owner of Sugar Hill Records, and Duke Bootee, a sometime member of the Furious Five. (Resident Sugar Hill percussionist Ed Fletcher composed the musical track, using a Roland 808 digital drum machine and keyboard synthesizer, embellished with various studio effects.) On top of the stark, cold electronic groove Grandmaster Flash intones the rap's grim opening **hook**:

> *It's like a jungle sometimes, makes me wonder how I keep from goin' under*

The sudden sound of glass shattering (produced on the drum machine) introduces a rhythmically complex and carefully articulated performance that alternates the smooth, slyly humorous style of Grandmaster Flash with the edgy, frustrated tone of MC Melle Mel:

> *Don't push me 'cause I'm close to the edge*
> *I'm tryin' not to lose my head*
> *Ah huh huh huh huh*

The two MCs—Melle Mel in particular—time their performances with great precision, speeding up and slowing down, compressing and stretching the spaces between words, and creating **polyrhythms** against the steady musical pulse. The lyric alternates between the humorous wordplay typical of hip-hop MC performances and various images of desperation—threatening bill collectors, a homeless woman "living in a bag," violent encounters in Central Park, a young child alienated by deteriorating public schools. The relationship between the grim reality of ghetto life and the tough-minded humor that is its essential antidote is summed up by Melle Mel's humorless quasi-laugh: "Ah huh huh huh huh."

The second half of "The Message"—a *Hustler's Convention*–style toast written and performed by Melle Mel—paints an even more chilling picture, an account of the life and death of a child born into poverty in the South Bronx:

> *A child is born with no state of mind*
> *Blind unto the ways of Mankind*
> *God is smiling on you, but he's frowning too*
> *Because only God knows what you'll go through . . .*
>
> *You'll admire all the number-book takers,*
> *Thugs, pimps and pushers, and the big money makers*
> *Driving big cars, spendin' 20s and 10s*
> *And you want to grow up to be just like them, huh-huh . . .*
>
> *Now you're unemployed, all null and void*
> *Walkin' round like you're Pretty Boy Floyd*
> *Turned stick-up kid, but look what you done did*
> *Got sent up for a eight year bid* [prison term] . . .

It was plain to see that your life was lost
You was cold and your body swung back and forth
But now your eyes sing the sad, sad song
Of how you lived so fast and died so young.

This recitation is followed by the sound of the Furious Five—MCs Cowboy, Kidd Creole, Rahiem, Scorpio, and Mel—meeting and greeting on a street corner and discussing the evening's plans. Suddenly a police car screeches up and officers emerge, barking orders at the young black men. "What are you, a *gang*?," one of the policemen shouts. "Nah, man, we're with Grandmaster Flash and the Furious Five." Flash enters from one side to defend his friends: "Officer, officer, what's the problem?" "You're the problem," the cop shouts back, "get in the car!" We hear the car driving away with the Furious Five in custody, arrested evidently for the crime of assembling on a street corner, and the track quickly "fades to black."

A whole stream within the subsequent history of rap music can be traced from this gritty record, ranging from the explicitly political raps of KRS-One and Public Enemy to the "gangsta" style of Los Angeles MCs like N.W.A., Snoop Doggy Dogg, and 2Pac Shakur. As the first honest description of life on the streets of the nation's urban ghettos in the 1980s to achieve wide commercial circulation, "The Message" helped to establish canons of realness and street credibility that are still vitally important to rap musicians and audiences.

Gold records like "Rapper's Delight" and "The Message" created opportunities for New York rappers to perform at venues outside their own neighborhoods and thereby widen their audience. They also alerted the major record companies to the commercial potential of hip-hop, eventually leading to the transition from the twelve-inch dance single as the primary medium for recorded rap (an inheritance from disco) to the rap album. The mid-1980s saw a rapid acceleration of rap's movement into the popular mainstream. In 1983 the jazz fusion musician Herbie Hancock collaborated with DJ Grandmixer DST on "Rockit," which made the R&B Top 10 and was played frequently on the still-young MTV channel. The following year, the popular soul singer Chaka Khan invited Melle Mel to provide a rap introduction for her hit single "I Feel for You," an adaptation of a Prince song that went to Number One R&B and Number Three pop.

The year 1986 saw the release of the first two multiplatinum rap albums, *Raising Hell* by Run-D.M.C. (which reached Number Three on *Billboard*'s Top Pop Albums chart and sold over three million copies) and *Licensed to Ill* by the Beastie Boys (Number One for seven weeks, with over seven million copies sold). That neither Run-D.M.C. nor the Beastie Boys hailed from the Bronx indicates the expanding appeal of rap music in the New York area. The key to the commercial success of these albums, however, was the expansion of the audience for hip-hop music, which now included millions of young white fans, attracted by the transgressive, rebellious sensibility of the genre. Both *Raising Hell* and *Licensed to Ill* were released on a new independent label called Def Jam, cofounded in 1984 by the hip-hop promoter Russell Simmons and the musician-producer Rick Rubin. During the 1980s Def Jam took up where Sugar Hill Records left off, cross-promoting a new generation of artists, expanding and diversifying the national audience for hip-hop, and in 1986 becoming the first rap-oriented independent label to sign a distribution deal with one of the "Big Five" record companies, Columbia Records.

Run-D.M.C.—a trio consisting of the MCs <u>Run</u> (Joseph Simmons, b. 1964) and <u>D.M.C.</u> (Darryl McDaniels, b. 1964), and the DJ <u>Jam Master Jay</u> (Jason Mizell, 1965–2002)—was perhaps the most influential act in the history of rap music. Simmons, McDaniels, and Mizell were college-educated black men, raised in a middle-class neighborhood in the borough of Queens. Working with Russell Simmons (Run's older brother) and producer Rick Rubin, they established a hard-edged, rock-influenced style that was to influence profoundly the sound and sensibility of later rap music. Their raps were literate and rhythmically skilled, with Run and D.M.C. weaving their phrases together and sometimes even completing the last few words of one another's lines. The "beats" produced by Rubin and Jam Master Jay were stark and powerful, mixing digitized loops of hard rock drumming with searing guitar sounds from heavy metal. Run-D.M.C. was the first rap group to headline a national tour and the first to appear on MTV. They popularized rap among the young, predominantly white audience for rock music; gave the genre a more rebellious image; and introduced hip-hop sartorial style—hats, gold chains, and untied Adidas sports shoes with fat laces—to millions of young Americans. The now familiar connection between rap music and athletic wear was established in 1986 when the Adidas corporation and Run-D.M.C. signed a $1.5 million promotional deal.

Run-D.M.C. Courtesy BMI Archives.

The creative and commercially successful synergy between rock music and hip-hop pioneered by Def Jam Records and Run-D.M.C. is well illustrated in "Walk This Way" (Number Four pop, Number Eight R&B in 1986), the gold single that propelled *Raising Hell* nearly to the top of the album charts. "Walk This Way," a collaboration between Run-D.M.C. and the popular hard rock group Aerosmith, was a cover version of a song written and previously recorded by Aerosmith. (Aerosmith brought a large portion of the hard rock audience to the table, having sold over twenty-five million albums since the early 1970s.) The recording opens with a sample of rock drumming from the original recording, interrupted by the sound of a turntable scratching, and the main **riff** of the song, played by Aerosmith's guitarist Joe Perry. Run and D.M.C. trade lines of the song's verses in an aggressive, shouted style that matches the intensity of the rock rhythm section. The chorus ("Walk this way, talk this way . . . ") is performed by Aerosmith's Steven Tyler, who sings the lyrics in a high, strained voice, a **timbre** associated with heavy metal music. As the track progresses, Run, D.M.C., and Tyler combine vocal forces in the interest of collective mayhem, and the recording ends with a virtuoso guitar solo by Joe Perry.

The video version of "Walk This Way"—the first rap video to be put into heavy rotation by MTV—gives visual substance to the musical image of a tense conversation between the worlds of hard rock and rap, unified by the sizzling textures of hip-hop scratching and hard rock guitar, the contrasting but similarly aggressive vocal timbres of Run-D.M.C. and Steven Tyler, and the over-the-top male braggadocio of the song's text. (The lyrics to "Walk This Way," with references to horny cheerleaders and high school locker room voyeurism, suggest that one of the few things shared by the predominantly male audiences for rap and rock was a decidedly adolescent approach to sex.) The video opens with Run-D.M.C. performing in a small sound studio. The amplified sound of turntable scratching penetrates a wall that separates this intimate but restricted musical world from that of a hard rock concert, held on the stage of a huge arena. Disturbed by the noise, the members of Aerosmith use their guitars to punch a hole in the wall, through which Run-D.M.C. run onto the stage of the concert and basically take over the show. Initially met with scowls from Tyler and Perry, the rappers succeed in winning them over, and the video ends in discordant harmony, with the huge, largely white crowd cheering. It is difficult to think of a more explicit (or more calculated) acting out of the process of black-white crossover in the history of American popular music, and the video of "Walk This Way" doubtless played a pivotal role in the mainstreaming of rap music. (Run-D.M.C. was not the first rap group to incorporate textures and grooves from rock music. Early hip-hop DJs Kool Herc and Afrika Bambaata regularly used breaks from groups like the Rolling Stones and Led Zeppelin.)

The Beastie Boys, the rap trio whose album *Licensed to Ill* topped the pop charts a few months after the release of *Raising Hell,* were the first commercially successful white act in hip-hop. Like Run-D.M.C., their recordings were produced by Rick Rubin, released on Def Jam Records, and benefited greatly from the distribution deal signed by Russell Simmons with industry giant Columbia Records. Although they received a great deal of criticism for ripping off a black style, it is perhaps more accurate to suggest that their early recordings represent a fusion of the youth-oriented rebelliousness of hardcore punk rock—the style that they began playing in 1981—with the sensibility and techniques of hip-hop. In 1985 the Beastie Boys were signed by Def Jam Records, appeared in *Krush Groove*—one of the first films to deal with hip-hop culture—and toured as the opening act for both Madonna and Run-D.M.C. The following year *Licensed to Ill,* their first album, sold 720,000 copies in six weeks and thereby became Columbia Records' fastest-selling debut album up to that point. The most popular track on the album, the Top 10 frat-boy anthem "(You Gotta) Fight for Your Right (To Party)" (a hit in 1987), established the Beastie Boys' appeal for the most rapidly expanding segment of the rap audience, young white males. After leaving Def Jam Records in 1988, the Beastie Boys continued to experiment with combinations of rap, heavy metal, punk, and psychedelic rock, and they scored a series of critical and commercial successes in the 1990s, culminating with the release of their 1998 album *Hello Nasty.*

By 1987 a series of million-selling singles had proven rap's commercial potential on the pop and R&B charts; the hits included rap ballads (L.L. Cool J's "I Need Love," Number One R&B, Number Nine pop in 1987), women's rap (Salt-N-Pepa's "Push It," Number Nineteen pop, Number Twenty-eight R&B in 1987), humorous party records (Tone-Lōc's "Wild Thing," Number Two pop, Number Three R&B in 1987), and rap specifically targeted at a young adolescent audience ("Parents Just Don't Understand" by D.J. Jazzy Jeff and the Fresh Prince, the gold single that established the career of actor Will Smith, which reached Number Twelve pop and Number Ten R&B in 1988). A number of the small independent labels that had sprung up to feed the growing demand for hip-hop music—Jive Records, Cold Chillin' Records, Tommy Boy Records, and Priority Records—followed the lead of Def Jam, signing distribution deals with the multinational entertainment conglomerates.

If 1986 and 1987 saw the emergence of new markets for hip-hop music, 1988 brought possibly an even more important milestone: the launching of MTV's first show dedicated entirely to hip-hop music. Hosted by hip-hop raconteur Fab Five Freddie Braithwaite, *Yo! MTV Raps* immediately attracted the largest audience in the network's history and was soon being broadcast on a daily basis. The mass popularity of rap was also reflected in the appearance of *The Source,* the first periodical devoted solely to hip-hop music and fashion. Over the subsequent decade *The Source* became the largest-selling music periodical in America, surpassing by a wide margin even such long-established publications as *Rolling Stone.* In 1988 the National Academy of Recording Arts and Sciences added a rap category to the Grammy Awards, and *Billboard* added a rap singles chart. This mainstreaming of rap music had a number of interesting consequences. While some rappers and producers focused their energies on creating multiplatinum crossover hits, others reacted against the commercialism of "pop rap," reanimating the tradition of social realism that had informed recordings like "The Message" and creating a more hardcore sound that paradoxically ended up generating some of the biggest crossover hits of all.

The tradition of socially engaged rap, chronicling the declining fortunes of urban black communities, received its strongest new impetus from the New York–based group Public Enemy. Founded in 1982, Public Enemy was organized around a core set of members who met as college students, drawn together by their interest in hip-hop culture and political activism. The standard hip-hop configuration of two MCs—Chuck D (a.k.a. Carlton Ridenhour, b. 1960) and Flavor Flav (William Drayton, b. 1959)—plus a DJ—Terminator X (Norman Lee Rogers, b. 1966)—was augmented by a "Minister of Information" (Professor Griff, a.k.a.

Public Enemy. Courtesy BMI Archives.

Richard Griffin) and by the Security of the First World (S1W), a cohort of dancers who dressed in paramilitary uniforms, carried Uzi machine guns, and performed a martial arts–inspired parody of Motown choreography.

The release of Public Enemy's second album in 1988—*It Takes a Nation of Millions to Hold Us Back* (Number One R&B, Number Forty-two pop)—was a breakthrough event for rap music. The album fused the trenchant social and political analyses of Chuck D—delivered in a deep, authoritative voice—with the streetwise interjections of his sidekick Flavor Flav, who wore comical glasses and an oversized clock around his neck. Their complex verbal interplay was situated within a dense, multilayered sonic web created by the group's production team, the Bomb Squad (Hank Shocklee, Keith Shocklee, and Eric "Vietnam" Sadler). Tracks like "Countdown to Armageddon" (an apocalyptic opening instrumental track, taped at a live concert in London), "Don't Believe the Hype" (a critique of white-dominated mass media), and "Party for Your Right to Fight" (a parody of the Beastie Boys' hit "Fight for Your Right (To Party)," from the previous year) turned the technology of digital sampling to new artistic purposes and insisted in effect that rap music continue to engage with the real-life conditions of urban black communities.

"Night of the Living Baseheads" is an instructive example of the moral authority and musical complexity of many of Public Enemy's recordings. The lyrics for "Night of the Living Baseheads" combine images of corpselike zombies with a commentary on the crack cocaine epidemic that was sweeping through America's inner cities during the 1980s. The track opens with the voice of the black nationalist leader Louis Farrakhan, sampled from one of his speeches:

> Have you forgotten that once we were brought here, we were robbed of our names, robbed of our language, we lost our religion, our culture, our God? And many of us, by the way we act, we even lost our minds.

With these words still ringing in our ears, we are suddenly dropped into the middle of a complexly textured groove. The lead MC of Public Enemy, Chuck D, opens with a verbal explosion, a play on words derived from hip-hop slang:

> *Here it is*
> *BAMMM*
> *And you say, Goddamn*
> *This is the dope jam*
> *But lets define the term called dope*
> *And you think it mean funky now, no*

In hip-hop argot the term "dope" carries a double meaning: it can function as a positive adjective, broadly equivalent to older terms such as "cool," "hip," or "funky"; or as a reference to psychoactive drugs, ranging from marijuana to the new, more devastating drug being critiqued by Chuck D in "Night of the Living Baseheads," crack cocaine. The rhetorical tactic of announcing the arrival of a compelling performance (a "dope jam") and thereby laying claim to the listener's attention is common in rap recordings. Chuck D takes this opening gambit and plays with it, redefining the term "dope jam" as a message about drug use and its effects on the black community. At the end of each stanza of his rap, Chuck D uses another pun, based on the homonyms "bass" (the deep, booming tones favored by rap producers) and "base" (a shorthand reference to "freebase," or crack cocaine).

> *Sellin', smellin'*
> *Sniffin', riffin'*
> *And brothers try to get swift an'*
> *Sell to their own, rob a home*
> *While some shrivel to bone*
> *Like comatose walkin' around*
> *Please don't confuse this with the sound*
> *I'm talking about . . . BASE*

Chuck D presents here a chilling snapshot of the effects of crack on the human body ("Some shrivel to bone, like comatose walkin' around"), and uses the bass/base pun to draw a contrast between the aesthetics of hip-hop and the devastating scourge of crack cocaine ("please don't confuse this [base] with the sound [bass]"). After this first occurrence, the bass/base homonym returns periodically in a syncopated, digitally sampled loop that punctuates the thickly layered sonic texture created by the Bomb Squad. Chuck D goes on to scold black drug dealers for victimizing members of their own community ("Shame on a brother when he dealin' [drugs on] the same block where my [Oldsmobile] 98 be wheelin'"). A sampled verbal phrase ("How low can you go?") is used as a rhythmic and rhetorical device to set up the final sequence of Chuck D's rap, which concludes with the story of a crack addict, a former hip-hop MC fallen on bad times:

> *Daddy-O once said to me*
> *He knew a brother who stayed all day in his jeep*
> *And at night he went to sleep*
> *And in the mornin' all he had was*
> *The sneakers on his feet*
> *The culprit used to jam and rock the mike, yo*
> *He stripped the jeep to fill his pipe*
> *And wander around to find a place*
> *Where they rocked to a different kind of . . . come on, y'all*
> [Samples of voices]
> *I'm talkin' 'bout BASE*

The grim message of "Night" is enveloped in a jagged, stark sonic landscape, layered with fractured words and vocal noises, bits and pieces of music and other sounds sewn together like a crazy quilt. The producers incorporated digital samples from no fewer than thirteen different recorded sources, among them an early twelve-inch rap single, several soul music records, a gospel music group, a glam rock record, and the sound of drums and air-raid sirens. In musical terms, "Night of the Living Baseheads" is like a complex archeological dig, a site richly layered with sonic objects, the cumulative meaning of which depends on the cultural and musical expertise of the listener.

Although rap is often regarded primarily as a verbal genre, a recording like "Night of the Living Baseheads," with its carefully constructed pastiche of sampled sound sources, compels us to consider rap *as music*. Hank Shocklee has argued vociferously for a broader conception of music and musicianship:

> Music is nothing but organized noise. You can take anything—street sounds, us talking, whatever you want—and make it music by organizing it. That's still our philosophy, to show people that this thing you call music is a lot broader than you think it is. (Rose 1994, p. 82)

This philosophy is similar to that expressed by certain art music composers throughout the twentieth century who have used tape recorders, digital technology, and elements of noise in their works. But it could be argued that the most extensive and creative use of the technology of digital sampling has been made in dance music—hip-hop, R&B, house music, and techno—rather than in contemporary art music composition. Rather than creating a cold, disembodied form of self-expression—as many critics of the new technologies had feared—digital technology in pop music has often been used to create communal experiences on the dance floor. On the other hand, some critics bemoan what they see as a lack of creativity in much contemporary rap music, referring to the practice of sampling as "artistic necrophilia" and the end product as "Memorex music." Whatever one's position on these matters, Public Enemy's "Night of the Living Baseheads" stands as a pioneering example of the creative and social potential of digital sound technologies.

Commercialization, Diversification, and the Rise of Gangsta Rap (1990s)

The expanding nationwide appeal of rap music during the late 1980s and early 1990s followed a familiar pattern. At the same time that some artists moved toward the pop mainstream, developing styles that blended the verbal cadences of rap and the techniques of digital sampling with R&B-derived dance rhythms and vocal styles, a variety of alternative rap styles emerged, reflecting the attitudes, experiences, and dialects of particular segments of the hip-hop audience. Interestingly, these marginal variants of hip-hop—especially so-called *gangsta rap*—ended up generating millions and millions of dollars in profits for the record industry.

The year 1990 was a watershed year for the mainstreaming of hip-hop. M. C. Hammer (Stanley Kirk Burrell, b. 1962), a rapper from Oakland, California, hit the charts in March of that year with *Please Hammer Don't Hurt 'Em*, which held the Number One position for twenty-one weeks and sold over ten million copies, becoming the bestselling rap album of all time. Hammer's celebrity was boosted by music videos that highlighted his impressive abilities as a dancer, by his appearances in corporate soft drink advertisements, and even by a short-lived children's cartoon show, called *Hammerman.* At the height of his popularity, Hammer was attacked by many in the hip-hop community for his lack of skill as a rapper and for pandering to a mass audience. There can be no denying that Hammer's success pushed rap fully into the mainstream, continuing a trend started in the mid-1980s by Run-D.M.C. and the Beastie Boys. At the same time, Hammer's pop-friendly rap style opened the door for an artist widely considered hip-hop's icon of "wackness" (weakness), the white rapper Vanilla Ice (Robert Van Winkle, born 1968 in Florida). Ice's first album, *To the Extreme* (1990), monopolized the Number One position for sixteen weeks in early 1991, selling seven million copies. In hip-hop culture, a performer's credibility is correlated by fans not only with musical and verbal skill but also with the degree to which the artist in question possesses "street knowledge," that is, firsthand experience of the urban culture that spawned rap music. When it was discovered that Van Winkle, raised in reasonably comfortable circumstances in a middle-class neighborhood, had essentially invented a gangster persona for himself—a form of misrepresentation known in hip-hop parlance as "perpetrating"—many fans turned their backs on him. It is undeniable that race was also a factor in the rejection of Vanilla Ice, for he was widely regarded as being merely the latest in a long line of untalented white artists seeking to make a living off the fruits of black creativity. Yet some white rappers and producers—for example, the Beastie Boys—have managed to gain acceptance as legitimate hip-hop artists, largely by virtue of their ability to forge a distinctive style within the parameters of an African American tradition.

By the late 1980s a number of distinctive regional variations on the formula of hip-hop music were well established in cities such as Philadelphia, Cleveland, Miami, Atlanta, Houston, Seattle, Oakland, and Los Angeles. The music critic Nelson George noted this process of regionalization:

> The rap that'll flow from down South, the Midwest and the West Coast will not, and should not, feel beholden to what came before. Just as hip-hop spit in the face of disco (and funk too), non–New York hip-hop will have its own accent, its own version of b-boy wisdom, if it's to mean anything. (George 1998, p. 132)

During this period southern California became a primary center of hip-hop innovation, supported by a handful of independent labels and one of the few commercial AM stations nationwide to feature hip-hop programming (KDAY). The sound of "new school" West Coast rap differed from "old school" New York hip-hop in a number of regards. The edgy, rapid-fire delivery of Melle Mel and Run-D.M.C. remained influential but was augmented by a smoother, more laid-back style of rapping. The dialects of southern California rappers, many of them the offspring of migrants from Louisiana and Texas, also contributed to the distinctive flavor of West Coast rap. And if the verbal delivery of West Coast rap was sometimes cooler, the content of the MCs' recitations themselves became angrier, darker, and more menacing, the social commitment of Public Enemy supplanted by the outlaw swagger of artists such as Ice-T (Tracy Marrow), who in 1987 recorded the theme song for *Colors,* Dennis Hopper's violent film about gang versus police warfare in South Central Los Angeles. Both the film and Ice-T's raps reflected ongoing changes in southern California's urban communities, including a decline in industrial production and rising rates of joblessness, the continuing effects of crack cocaine, and a concomitant growth of drug-related gang violence.

The emergence of West Coast gangsta rap was heralded nationwide by the release of the album *Straight Outta Compton* by N.W.A. (Niggaz with Attitude). While rap artists had previously dealt with aspects of urban street life in brutally straightforward terms, N.W.A. upped the ante with recordings that expressed the gangsta lifestyle, saturated with images of sex and violence straight out of the prison toast tradition. The nucleus of the group was formed in 1986, when O'Shea "Ice Cube" Jackson (b. 1969), the product of a middle-class home in South Central Los Angeles, met Andre "Dr. Dre" Young (b. 1965), a sometime member of a local funk group called the World Class Wreckin' Cru. Jackson and Young shared an interest in writing rap songs, an ambition that was realized when they teamed up with Eric "Eazy-E" Wright (1973–95), a former drug dealer who was using the proceeds of his occupation to fund a record label, Ruthless Records. Soon, the three began working together as N.W.A., eventually adding D.J. Yella (Antoine Carraby) and M.C. Ren (Lorenzo Patterson) to the group.

When the group started work on their second album, *Straight Outta Compton,* the idea of establishing a distinctive West Coast identity within hip-hop was clearly in their minds. As M.C. Ren put it in a 1994 interview in *The Source*:

> When we did N.W.A . . . New York had all'a the bomb groups. New York was on the map and all we was thinking, man—I ain't gonna lie, no matter what nobody in the group say—I think we was all thinking about making a name for Compton and L.A. (George 1998, p. 135)

Released in 1989, the album was more than a local success, selling 750,000 copies nationwide even before N.W.A. started a promotional tour. The album's attitude, sound, and sensibility was clearly indebted to earlier hip-hop recordings—particularly Public Enemy's *It Takes a Nation of Millions to Hold Us Back,* released the year before—but was in some ways unlike anything heard before, featuring tracks with titles like "F—— the Police" and "Gangsta Gangsta," underlain by a soundtrack that mixed the sound of automatic weapon fire and police sirens with samples from funk masters such as George Clinton and James Brown, a bouncy drum machine–generated dance groove called new jack swing, and high-pitched, thin-sounding synthesizer lines. The raps themselves were harrowing egocentric accounts of gang life, hearkening back to the bleakest aspects of the prison toast tradition. The cover of the CD—with the posse staring implacably down at, and holding a gun to the head of, the prospective purchaser—reinforced the aura of danger, one of the main appeals of the group for the young suburban audience that pushed the album to multiplatinum sales.

The acrimonious breakup of N.W.A., beginning in 1989, had the effect of disseminating the group's influence over a wider territory. During the 1990s Ice Cube went on to make a series of platinum albums totaling almost six million in sales, including the brilliant *AmeriKKKa's Most Wanted* (Number Nineteen in 1990), a more explicitly political album recorded in New York with Public Enemy and the Bomb Squad, and *The Predator*, which reached Number One in 1992. Eazy-E sold over five million albums in the 1990s, all released on his Ruthless Records label, and M.C. Ren sold one million copies of his *Kizz My Black Azz* (Number Twelve in 1992). But the most influential and economically successful member of N.W.A. turned out to be Andre Young (Dr. Dre), who founded an independent record label (Death Row/Interscope), cultivated a number of younger rappers, and continued to develop a distinctive hip-hop production style, christened "G-Funk" in homage to the P-funk style developed in the 1970s by George Clinton, often sampled on Dre's productions. Dr. Dre's 1992 album *The Chronic*—named after a particularly potent strain of marijuana—sold over three million copies and introduced his protégé, Snoop Doggy Dogg (Calvin Broadus, born in Long Beach in 1972).

Snoop's soft drawl and laid-back-but-lethal gangster persona were featured on *Doggystyle* (1993), which made its debut at the top of the album charts. The gold single—"What's My Name?," a so-called clean remix of the opening track on the *Doggystyle* album—will give us a sense of Snoop Doggy Dogg's prowess as a rapper and of Dr. Dre's distinctive G-funk production style. (Like many rap recordings intended to cross over to the pop charts, "What's My Name" was released on the album in its original, unexpurgated version and in a "clean" version on a single designed for radio airplay and mass distribution. We will analyze the remix here, which reached Number Eight on the *Billboard* Hot 100 singles chart in 1993.) Although the track opens with a dense, scratchy sample reminiscent of a Public Enemy/Bomb Squad recording—actually a brief sequence from an old Parliament track, looped to create a syncopated pattern—the texture soon shifts to a smoother, more dance-oriented sound. A relaxed, medium-tempo dance groove is established by drum machine and keyboard synthesizers (including a weighty and sinuous keyboard bass part), over which a digitally processed, nasal-sounding human voice floats, singing a **melismatic** phrase:

Eee-yi-yi-yi-yi-yah, the Dogg Pound's in the hou-ouse

A female choir enters, repeating the phrase "Snoop Doggy Dogg" in soul music style, and is answered by the sampled voice of George Clinton, intoning "Da Bomb" (a phrase commonly used to describe compelling grooves and other pleasurable experiences). After this brief mood-setting introduction, Snoop's drawling, laconic voice enters:

From the depths of the sea, back to the block [the neighborhood]
Snoop Doggy Dogg, funky as the, the, the Doc [Dr. Dre]

Went solo on that ass, but it's still the same
Long Beach is the spot where I served my cane [prison term]

Snoop Doggy Dogg. Courtesy BMI Archives.

These two stanzas immediately establish Snoop's local identity, his indebtedness to his mentor Dr. Dre, and his street credibility, referring to the time he spent in jail.

He then explodes into a rapid-fire, percussively articulated sequence of tongue-twisting wordplay:

> *Follow me, follow me, follow me, follow me, but you betta not slip*
> *'Cause Nine-trizzay's the yizzear* [1993's the year] *for me to f—— up sh——* [make an impact]
>
> *So I ain't holdin nuttin back*
> *And once again I got five on the twenty sack* [sentenced to five years in prison for possession of a twenty-dollar bag of marijuana]

Snoop declares his arrival in no uncertain terms, asserting that 1993 is the year for him to make a major impact on the music scene. He refers to a more recent conviction on marijuana possession charges and then shifts to a more threatening posture—aided by Dr. Dre's interjection of an automatic weapon-like sound effect:

> *It's like that and as a matter of fact* (Dr. Dre: *rat-tat-tat-tat*)
> *'Cause I never hesitate to put a fool on his back* [imitating Muhammad Ali]

(Dr. Dre: *Yeah, so peep out the manuscript* [pay close attention to the words]
You see that it's a must we drop gangsta sh—— [talk gangster talk])

Hold on, wha's my name?

The female choir reenters, introducing a bit of hip-hop history, a melodic line from
Parliament's "Give Up the Funk (Tear the Roof off the Sucker)" (see the discussion
of this recording in Chapter 7). Then Snoop continues to add verbal layers to his
gangsta persona, boasting about his potential for lethal violence, referring to himself
as "Mr. One Eight Seven"—a reference to the California penal code for homicide—and
departing the scene of a bloody massacre by disappearing mysteriously
into the night ("I step through the fog and I creep through the smog").

The following interlude between verses introduces a digitally processed voice
chanting "Bow-wow-wow, yippie-yo-yippie-yay," a sly reference to country and
western music and cowboy films. (References to cowboys and country music are
not at all unknown in rap music; for example, Seattle-based rapper Sir Mix-A-Lot's
"Buttermilk Biscuits," recorded in 1988, is a parody of square dance music.) In the
third and final section, Snoop moves on to another favorite subject, his sexual potency.
He begins with a catchphrase that goes back to the South Bronx origins of
hip-hop and MCs like Kool Herc and Grandmaster Flash:

Now just throw your hands way up in the air
And wave them all around like ya just don't care

Yeah roll up the dank [marijuana], *and pour the drank*
And watch your step (why?) 'cause Doggy's on the gank [ready to injure anyone
who disrespects him]

My bank roll's on swoll [swollen]
I'm standin' on hit, legit, now I'm on parole, stroll

With the Dogg Pound right behind me
And rollin' with my b—— [woman], *is where ya might find me*

Layin' that, playin' that G Thang
She want the G with the biggest sack [testicles], *and who's that?*

He is I, and I am him, slim with the tilted brim

Wha's yo name?

Read as words on a page, divorced of their musical context, "What's My Name?"
is simply an updated version of "Stagger Lee," a traditional African American ballad
about a powerful and amoral black desperado of prison toast fame. But the commercial
success of "What's My Name?" had as much to do with the musical groove and
texture of the recording as with the content and flow (rhyme and rhythm) of Snoop
Doggy Dogg's verbal performance. "What's My Name?" is in fact a club dance record,
more than half of which is taken up by instrumental music or singing. (It could be argued
that most of the people that bought this record could not have interpreted por-

tions of the text in any case, given the use of local references and gang jargon.) This recording is obviously less musically complex than Public Enemy's "Night of the Living Baseheads," judged from the viewpoints of textural complexity, tone color, or historical references. Dr. Dre's G-funk sound, while indebted to the innovations of Public Enemy's production team, the Bomb Squad, has an entirely different aesthetic and commercial goal. Dre's approach to the use of digital sampling is much less ambitious than Public Enemy's: he uses here only three prerecorded sources—George Clinton recordings from the 1970s and early 1980s—and generally seems to aim for a clean, crisp studio sound. (The less ambitious use of digital samples may have to do with the court cases discussed in Box 9.1, which by the mid-1990s made it much more difficult for hip-hop producers to experiment with prerecorded sources.) Despite its controversial verbal content, "What's My Name?" is a quintessential pop record, bristling with hooks, catchy melodies, riffs, and verbal mottoes, organized around a medium-tempo groove, and carefully calibrated for dance club consumption.

While the conflation of gangsta rhetoric and reality at least temporarily boosted the sales of rap recordings, it also had terrible real-life consequences, as the matrix of conflict between posses—one source of the creative energy that gave birth to hip-hop in the 1970s—turned viciously in on itself during the mid-1990s. Such conflicts—evoked constantly in gangsta rap—can develop at many levels: between members of the same posse ("set trippin'"), among posses representing different 'hoods, between gangs of different ethnicity (as for example between Chicano and black gangs in Los Angeles), among larger organizations (for example, national gangs like the Crips, Hoods, and Black Gangster Disciples), and between entire cities or regions of the country.

The mid-1990s saw the violent eruption of conflicts between East and West Coast factions within the hip-hop business. Standing in one corner was Marion "Suge" Knight, CEO of Los Angeles–based Death Row Records, and Death Row's up-and-coming star <u>Tupac (2pac) Shakur</u> (1971–96). In the other corner stood the producer and rapper <u>Sean "Puffy" Combs</u> (a.k.a. Puff Daddy, P. Diddy), CEO of the New York independent label Bad Boy Records, and the up-and-coming star <u>the Notorious B.I.G.</u> (Christopher Wallace, a.k.a. Biggie Smalls, 1972–97). By the time the stranger-than-fiction scenario played itself out at the end of the 1990s, Tupac Shakur and Christopher Wallace had been shot to death; Suge Knight, already on parole for a 1992 assault conviction, was reincarcerated after an attack on two rappers in a Las Vegas casino and had come under federal investigation for racketeering; Interscope, a subdivision of Time Warner Entertainment, had severed its formerly lucrative promotion and distribution deal with Death Row Records; Tupac Shakur's mother had sued Death Row for the rights to her dead son's tapes; and Dr. Dre and Snoop Doggy Dogg, Death Row's biggest stars, had severed ties with the label. In January 1998 Snoop told the *Long Beach Press-Telegram* (as quoted in RockOnTheNet.com) that he was leaving Death Row Records for fear of his life:

> I definitely feel my life is in danger if I stay in Death Row Records. That's part of the reason why I'm leaving . . . there's nothing over there. Suge Knight is in jail, the president; Dr. Dre left and 2Pac is dead. It's telling me that I'm either going to be dead or in jail or I'm going to be nothing.

Chillingly, both 2Pac and the Notorious B.I.G. had recorded prophetic raps that ended with the narrator speaking from the grave rather than standing in bloody

Box 9.1 Hip-Hop, Sampling, and the Law

As we have seen, the tradition of incorporating beats from secondary sources is as old as hip-hop itself. However, the increasing sophistication and afford-ability of digital sampling technology had, by the late 1980s, made it possible for rap producers to go much farther, weaving entire sound textures out of prerecorded materials. This development triggered some interesting court cases, as some of the artists being sampled sought to protect their rights.

In 1989 the Miami-based rap group 2 Live Crew released a song called "Pretty Woman," which borrowed from the rock 'n' roll hit "Oh, Pretty Woman" (Number One pop in 1964), written by Roy Orbison and William Dees. Although 2 Live Crew had tried to get permission from the music pub-lisher of the song, Acuff-Rose Music, to make a rap version of the song, per-mission had been denied. A lawsuit ensued over rapper Luther R. Campbell's (a.k.a. Luke Skyywalker's) raunchy send-up of the tune, and Campbell took the position that his use of the song was a parody that was legally protected as a fair use. The Supreme Court recognized the satirical intent of Campbell's version and held that 2 Live Crew's copying of portions of the original lyric was not excessive in relation to the song's satirical purpose.

Although the 2 Live Crew decision upheld the rights of rap musicians and producers to parody preexisting recorded material, control over actual digital sampling tightened up during the 1990s, as a result of a few well-publicized court cases. In 1991 the 1960s folk rock group the Turtles sued the hip-hop group De La Soul for using a snippet of the Turtles' song "You Showed Me" on a track called "Transmitting Live from Mars." The Turtles won a costly out-of-court settlement. That same year, an up-and-coming hip-hop artist named Biz Markie recorded a track that sampled the sentimental pop song "Alone Again (Naturally)," a Number One pop hit for the Irish song-writer Gilbert O'Sullivan in 1972. O'Sullivan was not pleased and pursued the case, eventually forcing Warner Brothers to remove Biz Markie's album from the market until the offending track was itself removed from the album. These decisions sent a chill through the rap music industry and encouraged pro-ducers to be less ambitious in their use of sampled materials. As the hip-hop historian Nelson George phrases it, "The high-intensity sound tapestries of Public Enemy have given way to often simpleminded loops of beats and vo-cal hooks from familiar songs—a formula that has grossed [M.C.] Hammer, Coolio, and Puff Daddy millions in sales and made old R&B song catalogs potential gold mines" (George 1998, p. 95).

triumph over his victims. (True to the logic of the popular music business, these voices were manifested in highly profitable posthumous albums with titles like *Life after Death, Born Again, Still I Rise,* and *Here After*).

Since the late 1980s the highly stylized narratives of gangsta rap have provided a chronicle of the dilemmas faced by urban communities—poverty, drug addiction, and violence—from a first-person, present-tense viewpoint. The recordings of artists like Ice-T, N.W.A., Snoop Doggy Dogg, 2Pac Shakur, and the Notorious B.I.G. com-bine a grim, survivalist outlook on life with a gleeful celebration of the gangster lifestyle. This celebratory nihilism, propelled by funk-derived, digitally sampled grooves and surrounded in the video versions of rap recordings with a continual flow of images of hip-hop fashion, champagne, expensive cars, and sexy women (characterized as "bitches" and "whores"), provokes an understandable ambivalence toward gangsta rap on the part of observers genuinely sympathetic to the plight of people struggling for economic and cultural survival in America's cities. How, such critics ask, could a genre of music that presents itself as being committed to "keeping it real" so deeply indulge itself in the escapism of consumer capitalism and in the exploitation of women as sex objects?

Part of the answer may lie in the fact that rap music is a part not only of African American culture but also of American culture as a whole. Rap reflects the positive qualities of American culture—its creative energy, regional diversity, and technological acumen—just as it expresses American society's dark side: the obsession with guns and violence, material wealth and status symbols, and long-standing traditions of racism, homophobia, and sexism. (And, as a number of observers have pointed out, folk tales of black outlaws like Stagger Lee have always existed in a dialogue with popular images of white gangsters like Capone and Derringer, and with violent Hollywood films like *Little Caesar, Scarface,* and *Natural Born Killers.*)

On the one hand, rap has provided an unvarnished view of the dystopia that infects many urban communities—what Cornel West, the prominent African American cultural critic, has called "the lived experience of coping with a life of horrifying meaninglessness, hopelessness, and lovelessness . . . a numbing detachment from others and a self-destructive disposition toward the world" (West 1993, p. 14). On the other hand, it is also clear that gangsta recordings, promoted by huge entertainment corporations to a predominantly white mass audience, may have served inadvertently to reinforce some old and pernicious stereotypes of black masculinity, dating back to the knife-toting dandy seen in nineteenth-century stage shows. Perhaps this is what Chuck D was referring to when in 1998 he told an interviewer, "Ten years ago, I called rap music black America's CNN. My biggest concern now is keeping it from becoming the Cartoon Network."

TECHNO: DANCE MUSIC IN THE DIGITAL AGE

During the 1980s, following on the heels of disco and paralleling the emergence of hip-hop, new forms of up-tempo, repetitive, electronic dance music developed in the club scenes of cities such as New York, Chicago, and Detroit, cross-fertilized with developments in London, Düsseldorf, and other European cities. These styles, generally traced to early 1980s genres such as garage and house music, and loosely lumped together under the general term *techno,* are in fact quite varied. There are literally dozens of subcategories, including jungle, drum'n'bass, funky breaks, tribal, 'ardcore, gabba, happy hardcore, trance, trip-hop, acid jazz, electro-techno, intelligent techno, ambient, and ever more subtly defined sub-subcategories (ambient house, dark ambient, ambient breakbeat, ambient dub, and so on), each patronized by a loyal cadre of fans. As Simon Reynolds puts it in his book *Generation Ecstasy:*

> For the newcomer to electronic dance music, the profusion of scenes and subgenres can seem at best bewildering, at worst willful obfuscation. Partly, this is a trick of perspective: kids who've grown up with techno feel it's **rock** that "all sounds

the same." The urgent distinctions rock fans take for granted—that Pantera, Pearl Jam, and Pavement operate in separate aesthetic universes—makes sense only if you're already a participant in the ongoing rock discourse. The same applies to dance music: step inside and the genre-itis begins to make sense. (Reynolds 1998, p. 7)

In essence, techno is the musical dimension of a whole youth culture, within which arguments about the difference between good music and bad music are informed by a set of shared assumptions and shared knowledge of the genre's history. Techno culture is focused on DJ/producers—who, unlike disco and hip-hop DJs, often attempt to remain anonymous, operating their equipment in the dark behind a web of wiring. (Most techno "groups"—such as the Orb, Orbital, Prodigy, and Moby—are in fact solo acts, or teams of two or three DJs.)

The main venues for techno are dance clubs and semipublic events called *raves*, partly modeled on the be-ins of the 1960s **counterculture**. A controversial aspect of raves—which started in England in the late 1980s and spread, in a more limited fashion, to the United States soon thereafter—is the prevalent use by participants of a psychoactive drug called Ecstacy (MDMA), which creates visceral sensations of warmth and euphoria. Matthew Collin, a British journalist who has written extensively about the drug-rave-music connection that emerged in his country in the 1980s, has described the drug's sensation:

> The world had opened up all around, the blank warehouse somehow changed into a wonderland designed just for us, glistening with a magic iridescence that I couldn't see earlier. New world. New sound. New life. Everything felt so right. A huge, glowing, magical YES. (Collin 1997, p. 3)

Unfortunately, this YES eventually mutated into a resounding NO, for one of the documented long-term effects of MDMA is an alteration of brain chemistry that makes it harder and harder to get high, leading to severe depression. Added to this was the banning of Ecstacy by the FDA in the United States, which drove the drug underground, exacerbated the problem of worse drugs being circulated under the guise of Ecstacy, and led to a number of fatal overdoses. In any case, by the mid-1990s increasing numbers of DJs and fans had rejected the use of Ecstacy. As one insider put it, "the *music* drugs the listeners."

The roots of techno are often traced to the Detroit area, home of Motown, the Stooges, and George Clinton. During the early 1980s a group of young, middle-class African American men living in the predominantly white suburban town of Belleville developed a form of electronic dance music that Derrick May, a pioneer of the genre, described as being like George Clinton and Kraftwerk "stuck in an elevator" with just a sequencer. Detroit techno was grounded in a different cultural scene from that which had spawned the Motown sound; young men like May and Juan Atkins were obsessed with symbols of class mobility, Italian fashions, and European disco recordings, and they developed a form of electronic dance music that featured futuristic imagery, samples from European records, and a dry, minimalist sound, underlain by a subliminal funk pulse.

At around the same time a genre called *house music* (named after the Warehouse, a popular gay dance club) was developing in Chicago. The Chicago house scene was pioneered by Frankie Knuckles, a DJ from New York who worked at the Warehouse from 1979 until 1983. Knuckles introduced New York turntable techniques to Chicago, manipulating disco records to emphasize the dance beat—the drums and bass—even more strongly. Many house recordings were purely instrumental, with elements of European synth-pop, Latin soul, reggae, rap, and jazz grafted over an insistent dance beat. By the mid-1980s house music scenes had emerged in New York and London, and in the late 1980s the genre made its first appearances on the pop charts, under the guise of artists like M/A/R/R/S and Madonna.

In the 1990s techno music began to diversify into the dozens of specialized subcategories mentioned above. These branches of techno were often distinguished by their relative "hardness," a quality connected with the tempo or b.p.m. (beats per minute) of recordings. Some forms of techno were influenced by punk rock, others by experimental art music, and still others by black popular music, including funk and hip-hop. The sensual and emotional tone of the music also varied widely from the stark, futuristic sound of Belgian gabba and the energetic funkiness of jungle to the world music influences of tribal and the otherworldly sonic atmospheres of ambient. Although techno has produced few big commercial hits throughout its history, the recordings of musicians like Prodigy, Orbital, and Moby did make inroads into the charts during the late 1990s, and techno recordings were increasingly being licensed as the soundtracks for technologically oriented television commercials and films.

ALTERNATE CURRENTS

In the 1990s the marketplace for popular music continued to metastasize into hundreds of named genres, each correlated with a particular segment of the audience. From jangle pop to trip hop, psychobilly to thrashcore, the decade saw a splintering of genres that exceeded anything previously experienced in the history of American popular music. While many of these styles sprang from the ground up, as it were, nurtured by local audiences, regional networks of clubs, and low-profit independent labels, the entertainment industry had refined its ability to identify such "alternative" genres and their specialized audiences.

By the end of the 1990s, almost every major genre had sprouted an alternative subcategory. According to the *All Music Guide* (www.allmusic.com), a widely consulted Internet guide to popular music, the range of alternative genres included alternative dance (including techno, which often forms its own category, and groups such as Pop Will Eat Itself and Everything but the Girl), adult alternative pop/rock (Alanis Morissette, Dave Matthews Band), alternative country (k.d. lang, Dwight Yoakam, Lyle Lovett), alternative country rock (Uncle Tupelo, the Jayhawks), alternative contemporary Christian music (Sixpence None the Richer, Jars of Clay), alternative metal (Rage against the Machine, Korn, Limp Bizkit), alternative rap (De La Soul, Arrested Development, Lauryn Hill), and a variety of styles broadly lumped under the heading of alternative pop/rock (R.E.M., Sonic Youth, Living Colour, Soundgarden, Nirvana, Nine Inch Nails, Red Hot Chili Peppers, Phish, and many other groups). Some artists classified under the "alternative pop/rock" rubric sound similar, while others seem to have come from different musical planets entirely. Some record for small independent labels, while others sign contracts with major record companies. Some have a strong social, moral, or political outlook—right-wing or left-wing—that shapes their music, and others do not. And to all these subcategories, still others could be added, such as "alternative singer-songwriters"

(Sinéad O'Connor, Ani DiFranco, Tracy Chapman). What, then, defines them all as "alternative" musicians?

Our difficulty in coming up with a one-size-fits-all definition of "alternative music" stems partly from the use of this term to advance two different and often conflicting agendas. On the one hand, the term "alternative"—like the broadly equivalent terms "underground" and "independent"—is used to describe (and to positively valorize) music that, in one regard or another, challenges the status quo. From this perspective alternative music is fiercely iconoclastic, anticommercial, and antimainstream; it is thought by its supporters to be local as opposed to corporate, homemade as opposed to mass-produced, and genuine as opposed to artificial.

An entirely different sense of the term underlies the music industry's use of "alternative" to denote the choices available to consumers via record stores, radio, cable television, and the Internet. This sense of the term is bound up with the need of the music business to identify and exploit new trends, styles, and audiences. In an interview conducted during the late 1980s, a senior executive for a major record company revealed that

> there's a whole indie section [of our company. There are] . . . kids—that will only buy records that are on an indie label . . . which is why we sometimes concoct labels to try and fool them. (Negus 1992, p. 16)

The notion of a huge entertainment corporation cooking up a fake independent record label to satisfy an audience hungry for musical expressions of authenticity and rebellion may seem a bizarre contradiction at first glance. From our long-term historical perspective, however, we can see this institutional development as the culmination of a decades-old trend within the music business. In the days before rock 'n' roll, genres such as race music, hillbilly music, and other genres were predominantly the bailiwick of small independently owned and operated record labels. By the 1980s and 1990s, however, the major record companies had fully internalized the hard lesson of rock 'n' roll and had come to view independent labels as the functional equivalent of baseball farm teams: small, specialized, close-to-the-ground operations perfectly situated to sniff out the next big thing. In an era when most so-called independent labels are distributed, promoted, and even owned outright by huge entertainment corporations, it became difficult to sustain a purely economic definition of alternative music as music that doesn't make money. To put it another way, the fact that a band's music, song lyrics, appearance, and ideological stance are anticommercial doesn't mean that they can't sell millions of records and thereby help to generate huge corporate profits.

Alternative Rock, 1980s–1990s

In the wake of punk rock's collapse—symbolized by the breakup of the Sex Pistols in 1978 (see Chapter 7)—a number of distinctive streams of "indie rock" or "underground rock" bubbled up in cities and towns across the United States. Strong underground rock scenes developed in towns such as Boston, Massachusetts; Athens, Georgia; Ann Arbor, Michigan; Minneapolis, Minnesota; Austin, Texas; San Francisco, California; and Seattle, Washington. Many of these communities are home to large populations of college students and to student-programmed college radio stations, both key ingredients for a regional underground scene. Starting out as local phenomena, supported by small but devoted audiences, touring within regional networks of clubs, and releasing recordings on tiny, hand-to-mouth independent labels, bands such as Sonic Youth, R.E.M., the Dead Kennedys, and Nirvana came to symbolize the essence of indie rock—local, anticommercial, guitar-based music blending the abrasive, do-it-yourself sensibility of 1970s punk with the thick, heavy sonic textures of heavy metal. In general, underground rock bands maintained a defiant stance toward the conformity and commercialism of the music industry. They were committed to songwriting that explored taboo issues (drug use, depression, incest, suicide); interested in social and political movements such as environmentalism, abortion rights, and AIDS activism; and identified with unconventional (and soon merchandised) styles of self-presentation that included "dressing down" in torn jeans, flannel shirts, and work boots. Despite their avowed opposition to mainstream rock music, genres such as indie rock, hardcore, and thrash were supported by a predominantly white, middle- and working-class, male audience.

As time wore on, some of these groups went on to achieve commercial success on an international scale, signing deals with major record companies and moving toward a more pop-influenced sound. Others, driven by the ideology of authenticity through nonconformity, remained small, intensely local, and close to their fan base. For the underground bands who made it big—leading to the emergence of alternative rock as a marketing category around 1990—there were many contradictions to face, not least the problem of maintaining an outsider identity as their albums rose to the top of the *Billboard* charts, received Grammy Awards, and were promoted on the mainstream mass media. For many of these groups, the sensation of being on the inside looking out was new and unnerving. For a few musicians, it proved fatal.

The most influential indie rock bands of the 1980s were R.E.M. (formed in 1980 in Athens, Georgia) and New York's Sonic Youth (formed in 1981). While both bands were influenced by the 1970s New York punk scene, they developed this musical impetus in different directions. R.E.M.'s reinterpretation of the punk aesthetic incorporated aspects of folk rock—particularly a ringing acoustic guitar sound reminiscent of the 1960s group the Byrds—and a propensity for catchy melodic hooks. Touring almost constantly and releasing a series of critically acclaimed and increasingly profitable albums on the independent label IRS, R.E.M. gradually grew from its roots as a regional cult phenomenon to command a large national audience. This process culminated in the release of *Document*, the band's first Top 10 album, in 1987. In 1988 R.E.M. signed a ten-million-dollar, five-album agreement with Warner Brothers, becoming one of the first underground bands of the 1980s to receive such a deal. By 1991, when alternative rock seemed to many observers to have suddenly erupted onto the pop music scene, R.E.M. had already been working steadily for over ten years to develop its idiosyncratic sound. That year the band released the album *Out of Time*, which shot to Number One on the album chart, sold four million copies, generated two Top 10 singles, and won a Grammy award for Best Alternative Music LP. (The alternative category had been established just the year before, an indication of the music industry's awakening interest in underground rock music.)

Sonic Youth, formed in New York City in 1981, pushed underground rock music in a quite different direction. Influenced by avant-garde experimentalists such as the Velvet Underground, Sonic Youth developed a dark, menacing, **feedback**-drenched sound, altering the tuning of their guitars by inserting screwdrivers and drumsticks under the strings at random intervals, and ignoring the conventional song structures of rock and pop music. On a series of influential (though commercially unsuccessful) recordings, released during the mid-1980s on the independent label SST, Sonic Youth began to experiment with more conventional pop song forms while maintaining the discordant sound with which they were so closely identified by fans and other musicians. By the early 1990s Sonic Youth, the former underground phenomenon, had signed with the major label DGC (owned by the media magnate David Geffen) and was being widely hailed as a pioneer of the alternative movement in rock. The magazine *Vanity Fair* went so far as to proclaim Sonic Youth's lead singer, Kim Gordon, the "godmother of alternative rock." The 1994 album *Experimental Jet Set, Trash, and No Star*, their third release on DGC, reached Number Thirty-four on the Top 100 album chart, proof that their national audience, like R.E.M.'s, had expanded beyond all expectations.

Around the same time that R.E.M. and Sonic Youth were formulating (and re-formulating) their distinctive underground sounds, another influential branch of postpunk music was developing in clubs on the West Coast. *Hardcore* was an extreme variation of punk, pioneered during the early 1980s by bands in San Francisco (the Dead Kennedys) and Los Angeles (the Germs, Black Flag, X, and the Circle Jerks). These groups—and others, such as the Texas-based Butthole Surfers—took the frenzied energy of the Ramones and the Sex Pistols and pushed it to the limit, playing simple riff-based songs at impossibly fast tempos and screaming nihilistic lyrics over a chaotic wall of guitar chords. Audiences at hardcore clubs—typically adorned in tattoos, buzz cuts, and combat boots—developed the practice of *slam dancing* or *moshing*, in which members of the audience pushed their way up to a *mosh pit*, an area situated directly in front of the stage, and smashed into one another, sometimes climbing onto the stage and diving off into the crowd. Most hardcore recordings were released by independent labels like SST, Alternative Tentacles, and IRS, and the typical hardcore disc was produced to look and sound as though it had been made in someone's basement. Few of these bands managed to score contracts with major labels, a fact proudly pointed out by fans as proof of their genuine underground status.

"Holiday in Cambodia" by the Dead Kennedys, released on the independent label Alternative Tentacles in 1981, is a good example of the sensibility of early 1980s hardcore. The lyrics—written by the band's lead singer, Jello Biafra (Eric Boucher, b. 1959 in Boulder, Colorado)—brim with merciless sarcasm. The song is directed at the spoiled children of suburban yuppies, who Biafra suggests ought to be sent to forced labor camps in Cambodia—then in the grip of Pol Pot's genocidal regime—to gain some perspective on the magnitude of their own problems. The recording opens with a nightmarish display of guitar pyrotechnics, a series of Hendrix-inspired whoops, slides, scratches, and feedback, evocative of a war zone. The band—guitar, electric bass, and drums—gradually builds to an extremely fast tempo (around 208 beats per minute). Over this chaotic din, Jello Biafra's quavering voice sneers out the caustic lyrics:

> *So you been to school for a year or two*
> *And you know you've seen it all*
> *In daddy's car, thinkin' you'll go far*
> *Back east your type don't crawl*

Play ethnicky jazz to parade your snazz [coolness]
On your five grand stereo
Braggin' that you know how the niggers feel cold
And the slums got so much soul . . .

Well you'll work harder with a gun in your back
For a bowl of rice a day
Slave for soldiers till you starve
Then your head is skewered on a stake . . .

Pol Pot, Pol Pot, Pol Pot, Pol Pot . . .

And it's a holiday in Cambodia
Where you'll do what you're told
A holiday in Cambodia
Where the slums got so much soul . . .

The Dead Kennedys' variant of hardcore was lent focus by the band's political stance, which opposed American imperialism overseas, the destruction of human rights and the environment, and what the band saw as a hypocritical and soulless suburban lifestyle. Jello Biafra composed songs with titles like "California über Alles," "Kill the Poor" (a Jonathan Swift–like suggestion for the practical application of neutron bombs), and "Chemical Warfare." As the hardcore scene began to attract right-wing racial supremacists—a problem that the genre shared with 1970s punk rock—Biafra penned a song entitled "Nazi Punks F—— Off" (1981), in an attempt to distance the progressive hardcore skinheads from their fascist counterparts.

By the mid-1980s the hardcore movement had largely played itself out, though aspects of the music's style and attitude were carried on by bands playing *thrash,* which blended the fast tempos and rebellious attitude of hardcore with the technical virtuosity of heavy metal guitar playing. Thrash was a harder, faster version of the commercially successful *speed metal* style played by bands such as Metallica, Megadeath, and Anthrax. (The 1991 album *Metallica* was the ultimate confirmation of heavy metal's mass popularity and newfound importance to the music industry: it streaked to Number One on the album charts, sold over five million copies, and stayed on the charts for an incredible 266 weeks.) Unlike speed metal, thrash didn't produce any superstars—the Los Angeles band Suicidal Tendencies was the most recognizable name to emerge from the genre—but it did exert an influence on alternative rock bands of the 1990s. Although thrash never developed a mass audience, its fans remained dedicated, keeping the style alive as an underground club-based phenomenon through the 1990s.

Although underground bands began to appear on the charts during the late 1980s, the commercial breakthrough for alternative rock—and the occasion of its enshrinement as a privileged category in the pop music marketplace—was achieved in 1992 by Nirvana, a band from the Pacific Northwest. Between 1992 and 1994, Nirvana—a trio centered on singer and guitarist Kurt Cobain (b. 1967 in Hoquiam, Washington; d. 1994) and bassist Krist Novoselic (b. 1965 in Compton, California)—released two multiplatinum albums that moved alternative rock's blend of hardcore punk and heavy metal out of the back corners of specialty record stores and into the commercial mainstream. The rise of so-called *grunge rock*—and the tragic demise of Kurt Cobain, who committed suicide in 1994 at the age of twenty-seven—provide some insight into the opportunities and the pressures facing alternative rock musicians in the early 1990s.

Cobain and Novoselic met in 1985 in the town of Aberdeen, an economically depressed logging town some one hundred miles from Seattle. (Cobain's parents had divorced when he was eight years old, an event that by his own account troubled him deeply and left him shy and introspective.) Inspired by the records of underground rock and hardcore bands and the creativity of the Beatles, and frustrated with the limitations of small-town working-class life, they formed Nirvana in 1987 and began playing gigs at local colleges and clubs. The following year they were signed by the independent label Sub Pop Records, formed in 1987 by the entrepreneurs Bruce Pavitt and Jonathan Poneman. (Sub Pop started out as a mimeographed fanzine for local bands before mutating into a record label.) Nirvana's debut album, *Bleach* (1989), cost slightly over six hundred dollars to record—less than the cost of thirty minutes of recording time at a major New York or Los Angeles recording studio—and sold thirty-five thousand copies, an impressive amount for a regional indie rock release. In 1991 the group signed with major label DGC. Following a European tour with Sonic Youth, the album *Nevermind* was released in September 1991, quickly selling out its initial shipment of fifty thousand copies and creating a shortage in record stores across America. By the beginning of 1992 *Nevermind* had reached Number One, displacing Michael Jackson's highly publicized comeback album *Dangerous*. The album stayed on the charts for almost five years, eventually selling more than ten million copies.

One source of *Nevermind*'s success was the platinum single "Smells Like Teen Spirit," a Top 10 hit. One of the most striking aspects of "Teen Spirit" is its combination of heavy metal instrumental textures and pop songwriting techniques, including a number of memorable verbal and melodic hooks. The band's sound, which had been thick and plodding on its Sub Pop recordings, is sleek and well focused (thanks in part to the production of Butch Vig and the mixing of engineer Andy Wallace). The song itself combines a four-chord heavy metal harmonic progression with a somewhat conventional formal structure, made up of four-, eight-, and twelve-bar sections. The overall structure of the song includes a verse of eight bars ("Load up on guns . . . "), which we are calling A, and two repeated sections, or choruses, which we have labeled B (eight bars in length) and C (twelve bars). These sections are marked off by distinctive instrumental textures, shifting from the quiet, reflective, even somewhat depressed quality of A, through the crescendo of B, with its spacey one-word mantra and continuous carpet of thick guitar chords, into the C section, where Cobain bellows his unfocused feelings of discontent and the group slams out heavy metal–style power chords. This ABC structure is repeated three times in the course of the five-minute recording, with room created between the second and final iterations for a sixteen-bar guitar solo.

Nirvana's "Smells Like Teen Spirit," the first alternative rock single of the 1990s to enter the Top 10, is a carefully crafted pop record. The sleek, glistening studio sound; Cobain's liberal use of melodic and verbal hooks; the trio's careful attention to textural shifts as a means of marking off formal sections of the song; and the fact that Cobain's guitar solo consists of an almost note-for-note restatement of the

LISTENING CHART "SMELLS LIKE TEEN SPIRIT"

Music by Nirvana; lyrics by Kurt Cobain; performed by Nirvana; recorded 1991

FORM	LYRICS	DESCRIPTIVE COMMENTS
Intro (16 = 4 + 8 + 4)		Bars 1–4: solo guitar plays progression (quiet); bars 5–12: whole band plays progression (loud, intense); bars 13–16: bass plays progression with guitar chimes (soft).
A (8)	*Load up . . .*	Lead vocal enters; quiet, somewhat depressed tone; gentle instrumental texture.
B (8)	*Hello, hello . . .*	Spacey one-word vocal, backed with continuous guitar chords; gradual crescendo.
C (12)	*With the lights out*	Vocal angry, growling; heavy metal power chords, loud and distorted.
Interlude (4)		Stoptime effect with guitar response.
Intro (4)		Last four bars of Introduction; bass plays progression with guitar chimes (soft).
A (8)	*I'm worse . . .*	
B (8)	*Hello, hello . . .*	Dreamy vocal (like Beatles); continuous bed of distorted guitar chords.
C (12)	*With the lights out*	Vocal angry, growling; heavy metal power chords, loud and distorted.
Interlude (4)		Stoptime effect, answered by guitar.
Guitar solo (16)		Guitar plays melody of sections A and B (little if any improvisation).
Intro (4)		Last four bars of Introduction.
A (8)	*And I forget . . .*	
B (8)	*Hello, hello . . .*	Crescendo, spacey one-word vocal.
C (20 = 12 + 8)	*With the lights out . . .*	Vocal angry, growling; heavy metal power chords, loud and distorted.

melodies of the A and B sections, driving these hooks even deeper into the listener's memory—all serve to remind us that the Beatles were as profound an influence on 1990s alternative rock as were bands like the Velvet Underground.

Although alternative bands like R.E.M. and Sonic Youth handled their rise to fame with relative aplomb, success destroyed Nirvana. The group's attitude toward the music industry appears to have crystallized early on, as this 1989 Sub Pop press release (reproduced at Sub Pop Records' website) indicates:

NIRVANA sees the underground scene as becoming stagnant and more accessible to big league capitalist pig major record labels. But does NIRVANA feel a moral duty to fight this cancerous evil? NO WAY! We want to cash in and suck up to the big wigs in hopes that we too can GET HIGH AND F—— . . . SOON we will need groupie repellant. SOON we will be coming to your town and asking if we can stay over at your house and use the stove. SOON we will do encores of "GLORIA" and "LOUIE LOUIE" at benefit concerts with all our celebrity friends.

The sardonic humor of this public relations document only partially masks the band's intensely ambivalent attitude toward rock celebrity, a kind of "listen to us, don't listen to us" stance. As *Nevermind* rose up the charts, Nirvana had begun to attract a mass audience that included millions of fans of hard rock and commercial heavy metal music, genres to which their own music was explicitly opposed. This realization impelled the group to ever more outrageous behavior, including baiting their audiences, wearing women's clothing, and kissing one another onstage. In 1992 Cobain married Courtney Love, the leader of an all-female alternative rock (a.k.a. "foxcore") group called Hole. Rumors concerning the couple's use of heroin began to circulate, and an article in *Vanity Fair* charged that Love had used the narcotic while pregnant with the couple's child, leading to a public struggle with the Los Angeles child services bureau over custody of the baby. In the midst of this adverse publicity, Nirvana released the album *In Utero*, a return to the raw sound of Nirvana's early Sub Pop recordings, which shot to Number One in 1993 and sold four million copies.

In 1994, after the band had interrupted a concert tour of Europe, Kurt Cobain overdosed on champagne and tranquilizers, remaining in a coma for twenty hours. Although the event was initially described as an accident, a suicide note was later discovered. He returned to Seattle and entered a detoxification program, only to check out two days later. On April 8, 1994, Cobain's body was discovered in his home; he had died three days earlier of a self-inflicted shotgun wound. While there is a diversity of opinion concerning the ultimate meaning of Cobain's suicide—he is viewed on the one hand as a martyr of alternative rock, and on the other as a self-indulgent, hypocritical rock star—his death has widely come to be viewed as evidence of the pressures faced by alternative musicians who are pulled into the mainstream.

Although the term "alternative rock" is most often used to describe bands like R.E.M., Sonic Youth, Dead Kennedys, and Nirvana—inspired by the 1970s punk rock movement—some forms of alternative rock found their inspiration elsewhere. The band Phish created a loyal following by extending the approach of the quintessential 1960s concert band, the Grateful Dead. Like the Dead, the members of Phish embraced eclectic tastes and influences. A typical Phish concert would weave together strands of rock, folk, jazz, country, bluegrass, and pop. A band devoted to improvisation, Phish required a live performance environment to be fully appreciated. There are some obvious differences between Phish and the Dead—Phish being a smaller and in some regards a more technically adept band, with a range of stylistic references arguably even broader than that of the Grateful Dead. Be that as it may, bands like Phish, Blues Traveler, and Dave Matthews Band, inspired by the counterculture of the 1960s and by the improvisational work of jazz musicians such as Miles Davis and Sun Ra, provide an optimistic, energetic, and open-minded alternative to the nihilism and relentless self-absorption of many alternative rock bands. The fact that Phish was often dismissed by rock critics—in part because their music doesn't make sense in terms of the rock-as-rebellion scenario that dominates

Box 9.2   The "Seattle Sound"

Regional "sounds" have played an important part in the history of popular music, from the Chicago blues of Muddy Waters to the Memphis **rockabilly** style of Elvis Presley and the southern California inflections of gangsta rap. Seattle, where Nirvana honed their sound and built a local fan base, was already home to a thriving alternative rock scene by the late 1980s. (The Pacific Northwest, while at somewhat of a remove from the main centers of the recording industry, had twenty-five years earlier played a role in the development of garage band rock, an important predecessor of punk rock.) The group often singled out as an originator of the "Seattle sound" was Green River (formed in 1983), whose 1988 album *Rehab Doll*, released on Sub Pop, helped to popularize grunge rock, blending heavy metal guitar textures with hardcore punk. Green River was also the training ground for members of later, more widely known Northwest bands such as Mudhoney (formed 1988), which was Sub Pop's biggest act until Nirvana came along, and Pearl Jam (formed 1990), who went on to become one of the most popular rock bands of the 1990s. One of the first bands signed to the fledgling Sub Pop label was Soundgarden (formed 1984), a heavy metal band that many insiders expected to be the first group to break the Seattle grunge sound on the national market. However, Soundgarden's first across-the-boards success—the album *Superunknown,* which reached Number One on the charts and sold five million copies—was not released until 1994.

Today, the push to define a regional style often comes as much from the promotion departments of record companies as from the local artists and fans themselves. The documentary video *Hype!* (1996), a revealing portrait of the role of Sub Pop Records in the Seattle alternative rock scene, suggests that many Seattle-based musicians and fans rejected the grunge label as a commercial gimmick, especially when it was adopted by advertising agencies and upscale fashion designers. This tension between commercialism and authenticity continues to play a central role in the creation and promotion of alternative rock music.

such criticism—didn't impede their success as a live act. Unlike bands such as R.E.M., Nirvana, and Pearl Jam, however, their popularity as a touring act never translated into massive record sales. By the mid-1990s Phish was able to pack stadiums—selling out Madison Square Garden in merely four hours—but none of their albums has sold as many as a million copies.

The twelve-and-a-half-minute track "Stash," from the concert album *Phish: A Live One* (1995), exemplifies the band's loose-jointed, freewheeling approach to collective improvisation. (This is, it must be admitted, a relatively brief selection. For an even better sense of the band's improvisational prowess, we would advise that you listen to one of the longer tracks, perhaps the half-hour-long "Tweezer.") The song—in the sense of a verse-chorus structure with a more or less fixed melody and lyrics—takes up only a small proportion of the track, which is an extended

collective exploration of the improvisational possibilities of a minor-key chord progression, carried along on a rhythmic groove indebted to Latin American music.
Certain relatively fixed elements create a sense of structure—for example, the tan-
golike melody played by guitarist Trey Anastasio at the beginning of the track and
periodically throughout. (The audience's familiarity with these structural points is
evidenced by the fact that they fill in one part of the melody with collective, and
reasonably precise, clapping.) At some points these structural elements seem to
melt away completely, as the guitar, acoustic piano, electric bass, and drums develop a subtle interplay, taking the performance in unexpected directions. While
Anastasio's guitar is generally the dominant instrument in the mix, Phish's approach to improvisation resembles that found in early (New Orleans) jazz more
than it reflects the hierarchical structure of rock bands, in which the soloist becomes the more or less exclusive center of attention and the rest of the band plays
a subservient role.

In an interview in *Addicted to Noise* (issue 1.07, June 1995), guitarist Trey Anastasio talked about the fact that Phish has never in over a decade of touring had a
hit album or single:

> Lately I've been thinking . . . the worst thing that could happen to a band is to have
> a hit single. . . . Because you weaken your fan base. People start coming in that aren't
> interested in the whole thing. And then they're expecting to hear that one song. . . .
>
> Kind of like life. You don't go from being 13 to being 30, you gotta go through
> everything in between. Music is life to a musician. Having a hit single is very simi-
> lar to going up to someone in eighth grade and saying, "Wow, that thing you did
> in eighth grade was really great. We're going to skip you to college. Here you go!
> Good luck!" Take it slow. Life is long.

Life is long, but lives are sometimes short. It is in the end difficult to explain
why musicians such as Ray Charles, Willie Nelson, Paul Simon, and the
Grateful Dead managed to sustain a pattern of creative growth over several
decades, while others—for instance, Hank Williams, Jimi Hendrix, Janis Joplin, or
Kurt Cobain—burned out almost overnight, consumed by social pressures or
personal demons. Anastasio's quote suggests that the key to musical longevity
may be the ability to balance the passionate involvement of music making with a
philosophical, even somewhat distanced perspective on the business of making
a living from music.

Women's Voices: Alternative Folk, Hip-Hop, and Country

While the term is most frequently associated with rock music, there are "alternative" artists in almost all genres of popular music. In this section we will look at
the work of three women who have established an alternative identity in their respective genres: Ani DiFranco (a folk singer-songwriter); Lauryn Hill (a hip-hop
artist); and k.d. lang (a country singer). In each case, the music industry's application of the term "alternative" to these performers has to do with the fact that
women's perspectives—and feminist values—play an important role in their
recorded work. While DiFranco, Hill, and lang share this commitment, they differ
in their relationships to the corporate music business, in their performance styles,
and in the degree of commercial success they have enjoyed.

A folk singer dressed in punk rock clothing, Ani DiFranco (b. 1970 in Buffalo,
New York) has spent her career resisting the lure of the corporate music business,
releasing an album and playing upward of two hundred live dates every year, and

Ani DiFranco. Courtesy BMI Archives.

building up a successful independent record label (Righteous Babe Records) and a substantial grassroots following. DiFranco began performing publicly at nine, performing covers of Beatles songs at a local coffeehouse. By the age of nineteen DiFranco had written over one hundred original songs and relocated from her native Buffalo to New York City to pursue a musical career. In 1989 she recorded a demo album and pressed five hundred copies of an eponymous cassette to sell at shows. The tape—a spare collection of intensely personal songs about failed relationships and gender inequality, accompanied with acoustic guitar—quickly sold out, and in 1990 DiFranco founded the independent label Righteous Babe Records to distribute her recordings more effectively.

By the mid-1990s the mainstream media had begun to take notice of DiFranco's homespun, low-tech music. Her 1995 album *Not a Pretty Girl* garnered notice from CNN and the *New York Times,* though it did not appear in the *Billboard* charts. But 1996 brought *Dilate,* an eclectic work recounting a love affair with a man, which debuted in the Top 100 of the *Billboard* charts, an unusual achievement for an independent release. The live album *Living in Clip,* released in 1997, became her first gold album. In 1998 DiFranco released the studio effort *Little Plastic Castle,* her highest-charting album to that date, which debuted at Number Twenty-two on the Top 200 chart. All of these albums were released on the Righteous Babe label, despite many offers from major record companies.

"Not a Pretty Girl," from the album *Not a Pretty Girl* (1995), is a typical Ani DiFranco recording, with self-revealing lyrics and an austere, minimalist studio sound, focused on DiFranco's voice and acoustic guitar. Because—as is often the case in urban folk music—the words are so important to the effect of this song, we must pay particularly close attention to their construction and how they are performed. The lyrics operate on at least two levels: first, as a response to an individual, a man who has wronged the singer in some way; and second, as a more general indictment of society's treatment of women.

The track opens in a reflective mood, with the solo acoustic guitar playing a four-chord progression. The musical form of "Not a Pretty Girl" is not dissimilar to that of many Anglo-American folk songs, and the song's text, as printed on the CD's liner notes, suggests the format of a traditional folk ballad, made up of a series of stanzas. However, DiFranco's performance of the lyrics—which escalates from a sung whisper at the beginning to an assertive growl in the middle, then ends with gentle wordless singing—creates an effect entirely different from that of seeing the words laid out on the page. DiFranco lays her lyrics over the structure of the song like ropes, tightening them here, loosening them there, and creating a sense of emotional intensity and musical momentum. She begins the first verse of the song in a whisper, her dislike for the man to whom the song is addressed emerging clearly only on the word "punk," which she spits out derisively. The way the accents in the text are distributed around the strong waltz rhythm of the music—with its *one*-two-three pulsations—creates the sense of a woman who is impatient with the injustices of the world and who insists upon being treated as a person, not a stereotype. (Each numbered line below represents a unit of four three-beat measures.)

> *I am not a*
> (1) **pre**tty *girl,*
> (2) *that is not what I* **do,** *I ain't no* **dam-**
> (3) *sel in di***stress,** *and I don't* **need**
> (4) *to be rescued, so, so put me* **dowwwwn,**
> (5) **punk.** *Wouldn't you pre-*
> (6) **fer** *a maiden* **fair?** *Isn't there a*
> (7) **kit**ten *stuck up a* **tree** *somewhere?*
> (8)

At this point DiFranco's acoustic guitar is joined by electric guitar, bass, and drums, changing the texture of the recording to a blend of folk music and alternative rock. In the second verse DiFranco packs more syllables into each four-bar musical phrase, the words rushing out and then being held back, emphasizing the central point of the lyrics (i.e., that women who express themselves forcefully are too often dismissed as merely being "angry"). In the second half of the verse, the accents of her words coincide with the stressed beats of the music more frequently, creating a sense of urgency.

> *I am not an*
> (1) **an**gry *girl, but it seems like*
> (2) *I've got* **ev**eryone *fooled. Every time I say*
> (3) **some**thing *they find hard to* **hear,** *they chalk it* **up**
> (4) *to my* **an**ger, *and* **ne**ver *to their own fear. I-*
> (5) **ma**gine *you're a girl, just trying to*
> (6) **fi**nally *come* **clean,** *knowing full*
> (7) **well** *they'd prefer you were* **dirty**
> (8) *and* **smi-i-iling.** *And I am*
> (9) **sor**ry, *but I am*
> (10) **not** *a* **mai**den *fair, and I am not a*
> (11) **kit**ten *stuck up a tree somewhere*
> (12)

In the third verse the texture moves even further toward the rock side, and DiFranco further escalates the emotional tension. At the very end of the verse a slight shift in the lyric makes us more aware of the singer's mixture of defiance and vulnerability. Whereas, in the second verse DiFranco's character states emphatically that she is "not a kitten up a tree," at the end of the third verse that claim is pushed a bit off-center when she asks rhetorically, "Don't you think every kitten figures out how to get down, whether or not *you* ever show up?" Here we catch a glimpse of a wound that lies beneath the protagonist's emotional armor:

> *And* **gen***erally my*
> *(1)* **gen***eration wouldn't be caught* **dead**
> *(2)* **work***ing for the* **man,** *And generally I a-*
> *(3)* **gree** *with them,* **Trou***ble is, you've got to* **have**
> *(4)* *yourself an* **al***ternate plan, And I have* **ear** *. . .*
> *(5)* **ned** *my* **dis***illusionment, I have been*
> *(6)* **work***ing all of my* **life** *And I am a* **pa-**
> *(7)* *triot,* **I** *have been*
> *(8)* **fight***ing the good* **fight.** *And* **what** *if there are no*
> *(9)* **dam***sels in dis***tress?** **What** *if I knew*
> *(10)* **that,** *and I called your* **bluff?** *Don't you think every*
> *(11)* **kit***ten figures out how to get* **down**
> *(12)* **Whe***ther or not you ever* **show up***?*

The final stanza of "Not a Pretty Girl" reinforces the more general message of the text, a critique of the physical norms by which society, and men in particular, so often judge women.

> *I am* **not** *a* **pre***tty girl*
> *I don't really* **want** *to be* **pre***tty girl*
> *I want to be* **more** *than a* **pre***tty girl.*

The recording ends gently, with DiFranco's overdubbed voice singing two melodic patterns in a responsorial manner.

The impact of "Not a Pretty Girl" is closely tied up with its carefully controlled fluctuations in musical texture, verbal density, and emotional color. DiFranco artfully blends the progressive outlook of urban folk music with the rebellious energy of alternative rock. At the same time, her performance—a song-portrait of a woman whose experience of sexism has had profound emotional consequences—implies that matters of the heart cannot simply be reduced to political positions. This is where music can exceed the power of a speech or slogan, filling in the texture and nuance of emotions and demonstrating that social injustice is registered not only in the mind but also in the heart.

Lauryn Hill (b. 1975 in South Orange, New Jersey) is a hip-hop artist whose work is a self-conscious alternative to the violence and sexism of rap stars such as Dr. Dre, the Notorious B.I.G., and 2Pac Shakur. Hill started her recording career with the Fugees, a New Jersey–based hip-hop trio that scored a Number One hit in 1996 with their second album, *The Score.* Hill's debut solo album—*The Miseducation of Lauryn Hill* (1998)—extended the Fugees' successful blend of rap, reggae, and R&B. The album shot to Number One on the charts, selling seven million copies in a little over a year, and spawning the Number One hit "Doo Wop (That Thing)."

"Doo Wop" combines aspects of 1950s R&B—including a soulful lead vocal, four-part vocal harmony, and a horn section—with Hill's penetrating observations on male and female behavior. The cut opens with Hill and a few of her friends reminiscing about the good old days. Then the digital drum machine's groove enters, and Hill launches into the first half of her rap, directed to female listeners:

> *It's been three weeks since you were looking for your friend*
> *The one you let hit it* [have sex with you] *and never called you again*
> *Remember when he told you he was 'bout the benjamins?* [interested only in money]
> *You act like you ain't hear him, then gave him a little trim* [had sex with him] . . .
>
> *Talkin' out your neck* [being hypocritical], *sayin' you're a Christian*
> *A Muslim, sleeping with the Gin*
> *Now that was the sin that did Jezebel in* . . .

Hill admonishes the women in her audience to be more selective about their sexual relationships and to avoid being hypocritical about their personal conduct. She then turns to the men in her audience, opening up a rapid-fire volley of wordplay that strips the so-called gangstas of their tough-guy trappings, exposing them as mother-dependent, sneaky, woman-beating, sexually immature hypocrites:

> *The second verse is dedicated to the men* . . .
>
> *Let's stop pretendin' they wanna-pack-pistol-by-they-waist men*
> *Cristal* [champagne]*-by-the-case men, still* [living] *in they Mother's basemen'*
> *The pretty-face-men-claimin'-that-they-did-a-bid* [prison time] *men*
> *Need-to-take-care-of-their-3-and-4-kids men*
> *But they face a court case when the child support's late*
> *Money-takin', heart-breakin', now you wonder why women hate men*
> *The sneaky-silent men, the punk-domestic-violence men*
> *The quick-to-shoot-the-semen . . . Stop acting like boys and be men!*
>
> *How you gon' win when you ain't right within?!*

"Doo Wop (That Thing)" is essentially a moral parable, delivered in terms that leaven Hill's righteous anger with light-hearted and thoroughly up-to-date hip-hop jargon. She lowers her audience's potential defensiveness by admitting that she has found herself in similar situations and pleads with them to pay attention to the development of an inner life—*How you gon' win when you ain't right within?*—in order to avoid the twin traps of materialism and easy pleasure. The mixture of sweet soul singing and assertive rapping, R&B horns and a digital groove, moral seriousness and playful humor not only announced the arrival of a new and distinctive voice but also made the single "Doo Wop" a unique and important contribution to the hip-hop repertoire.

k.d. lang (b. 1961 in Alberta, Canada) has always occupied a marginal position in the conservative world of country music. Raised in an isolated rural town on the high plains of Canada, lang listened to classical and rock music as a young girl, discovering country music somewhat later, when she played a Patsy Cline–type character in a college play. She began her career in 1982 as a Cline imitator, going so far as to christen her band the Re-clines. During the early 1980s she released two albums on the Edmonton-based independent label Bumstead Records, but it was only in 1987, when Sire Records (former label of Patti Smith and the Ramones) released her *Angel with a Lariat,* that lang came to the attention of a broader audience. (The album was played on college radio stations and progressive country stations.) Her subsequent albums—1988's *Shadowland* and 1989's *Absolute Torch and Twang*—moved toward a more traditional honky-tonk sound, producing lang's first appearances on the country Top 40 chart, and a Grammy award for Best Female Country Vocal Performance. Even at that stage, however, lang never sat quite right with the Nashville establishment, who found her campy outfits (rhinestone suits and cat-eye glasses) and somewhat androgynous image off-putting.

A scandal over lang's appearance in a commercial for the "Meat Stinks" campaign of the People for Ethical Treatment of Animals led stations in the cattle-producing areas of the Midwest to boycott her records and generated an impressive volume of hate mail. In 1992 lang officially announced her homosexuality, a move that rather than hurting her career, led to lang being christened an "icon of lesbian chic" (*New York* magazine). During the 1990s lang moved in the direction of adult contemporary pop music, becoming an "alternative" star in that category as well. *Ingénue,* a 1992 album that owed little to country music, sold over a million copies in the United States and over two million in Canada. A single from *Ingénue,*

k.d. lang. Courtesy BMI Archives.

"Constant Craving," reached the pop Top 40 and won the Grammy award for Best Female Pop Vocal Performance. Although she was not able to repeat this commercial success, lang continued throughout the 1990s to maintain a dedicated following.

"Nowhere to Stand," from the 1989 album *Absolute Torch and Twang* (1989), is a traditional song in musical terms, with a series of four-line verses and a repeated chorus, all in triple meter. In fact, apart from lang's public image, the only thing that marks this as an alternative country song is the content of the lyrics, which are an indictment of the "traditional" practice of child abuse. The song begins quietly with lang's country-tinged alto voice, accompanied by acoustic guitar. The message of the song is not explicit in the first two verses, the second of which is accompanied by a solo fiddle:

> *As things start to surface, tears come on down*
> *Scars of a childhood in a small town*
> *The hurt she pushed inward, starting to show*
> *Now she'll do some talkin', but he'll never know*
>
> *Tables have turned now, with a child of her own*
> *But she's blind to the difference, what's taught is what's known*
> *Numbed by reaction, and stripped of the trust*
> *A young heart is broken, not aware that it's just*

The intensity of lang's performance builds through the second verse, but only in the chorus—which enters suddenly, a measure early—do we become aware that this is not the typical lovelorn country song and that something hidden, and deadly serious, is being revealed to us:

> *A family tradition, the strength of this land*
> *Where what's right and wrong is the back of a hand*
> *Turns girls into women, and a boy to a man*
> *The rights of the children have nowhere to stand.*

The characterization of child abuse as a "family tradition, the strength of this land"—in which moral values and gender identity are taught with "the back of a hand"—drives lang's message home without resorting to explicit descriptions of violence. The verse that follows sketches the psychological legacy of domestic violence as a deeply buried memory, "like a seed that's been planted and won't be denied," and the recording reaches its emotional peak in the second, final chorus. lang's juxtaposition of traditional Anglo-American song form and country music sensibility with a lyric that in essence questions the sanctity of the family—used by politicians and cultural commentators as the ultimate symbol of traditional values—creates a tender but powerful critique of American (and Canadian) culture.

Ani DiFranco, Lauryn Hill, and k.d. lang have all achieved the status of alternative artists in their respective genres, and it is worth taking a moment to consider why. The lyrics of DiFranco's "Not a Pretty Girl" don't depart totally from the norms of urban folk music, a genre long identified with social and political criticism. What makes this track an alternative folk recording is the introduction of instrumental textures and vocal style from punk rock, and the fact that it was released on a small independent label, managed by the artist herself. Hill's "Doo Wop (That Thing)" is classified as an alternative hip-hop recording not because it incorporates aspects of

R&B and soul music—many mainstream hip-hop records do this—but rather because the song's lyric challenges aspects of the materialistic and sexist ideology promoted on many of the most commercially successful rap recordings. k.d. lang's "Nowhere to Stand" hews quite closely to the norms of country and western music in its form, its vocal and instrumental style, and its emotional tone. Its status as an alternative country song has more to do with the singer's public persona (the only Jewish Canadian vegetarian lesbian in country music), and with the subject matter of the song, the secret of child abuse in "traditional" families.

While these three songs present an interesting series of contrasts, it is also worth noting the strong parallels among the careers of DiFranco, Hill, and lang. All three are innovative singer-songwriters, whose "alternative" perspectives are deeply informed by historical knowledge of the particular genres in which they have chosen to work. DiFranco refers to herself as "just a folk singer" and performs at tribute concerts for urban folk pioneers like Pete Seeger, while Hill demonstrates her "old school" credentials by evoking, and verbally citing, the sound of postwar rhythm and blues, and k.d. lang uses the 1960s country style of Patsy Cline to convey her social messages. All three artists are committed to creating popular music that engages with contemporary social issues, particularly the rights of women and children. And finally, in a business where the boundaries of acceptable nonconformity are narrowly drawn, and where even today any hint of a feminist perspective is generally enough to propel an artist into the "alternative" category, DiFranco, Hill, and lang have all been able to achieve a degree of commercial success while not compromising their passionate and distinctive voices.

Globalization and the Rise of World Music

During the 1980s the boundary between mainstream and marginal music became ever fuzzier, and the twin pressures to expand the global market for American popular music and create new alternative genres and audiences within the American market grew ever stronger. One of the most interesting results of these processes was the emergence of a category called *world music*. The term was first systematically adopted in the late 1980s by independent record label owners and concert promoters, and it entered the popular music marketplace as a replacement for longer-standing categories such as "traditional music," "international music," and "ethnic music." These sorts of records were traditionally positioned in the very back of record stores, in bins containing low-turnover items such as Irish folk song collections, Scottish bagpipe samplers, German polka records, recordings by tourist bands from the Caribbean and Hawai'i, and perhaps a few scholarly recordings of so-called primitive music from Africa, Native America, or Asia. International records were generally purchased by immigrants hungry for a taste of home, by cross-cultural music scholars such as ethnomusicologists, and by a handful of aficionados. In general, while transnational entertainment corporations became ever more successful at marketing American pop music around the globe, most of the world's music continued to have little or no direct influence on the American marketplace.

To be fair, we can point to some examples of international influence on the American pop mainstream before the 1980s—Cuban rumba, Hawai'ian guitar, and Mexican marimba records of the 1920s and 1930s; Indian classical musician Ravi Shankar's album *Live at the Monterey Pop Festival*, which reached Number Forty-three in 1967, as the counterculture was at its peak; "Grazing in the Grass" (1968), a Number One hit by the South African jazz musician Hugh Masekela; or "Soul Makossa" (1973), the Top 40 dance club single by the Cameroonian pop musician Manu Dibango, often cited as a primary influence on disco music. But these cosmopolitan influences were typically filtered through the sensibilities of Western musicians and channeled by the strategies of American and European record companies and publishing firms. A quintessential example of this is the Tokens' rock 'n' roll hit "The Lion Sleeps Tonight" (Number One in 1961), an adaptation of a hit single by the urban folk group the Weavers, entitled "Wimoweh" (a Number Fourteen pop single in 1952). "Wimoweh" had in turn been an adaptation of a 1939 South African recording by a vocal group made up of Zulu mine workers, Solomon Linda and the Evening Birds. By the time the Evening Birds' song reached the ears of Americans, it had undergone several bouts of invasive surgery, including the insertion of a pop-friendly melodic hook and English lyrics, and removal of all royalty rights pertaining to the original performers.

This sort of rip-off—a basic operating procedure for many years in the fields of American rhythm & blues and country music as well as in the international music market—reflected the global imbalances of power that had initially been created by Western colonialism. Later world fusion or world beat projects—including Paul Simon's pioneering albums *Graceland* (see Chapter 8) and *The Rhythm of the Saints,* the annual WOMAD (World Music and Dance) festival, initiated in 1982 by Peter Gabriel, and various recordings by David Byrne and Ry Cooder—helped to redress this imbalance to some degree. Nonetheless, the unequal economic relationship between "the West" and "the rest" continues to haunt such cross-cultural collaborations up to the present day.

The 1980s also saw musicians from Africa, South Asia, the Near East, Eastern Europe, and Latin America touring the United States with increasing frequency and appearing, if rarely, on the *Billboard* pop charts. The first indication that musicians from the so-called Third World might gain increased access to the American market was the release in 1982 of the album *Juju Music,* by a Nigerian group called the African Beats, led by the guitarist King Sunny Adé. Featuring an infectious brand of urban African dance music that blended electric guitars, Christian church hymns, and Afro-Caribbean rhythms with the pulsating sound of the Yoruba "talking drum," *Juju Music* sold over 100,000 copies and rose to Number 111 on *Billboard*'s album chart. The African Beats' next album, *Synchro System,* reached as high as Number 91 on the chart; however, the group was soon thereafter dropped by Island Records and never again appeared on the American pop charts.

In an article published in 1982 in the *Village Voice* by the popular music critic Greg Tate, entitled "Are You Ready for Juju?," the author explicitly identified King Sunny Adé as a potential replacement for Bob Marley, the Jamaican reggae superstar who had very recently died. On one level, this seems perfectly logical, and it probably reflects the strategic thinking of Island Records, who released the Adé albums. Adé might well have had a shot at equaling Marley's success, but the fact that he sang in Yoruba—a language spoken by precious few American listeners—rather than Marley's richly spiced version of Jamaican English doomed him to failure from the beginning. (Very few American Top 40 hits have not featured English lyrics. This is an insurmountable barrier for many international musicians, although this may change as the linguistic makeup of the United States continues to diversify.) Adé did succeed in establishing a market for so-called Afro-pop music, opening the door for African popular musicians such as Youssou N'dour (Senegal), Salif Keita (Mali), Thomas Mapfumo (Zimbabwe), and Ali Farka Toure (see below).

By 1990, when the heading "world music" first appeared above a *Billboard* record chart, it was as a subcategory of the broader heading "adult alternative albums." Interestingly, this latter category also included New Age music, a genre of instrumental music designed to facilitate contemplative and mystical moods, and sometimes loosely linked with the religious and healing practices of Native American, African, and Asian cultures. The larger category "adult alternative albums" suggests an effort on the industry's part to identify forms of alternative music that would appeal to an affluent baby boomer audience, rather than to the younger audience attracted by rock bands such as Nirvana. (Since 1991 the National Academy of Recording Arts and Sciences [NARAS] has limited its Grammy awards for world music, New Age, folk, Latin, reggae, blues, polka, and various other alternative genres to albums only, presumably on the assumption that such genres are unlikely to generate hit singles.) The world music sections of most record stores usually do not include Latin dance music (salsa) or reggae, genres that sell enough records to justify their own discrete territories.

What, then, is world music? In a strictly musical sense, it is a pseudo-genre, taking into its sweep styles as diverse as African urban pop (juju), Pakistani dance club music (bhangara), Australian Aboriginal rock music (the band Yothu Yindi), and even the Bulgarian State Radio and Television Female Vocal Choir, whose evocatively titled 1987 release *Le Mystère des Voix Bulgares* (*The Mystery of the Bulgarian Voices*) reached Number 165 on the *Billboard* album chart in 1988. Bestselling albums on *Billboard*'s world music chart have featured the Celtic group Clannad (whose popularity was boosted in the United States by their appearance in the soundtrack for a Volkswagen advertisement), Spanish flamenco music (played by the Gypsy Kings, a hotel band from France), Tibetan Buddhist chant (presented by Mickey Hart, drummer for the Grateful Dead), and diverse collaborations between American and English rock stars and musicians from Africa, Latin America, and South Asia. The overlap among various types of "adult alternative" music—including New Age, world music, techno, and certain forms of European sacred music—is reflected in the commercial success of albums like *Vision* (1994), a mélange of "12th-century chant, world beat rhythms, and electronic soundscapes," as one press release put it. (It's hard to imagine better confirmation of the historical saw that "the past is another country.") The attraction of world music for its contemporary American audience is bound up with stereotyped images of the "exotic," whether these be discovered on imaginary pilgrimages to Africa and the Himalayas, or in time travel back to the monastic Christianity of medieval Europe. Nonetheless, there are limits to the degree of musical exoticism most listeners are willing to tolerate. This may explain the almost total absence on the *Billboard* charts of music from East Asia, which many American listeners find particularly challenging.

We are all familiar with the assertion that music is a universal language, by which people usually mean to suggest that music can transcend the boundaries separating diverse nations, cultures, or languages. This statement, however comforting, does not stand up to close scrutiny—even within American culture, one person's music may be another person's noise. Nonetheless, the music industry has wasted no time in chaining the rhetoric of musical universalism to the profit motive, as for example in this mid-1990s advertisement for the E-mu Proteus/3 World, a digital device programmed with hundreds of samples of world music:

Enrich Your Music with a Global Texture. As borders dissolve, traditions are shared. And this sharing of cultures is most powerful in the richness of music. . . . E-mu has gathered these sounds and more—192 in all. Use them to emulate traditional world instruments or as raw material for creating one-of-a-kind synthesized sounds of your own. (Théberge 1997, p. 201)

Music, with its ability to flow over the boundaries of society and the borders of nations, holds open the possibility that we may glimpse something familiar and sympathetic in people strange to us—that the inequalities of the world in which we live may for a moment be suspended, or even undermined, in the act of making or listening to music. Still, the suggestion that installing a digital device in your home studio in order to emulate the "gathered sounds" of faraway people has anything to do with "sharing cultures" reveals a critically impoverished vision of cross-cultural communication. There is no denying that music has the potential to traverse the boundaries of culture and language and thereby add to our understanding of people very different from us. But the ultimate responsibility for interpreting its meanings, and determining its impact, lies with the listener.

Two World Music Collaborations: Ali Farka Toure and Nusrat Fateh Ali Khan

By the 1990s collaborations between American and foreign musicians had become more common, spurred on the one hand by folk and alternative music fans' search for a broader range of musical experiences, and on the other by the globalization of the music industry. Two particularly interesting examples of this sort of transnational collaboration are the album *Talking Timbuktu,* which won the Grammy award for Best World Music Recording in 1994, and a sampler album inspired by the film *Dead Man Walking,* which reached Number Sixty-one on the album charts in 1996.

Talking Timbuktu was produced by the singer and guitarist <u>Ry Cooder</u> (b. 1947 in Los Angeles), whose career as a session musician and bandleader had already encompassed a wide array of styles, including blues, reggae, Tex-Mex music, urban folk song, Hawai'ian guitar music, Dixieland jazz, and gospel music. The sound and sensibility of *Talking Timbuktu* are derived from the music of <u>Ali Farka Toure</u> (b. 1950), a guitarist and traditional praise singer (*griot*) from the West African nation of Mali.

Encountering a track like "Diaraby," an American listener is likely to be struck by the music's close affinities with the blues. This is no accident. To begin with, the blues styles of Mississippi, Texas, and other southern states were strongly influenced by the traditions of African slaves, many of whom came precisely from the Sahel region of West Africa, homeland of Ali Farka Toure's people, the Bambara. The high-pitched, almost wailing sound of Toure's singing; the percussive, ostinato-driven guitar patterns; and the use of song as a medium for social and personal commentary—all of these features represent an evolution of centuries-old links between the West African griot tradition and the blues created by black musicians in America's Deep South. In point of fact, it turns out that Toure's style was directly influenced by American blues musicians such as John Lee Hooker, whose records he discovered after his career was established in Africa.

Talking Timbuktu features contributions by the blues guitarist and fiddler Clarence "Gatemouth" Brown and various prominent session musicians. The result, as exemplified by "Diaraby," sung in the Bambara language, hews close to its African roots, with the American musicians playing in support of Toure. The lyric of the song is itself reminiscent of the bittersweet emotion of some American blues:

> *What is wrong my love? It is you I love*
> *Your mother has told you not to marry me, because I have nothing. But I love you.*
> *Your friends have told you not to marry me, because I have nothing. But I love you.*
> *Your father has told you not to marry me, because I have nothing. But I love you.*
> *What is wrong my love? It is you I love.*
> *Do not be angry, do not cry, do not be sad because of love.*

The sound and sensibility of "Diaraby" provide additional evidence, if any were needed, of the deep links between African and American music. This is not music functioning as a universal language, but rather a conversation between two dialects of a complexly unified Afro-Atlantic musical language.

The track "The Face of Love" is a different sort of collaboration, featuring the lead singer for the Seattle-based alternative rock band Pearl Jam, Eddie Vedder (b. 1966 in Chicago), and the great Pakistani musician Nusrat Fateh Ali Khan (1948–97), and produced by Ry Cooder. Khan was a leading performer of *qawwali,* a genre of mystical singing practiced by Sufi Muslims in Pakistan and India. (Sufism was founded in Iran between the ninth and twelfth centuries C.E. A response to orthodox Islam, Sufism emphasizes the inner kinship between God and human beings and seeks to bridge the distance between them through the force of love.)

Nusrat Fateh Ali Khan and Ensemble. Photo by S. T. Sakata.

Qawwali singing is traditionally accompanied by a double-headed drum called the *dholak* (or a *tabla,* used in Indian classical music) and a portable keyboard instrument called the harmonium, which creates a continuous drone under the singing. In traditional settings the lead singer (or *qawwal*) alternates stanzas of traditional poetic texts (sung in unison with a choir) with spectacular and elaborate melodic improvisations, in an attempt to spiritually arouse his listeners and move them into emotional proximity with the Divine.

During the 1990s Nusrat Fateh Ali Khan became the first *qawwali* artist to command a large international following, owing to his performances at the annual WOMAD festivals curated by the rock star Peter Gabriel, and to a series of recordings released on Gabriel's Real World label. Khan began to experiment with non-traditional instruments and to work with musicians outside the *qawwali* tradition, leading some critics to charge that the music had moved away from its spiritual roots. "All these albums are experiments," Khan told the interviewer Ken Hunt in 1993. "There are some people who do not understand at all but just like my voice. I add new lyrics and modern instruments to attract the audience. This has been very successful" (see the web version of *All Music Guide*).

Most American listeners first heard Khan in the soundtracks to *The Last Temptation of Christ* and *Natural Born Killers,* though without knowing it, since he was part of the overall blend. (Khan was unhappy about being included in the soundtrack for *Natural Born Killers,* since it did not reflect the spiritual goals of *qawwali.*) The 1996 film *Dead Man Walking*—the story of a nun's attempt to redeem the soul of a convicted murderer on the verge of execution—was the first to foreground Khan's contributions. Many reviews of *Dead Man Walking* stressed the contribution of Khan's voice to the haunting, mystical, and spiritual atmosphere of the film. The song "The Face of Love" is based on a simple melody, sung first by Khan with lyrics in the Urdu language, and then with English lyrics by Pearl Jam's lead singer Eddie Vedder:

> *Jeena kaisa Pyar bina* [What is life without love]—
> *Is Duniya Mein Aaye ho to* [Now that you have come to this world] *(2x)*
> *Ek Duje se pyar karo* [Love each other, one another]
>
> *Look in the eyes of the face of love*
> *Look in her eyes, oh, there is peace*
> *No, nothing dies within pure light*
>
> *Only one hour of this pure love*
> *To last a life of thirty years*
> *Only one hour, so come and go*

In this case the sound of the music (particularly the drone of the harmonium) and the mysticism of the Sufi poetic text resonate with the transcendental atmosphere of the film—the contemplative mood of a man sentenced to die by lethal injection. The filmmaker does not make an explicit argument for or against the death penalty, and the music, with its subtly shifting textures, embodies the complexity and ambivalence of the film's subject. Although Eddie Vedder could not be expected to possess the formidable vocal improvisatory technique that Khan unleashes briefly in the middle of this track, he nonetheless manages to blend the timbre of his voice (and his acoustic guitar playing) with the mood and texture of the *qawwali* ensemble. In addition, Vedder's English lyrics do evoke the theme of mystical love so central to *qawwali* singing. This is not an example of music's functioning as a universal language, for most members of the film's American audience neither understood the words that Khan sang nor possessed any knowledge of the centuries-long history of Sufi mystical traditions. Nonetheless, it could be argued that this is a case where the well-meaning effort of artists to reach across cultural and musical boundaries does produce something like an aesthetic communion, a common purpose embodied in musical texture and poetry, provisional though it might be.

Khan's appearance on the soundtrack of *Dead Man Walking* led to his being signed by the indie label American Recordings, managed by Rick Rubin, formerly the mastermind behind the rappers Run-D.M.C. and the Beastie Boys. The American music industry's market positioning of world music as yet another variant of alternative music is indicated by that label's roster of artists, which included not only Nusrat Fateh Ali Khan but also the "death metal" band Slayer, the rap artist Sir Mix-A-Lot, and the country music icon Johnny Cash.

———

We have completed our historical journey through the rock era of American popular music, from the birth of rock 'n' roll, into the age of rock music, rap, digital technology, and global pop. In our concluding chapter, we return to the underlying themes that were presented at the beginning of this book: the relationship between music and identity, the effect of technology on music, the operations of the music business, and the complex, shifting relationship between the mainstream and the margins of popular taste and the marketplace for popular music.

CHAPTER TEN

CONCLUSION

At the beginning of our survey of American popular music in the rock era we suggested that this history is best thought of, not as a single story told in a single voice, but as a variegated and continually shifting landscape, characterized by the complex interaction of various styles, performers, audiences, and institutions. We provided surveying tools to help orient ourselves, a set of thematic sightlines that run right across the expansive terrain of America's popular music. These included the relationship between music and identity; the evolving role of musical technology; the institutions and strategies of the music business; and the notion that the marketplace for popular music can usefully be divided into a center or mainstream, on the one hand, and various margins or peripheries, on the other. In this concluding section we will revisit these themes and discuss some trends that are likely to influence the future development of popular music in the United States.

MUSIC AND IDENTITY

In the course of our study of American popular music in the rock era we have encountered many examples of the complex relationship between music and identity. One of the most prominent of these has been the long, complicated history of white fascination with black music—and of the relationship between black and white musicians, and between African American and European American musical traditions. Many metaphors have been used to describe this relationship—homage, borrowing, syncretism, crossover, exchange, exploitation, rip-off—but none of them adequately captures the shifting, sometimes tensely ambivalent and sometimes joyously synergistic relationship between these two great musical streams and the cultures that gave them birth.

The role of race and ethnicity in American music must be situated within a broader context. The very fact that Americans speak of black and white music as though these were self-evident, well-defined entities stems from a particular history of racial segregation—and from the so-called Jim Crow laws designed during the early twentieth century to prevent racial commingling in the American South. This way of classifying human beings into racial categories is not universal and in fact differs substantially from perceptions of human diversity in many other parts of the world. Of course, if race is more a social fiction than a biological fact, it is a fiction that has taken on a powerful life of its own, advantaging some people and disadvantaging others on the basis of their physical appearance and ancestry. If we accept the statement that "music has no color"—an assertion made in full sincerity by many musicians of all hues—we nonetheless cannot escape the fact that racial stereotypes carry a great deal of force in contemporary popular culture.

A pernicious by-product of any relentless focus on differences and interactions between black and white music and musicians is the tendency to forget about our third stream, a diverse Latin American tradition that has reasserted itself again and again throughout the history of American popular music. (We need only recall the Latin rock recordings of Carlos Santana, who created one of the most distinctive sounds of the 1960s counterculture and resurfaced some thirty years later to receive the first Grammy of the new millennium.) At the beginning of the twenty-first century, many of the top-selling albums in the United States were by Latino artists such as Jennifer Lopez and Ricky Martin, a reflection of America's growing Latino population and the rise of Spanish-language broadcasting corporations such as Univision and Telemundo. This phenomenon pushes us toward a wider view of "American music," rooted in a transcontinental zone of cultural interaction that reaches from Canada to South America.

In the end, much of the music that we have examined does not admit easily of straightforward racial or ethnic classification—think, for example, of Elvis Presley's two-sided hit "Don't Be Cruel"/"Hound Dog" (the only record ever to top the pop, country, and R&B charts at the same time); Ray Charles's rural twang on "I Can't Stop Loving You"; the Beatles' emulation of Chuck Berry's country-tinged rock 'n' roll style; or the wildly eclectic juxtaposition of funk, rock, and European synth-pop in hip-hop breakbeats. To argue that there is a broad body of music that can reasonably and simply be labeled American is not, however, to deny the continuing existence of racism in American society, or the effect of racial identities on popular music.

Sexuality and gender are other aspects of identity that are also central to the history of American popular music. During our journey we have encountered many strikingly stylized images—or stereotypes—of American men, including the lonely wanderer of Hank Williams's "I'm So Lonesome I Could Cry" (1949); the mythological super-male of Muddy Waters's blues anthem "Hoochie Coochie Man" (1954); the young working-class rebels who feature centrally in so many rock songs, from Elvis Presley to the Ramones, Bruce Springsteen to the Beastie Boys; and the tough-talking street hustler persona of gangsta rap tracks like Snoop Doggy Dogg's "What's My Name?" (1993). We have met many memorable women along the way as well—the malevolent super-female of Big Mama Thornton's "Hound Dog" (1953); the mature, world-weary persona of Tina Turner's "What's Love Got to Do with It" (1984); the complex, shifting, and self-consciously constructed persona of Madonna;

and the young feminist in Ani DiFranco's "Not a Pretty Girl" (1995), whose critique of sexist stereotypes combines the personal with the political.

A large proportion of American popular music has been concerned, in one way or another, with relationships between men and women. This polyphonic public conversation has represented many voices, attitudes, and viewpoints: the mature resignation of Carole King's "It's Too Late" (1971); the old-fashioned chivalry of Kenny Rogers's "Lady" (1980); the Freudian angst of Prince's "When Doves Cry" (1984); and the hip moralizing of Lauryn Hill's "Doo-Wop (That Thing)" (1998), a didactic song that urges both men and women to clean up their acts. The history of American pop music is a history of popular attitudes toward romance, love, and sex.

Since so much popular music deals with love and sex, it is not surprising that public authorities of various sorts have been concerned to monitor representations of sexuality. There are many examples of censorship in the history of American popular music—for example, the cover version of Big Joe Turner's "Shake, Rattle, and Roll" by Bill Haley and the Comets, or the production of "childproofed" versions of hip-hop and alternative rock hits, with the offensive references "bleeped" out. In particular, the depiction of homosexual and bisexual relationships has always been treated gingerly by the music industry. Even Top 10 singles like the Village People's "YMCA" and "In the Navy" (Number Two and Three respectively in 1979), which can be interpreted on one level as a defiantly out-of-the-closet celebration of gay popular culture, function on another level to reaffirm gay stereotypes (conveyed onstage and in music videos by the band's adornment in campy costumes—the cowboy, the construction worker, the sailor, the leather-clad biker, the Indian chief, and so on). The question of what the Navy thought it was doing when it sought to use the song "In the Navy" for a recruitment campaign, or what millions of straight Americans think they're up to when they mime the song "YMCA" at sporting events, raises a number of interesting issues that we cannot probe here. It must also be noted that a number of prominent pop music stars—including Little Richard, David Bowie, Prince, and Madonna—have fashioned personas that seem purposefully to *blur* public perceptions of their sexual orientation. In regard to sexuality, as with other dimensions of social identity, music seems particularly well suited to carrying multiple meanings, depending in substantial measure upon who is doing the listening.

Although Americans, unlike the English, are often characterized as being oblivious to class distinctions, the expression of working-class, middle-class, and upper-class identities and experiences runs right through the history of American popular music. Class identity has often bubbled just below the sleek surfaces of American pop music. In Chuck Berry's "Maybellene" (1955), the protagonist's automotive pursuit of a young woman is given a distinctive flavor by the distinction between his working-class V-8 Ford and the girl's more expensive Cadillac Coupe de Ville. (The use of a French name—always a marker of elite culture—drives the point home, we might say.) The Crystals' 1962 hit "Uptown" sketches the social geography of New York City, tracing the daily path of a young man who works "downtown," where he "don't get no breaks," and comes home every evening to his lover's "uptown" tenement, where he feels like a "king." Although Americans do not tend to wear their class affiliations on their sleeve, popular music is full of references to wealth, poverty, and the effect of economic matters on the human heart.

Generational identity has, perhaps naturally, been a constant theme in an industry that relies to a great degree on the exploitation and creation of new styles, or at least the appearance of novelty. Since its inception in the 1950s, rock music has played a major role in creating youth cultures and in shaping Americans' conceptions of adolescence. The music industry now draws a broad distinction between kids in the twelve to sixteen age bracket—the patrons of teenybopper acts like the Backstreet Boys, the Spice Girls, and Britney Spears—and young adults in the seventeen- to twenty-five-year-old range, whom the industry relies on to buy millions upon millions of rock, rap, and alternative music CDs. Popular music provides us with a unique window onto changing conceptions of adolescence, ranging from the mild rebellion of the Beach Boys' "Fun, Fun, Fun" (1964) to the Beastie Boys' rowdy party anthem "(You Gotta) Fight for Your Right (To Party)" (1987) and Nirvana's sardonic, depression-tinged "Smells Like Teen Spirit" (1991). It is no exaggeration to say that popular music is one of the main media through which we learn how to "act our age."

TECHNOLOGY AND THE MUSIC BUSINESS

We have traced shifts in technology for the recording, reproduction, and mass dissemination of sound, from magnetic tape recording and the long-playing disc (1940s), through FM radio and 45s (1950s), to the innovations of the 1970s and 1980s (home video, cable television, portable tape players, digital recording, and the compact disc). At each stage in the development of popular music, new technologies have opened up creative possibilities for musicians and created a wider range of choices for consumers. Of course, there is no guarantee that a given technological innovation will automatically provide greater freedom and flexibility for musicians and consumers or lead to more creative, interesting, and satisfying music. (We have noted elsewhere the nostalgia that crops up from time to time for older, more "human" technologies, a sentiment that motivates many alternative music scenes and the contemporary "lo-fi" movement.)

We are accustomed to thinking of technology as an agent of change. In some cases, however, the new digital technologies have allowed musicians to excavate the musical past. The techno musician Moby did precisely this on his bestselling 1999 album *Play,* when he sampled segments of performances by Georgia Sea Islands singer Bessie Jones, Texas blues singer Boy Blue, and the Shining Light Gospel Choir, recorded in the field some forty years earlier by the folk music scholar Alan Lomax. What goes around comes around, but never in precisely the same form.

As we move into the twenty-first century, technology continues to affect how popular music is made, recorded, reproduced, marketed to, and enjoyed by listeners. A new standard for digital music making was introduced in 1992 with the Alesis ADAT. The core of the ADAT system was an eight-track digital synthesizer/recorder that could expand to 128 tracks by adding additional units. This meant that a consumer could set up a basic home studio at relatively small expense, while professionals could use the same technology to build highly sophisticated digital sound facilities. *Electronic Musician* magazine declared in 1992 that "ADAT is more than a technological innovation; it's a social force."

The 1990s also saw the introduction of music software programs such as Pro-Tools, designed to run on personal computers. This software allowed recording engineers and musicians to gain even more control over every parameter of musical sound, including not only pitch and tempo but also the quality of a singer's voice or an instrumentalist's timbre. One of the most obvious examples of ProTools' potential for altering the sound of the human voice was Cher's Number One hit "Believe" (the best-selling single of 1998), which featured a highly processed vocal sound and a variety of post-production effects.

One of the complaints voiced against ProTools and similar software by some musicians is that it allows the correction of musical errors—including not only the erasure and substitution of individual notes and phrases, but also the alteration of a musician's sonic identity, the very aspect of their sound that makes them recognizable and unique. From this perspective, "imperfection" is a necessary part of music as a form of human expression. As the drummer Matt Cameron put it in an interview about Pearl Jam's 2002 album *Riot Act*, recorded "live" in a studio:

> This is definitely our anti-ProTools record. . . . it's more interesting hearing musicians in a room playing hard, with the tempo fluctuating slightly as the band heats up. Perfection is boring. (*Philadelphia Inquirer*, November 10, 2002)

In the arena of radio broadcasting and concert promotion, intense debates have arisen in response to the increasing integration of aspects of the music business by corporations. Much of the controversy has centered on Clear Channel, a publicly traded corporation that owns over 1,200 radio stations, 39 television stations, more than 100,000 advertising billboards, and over 100 live performance venues, ranging from huge amphitheaters to dance clubs, allowing them to present more than 70 percent of all live events nationwide. (This is a strategy referred to as "vertical integration," in which a corporation gains control over all aspects of the production of a commodity and its promotion and delivery to consumers.)

Critics have asserted that Clear Channel's use of its radio stations and billboards to advertise Clear Channel–booked shows at Clear Channel–owned venues is in essence a monopoly. The corporation has also drawn criticism for using "voice tracking," in which DJs at the company's headquarters in Texas record radio shows that are played on Clear Channel stations nationwide but presented as though they were being broadcast locally. It is argued that the company's dominance of radio markets makes it harder for local musicians and artists to get their music played on local stations, leading to a homogenization of music broadcasting nationwide. Defenders of Clear Channel argue that they are simply giving consumers what they want. Whatever one's viewpoint on the matter, it seems undeniable that this controversy is a direct descendant of the introduction of standardized Top 40 playlists and the payola scandals of the 1950s, only on a much larger scale.

Despite this evidence of a trend toward corporate consolidation of the music business, it can be argued that the most profound transformations in the dissemination and consumption of popular music have been catalyzed by the Internet, a vast concatenation of millions of computers linked together by a global network. In musical terms, the most influential new medium associated with the Internet is **MP3**, a variant of MPEG. (MPEG was a digital file compression system originally applied in the development of DVDs, or digital video disks.) MP3 allows sound files to be compressed to as little as one-twelfth of their original size. Let's assume that you would like to download a four-minute track of music from a Web site featuring original music. In its uncompressed, digitally encoded form, this track would require forty megabytes of data, creating a file that would take hours to download over a modem. With MP3 compression, this file could be squeezed down to only four megabytes, while still retaining something approaching the sound quality of a CD.

The introduction of MP3 technology spurred a series of bitter struggles between entertainment corporations and small-scale entrepreneurs, echoing past conflicts between major and indie record labels, though on an even larger scale. In 1997 a firm called MP3.com was founded by Michael Robertson, who started by making three thousand songs available for free downloading over the Internet. By the year 2000 MP3.com had become by far the most successful music site on the World Wide Web, with over ten million registered members. As with digital sampling, this new way of disseminating musical materials raised a host of thorny legal problems, centered on the issue of copyright. While MP3 files are not inherently illegal, the practice of digitally reproducing music from a copyrighted compact disc and giving it away for free without the artist's or record company's permission arguably is illegal.

In January 2000 a lawsuit was filed against MP3.com by the Recording Industry Association of America (RIAA), the trade association whose member companies—Universal, Sony, Warner Brothers, Arista, Atlantic, BMG, RCA, Capitol, Elektra, Interscope, and Sire Records—control the sale and distribution of approximately 90 percent of the offline music in the United States. The suit charged Robinson with copying forty-five thousand compact discs produced by these companies and making them available for free. MP3.com immediately issued a countersuit against the RIAA, but a court injunction forced them to remove all files owned by the corporations.

The year before, in 1999, an eighteen-year-old college dropout named Shawn Fanning had developed Napster, an Internet-based software program that allowed computer users to share and swap files, specifically music, through a centralized file server. Once again, the RIAA filed suit, charging Napster with tributary copyright infringement (meaning that the firm was accused not of violating copyright itself but of contributing to and facilitating other people's violation of the law). In its countersuit the firm argued that because the actual files were not permanently stored on its servers but rather transferred from user to user, Napster was not acting illegally. A federal court injunction finally forced Napster to shut down operations in February 2001, and users exchanged some 2.79 billion files in the closing days of Napster's existence as a free service.

In the wake of Napster's closure a number of companies specializing in "peer-to-peer" (p2p) file-sharing networks were established, including FastTrack, Gnutella, Audio Galaxy, and Grokster. These services' claim to exemption from copyright law is based on the fact that in a peer-to-peer network there is no central server on which files are even temporarily stored, and thus no "place" in cyberspace to which the act of copyright violation can be traced, apart from the millions of computers of the network's users. From the viewpoint of these users—including many musicians attempting to promote their recordings outside the corporate framework—p2p is the ultimate expression of musical democracy, a decentralized system made up of millions of individuals expressing free choice. From the RIAA's viewpoint, peer-to-peer music sharing is a case of mass theft, a maddeningly complex cybernetwork that challenges the ability of corporations (and the courts) to apply traditional conceptions of music as a form of property. The MP3 debates have raised fundamental questions about American culture, particularly in regard to the not always harmonious relationship between representative democracy and corporate capitalism.

The development of new personal listening devices came hand-in-hand with the rise of file-sharing on the Internet. In 2001 Apple Computer introduced the first-generation iPod player, which could store up to one thousand CD-quality songs on its internal hard drive. The iPod and other MP3 players have come to dominate the market for portable listening devices, in part because they provide the listener with the ability to build a unique library of music reflecting his or her personal tastes. (This trend was initiated half a century earlier with the introduction of the 45 r.p.m. record changer, which allowed consumers to play their favorite songs in whatever order they chose; see Chapter 2.) The ability of the iPod to "shuffle" music—that is, to play tracks in random order, mixing genres, performers, and historical periods—has not only exerted an influence on personal listening habits but also provided a metaphor for the contemporary (some would say postmodern) state of consumer culture. (In 2005, Apple introduced a device called the iPod Shuffle, promoted with the advertising slogans "Random Is the New Order" and "Lose Control. Love It.")

Studies of the intimate relationship between the iPod and its users suggest that for many listeners the device functions as a kind of aural prosthetic—an extension of the ears and musical mind and a point of connection to wider circuits for the circulation of digital information. Through these portable devices contemporary con-

New music technology for the new century. © Royalty-Free/CORBIS sumers of popular music are connected to a global entertainment matrix that includes home computers, the Internet, music download services such as the new Napster, and new services that are beginning to supplant the traditional functions of broadcasting. The rise of "podcasting"—a method of online audio distribution in which digital sound files are uploaded to a website, and listeners can automatically load files onto a portable player as they're made available—even has some cultural observers forecasting the demise of radio.

Of course there is no way for us to provide the final word on the rapidly shifting landscape of music technology. At the time of this writing (mid-2005) Napster has "gone legit," paying a multimillion-dollar settlement to music publishers for past copyright infringements, signing licensing agreements with the corporations represented by the RIAA, and reopening as a fee-based service. In June 2005 the Supreme Court of the United States handed down a ruling in the case *MGM Studios v. Grokster.* MGM was supported in its cause by other film studios, the RIAA, Major League Baseball, and intellectual property advocates. Grokster and allied software companies contended they should not be held responsible for the illegal acts of their customers, since their software is intended to download and share legal or non-protected files, and therefore meets the legal standard for protection from liability. In the end, the Supreme Court sided unanimously with the music and film corporations, holding that the software companies had in fact actively encouraged copyright infringement. While the ruling provided immediate support for the battle against file-sharing, many "insiders" agreed that the entertainment industry was simply staving off inevitable changes in the business model for selling popular music.

As you might expect, the *MGM Studios v. Grokster* case provoked intense responses among musicians and music fans as well as corporate lawyers. Speaking on the steps of the Supreme Court, Lamont Dozier, the great Motown songwriter and producer, said, "If I was back in Detroit, if we had this problem then, in the sixties there never would have been a Motown, I would have been at Ford's car factory, because I couldn't make a living in the music business" (*Money.CNN.com*, March 29, 2005). At the same time that Dozier was defending the rights of composers, musicians, and record companies to the fruits of their labor, hundreds of mostly young people gathered to support the p2p file-sharing companies, chanting and carrying signs. Some camped out overnight to attend the oral arguments, and it is easy to imagine that they passed the time listening to and exchanging music on their iPods—perhaps even some of Dozier's classic Motown tracks! One thing seems clear: the *MGM Studios v. Grokster* decision will not end the struggle between the entertainment conglomerates, on the one hand, and Internet entrepreneurs, fans, and independent musicians, on the other.

It is worth returning to the basic issue that underlies these controversies and others surely yet to come—the fact that digital technology allows the content of a recording to be liberated from its physical medium. Earlier recording technologies involve a process of "translation" from one medium to another: analog recording, for example, translates sound waves in the air into physical impressions on the surface of a disc or arrangements of iron oxide molecules on a magnetic tape. But digital recording involves the translation of musical sound into pure information, encoded in streams of ones and zeros. This in turn means that music can be transmitted, reproduced, and manipulated in a "virtual" form, free of the constraints of any particular technology (compact disc, magnetic tape, etc.). This development has raised questions that will no doubt shape the course of American popular music for years to come: What does it mean when a consumer licenses the right to use the contents of an album, rather than buying a single copy of it in a store? How can copyright be enforced—indeed, what is the meaning of the term "copyright"—when thousands of consumers can download the same piece of music simultaneously over the Internet? How will the transformation of music into pure information affect musicians and consumers? If "Video Killed the Radio Star"—to cite the first song promoted on MTV—will the Internet kill the CD store? What will the music industry of tomorrow look like?

CENTERS AND PERIPHERIES

As we have charted the growth of the marketplace for recorded music—which had by the close of the twentieth century reached an annual sales total of fourteen billion dollars nationally and forty billion dollars worldwide—it has become increasingly difficult to sustain the distinction that we initially drew between the mainstream of popular music and its margins. In part this is because at the outset we were able to conflate two quite different concepts: on the one hand, the idea of a musical mainstream and margins, involving cultural and stylistic distinctions that have grown more and more blurry over time; and, on the other, the idea that the market for popular music has an economic and institutional center and periphery. In the early twentieth century these two dichotomies fit together rather neatly, for the mainstream of popular music coincided to a great degree with the central institutions of the music business (publishing firms, phonograph companies, and somewhat later, radio networks). But by the end of the century, the two dichotomies, as well as the correlation between them, had broken down almost completely.

What started out as marginal genres—R&B, country and western, urban folk music, soul music, disco, heavy metal, rap, and alternative rock—came in turn to occupy the mainstream, right alongside (and frequently displacing) "adult contemporary" music more directly descended from the Tin Pan Alley tradition. And this process was mirrored in turn by the economic evolution of the music business. Independent record labels, which once operated on the fringes of the industry, are today more and more closely tied in with (and sometimes even invented by) the major record companies. At the dawn of the rock 'n' roll era, New York City and Los Angeles were unquestionably the geographical centers of the American music industry. Fifty years later, the spread of digital technology seems to be completing a process of total decentralization, as anybody with a computer, anywhere, can with increasing ease produce and market his or her own recordings.

The rise of international pop superstars such as Julio Iglesias, Ricky Martin, Celine Dion, and Shakira, and the emergence of world music as a distinct category with its own Grammy award and *Billboard* chart, suggest that the center-periphery concept must now be recast in truly global terms. Although the United States is still the largest market for recorded music in the world, its preeminence as the nexus of the music industry is no longer indisputable. At the beginning of the twenty-first century five major conglomerates are responsible for as much as 90 percent of the sales of music worldwide, and only one of these corporations is officially head-quartered in the United States. With the unification of the European market and ongoing changes in Asia (including the rise of India and China as major centers for the production and consumption of popular music), it seems likely that the United States will remain an important, even indispensable part of the global music system, but not its dominant center.

Even if the United States can no longer cling to a mythology of manifest destiny in relation to the rapidly growing and diversifying global entertainment industry, there can be no doubt that the sounds and sensibilities of American popular music will continue to exert an enormous impact all over the world. Millions of people worldwide have come to know the United States through its popular culture, as disseminated in movie theaters, on television and radio, and on cassettes and discs. This image of America is a song-map: a set of narratives about being "Born in the U.S.A." and "Living in America," and a network of imaginary pathways juxtaposing street knowledge "Straight outta Compton" with the urban delights of "Spanish Harlem," and pitting the seductively mirrored "Hotel California" against the plain white city hall of "Muskogee," Oklahoma. Similarly, the popular narrative of America as a center of novelty, excitement, and mobility has been disseminated by mass-reproduced sonic images of Americans "rollin' on the river" on the "Proud Mary," "Waiting for a Train," "Leavin' on a Jet Plane," driving around in a "Pink Cadillac" or a "Little Deuce Coupe," and wandering footloose, "Like a Rolling Stone." Although music is by no means a universal language, the recurring themes of American popular music—love and sex, home and travel, materialism and morality, optimism and despair—have resonated with millions of listeners worldwide. (This may be why country and western music is extremely popular in Africa, a fact that surprises many Americans.)

We have reached the endpoint of our journey, but there is every reason to expect that the energy and creativity, the crassness and commercialism of American popular music—that messy product of almost four centuries of cultural miscegenation—will continue to impress themselves on the world's consciousness, provoking equal measures of admiration and disapproval. Whether one views this process as an extension of cultural imperialism or as proof positive of the unique value of American musical culture, there can be no denying that popular music—forged by sons and daughters of Africa and Europe, shaped by the diverse musical cultures of the Americas, hustled and hyped by generations of entrepreneurs, molded and remolded by the force fields of identity, technology, and the music industry—constitutes an epochal contribution not only to American culture but also to a wider, still-emerging world culture. Rock on!

GLOSSARY

This glossary consists of terms requiring specialized definitions that recur throughout the book. Such terms appear in the text in **boldface**. Important terms of local significance—that is, those relevant principally to particular chapters or to sections of chapters only—are *italicized* in the text and defined in context, and may also be located using the index.

a cappella   Vocal singing that involves no instrumental accompaniment.

A&R   Abbreviation for "artists and repertoire." This is the department of a record company whose responsibility it is to discover and cultivate new musical talent, and to find material for the artists to perform—naturally, with an eye toward commercial potential. As many artists today write and record their own material, the latter function of A&R has atrophied to some extent.

arranger   A person who adapts (or arranges) the melody and chords of a song to exploit the capabilities and instrumental resources of a particular musical ensemble. For example, a simple pop tune originally written for voice and piano may be arranged for a jazz "big band" with many horns and a rhythm section.

ballad   A type of song consisting usually of verses set to a repeating melody (see **strophic** form) in which a story, often romantic, historic, or tragic, is sung in narrative fashion.

blue notes   Expressive notes or scalar inflections found primarily in blues and jazz music. The blue notes derive from African musical practice; although they do not correspond exactly to the Western system of **major** and **minor** scales, it is helpful to imagine them as "flatter" or "lower" versions of the scale degrees to which they are related, and thus one speaks of "blue" thirds, fifths, and sevenths.

blues   A genre of music originating principally from the field hollers and work songs of rural blacks in the southern United States during the latter half of the nineteenth century. Themes treated by blues lyrics included the oppressive conditions suffered by African Americans; love gone wrong; alienation; misery; and the supernatural. The lyrics are often obscured by a coded, metaphorical language. The music of the blues is rich in Africanisms and earthy rhythms. Originally an acoustic music, the blues moved to the urban North in the mid-twentieth century, becoming electrified in the process.

bridge   A passage consisting of new, contrasting material that serves as a link between repeated sections of melodic material. A bridge is sometimes called a **release** (see discussion of AABA song form in Chapter 2).

cadence   A melodic or harmonic event that signals the end of a musical line or section, or of the piece as a whole.

call-and-response   A musical form in which a phrase performed by a single musician (the "call") is answered by a contrasting phrase performed by a group of musicians (the "response"). In African American music and related genres the call is typically improvised, while the response is repeated more or less exactly.

chord   The simultaneous sounding of different pitches.

chorus   A repeating section within a song consisting of a fixed melody *and* lyric that is repeated exactly each time that it occurs, typically following one or more verses.

coda   The "tail end" of a musical composition, typically a brief passage after the last complete section that serves to bring the piece to its conclusion

composer   A person who creates a piece of music. Although the term may be, and often is, used to describe the creators of popular songs, it is more commonly applied to those who create more extended, formally notated works of music.

counterculture   A subculture existing in opposition to and espousing values contrary to that of the dominant culture. The term is most often used to describe the values and lifestyle of young people during the late 1960s and early 1970s (see Chapter 5).

counterpoint   The sounding of two independent melodic lines or voices against one another.

cover version   The term "cover" or "cover version" refers to the second version, and all subsequent versions, of a song, performed by either another act than the one that originally recorded it or by anyone except its composer(s). In the early days of rock 'n' roll, white singers and groups frequently covered rhythm & blues hits by black artists. Because the white performers had easier access to radio airplay, the cover versions often outsold the original recordings.

dialect   A regional speech variant; one may allude to regional musical "dialects" to describe stylistic variants of the same basic musical genre, as with Mississippi Delta blues or East Texas blues.

dissonance   A harsh or grating sound. (The perception of dissonance is culturally conditioned. For example, the smaller intervals employed in certain Asian and Middle Eastern musics may sound "out of tune" and dissonant to Western ears; within their original context, however, they are regarded as perfectly consonant.)

distortion   A buzzing, crunchy, or "fuzzy" tone color originally achieved by over-driving the vacuum tubes of a guitar amplifier. This effect can be simulated today by solid state and digital sound processors. Distortion is often heard in a hard rock or heavy metal context.

DJ **Disc jockey** (deejay); one who plays recordings (as on a radio program).

feedback Technically, an out-of-control sound oscillation that occurs when the output of a loudspeaker finds its way back into a microphone or electric instrument pickup and is reamplified, creating a sound loop that grows in intensity and continues until deliberately broken. Although feedback can be difficult to manage, it becomes a powerful expressive device in the hands of certain blues and rock musicians, most notably the guitarist Jimi Hendrix. Feedback can be recognized as a "screaming" or "crying" sound.

groove Term originally employed by jazz , rhythm & blues, and funk musicians to describe the channeled flow of swinging, "funky," or "phat" rhythms.

hillbilly music An early term for what now would be called country music: music made by rural southerners that developed out of traditions originating in the British Isles.

hook A "catchy" or otherwise memorable musical phrase or pattern.

lyricist A person who supplies a poetic text (lyrics) to a piece of vocal music; not necessarily the composer.

major refers to one of the two scale systems central to Western music (see **minor**); a major scale is arranged in the following order of whole- and half-step intervals: $1-1-\frac{1}{2}-1-1-1-\frac{1}{2}$. (This pattern is easy to see if one begins at the pitch C on the piano keyboard and plays the next seven white notes in succession, which yields the C major scale: CDEFGABC.) A song is said to be in a major tonality or key if it uses melodies and chords that are constructed from the major scale. Of course, a song may (and frequently does) "borrow" notes and chords from outside a particular major scale, and it may "modulate" or shift from key to key within the course of the song.

melisma One syllable of text spread out over many musical tones.

minor Refers to one of the two scale systems central to Western music (see **major**); a minor scale is arranged in the following order of whole- and half-step intervals: $1-\frac{1}{2}-1-1-\frac{1}{2}-1-1$. (This pattern represents the so-called natural minor scale, often found in blues and blues-based popular music; it is easy to see if one begins at the pitch A on the piano keyboard and plays the next seven white notes in succession, which yields the A minor scale: ABCDEFGA. The two other minor scales in common usage—the melodic minor and harmonic minor scales—have ascending and descending forms that differ somewhat from the natural minor scale.) A song is said to be in a minor tonality or key if it uses melodies and chords that are constructed from the minor scale. Of course, a song may (and frequently does) "borrow" notes and chords from outside a particular minor scale, and it may "modulate" or shift from key to key within the course of the song. In comparison to the major scale, the minor scale is often described as having a "sad" or "melancholy" sound.

MP3 A variant of the MPEG compression system, which allows sound files to be compressed to as little as one-twelfth of their original size.

payola The illegal and historically widespread practice of offering money or other inducements to a radio station or deejay in order to insure the prominent airplay of a particular recording.

polyrhythm The simultaneous sounding of rhythms in two or more contrasting meters, such as three against two, or five against four. Polyrhythms are found in abundance in African and Asian musics and their derivatives.

producer   A person engaged either by a recording artist or, more often, a record company, who directs and assists the recording process. The producer's duties may include securing the services of session musicians; deciding on arrangements; making technical decisions; motivating the artist creatively; helping to realize the artistic vision in a commercially viable way; and not unimportantly, insuring that the project comes in under budget. A good producer often develops a distinctive signature sound, and successful producers are always in great demand. They are often rewarded handsomely for their efforts, garnering a substantial share of a recording's earnings, in addition to a commission.

R&B   **Rhythm & blues.** An African American musical genre emerging after World War II. It consisted of a loose cluster of styles derived from black musical traditions, characterized by energetic and hard-swinging rhythms. At first performed exclusively by black musicians and aimed at black audiences, R&B came to replace the older category of "race records" (see Chapter 2).

refrain   In the verse-refrain song , the refrain is the "main part" of the song, usually constructed in AABA or ABAC form (see discussion of "Love and Marriage" in Chapter 2).

release   *See* **bridge.**

reverb   Short for "reverberation"—a prolongation of a sound by virtue of an ambient acoustical space created by hard, reflective surfaces. The sound bounces off these surfaces and recombines with the original sound, slightly delayed (reverb is measured in terms of seconds and fractions of seconds). Reverberation can occur naturally or be simulated either electronically or by digital sound processors.

rhythm & blues   *See* **R & B.**

riff   A simple, repeating melodic idea or pattern that generates rhythmic momentum; typically played by the horns or the piano in a jazz ensemble, or by an electric guitar in a rock 'n' roll context.

rockabilly   A vigorous form of country and western music ("hillbilly" music) informed by the rhythms of black R&B and electric blues. It is exemplified by such artists as Carl Perkins and the young Elvis Presley.

sampling   A digital recording process wherein a sound source is recorded or "sampled" with a microphone, converted into a stream of binary numbers that represent the profile of the sound, quantized, and stored in computer memory. The digitized sound sample may then be retrieved in any number of ways, including "virtual recording studio" programs for the computer, or by activating the sound from an electronic keyboard or drum machine.

scat singing   A technique that involves the use of nonsense syllables as a vehicle for wordless vocal improvisation. It is most often found in a jazz context.

slap-back   A distinctive short reverberation with few repetitions, often heard in the recordings of rockabilly artists, such as the Sun Records recordings of Elvis Presley.

strophes   Poetic stanzas; often, a pair of stanzas of alternating form that constitute the structure of a poem. These could become the **verse** and **chorus** of a **strophic** song.

strophic   A song form that employs the same music for each poetic unit in the lyrics.

syncopation   Rhythmic patterns in which the stresses occur on what are ordinarily weak beats, thus displacing or suspending the sense of metric regularity.

tempo   Literally, "time" (from Italian). The rate at which a musical composition proceeds, regulated by the speed of the beat or pulse to which it is performed.

timbre   The "tone color" or characteristic sound of an instrument or voice, determined by its frequency and overtone components. Timbre is the aspect of sound that allows us, for example, to differentiate between the sound of a violin and a flute when both instruments are playing the same pitch.

Tin Pan Alley   Originally a name for the area in New York City where music publishing was centered, this phrase came to refer to the extremely popular style of music that was produced there during the first half of the twentieth century—and to later popular music obviously indebted to that style.

tonic   Refers to the central or "home" pitch, or chord, of a musical piece—or sometimes of just a section of the piece.

tremolo   The rapid reiteration of a single pitch to create a vibrating sound texture. This effect can be produced by acoustic instruments or by electronic means.

verse   In general usage, this term refers to a group of lines of poetic text, often rhyming, that usually exhibit regularly recurring metrical patterns. In the verse-refrain song, the verse refers to an introductory section that precedes the main body of the song, the **refrain** (see discussion of "Love and Marriage" in Chapter 2).

vibrato   An expressive musical technique that involves minute wavering or fluctuation of a pitch.

waltz   A dance in triple meter with a strong emphasis on the first beat of each bar.

BIBLIOGRAPHY

This list includes all works cited in the body of this book, along with a small number of others that may be recommended for further reading on individual topics and issues central to the material covered in the preceding pages. No attempt is made to offer a comprehensive bibliography here, or to list books of a general introductory nature in the area of American popular music.

Bashe, Philip. *Heavy Metal Thunder*. Garden City, N.Y., 1985.

Beatles, the. *Anthology*. San Francisco, 2000.

Berry, Chuck. *The Autobiography*. New York, 1987.

Bright, Spencer. *Peter Gabriel: An Authorized Biography*. London, 1999.

Chapple, Steve, and Reebee Garofalo. *Rock 'n' Roll Is Here to Pay: The History and Politics of the Music Industry*. Chicago, 1977.

Charles, Ray, and David Ritz. *Brother Ray: Ray Charles' Own Story*. New York, 1978.

Chilton, John. *Let the Good Times Roll: The Story of Louis Jordan and His Music*. Ann Arbor, 1994.

Clarke, Donald. *The Rise and Fall of Popular Music*. New York, 1995.

Collin, Matthew. *Altered State: The Story of Ecstasy Culture and Acid House*. London, 1997.

Deffaa, Chip. *Blue Rhythms: Six Lives in Rhythm and Blues*. Urbana, Ill., 1996.

Frith, Simon. *Sound Effects: Youth, Leisure, and the Politics of Rock 'n' Roll*. New York, 1981.

George, Nelson. *Hip Hop America*. New York, 1998.

George, Nelson, et al., eds. *Fresh: Hip-hop Don't Stop*. New York, 1985.

Gillett, Charlie. *The Sound of the City: The Rise of Rock and Roll*. New York, 1996.

Goodwin, Andrew. *Dancing in the Distraction Factory: Music Television and Popular Culture*. Minneapolis, 1992.

Guralnick, Peter. *Sweet Soul Music: Rhythm and Blues and the Southern Dream of Freedom*. New York, 1986.

——— *Last Train to Memphis: The Rise of Elvis Presley*. Boston, 1994.

——— *Careless Love: The Unmaking of Elvis Presley*. Boston, 1999.

Hager, Steven. *Hip Hop: The Illustrated History of Break Dancing, Rap Music, and Graffiti*. New York, 1984.

Jackson, Mahalia, and E. M. Wylie. *Movin' on Up*. New York, 1966.

Karlen, Neal. "Prince Talks." *Rolling Stone*, April 1985.

Keil, Charles. *Urban Blues*. Chicago, 1966.

Keil, Charles and Steven Feld. *Music Grooves*. Chicago, 1994.

Laing, Dave. *One-Chord Wonders*. Philadelphia, 1985.

Levine, Lawrence. *Black Culture and Black Consciousness: Afro-American Folk Thought from Slavery to Freedom*. New York, 1977.

Lhamon, W. T., Jr. *Raising Cain: Blackface Performance from Jim Crow to Hip Hop*. Cambridge, Mass., 1998.

Malone, Bill C. *Country Music, U.S.A.* Rev. ed. Austin, Tex., 1985.

Morse, Dave. *Motown and the Arrival of Black Music*. New York, 1971.

Negus, Keith. *Producing Pop: Culture and Conflict in the Popular Music Industry*. London, 1992.

Oliver, Paul. *Blues Fell This Morning: Meaning in the Blues*. Cambridge, England, 1990.

Palmer, Robert. *Deep Blues*. New York, 1981.

——— *Rock & Roll: An Unruly History*. New York, 1995.

Peterson, Richard A. *Creating Country Music: Fabricating Authenticity*. Chicago, 1997.

Petkov, Steven, and Leonard Mustazza, eds. *The Frank Sinatra Reader*. New York, 1995.

Pleasants, Henry. *The Great American Popular Singers*. New York, 1974.

Reynolds, Simon. *Generation Ecstasy: Into the World of Techno and Rave Culture*. New York, 1998.

Roberts, John Storm. *The Latin Tinge: The Impact of Latin American Music on the United States*. New York, 1979.

Rose, Tricia. *Black Noise: Rap Music and Black Culture in Contemporary America*. Middletown, Conn., 1994.

Sexton, Adam, ed. *Desperately Seeking Madonna*. New York, 1993.

Shaw, Arnold. *Honkers and Shouters: The Golden Years of Rhythm and Blues*. New York, 1986.

Taylor, Timothy D. *Global Pop: World Music, World Markets*. New York, 1997.

Théberge, Paul. *Any Sound You Can Imagine: Making Music/Consuming Technology*. Middletown, Conn., 1997.

Toop, David. *The Rap Attack 2: African Rap to Global Hip Hop*. London, 2000.

Walser, Robert. *Running with the Devil: Power, Gender, and Madness in Heavy Metal Music*. Middletown, Conn., 1993.

West, Cornel. *Race Matters*. Boston, 1993.

Wynn, Ron. *Tina: The Tina Turner Story*. New York, 1985.

INDEX

Bold numbers indicate photographs; "n" indicates a footnote

A&M Records, 215, 233
A&R personnel, 9, 67
AABA form, 3, 29–31, 52,
    61–62, 90, 108, 115–19,
    175, 180
ABC network, 21, 23
Abdul, Paula, 257
Abraxas, 187–88
Absolute Torch and Twang,
    305–6
A cappella singing, 61–62
Accent, 25, 27, 202
Ace of Base, 269
Acid jazz music, 223
"Act Naturally," 126
Acuff, Roy, 197
Adam Ant, 232
ADAT system, 317
"A Day in the Life," 155–56
Addicted to Noise, 300
Adé, King Sunny, 308–9
Adidas, 276
Adorno, Theodor, 9
Adult contemporary, 169–71,
    238. *See also specific artists*
Adventures of Ossie and
    Harriet, The, 57
Aerosmith, **6**, 268, 277
African Americans. *See also* Race
    counterculture and, 152
    dialect and, 4–5
    funkmaster image of,
        221–22
    identity of, 5–6, 270–71,
        314–15
    income of, postwar, 20
    musical traditions of,
        13–15, 42, 65, 270, 272,
        310–11, 314–15
    political influence of, 134
    record company ownership
        by, 101, 273
    slavery and, 13–14, 272
    stereotyping of, 5–6, 222,
        270, 289
    style and, 10–11, 15, 271
    in Vietnam War, 151
    WDIA and, 37
African Beats, 308
Afrika Bambaata, 271, 273, 277
Agogo, 194

"Ain't It a Shame," 78
Aladdin Records, 20
Album-oriented rock (AOR)
    format, 169, 208, 219–20,
    223, 226, 232
Albums. *See also specific titles*;
    Recordings
    on CD. *See* Compact discs
    concept. *See* Concept
        albums
    dust jackets for. *See* Dust
        jacket
    liner notes for. *See* Liner
        notes
    vs. singles, 22, 146, 184,
        198, 236–37, 248–49, 269,
        284, 309
    on tape. *See* Tapes
    on vinyl. *See* Phonograph
        records
Alesis ADAT system, 317
"Alfie," 142
Alien, 187
"All Around the World, or The
    Myth of Fingerprints," 254
"All I Really Want to Do," 145
"All I Want," 185
All Music Guide, 291
"All My Love," 48
All Summer Long, 109
"All You Need Is Love," 157
"Alone Again (Naturally),)" 288
Alternative music. *See also
    specific artists*
    agendas, 292
    audience for, 293
    business savvy and, 158,
        269, 292
    categories of, 291
    censorship and, 316
    childproof versions of, 316
    counterculture and,
        298–303, 306
    country music and, 304–7
    definition of, 269, 291–92
    grunge, 234, 295–99
    hardcore, 234, 293–95
    hip-hop music and, 303–4,
        306–7
    playlists and, 68, 157
    punk rock and, 2, 207–9,

    292–98
    radio and, 157, 169, 292
    regionalization of, 299
    sales of, 292
    speed metal, 234, 295
    thrash, 3, 234, 293, 295
    underground rock, 292–94
    urban folk music and,
        300–3, 306–7
    women in, 300–307
    world beat. *See* World
        music
Alternative Tentacles Records,
    294
Amazing Grace, 136
"America," 151
American Bandstand, 74, 93, **95**,
    222
American Broadcasting
    Company (ABC), 21, 23
American Graffiti, 168
"American Pie," 5, 177–78
American Recordings, 313
American Society of
    Composers, Authors, and
    Publishers (ASCAP),
    20–21
AmeriKKKa's Most Wanted, 284
Ampex Corporation, 22
AM radio stations
    counterculture and, 157–58,
        167
    vs. FM, 22
    hip-hop music and, 283
    payola to, 20, 38, 55
    R&B and, 38, 43
    Top 40 programming by,
        19, 68, 157, 169
Analog recordings, 7, 231–32,
    234, 321
*An American Werewolf in
    London*, 233
"Anarchy in the UK," 214
Anastasio, Trey, 300. *See also*
    Phish
"And I Love Her," 118
An Evening with John Denver,
    181
"Angel," 258
Angel with a Lariat, 305
Animals, The, 113

Anka, Paul, 57
Anthony, Michael, 242. *See also*
    Van Halen (group)
Anthrax, 242, 295
"Anyone Who Had a Heart,"
    142
Apollonia, 261, 263
Apple iPods, 320–21
Areas, Jose, 193. *See also*
    Santana (group)
Are You Experienced?, 163
"Are You Lonely for Me," 127
Arista, 211, 319
Armadillo World
    Headquarters, 197
Arnaz, Desi, 16
Around the World in a Day, 261
Arp synthesizer, 235
Arrangers, 9
Arrested Development, 291
The Artist formerly known as
    Prince, 262. *See also*
    Prince
Artists and repertoire
    personnel (A&R), 9, 67
Art music, 14, 135, 142, 163,
    169, 186, 209, 216, 281.
    See also specific artists
ASCAP, 20–21
Asheton, Ron, 210. *See also*
    Stooges, The (group)
Ashford, Nickolas, 103
Asian Americans, 5. *See also*
    Race
Association of Country
    Entertainers, 174
"As Tears Go By," 113
Atkins, Chet, **51**, 82, 197
Atkins, Juan, 290
Atlantic Records, 10, 20, 44–45,
    59, 135, 170, 189, 233, 319
"At the Hop," 57
Audio Galaxy, 319
Audiotapes. *See* Tapes
Avalon Ballroom, 152, 158
Average White Band, 222
Ayler, Albert, 211
Azpiazú, Don, 16

"Baby Be Mine," 249
Baby boom generation, 53–58,

139–40
Bacharach, Burt, 142, 170–71
"Back in the Day," 5
Backstreet Boys, The, 317
Bad Boy Records, 287
"Bad Girls," 227–29
"Bad Moon Rising," 165
Baez, Joan, 140
Baion rhythm, 101
Baker, Ginger, 164
Bakersfield sound, 172, 196
Ballads
    Brown (Charles) and, 41
    Cole and, 34
    country music and, 13,
        200–201
    definition of, 11
    DiFranco and, 302–3
    Dylan and, 120, 152
    "Eleanor Rigby" and, 120
    folk music and, 11–13
    heavy metal music and,
        189–92
    Kingston Trio and, 89
    Latin influence on, 200
    Motown and, 104
    opera and, 12
    rap music and, 278
Ballard, Hank, 93–94
"Ball of Confusion," 122, 161
Ballroom dancing, 12, 16, 67
Band of Gypsys, 187
Banjo, invention of, 14
Barrett, Aston and Carlton,
    203, 205, 207
Barry, Jeff, 98–101
Bars, definition of, 25
Bartholomew, Dave, 78
Batman (album), 261
Batman (TV show), 3
Battle of the Speeds, 22
Beach Boys, The, 106–10, 107,
    122–25, 181, 184, 317
Beastie Boys, The, 275, 277–79,
    282, 317
"Beat It," 233, 248–49
Beatles, The, 112, 155
    albums by, 99, 111, 113–14,
        122, 154–57, 184, 187
    Berry and, 114, 315
    breakup of, 168
    career of, 108, 110–22
    concerts by, 183
    counterculture and, 154–57
    The Crickets and, 85, 114
    Everly Brothers and, 114
    Fats Domino and, 116
    ideology of, 158
    image manipulation by,
        256
    Jennings and, 197
    King and, 176
    Little Richard and, 78, 114
    in movies, 115, 118
    Nirvana and, 296–97
    Perkins and, 114
    Rolling Stones and, 154,
        188
    Sinatra and, 183
    songs by, 3, 5, 110–11,
        113–21, 126, 149, 153–57,
        197
    Spector and, 99
    on TV, 255
    Wilson (Brian) and, 122
The Beatles (album), 187
Beats, 14, 25–26, 91, 202, 207,
    220, 227–29, 276
Bebop style, 70

Beck, 4
Beck, Jeff, 162, 164. See also
    Yardbirds
Bedtime Stories, 259
Bee Gees, The, 170, 224–25
Beggar's Opera, The, 12
Belafonte, Harry, 89
"Believe," 318
"Be My Baby," 97, 100–101,
    143, 260
Benjamin, Benny, 103
Bennett, Tony, 48, 50, 67, 142
Berlin, Irving, 30, 132
Berry, Charles "Chuck," 72
    Beatles and, 114, 315
    career of, 71, 75–76, 170,
        177
    Chess Records and, 81
    classification of, 56
    country music and, 71,
        74–75
    dialect and, 4
    vs. Domino, 78–79
    influence of, 85, 108–9, 114,
        162
    on Jordan, 39
    Motown and, 102
    rock 'n' roll and, 71, 76
    songs by, 69, 71–76, 108–9,
        170, 316
    stage devices of, 76
Berry, Jan, 110
Bertelsmann, 233
Bhangara music, 309
Big Bank Hank, 273. See also
    Sugarhill Gang
The Big Beat, 79
Big Bopper, The, 85
Big Brother and the Holding
    Company, 158–59
Biggie Smalls, 268, 287–88
Big Mama Thornton: Hound
    Dog/The Peacock
    Recordings, 46
Billboard magazine, 36–37, 67,
    127n1, 278
Bill Haley and the Comets,
    59–60, 67, 68, 69, 177, 316
Bill Haley and the Saddlemen,
    69
"Billie Jean," 233, 249
Biz Markie, 288
Black, Bill, 63
Black, Clint, 234, 268
Black and Blue, 46
Blackboard Jungle, 69, 206
"Black Denim Trousers and
    Motorcycle Boots," 57
Black Flag, 1, 294
"Black Magic Woman," 192
"Black Night," 41
Blacks. See African Americans
Black Sabbath, 189
Black Swan Records, 101
Blackwell, Chris, 204–5
Blackwell, Otis, 86
Blackwell, Robert, 86
Blaine, Hal, 98
Bleach, 296
Blonde Ambition tour, 261
Blondie, 208, 211, 248
Blow, Kurtis, 14, 273
"Blowin' in the Wind," 139–41,
    147–48
Blue, 185
"Blueberry Hill," 79
"Blue Eyes Crying in the
    Rain," 198
Bluegrass, 48

Blue notes, 49, 65, 71, 84,
    90–91, 116
Blues crooners, 38, 40–42
Blues music. See Rhythm &
    blues music (R&B)
Blues Traveler, 298
"Blue Suede Shoes," 56
"Blue Yodel," 199
BMG Records, 233, 319
Bob and Earl, 113
Bobby soxers, 32
Bob Marley and the Wailers,
    204–7. See also Marley,
    Bob
The Bodyguard, 268
"Bohemian Rhapsody," 232
Bolero rhythm, 101
Bomb Squad, 279–80, 284, 287
Bonham, John, 188. See also
    Led Zeppelin
Bon Jovi, 242–43
Bono, 4
Boogie-woogie music, 40
Boone, Debby, 171
Boone, Pat, 56
Bootee, Duke, 274. See also
    Furious Five
Bootleg recordings, 160
"Borderline," 258
Born Again, 287
Born in the U.S.A. (album), 247,
    249–51, 263
"Born in the USA" (song), 250,
    323
Born to Run (album), 247
"Born to Run" (song), 249
Bossa nova, 17
Bottleneck slide guitar
    technique, 42
Boucher, Eric, 294–95. See also
    Dead Kennedys, The
Bowie, David, 78, 185, 187, 199,
    219, 242, 316
Boy Blue, 317
Boyd, Eva, 96
Boyd, Henry, 78
Boyd, Jimmy, 19
Boyz II Men, 268–69
"Brain Damage," 186
Brain Salad Surgery, 187
Braithwaite, Freddie, 271, 278
Brando, Marlon, 208
Breakbeat music, 271
Breakdancing, 270–71
Breaks, 271–72
"The Breaks," 273
Brenston, Jackie, 241
Bridge over Troubled Water
    (album), 252
"Bridge over Troubled Water"
    (song), 151, 252
Bridge section, 30, 62, 90–91,
    180, 229
Brill Building, 98
Bringing It All Back Home, 144
British Invasion, 111, 113. See
    also specific artists
Britten, Terry, 240–41
Broadcaster guitar, 70
Broadcast Music, Inc. (BMI), 21
Broadsides, 11–12
Broadus, Calvin, 268, 275,
    284–87, 285, 315
Broadway musicals, 22, 46
Brooks, Garth, 233–34, 268
Brooks, Harvey, 59
Brown, Charles, 40–41
Brown, Clarence "Gatemouth,"
    310
Brown, Dave, 193. See also

Santana (group)
Brown, James, 133
    albums by, 135
    career of, 132–35, 170, 220
    Charles and, 131
    concerts by, 135
    disco and, 225–26
    Dominoes and, 44
    funk music and, 220
    hip-hop music and, 134,
        271–72
    on Jordan influence, 40
    minimalism and, 135, 216
    N.W.A. and, 283
    politics and, 134
    polyrhythms and, 14
    rap music and, 134, 271–72
    reggae and, 203
    songs by, 3, 6, 133–35,
        137–38, 220, 226, 271–72
    Talking Heads and, 216,
        218
    Wonder and, 177
    world music and, 134
Brown, Roy, 55
Brown, Ruth, 44–47, 45
Brubeck, Dave, 142
Bruce, Jack, 164
Brunswick Records, 82
Bubblegum music, 170, 213
Bullock, Annie, 237, 240,
    240–42, 259, 315
Bumstead Records, 305
Bunny hug, 12
Burke, Solomon, 129
Burnin', 207
"Burning Love," 177
Burrell, Stanley, 282, 288
Burru, 203
Butch Cassidy and the Sundance
    Kid, 171
"Buttermilk Biscuits," 286
Butthole Surfers, 294
"Bye, Bye, Love," 132
Byrd, Henry, 78
Byrds, The, 144–45, 293
Byrne, David, 4, 16, 209, 216,
    219, 308. See also Talking
    Heads
"By the Time I Get to
    Phoenix," 173

Cadence, 25–26, 29–30, 115, 141
Cahn, Sammy, 30
Cajun music, 13
Cale, John, 209–10. See also
    Velvet Underground, The
Calhoun, Charles, 59–60
"California Girls," 108
"California über Alles," 295
Call-and-response, 14, 88, 90,
    130–32, 137–39, 222, 239,
    245
Cameron, Matt, 318. See also
    Pearl Jam
Campbell, Clive, 271, 277, 286
Campbell, Glen, 171–73
Campbell, Luther, 288
"Candle in the Wind (1997),"
    269
"Can't Get Enough of Your
    Love, Babe," 180
"Can't Help Falling in Love,"
    129
Capitol Records
    Beatles and, 110–11
    Cole and, 34
    country music and, 48
    Haggard and, 172

"Learning the Blues," 67
ownership of, 168, 233
in postwar years, 20, 34
Prince and, 262
rock 'n' roll and, 67
sampling and, 319
Sinatra and, 80
Turner (Tina) and, 241
Carabello, Mike, 193. *See also*
Santana (group)
"Carey," 185
Carey, Mariah, 268–69
Caribbean Americans, 201–7,
270–71. *See also* Race
Carioca, 16–17
Carmichael, Hoagy, 129
"Caroline, No," 122
Carpenters, The, 169
Carraby, Antoine, 283. *See also*
N.W.A.
Cars, 73–75, 108–9, 316
Casablanca Records, 222,
224–25
Cash, Johnny, 171, 313
Cashbox magazine, 67
Castle, Irene and Vernon, 16,
255
Categories of popular music,
2–3, 37, 168–69
Catero, Fred, 193
CBGB & OMFUG Club, 211,
216
CBS network, 21, 23, 168
Celebrity, production of,
255–56, 297–98
Centers of popular music,
10–11, 322–23
Cha-cha-chá, 16
Chad Mitchell Trio, 180
"Chances Are," 80
Chandler, Chas, 163
Chantays, The, 110, 225
Chants, 309
"Chapel of Love," 99
Chapman, Tracy, 292
Charles, Ray, 15, 44, 129–32,
130, 300, 315
Charleston (dance), 12
"Charlie Brown," 78, 88–91
Cheap Thrills, 158–59
Checker, Chubby, 94–96, **95**
"Chemical Warfare," 295
Cher, 145, 318
"Cherry Pink and Apple
Blossom White," 67
Chess, Leonard and Phil, 74
Chess Records, 20, 42–43, 74,
81
Chic, 170, 220, 227–30, **228**,
258, 273
Chicago, riot in, 226
Chicago electric blues, 41–43,
45, 74
Chicago (group), 169, 193
Chirac, Jacques, 257
"Choo Choo Ch'Boogie," 23,
26–29, 40
Chords, 26–28, 63, 115–21, 124,
133–34, 138, 203, 235, 245
Chords, The, 61–62, 82
Chorus, 12, 24–30, 73–75, 78,
86–87, 90, 120–21, 264–67
Christian, Charlie, 70
Christmas music, 19, 94
The Chronic, 10, 284
Chuck D, 270, 278–81, **279**, 289.
See also Public Enemy
Chudd, Lew, 79
Chung House of Metal, 4

Ciccone, Madonna. *See*
Madonna
Circle Jerks, 294
Civil rights movement, 6, 134,
149–51
Clannad, 309
Clapton, Eric
career of, 111, 164–66
influence of, 162
on Muddy Waters, 42
Page and, 188
R&B and, 113
reggae and, 201
songs by, 205–7
soundprint of, 4
on *Unplugged*, 7
Clark, Dick, 55, **95**
Clash, The, 211–12, 214
Class, 10–11, 57, 316
Classical music, 186
Clavinet, 177
Clean remix versions, 284
Clear Channel Corporation,
318
Cliff, Jimmy, 201, 204, 206
Cline, Patsy, 128, 197, 304–5,
307
Clinton, George, 183, 222–23,
236, 248, 261, 283–84,
286–87, 290
Clooney, Rosemary, 31
"Cloud Nine," 161
Coal Miner's Daughter, 171
Coasters, The, 78, 88–91
Cobain, Kurt, 295–98, 300. *See
also* Nirvana
Cocktail blues, 40
Coda, 117, 217–19, 229
"Cold, Cold Heart," 19, 48, 50
Cold Chillin' Records, 278
Cole, Eddie, 34
Cole, Nat "King," 23, 31, **33**,
32–34, 39, 80, 130
Collaboration, 253–54
Collins, Judy, 140
Collins, Phil, 231–33. *See also*
Genesis
Collins, William "Bootsy," 222.
See also James Brown and
the Famous Flames;
Parliament
Colors, 283
Coltrane, John, 192
Columbia Broadcasting System
(CBS), 21, 23, 168
Columbia Records. *See also* Sony
in "Battle of the Speeds,"
22
Beastie Boys and, 277–78
Big Brother and the
Holding Company and,
158
counterculture and, 152
Def Jam Records and, 275
Franklin and, 135, 137
Jackson and, 233
Miller and, 67
MTV and, 233
ownership of, 168, 233
"Oye Como Va" and, 194
in postwar years, 20, 22
rock 'n' roll and, 67
Santana and, 192
Sinatra and, 80
Columbus Day Riot, 31–32
Colvin, Douglas, 211, **212**. *See
also* Ramones (group)
Combs, Sean "Puffy," 287–88
Come Dance with Me, 81

Commodores, 238
Como, Perry, 23, 31
Compact discs (CDs), 22,
231–32, 236–37, 262, 275,
319
Composers, 8–9, 12, 20–21, 38,
87, 98, 158, 258
Concept albums
approaches to, 182–86
Beach Boys and, 122, 184
Beatles and, 154–57, 184
Bowie and, 185
Charles and, 131–32
concert tours and, 183, 185
country music and, 198–99
digital sampling and, 122,
262
Eagles and, 182
ELP and, 186
Gaye and, 186
Jackson and, 249
Mitchell and, 185
Nelson and, 198–99
Parliament and, 222
Pink Floyd and, 185–86
Prince and, 262
Rolling Stones and, 188
Simon and, 253
Sinatra and, 81
Springsteen and, 251
Who and, 184
Concert albums, 135
Congas, 194
Conjunto acordeon style, 17
"Constant Craving," 306
Contours, The, 102–3
Contradances, 12
"Convoy," 171
Cooder, Ry, 308, 310–11
Cook, Paul, 214. *See also* Sex
Pistols, The
Coolio, 288
Cool Runnings, 206
Copyright. *See* Licensing and
copyright
Corridos, 200
Costello, Elvis, 201
Count Basie, 31, 202
"Countdown to Armageddon,"
279
Counterculture
alternative music and,
298–303, 306
Beatles and, 154–57
characteristics of, 152
country music and, 196–97
dancing and, 220
drug use and, 153–55,
160–62
Haggard on, 127
mainstreaming of, 167
members of, 151–52
punk rock and, 207–9
radio stations and, 157–58,
167
San Francisco and, 157–62
techno music and, 290
TV and, 167
world music and, 152, 154
Counterpoint, 121, 239, 243
Country, Bluegrass, Blues &
Other Music for Urban
Gourmandizers club, 211,
216
Country crooners, 48, 80
Country music. *See also* specific
artists
alternative music and,
304–7

audience for, 20, 126–27,
171, 233
Bakersfield sound, 172, 196
Billboard and, 37, 127n1
categories of, 168–69
counterculture and, 196–97
countrypolitan sound, 127,
173
cover versions and, 48, 58
crooners of, 48, 80
dialect and, 4
honky-tonk, 48–50, 172, 196
influences on, 12–13, 15,
17, 20, 36, 200–201
Nashville sound, 82,
127–29, 196
the outlaws of, 196–201
in postwar years, 36–37,
47–52
progressive, 196–201
rap music and, 286
rockabilly. *See* Rockabilly
rock 'n' roll and, 59–60, 69,
71, 74–75
royalties for, 20–21, 308
soft rock and, 170–74, 181
soundprint of, 13
style of, 2
Country Music Association,
173–74, 237–38
"Cover Me," 249
Cover versions, 16, 31, 38,
58–66
Coward of the County, 237
Cowboy, 275. *See also* Furious
Five
Cracked Rear View, 269
Cramer, Floyd, 128
"Crazy," 128, 197
"Crazy, Man, Crazy," 69
"Crazy Blues," 14
Cream, 164–66
Creedence Clearwater Revival
(CCR), 78, 165, 241
Crew Cuts, The, 61–62, 82
Crews, 271
Crickets, The, 84–85, 114, 197.
See also Holly, Buddy
Critical listening, 3
"Crocodile Rock," 175, 177–79
Crooners, 18, 31–34, 38, 40–42,
48, 62, 80. *See also* specific
artists
Crosby, Bing, 21–22, 31, 48, 94,
255–56
Crosby Stills and Nash (album),
187
Crosby, Stills, and Nash
(group), 183, 187
"Cross over the Bridge," 61
"Cross Road Blues," 164
"Crossroads," 164
Crowley, Aleister, 189
Crumb, Robert, 158
Cruz, Celia, 16
"Cry," 19
"Crying in the Chapel," 129
Crystals, The, 97, 100–101, 316
"Cry to Me," 129
Cuban habanera style, 16
Cummings, John, 211, **212**, 213.
See also Ramones (group)
Curtis, King, 4, 90–91

Dale, Dick, 110
Damned, The, 212, 214
Dance bands, 15, 40
Dance music. *See also* Disco
music

on *American Bandstand*, 74, 93–94
AOR format and, 219–20, 223, 226
cataloging of, 15
country music and, 12, 49
funk music and, 137–38, 219–23
at hardcore clubs, 294
hip-hop music and, 270–71
in honky-tonks, 49
influences on, 12, 15–17
"Love's Theme," 175, 179–80
marching band music and, 12
Motown and, 96, 102–3
new jack swing, 283
Pakistani, 309
R&B, 28
rap music and, 283–87
rock and, 220
rock 'n' roll and, 59–60, 93–96
sampling and, 281
Santana and, 193
segregation and, 40
Danceteria, 258
"Dance to the Music," 221
"Dancing in the Dark," 251
Dangerous, 296
"Darkness on the Edge of Town," 249
Dark Side of the Moon, 185–86
Darling, Denver, 28
Dave Matthews Band, 291, 298
David, Hal, 142, 170–71
Davis, Clive, 211
Davis, Miles, 192, 261, 298
Day, Doris, 31, 67
Day, Morris, 263
The Day the Earth Stood Still, 235
Deadheads, 160–62. *See also* Grateful Dead, The
Dead Kennedys, The, 293–95, 298
Dead Man Walking, 310, 312–13
Death Row Records, 284, 287
Decca Records, 20, 23, 26–29, 36, 39–40, 58–60, 67, 69. *See also* Brunswick Records
Dee, Joey, 94
Deep Purple, 169, 183, 187, 189
Dees, William, 288
Def Jam Records, 275–78
Def Leppard, 242
Dekker, Desmond, 206
DeKnight, Jimmy, 69
De La Soul, 288, 291
Delfonics, The, 179
Del-Tones, The, 110
DeMann, Freddie, 258
Denver, John, 170–71, 173–75, 180, 180–81, 257
De Shannon, Jackie, 142
Desmond Dekker and the Aces, 206
"Desperado," 182
Desperately Seeking Susan, 258
Deutschendorf, John. *See* Denver, John
DGC Records, 294, 296
Dholak, 312
Dialect, 4–5
Diamond, Neil, 99, 169, 171, 183

Diamond Dogs, 187
"Diaraby," 310–11
Dibango, Manu, 308
Diddley, Bo, 14, 81
DiFranco, Ani, 269, 292, 300–303, **301**, 306–7, 315–16
Digital recordings, 7, 22, 59, 231–32, 234, 236, 317–21
Dilate, 301
Dion, Celine, 234, 261, 268, 322
Dirty Dancing, 103
"Dirty Water," 209
Disc jockey (DJ)
alternative music and, 157, 169, 292
disco and, 223, 271
hip-hop music and, 271–72
location of, 318
payola to, 20, 38, 55
racism and, 37
techno music and, 290
Top 40 programming by, 19, 68, 157, 169
turntable techniques of, 223, 271–72, 290–91
voice tracking by, 318
The Disco Box, 180
"Disco Duck," 225
Disco music. *See also* specific artists
AOR format and, 223
Brown (James) and, 225–26
definition of, 170
disc jockeys and, 223, 271
Eurodisco, 225, 234, 269, 290
funk music and, 220–26
hip-hop music and, 223, 271
house music and, 223, 290–91
influences on, 308
The Last Days of Disco, 225
"Love's Theme," 175, 179–80
Motown and, 225
movies and, 224–25
rap music and, 229, 271
rock music and, 225–26
rock 'n' roll and, 94–96
salsa and, 16
studio technology and, 224–25
techno music and, 223, 225, 234, 289–90
Discotheques, 94, 223–25, 258, 273
"Dis-Gorilla," 225
Dissonance, 117, 163
Distortion, 158, 163
Dixie Cups, The, 99
Dixon, Willie, 42, 74
D.M.C., 276, **276**. *See also* Run-D.M.C.
Document, 293
Dodd, Coxsone, 202, 204
"The Doggie in the Window," 19, 48
Doggystyle, 284
Dolby, Thomas, 232
Dominant chord, 27
Domino, Antoine "Fats," 56, 75–76, 78–80, **79**, 94, 102, 116, 131, 202
Dominoes, The, 43, 43–44, 55
Donahue, Tom, 157
Donovan, Kevin, 271, 273, 277

Don't Be Cruel," 78, 82, 84, 86–87, 237, 315
"Don't Believe the Hype," 279
"Don't Bogart That Joint," 153
Don't Knock the Rock, 77
Don't Shoot Me I'm Only the Piano Player, 177
"Don't Think Twice, It's All Right," 141–43
Doors, The, 3
"Doo-wop" music, 43. *See also* Vocal harmony groups
"Doo Wop (That Thing)," 303–4, 316
Dorsey, Tommy, 23, 31
"Do the Bird," 96
Double-tracking, 85, 97
"Do You Know the way to San Jose," 142
"Do You Love Me," 102–3
"Do You Remember?," 109
Dozier, Lamont, 103–6, 321
Drayton, William, 278–79, **279**. *See also* Public Enemy
Dr. Dre, 4, 10, 223, 283–87. *See also* N.W.A.
"Dress You Up," 258
Dr. Funkenstein. *See* Clinton, George
Drifters, The, 44, 88, 98, 101, 187
"Drifting Blues," 40–41
Drifting Cowboys, The, 50
Drug use
counterculture and, 153–55, 160–62
country music and, 172
grunge and, 298
punk rock and, 208–9, 213, 215
rap music and, 280–81, 283–86
by Rastafarians, 203–4
at raves, 290
underground rock bands and, 293
Drum machines, 235
Drummond, Don, 202
Dub, 201
Duke Records, 20
Dumont network, 21, 23
Dunbar, Sly, 203
Dust jacket
for *Abraxas*, 187
for *Band of Gypsys*, 187
for *The Beatles* (album), 187
for *Brain Salad Surgery*, 187
for *Cheap Thrills*, 158
for *Crosby Stills and Nash*, 187
for *Diamond Dogs*, 187
for Drifters' *Greatest Recordings*, 187
for *Exile on Main Street*, 188
images, 187
for *Led Zeppelin IV*, 189, 192
liner notes on. *See* Liner notes
for *Made in Japan*, 187
for *Red-Headed Stranger*, 198
for *Sgt. Pepper's Lonely Hearts Club Band* (album), 154, 187
for *Sticky Fingers*, 187
for *Straight outta Compton*, 284

for Velvet Underground, 209
for *What's Going On*, 187
Dwight, Reginald. *See* John, Elton
DX-7 synthesizer, 235
Dylan, Bob
acid rock and, 158
albums by, 141, 144, 146
ballads and, 120, 152
career of, 139–46
CCR and, 165
country music and, 146, 196, 201
image manipulation by, 256
Jefferson Airplane and, 158
lyrics of, 4, 140–41, 143, 147–48
reggae and, 203
songs by, 139–49, 153, 157
urban folk music and, 36, 139–46, 169

Eagles, The, 175, 180–82
Eagles/Their Greatest Hits, 182
"Earth Angel," 3
Eazy-E, 283–84. *See also* N.W.A.
Eberle, Ray, 79
Echo, 4, 9, 82, 97
"El Condor Pasa," 251–52
"Eleanor Rigby," 113–14, 119–21
The Electric Kool-Aid Acid Test, 160
Electro String Instrument Company, 70
Elektra Records, 233, 319
Elliott, Missy, 5
Ellis, Alton, 203
"El Manicero," 16
"El Paso," 92–93
Emerson, Keith, 186. *See also* Emerson, Lake, and Palmer (ELP)
Emerson, Lake, and Palmer (ELP), 169, 186–87
EMI Records, 110, 168, 214, 233, 262
Engineers, 9, 318
Environmental music, 3
Epstein, Brian, 114
Erdelyi, Tom, 209, 211, **212**. *See also* Ramones (group)
Erotica, 259
Ertegun, Ahmet, 135
E Street Band, 249–50. *See also* Springsteen, Bruce
Ethnicity, 4–6, 314–15
Ett, Steve, 4
Eurodisco, 225, 234, 269, 290. *See also* Disco music
European Americans, 4–6, 10–13, 15, 65, 314–15. *See also* Race
Eurythmics, 137, 232, 238–40
Evans, Bill, 34
Evans, Ernest, 94–96, **95**
"Eve of Destruction," 145–46
Everly Brothers, The, 56, 114, 132
"Everybody," 258
"Everybody is a Star," 221
"Everyday," 85
"Everyday People," 221
Everything but the Girl, 291

Evita, 259
Exile on Main Street, 186–87
Experimental Jet Set, Trash, and No Star, 294
"Express Yourself," 258

Fab Five Freddie, 271, 278
Fab Four. *See* Beatles, The
"The Face of Love," 311–13
Faith, Percy, 19
"Family Affair," 221
Fanning, Shawn, 319
Farrakhan, Louis, 280
Fast Track, 319
Fat Boys, 96
"The Fat Man," 75
Federal Records, 43
Feedback, 163, 165–66, 218, 293–94
Felder, Don, 181. *See also* Eagles, The
Fender, Leo, 70
Fender guitars, 70
Fields, Danny, 211
Fifth Dimension, 142
"(You Gotta) Fight for Your Right (To Party)," 278, 278–79, 317
Fillmore, The, 152, 158
Films. *See* Movies
"Fire," 221
First Edition, The, 237
Flack, Roberta, 169, 171
Flamenco music, 309
Flavor Flav, 278–79, **279**. *See also* Public Enemy
Fleetwood Mac, 192
Fletcher, Ed, 274
Flintstones, The, 3
Flock of Seagulls, 232
"Fly, Robin, Fly," 179
FM radio stations, **8**, 22, 68, 157, 169. *See also* Album-oriented rock (AOR) format
Fogerty, John, 165. *See also* Creedence Clearwater Revival (CCR)
Folk music, 11–15, 20, 24, 89, 139–40, 184, 189–92. *See also specific artists*; Urban folk music
"A Fool in Love," 241
"(I Love You) For Sentimental Reasons," 19, 34
"Fortunate Son," 165
45 r.p.m. disks, 7, 22, 149, 320
"Four Bitches Is What I Got," 272
"409," 108
461 Ocean Boulevard, 206
Four Tops, The, 103
Foxcore bands, 298
Fox-trot, 12
Frampton, Peter, 169
Francis, Connie, 128
Franklin, Aretha, 4, 44, 131–32, 135–39, **136**, 170, 186, 203
Franklin, Erma, 159
Frantz, Chris, 216. *See also* Talking Heads
Fratto, Russel, 75n1
Freak (dance), 270
Freed, Alan, 54–56, **56**, 75n1
Freedman, Max, 69
"Freeway of Love," 135
The Freewheelin' Bob Dylan, 141
Fresh Prince, 278

Frey, Glenn, 181. *See also* Eagles, The
Frizzell, Lefty, 49
"F– the Police," 283
Fugees, The, 303
"The Fugitive," 172
Fullerton, George, 70
Funicello, Annette, 57
Funkadelic, 222–23
Funk Brothers, 103
Funk music. *See also specific artists*
    audience for, 219–20, 248
    characteristics of, 220
    development of, 2, 220–23
    disco music and, 220–26
    heavy metal music and, 264
    hip-hop music and, 271
    jazz and, 220
    listening to, 3
    polyrhythms in, 14
    rap music and, 223, 283–87
    rock music and, 219–23
    soul music and, 220
    techno music and, 290
    on TV, 221–22
Furious Five, 273–75

Gabler, Milt, 28, 40, 69
Gabriel, Peter, 203, 237, 243–46, **244**, 308, 312
Gadd, Steve, 4
Galops, 12
Gamble, Kenny, 170
The Gambler, 237
"Gangsta Gangsta," 283
Gangsta rap music, 43, 234, 282–88. *See also* Rap music; *specific artists*
Garage bands, 209, 299
Garcia, Jerry, 160–62. *See also* Grateful Dead, The
Gardel, Carlos, 16
Garfunkel, Arthur, **150**, 150–51. *See also* Simon and Garfunkel
Garvey, Josiah, 202
Gay, John, 12
Gaye, Marvin, 103, 169–70, 183, 186–87
Gaynor, Gloria, 224
Geffen, David, 294
Geffen Records, 233
Gender, 5–6, 169, 315. *See also* Sexuality
General M.D. Shirinda and the Gaza Sisters, 253
Genesis, 243
Genius & Soul, 132
"Gentle on My Mind," 173
"Georgia on My Mind," 129, 131
Georgia Sea Islands, 317
Germs, The, 294
Gershwin, George, 30, 142, 159
"Get on the Good Foot," 220, 271
G-Funk style, 284, 287
Gibb, Barry, 225. *See also* Bee Gees, The
Gibson, Don, 129
Gibson Company, 70
Giger, H.R., 187
Gilbert, Ronnie, **35**. *See also* Weavers, The
Gillespie, Dizzy, 16
The Girl Can't Help It, 77

"The Girl from Ipanema," 17
Girl groups, 98. *See also specific artists*
"The Girl Is Mine," 248–49
"Give Up the Funk (Tear the Roof off the Sucker)," 222, 286
Gladys Knight and the Pips, 103
Glam rock, 185, 211
Glass, Philip, 135, 216
Gleason, Jackie, 19, 23
The Glen Campbell Goodtime Hour, 171, 173
"Gloria," 298
Gnutella, 319
"God Save the Queen (It's a Fascist Regime)," 215
Goffin, Gerry, 98–99, 176
Go-go dancers, 94
Goldberg, Morris, 254
Gold Star Studios, 97–98
Good as I Been to You, 146
Goodman, Benny, 31–32, 70, 202
"Good Morning Good Morning," 156
Good Rockin' Dopsie and the Twisters, 254
"Good Rockin' Tonight," 55
"Good Times," 227–30, 258, 273
"Good Vibrations," 122–25, 235
Gordon, Kim, 294. *See also* Sonic Youth
Gordy, Barry, Jr., 101–3, 186. *See also* Motown Records
Gordy Records, 102
Gorrell, Stuart, 129
Gospel music, 13–15, 43–46, 50, 62, 102, 130–31, 136
Graceland, 151, 247, 251–55, 308
Graffiti, 270–71
Graham, Bill, 157–58
Graham, Larry, 221. *See also* Sly and the Family Stone
Grand Funk Railroad, 96
Grandmaster Flash, 271–75, 286
Grandmixer DST, 275
Grand Ole Opry, 37, 47, 50, 171
Grateful Dead, The, 146, 152–53, 160–62, 195, 298, 300
"Grazing in the Grass," 307–8
Grease, 168, 174
The Great Rock 'n' Roll Swindle, 215
Green, Al, 170
Green, Jerome, 74
Green River, 299
"Greensleeves," 12
Greenwich, Ellie, 98–101
Griffin, Richard, 278–79. *See also* Public Enemy
Griot, 14, 310
Grokster, 319, 321
Groove
    Brown (James) and, 220
    definition of, 4
    in "Maybellene," 74
    Motown and, 103
    in "Oye Como Va," 194–95
    in "Papa's Got a Brand New Bag," 138
    in "Psycho Killer," 217–19

    in rap music, 284
    sequencers and, 235
    in "Sledgehammer," 245
    in "When Doves Cry," 266–67
Grunge music, 234, 295–99
Guard, Dave, 89. *See also* Kingston Trio (group)
Guilty, 225
Guiro, 194
Guitars
    acoustic vs. electric, 7, 42, 70–71, 118
    in country music, 49, 52, 70
    power chords on, 243, 296
    in R&B bands, 39, 42, 70
    in rock 'n' roll bands, 52, 70–71
    sex and, 71
    in surf music, 110
    in swing bands, 39, 70
    synthesizers and, 243
    in "Uptown," 101
Guitar Slim, 81
Gypsy Kings, 309
"Gypsy Queen," 193

Habanera rhythm, 16
Haggard, Merle, 6, 126–27, 171–73, 200
Haley, Alex, 14
Haley, Bill, 59–60, 67, 69, 177
Hall, Tom T., 197
"Hallelujah I Love Her So," 130
"Hambone" riffs, 14
Hammerman, 282
Hammond organ, 194, 235
Hancock, Herbie, 275
Hank Ballard and the Midnighters, 93
Happy Days, 168
Hardcore music, 234, 293–95. *See also specific artists*
A Hard Day's Night (movie), 115, 118
"A Hard Day's Night" (song), 115–17
The Harder They Come (movie), 201, 203–6
"The Harder They Come" (song), 204
"A Hard Rain's A-Gonna Fall," 143–44
"Harlem Shuffle," 113
Harmonium, 312
Harmony, 25, 27, 29–30, 134–35, 138, 228–29, 245, 264
Harold Melvin and the Blue Notes, 170
"Harper Valley PTA," 197
Harris, Phil, 19
Harrison, George, **112**, 114, **155**, 162. *See also* Beatles, The
Hart, Mickey, 309. *See also* Grateful Dead, The
"Have Mercy Baby," 43–44
"Have You Never Been Mellow," 174
Hawai'ian Americans, 70, 307
Hayloft Jamboree, 47
Hayman, Jeffrey, 211, **212**, 213. *See also* Ramones (group)
Hays, Lee, **35**. *See also* Weavers, The
"A Hazy Shade of Winter, 151

Heavy metal music. *See also specific artists*
audience for, 169, 189, 242, 247–48
folk music and, 189–92
format for, 169
funk music and, 264
grunge and, 298
guitar virtuosity and, 162–64, 242–43
influences on, 15, 164, 188–91
listening to, 3
rap music and, 277
sales of, 243
thrash and, 234, 295
underground music and, 293
Hee-Haw, 171
Hell, Richard, 211. *See also* Television (group); Voidoids, The
Hellerman, Fred, **35**. *See also* Weavers, The
"He'll Have to Go," 128
Hello Nasty, 278
Helms, Chet, 158
"Help Me Make It through the Night," 197
Hendrix, Jimi, 4, 153, **162**, 162–64, 168, 187, 189, 192, 262, 300
Henley, Don, 181. *See also* Eagles, The
Here After, 287
"Here You Come Again," 174
"Hey, Good Lookin'," 50, 52, 127, 132
"Hey, Jude," 149
Hill, Lauryn, 269, 291, 300, 303–4, 306–7, 316
Hillbilly music, 13, 20, 24, 36. *See also* Country music
Hip-hop music. *See also specific artists*
alternative music and, 303–4, 306–7
audience for, 270–71
Brown (James) and, 134, 271–72
censorship and, 316
credibility in, 282
disco music and, 223, 271
funk music and, 271
identity and, 270–71
influences on, 270–73
PCs and, 232
politics and, 270–71
on radio, 283
rap music and, 234, 270–89
regionalization of, 282–83, 287
salsa music and, 271
sartorial style of, 276
sexuality and, 273, 303–4, 307
The Source, 278
structure of, 14
style and, 271
technology and, 7
techno music and, 289–90
violence and, 287
vocal harmony groups and, 269
women in, 269, 278, 291, 300, 303–4, 306–7, 316
"Hold Me Tight," 206
Hole, 298
"Holiday," 258

"Holiday in Cambodia," 294
Holland, Brian and Eddie, 103–6
Holley, Charles. *See* Holly, Buddy
Holly, Buddy, 14, 82, 84–85, **85**, 114, 162, 216. *See also* Crickets, The
"Hollywood Swinging," 221
"Homeless," 253
Hometown Jamboree, 47
Honky-tonk music, 48–50, 172, 196. *See also* Country music
"Hoochie Coochie Man," 42–43, 45, 315
Hook
in AABA songs, 29
in "Charlie Brown," 88
definition of, 4
in disco music, 224, 227–28
in "Don't Be Cruel," 86
in "A Hard Day's Night" (song), 117
in "(I Can't Get No) Satisfaction," 113
in "Like a Virgin" (song), 260
in "Love to Love You Baby," 224
in "Maybellene," 75
in "The Message," 274
in "My Girl," 104
in "Please Please Me," 116
in "Smells Like Teen Spirit," 296–97
in strophic songs, 24
in "Superstition," 177
in Talking Heads songs, 216
in "Uptown," 100
in "Yesterday," 118–19
Hooker, John Lee, 310
Hootie and the Blowfish, 269
Horses, 211
Horton, Vaughan, 28
Hoskyns, Barney, 262
Hotel California (album), 182
"Hotel California" (song), 175, 181–82, 323
"Hot Pants (She Got to Use What She Got to Get What She Wants)," 220
"Hound Dog," 46–47, 83–84, 237, 315
House music, 223, 290–91. *See also specific artists*
House Un-American Activities Committee, 36n1, 54
Houston, Whitney, 15, 231
"How Can You Mend a Broken Heart," 224
Howlin' Wolf, 15, 74, 145
Huff, Leon, 170
Humphrey, Hubert, 134
"Hungry Heart," 249
"The Hustle," 179
Hustler's Convention, 272–74
Hype!, 299

"I Can See Clearly Now," 206
"(I Can't Get No) Satisfaction," 113
"I Can't Stop Loving You," 129, 132, 315
Ice Cube, 283–84. *See also* N.W.A.
Ice-T, 4, 283
"Ida Red," 71

Identity, 5–6, 15, 270–71, 314–17
"I Dig Rock and Roll Music," 139
Idol, Billy, 232
"I Fall to Pieces," 128
"I Feel Like Going Home," 42
"I Feel the Earth Move," 176
"If I Fell," 118
"If I Only Had a Brain," 186
"If We Make it through December," 173, 213
"If You Don't Know Me by Now," 170
"If You Love Me (Let Me Know)," 174
"I Get Around," 109
Iggy Pop, 210. *See also* Stooges, The (group)
Iglesias, Julio, 322
"I Got You (I Feel Good)," 3
"I Just Wasn't Made for These Times," 122
Ike and Tina Turner Revue, 240–41
"I Knew You Were Waiting (For Me)," 135
"I Know What I Know," 253–54
I Love Lucy, 16
"(I Love You) For Sentimental Reasons," 19, 34
"I'm against It," 208
"I'm in Love Again," 78
"I'm Movin' On," 129
"I'm on Fire," 251
Imperial Records, 79
"I'm So Lonesome I Could Cry," 50–52, 127, 315
"I'm Sorry," 128
"I'm Walkin'," 78
Independent music, 292
Indian music, 111, 152, 154, 307
"I Need Love," 278
"I Never Loved a Man (The Way I Love You)," 135
Ingénue, 305–6
"In My Life," 5
"Inner City Blues (Make Me Wanna Holler)," 186
Interscope Records, 284, 287, 319
In the Dark, 160
"In the Navy," 225, 316
In the Wee Small Hours, 81
In Utero, 298
iPods, 320–21
IRS Records, 293–94
"I Saw Mommy Kissing Santa Claus," 19
"I Say a Little Prayer," 142
"I Shot the Sheriff," 203, 205–7
Island Records, 204–5, 233, 308
Isley Brothers, 114, 152
"Israelites," 206
"It's Gonna Work Out Fine," 241
"It's Not for Me to Say," 80
"It's Too Funky in Here," 226
"It's Too Late," 175–76, 316
"Itsy Bitsy Teenie Weenie Yellow Polkadot Bikini," 57
It Takes a Nation of Millions to Hold Us Back, 279, 283
"I've Got a Tiger by the Tail," 127
"I've Got a Woman," 130

"I've Got You under My Skin," 80–81
"I Wanna Be Sedated," 213
"I Wanted Everything," 213–16
"I Want to Hold Your Hand," 110–11, 115
"I Want You," 153
"I Want You, I Need You, I Love You," 153

Jackson, Henry, 273. *See also* Sugarhill Gang
Jackson, Janet, 231, 268
Jackson, Michael. *See also* Jackson Five, The
albums by, 10, 233, 246–49, 265, 296
DeMann and, 258
image manipulation by, 185
Madonna and, 256–58
McCartney and, 233, 248
moonwalk dance of, 249
Motown and, 103
MTV and, 232–33
origins of, 256
Prince and, 262, 265
recession and, 231
songs by, 233, 248–49
soul music and, 15, 183
Van Halen and, 233, 248, 265
Jackson, O'Shea, 283–84. *See also* N.W.A.
Jackson, Wayne, 244
Jackson Five, The, 103, 170, 246
Jagged Little Pill, 269
Jagger, Mick, 113, 187–88, 203. *See also* Rolling Stones, The
"Jambalaya (On the Bayou)," 50
Jamerson, James, 4, 103
James, Harry, 31
James, Rick, 232
James, Sonny, 126–27
James Brown and the Famous Flames, **133**, 137–38. *See also* Brown, James
Jam Master Jay, 276, **276**. *See also* Run-D.M.C.
Jan and Dean, 110
Jars of Clay, 291
Jayhawks, The, 291
Jazz
"acid," 223
audience for, 15
Bacharach and, 142
bebop style, 70
cataloging of, 15
funk music and, 220
influences on, 14–15
"Latin tinge" in, 16
Phish and, 300
politics and, 167
Prince and, 256
rumba and, 16
Santana and, 192
sex and, 55
Television (group) and, 211
tonal techniques in, 14
Jazzy Jeff, 278
"Jeanie with the Light Brown Hair," 238
Jefferson Airplane, 152–53, 158
Jello Biafra, 294–95. *See also* Dead Kennedys, The
Jenkins, Gordon, 36
Jennings, Waylon, 197–99

The Jimi Hendrix Experience, **162**, 163. *See also* Hendrix, Jimi
Jive Records, 278
Joey Dee and the Starliters, 94
John, Elton, 78, 111, 168–69, 175, 177–79, **178**, 183, 269
"Johnny B. Goode," 76, 109
The Johnny Cash Show, 171
Johnny Rotten, 214. *See also* Sex Pistols, The
Johnson, Enotris, 86
Johnson, Johnny, 74
Johnson, Lyndon, 134
Johnson, Robert, 41, 164–65
Johnston, Bruce, 225. *See also* Beach Boys, The
Johnston, Steven, 246
Jones, Bessie, 317
Jones, George, 49, 126
Jones, John Paul, 188–89. *See also* Led Zeppelin
Jones, Quincy, 9, 247
Jones, Steve, 214. *See also* Sex Pistols, The
Joplin, Janis, 153, 158–60, **159**, 168, 192, 300
Jordan, Louis, 23, 26–29, 34, **39**, 39–40, 69, 202
Jordanaires, The, 82
Journey, 183
Jug-and-washboard bands, 15
Juju Music, 308
Juju music, 308–9
Jukeboxes, 37, 49, **55**
"Jump," 242–43
Jump bands, 23, 26–29, 38–40, 59–60, 69, 78
"Jungle Boogie," 221
Junior Walker and the All Stars, 103
"Just Make Love to Me," 42
"Just Out of Reach (Of My Two Open Arms)," 129

Kamins, Mark, 258
Kansas, 183
Karaoke, 7
Kaye, Carol, 98
KDAY, 283
Keita, Salif, 309
Kelly, Tom, 259
Kennedy, John F., 110, 167
Kenny Rogers's Greatest Hits, 237
Kern, Jerome, 132
Key, 100, 125, 142, 245, 264, 300
Khan, Chaka, 275
Khan, Nusrat, **311**, 311–13
Kidd Creole, 275. *See also* Furious Five
"Killing Me Softly with His Song," 171
"Kill the Poor," 295
King, B.B., 37, 162, 164
King, Ben E., 101
King, Carole, 96, 98–99, **99**, 137, 169, 175–76, 183, 316
King, Martin Luther, Jr., 134
King, Pee Wee, 48
King Cole Trio, 34
King Crimson, 169
King Records, 20, 93
Kingsmen, 209
The Kingston Trio (album), 89
Kingston Trio (group), 36, 89, 140
Kinks, The, 111, 113

Kiss, 185
Kizz My Black Azz, 284
Klezmer music, 13
KMPX, 157
Knight, Evelyn, 58
Knight, Marion "Suge," 287
"Knock on Wood," 244
Knuckles, Frankie, 290–91
KOKE, 197
"Kokomo," 106
Kong, Leslie, 202, 204
Kool and the Gang, 220–22
Kool Herc, 271, 277, 286
Korn, 291
Kraftwerk, 225, 290
Kristofferson, Kris, 197
KRS-One, 275
Krush Groove, 278
KYA, 157
Kyser, Kay, 19

"La Bamba," 17, 192
Ladies Love Outlaws, 197
"Lady," 237–38, 316
"The Lady in My Life," 249
"Lady Madonna," 116
Ladysmith Black Mambazo, 253
Laine, Frankie, 31, 67
Landis, John, 233
lang, k.d., 200, 269, 291, 300, 304–7, **305**
"Last Date," 128
The Last Days of Disco, 225
Last Poets, 272
The Last Temptation of Christ, 312
"The Last Time I Saw Richard," 185
The Late, Great Townes Van Zandt, 200–201
Latin Americans. *See also* Race
  dialect and, 4–5
  identity of, 5–6, 315
  musical influence of, 15–17, 19, 37, 70, 100–101, 315
  stereotyping of, 5
  style and, 11
"Learning the Blues," 67
"Leaving' on a Jet Plane," 323
Ledbetter, Huddie "Leadbelly," **35**, 36
Led Zeppelin, 146, 169–70, 183, 188–92, 189, 277
Led Zeppelin IV, 188–90
Lee, Brenda, 128
Lee, Peggy, 31
Legend, 207
The Legend of Tom Dooley, 89
Leiber, Jerry, 46, 88–91, 98–99
Le Mystère des Voix Bulgares, 309
Lennon, John, 4, **112**, 114, 116–17, 119, 121, 153, **155**. *See also* Beatles, The
Lennox, Annie, 238–39. *See also* Eurythmics
Les Paul guitar, 70
Let It Be, 99
"Let Me Be There," 174
"Let's Go Away for Awhile," 122
"Let's Go Crazy," 263
"Let's Twist Again," 96
Lewis, Jerry Lee, 78, 209
Library of Congress, 41
Licensed to Ill, 275
Licensing and copyright, 20–21, 59, 231–32, 236, 319–22

Life after Death, 287
Lifestyles of the Rich and Famous, 9
Like a Prayer (album), 257
"Like a Prayer" (song), 258
"Like a Rolling Stone," 144, 146–49, 157, 323
Like a Virgin (album), 10, 257–58
"Like a Virgin" (song), 258–61
Limp Bizkit, 291
Line dances, 12
Liner notes, 139, 141, 157, 254
"The Lion Sleeps Tonight," 308
Listening to music, 3–4, 7, 316
"A Little Bird Told Me," 58–59
"Little Deuce Coupe," 108, 323
Little Eva, 96
"Little Green," 185
"A Little Help from My Friends," 155
"Little Honda," 108
Little Junior's Blue Flames, 63–65
Little Plastic Castle, 301
Little Richard, 3, 75–79, **77**, 86, 102, 114, 209, 262, 316
Live at the Apollo, 135
Live at the Monterey Pop Festival, 307
Live performances
  by Allman Brothers, 195
  bootleg recordings of, 160
  Brown (James) and, 135
  by Clapton, 166
  by Grateful Dead, 160, 195
  by Motown artists, 102
  by Parliament, 222
  by Phish, 298–300
  vs. records, 7, 74, 223
  royalties for, 20–21, 23
  by Santana, 194–95
  by Shankar, 307
  by Turner (Tina), 241–42
  on TV, 74, 76, 232
  venue ownership and, 318
Living Colour, 291
"Living in America," 323
Living in Clip, 301
L.L. Cool J, 278
"The Loco-Motion," 96
Loft, The, 226
Lomax, Alan and John, 41, 317
"Lonely Days," 224
"Long Tall Sally," 77–78, 86, 90
"The Look of Love," 142
Loops, 235
Lopez, Jennifer, 315
"Lord Randall," 144
Los Incas, 252
Los Lobos, 17, 254
"Louie, Louie," 209, 298
Louisiana Hayride, 47
Louis Jordan and His Tympany Five, 23, 26–29, **39**, 40, 69
Love, Courtney, 298
Love, Mike, 125. *See also* Beach Boys, The
"Love and Marriage," 3, 23, 29–31, 81, 142
"Love Hangover," 225
"Love Me Tender," 82
"Love Rollercoaster," 221
"Lovesick Blues," 50
"Love's Theme," 175, 179–80
"Love the One You're With," 152
"Love to Love You Baby," 224

"Love Train," 170
Lovett, Lyle, 200–201, 291
Love Unlimited Orchestra, 175, 179–80
"Lucky Star," 258
"Lucy in the Sky with Diamonds," 153
Luke the Drifter. *See* Williams, Hank
Luke Skyywalker, 288
Lydon, John, 214. *See also* Sex Pistols, The
"Lyin' Eyes," 181
Lyle, Graham, 240
Lymon, Frankie, 55, 57
Lynn, Loretta, 126, 152, 171
Lyricists
  of ballads, 12, 152
  in Brill Building, 98
  listening to, 4
  production, roles in, 8–9
  punk rock and, 209
  rock 'n' roll and, 87

"The Macarena," 269
Machito, 16
"Macho Man," 225
Made in Japan, 187
Madonna, 10, 185, 231, 242, **256**, 256–61, 264, 278, 291, 315–16
Major Bowes' Amateur Hour, 31
The Making of Michael Jackson's Thriller, 233
"Mama, He Treats Your Daughter Mean," 45, 47
Mambo, 16
Mann, Barry, 98–101, **99**, 174
Mann, Carl, 80
"Mannish Boy," 42
Mantovani, 19
"Many Rivers to Cross," 204
Mapfumo, Thomas, 309
Marching band music, 12, 14
Mariachi music, 17
Mariah Carey, 269
Markoe, Merrill, 257
Marley, Bob, 201, 203–7, **205**, 308
Married with Children, 81
Marrow, Tracy, 4, 283
M/A/R/R/S, 291
Martha and the Vandellas, 103
Martin, Dean, 62
Martin, George, 97, 114, 156
Martin, Ricky, 234, 315, 322
Martin, Vincent, 203
Marvelettes, The, 102–3
Masekela, Hugh, 307–8
"Mashed Potato Time," 96
Mason, Barbara, 171
Master Gee, 273. *See also* Sugarhill Gang
Master of ceremonies, 273
"Matchbox," 114
"Material Girl," 258
Mathis, Johnny, 80, 142
Matlock, Glen, 214–15. *See also* Sex Pistols, The
Matrix Club, 158
Matsushita, 233
May, Billy, 80
May, Derrick, 290
"Maybellene," 71–75, 316
Mayfield, Curtis, 131
Mayfield, Percy, 81

MCA Records, 46, 168, 233
McCall, C.W., 171
McCartney, Paul, 4, **112**, 114–21, **155**, 168–69, 199, 233, 248–49. *See also* Beatles, The
McCoy, Van, 179
McDaniels, Darryl, 276, **276**. *See also* Run-D.M.C.
McEntire, Reba, 234, 268
McGovern, George, 171
McGuire, Barry, 146
M.C. Hammer, 282, 288
McLaren, Malcolm, 214–15
McLean, Don, 5, 177–78
McPhatter, Clyde, 43. *See also* Dominoes, The; Drifters, The
MCs, 273
"Me and Paul," 199
Measures, 25–26
The Me Decade, 167
Medley, Phil, 114
Meet the Beatles, 111
Megadeath, 242, 295
Melisma, 49, 239, 284
Melle Mel, 274–75, 283. *See also* Furious Five
Melody, 12, 24–26, 264
Melotron, 184
Memphis Horns, 244
Mento, 202
Mercury Records, 48, 67, 233
"Mercy Mercy Me (The Ecology)," 186
"The Message," 273–75, 278
Metallica (album), 295
Metallica (group), 242, 268, 295
Meter, 25–26, 50
MFSB, 179
MGM Records, 67, 168, 321
Miami Sound Machine, 16
Michael, George, 135
Mickey Mouse Club, The, 57
MIDI specification, 232, 235
Miller, Glenn, 31, 79, 202
Miller, Jimmy, 188
Miller, Mitch, 67–68
Mills Brothers, 34
Minimalism, 135, 216
Minimoog synthesizer, 235
Minogue, Kylie, 96
Minstrel shows, 14, 67
Miracles, The, 96
Mirage keyboard sampler, 235
Miranda, Carmen, 17
The Miseducation of Lauryn Hill, 303
"Misirlou," 1, 110
Miss Rhythm. *See* Brown, Ruth
"Miss You," 225
Mister Rock 'n' Roll, 77
Mitchell, Joni, 137, 146, 185, 255, 261
Mitchell, Mitch, 163
Mitch Miller Singers, 67
Mizell, Jason, 276, **276**. *See also* Run-D.M.C.
Moby, 290–91, 317
Modern Sounds in Country and Western Music, 131–32
Mojo, definition of, 42
"Mona Lisa," 34, 80
"Money," 185
Monterey Pop Festival, 158, 163, 183, 307
Monterey Pop (movie), 163
Moondog Show, 54
Moonglows, The, 81

Moore, Scotty, 63
Morali, Jacques, 225
Morganfield, McKinley. *See* Muddy Waters
Morissette, Alanis, 268–69, 291
Moroder, Giorgio, 224
Morrison, Jim, 168. *See also* Doors, The
Morton, Ferdinand "Jelly Roll," 16
Mosh pits, 94, 294
"The Most Beautiful Girl," 171
Mothership Connection, 222
Mothers of Invention, 183
Mötley Crüe, 242
Motown Records
  audience for, 101
  ballads and, 104
  dance music and, 96, 102–3
  development of, 2
  disco and, 225
  Gordy and, 101–3
  Jackson Five and, 103, 246
  labels, 102
  psychedelic rock music and, 161
  soft soul music and, 170
  soundprint of, 102
  Top 40 playlists and, 170
  25 Years of Motown, 249
  urban folk music and, 161
  Wonder and, 103, 176
Movieolas, 37
Movies. *See also specific titles*
  concept albums and, 186
  counterculture and, 163, 167
  disco and, 224–25
  gangster lifestyle and, 288
  hip-hop music and, 278
  individualism and, 9
  Little Richard in, 77
  music videos and, 233
  Presley and, 82
  rap music and, 278, 283
  reggae and, 201
  "Rock around the Clock" in, 69
  rock 'n' roll and, 69, 76, 206
  royalties from, 20
  techno music and, 291
  teen culture and, 57
  world music and, 312
MP3 and MPEG, 318–21
"Mr. Tambourine Man," 144
MTV. *See also* Videos, music
  AOR format and, 232
  Columbia Records and, 233
  Eurythmics and, 239
  Headbangers' Ball, 243
  Purple Rain (film) on, 263
  racism and, 232–33
  "Rockit" on, 275
  Run-D.M.C. and, 276–77
  "Sledgehammer" and, 245–46
  Unplugged, 7
  Yo! MTV Raps, 278
Muddy Waters, 15, 41–43, 70, 74, 145, 162, 315
Mudhoney, 299
Multiphonics, 159
Muscle Shoals Sound Rhythm Section, 135
Musical instrument digital interface specification, 232, 235
Musical instruments

acoustic vs. electric, 7, 70, 118
African influence on, 14
in Chicago electric blues bands, 42
in country bands, 13, 49, 70
digital technology and, 232, 234–35, 317–18
European influence on, 13, 71
in funk bands, 220
Hawai'ian influence on, 70, 307
in honky-tonk bands, 49
Indian influence on, 111, 154, 307
in jump bands, 39
Latin influence on, 70, 193–94, 307
in mariachi bands, 17
placement of, in studio, 193–94
playing vs. passive listening, 7
in R&B bands, 39, 42, 64, 70
in rock 'n' roll bands, 52, 70–71, 111, 119, 124
in ska bands, 202
Spector and, 97
in swing bands, 39, 70
turntables as, 271–72
Musical structure
  12-bar blues. *See* Twelve-bar blues
  16-bar blues, 42, 45, 109
  AABA form, 3, 29–31, 52, 61–62, 90, 108, 115–19, 175, 180
  ABAC form, 30
  call-and-response. *See* Call-and-response
  in "Good Vibrations," 123–25
  habanera rhythm, 16
  strophic. *See* Strophic form
Music industry, 8–10
  1950s era, 67–68
  alternative music and, 292
  deregulation of, 232
  DJs. *See* Disc jockey (DJ)
  licensing and copyright by, 20–21, 59, 231–32, 236, 319–22
  payola and, 20, 38, 55
  in postwar years, 19–20, 66–67
  publishers. *See* Publishing firms
  radio stations. *See* Radio stations
  record companies. *See* Record companies
  royalties and, 20, 308
  vertical integration in, 318
Music television. *See* MTV; VH-1
Musorgsky, Modest, 186
Muzak Corporation, 3, 19
"My Blue Heaven," 79, 116, 131
"My Boy Lollipop," 206
"My Darling, My Darling," 19
"My Ding-a-Ling," 170
"(My Friends Are Gonna Be) Strangers," 172
"My Generation," 208
"My Girl," 103–5
"My Heart Has a Mind of Its Own," 128

"My Hometown," 251
"My Old Man," 185
"My Prayer," 80
The Mystery of the Bulgarian Voices, 309
"Mystery Train," 62–66, 83–84

Napster, 319, 321
Nash, Johnny, 206
Nashville, 171
Nashville Skyline, 146
Nashville sound, 82, 127–29, 196
National Academy of Recording Arts and Sciences, 278, 293, 309
National Broadcasting Company (NBC), 21, 23
Natural Born Killers, 312
"Nature Boy," 34
"Nazi Punks F– Off," 295
NBC network, 21, 23
N'dour, Youssou, 309
Nebraska, 250
Nelson, Prince. *See* Prince
Nelson, Ricky, 56–57, 177
Nelson, Willie, 15, 128, 132, 197–200, **199**, 300
Nevermind, 10, 296–98
Never Mind the Bollocks, Here's the Sex Pistols, 215
New age music, 309
New Christy Minstrels, 146, 237
New jack swing, 283
New Orleans sound, 78
Newport Folk Festival, 144
The New Republic magazine, 257
Newsweek magazine, 171
Newton, Ernie, **51**
Newton-John, Olivia, 170, 174
New wave music, 208–10, 216, 239, 247–48. *See also specific artists*
New York Dolls, The, 209, **210**, 211, 214
Niggaz with Attitude (N.W.A.), 1, 275, 283–84
"Night Fever," 224
"Night Moves," 5
"Night of the Living Baseheads," 280–81, 287
Nine Inch Nails, 291
1984, 242
"1969," 210–11
"96 Tears," 209
Nirvana, 7, 10, 268, 291, 293, 295–99, 317
Nitzsche, Jack, 98
Nixon, Richard, 167, 171–72
"No Other Love," 19
"Norwegian Wood," 111, 197
Norworth, Jack, 269
"No Surrender," 251
Not a Pretty Girl (album), 301
"Not a Pretty Girl" (song), 301–3
"Not Fade Away," 85
Notorious B.I.G., 268, 287–88
Novoselic, Krist, 295–96. *See also* Nirvana
"Nowhere to Stand," 306
NPG Records, 262
Nutcracker Suite, 186
"Nutrocker," 186
N.W.A., 1, 275, 283–84
Nyro, Laura, 137

Oasis, 111
O'Brien, Guy, 273. *See also* Sugarhill Gang
Ochs, Phil, 140
O'Connor, Sinéad, 292
"Oh, Boy!," 85
"Oh, Pretty Woman," 288
Ohio Players, 220–22
O'Jays, The, 170
Okeh Records, 14–15
"Okie from Muskogee," 6, 127, 172–73, 323
Oldies radio, 170
"Old Shep," 62
"On Broadway," 98
"One Less Bell to Answer," 142
"One of These Nights," 182
One-step (dance), 12
"One Sweet Day," 269
"Open Your Heart," 258
Opera, 12, 159
Orb, The, 290
Orbison, Roy, 288
Orbital, 290–91
Osmonds, The, 170
Osterburg, James, 210. *See also* Stooges, The (group)
O'Sullivan, Gilbert, 288
Otis, Johnny, 14, 46
Otis Redding Soul Revue, 244
Our Town, 81
Outlaws of country music, 197–99. *See also* Nelson, Willie
Out of Time, 293
Overdubbing, 21, 176, 184
Owens, Buck, 126–27, 172
"Oye Como Va," 188, 192–95, 235

Page, Jimmy, 162, 164, 188–91. *See also* Led Zeppelin; Yardbirds
Page, Patti, 19, 48, **49**, 56, 61, 171
Paglia, Camille, 257
Paisley Park studio, 256, 261–62
"Pancho and Lefty," 200–201
Pantera, 290
"Papa Don't Preach," 258
"Papa's Got a Brand New Bag," 137–38
"Papa Was a Rollin' Stone," 161
"Parents Just Don't Understand," 278
Parents' Music Resource Center (PMRC), 257
Parker, Charlie, 153
Parker, Herman "Little Junior," 62–65, 83–84
Parker, Maceo, 222. *See also* James Brown and the Famous Flames; Parliament
Parker, Thomas "Colonel," 82
Parkway Records, 93
Parliament, 222–23, 284, 286
Parsons, Alan, 185
Parsons, Gram, 196. *See also* Byrds, The
Parton, Dolly, 174
"Party for Your Right to Fight," 279
Patch cords, 235
Patterson, Lorenzo, 283–84. *See also* N.W.A.

Patti Smith Group, 213
Patton, Charley, 41
Paul, Les, 21, 70, 162
Pavement, 290
Pavitt, Bruce, 296
Paxton, Tom, 140
"The Payback," 220
Payne, Rufe "Tee-Tot," 50
Payola, 20, 38, 55
P. Diddy, 287
"Peaceful Easy Feeling," 182
Peacock Records, 20
"The Peanut Vendor," 16
Pearl Jam, 268, 290, 299, 311–12, 318
Peer, Ralph, 15
"Peggy Sue," 85
Penguins, The, 3
Penn, Sean, 258
Penniman, Richard. *See* Little Richard
People for Ethical Treatment of Animals (PETA), 305
Peppermint Lounge, 94
"Peppermint Twist," 94
Pepsi-Cola, 258
Perkins, Carl, 56, 114
Perry, Joe, 277. *See also* Aerosmith
Perry, Lee, 205
Personal computers, 232, 318–21
Peter, Paul, and Mary (album), 139
Peter, Paul, and Mary (group), 36, 139–41, 169
Peterson, Oscar, 34
Pet Sounds, 122, 184
Pettibone, Shep, 260
P-Funk style, 222–23, 284. *See also* Clinton, George
Philles Records, 97–99, 102
Phillips, Sam, 63
Phil Spector: Back to Mono (1958–1969), 97
Phish, 291, 298–300
Phish: A Live One, 299
Phonograph records. *See also* Albums
   analog vs. digital, 7, 231–32
   in "Battle of the Speeds," 22
   vs. CDs, 232, 275
   copying of, 231–32
   disco and, 223, 271–72
   dust jacket for. *See* Dust jacket
   hip-hop music and, 275
   materials used in, 22, 168
   studio technology and, 184
   vs. tapes, 21, 231
Phrases, 25–27, 115, 118–21, 224
Pictures at an Exhibition, 186
"Piece of My Heart," 159
Pierce, Webb, 49, 126
"The Pill," 152
"Pink Cadillac," 323
Pink Floyd, 169, 183, 185–86
"Pipeline," 110, 225
Pitch, 14, 25, 29, 134, 235
"Planet Rock," 273
Plant, Robert, 189–91. *See also* Led Zeppelin
Platters, The, 80
Play, 317
Playlists, 19, 68, 157–58, 167, 169–70, 318
"Play That Funky Music," 221
Please Hammer Don't Hurt 'Em,

282
"Please Mr. Postman," 102–3
Please, Please Me (album), 114
"Please Please Me" (song), 115–16
"Please, Please, Please," 133, 135
Pleasure gardens, 12
Police, The, 201
Politics
   1950s era, 34–36, 54
   ballads and, 11–12
   Beatles and, 110
   "Blowin' in the Wind" and, 140–41
   Brown (James) and, 134
   civil rights movement, 6, 134, 149–51
   Dead Kennedys and, 294–95
   Gaye and, 186
   hip-hop music and, 270–71
   House Un-American Activities Committee, 36n1, 54
   Ice-T and, 283
   N.W.A. and, 283
   postwar, 19
   Public Enemy and, 279–81, 284
   punk rock and, 208–14
   reggae and, 203–5
   rock steady music and, 203
   Simon and, 252–53
   Springsteen and, 250–51
   underground rock bands and, 293
   urban folk music and, 34–36, 140–41, 145
   Vietnam War, 149–51, 167, 186
   Watergate, 167
Polkas, 12–13, 37
Polydor Records, 233
Polygram, 233
Polyrhythms, 14, 134, 203, 245, 274
Pomus, Doc, 98
Poneman, Jonathan, 296
"Poor Little Fool," 57
Popular music, definition of, 2, 269
Pop Will Eat Itself, 291
Porgy and Bess, 159
Porter, Cole, 81
Posses, 271, 287
Power chords, 243, 296
Prado, Perez, 67
Precision Bass guitar, 70
The Predator, 284
Presley, Elvis, **66**, **83**
   career of, 62–66, 81–84, 170, 177
   death of, 153
   Nashville sound and, 82, 128–29
   RCA and, 46, 63, 67, 82
   Rolling Stones and, 188
   slapback echo and, 4
   songs by, 46, 56, 62–66, 78, 82–84, 86–87, 129, 153, 177, 199, 237, 315
   songwriting and, 86–87
   soundprint of, 64–65, 82
   Sun Records and, 63, 80–82
   Tin Pan Alley songs and, 80
   on TV, 82, 255
"Pretty Woman," 288

Price, Lloyd, 81
Price, Vincent, 248
Pride, Charley, 6, 15, 129
Prince, **256**
   albums by, 261–63
   career of, 256–57, 261–63
   funk music and, 264
   image manipulation by, 185, 256–57, 262–63, 266, 316
   influences on, 262
   Jackson and, 262, 265
   Little Richard and, 78
   lyrics of, 4
   in movies, 262–63
   recession and, 231
   roles of, 9
   songs by, 263–67, 275, 316
   soul music and, 183
Priority Records, 278
"Prisoner of Love," 19
Private Dancer, 241
Prodigy, 290–91
Producer, record, 9, 87, 96–99, 223–24, 273
Professor Griff, 278–79. *See also* Public Enemy
Professor Longhair, 78
Progressive country, 196–201
"Promises, Promises," 142
Prophet-5 synthesizer, 235
ProTools, 318
"Proud Mary," 241, 323
Psychedelic rock music, 157–62
"Psychedelic Shack," 161
Psycho, 216
"Psycho Killer," 216–19
Public Enemy, 275, 278–81, **279**, 283–84, 287–88
Publishing firms, 8, 20–21, 59, 288, 321
Puente, Tito, 16, 192, 195
Puff Daddy, 287–88
Pulp Fiction, 1
Punk rock, 2–4, 184, 207–14, 234, 277, 292–98. *See also* specific artists
"Puppy Love," 57
"Purple Haze," 163
Purple Rain (album), 261–63
Purple Rain (film), 262
"Purple Rain" (song), 263
"Push It," 278
"Put It Right Here (Or Keep It Out There)," 73

Qawwali, 311–13
Queen, 232, 269
? and the Mysterians, 209
Quicksilver Messenger Service, 158

Race
   Brown v. Board of Education and, 54
   dialect and, 4–5
   employment opportunities and, 40
   gangster lifestyle and, 288
   identity and, 5–6, 15, 314–15
   MTV and, 232–33
   musical categories and, 2, 15, 36, 40, 54–57, 169, 208, 270, 314–15
   stereotyping and, 5–6, 222, 270, 289
   style and, 10–11
Race music, 15, 36, 58

"Racing in the Street," 249
Radio stations. *See also specific call signs*
  AM. *See* AM radio stations
  BMI and, 21
  censorship and, 60, 316
  counterculture and, 157–58, 167
  FM. *See* FM radio stations
  hip-hop music and, 283
  iPods and, 321
  ownership of, 37, 318
  payola to, 20, 38, 55
  in postwar years, 37, 47
  R&B and, 38, 43
  royalties from, 20–21
  stereo broadcasting by, 22
  student-programmed, 157, 169, 292
  Top 40 programming by, 19, 68, 157, 169
Rage against the Machine, 291
Ragtime music, 16
Rahiem, 275. *See also* Furious Five
"Raindrops Keep Fallin' on My Head," 170–71
Raising Hell, 275
Raitt, Bonnie, 4, 15, 261
The Ramones (album), 212
Ramones (group), 208–9, 211–16, **212**, 294
Randolph, Boots, 91
Rap music. *See also specific artists*
  art music and, 281
  audience for, 248, 270–71, 276–78
  Brown (James) and, 134, 271–72
  country music and, 286
  dialect and, 4
  disco music and, 229, 271
  funk music and, 223
  hip-hop and, 234, 270–89
  identity and, 270–71
  influences on, 15, 43, 270–73
  listening to, 3, 15
  mainstreaming of, 278, 282
  MCs and, 273
  reggae and, 201
  regionalization of, 282–83, 287
  structure of, 14
  style and, 271
  "Thriller" and, 248
  violence and, 287
"Rapper's Delight," 229, 273, 275
Rastafarianism, 202–4
Rastaman Vibration, 205
"Rave On," 85
Raves, 290
Ray of Light, 259
RCA Victor. *See also* Bertelsmann
  in "Battle of the Speeds," 22
  "Cherry Pink and Apple Blossom White," 67
  "Hound Dog," 46, 84
  Jefferson Airplane and, 158
  Jennings and, 197, 199
  ownership of, 168, 233
  in postwar years, 20, 22
  Presley and, 46, 63, 67, 82
  rock 'n' roll and, 67, 82
  sampling and, 319
  slapback echo and, 82

Real World Records, 312
Record companies. *See also specific companies*
  1973 energy crisis and, 168
  consolidation of, 168, 230, 233
  independent vs. major, 10, 21, 37, 47–48, 58, 67, 82, 168, 292, 319
  marketing by, 9, 233, 292
  payola from, 20, 38, 55
  in postwar years, 18–21, 37, 47–48
  race music and, 15, 37, 58
  sales. *See* Sales
  saturation distribution by, 20, 97
  TV and, 23
Recording Industry Association of America (RIAA), 182, 319–21
Recordings
  analog. *See* Analog recordings
  bootleg, 160
  digital. *See* Digital recordings
  licensing and copyright of, 20–21, 59, 231–32, 236, 319–22
  vs. live performances, 7, 74, 223
  pirating of, 231–32
  playing time of, 22, 149, 184
  sampling of. *See* Sampling, digital
  unified groups of. *See* Concept albums
  of world music, 309
Records, production of
  "Battle of the Speeds" and, 22
  LPs vs. CDs, 232, 275
  Madonna and, 258
  materials used in, 22, 168
  roles in, 8–9
  software for, 318
  soundprints and, 4, 318
  technology and, 6–7, 184, 232, 317–22
  vertical integration in, 318
Redding, Noel, 163
Redding, Otis, 131, 137–39. *See also* Otis Redding Soul Revue
Red-Headed Stranger, 198–99
Red Hot Chili Peppers, 223, 268, 291
Reed, Lou, 209, 211. *See also* Velvet Underground, The
Reeves, Jim, 128
Reeves, Martha, 102. *See also* Martha and the Vandellas
"Reflections," 161
Refrains, 30
Reggae, 201–7, 309
Rehab Doll, 299
Reich, Steve, 135, 216
Release, 30
Religion, 5, 10–11. *See also* Gospel music
R.E.M., 7, 291, 293–94, 297–99
Ren, 283–84. *See also* N.W.A.
REO Speedwagon, 183
"Respect," 137–39
Rests, 25
Reverb, 9, 82, 110, 224

Revolver, 156
Reynold, Nick, 89. *See also* Kingston Trio (group)
Rhapsody in White, 179
"Rhinestone Cowboy," 171
Rhythm
  bass and, 264
  in breaks, 271
  Brown (James) and, 133–34, 138
  in disco music, 227–29
  in "Goodnight, Irene," 25–26
  in "Maybellene," 74
  minimalism and, 135
  in "Mystery Train," 64
  in "Papa's Got a Brand New Bag," 138
  in reggae, 203
  in strophic songs, 25–26
  in twelve-bar blues, 26–28
Rhythm & blues music (R&B). *See also specific artists*
  in 1953 *Billboard* survey, 37
  audience for, 15, 20
  Berry and, 71
  categories of, 168–69
  Chicago electric blues, 41–43, 45, 74
  Clapton and, 164
  cover versions and, 38, 46, 58
  crooners of, 38, 40–42
  gospel music and, 43–46
  Hendrix and, 163–64
  honky-tonk music and, 49
  influences on, 14–15, 20, 36, 310
  jump bands. *See* Jump bands
  Motown and, 102
  Nashville sound and, 129
  in postwar years, 36–47
  rap music and, 43
  rockabilly and, 78
  rock music and, 249
  rock 'n' roll and, 15, 40, 54–65, 75–78
  royalties for, 20–21, 308
  sex and, 42–43, 60, 84
  sixteen-bar, 42, 45, 109
  social criticism in, 14
  soft soul and, 170
  strophic form in, 24, 26–29, 41
  tonal techniques in, 14, 42, 62
  twelve-bar. *See* Twelve-bar blues
  vocal harmony groups and, 43–44, 61
The Rhythm of the Saints, 151, 254, 308
Rich, Charlie, 171, 173
Richards, Keith, 113, 188. *See also* Rolling Stones, The
Richardson, J.P., 85
Richie, Lionel, 237–38
Rick Dees and his Gang of Idiots, 225
Rickenbacker, 70
Riddle, Nelson, 67, 80
Ridenhour, Carlton, 270, 278–81, **279**, 289. *See also* Public Enemy
"Riders on the Storm," 3
Riffs, 4, 14, 28, 134, 138, 177
Righteous Babe Records, 301
Riley, Jeannie, 197

Riley, Terry, 216
Riot Act, 318
The Rise and Fall of Ziggy Stardust and the Spiders from Mars, 185, 199, 219
Ritchie, John, 215. *See also* Sex Pistols, The
Road bands, Jamaican, 202
Road to Ruin, 213
Robbins, Marty, 92–93
Robertson, Michael, 319
Robinson, Jackie, 34
Robinson, Ray Charles. *See* Charles, Ray
Robinson, Sylvia, 274
Robinson, William "Smokey," 102–5. *See also* Miracles, The
Rock & Roll, 209
Rock & Soul, 261
Rockabilly, 50, 78, 127, 172, 196
"Rock and Roll Is Here to Stay," 57
"Rock and Roll Music," 76
"Rock around the Clock," 67, 69, 177
"Rocket 88," 241
Rock music. *See also specific artists*
  aboriginal, 309
  audience for, 149–54, 163, 169, 219–20, 234, 317
  broadcasting of, 157, 167–69
  career in, model of, 107
  categories of, 2–3, 168–69, 183
  definition of, 2
  disco music and, 225–26
  funk music and, 219–23
  grunge, 234, 295–99
  hardcore, 234, 293–95
  influences on, 11–17
  psychedelic, 157–62
  punk. *See* Punk rock
  R&B and, 249
  vs. rock 'n' roll, 57, 145
  soloist vs. group, 162–64, 242–43, 300
  studio technology and, 184
  techno music and, 289–90
Rock 'n' roll music. *See also specific artists*
  audience for, 15, 53–58
  business savvy and, 66–68
  censorship and, 60, 316
  country music and, 59–60, 69, 71, 74–75
  cover versions and, 58–66
  crooners of, 62, 80
  dance music and, 59–60, 93–96
  disco music and, 94–96
  Freed and, 54
  instruments for, 52, 70–71, 111, 119, 124
  live vs. records, 74
  movies and, 69, 76, 206
  nostalgia for, 168, 170, 177
  punk rock and, 207–8
  R&B and, 15, 40, 54–65, 75–78
  vs. rock music, 57, 145
  sex and, 55
  teen culture and, 57
  Tin Pan Alley and, 80–81
"Rock 'n' Roll Suicide," 185
"Rocks Off," 188
Rock steady music, 203

"Rocky Mountain High," 181
Rodgers, Jimmie, 199
Rodgers, Nile, 227–30, 258, 260
Rogers, Kenny, 170, 237–38, 316
Rogers, Norman Lee, 278. *See also* Public Enemy
Rolling Stone magazine, 146, 216, 257, 263, 278
Rolling Stones, The
 albums by, 186–87
 Beatles and, 154, 188
 career of, 108, 111, 113, 188
 classification of, 183
 disco and, 225
 on Muddy Waters, 42
 Presley and, 188
 R&B and, 113
 rap music and, 277
 Sgt. Pepper's Lonely Hearts Club Band and, 154
 songs by, 113, 188, 225
 soul music and, 183
 Turner (Tina) and, 241
"Roll over Beethoven," 57, 76, 109
Ronettes, The, 97, 100–101, 260
Ronstadt, Linda, 17, 254
Roots (book), 14
Ross, Diana, 4, 102, **105**, 170, 186, 225. *See also* Supremes, The
Roth, David Lee, 242. *See also* Van Halen (group)
Rubber Soul, 111, 122
Rubin, Rick, 275–77, 313
Rude Boys, 203
Rumba, 16, 201, 307
Run, 276, **276**. *See also* Run-D.M.C.
"Run Away Child, Running Wild," 161
Run-D.M.C., 73, 275–78, **276**, 283
Rupe, Art, 79
Rush, 183
Russell, Bert, 114
Ruthless Records, 283–84

Sacred Harp singers, 13
Saddler, Joseph, 271–75, 286
Sadler, Eric "Vietnam," 279. *See also* Bomb Squad
Sales
 1958 survey on, 68
 1973 survey on, 168
 1978 survey on, 168, 230
 1979 survey on, 230
 1982 survey on, 230
 1990 survey on, 233
 2000 survey on, 322
 of alternative music, 292
 celebrity and, production of, 255–56, 297–98
 of heavy metal music, 243
 in postwar years, 18
 predicting trends in, 9–10, 230
 profit from, 10, 14–15, 168, 231–34, 255
 recession in, 231
 saturation distribution and, 20, 97
 store organization and, 168, 307
 of tapes, prerecorded, 168, 231
 urban market for, 10, 12
 of world music, 307–9

"Sally Goodin," 181
Salsa music, 16–17, 192, 194, 271, 309
Salt-N-Pepa, 278
Samba, 16
Sample Some of Disc, Sample Some of D.A.T., 236
Sampling, digital
 Brown (James) and, 134
 concept albums and, 122
 copyright and, 59, 236, 319–22
 dance music and, 281
 Dr. Dre and, 287
 Dr. Funkenstein and, 223, 236, 287
 equipment for, 235–36, 318–21
 hip-hop music and, 232, 236, 279–81, 287–88
 Moby and, 317
 Napster and, 319–21
 peer-to-peer file sharing and, 319–21
 Prince and, 262
 Public Enemy and, 279–81, 287
 technology for, 232
 techno music and, 232, 236
 turntable techniques and, 272
 of world music, 309–10
Santana, Carlos, 17, 192–94, **193**, 262, 315. *See also* Santana (group)
Santana (album), 192
Santana (group), 183, 187–88, 192–95, 235
Sante, Luc, 257
"(I Can't Get No) Satisfaction," 113
Saturday Night Fever, 224–25
Saturday Night Shindig, 47
"Save the Children," 186
"Save the Last Dance for Me," 57, 98, 101
"Say It Loud, I'm Black and Proud," 6, 134
Scat singing, 61–62
"School Day," 57, 76
Schottisches, 12
The Score, 303
Scorpio, 275. *See also* Furious Five
Scott, Freddie, 127
Scratching technique, 272
Scruggs, Earl, 197
Security of the First World ($1W), 279. *See also* Public Enemy
Sedaka, Neil, 98
Seeger, Pete, 34–36, **35**, 140, 307. *See also* Weavers, The
"See You Later, Alligator," 69
Seger, Bob, 5
Selassie, Haile, 202
"Sentenced to the Chair," 272–73
Sequencers, digital, 235
78 r.p.m. disks, 7, 22
Sex, 259
"Sex Machine," 272
Sex Pistols, The, 211–12, 214–16, **215**, 294
Sexuality
 Bowie and, 185, 187
 counterculture and, 152–53
 disco and, 225–26
 dust jackets and, 187

Hill and, 303–4, 307
 hip-hop music and, 273, 303–4, 307
 identity and, 315
 lang and, 305
 Lennox and, 239
 Little Richard and, 78
 R&B and, 39–44
 Snoop Doggy Dogg and, 286
 stereotyping of, 6
 Village People and, 6, 225, 316
Sgt. Pepper's Lonely Hearts Club Band (album), 111, 113, 122, 154–57, 184
"Sgt. Pepper's Lonely Hearts Club Band" (song), 156
Shabalala, Joseph, 253
Shadowland, 305
"Shake, Rattle, and Roll," 59–60, 69, 316
Shakespeare, Robbie, 203
"Shake Your Hips," 188
Shakira, 322
Shakuhachi, 245
Shakur, Tupac. *See* 2Pac Shakur
Shane, Bob, 89. *See also* Kingston Trio (group)
Shankar, Ravi, 307
Sharp, Dee Dee, 96
"Sh-Boom," 61–62, 82
"Sheena Is a Punk Rocker," 212
Sheet music, 8, 11–12, 59, 74
Sheila E., 261
"She Loves You," 115
Shining Light Gospel Choir, 317
Shirelles, The, 99
Shirinda, M.D., 253
Shocklee, Hank, 279, 281. *See also* Bomb Squad
Shocklee, Keith, 279. *See also* Bomb Squad
Shout Records, 127
Shrieve, Mike, 193. *See also* Santana (group)
Shuffle, 28
Shuman, Mort, 98
"Shut Down," 108
Shut Down, Volume 2, 109
Sid Vicious, 215
The Sign, 269
Silver Convention, 179
Silver Fox. *See* Rich, Charlie
Simmons, Joseph, 276, **276**. *See also* Run-D.M.C.
Simmons, Russell, 275–77
Simon, Paul. *See also* Simon and Garfunkel
 African influence on, 16, 252–54
 albums by, 151, 247, 251–55, 308
 career of, 247, 251–53, 300
 classification of, 169, 183
 Gadd and, 4
 reggae and, 201
 songs by, 253–54
 world music and, 16, 247, 251–55, 308
Simon and Garfunkel, **150**, 150–51, 247, 251–52
Simpson, Valerie, 103
Sinatra, Frank, **32**, **33**, **83**
 albums by, 81
 audience for, 142
 Beatles and, 32, 183

career of, 31–32, 80–81
 classification of, 56
 media promotion of, 31–32, 255
 songs by, 3, 23, 29–31, 67, 80–81
"Sing a Simple Song," 221
Singer-songwriters, 169
Singing Kid, The. *See* Williams, Hank
"Singing Winds, Crying Beasts," 193
Singles. *See also specific titles*; Recordings
 vs. albums, 22, 146, 184, 198, 236–37, 248–49, 269, 284, 309
 "Battle of the Speeds" and, 22
 clean remix versions for, 284
 demand for, 300
 playing time of, 22, 149
"Sioux City Sue," 48
Sire Records, 211, 216, 257–58, 305, 319
Sir Mix-A-Lot, 286, 313
"Sisters Are Doin' It for Themselves," 137
Sitar, 111
Sixpence None the Richer, 291
Sixteen-bar blues, 42, 45, 109
"Sixty Minute Man," 43, 55
Ska music, 202–4, 245
Skatalites, The, 202
Slam dancing, 294
Slayer, 242, 313
"Sledgehammer," 237, 243–46
Slick, Grace, 158
Sloan, P.F., 145
Slow Train Coming, 146
"Slow Twistin'," 96
Sly and the Family Stone, 161, 169, 192, 220–21, **221**
Small, Millie, 206
"Smells Like Teen Spirit," 296–97, 317
Smile, 122
Smith, Bessie, 73, 159
Smith, Mamie, 14–15
Smith, Patti, 211. *See also* Patti Smith Group
Smith, Sammi, 197
Smith, Will, 278
"Smoke Gets in Your Eyes," 80
Snoop Doggy Dogg, 268, 275, 284–87, **285**, 315
Snow, Hank, 49, 129
So, 243
Sock rhythm, 49
Soft soul music, 170
Software, 318
Solid Swingers, 34
Solomon Linda and the Evening Birds, 308
"Somebody to Love," 158
Something to Remember, 259
Sommers, John, 180
Songs for Swingin' Lovers, 81
Sonic Youth, 291, 293–94, 296–97, 298
Son music, 16
Sony, 233, 319
Soul City Symphony, 179
"Soul Makossa," 308
"Soul Man," 244
Soul music, 15, 44, 131–35, 170, 220, 243–44. *See also specific artists*
Soul Records, 102

Soul Sonic Force, 273
Soul Train, 222
Soundgarden, 291, 299
"The Sounds of Silence,"
  150–51
The Source, 278
"Spanish Harlem," 101, 323
Spears, Britney, 317
Specialty Records, 79–81
Spector, Phil, 4, **96**, 96–102, 106
Spector, Ronnie, 260. *See also*
  Ronettes, The
Speed metal music, 234, 295.
  See also specific artists
Spice, 269
Spice Girls, The, 269, 317
Spinners, The, 170, 179
Sports, music and, 269, 316
Springsteen, Bruce, 4, 15,
  213–16, 231, 247, 249–51,
  250, 263
Square dancing, 12, 286
SST Records, 294
"Stagger Lee," 286, 288
Standells, 209
Starlite Wranglers, The, 63
Starr, Edwin, 161
Starr, Kay, 67
Starr, Ringo, **112**, 114, **155**. *See
  also* Beatles, The
"Stash," 299–300
Stax Records, 4
"Stayin' Alive," 224
Steely Dan, 4
Steinberg, Billy, 259
Stereo recordings, 22
Sterne, Toni, 175
Stewart, Dave, 238–39. *See also*
  Eurythmics
Stewart, Rod, 169, 241
Stewart, Sylvester. *See* Stone, Sly
Sticky Fingers, 187
"Still a Fool," 42
Still Crazy after All These Years,
  253
Still I Rise, 287
Stills, Stephen, 152. *See also*
  Crosby, Stills, and Nash
  (group)
Sting, 111. *See also* Police, The
"Stir It Up," 206
Stoller, Mike, 46, 88–91, 98–99
Stone, Jesse, 59–60
Stone, Sly, 131, 161, 183, 186,
  220–21, 262. *See also* Sly
  and the Family Stone
"Stoned Love," 161
Stoners, The, 221
Stooges, The (group), 209–11,
  222
The Stooges (album), 210–11
Stop Making Sense, 219
Stoptime technique, 42, 138–39,
  227
Storz, Todd, 19
Straight outta Compton (album),
  1, 283
"Straight outta Compton"
  (song), 323
"(My Friends Are Gonna Be)
  Strangers," 172
Stratocaster guitar, 70
Streisand, Barbra, 4, 169, 171,
  225
String bands, 13–15
Strong, Barrett, 103, 161
Strophic form
  AABA form and, 30
  in "A Hard Rain's A-
    Gonna Fall," 144

in ballads, 11, 24–26
in "Blowin' in the Wind,"
  140–41, 147–48
in "Choo Choo
  Ch'Boogie," 26–29
chorus-verse arrangement
  in, 24–26
definition of, 24
in "Eleanor Rigby," 121
in "Fun, Fun, Fun," 109
in "Goodnight, Irene,"
  24–26
in "I'm So Lonesome I
  Could Cry," 50
in "Like a Rolling Stone,"
  147–48
melody in, 24–26
in "Mystery Train," 63–65
in "Please, Please, Please,"
  133
in "Purple Haze," 163
in R&B, 24, 26–29, 41
sixteen-bar blues and, 42
in Tin Pan Alley songs, 30
in "Tom Dooley," 89
twelve-bar blues and, 26–28
units in, 24
Stylistics, The, 179
Styx, 183
Subdominant chord, 27, 63
Sub Pop Records, 296–99
"Sucker M.C.'s," 73
Sugarhill Gang, 229, 273, 275
Sugar Hill Records, 273–74
Suicidal Tendencies, 295
Summer, Donna, 170, 224–25,
  227–29, **228**
Summer of Love, 154
"Summertime," 159
"Summertime Blues," 57
Sun Ra, 298
Sun Records, 4, 20, 62–65, 80,
  82–84, 173
"Super Bad," 220
"Superstition," 175–77
Superunknown, 299
Supreme Records, 58–59
Supremes, The, 102–6, **105**, 161,
  233
"Surf City," 110
"Surfer Girl," 108
"Surfin' Safari," 108
"Surfin' USA," 108
Surrealistic Pillow, 158
"Suspicious Minds," 199
"Sweet Black Angel," 188
Sweet Dreams (Are Made of This)
  (album), 238
"Sweet Dreams (Are Made of
  This)" (song), 238–40
"Sweet Little Sixteen," 76, 108
"Sweet Nothin's," 128
"Sweet Virginia," 188
Swing music, 15, 19–20, 70. *See
  also specific artists*
Synchro System, 308
Synclavier, 235
Syncopation, 131, 141, 207
Syncretism, 13
Synthesizers, 177, 234–35,
  264–67, 317
Synth-pop music, 238–40,
  258–59, 291. *See also
  specific artists*
Szabo, Gabor, 193

Tabla, 312
Tag, 28
"Take a Bow," 259
"Take Good Care of My

Baby," 176
"Take It Easy," 182
"Take Me Home, Country
  Roads," 180–81
"Take Me Out to the
  Ballgame," 269
Talking Heads, 185, 209, 216–19
Talking Heads '77, 216
Talking Timbuktu, 310–11
Tamla Records, 102
Tango, 16, 201, 300
Tapes, 7, 21–22, 38, 168, 231–32
Tapestry, 175–76
Taupin, Bernie, 177
Taylor, James, 169
Tchaikovsky, Peter, 186
"Teardrops on Your Letter," 93
Techno music, 223, 225, 232,
  234, 238–40, 289–90. *See
  also specific artists*
Teddy Bears, The, 96
"Teen-Age Crush," 57
"A Teenager in Love," 57
Teenage symphonies, 97,
  100–101, 103
Telecaster guitar, 70
Television (group), 211, 213
Television (TV). *See also specific
  shows*
  BMI and, 21
  cable channels on, 232
  counterculture and, 167
  country music and, 171,
    174
  development of, 23
  documentaries on, 209
  individualism and, 9
  Latin influence on, 16
  Presley and, 82
  records and, 23
  royalties from, 20–21, 23
  segregation and, 55
  Sex Pistols and, 214
  stations, ownership of, 318
  techno music and, 291
  teen culture and, 57
  Watergate hearings on, 167
  world music and, 309
Tempo, 64–65, 72–73, 100,
  202–4, 227, 229, 272, 294
Temptations, The, 102–5, 122,
  161
"Tennessee Waltz," 48
Tenth Floor, The, 226
"Tequila Sunrise," 182
Terminator X, 278. *See also*
  Public Enemy
"T for Texas," 199
"Thank God I'm a Country
  Boy," 171, 175, 180–81
"Thank You (Falletinme Be
  Mice Elf Again)," 221
"That'll Be the Day," 84–85
"That Was Your Mother," 254
Theodore, 272
Theremin, 124, 235
"There Was a Time," 133–34
"The Sound of Philadelphia
  (TSOP)," 179
"The Thing," 19
"Think," 136
33[1/3] r.p.m. disks, 22, 184
Thomas, B.J., 170–71
Thomas, Dylan, 140
Thorn, 233
Thornton, Willie Mae "Big
  Mama," 44, 46–47, 83–84,
  159, 315
Thrash metal music, 3, 234,
  293, 295. *See also specific*

artists
Thriller (album), 10, 233,
  246–49
"Thriller" (song), 233, 248–49
Timbales, 194
Timbre, 4, 14, 62, 70, 117, 224,
  235, 277
Time, The, 261, 263
Time magazine, 171
"Time of the Preacher," 198–99
Time-Warner, 233, 287
Tin Pan Alley
  Bacharach-David and, 142,
    170–71
  Brill Building and, 98
  country music and, 52, 58,
    129, 131
  definition of, 30
  Domino and, 79–80
  forms used by, 30
  Presley and, 80
  race music and, 38, 58
  record companies and, 67
  rock 'n' roll and, 80–81
  sports music and, 269
Titanic, 268
Tokens, The, 308
"To Know Him Is to Love
  Him," 96
"Tom Dooley," 89
Tommy, 184
Tommy Boy Records, 278
Tone color, 4, 42, 270
Tone-Lōc, 278
Tones, 13–14
Tonic, 27–28, 63, 73, 116–17,
  120, 245
"Too Young," 34
Torrence, Dean, 110
To the Extreme, 282
"Touch of Gray," 162
Toure, Ali Farka, 309–11
"Transmitting Live from
  Mars," 288
Travis, Merle, 70
Tremolo, 110
True Blue, 257
"TSOP," 179
Tubb, Ernest, 49, 172
"Tumbling Dice," 188
Turner, Big Joe, 59–60, 316
Turner, Ike, 240–41
Turner, Tina, 237, **240**, 240–42,
  259, 315
Turtles, The, 288
"Tutti Frutti," 3, 77
TV. *See* Television (TV)
Twain, Shania, 268
"Tweezer," 299
Twelve-bar blues
  in *Batman* theme song, 3
  in "Black Night," 41
  in "Charlie Brown," 90–91
  in "Choo Choo
    Ch'Boogie," 26–29
  in "Cover Me," 249
  definition of, 27
  "Don't Be Cruel" and, 82,
    86–87
  in "Fun, Fun, Fun," 109
  "A Hard Day's Night"
    and, 116–17
  in "Have Mercy Baby,"
    43–44
  in "Hound Dog," 46–47
  in "I Got You (I Feel
    Good)," 3
  "Long Tall Sally" and, 78,
    86, 90
  "Maybellene" and, 71,

73–75
in Motown records, 102
in "Mystery Train," 63–65
in "Oh, Boy!," 85
in "Papa's Got a Brand
   New Bag," 137–38
in "Peggy Sue," 85
in "Riders on the Storm," 3
in "Shake, Rattle, and
   Roll," 59
in "Shut Down," 108
"Sledgehammer" and,
   244–45
"Superstition" and, 177
"That'll Be the Day" and,
   85
"Tutti Frutti" and, 3, 77
in "The Twist," 93
25 Years of Motown, 249
"Twilight Time," 80
"The Twist," 93–96
"Twist and Shout," 114
Twitty, Conway, **95**
2 Live Crew, 288
2Pac Shakur, 268, 275, 287–88
Two-step (dance), 12
Tyler, Steven, **6**, 277. *See also*
   Aerosmith
Tympany Five, 23, 26–29, **39**,
   40, 69

Uncle Tupelo, 291
"Under African Skies," 254
Underground music, 292–94
"Unforgettable," 34
Unions, 31, 37, 171
United Artists-MGM, 168
Universal, 319
Unplugged, 7
"Up on the Roof," 98
"Upside Down," 225
"Uptown," 97, 100–101, 316
Urban contemporary, 169
Urban folk music, 34, 36,
   139–46, 158, 160–61, 169,
   300–3, 306–7. *See also*
   specific artists
Uridin, Jala, 272–73

"Vacation," 128
Valens, Richie, 17, 85, 192
Valentino, Rudolph, 16
Van Dyke, Earl, 103
Van Halen, Alex, 242. *See also*
   Van Halen (group)
Van Halen, Eddie, 4, 233,
   242–43, 248–49, 265
Van Halen (group), 242–43
Van Heusen, James, 30
Vanilla Ice, 282
Vanity Fair magazine, 294, 298
Van Winkle, Robert, 282
Van Zandt, Townes, 197,
   200–201
Vaudeville, 14, 46
Vaughan, Stevie Ray, 6
Vedder, Eddie, 311–13. *See also*
   Pearl Jam
Vee-Jay Records, 115
Veliotes. *See* Otis, Johnny
Velvet Underground, The,
   209–11, 293, 297
Ventures, The, 110
Verses
   in "Charlie Brown," 90
   in "Choo Choo
      Ch'Boogie," 26–29
   in "Don't Be Cruel," 86–87

in "Goodnight, Irene,"
   24–26
in "Long Tall Sally," 78, 86,
   90
in "Maybellene," 73–75
in strophic songs, 24–29
in Tin Pan Alley songs, 30
twelve-bar blues and,
   26–29
in "When Doves Cry,"
   264–67
VH-1, 232. *See also* MTV;
   Videos, music
"Video Killed the Radio Star,"
   232
Videos, music
   audience for, 232
   Hype!, 299
   Jackson and, 233, 248–49
   Madonna and, 258–61
   Movieolas and, 37
   movies and, 233, 262
   MP3 and MPEG, 318–19
   MTV. *See* MTV
   Queen and, 232
   of "Rockit," 275
   Run-D.M.C. and, 276–77
   Simon and, 255
   Springsteen and, 251
Vietnam War, 149–51, 167, 186
Vig, Butch, 296
Village People, The, 6, 170,
   225–26, 269, 316
Village Voice newspaper, 308
Vincent, Gene, 82
Virgin Records, 215, 233
Vision, 309
Vocal harmony groups, 43–44,
   61, 80, 82, 98, 102–3. *See
   also specific artists*
Voidoids, The, 211
Von Tilzer, Albert, 269

"Waiting for a Train," 323
WAKR, **56**
Walker, Aaron "T-Bone," 70,
   79, 162
Walker Brothers, 111
"Walkin' after Midnight," 128
"Walk on By," 142
"Walk This Way," 277
Wallace, Andy, 296
Wallace, Christopher, 268,
   287–88
Wallace and Gromit, 246
Wall of sound, 97, 100–101
Waltzes, 12, 26, 48, 50, 67, 302
Wanted: The Outlaws, 199
"War," 161
Ward, Billy, 43
Warhol, Andy, 209
"The Warmth of the Sun,"
   108–9
Warner Communications, 168.
   See also Time-Warner
Warner Records, 233, 257,
   262–63, 288, 293, 319
Warwick, Dionne, 142
Watergate, 167
Watson, Paula, 58
"The Way We Were," 171
WDIA, 37
Weavers, The, 23–26, 34–36, **35**,
   89, 140, 308
Wednesday Morning, 3 A.M.,
   150–51
Weil, Cynthia, 98–101, **99**, 174
Wells, Kitty, 126

Wells, Mary, 103
Wesley, Fred, 222. *See also*
   James Brown and the
   Famous Flames;
   Parliament
Western swing music, 59–60, 69
"We Will Rock You," 269
Wexler, Jerry, 135
Weymouth, Tina, 216. *See also*
   Talking Heads
"What'd I Say," 129–31
What's Going On, 186–87
What's Love Got to Do With It
   (movie), 241
"What's Love Got to Do with
   It" (song), 237, 240–42,
   259
"What's My Name?," 284–87,
   315
"What the World Needs Now
   Is Love," 142
"When Doves Cry," 263–67,
   316
"Where Have All the Flowers
   Gone," 140
White, Barry, 170, 175, **178**,
   179–80
White, Ronald, 104
"White Christmas," 94
Whites. *See* European
   Americans
Whitfield, Norman, 103, 161
Who, The, 111, 113, 184, 208
"Wholy Holy," 186
"Who's That Girl," 239
"Why Do Fools Fall in Love?,"
   57
"Wichita Lineman," 173
Wild Cherry, 221–22
The Wild One, 208
"Wild Thing," 278
Williams, Hank, 15, 49–52, **51**,
   127, 132, 153, 172, 300,
   315
"Will You Love Me
   Tomorrow?," 99, 176
Wilson, Brian, 103, 106–10, **107**,
   122–25, 158. *See also*
   Beach Boys, The
Wilson, Jackie, 82, 102
Wilson, Tom, 150
"Wimoweh," 308
Wings, 248
WINS, 55
Winter, Edgar, 184
"Within You without You,"
   111, 154
The Wizard of Oz, 186
Wolfe, Tom, 97, 160, 167
Women
   acid rock and, 158
   alternative music and,
      300–307
   birth-control pills for, 152
   performance style of, 136
   R&B and, 44–47
   in rap music, 278
   stereotyping of, 5
Wonder, Stevie
   AOR format and, 169
   Brown (James) and, 177
   career of, 168, 176–77
   classification of, 183, 186
   Gadd and, 4
   Motown and, 103, 176
   Prince and, 256, 262
   rock music and, 183
   roles of, 9, 103, 176, 184

"Superstition," 175–77
Talking Book, 176
"Wonderful World, Beautiful
   People," 206
Wonder Mike, 273. *See also*
   Sugarhill Gang
Woodstock Festival, 163, 183,
   192, 221
"Woody Woodpecker," 19
World Class Wreckin' Cru, 283
World music. *See also specific
   artists*
   Beatles and, 111–12
   Brown (James) and, 134
   Byrne and, 16, 219
   colonialism and, 308
   definition of, 270, 307
   Gabriel and, 243, 245, 312
   Latin influence on, 16
   reggae and, 201–2
   royalties for, 308
   sales of, 307–9
   Simon (Paul) and, 16, 247,
      308
   Weavers and, 36
World Music and Dance
   festival, 308, 312
Worrell, Bernie, 223. *See also*
   Parliament
"Wouldn't It Be Nice," 122
Wrecking crew, 98
"Wreck on the Highway," 249
Wright, Eric, 283–84. *See also*
   N.W.A.
Wright, Michael, 273. *See also*
   Sugarhill Gang

X, 1, 294

Yardbirds, 164, 188
Yella, 283. *See also* N.W.A.
"The Yellow Rose of Texas,"
   67
"Yellow Submarine," 119
"Yesterday," 3, 114, 118–19,
   126
"(At the) YMCA," 6, 225–26,
   269, 316
"Yo, Twist!," 96
Yoakam, Dwight, 200, 291
Yo! MVT Raps, 278
Yothu Yindi, 309
"You Can Call Me Al," 254
"You Can't Hurry Love,"
   103–6, 232–33
"(You Gotta) Fight for Your
   Right (To Party)," 278,
   278–79, 317
"You Light Up My Life," 171
Young, Andre. *See* Dr. Dre
Young, Neil, 201
"Your Cheatin' Heart," 50
"You're Breaking My Heart," 19
"You Showed Me," 288
"You Still Believe in Me," 122
"You've Got to Hide Your
   Love Away," 197
"You You You," 19

Zappa, Frank, 146, 154, 183,
   257
Ziggy Stardust concert tour,
   185, 219
Zimmerman, Robert. *See*
   Dylan, Bob
Zoso, 188–90
Zydeco bands, 254
ZZ Top, 183